# Digital Control System Design

# Digital Control System Design

**Gene H. Hostetter**
UNIVERSITY OF CALIFORNIA, IRVINE

**Holt, Rinehart and Winston, Inc.**
New York   Chicago   San Francisco
Philadelphia   Montreal   Toronto
London   Sydney   Tokyo

Printed in the United States of America
8  9  0  038  9  8  7  6  5  4  3

ISBN 0-03-070617-3

**Library of Congress Cataloging-in-Publication Data**

Hostetter, G. H., 1939–
  Digital control system design.

  Bibliography: p.
  Includes index.
  1. Digital control systems.   I. Title.
TJ223.M53H66   1987                 629.8              86-33642


Holt, Rinehart and Winston, Inc.
The Dryden Press
Saunders College Publishing

For my father, JOHN
and for
DONNA, COLLEEN, and KRISTEN

# Contents

# 3   State Descriptions of Discrete-Time Systems

# 4   Discrete-Time Observation, Control and Feedback

# 5   Digital Regulator Design

# Preface

The dramatic development of small, inexpensive, and highly capable digital computers is changing the nature of most control system design from analog-based to digital. At the same time, powerful digital computation tools for control system design are increasingly accessible, making sophisticated design methods cost-effective. These advancements have already had a tremendous impact in some areas such as the aerospace industry. For most of industry though, the flourishing of digital control is really just beginning, and today's engineering and scientific graduates will be those responsible for its design.

This is a design-oriented digital control systems text for use in an academic course at the advanced undergraduate or beginning graduate level and for self-study and reference by practicing engineers in industry. It is intended to convey those fundamental and general concepts that are most effectively taught in the classroom, in intensive short courses, and by self-study. Of course much more, especially experience and common sense, is expected of a seasoned designer. Our orientation is that of state space, but with an appreciation for classical viewpoints and methods.

In developing a textbook as in preparing a course, it is usually hardest to decide what *not* to include. There is a temptation to try to teach too many things in parallel. With reluctance, I have not included stochastic concepts. For many, perhaps most, students it is far more efficient to obtain a thorough grounding in deterministic systems before studying deterministic controllers that perform particularly well when the plant model involves noise. The concluding sections of the text concern least squares estimation and optimal control, and this is a good point for transition to stochastic control.

The book is organized into eight chapters, as follows:

**Chapter 1: Introductory Concepts**
Concepts and terminology of classical continuous-time control system design. Summary of the fundamentals of linear algebra. Introduction to state variables for continuous-time systems.

**Chapter 2: Discrete-Time Systems and the Z-Transformation**
Discrete-time signals and systems. Sampling and reconstruction. Controller design by approximation and an overview of classical pole-zero design methods.

**Chapter 3: State Descriptions of Discrete-Time Systems**
Step-invariant discrete-time system models and response. Review of the characteristic value problem with application to decoupling state equations. Observability and controllability.

**Chapter 4: Discrete-Time Observation, Control and Feedback**
Observing and controlling the state of a system. Introduction to least squares state estimation and parameter identification. State feedback, eigenvalue placement, and output feedback.

**Chapter 5: Digital Regulator Design**
Observer concepts and properties. Design of state and observer feedback for acceptable transient response.

**Chapter 6: Digital Tracking System Design**
Design for acceptable reference input tracking via inverse filtering, response model, and reference model methods. Introduction to disturbance rejection.

**Chapter 7: Controlling Continuous-Time Systems**
Discrete-time models of continuous-time systems. Design of between-sample response when a continuous-time plant is controlled digitally. Introduction to digital hardware and software considerations.

**Chapter 8: Step-Varying Systems**
Description and control of linear, step-varying systems. Recursive least squares state estimation and optimal control.

It is expected that most readers will have had background in classical control concepts and an understanding of the basics of linear algebra. For these students, the first chapter serves as a concise review and a convenient way of initiating study. For the student who initially lacks this preparation, the chapter is sufficiently detailed to serve as tutor for the diligent.

The design of digital tracking feedback controllers for known linear plants is composed of two fundamental parts:

1. Design for acceptable feedback system zero-input (or transient) response;
2. Design for acceptable feedback system zero-state response for a relevant or representative class of reference inputs to be tracked.

Additionally, if the plant to be controlled is continuous-time, it is necessary to

3. Design for acceptable between-sample response of the plant.

This is our agenda. At the appropriate time we also consider some aspects of digital hardware and software that are not likely to be obsolete in the near future.

The desirability of connecting a text such as this too closely with specific computational programs is doubtful. The computer-aided design (CAD) support available at universities and in industry varies widely in its capabilities and idiosyncrasies. Those with good and easily accessed digital computer support for modern control system design should simply apply the tools in place, with what are probably already-familiar formats. For those desiring decentralization and quick startup of accompanying CAD experience, and for those who are just beginning to develop CAD capability, a fully documented package of fundamental design-oriented software for personal computers, keyed to the text, is available. The text, however, is software-independent.

A large number of students and colleagues have enthusiastically contributed to this work. I am especially indebted to William Ballance, Behnam Bavarian, Jeffrey Burl, C. W. Barnes, John Duffy, Iman Foroutan, Anton Horvath, Claude Lindquist, Alan Ross, and Allen R. Stubberud. A distinguished group of reviewers also contributed greatly to this effort. They were John E. Bennett, Clemson University; Richard Christiansen, Brigham Young University; Robert E. Fenton, Ohio State University; Ralph Hippenstiel, US Naval Postgraduate School; W. Richard Kolk, Hartford Graduate Center; Harris McClamrock, University of Michigan; Robert Mulholland, University of Oklahoma; Vijay Raman, Florida International University; Michael Rekoff, University of Alabama; and Lal Tummala, Michigan State University. Special thanks are due to Mrs. Sarah Yap who supervised the manuscript typing, to Richard Oxford who did many of the original drawings, to Mohammed Santina who compiled the excellent manual of problem solutions, and to Paul D'Carpio-Montalvo who developed the computer software.

# About the Author

Gene H. Hostetter lives in Huntington Beach, California with his wife, Donna, and their two teenage daughters. The family enjoys and is involved with many outdoor and church activities. They vacation regularly in the Pacific Northwest and western Canada.

Professor Hostetter's research interests are in the areas of microprocessor-based digital signal processing and control, digital and linear electronic system design, and electrooptics. He came to the University of California, Irvine, after ten years of industrial experience, at Seattle Broadcasting Company, the Boeing Company, and as founder and cofounder of several small electronics firms. He is consultant to Battelle Institute, Meditek, Sundstrand Corporation, and Western Digital Corporation, among other organizations.

At UCI, Professor Hostetter teaches classes in digital control system design, microprocessor system design, advanced electronic design, and electromagnetic theory. He and A. R. Stubberud are codirectors of the Intelligent Control Laboratory, which currently supports the work of nine Ph.D. graduate students.

Dr. Hostetter is a Fellow of the IEEE and an IEEE Centennial Medal recipient. He is the author of four electrical engineering textbooks, over a hundred scholarly technical papers, and numerous reviews and review articles.

*The whole art of teaching is only the art of
awakening the natural curiosity of young minds.*

—ANATOLE FRANCE (1844–1924)

# Digital Control System Design

# Introductory Concepts

## 1.1 Preview

This is a book about fundamental concepts in modern digital control system design. The rapid development of digital technology, made possible by the invention of the transistor and the integrated circuit, has radically changed the boundaries of practical control system design options. It is now routinely feasible to employ very complicated high-order digital controllers and to carry out the extensive calculations required for their design. These advances in implementation and design capability can be achieved at low cost because of the widespread availability of inexpensive, powerful digital computers and related devices.

This first chapter outlines some of the background necessary for a good understanding of the ideas to follow. The following section consists of a brief overview of classical control viewpoints and methods that is intended to aid the reader in making connections between classical and state variable results. The next section is a concise presentation of key topics in linear algebra. This material serves to establish style and notation, and to provide a summary of necessary background. Further topics in linear algebra are discussed in later chapters, as the need for them arises.

We then make the transition from classical system description and design to state variable methods. Continuous-time state descriptions are introduced through synthesis of systems with specified transfer functions. Once the form of the equations is established, system response is described in terms of the state transition matrix and convolution, and the matrix of transfer functions describing multiple-input, multiple-output systems is found in terms of the state equations. As our main objective is digital control, the emphasis is on those concepts with direct bearing on digital control system design. Much more can be said about the use of state variables in continuous-time control; when the topics here have been carried over to discrete-time systems, it will be apparent to the interested reader how similar methods also apply to strictly continuous-time control.

The chapter concludes with discussion of two example systems. The first involves a chamber where it is desired to precisely control temperature. The physical plant to be controlled is nonlinear, and a linear model, adequate for sufficiently small deviations from a nominal operating point, is derived. The model parameters are determined from records of plant input and output data. The second system is a simple model of a monorail train consisting of an engine and two cars. A sixth-order state variable model is derived from physical principles.

# 1.2  Classical Control System Design

The focus of our study is modern, state space-based design of digital control systems. To begin, we review basic control system terminology and outline the classical approach to continuous-time tracking system design. The key concepts, involving specification of transient and steady state response requirements are also much a part of the modern approach. While our concern is with digital control, digital controllers are most often used to control continuous-time plants. It is important then to have a good understanding of the plant to be controlled as well as of the controller and its interfaces with the plant.

## 1.2.1  Control System Terminology

A *control system* is an interconnection of components to provide a desired function. The portion of the system to be controlled is called the *plant*, and the part doing the controlling is the *controller*. Often, a control system designer has little or no design freedom with the plant; it is fixed. A controller is to be developed that will control the given plant acceptably. When measurements of plant response are available to the controller (which in turn generates signals affecting the plant), the configuration is a *feedback* control system.

A *digital control system* uses digital hardware, usually in the form of a programmed digital computer, as the heart of the controller. In contrast, the controller in an *analog control system* is composed of analog hardware, typically analog electronic, mechanical, electromechanical, and hydraulic devices. Digital controllers normally have analog elements at their periphery to interface with the plant; it is the internal workings of the controller that distinguishes digital from analog control.

A general control system diagram appears in Figure 1-1. The plant is affected by input signals, some of which (the control inputs) are accessible to the controller, and some of which (the disturbance inputs) are not. Some of the plant signals (the tracking outputs) are to be controlled and some of the plant signals (the measurement outputs) are available to the controller. A controller generates control inputs to the plant with the objective of having the tracking outputs closely approximate the reference inputs.

The signals used in the description of control systems are classified as *continuous-time* or *discrete-time*. Continuous-time signals are functions of a continuous variable, while discrete-time signals are defined only for discrete values of the variable, usually evenly-spaced ones. Discrete-time signals and their manipulations are inherently well-suited to digital computation and are used in describing the digital portions of a control system. Most often, continuous-time signals are involved in describing the plant and the interfaces between a controller and the plant it controls. Signals are further classified as being of *continuous-amplitude* or *discrete-amplitude*. Discrete-amplitude (or *quantized*) signals can attain only discrete values, usually evenly-spaced. For example, an 8-bit binary code can represent only 256 different values. Because of the complexity of dealing with quantized signals, digital control system design proceeds as if computer-generated signals were not of discrete-amplitude. Then further analysis is done if necessary to determine if a proposed level of quantization is acceptable.

Systems and system components are classified as to the nature of their mathematical model. They are termed "continuous-time" or "discrete-time" according to the type of signals they involve. They are classified as being *linear* if signal components in them can be superimposed. Any linear combination of signal components applied to an input produces the same linear combination of corresponding output components; otherwise, a system

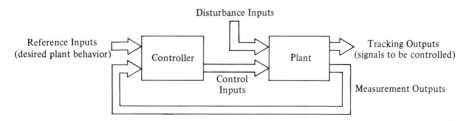

**FIGURE 1-1   A control system.**

is *nonlinear*. A system or component is *time-invariant* (or *constant-parameter*) if its properties do not change with time. Any time shift of the inputs produces an equal time shift of every corresponding signal.

Two important classes of control systems are the *regulator* and the *tracking system* (or *servosystem*). In the former, the objective is to bring the system tracking outputs near to zero in an acceptable manner, often in the face of disturbances. For example, a regulator might be used to keep a motor-driven satellite dish antenna on a moving vehicle accurately pointed in a fixed direction, even when the antenna base is moving and vibrating and when the antenna itself is buffeted by winds. In a tracking system, the objective is for system tracking outputs to, as nearly as possible, equal (or "track" or "follow") an equal number of reference input signals. Regulation is a special case of tracking, where the desired tracking is of zero.

## 1.2.2  An Overview of Classical Control

The starting point of most beginning study of classical and state space control is with a linear, time-invariant model of the plant to be controlled. But, in fact, most plants have nonlinearities and many have significantly time-varying parameters.

Practical, tractable design methods exist only for very limited classes of nonlinear systems, so it is usually expedient to approximate the plant with a linear model. To obtain a linear plant model to which linear control system design methods apply, a linear approximation about the nominal plant operating conditions (the *operating point*) is made. The nominal conditions are supplied by separate *set point* signals, and the linear controller adds to, or subtracts from, these to control relatively small excursions of the plant from the operating point. If it is necessary to change the operating point, as when control objectives are changed or when the plant parameters change appreciably, the set point signals, plant model, and controller change.

The tools of classical linear control system design are the Laplace transform, stability testing, root locus, and frequency response. Laplace transform is used to convert system descriptions in terms of integrodifferential equations to equivalent algebraic relations involving rational functions. These are conveniently manipulated in the form of transfer functions with block diagrams and signal flow graphs. Through superposition, the *zero-input response*, that due to initial conditions, and the individual *zero-state response* contributions of each input can be dealt with separately. Alternatively, one can deal with *natural* (or *transient*) and *forced* (or *steady state*) response components.

When the transfer functions describing a linear, time-invariant system are rational, the locations of denominator roots, the *poles*, indicate whether or not the system is input-output stable, according to whether or not all transfer function poles are in the left half of the complex plane. Stability is tested by factoring the transfer function denominator polynomials or with a simpler method such as the Routh-Hurwitz test. A pole-zero plot is a plot, on the complex plane, of the poles (denominator roots) and the zeros (numerator roots) of a transfer function.

Simple feedback systems can be described by either their *open-loop* transfer functions, their transfer functions when the feedback is not connected, or by their overall *closed-loop* transfer functions. Usually it is easier for the designer to deal directly with open-loop quantities than with closed-loop ones because the open-loop poles and zeros are known or can be easily found. A root locus plot consists of a pole-zero plot of the open-loop transfer function of a feedback system, upon which is superimposed the locus of the poles of the closed-loop transfer function as some parameter is varied.

Frequency response characterizations of systems have long been popular because of the ease and practicality of steady-state sinusoidal response measurements. These methods apply to systems with irrational transfer functions such as those involving time delays. They do not require explicit knowledge of system transfer function models. A stability test, the Nyquist criterion, is available but its principal measures of zero-input system performance, gain margin and phase margin, are difficult to relate closely to the character of the feedback system's response. Frequency response methods are most useful in developing models from experimental data, in verifying the performance of a system designed by other methods, and in dealing with those systems and situations where rational transfer function models are not adequate.

### 1.2.3 Tracking System Design

A typical classical control system design problem is to determine and specify the transfer function $G_c(s)$ of a cascade compensator that will result in a unity feedback tracking system with prescribed performance requirements. This is only a part of complete control system design, of course. It applies after a suitable model has been found and when the performance requirements are quantified. In learning solution methods for idealized problems such as these, we separate general design principles from the highly specialized details of a particular application.

The basic system configuration for this problem is shown in Figure 1-2. There are, of course, many variations on the theme, including situations where the system structure is more involved, where it is not a tracking system, where there are disturbance inputs to be considered, and where the designer specifies portions of the plant.

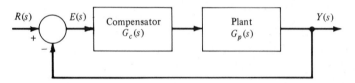

**FIGURE 1-2.   Cascade compensation of a unity feedback system.**

Tracking system design has two basic concerns:

1. Obtaining acceptable zero-input system response;
2. Obtaining acceptable zero-state system response to reference inputs.

The character of a system's zero-input response is determined by its pole locations, so the first concern of tracking system design is met by choosing a compensator $G_c(s)$ that results in acceptable pole locations for the overall transfer function

$$T(s) = \left.\frac{Y(s)}{R(s)}\right|_{\text{zero initial conditions}} = \frac{G_c(s)G_p(s)}{1 + G_c(s)G_p(s)}$$

Root locus is an important design tool because, with it, the effects upon closed-loop system pole locations of varying a design parameter are quickly and easily visualized.

If only the rate of decay of the plant's zero-input response is of concern, then for the zero-input response to decay at least as fast as $\exp(-\sigma t)$, all poles of $T(s)$ must be to the left of $s = -\sigma$ on the complex plane. If, in addition, all oscillatory zero-input response terms are to have damping ratios larger than some specific ratio $\zeta$, then all complex conjugate pairs of poles of $T(s)$ must lie between angles 180 deg $\pm$ arc cos $\zeta$ in the left half of the complex plane.

The second concern of tracking system design is obtaining acceptable closed-loop zero-state response. Zero-state performance is particularly simple to deal with if it can be expressed as a maximum steady state error to a power-of-time input. The transfer function that relates the error between the plant output and input

$$E(s) = R(s) - Y(s)$$

is

$$T_E(s) = \left.\frac{E(s)}{R(s)}\right|_{\text{zero initial conditions}} = 1 - T(s)$$

If we denote the open-loop transfer function numerator and denominator polynomials by

$$G_c(s)G_p(s) = \frac{n(s)}{d(s)}$$

then

$$T(s) = \frac{n(s)}{d(s) + n(s)}; \qquad T_E(s) = \frac{d(s)}{d(s) + n(s)}$$

The plant and error transfer functions have the same poles.

Assuming the plant is stable, the steady state error to a power-of-time input of the form

$$r(t) = \frac{1}{i!} t^i u(t); \qquad R(s) = \frac{1}{s^{i+1}} \tag{1-1}$$

where $u(t)$ is the unit step function, is given by the final value theorem

$$\text{limit}_{t \to \infty} e(t) = \text{limit}_{s \to 0} [sE(s)] = \text{limit}_{s \to 0} [sT_E(s)R(s)] = \text{limit}_{s \to 0} \left\{ \frac{d(s)}{s^i[n(s) + d(s)]} \right\}$$

The steady state error is finite if the open-loop transfer function has $i$ poles (the roots of $d(s)$) at $s = 0$. If the open-loop transfer function has more than $i$ poles at $s = 0$, the steady state error to an input (1-1) is zero; if there are less than $i$ open-loop poles at $s = 0$, the steady state error is infinite.

In practice, if necessary, compensator poles are placed at or near $s = 0$ to achieve the required steady state performance. The compensator gain and its zero locations are selected so that the resulting closed-loop system pole locations result in acceptable zero-input response. One generally begins with a simple compensator and analyzes the possibilities, increasing the compensator order until the performance requirements are met.

As a simple numerical example, consider the unity feedback system of Figure 1-3 which has a plant with transfer function

$$G_p(s) = \frac{1}{s + 4}$$

The feedback system consists of a loop with the error between input and output, amplified by a gain $K$, driving the plant. The overall transfer function

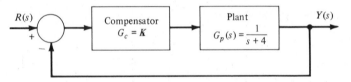

**FIGURE 1-3.** Compensator with constant gain in a unity feedback system.

is, in terms of $K$:

$$T(s) = \frac{K G_p(s)}{1 + K G_p(s)} = \frac{K}{s + 4 + K}$$

The error transfer function is

$$T_E(s) = 1 - T(s) = \frac{s + 4}{s + 4 + K}$$

and the steady state error to a unit step input is

$$e_{\text{step}} = \lim_{s \to 0} s \left(\frac{1}{s}\right) \left(\frac{s + 4}{s + 4 + K}\right) = \frac{4}{4 + K}$$

The zero-input response of this feedback system is of the form $e^{-(4 + K)t}$. The larger the value of $K$, the smaller the steady state step error and the more rapidly the system's zero-input response decays with time.

Suppose it is desired that the plant be controlled so that its steady state error to a unit ramp is no more than 1 percent and also that the zero-input response of the system decays at least as quickly as $e^{-10t}$. The compensator of Figure 1-3 will not suffice because it has finite steady state error to a step input and thus infinite steady state ramp input error. For zero step input error, the open-loop system must have at least one pole at $s = 0$, as it does for the compensator of Figure 1-4(a). The overall transfer function of this system is

$$T(s) = \frac{\left(\dfrac{K}{s}\right)\left(\dfrac{1}{s + 4}\right)}{1 + \left(\dfrac{K}{s}\right)\left(\dfrac{1}{s + 4}\right)} = \frac{K}{s^2 + 4s + K}$$

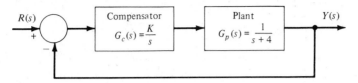

(a) Compensator with a single pole at $s = 0$.

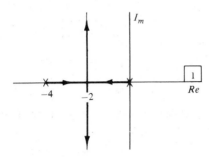

(b) Root locus plot for variable $K$ with the compensator of $(a)$. The pole location requirement cannot be met.

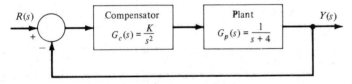

(c) Another compensator. This system is unstable.

**FIGURE 1-4. Compensators with $s = 0$ poles.**

and the error transfer function is

$$T_E(s) = 1 - T(s) = \frac{s^2 + 4s}{s^2 + 4s + K}$$

This system has zero steady state error to a step input, and the steady state error

$$e_{ramp} = \underset{s \to 0}{\text{limit }} s \left(\frac{1}{s^2}\right)\left(\frac{s^2 + 4s}{s^2 + 4s + K}\right) = \frac{4}{K}$$

to a ramp input. For less than 1 percent ramp error, $K$ must be greater than 400. However, the root locus plot of Figure 1-4(b) shows that the requirement that all poles of the closed-loop system be at, or to the left of, $s = -10$ can never be met.

Changing the compensator to include a double pole at $s = 0$, as in Figure 1-4(c), to potentially obtain zero steady state ramp error, gives the overall transfer function

$$T(s) = \frac{\left(\dfrac{K}{s^2}\right)\left(\dfrac{1}{s+4}\right)}{1 + \left(\dfrac{K}{s^2}\right)\left(\dfrac{1}{s+4}\right)} = \frac{K}{s^3 + 4s^2 + K}$$

which unfortunately is unstable for all values of $K$.

The compensator of Figure 1-5(a), with a single $s = 0$ pole and a zero at $s = -a$, results in the overall transfer function

$$T(s) = \frac{K(s+a)}{s^2 + (4+K)s + Ka}$$

and the error transfer function

$$T_E(s) = 1 - T(s) = \frac{s^2 + 4s}{s^2 + (4+K)s + Ka}$$

Its steady state error to a ramp input is

$$e_{\text{ramp}} = \lim_{s \to 0} \left[ s\left(\frac{1}{s^2}\right) \frac{s^2 + 4s}{s^2 + (4+K)s + Ka} \right] = \frac{4}{Ka}$$

The effect of adding the compensator zero is to draw the closed-loop system poles into the left half of the complex plane, as can be seen from the root locus plot of Figure 1-5(b), which has been sketched for an arbitrary zero location. If $K$ is large and the zero location is at $s = -10$, the closed-loop system poles will be to the left of $s = -10$ on the complex plane.

With this choice of $a = 10$ and the choice $K = 40$ to meet the steady state ramp error requirement, the designed compensator, Figure 1-5(c), has

$$G_c(s) = \frac{40(s+10)}{s}$$

The overall system transfer function is

$$T(s) = \frac{40(s+10)}{s^2 + 44s + 400}$$

and has poles at $s = -12.83$ and $s = -31.17$.

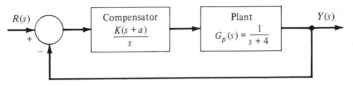

(a)  Block diagram.

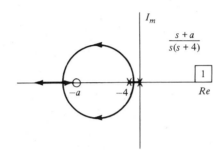

(b)  Character of the root locus plot for fixed *a* and variable *K*.

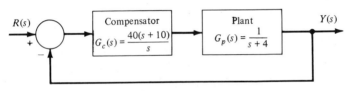

(c)  Completed design.

**FIGURE 1-5.   Compensator with an $s = 0$ pole and a zero.**

The extension of methods such as these to the control of complicated feedback structures involving many loops, each of which might include a compensator, is not easy. Put another way, we nowadays want to design compensators having multiple inputs and multiple outputs, sometimes dozens of each. Design *is* iterative and it does involve trial and error. But when there are many design variables, it is important to deal efficiently with those design decisions that need not be iterative. The powerful methods of linear algebra offer new insights as to what is possible and what is not. And, they provide an excellent framework for general methods of approaching and accomplishing our objectives.

## 1.3  Elements of Linear Algebra

Linear algebra is the language of modern control system design. We now present topics in linear algebra that have immediate application in sections to follow. Our emphasis is on summarizing needed concepts and results and on establishing terminology and notation that will continue throughout this book.

## 1.3.1 Matrix Methods

A *matrix* is a rectangular array of elements, most often numbers. Matrices are symbolized by letters, and the elements that comprise a matrix are denoted by a subscripted letter, usually the lower case of the symbol for the matrix itself. The first subscript is the row of the element and the second subscript is the column of the element. A matrix with $m$ rows and $n$ columns is of dimension $m \times n$. A *square* matrix has the same number of rows as columns. A *column vector* (or just "vector") is a matrix with just one column. The elements of a column vector, called an *m-vector*, where $m$ is the number of its elements, are labeled with a single subscript.

A matrix with all elements zero is a *zero* (or *null*) matrix. An $m \times n$ zero matrix is denoted by just $\mathbf{0}$ or by $\mathbf{0}_{mn}$ when its dimensions are not obvious. A square matrix with all elements zero except perhaps on the diagonal is a *diagonal* matrix. A diagonal matrix with all diagonal elements unity is an *identity* matrix. The $n \times n$ identity matrix is denoted by $\mathbf{I}$, or by $\mathbf{I}_n$.

Two matrices are equal,

$$\mathbf{A} = \mathbf{B}$$

if and only if they have the same dimensions as one another (they are then said to be *conformable*) and all corresponding elements in the two matrices are equal. The product of a matrix $\mathbf{A}$ with a scalar $k$ is another matrix $\mathbf{B} = k\mathbf{A}$ of the same dimensions as $\mathbf{A}$ but with corresponding elements $k$ times those of $\mathbf{A}$:

$$b_{ij} = ka_{ij}$$

The sum or difference of two matrices, $\mathbf{C} = \mathbf{A} \pm \mathbf{B}$, only makes sense if $\mathbf{A}$ and $\mathbf{B}$ are conformable. The sum $\mathbf{C}$ has the same dimensions as $\mathbf{A}$ and $\mathbf{B}$ and has elements that are the sums or differences of the corresponding elements of $\mathbf{A}$ and $\mathbf{B}$:

$$c_{ij} = a_{ij} \pm b_{ij}$$

The order that several conformable matrices are added or subtracted is of no consequence.

A square matrix $\mathbf{A}$ for which $a_{ij} = a_{ji}$ is called *symmetric*. The definition does not restrict the diagonal elements; they can be any numbers. A square matrix $\mathbf{A}$ for which $a_{ij} = -a_{ji}$ is called *skew-symmetric*. The skew-symmetric definition requires that the diagonal elements be negatives of themselves, which means they must be zero. Any square matrix can be expressed as the sum of a symmetric matrix plus a skew-symmetric matrix.

A *dagger* symbol, as in $\mathbf{B} = \mathbf{A}^\dagger$ denotes an interchange of the rows and columns of a matrix. The matrix $\mathbf{B}$ is the *transpose* of the matrix $\mathbf{A}$. The transpose of the transpose is the matrix itself:

$$(\mathbf{A}^\dagger)^\dagger = \mathbf{A}$$

The transpose of a column vector is a *row vector*:

$$\mathbf{b}^\dagger = \begin{bmatrix} b_1 \\ b_2 \\ b_3 \\ \vdots \end{bmatrix}^\dagger = [b_1 \quad b_2 \quad b_3 \cdots]$$

The notation to be used here, which is common, is that lower case symbols represent column vectors. A row vector is then represented as the transpose of the corresponding column vector.

The *product* of two matrices, $\mathbf{C} = \mathbf{AB}$, only makes sense if

(no. columns of $\mathbf{A}$) = (no. rows of $\mathbf{B}$)

The matrices are then said to be *conformable for multiplication*. If $\mathbf{A}$ is $m \times n$ and $\mathbf{B}$ is $n \times p$, the product is $m \times p$:

$$\begin{array}{ccc} \mathbf{C} & = & \mathbf{A} & \mathbf{B} \\ m \times p & & m \times n & n \times p \end{array}$$

For conformable matrices:

$$c_{ij} = a_{i1}b_{1j} + a_{i2}b_{2j} + \cdots + a_{in}b_{nj} = \sum_{k=1}^{n} a_{ik}b_{kj}$$

Multiplication of a matrix on the left (*premultiplication*) or on the right (*postmultiplication*) by an identity matrix of proper dimension for conformability has no effect:

$$\mathbf{IA} = \mathbf{A} \quad \text{and} \quad \mathbf{AI} = \mathbf{A}$$

In general, however, products of conformable matrices have these differences from scalar products:

$\mathbf{AB}$ does *not* necessarily equal $\mathbf{BA}$

$\mathbf{AB} = \mathbf{AC}$ does *not* generally imply that $\mathbf{B} = \mathbf{C}$

$\mathbf{AB} = \mathbf{0}$ does *not* generally imply that $\mathbf{B} = \mathbf{0}$ or $\mathbf{A} = \mathbf{0}$

For multiple products, the ordering of the product is important but the order in which the operations are carried out is of no consequence:

$$\mathbf{ABC} = \mathbf{A}(\mathbf{BC}) = (\mathbf{AB})\mathbf{C}$$

Premultiplication and postmultiplication have the distributive property

$$\mathbf{A}(\mathbf{B} + \mathbf{C}) = \mathbf{AB} + \mathbf{AC}$$

$$(\mathbf{A} + \mathbf{B})\mathbf{C} = \mathbf{AC} + \mathbf{BC}$$

and

$$\mathbf{A0} = \mathbf{0A} = \mathbf{0}$$

Partitioning of a matrix is indicated by dashed lines and is a way of indicating how a matrix is composed of smaller *submatrices*, that is, how matrices are joined to form larger matrices. For example:

$$\mathbf{A} = \begin{bmatrix} a_{11} & a_{12} & a_{13} & a_{14} & a_{15} \\ a_{21} & a_{22} & a_{23} & a_{24} & a_{25} \\ a_{31} & a_{32} & a_{33} & a_{34} & a_{35} \\ a_{41} & a_{42} & a_{43} & a_{44} & a_{45} \end{bmatrix} = \begin{bmatrix} \mathbf{A}_{11} & \mathbf{A}_{12} \\ \mathbf{A}_{21} & \mathbf{A}_{22} \end{bmatrix}$$

indicates that the matrix $\mathbf{A}$ is considered to be composed of the submatrices $\mathbf{A}_{11}$, $\mathbf{A}_{12}$, $\mathbf{A}_{21}$, and $\mathbf{A}_{22}$.

The partitioning

$$\mathbf{A} = [\mathbf{a} \mid \mathbf{b} \mid \cdots]$$

indicates that the columns of $\mathbf{A}$ are the vectors $\mathbf{a}$, $\mathbf{b}$, . . . . The partitioning

$$\mathbf{A} = \begin{bmatrix} \mathbf{x}^\dagger \\ \mathbf{y}^\dagger \\ \vdots \end{bmatrix}$$

indicates that the rows of $\mathbf{A}$ are the row vectors $\mathbf{x}^\dagger$, $\mathbf{y}^\dagger$, . . . . Matrix products, when the matrices involved are partitioned so that the submatrices are conformable for multiplication, have multiplication relations as if the submatrices were numbers, paying due respect to the ordering of the products.

The transpose of a matrix product is the product of the transposed matrices in reverse order,

$$(\mathbf{AB})^\dagger = \mathbf{B}^\dagger \mathbf{A}^\dagger$$

Applying this result successively

$$(\mathbf{AB} \ldots \mathbf{PQ})^\dagger = \mathbf{Q}^\dagger \mathbf{P}^\dagger \ldots \mathbf{B}^\dagger \mathbf{A}^\dagger$$

The trace of a square matrix $\mathbf{A}$ is denoted by trace $(\mathbf{A})$ and is the sum of the diagonal elements:

$$\text{trace } (\mathbf{A}) = a_{11} + a_{22} + \cdots + a_{nn} = \sum_{i=1}^{n} a_{ii}$$

The complex conjugate $\mathbf{A}^*$ of a matrix $\mathbf{A}$ is simply the matrix composed of the complex conjugates of the elements of $\mathbf{A}$.

The derivative of a matrix $\mathbf{A}$ with respect to a scalar is the matrix composed of elements that are the derivatives of the corresponding elements of $\mathbf{A}$. Higher derivatives, partial derivatives, and integrals are defined similarly, as matrices of the same dimension, composed of the corresponding derivatives or integrals of the original elements.

The partial derivative of a scalar function $f$ with respect to a vector $\mathbf{x}$ is denoted by

$$\frac{\partial f}{\partial \mathbf{x}} = \left[ \frac{\partial f}{\partial x_1} \quad \frac{\partial f}{\partial x_2} \quad \cdots \quad \frac{\partial f}{\partial x_n} \right]$$

and is a *row* vector composed of the derivatives of $f$ with respect to each of the components of $\mathbf{x}$. The derivative of a scalar function with respect to a vector is also termed the *gradient* operation. The partial derivative of a vector $\mathbf{y}$ with respect to a vector $\mathbf{x}$ is

$$\frac{\partial \mathbf{y}}{\partial \mathbf{x}} = \begin{bmatrix} \dfrac{\partial y_1}{\partial \mathbf{x}} \\[2mm] \dfrac{\partial y_2}{\partial \mathbf{x}} \\[2mm] \vdots \\[2mm] \dfrac{\partial y_m}{\partial \mathbf{x}} \end{bmatrix} = \begin{bmatrix} \dfrac{\partial y_1}{\partial x_1} & \dfrac{\partial y_1}{\partial x_2} & \cdots & \dfrac{\partial y_1}{\partial x_n} \\[2mm] \dfrac{\partial y_2}{\partial x_1} & \dfrac{\partial y_2}{\partial x_2} & \cdots & \dfrac{\partial y_2}{\partial x_n} \\[2mm] \vdots & & & \\[2mm] \dfrac{\partial y_m}{\partial x_1} & \dfrac{\partial y_m}{\partial x_2} & \cdots & \dfrac{\partial y_m}{\partial x_n} \end{bmatrix}$$

The partial derivative of a scalar function $f$ with respect to an $n \times n$ matrix

$$A = [a_1 \mid a_2 \mid \cdots \mid a_m]$$

is

$$\frac{\partial f}{\partial A} = \begin{bmatrix} \dfrac{\partial f}{\partial a_1} \\ \dfrac{\partial f}{\partial a_2} \\ \vdots \\ \dfrac{\partial f}{\partial a_m} \end{bmatrix} = \begin{bmatrix} \dfrac{\partial f}{\partial a_{11}} & \dfrac{\partial f}{\partial a_{21}} & \cdots & \dfrac{\partial f}{\partial a_{n1}} \\ \dfrac{\partial f}{\partial a_{12}} & \dfrac{\partial f}{\partial a_{22}} & \cdots & \dfrac{\partial f}{\partial a_{n2}} \\ \vdots \\ \dfrac{\partial f}{\partial a_{1m}} & \dfrac{\partial f}{\partial a_{2m}} & \cdots & \dfrac{\partial f}{\partial a_{nm}} \end{bmatrix}$$

Some important properties of derivatives involving matrices are listed in Table 1-1. It is assumed that each of the variables involved in the partial derivatives are independent of one another.

The determinant of a square matrix $A$, denoted $|A|$, is uniquely defined by the three properties listed in Table 1-2. Important further properties that follow from the defining ones are also listed in the table. The determinant of a $2 \times 2$ matrix is

$$\begin{vmatrix} a_{11} & a_{12} \\ a_{21} & a_{22} \end{vmatrix} = a_{11}a_{22} - a_{12}a_{21}$$

Determinants of square matrices of larger dimension can be found by manipulation, using these properties, or by expanding the determinant of a larger matrix into determinants of smaller matrices.

The $i$th row, $j$th column *minor* of a matrix, $|M_{ij}|$, is the determinant of the matrix formed by deleting the $i$th row and the $j$th column of the original matrix. The $i$th row, $j$th column *cofactor* of a matrix, $|A_{ij}|$, is the same as the minor $|M_{ij}|$ except for a possible difference in algebraic sign:

$$|A_{ij}| = (-1)^{i+j}|M_{ij}|$$

Cofactors are used in Laplace's expansion, which is a systematic method of finding the value of a determinant. In Laplace expansion, a determinant is expressed in terms of cofactors. The cofactors involve determinants of smaller dimension than the original matrix and their values in turn can be expressed in terms of *their* cofactors, and so on until the result is in terms of determinants of small matrices. A determinant can be Laplace-expanded along any row or along any column. If it is expanded along the $i$th row, then

**TABLE 1-1    Some Properties of Matrix Derivatives**

### Derivative of a Matrix With Respect to a Scalar

**A.** $\dfrac{d}{dt}(k\mathbf{A}) = k\dfrac{d\mathbf{A}}{dt} + \dfrac{dk}{dt}\mathbf{A},$   if $k$ is a scalar

$\dfrac{\partial}{\partial t}(k\mathbf{A}) = k\dfrac{\partial \mathbf{A}}{\partial t} + \dfrac{\partial k}{\partial t}\mathbf{A},$   if $k$ is a scalar

**B.** $\dfrac{d}{dt}(\mathbf{A} + \mathbf{B}) = \dfrac{d\mathbf{A}}{dt} + \dfrac{d\mathbf{B}}{dt}$

$\dfrac{\partial}{\partial t}(\mathbf{A} + \mathbf{B}) = \dfrac{\partial \mathbf{A}}{\partial t} + \dfrac{\partial \mathbf{B}}{\partial t}$

**C.** $\dfrac{d}{dt}(\mathbf{AB}) = \dfrac{d\mathbf{A}}{dt}\mathbf{B} + \mathbf{A}\dfrac{d\mathbf{B}}{dt}$

$\dfrac{\partial}{\partial t}(\mathbf{AB}) = \dfrac{\partial \mathbf{A}}{\partial t}\mathbf{B} + \mathbf{A}\dfrac{\partial \mathbf{B}}{\partial t}$

### Derivative of a Scalar With Respect to a Vector

**D.** $\dfrac{\partial}{\partial \mathbf{x}}(\mathbf{x}^\dagger \mathbf{y}) = \dfrac{\partial}{\partial \mathbf{x}}(\mathbf{y}^\dagger \mathbf{x}) = \mathbf{y}^\dagger$

**E.** $\dfrac{\partial}{\partial \mathbf{x}}(\mathbf{x}^\dagger \mathbf{A}\mathbf{x}) = \mathbf{x}^\dagger \mathbf{A}^\dagger + \mathbf{x}^\dagger \mathbf{A}$

### Derivative of a Vector With Respect to a Vector

**F.** $\dfrac{\partial}{\partial \mathbf{x}}(\mathbf{A}\mathbf{x}) = \mathbf{A}$

### Derivative of a Scalar With Respect to a Matrix

**G.** $\dfrac{\partial}{\partial \mathbf{A}}[\text{trace }(\mathbf{BA})] = \mathbf{B}$

## TABLE 1-2 Properties of Determinants

### Defining Properties

**A.** $|\mathbf{A}|$ is unchanged if the elements of any row (or column) are replaced by the sums of the elements of that row (column) and the corresponding ones of another row (column).

**B.** The value of the determinant is multiplied by $k$ if all of the elements of any row or column are each multiplied by a scalar $k$.

**C.** The determinant of an identity matrix is unity.

### Further Properties

These further properties of determinants follow from the defining properties:

**D.** $|\mathbf{A}|$ is unchanged if the elements of any row (or column) are replaced by the sums of each of these elements with any number times the corresponding elements of another row (column).

**E.** The algebraic sign of $|\mathbf{A}|$ is reversed if any two rows or columns are interchanged.

**F.** $|\mathbf{A}| = 0$ if all elements of a row or column are zero or if the corresponding elements of any two rows or columns are identical or have a common ratio.

**G.** The determinant of a diagonal matrix is the product of the diagonal elements.

**H.** $|\mathbf{A}^{t}| = |\mathbf{A}|$

---

$$|\mathbf{A}| = a_{i1}|\mathbf{A}_{i1}| + a_{i2}|\mathbf{A}_{i2}| + \cdots + a_{in}|\mathbf{A}_{in}| = \sum_{j=1}^{n} a_{ij}|\mathbf{A}_{ij}|$$

Expansion along the $j$th column is similar:

$$|\mathbf{A}| = a_{1j}|\mathbf{A}_{1j}| + a_{2j}|\mathbf{A}_{2j}| + \cdots + a_{nj}|\mathbf{A}_{nj}| = \sum_{i=1}^{n} a_{ij}|\mathbf{A}_{ij}|$$

If $\mathbf{A}$ and $\mathbf{B}$ are each square and of the same dimensions, then

$$|\mathbf{AB}| = |\mathbf{A}||\mathbf{B}|$$

as can be verified by comparing the Laplace expansions of each side. In general, for $\mathbf{A}, \mathbf{B}, \ldots, \mathbf{P}, \mathbf{Q}$, all $n \times n$,

$$|\mathbf{AB} \ldots \mathbf{PQ}| = |\mathbf{A}||\mathbf{B}| \ldots |\mathbf{P}||\mathbf{Q}|$$

The rank of a matrix, denoted by rank($\mathbf{A}$) is the dimension of the largest square array having nonzero determinant within the matrix $\mathbf{A}$ formed by deleting rows and/or columns as necessary. A matrix of the largest possible rank for its dimension is said to be of *full rank*. A matrix $\mathbf{A}$ and its transpose have the same rank:

$$\text{rank}(\mathbf{A}^\dagger) = \text{rank}(\mathbf{A})$$

A square matrix $\mathbf{A}$ that is not of full rank has $|\mathbf{A}| = 0$ and is said to be *singular*.

## 1.3.2 Linear Algebraic Equations

We now review the properties of linear algebraic equations and the use of matrices to represent them. A set of $m$ simultaneous linear algebraic equations in the $n$ variables $x_1, x_2, \ldots, x_n$ has the form

$$\begin{cases} a_{11}x_1 + a_{12}x_2 + \cdots + a_{1n}x_n = y_1 \\ a_{21}x_1 + a_{22}x_2 + \cdots + a_{2n}x_n = y_2 \\ \vdots \\ a_{m1}x_1 + a_{m2}x_2 + \cdots + a_{mn}x_n = y_m \end{cases} \tag{1-2}$$

where the $a$'s are the *coefficients* of the equations. The left side of each equation is referred to as the "unknowns" side; it involves the $x$'s which are the "unknowns." The right side is the "knowns" side and consists of the $y$'s, which are the "knowns." A set of variables $(x_1, x_2, \ldots, x_n)$, satisfying all of the equations is a *solution* of the equations. A set of equations might have no solution, as is the case for the set

$$\begin{cases} x_1 + 2x_2 = 4 \\ 3x_1 + 6x_2 = -5 \end{cases}$$

It might have a unique solution, as does

$$\begin{cases} x_1 + x_2 = 1 \\ 2x_1 - x_2 = 8 \end{cases}$$

Or, a set may have numerous solutions, as does

$$\begin{cases} x_1 + 3x_2 = 4 \\ -2x_1 - 6x_2 = -8 \end{cases}$$

One method of solving a set of linear algebraic equations is to replace the original set of equations with a new set that has the same solution but is simpler than the original set. Any equation in a set can be replaced by the sum of that equation and a nonzero constant times any other equation in the set. The new set of equations is equivalent to the original set; that is, it has the same solution(s).

*Gauss-Jordan pivoting* is a systematic procedure for obtaining a simplest set of equivalent algebraic equations. Multiples of one equation in the set are added to each other equation in the set to make the coefficients of the first variable in the other equations zero. The equation used to eliminate terms in the other equations is called the *pivot equation* for this *pivot cycle*. Then another equation (the next pivot equation) is selected and multiples of that equation are added to each other equation to make the coefficients of the second variable in all other equations zero. The second pivot cycle is then complete. The process is continued until all equations have been used as pivots or until each variable has been eliminated from all but one equation, or both.

An equation

$$a_{11}x_1 + a_{12}x_2 + \cdots + a_{1n}x_n = y_1 \tag{1-3}$$

is *linearly dependent* on other equations

$$a_{21}x_1 + a_{22}x_2 + \cdots + a_{2n}x_n = y_2$$
$$a_{31}x_1 + a_{32}x_2 + \cdots + a_{3n}x_n = y_3$$
$$\vdots$$
$$a_{m1}x_1 + a_{m2}x_2 + \cdots + a_{mn}x_n = y_m \tag{1-4}$$

if it can be expressed as a linear combination of the other equations:

$$a_{11}x_1 + a_{12}x_2 + \cdots + a_{1n}x_n$$
$$= k_1(a_{21}x_1 + a_{22}x_2 + \cdots + a_{2n}x_n)$$
$$+ k_2(a_{31}x_1 + a_{32}x_2 + \cdots + a_{3n}x_n)$$
$$+ \cdots + k_{m-1}(a_{m1}x_1 + a_{m2}x_2 + \cdots + a_{mn}x_n) \tag{1-5}$$

and

$$y_1 = k_1 y_2 + k_2 y_3 + \cdots + k_{m-1} y_m \tag{1-6}$$

for some constants $k_1, k_2, \ldots, k_{m-1}$. A linearly dependent equation is redundant and can be deleted from a set of equations without affecting any solution. Indeed, it is highly desirable to make such deletions to simplify the set of equations and to place the set in a nonredundant form. A linearly dependent equation is indicated by an equation with an entire row of zero coefficients and a zero "known" after Gauss-Jordan pivoting.

Equation (1-3) is said to be *inconsistent* with other equations (1-4) if the "unknowns" side of that equation can be expressed as a linear combination of the "unknowns" sides of the other equations, as in equation (1-5), but the same linear combination on the "knowns" side (1-6) is *not* equal:

$$y_1 \neq k_1 y_2 + k_2 y_3 + \cdots + k_{m-1} y_m$$

The presence of one or more inconsistent equations in a set means that the set has no solution. Inconsistent equations are indicated by an equation with an entire row of zero coefficients and a nonzero "known" after Gauss-Jordan pivoting.

A set of *homogeneous* equations, a set with all the "knowns" zero,

$$\begin{cases} a_{11}x_1 + a_{21}x_2 + \cdots + a_{1n}x_n = 0 \\ a_{21}x_1 + a_{22}x_2 + \cdots + a_{2n}x_n = 0 \\ \vdots \\ a_{m1}x_1 + a_{m2}x_2 + \cdots + a_{mn}x_n = 0 \end{cases}$$

cannot be inconsistent since any linear combination of elements on the "knowns" side always gives zero. Another way of viewing this result is that for homogeneous equations, there is always the *trivial solution*

$$\begin{cases} x_1 = 0 \\ x_2 = 0 \\ \vdots \\ x_n = 0 \end{cases}$$

There might be other *nontrivial* solutions as well.

Suppose a set of linear algebraic equations is consistent and suppose that any linearly dependent equations have been deleted so that the set consists entirely of linearly independent equations. If there are $n$ variables, the set cannot consist of more than $n$ linearly independent equations because those equations in excess of $n$ equations can be shown, using pivoting, to be linearly dependent on the others. If there are exactly $n$ equations in the set, there is a *unique* solution to the set. If, instead, there are less than $n$ equations, the set has a whole family of different solutions. If there are $(n - p)$ linearly independent equations in the set, the solutions can be found by assigning arbitrary values to $p$ of the variables and solving the resulting $(n - p)$ linearly independent equations in $(n - p)$ variables. For example, in the set of equations

$$\begin{cases} x_1 + x_2 & = \ \ \ 2 \\ x_1 - x_2 & = -3 \\ \quad\ \ x_2 - x_3 + x_4 = \ \ \ 0 \end{cases}$$

the variables $x_1$ and $x_2$ are determined by the first two equations, but either of the variables $x_3$ or $x_4$ can be assigned an arbitrary value.

A set of $m$ equations in $n$ variables as in equation (1-2) is written in matrix notation as

$$\mathbf{Ax} = \mathbf{y}$$

Matrix notation is useful because it saves a lot of writing and because it greatly simplifies descriptions of equation manipulations.

When a unique solution exists to a set of $n$ linear algebraic equations in $n$ variables

$$\mathbf{Ax} = \mathbf{y}$$

where $\mathbf{A}$ is $n \times n$, it is given by *Cramer's rule*. The solution for the $i$th variable is

$$x_i = \frac{|\mathbf{A}_i|}{|\mathbf{A}|}$$

where the $i$th row *cofactor* $|\mathbf{A}_i|$ is the same as $|\mathbf{A}|$ except that the $i$th column is replaced by the column of "knowns."

Because some pairs of matrices are not conformable for multiplication and because, when they are conformable, the order in which two matrices are multiplied generally makes a difference to the product, matrix division is not defined. Instead, for square matrices with nonzero determinants, the *inverse* matrix is used. The product of a matrix with its inverse is an identity matrix:

$$\mathbf{AA}^{-1} = \mathbf{I} \tag{1-7}$$

The inverse of a matrix can be found by using Cramer's rule to solve (1-7), obtaining

$$\mathbf{A}^{-1} = \frac{1}{|\mathbf{A}|} \begin{bmatrix} |\mathbf{A}_{11}| & |\mathbf{A}_{21}| & \cdots & |\mathbf{A}_{n1}| \\ |\mathbf{A}_{12}| & |\mathbf{A}_{22}| & \cdots & |\mathbf{A}_{n2}| \\ \vdots & & & \\ |\mathbf{A}_{1n}| & |\mathbf{A}_{2n}| & \cdots & |\mathbf{A}_{nn}| \end{bmatrix} = \frac{\text{adj. } \mathbf{A}}{|\mathbf{A}|}$$

The *adjugate* (or *adjoint*) of a square matrix $\mathbf{A}$, denoted by adj $\mathbf{A}$, is the transpose of the matrix where each element of $\mathbf{A}$ is replaced by its cofactor. If $|\mathbf{A}| = 0$, $\mathbf{A}^{-1}$ does not exist and the matrix $\mathbf{A}$ is *singular*. Some properties of inverse matrices are listed in Table 1-3.

Integer powers of a square matrix are defined according to

$$\mathbf{A}^i = \underbrace{\mathbf{A} \cdots \mathbf{A}}_{i\,\text{terms}}$$

The additional definitions

$$\mathbf{A}^0 = \mathbf{I}$$

and, (providing $\mathbf{A}$ is nonsingular)

$$\mathbf{A}^{-i} = \underbrace{(\mathbf{A}^{-1})(\mathbf{A}^{-1}) \cdots (\mathbf{A}^{-1})}_{i\,\text{terms}}$$

## TABLE 1-3 Properties of Inverse Matrices

### Defining Property

A. $\mathbf{A}\,\mathbf{A}^{-1} = \mathbf{I}$

### Further Properties

These properties follow from the defining property:

B. $\mathbf{A}^{-1}\,\mathbf{A} = \mathbf{I}$
C. $\mathbf{I}^{-1} = \mathbf{I}$
D. $[\mathbf{A}^{-1}]^{-1} = \mathbf{A}$
E. $[\mathbf{A}^{-1}]^{\dagger} = [\mathbf{A}^{\dagger}]^{-1}$
F. The inverse of a nonsingular diagonal matrix $\mathbf{D}$ is diagonal. It has diagonal elements that are the reciprocals of the diagonal elements of $\mathbf{D}$
G. $(k\mathbf{A})^{-1} = \dfrac{1}{k}\mathbf{A}^{-1}$  for $k$ a nonzero scalar
H. $(\mathbf{AB})^{-1} = \mathbf{B}^{-1}\mathbf{A}^{-1}$, provided that $\mathbf{A}$ and $\mathbf{B}$ are each square and nonsingular.

   Applying this result repeatedly

$$(\mathbf{AB}\dots\mathbf{PQ})^{-1} = \mathbf{Q}^{-1}\mathbf{P}^{-1}\dots\mathbf{B}^{-1}\mathbf{A}^{-1}$$

I. $\dfrac{d}{dt}(\mathbf{A}^{-1}) = -\mathbf{A}^{-1}\dfrac{d\mathbf{A}}{dt}\mathbf{A}^{-1}$

are useful to make, so that

$$\mathbf{A}^{i_1}\mathbf{A}^{i_2} = \mathbf{A}^{(i_1+i_2)}$$

for all integers $i_1$ and $i_2$. A matrix polynomial is a function of a square matrix $\mathbf{A}$ of the form

$$\mathbf{F}(\mathbf{A}) = c_0\mathbf{I} + c_1\mathbf{A} + c_2\mathbf{A}^2 + c_3\mathbf{A}^3 + \cdots$$

where $c_1, c_2, c_3, \ldots$, are scalars. If there is a finite number of terms in the polynomial, the polynomial is said to be finite. Otherwise, it is an infinite polynomial.

### 1.3.3 Vectors and Transformations

Solutions to linear equations are represented by vectors, as are many other quantities of special importance in linear algebra. Assignment of scalar size to each vector $\mathbf{x}$ in a set is termed a vector *norm*, denoted by $\|\mathbf{x}\|$, and required to have the four properties listed in Table 1-4. The most commonly used norm is the *Euclidean norm*, which for real vector elements $x_1, x_2, \ldots, x_n$ is the vector magnitude or length:

$$\|\mathbf{x}\| = \sqrt{x_1^2 + x_2^2 + \cdots + x_n^2} = \sqrt{\mathbf{x}^\dagger\mathbf{x}}$$

Norms other than the Euclidean norm find occasional uses. One possibility is the sum of the magnitudes of the elements of $\mathbf{x}$. Another is the maximum of the magnitudes of the elements of $\mathbf{x}$. Hereafter, as is common usage, the term *norm* will mean Euclidean norm unless otherwise noted. If the norm of a vector is unity, the vector is called a *unit vector*.

An *inner product* assigns a scalar measure of closeness in direction of two vectors of the same dimension. For two vectors $\mathbf{x}$ and $\mathbf{y}$, the inner product is denoted by $\langle \mathbf{x}, \mathbf{y} \rangle$ and is a scalar function of the elements of the two vectors. It is required to have the four properties listed in Table 1-5. The most

**TABLE 1-4   Requirements of a Vector Norm**

**A.** $\|\mathbf{x}\| > 0$   for $\mathbf{x} \neq 0$
**B.** $\|\mathbf{x}\| = 0$   for $\mathbf{x} = 0$
**C.** $\|k\mathbf{x}\| = |k|\mathbf{Ex}\|$   for any scalar $k$
**D.** $\|\mathbf{x}\| + \|\mathbf{y}\| \geq \|\mathbf{x} + \mathbf{y}\|$ (triangle inequality)

**TABLE 1-5    Requirements of a Vector Inner Product**

**A.** $\langle \mathbf{y}, \mathbf{x} \rangle = \langle \mathbf{x}, \mathbf{y} \rangle^*$    where * denotes the complex conjugate
**B.** $\langle k\mathbf{x}, \mathbf{y} \rangle = k^* \langle \mathbf{x}, \mathbf{y} \rangle = \langle \mathbf{x}, k^* \mathbf{y} \rangle$    where $k$ is a scalar
**C.** $\langle \mathbf{x}, \mathbf{x} \rangle > 0$    for    $x \neq 0$
**D.** $\langle \mathbf{x} + \mathbf{u}, \mathbf{y} + \mathbf{v} \rangle = \langle \mathbf{x}, \mathbf{y} \rangle + \langle \mathbf{x}, \mathbf{v} \rangle + \langle \mathbf{u}, \mathbf{y} \rangle + \langle \mathbf{u}, \mathbf{v} \rangle$

commonly used inner product is the Euclidean inner product, which for real vector elements is

$$\langle \mathbf{x}, \mathbf{y} \rangle = \mathbf{x}^\dagger \mathbf{y} = x_1 y_1 + x_2 y_2 + \cdots + x_n y_n$$

While other inner products are sometimes useful, the term *inner product* ordinarily means the Euclidean inner product unless otherwise noted.

Two vectors of nonzero norm, $\mathbf{x}$ and $\mathbf{y}$, are *orthogonal* if

$$\langle \mathbf{x}, \mathbf{y} \rangle = 0$$

Orthogonality is the same as perpendicularity for vectors with real elements when the inner product used is the usual Euclidean one. For example, the 3-vectors

$$\mathbf{x} = \begin{bmatrix} 1 \\ -1 \\ 0 \end{bmatrix} \quad \mathbf{y} = \begin{bmatrix} 1 \\ 1 \\ 0 \end{bmatrix} \quad \text{and} \quad \mathbf{z} = \begin{bmatrix} 0 \\ 0 \\ 3 \end{bmatrix}$$

are *mutually orthogonal,* since

$$\begin{cases} \langle \mathbf{x}, \mathbf{y} \rangle = \mathbf{x}^\dagger \mathbf{y} = 0 \\ \langle \mathbf{x}, \mathbf{z} \rangle = \mathbf{x}^\dagger \mathbf{z} = 0 \\ \langle \mathbf{y}, \mathbf{z} \rangle = \mathbf{y}^\dagger \mathbf{z} = 0 \end{cases}$$

It is occasionally convenient to introduce superscript indices on vector symbols. Since $x_i$ is used to denote the $i$th element of the vector $\mathbf{x}$, a superscript, for example $\mathbf{x}^j$, is used to indicate the $j$th vector in some set of vectors. There is no conflict with the notation for an exponent here because a vector is not conformable for multiplication with itself. A set of $m$ vectors, $\mathbf{x}^1$, $\mathbf{x}^2, \ldots, \mathbf{x}^m$, is said to be *linearly independent* if there are no scalars $k_1, k_2, \ldots,$ $k_m$ except all $k$'s zero for which

$$k_1 \mathbf{x}^1 + k_2 \mathbf{x}^2 + \cdots + k_m \mathbf{x}^m = \mathbf{0}$$

Otherwise, the set of vectors is *linearly dependent*. Linear independence means that no vector in the set is a linear combination of the other vectors in the set. No more than $n$ $n$-vectors can be linearly independent of one another. A set of $n$ linearly independent $n$-vectors can always be found; for example the *unit coordinate vectors*

$$\mathbf{i}_1 = \begin{bmatrix} 1 \\ 0 \\ 0 \\ \vdots \\ 0 \\ 0 \end{bmatrix} \quad \mathbf{i}_2 = \begin{bmatrix} 0 \\ 1 \\ 0 \\ \vdots \\ 0 \\ 0 \end{bmatrix} \quad \cdots \quad \mathbf{i}_n = \begin{bmatrix} 0 \\ 0 \\ 0 \\ \vdots \\ 0 \\ 1 \end{bmatrix}$$

are obviously linearly independent. Any set of $n$-linearly independent $n$-vectors is said to form a *basis* for the $n$ dimensional space of all $n$-vectors, and any $n$-vector can be expressed as a unique linear combination of a set of basis vectors.

In a set of linear algebraic equations

$$\mathbf{Ax} = \mathbf{y}$$

one may think of the rows of $\mathbf{A}$ as vectors:

$$\mathbf{A} = \begin{bmatrix} \mathbf{a}_1^\dagger \\ \hline \mathbf{a}_2^\dagger \\ \hline \vdots \\ \hline \mathbf{a}_m^\dagger \end{bmatrix}$$

A solution $\mathbf{x}$ then has the property

$$\begin{cases} \langle \mathbf{a}_1, \mathbf{x} \rangle = \mathbf{a}_1^\dagger \mathbf{x} = y_1 \\ \langle \mathbf{a}_2, \mathbf{x} \rangle = \mathbf{a}_2^\dagger \mathbf{x} = y_2 \\ \vdots \\ \langle \mathbf{a}_m, \mathbf{x} \rangle = \mathbf{a}_m^\dagger \mathbf{x} = y_m \end{cases} \tag{1-8}$$

That is, the inner products of $\mathbf{x}$ with each of the vectors $\mathbf{a}_1, \mathbf{a}_2, \ldots, \mathbf{a}_m$ are $y_1, y_2, \ldots, y_m$.

For a set of homogeneous equations

$$\mathbf{Ax} = \mathbf{0} \tag{1-9}$$

relation (1-8) with $\mathbf{y} = \mathbf{0}$ shows that a nontrivial solution $\mathbf{x}$, if it exists, is orthogonal to each of the vectors $\mathbf{a}_1, \mathbf{a}_2, \ldots, \mathbf{a}_m$. As no more than $n$ $n$-vectors can be linearly independent, if there are $n$ linearly independent $n$-vectors among the $\mathbf{a}$'s, that is, if the rank of $\mathbf{A}$ is $n$, the trivial solution

$$\mathbf{x} = \mathbf{0}$$

is the only possible solution of (1-9). If there are not $n$ linearly independent $n$-vectors among the $\mathbf{a}$'s, then a nontrivial solution for $\mathbf{x}$ exists because it is always possible to find an $n$-vector that is orthogonal to less than $n$ different $n$-vectors. The norm of any nontrivial solution is arbitrary since its only requirement is that it must be orthogonal to each of the $\mathbf{a}$'s. If only $n - p$ of the rows of $\mathbf{A}$ are linearly independent, that is, if $\mathbf{A}$ is of rank $n - p$, then $p$ linearly independent $n$-vectors can be found that are orthogonal to each of the rows of $\mathbf{A}$.

Linear transformations are of special importance in the analysis of many problems because the description of system properties is often greatly simplified by judicious choice of a coordinate system. What a tremendous simplification the simple change in coordinates attributed to Copernicus was! The multiplication of a vector $\mathbf{x}$ by a square matrix to form another vector $\mathbf{y}$,

$$\mathbf{Ax} = \mathbf{y}$$

can be thought of as a transformation that converts the vector $\mathbf{x}$ to the vector $\mathbf{y}$. The transformation is linear because it always maps any scaled vector $\mathbf{x}$ to the $\mathbf{y}$ vector scaled by the same factor

$$\mathbf{A}(k\mathbf{x}) = (k\mathbf{y})$$

and sums of vectors map to the corresponding sums of individual results. If

$$\mathbf{Ax}^1 = \mathbf{y}^1 \qquad \text{and} \qquad \mathbf{Ax}^2 = \mathbf{y}^2$$

then

$$\mathbf{A}(\mathbf{x}^1 + \mathbf{x}^2) = \mathbf{y}^1 + \mathbf{y}^2$$

If the matrix $\mathbf{A}$ is square and nonsingular, the vector $\mathbf{x}$ can be recovered from $\mathbf{y}$ through

$$\mathbf{x} = \mathbf{A}^{-1}\mathbf{y}$$

Each possible vector $\mathbf{x}$ is transformed to a unique vector $\mathbf{y}$ by a nonsingular

$n \times n$ transformation $\mathbf{A}$, and each $\mathbf{y}$ corresponds to a unique $\mathbf{x}$. If, instead, the rank of $\mathbf{A}$ is $m < n$ so that just $m$ of the rows of $\mathbf{A}$ are linearly independent, then the space of possible vectors $\mathbf{y}$ is $m$-dimensional. This space is called the *range space* of $\mathbf{A}$. A basis for the range space of $\mathbf{A}$ is a largest set of linearly independent *columns* of $\mathbf{A}$:

$$\mathbf{A} = [\mathbf{c}_1 \mid \mathbf{c}_2 \mid \cdots \mid \mathbf{c}_n]$$

since a general vector $\mathbf{x}$ maps to

$$\mathbf{y} = x_1\mathbf{c}_1 + x_2\mathbf{c}_2 + \cdots + x_n\mathbf{c}_n$$

If the matrix $\mathbf{A}$ of a linear transformation is not of full rank, different vectors $\mathbf{x}$ are transformed to the same vector $\mathbf{y}$. The space of vectors $\mathbf{x}$ for which

$$\mathbf{A}\mathbf{x} = \mathbf{0} \tag{1-10}$$

is called the *null space* of the matrix $\mathbf{A}$. Any vector $\mathbf{x}^0$ in this space can be added to any vector $\mathbf{x}$ with no effect on the resulting $\mathbf{y}$:

$$\mathbf{y} = \mathbf{A}\mathbf{x} = \mathbf{A}(\mathbf{x} + \mathbf{x}^0)$$

A basis for the null space of $\mathbf{A}$ is a largest set of linearly independent vectors $\mathbf{x}$ satisfying equation (1-10).

If a matrix $\mathbf{A}$, which need not be square, is premultiplied or postmultiplied by a square nonsingular matrix $\mathbf{Q}$, the rank of the product is the same as the rank of $\mathbf{A}$. If the matrix $\mathbf{A}$ is taken to be the coefficient matrix for a set of homogeneous equations

$$\mathbf{A}\mathbf{x} = \mathbf{0}$$

the rank of $\mathbf{A}$ is the number of linearly independent equations in the set. Postmultiplication of $\mathbf{A}$ by a conformable, nonsingular matrix $\mathbf{Q}$ can be interpreted as a change of variables

$$\mathbf{x} = \mathbf{Q}\mathbf{x}'$$
$$\mathbf{A}\mathbf{x} = (\mathbf{A}\mathbf{Q})\mathbf{x}' = \mathbf{0}$$

in the equations. Since the old variables can be recovered from the new ones through

$$\mathbf{x}' = \mathbf{Q}^{-1}\mathbf{x}$$

the change of variables cannot change the intrinsic number of linearly independent equations in the set. Premultiplication by a nonsingular matrix leaves the rank unchanged, too.

# 1.4 Continuous-Time State Equations

State variable (or *state space*) descriptions of systems provide an important means of efficiently describing and dealing with complex systems. They give standard representations that offer economy of notation, direct applicability of matrix algebra, and ease of entry for computer-aided design. They are also well suited for extensions to time-varying and nonlinear systems.

In this section, we review the fundamentals of state variables for linear, time-invariant continuous-time systems with an eye toward carrying these over to the discrete-time case in Chapter 3 and to later using these results in designing digital controllers for continuous-time systems.

## 1.4.1 Integration Diagrams and State Equations

Continuous-time state variable descriptions are mathematical models of systems in terms of coupled first-order differential equations. The signals involved are the system inputs, the system outputs, and internal signals. The internal signals are the state variables. For linear, time-invariant, continuous-time systems, state variable models involve the operations of summation,

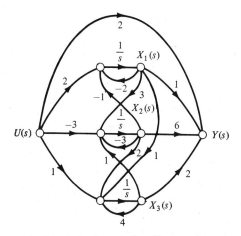

**FIGURE 1-6.  Integration diagram in terms of Laplace transforms.**

multiplication by a constant, and integration. A block diagram or signal flow graph representing a state variable model is called an *integration diagram* (or a *simulation diagram*). The output of each integrator is a state variable, and the order of the system is the number of integrators, which is the number of state variables. The diagram is arranged so that the input to each integrator is a linear combination of the system inputs and the state variables. Each system output is also a linear combination of the system inputs and the state variables.

Figure 1-6 shows an example of an integration diagram, in signal flow graph form in terms of Laplace transformed signals, for a single-input, single-output system. For this system, there are three integrators, so the system represented is third-order. The internal system signals, the state variables, are the integrator outputs, and the integrator inputs are each a linear combination of the state variables and the external input, $U(s)$. From the diagram, the three Laplace transformed *state equations* for this system are

$$\begin{cases} X_1(s) = \dfrac{1}{s}[-2X_1(s) - X_2(s) + 2U(s)] \\[2mm] X_2(s) = \dfrac{1}{s}[3X_1(s) - 3X_2(s) + X_3(s) - 3U(s)] \\[2mm] X_3(s) = \dfrac{1}{s}[X_1(s) + 2X_2(s) + 4X_3(s) + U(s)] \end{cases}$$

or

$$\begin{cases} sX_1(s) = -2X_1(s) - X_2(s) + 2U(s) \\ sX_2(s) = 3X_1(s) - 3X_2(s) + X_3(s) - 3U(s) \\ sX_3(s) = X_1(s) + 2X_2(s) + 4X_3(s) + U(s) \end{cases}$$

which, as functions of time, are

$$\begin{cases} \dfrac{dx_1}{dt} = -2x_1(t) - x_2(t) + 2u(t) \\[2mm] \dfrac{dx_2}{dt} = 3x_1(t) - 3x_2(t) + x_3(t) - 3u(t) \\[2mm] \dfrac{dx_3}{dt} = x_1(t) + 2x_2(t) + 4x_3(t) + u(t) \end{cases}$$

In matrix form:

$$\begin{bmatrix} \dot{x}_1(t) \\ \dot{x}_2(t) \\ \dot{x}_3(t) \end{bmatrix} = \begin{bmatrix} -2 & -1 & 0 \\ 3 & -3 & 1 \\ 1 & 2 & 4 \end{bmatrix} \begin{bmatrix} x_1(t) \\ x_2(t) \\ x_3(t) \end{bmatrix} + \begin{bmatrix} 2 \\ -3 \\ 1 \end{bmatrix} u(t)$$

where the dot over the symbol for a function denotes differentiation with respect to time, $t$. The system's output is a linear combination of the state variables and the input

$$Y(s) = X_1(s) + 6X_2(s) + 2X_3(s) + 2U(s)$$

or

$$y(t) = x_1(t) + 6x_2(t) + 2x_3(t) + 2u(t)$$

In matrix form, the *output equation* for this system is

$$y(t) = \begin{bmatrix} 1 & 6 & 2 \end{bmatrix} \begin{bmatrix} x_1(t) \\ x_2(t) \\ x_3(t) \end{bmatrix} + 2u(t)$$

An integration diagram shows how the system can be constructed in hardware, with operational amplifiers connected to form scaled summations and integrals of signals, and in software, where the integration operations represent numerical integrations. Alternatively, integration diagrams can relate signals in the time domain rather than the transform domain, as in the block diagram of Figure 1-7. The collection of integrator outputs at time $t = 0$ is the initial state, $\mathbf{x}(0)$.

Even though the symbol $u$ is sometimes used to denote the unit step function, it is common practice to also use $u$ to represent inputs in state variable models. The ambiguity is easily resolved by context, and is preferable to using nonstandard notation.

Another integration diagram, a second-order one with multiple inputs and outputs, is shown in Figure 1-8. For this system, the state and output equations are

$$\begin{bmatrix} \dot{x}_1(t) \\ \dot{x}_2(t) \end{bmatrix} = \begin{bmatrix} -10 & -9 \\ 3 & 2 \end{bmatrix} \begin{bmatrix} x_1(t) \\ x_2(t) \end{bmatrix} + \begin{bmatrix} 1 & -2 & -5 \\ 3 & 1 & 0 \end{bmatrix} \begin{bmatrix} u_1(t) \\ u_2(t) \\ u_3(t) \end{bmatrix}$$

$$\begin{bmatrix} y_1(t) \\ y_2(t) \end{bmatrix} = \begin{bmatrix} 0 & 4 \\ -6 & 5 \end{bmatrix} \begin{bmatrix} x_1(t) \\ x_2(t) \end{bmatrix} + \begin{bmatrix} -4 & 0 & 0 \\ 0 & 0 & 7 \end{bmatrix} \begin{bmatrix} u_1(t) \\ u_2(t) \\ u_3(t) \end{bmatrix}$$

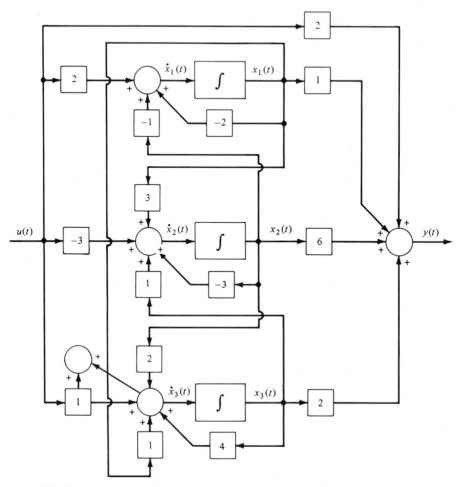

**FIGURE 1-7.** Integration diagram in terms of time-domain signals.

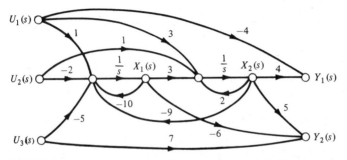

**FIGURE 1-8.** An integration diagram with multiple inputs and outputs.

In general, continuous-time state equations are of the form

$$
\begin{bmatrix} \dot{x}_1(t) \\ \dot{x}_2(t) \\ \vdots \\ \dot{x}_n(t) \end{bmatrix} = \begin{bmatrix} a_{11} & a_{12} & \cdots & a_{1n} \\ a_{21} & a_{22} & \cdots & a_{2n} \\ \vdots & & & \\ a_{n1} & a_{n2} & \cdots & a_{nn} \end{bmatrix} \begin{bmatrix} x_1(t) \\ x_2(t) \\ \vdots \\ x_n(t) \end{bmatrix} + \begin{bmatrix} b_{11} & b_{12} & \cdots & b_{1r} \\ b_{21} & b_{22} & \cdots & b_{2r} \\ \vdots & & & \\ b_{n1} & b_{n2} & \cdots & b_{nr} \end{bmatrix} \begin{bmatrix} u_1(t) \\ u_2(t) \\ \vdots \\ u_r(t) \end{bmatrix} \tag{1-11}
$$

or

$$
\dot{\mathbf{x}}(t) = \mathbf{A}\mathbf{x}(t) + \mathbf{B}\mathbf{u}(t) \tag{1-12}
$$

where the *state vector* $\mathbf{x}(t)$ is an $n$-vector, the *state coupling matrix* $\mathbf{A}$ is $n \times n$ the *input vector* $\mathbf{u}(t)$ is an $r$-vector of input signals, and the *input coupling matrix* $\mathbf{B}$ is $n \times r$. The order of the system is the dimension of the state vector, $n$. The general form of the output equations is

$$
\begin{bmatrix} y_1(t) \\ y_2(t) \\ \vdots \\ y_m(t) \end{bmatrix} = \begin{bmatrix} c_{11} & c_{12} & \cdots & c_{1n} \\ c_{21} & c_{22} & \cdots & c_{2n} \\ \vdots & & & \\ c_{m1} & c_{m2} & \cdots & c_{mn} \end{bmatrix} \begin{bmatrix} x_1(t) \\ x_2(t) \\ \vdots \\ x_n(t) \end{bmatrix} + \begin{bmatrix} d_{11} & d_{12} & \cdots & d_{1r} \\ d_{21} & d_{22} & \cdots & d_{2r} \\ \vdots & & & \vdots \\ d_{m1} & d_{m2} & \cdots & d_{mr} \end{bmatrix} \begin{bmatrix} u_1(t) \\ u_2(t) \\ \vdots \\ u_r(t) \end{bmatrix} \tag{1-13}
$$

or

$$
\mathbf{y}(t) = \mathbf{C}\mathbf{x}(t) + \mathbf{D}\mathbf{u}(t) \tag{1-14}
$$

where the *output vector* $\mathbf{y}(t)$ is an $m$-vector of output signals, the *output coupling matrix* $\mathbf{C}$ is $m \times n$, and the *input-to-output coupling matrix* $\mathbf{D}$ is $m \times r$.

A block diagram that shows how the input, output, and state vectors are related in general in a continuous-time state variable system is given in Figure 1-9. The wide arrows in that diagram represent vectors of signals.

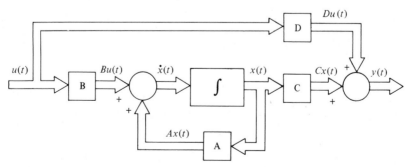

**FIGURE 1-9. Block diagram showing the relations between signal vectors in a continuous-time state variable model.**

## 1.4.2 Laplace Transformed Signals

The emphasis of state variable methods is on the time domain rather than a transform domain. However for linear, time-invariant systems, the Laplace transform helps relate state variables to classical concepts and gives easy derivations of important time domain results. When Laplace transformed, the state and output equations of a state variable system model, equations (1-11) and (1-13) or equations (1-12) and (1-14), become

$$
\begin{bmatrix} sX_1(s) \\ sX_2(s) \\ \vdots \\ sX_n(s) \end{bmatrix} - \begin{bmatrix} x_1(0^-) \\ x_2(0^-) \\ \vdots \\ x_n(0^-) \end{bmatrix} = \begin{bmatrix} a_{11} & a_{12} & \cdots & a_{1n} \\ a_{21} & a_{22} & \cdots & a_{2n} \\ & & \vdots & \\ a_{n1} & a_{n2} & \cdots & a_{nn} \end{bmatrix} \begin{bmatrix} X_1(s) \\ X_2(s) \\ \vdots \\ X_n(s) \end{bmatrix}
$$

$$
+ \begin{bmatrix} b_{11} & b_{12} & \cdots & b_{1r} \\ b_{21} & b_{22} & \cdots & b_{2r} \\ & & \vdots & \\ b_{n1} & b_{n2} & \cdots & b_{nr} \end{bmatrix} \begin{bmatrix} U_1(s) \\ U_2(s) \\ \vdots \\ U_r(s) \end{bmatrix}
$$

$$
\begin{bmatrix} Y_1(s) \\ Y_2(s) \\ \vdots \\ Y_m(s) \end{bmatrix} = \begin{bmatrix} c_{11} & c_{12} & \cdots & c_{1n} \\ c_{21} & c_{22} & \cdots & c_{2n} \\ & & \vdots & \\ c_{m1} & c_{m2} & \cdots & c_{mn} \end{bmatrix} \begin{bmatrix} X_1(s) \\ X_2(s) \\ \vdots \\ X_n(s) \end{bmatrix} + \begin{bmatrix} d_{11} & d_{12} & \cdots & d_{1r} \\ d_{21} & d_{22} & \cdots & d_{2r} \\ & & \vdots & \\ d_{m1} & d_{m2} & \cdots & d_{mr} \end{bmatrix} \begin{bmatrix} U_1(s) \\ U_2(s) \\ \vdots \\ U_r(s) \end{bmatrix}
$$

or

$$ sX(s) - x(0^-) = AX(s) + BU(s) $$

$$ Y(s) = CX(s) + DU(s) $$

Here, the initial conditions $x(0^-)$ have been included. Solving for the transform of the state vector gives

$$ (sI - A)X(s) = x(0^-) + BU(s) $$

$$ X(s) = \underbrace{(sI - A)^{-1}x(0^-)}_{\text{Zero-Input Component of State Vector}} + \underbrace{(sI - A)^{-1}BU(s)}_{\text{Zero-State Component of State Vector}} $$

where the zero-input and zero-state components of the state vector are evident. The zero-input component is the solution when the input is zero, and the zero-state component is the solution when the initial conditions are zero.

The transform of the system output is then

$$Y(s) = CX(s) + DU(s) = \underbrace{C(sI - A)^{-1}x(0^-)}_{\text{Zero-Input Component of Output}} + \underbrace{[C(sI - A)^{-1}B + D]U(s)}_{\text{Zero-State Component of Output}}$$

As a numerical example of finding signals in state variable models using Laplace transformation, consider the second order single-input, single-output system

$$\begin{bmatrix} \dot{x}_1(t) \\ \dot{x}_2(t) \end{bmatrix} = \begin{bmatrix} -7 & 1 \\ -12 & 0 \end{bmatrix} \begin{bmatrix} x_1(t) \\ x_2(t) \end{bmatrix} + \begin{bmatrix} 2 \\ -1 \end{bmatrix} u(t) = Ax(t) + bu(t)$$

$$y(t) = \begin{bmatrix} 3 & -4 \end{bmatrix} \begin{bmatrix} x_1(t) \\ x_2(t) \end{bmatrix} - 2u(t) = c^t x(t) + du(t)$$

The output coupling matrix $C$ is, in this case, a single row, which is represented as the transpose of a column vector $c$. The integration diagram for this system is shown in Figure 1-10(a). Let the system input be

$$u(t) = 3e^{-t}$$

and let the initial system state be

$$\begin{bmatrix} x_1(0^-) \\ x_2(0^-) \end{bmatrix} = \begin{bmatrix} -6 \\ 1 \end{bmatrix}$$

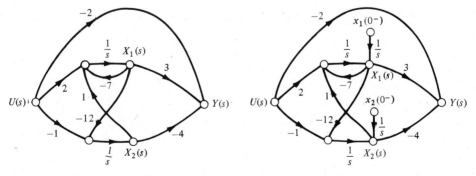

(a) Simulation diagram.        (b) Simulation diagram including initial conditions.

FIGURE 1-10.    Finding the response of a continuous-time state variable system.

The Laplace transformed state equations are

$$\begin{cases} sX_1(s) - x_1(0^-) = -7X_1(s) + X_2(s) + 2U(s) \\ sX_2(s) - x_2(0^-) = -12X_1(s) - U(s) \end{cases}$$

If desired, the initial conditions can be included as part of the integration diagram, as in Figure 1-10(b). In matrix form,

$$\begin{bmatrix} (s+7) & -1 \\ 12 & s \end{bmatrix} \begin{bmatrix} X_1(s) \\ X_2(s) \end{bmatrix} = \begin{bmatrix} x_1(0^-) \\ x_2(0^-) \end{bmatrix} + \begin{bmatrix} 2 \\ -1 \end{bmatrix} U(s)$$

or

$$(s\mathbf{I} - \mathbf{A})\mathbf{X}(s) = \mathbf{x}(0^-) + \mathbf{b}U(s)$$

The solution for the transform of the state vector is given by

$$\begin{bmatrix} X_1(s) \\ X_2(s) \end{bmatrix} = \begin{bmatrix} (s+7) & -1 \\ 12 & s \end{bmatrix}^{-1} \begin{bmatrix} x_1(0^-) \\ x_2(0^-) \end{bmatrix} + \begin{bmatrix} (s+7) & -1 \\ 12 & s \end{bmatrix}^{-1} \begin{bmatrix} 2 \\ -1 \end{bmatrix} U(s)$$

$$= \underbrace{\frac{\begin{bmatrix} s & 1 \\ -12 & (s+7) \end{bmatrix} \begin{bmatrix} -6 \\ 1 \end{bmatrix}}{s^2 + 7s + 12}}_{\text{Zero-Input Component of State Vector}} + \underbrace{\frac{\begin{bmatrix} s & 1 \\ -12 & (s+7) \end{bmatrix} \begin{bmatrix} 2 \\ -1 \end{bmatrix} \left( \dfrac{3}{s+1} \right)}{s^2 + 7s + 12}}_{\text{Zero-State Component of State Vector}}$$

$$= \begin{bmatrix} \dfrac{-6s^2 + s - 2}{(s+1)(s+3)(s+4)} \\ \dfrac{s^2 + 77s - 14}{(s+1)(s+3)(s+4)} \end{bmatrix}$$

which could be inverted to find $x_1(t)$ and $x_2(t)$. The system output has transform

$$Y(s) = \mathbf{c}^\dagger \mathbf{X}(s) + dU(s) = \begin{bmatrix} 3 & -4 \end{bmatrix} \begin{bmatrix} \dfrac{-6s^2 + s - 2}{(s+1)(s+3)(s+4)} \\ \dfrac{s^2 + 77s - 14}{(s+1)(s+3)(s+4)} \end{bmatrix} - 2 \left( \dfrac{3}{s+1} \right)$$

$$= \frac{-22s^2 - 305s + 50}{(s+1)(s+3)(s+4)} - \frac{6}{s+1} = \frac{\dfrac{297}{6}}{s+1} + \frac{\dfrac{767}{2}}{s+3} + \frac{\dfrac{918}{3}}{s+4}$$

so that

$$y(t) = \frac{297}{6} e^{-t} + \frac{-767}{2} e^{-3t} + \frac{918}{3} e^{-4t}, \quad t \geqslant 0$$

The transfer functions of a state variable system are found by expressing the Laplace transform of the output vector in terms of the Laplace transform of the input vector when the initial conditions are zero. Laplace transforming the state equations

$$\dot{\mathbf{x}}(t) = \mathbf{A}\mathbf{x}(t) + \mathbf{B}\mathbf{u}(t)$$

with zero initial conditions gives

$$s\mathbf{X}(s) = \mathbf{A}\mathbf{X}(s) + \mathbf{B}\mathbf{U}(s)$$

or

$$(s\mathbf{I} - \mathbf{A})\mathbf{X}(s) = \mathbf{B}\mathbf{U}(s)$$
$$\mathbf{X}(s) = (s\mathbf{I} - \mathbf{A})^{-1}\mathbf{B}\mathbf{U}(s)$$

Using

$$\mathbf{y}(t) = \mathbf{C}\mathbf{x}(t) + \mathbf{D}\mathbf{u}(t)$$

there results

$$\mathbf{Y}(s) = [\mathbf{C}(s\mathbf{I} - \mathbf{A})^{-1}\mathbf{B} + \mathbf{D}]\mathbf{U}(s)$$

The quantity

$$\mathbf{T}(s) = \mathbf{C}(s\mathbf{I} - \mathbf{A})^{-1}\mathbf{B} + \mathbf{D}$$

is an $m \times r$ matrix, where $m$ is the number of outputs in $\mathbf{y}(t)$ and $r$ is the number of inputs in $\mathbf{u}(t)$. The elements of $\mathbf{T}(s)$ are functions of the variable $s$, and the element in the $i$th row and $j$th column of $\mathbf{T}(s)$ is the transfer function relating the $i$th output to the $j$th input:

$$T_{ij}(s) = \left. \frac{Y_i(s)}{U_j(s)} \right|_{\text{zero initial conditions and all other inputs zero}}$$

Since

$$(s\mathbf{I} - \mathbf{A})^{-1} = \frac{\text{adj}(s\mathbf{I} - \mathbf{A})}{|s\mathbf{I} - \mathbf{A}|}$$

the *n*th degree *characteristic polynomial*

$$q(s) = |s\mathbf{I} - \mathbf{A}|$$

always occurs as the denominator polynomial of each individual transfer function. The roots of the *characteristic equation*

$$|s\mathbf{I} - \mathbf{A}| = 0 \qquad (1\text{-}15)$$

are thus the poles of each of the system transfer functions. The system's poles are also called its *eigenvalues* because the solutions of equation (1-15) are the eigenvalues of the matrix **A**. The system is stable if and only if all the eigenvalues of **A** are in the left half of the complex plane (LHP). This definition of stability of a linear, time-invariant system is more restrictive than the input-output stability that is usually considered in classical control because it requires that all *possible* transfer functions have all their poles in the LHP.

The three-input, two-output second-order system

$$\begin{bmatrix} \dot{x}_1(t) \\ \dot{x}_2(t) \end{bmatrix} = \begin{bmatrix} 0 & 1 \\ -5 & -2 \end{bmatrix} \begin{bmatrix} x_1(t) \\ x_2(t) \end{bmatrix} + \begin{bmatrix} 1 & 0 & -1 \\ 0 & -2 & 3 \end{bmatrix} \begin{bmatrix} u_1(t) \\ u_2(t) \\ u_3(t) \end{bmatrix}$$

$$= \mathbf{A}\mathbf{x}(t) + \mathbf{B}\mathbf{u}(t)$$

$$\begin{bmatrix} y_1(t) \\ y_2(t) \end{bmatrix} = \begin{bmatrix} 0 & -3 \\ 2 & -4 \end{bmatrix} \begin{bmatrix} x_1(t) \\ x_2(t) \end{bmatrix} + \begin{bmatrix} 1 & -2 & 0 \\ 0 & 0 & 0 \end{bmatrix} \begin{bmatrix} u_1(t) \\ u_2(t) \\ u_3(t) \end{bmatrix}$$

$$= \mathbf{C}\mathbf{x}(t) + \mathbf{D}\mathbf{u}(t)$$

has the integration diagram of Figure 1-11 and has a transfer function matrix given by

$$\mathbf{T}(s) = \mathbf{C}(s\mathbf{I} - \mathbf{A})^{-1}\mathbf{B} + \mathbf{D}$$

$$= \begin{bmatrix} 0 & -3 \\ 2 & -4 \end{bmatrix} \begin{bmatrix} s & -1 \\ 5 & (s+2) \end{bmatrix}^{-1} \begin{bmatrix} 1 & 0 & -1 \\ 0 & -2 & 3 \end{bmatrix} + \begin{bmatrix} 1 & -2 & 0 \\ 0 & 0 & 0 \end{bmatrix}$$

$$= \frac{\begin{bmatrix} 0 & -3 \\ 2 & -4 \end{bmatrix} \begin{bmatrix} (s+2) & 1 \\ -5 & s \end{bmatrix} \begin{bmatrix} 1 & 0 & -1 \\ 0 & -2 & 3 \end{bmatrix}}{s^2 + 2s + 5} + \begin{bmatrix} 1 & -2 & 0 \\ 0 & 0 & 0 \end{bmatrix}$$

$$= \begin{bmatrix} \dfrac{s^2 + 2s + 20}{s^2 + 2s + 5} & \dfrac{-2s^2 + 2s - 10}{s^2 + 2s + 5} & \dfrac{-9s - 15}{s^2 + 2s + 5} \\ \dfrac{2s + 24}{s^2 + 2s + 5} & \dfrac{8s - 4}{s^2 + 2s + 5} & \dfrac{-14s - 18}{s^2 + 2s + 5} \end{bmatrix}$$

$$= \begin{bmatrix} T_{11}(s) & T_{12}(s) & T_{13}(s) \\ T_{21}(s) & T_{22}(s) & T_{23}(s) \end{bmatrix}$$

The six individual transfer functions that are elements of this transfer function matrix are the usual ratios of Laplace transformed signals

$$T_{11}(s) = \frac{Y_1(s)}{U_1(s)}; \qquad T_{12}(s) = \frac{Y_1(s)}{U_2(s)}; \qquad T_{13}(s) = \frac{Y_1(s)}{U_3(s)};$$

$$T_{21}(s) = \frac{Y_2(s)}{U_1(s)}; \qquad T_{22}(s) = \frac{Y_2(s)}{U_2(s)}; \qquad T_{23}(s) = \frac{Y_2(s)}{U_3(s)}$$

when the initial conditions and all other inputs are zero.

Alternatively, the transfer functions can be found from the integration diagram, using Mason's gain rule or block diagram reduction.

When the vector of outputs of one system is the vector of inputs to a second system, the overall composite system has a transfer function matrix that is the product of the individual system transfer function matrices.

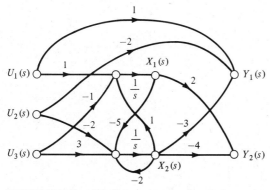

**FIGURE 1-11.  Finding a transfer function matrix.**

### 1.4.3 *Time Domain Solution*

It is advantageous to have an expression for the solution for the state of a system as a function of time rather than in terms of Laplace transforms. For a first-order system with state equation

$$\frac{dx}{dt} = ax(t) + bu(t)$$

this solution can be obtained as follows. Multiplying both sides of the equation by the "integrating factor" $e^{-at}$ gives

$$e^{-at}\frac{dx}{dt} - ax(t)e^{-at} = e^{-at}bu(t)$$

The left side of the equation is then the derivative of a product:

$$\frac{d}{dt}[e^{-at}x(t)] = e^{-at}b\, u(t)$$

Integrating both sides, and

$$e^{-at}x(t) = \int e^{-at}bu(t)dt + \text{(arbitrary constant)}$$

If the integration is begun at time $t = 0^-$, then

$$e^{-at}x(t) = \int_{0^-}^{t} e^{-a\tau}bu(\tau)d\tau + x(0^-), \qquad t \geqslant 0$$

where the variable of integration has been distinguished from the time, $t$, which occurs as a limit of integration. Solving for $x(t)$,

$$x(t) = e^{at}x(0^-) + \int_{0^-}^{t} e^{a(t-\tau)}bu(\tau)d\tau, \qquad t \geqslant 0$$

The integral is the *convolution* of the function $e^{-at}$ and the input term $bu(t)$. In terms of Laplace transforms, the state of this first-order system is given by

$$sX(s) - x(0^-) = aX(s) + bU(s)$$

$$X(s) = \frac{1}{s - a} x(0^-) + \frac{1}{s - a} b\, U(s)$$

$$x(t) = \mathscr{L}^{-1} \left[ \frac{1}{s - a} x(0^-) + \frac{1}{s - a} bU(s) \right]$$

$$= e^{at} x(0^-) + \mathscr{L}^{-1} \left[ \frac{1}{s - a} bU(s) \right], \qquad t \geq 0$$

so that

$$\mathscr{L}^{-1} \left[ \frac{1}{s - a} bU(s) \right] = \int_{0^-}^{t} e^{a(t - \tau)} bu(\tau) d\tau, \qquad t \geq 0$$

$$= \text{convolution}[e^{at}, bu(t)]$$

For digital computation, convolution using numerical integration is generally easier than dealing with Laplace transforms.

In general, the $n$th order state equations

$$\dot{\mathbf{x}}(t) = \mathbf{A}\mathbf{x}(t) + \mathbf{B}\mathbf{u}(t)$$

have solution given by

$$s\mathbf{X}(s) - \mathbf{x}(0^-) = \mathbf{A}\mathbf{X}(s) + \mathbf{B}\mathbf{U}(s)$$

$$(s\mathbf{I} - \mathbf{A})\mathbf{X}(s) = \mathbf{x}(0^-) + \mathbf{B}\mathbf{U}(s)$$

$$\mathbf{X}(s) = (s\mathbf{I} - \mathbf{A})^{-1}\mathbf{x}(0^-) + (s\mathbf{I} - \mathbf{A})^{-1}\mathbf{B}\mathbf{U}(s)$$

or

$$\mathbf{x}(t) = \mathscr{L}^{-1}[(s\mathbf{I} - \mathbf{A})^{-1}]\mathbf{x}(0^-) + \text{convolution}\{\mathscr{L}^{-1}[(s\mathbf{I} - \mathbf{A})^{-1}], \mathbf{B}\mathbf{u}(t)\}$$

Denoting the *state transition matrix* by

$$\mathbf{\Phi}(t) = \mathscr{L}^{-1}[(s\mathbf{I} - \mathbf{A})^{-1}] \qquad\qquad (1\text{-}16)$$

then

$$\mathbf{x}(t) = \mathbf{\Phi}(t)\mathbf{x}(0^-) + \text{convolution}[\mathbf{\Phi}(t), \mathbf{Bu}(t)]$$

$$= \mathbf{\Phi}(t)\mathbf{x}(0^-) + \int_{0^-}^{t} \mathbf{\Phi}(t - \tau)\mathbf{Bu}(\tau)d\tau$$

The state transition matrix of a linear, time-invariant continuous-time system is the matrix exponential function

$$\mathbf{\Phi}(t) = \exp(\mathbf{A}t) = \mathbf{I} + \mathbf{A}t + \frac{1}{2!}\mathbf{A}^2 t^2 + \cdots + \frac{1}{i!}\mathbf{A}^i t^i + \cdots$$

Matrix exponential functions play much the same role in the solution of higher-order linear time-invariant differential equations as scalar exponential functions

$$e^{at} = 1 + (at) + \frac{(at)^2}{2!} + \frac{(at)^3}{3!} + \cdots$$

do in the solution of first-order equations. That the function $\exp(\mathbf{A}t)$ is the state transition matrix can be shown as follows. Laplace transforming equation (1-16):

$$\mathbf{\Phi}(s) = (s\mathbf{I} - \mathbf{A})^{-1}$$

so that

$$s\mathbf{\Phi}(s) - \mathbf{I} = \mathbf{A}\mathbf{\Phi}(s)$$

or

$$\dot{\mathbf{\Phi}}(t) = \mathbf{A}\mathbf{\Phi}(t)$$

with

$$\mathbf{\Phi}(0) = \mathbf{I}$$

This set of differential equations and boundary conditions has solution

$$\mathbf{\Phi}(t) = \exp(\mathbf{A}t)$$

since

$$\frac{d}{dt}[\exp(\mathbf{A}t)] = \mathbf{A}\exp(\mathbf{A}t)$$

and

$$\exp(O) = \mathbf{I}$$

Some important properties of state transition matrices are summarized in Table 1-6.

One method of calculating the state transition matrix for a linear, time-invariant continuous-time system is to use the relation

$$\mathbf{\Phi}(t) = \exp(\mathbf{A}t) = \mathscr{L}^{-1}[(s\mathbf{I} - \mathbf{A})^{-1}]$$

## TABLE 1-6   Properties of State Transition Matrices

For the linear, time-invariant continuous-time system with state equations

$$\dot{\mathbf{x}}(t) = \mathbf{A}\mathbf{x}(t) + \mathbf{B}\mathbf{u}(t)$$

$$\mathbf{x}(t) = \mathbf{\Phi}(t)\mathbf{x}(0^-) + \int_{0^-}^{t} \mathbf{\Phi}(t - \tau)\mathbf{B}\mathbf{u}(\tau)d\tau$$

the state transition matrix $\mathbf{\Phi}(t)$ has these properties:

**A.** $\mathbf{\Phi}(t) = \mathscr{L}^{-1}[(s\mathbf{I} - \mathbf{A})^{-1}]$

**B.** $\mathbf{\Phi}(t) = \exp(\mathbf{A}t) = \mathbf{I} + \mathbf{A}t + \dfrac{1}{2!}\mathbf{A}^2 t^2 + \cdots + \dfrac{1}{i!}\mathbf{A}^i t^i + \cdots$

**C.** $\mathbf{\Phi}(0) = \mathbf{I}$

**D.** $\mathbf{\Phi}(t + \tau) = \mathbf{\Phi}(t)\mathbf{\Phi}(\tau) = \mathbf{\Phi}(\tau)\mathbf{\Phi}(t)$

**E.** The state transition matrix is the unique $n \times n$ solution to

$$\dot{\mathbf{\Phi}}(t) = \mathbf{A}\mathbf{\Phi}(t)$$

with

$$\mathbf{\Phi}(0) = \mathbf{I}$$

For example, for a system with state coupling matrix

$$A = \begin{bmatrix} 0 & 1 \\ -3 & -4 \end{bmatrix}$$

the state transition matrix is

$$\Phi(t) = \mathscr{L}^{-1}\left\{\begin{bmatrix} s & -1 \\ 3 & (s+4) \end{bmatrix}^{-1}\right\} = \mathscr{L}^{-1}\begin{bmatrix} \dfrac{s+4}{s^2+4s+3} & \dfrac{1}{s^2+4s+3} \\ \dfrac{-3}{s^2+4s+3} & \dfrac{s}{s^2+4s+3} \end{bmatrix}$$

$$= \mathscr{L}^{-1}\begin{bmatrix} \dfrac{\frac{3}{2}}{s+1} + \dfrac{-\frac{1}{2}}{s+3} & \dfrac{\frac{1}{2}}{s+1} + \dfrac{\frac{1}{2}}{s+3} \\ \dfrac{-\frac{3}{2}}{s+1} + \dfrac{\frac{3}{2}}{s+3} & \dfrac{-\frac{1}{2}}{s+1} + \dfrac{\frac{3}{2}}{s+3} \end{bmatrix}$$

$$= \begin{bmatrix} \frac{3}{2}e^{-t} - \frac{1}{2}e^{-3t} & \frac{1}{2}e^{-t} - \frac{1}{2}e^{-3t} \\ -\frac{3}{2}e^{-t} + \frac{3}{2}e^{-3t} & -\frac{1}{2}e^{-t} + \frac{3}{2}e^{-3t} \end{bmatrix}$$

# 1.5 Precision Temperature System

Precisely controlled temperatures are important in many applications. A chamber with an electric heater serves as a simple example of the determination of a plant model and the linearization of that model about an operating point.

### 1.5.1 Finding the Plant Model

Figure 1-12 shows a schematic diagram of a chamber (or oven) for precise temperature control, possibly one used for cell culture growth for the production of a medicine. A simple model of this plant, assuming good mixing of the heated air in the oven, is described as follows, with all quantities expressed in SI units. The rate of change of the temperature difference in the heat flow $Q_h$ supplied by the heater, and the flow rate

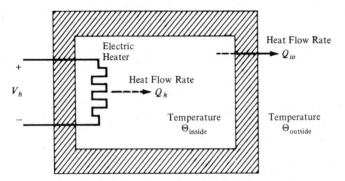

**FIGURE 1-12.   Schematic diagram of the oven.**

through the oven insulation, $Q_{io}$ are related by

$$c \frac{d}{dt} (\Theta_{inside} - \Theta_{outside}) = Q_h - Q_{io}$$

For constant (or very slowly varying) outside temperature, this relation becomes

$$c \frac{d\Theta_{inside}}{dt} = Q_h - Q_{io} \qquad (1\text{-}17)$$

The constant of proportionality $c$ is the thermal capacity of the oven (in joules per degree kelvin). $Q_h$ and $Q_{io}$ are heat flow rates (in joules per second = watts), and $\Theta_{inside}$ and $\Theta_{outside}$ are temperatures (in degrees kelvin). The heat flow rate supplied by the heater is

$$Q_h = \frac{V_h^2}{R} \text{ joules/second = watts} \qquad (1\text{-}18)$$

where $V_h$ is the heater voltage (in volts) and $R$ is the electrical resistance of the heater (in ohms). The rate of heat loss through the insulation is proportional to the temperature difference across the insulation

$$Q_{io} = \frac{\Theta_{inside} - \Theta_{outside}}{r} \qquad (1\text{-}19)$$

where $r$ is the thermal resistance of the insulation (in kelvin-seconds per joule = kelvins per watt).

Substituting from equations (1-18) and (1-19) into equation (1-17) gives

$$\frac{d\Theta_{\text{outside}}}{dt} + \frac{1}{rc} \Theta_{\text{inside}} = \frac{1}{rc} \Theta_{\text{outside}} + \frac{1}{Rc} V_h^2 \qquad (1\text{-}20)$$

As the derivative removes any reference level from $\Theta_{\text{outside}}$ and as the other temperature terms involve a temperature difference, degrees centigrade can be used for temperatures instead of degrees kelvin, if desired.

## 1.5.2 Identifying Model Parameters

Numerical values of the parameters $rc$ and $Rc$ in equation (1-20) could be estimated by the designer from the material properties and dimensions of the oven. For an oven already in existence, as we suppose this one to be, measurements can be used to determine the parameters. Table 1-7 gives temperature data for the oven when the heater has been turned off. An exponential decay curve has been fitted to the data, in Figure 1-13. The exponential curve has time constant

$$rc = 3000 \text{ seconds}$$

The outside temperature of about 30°C can also be inferred from this data, but this is of no direct use in determining $rc$.

Data that allow determination of the constant $Rc$ are given in Table 1-8. From equation (1-20), the steady state (or forced) oven temperature for constant heater voltage $V_h$ is given by

$$\Theta_{\text{inside}} = \Theta_{\text{outside}} + \left(\frac{r}{R}\right) V_h^2 \qquad (1\text{-}21)$$

**TABLE 1-7  Oven Temperature Decay Data**

| Time | Temperature (°C) |
|---|---|
| 14:23:10 | 120 |
| 14:31:00 | 108 |
| 14:39:30 | 92 |
| 14:48:35 | 80.5 |
| 15:05:00 | 63 |
| 15:34:00 | 40.5 |

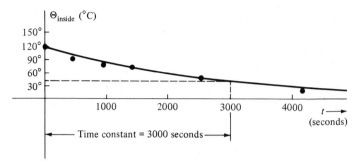

**FIGURE 1-13.   Plot of oven temperature decay data.**

**TABLE 1-8   Steady State Oven Temperature Data**

| Heater Voltage (volts) | Steady State Oven Temperature (°C) |
|---|---|
| 9.8 | 34.1 |
| 20.0 | 50.5 |
| 29.5 | 74.0 |
| 40.0 | 110 |

In Figure 1-14, the steady state oven temperature data is plotted versus the heater voltage, along with a curve of the form of equation (1-21). The outside temperature is again found to be about 30°C and

$$\frac{r}{R} = 5 \times 10^{-2}$$

giving

$$Rc = (rc)\left(\frac{R}{r}\right) = (3000)\left(\frac{1}{5 \times 10^{-2}}\right) = 60,000 \text{ seconds}$$

The oven model is thus established to be approximately

$$\frac{d\Theta_{inside}}{dt} + \frac{1}{3000}\Theta_{inside} = \frac{1}{3000}\Theta_{outside} + \frac{1}{60,000}V_h^2 \tag{1-22}$$

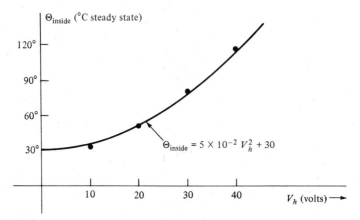

**FIGURE 1-14.   Plot of steady-state oven temperature data.**

### 1.5.3 Linearization About the Operating Point

For sufficiently small changes about an operating point, equation (1-22) can be linearized by expressing each of the signals involved as the sum of a constant nominal value plus a deviation from the nominal:

$$V_h(t) = \bar{V}_h + v_h(t)$$

$$\Theta_{inside}(t) = \bar{\Theta}_{inside} + \theta_{inside}(t)$$

$$\Theta_{outside}(t) = \bar{\Theta}_{outside} + \theta_{outside}(t) \tag{1-23}$$

The symbols with overbars are the constant nominal values and the lower case symbols represent deviations from the nominal.

Suppose that the nominal operation of the oven is to be with

$$\bar{\Theta}_{inside} = 50°C$$

$$\bar{\Theta}_{outside} = 30°C$$

With these inside and outside temperatures, the steady state solution of equation (1-22) for the heater voltage, its nominal value, is

$$\bar{V}_h = 20 \text{ volts}$$

The collection of nominal conditions is called the *operating point* (or *set point*) of the plant.

Substituting

$$V_h(t) = 20 + v_h(t)$$

$$\Theta_{inside}(t) = 50 + \theta_{inside}(t)$$

$$\Theta_{outside}(t) = 30 + \theta_{outside}(t)$$

in equation (1-22) gives

$$\frac{d\theta_{inside}}{dt} + \frac{1}{3000}\theta_{inside}(t) = \frac{1}{3000}\theta_{outside}(t) + \frac{40}{60,000}v_h(t) + \frac{1}{60,000}v_h^2(t) \quad (1\text{-}24)$$

For sufficiently small perturbations $v_h(t)$ of the heater voltage from the nominal value, the $v_h^2$ term in equation (1-24) can be neglected in comparison to the $v_h$ term. The linearized equation, valid for small deviations from the operating point, is

$$\frac{d\theta_{inside}}{dt} + \frac{1}{3000}\theta_{inside}(t) = \frac{1}{3000}\theta_{outside}(t) + \frac{40}{60,000}v_h(t) \quad (1\text{-}25)$$

The neglected $v_h^2$ term is less than 20 percent of the linear $v_h$ term for $v_h$ less than 8 volts. The effect of changing the operating point will be to change the coefficient of $v_h$ in equation (1-25).

This plant model is of first order and has linearized state equation

$$\dot{\theta}_{inside}(t) = -\frac{1}{3000}\theta_{inside}(t) + \frac{1}{3000}\theta_{outside}(t) + \frac{1}{1500}v_h(t)$$

where $\theta_{outside}(t)$ is a disturbance input and $v_h(t)$ is a control input. In practice, the nominal constant heater voltage $\bar{V}_h$ would be summed with $v_h(t)$ and applied to the heater. Necessary changes in the operating point, as when $\Theta_{outside}$ changes drastically or when the oven door has been left open, are made very slowly or in concert with changes in the opposite sense in $v_h(t)$. Provision is made to limit the maximum heater voltage to a safe value and not to allow negative applied voltages. A negative voltage would indicate that the control system is trying to *cool* the oven, but that cannot be done with a heater.

# 1.6 A Monorail System

A simple one-dimensional model of a two-car (plus engine) monorail train is shown in Figure 1-15(a). The engine is modeled as the mass $M_1$. Its air and drive system frictions are modeled by $B_1$, and the equivalent linear force

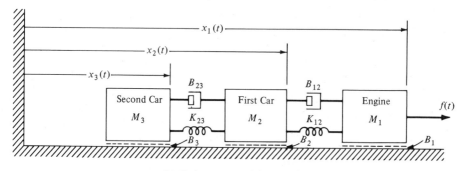

(a) Spring, mass, and damper model.

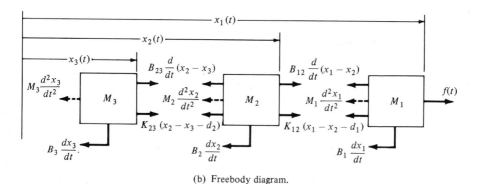

(b) Freebody diagram.

**FIGURE 1-15.   Monorail train model.**

produced by the engine's rotation of its drive wheels is represented by the applied force $f(t)$. The two cars also have masses and air and track frictions, and each is coupled to the others by devices having both spring $K$ and damping $B$ properties. The position of the engine from some stationary reference point is $x_1(t)$. Similarly, the positions of the cars are $x_2(t)$ and $x_3(t)$.

A freebody diagram for this model is drawn in Figure 1-15(b). The air and track frictional forces

$$B_1 \frac{dx_1}{dt}; \quad B_2 \frac{dx_2}{dt}; \quad B_3 \frac{dx_3}{dt}$$

are proportional to the velocity of each car. The frictional forces of the car couplings

$$B_{12} \frac{d}{dt}(x_1 - x_2); \quad B_{23} \frac{d}{dt}(x_2 - x_3)$$

are proportional to the difference in velocities of the two cars involved. The spring forces of the car coupling

$$K_{12}(x_1 - x_2 - d_1); \qquad K_{23}(x_2 - x_3 - d_2)$$

are proportional to the relative distances between adjacent cars, where $d_1$ and $d_2$ are the equilibrium distances for which there is no spring force. If the distances $x_2$ and $x_3$ are translated by $d_1$ and $(d_1 + d_2)$ respectively, the constants $d_1$ and $d_2$ in the force relations above become zero. We will assume this has been done. Equating the forces to the rate of change of momentum for each car gives the simultaneous differential equations

$$\begin{cases} M_1 \dfrac{d^2x_1}{dt^2} + (B_1 + B_{12})\dfrac{dx_1}{dt} - B_{12}\dfrac{dx_2}{dt} + K_{12}x_1 - K_{12}x_2 = f(t) \\[2mm] M_2 \dfrac{d^2x_2}{dt^2} + (B_2 + B_{23} + B_{12})\dfrac{dx_2}{dt} - B_{12}\dfrac{dx_1}{dt} - B_{23}\dfrac{dx_3}{dt} \\[2mm] \qquad + (K_{12} + K_{23})x_2 - K_{12}x_1 - K_{23}x_3 = 0 \\[2mm] M_3 \dfrac{d^2x_3}{dt^2} + (B_3 + B_{23})\dfrac{dx_3}{dt} - B_{23}\dfrac{dx_2}{dt} + K_{23}x_3 - K_{23}x_2 = 0 \end{cases} \qquad (1\text{-}26)$$

The equations (1-26) are not in state variable form. They involve second derivatives and they do not equate the derivative of each state variable to a linear combination of the state variables and the input. They can be converted to a form involving only first derivatives by defining the mass velocities as

$$v_1 = \frac{dx_1}{dt}; \qquad v_2 = \frac{dx_2}{dt}; \qquad v_3 = \frac{dx_3}{dt} \qquad (1\text{-}27)$$

and substituting, using

$$\frac{d^2x_1}{dt^2} = \frac{dv_1}{dt}; \qquad \frac{d^2x_2}{dt^2} = \frac{dv_2}{dt}; \qquad \frac{d^2x_3}{dt^2} = \frac{dv_3}{dt}$$

so that (1-26) becomes

$$\begin{cases} M_1 \dfrac{dv_1}{dt} + (B_1 + B_{12})v_1 - B_{12}v_2 + K_{12}x_1 - K_{12}x_2 = f(t) \\[2mm] M_2 \dfrac{dv_2}{dt} + (B_2 + B_{23} + B_{12})v_2 - B_{12}v_1 - B_{23}v_3 \\[2mm] \qquad + (K_{12} + K_{13})x_2 - K_{12}x_1 - K_{23}x_3 = 0 \\[2mm] M_3 \dfrac{dv_3}{dt} + (B_3 + B_{23})v_3 - B_{23}v_2 + K_{23}x_3 - K_{23}x_2 = 0 \end{cases} \qquad (1\text{-}28)$$

The collection of the three equations of (1-27) and the three equations of (1-28) constitute a set of six equations in the six variables $x_1, x_2, x_3, v_1, v_2,$ and $v_3$. Solving for the first derivative of each of these variables gives the state equations

$$
\begin{cases}
\dfrac{dx_1}{dt} = v_1 \\[2ex]
\dfrac{dv_1}{dt} = -\dfrac{B_1 + B_{12}}{M_1} v_1 + \dfrac{B_{12}}{M_1} v_2 - \dfrac{K_{12}}{M_1} x_1 + \dfrac{K_{12}}{M_1} x_2 + f(t) \\[2ex]
\dfrac{dx_2}{dt} = v_2 \\[2ex]
\dfrac{dv_2}{dt} = -\dfrac{B_2 + B_{23} + B_{12}}{M_2} v_2 + \dfrac{B_{12}}{M_2} v_1 + \dfrac{B_{23}}{M_2} v_3 - \dfrac{K_{12} + K_{13}}{M_2} x_2 \\[2ex]
\qquad\quad + \dfrac{K_{12}}{M_2} x_1 + \dfrac{K_{23}}{M_2} x_3 \\[2ex]
\dfrac{dx_3}{dt} = v_3 \\[2ex]
\dfrac{dv_3}{dt} = -\dfrac{B_3 + B_{23}}{M_3} v_3 + \dfrac{B_{23}}{M_3} v_2 - \dfrac{K_{23}}{M_3} x_3 + \dfrac{K_{23}}{M_3} x_2
\end{cases}
$$

or

$$
\begin{bmatrix} \dot{x}_1(t) \\ \dot{v}_1(t) \\ \dot{x}_2(t) \\ \dot{v}_2(t) \\ \dot{x}_3(t) \\ \dot{v}_3(t) \end{bmatrix}
=
\begin{bmatrix}
0 & 1 & 0 & 0 & 0 & 0 \\
-\left(\dfrac{K_{12}}{M_1}\right) & -\left(\dfrac{B_1 + B_{12}}{M_1}\right) & \left(\dfrac{K_{12}}{M_1}\right) & \left(\dfrac{B_{12}}{M_1}\right) & 0 & 0 \\
0 & 0 & 0 & 1 & 0 & 0 \\
\left(\dfrac{K_{12}}{M_2}\right) & \left(\dfrac{B_{12}}{M_2}\right) & -\left(\dfrac{K_{12} + K_{13}}{M_2}\right) & -\left(\dfrac{B_2 + B_{23} + B_{12}}{M_2}\right) & \left(\dfrac{K_{23}}{M_2}\right) & \left(\dfrac{B_{23}}{M_2}\right) \\
0 & 0 & 0 & 0 & 0 & 1 \\
0 & 0 & \left(\dfrac{K_{23}}{M_3}\right) & \left(\dfrac{B_{23}}{M_3}\right) & -\left(\dfrac{K_{23}}{M_3}\right) & -\left(\dfrac{B_3 + B_{23}}{M_3}\right)
\end{bmatrix}
$$

$$
\times
\begin{bmatrix} x_1(t) \\ v_1(t) \\ x_2(t) \\ v_2(t) \\ x_3(t) \\ v_3(t) \end{bmatrix}
+
\begin{bmatrix} 0 \\ 1 \\ 0 \\ 0 \\ 0 \\ 0 \end{bmatrix} f(t)
$$

If tachometers are placed on a wheel of each car, an electrical signal proportional to each car's velocity will be produced,

$$y_1(t) = \alpha v_1(t); \qquad y_2(t) = \alpha v_2(t); \qquad y_3(t) = \alpha v_3(t)$$

where $\alpha$ is the constant of proportionality relating tachometer voltage to car velocity. These outputs

$$\begin{bmatrix} y_1(t) \\ y_2(t) \\ y_3(t) \end{bmatrix} = \begin{bmatrix} 0 & \alpha & 0 & 0 & 0 & 0 \\ 0 & 0 & 0 & \alpha & 0 & 0 \\ 0 & 0 & 0 & 0 & 0 & \alpha \end{bmatrix} \begin{bmatrix} x_1(t) \\ v_1(t) \\ x_2(t) \\ v_2(t) \\ x_3(t) \\ v_3(t) \end{bmatrix}$$

might be used in a feedback arrangement to the engine controller to aid in giving a smooth ride.

Clearly, the model for a system of this kind could be of very high order if more cars were involved, if the dynamics of the engine were included, and if the rotational moments of the wheels were modeled.

## 1.7 Summary

In this first chapter, we outlined concepts important to a good understanding of the material to follow. Some control terminology was discussed and a brief survey of classical continuous-time feedback control system design was given. In the classical approach, the designer begins with a low-order controller and raises the controller order as necessary to meet the feedback system performance requirements. The controller poles, zeros, and multiplying constant are chosen so that the overall system has poles at locations for which the character of its zero-input response is acceptable. Simultaneously, it is required that the zero-state (or "steady state") response to a representative class of inputs, such as steps and ramps, be adequate.

Important aspects of linear algebra that are fundamental to modern control system design were reviewed, then continuous-time state variable models were discussed. For a linear, time-invariant system, these have the form

$$\dot{\mathbf{x}}(t) = \mathbf{A}\mathbf{x}(t) + \mathbf{B}\mathbf{u}(t)$$

$$\mathbf{y}(t) = \mathbf{C}\mathbf{x}(t) + \mathbf{D}\mathbf{u}(t)$$

where $\mathbf{u}(t)$ is an $r$-vector of inputs, $\mathbf{y}(t)$ is an $m$-vector of outputs, and $\mathbf{x}(t)$ is the *n*-vector state. The relations between signals in a state variable system can be visualized with an integration diagram, involving only the operations of integration, multiplication by a constant, and addition.

In terms of Laplace transforms, the solution for the state and output, in terms of an initial state and the inputs, is

$$\mathbf{X}(s) = (s\mathbf{I} - \mathbf{A})^{-1}\mathbf{x}(0^-) + (s\mathbf{I} - \mathbf{A})^{-1}\mathbf{B}\mathbf{U}(s)$$

$$\underbrace{\qquad\qquad}_{\text{zero-input component}} \quad \underbrace{\qquad\qquad}_{\text{zero-state component}}$$

$$\mathbf{Y}(s) = \mathbf{C}\mathbf{X}(s) + \mathbf{D}\mathbf{U}(s)$$

The matrix of transfer functions, each relating an output to an input, is given by

$$\mathbf{T}(s) = \mathbf{C}(s\mathbf{I} - \mathbf{A})^{-1}\mathbf{B} + \mathbf{D}$$

Each transfer function element shares the denominator polynomial

$$q(s) = |s\mathbf{I} - \mathbf{A}|$$

the roots of which are the transfer function poles and also the eigenvalues of the matrix **A**. The state variable model is stable if and only if the eigenvalues of **A** are in the left half of the complex plane.

The time domain solution for the state is

$$\mathbf{x}(t) = \mathbf{\Phi}(t)\mathbf{x}(0^-) + \int_0^t \mathbf{\Phi}(t - \tau)\mathbf{B}\mathbf{u}(\tau)d\tau$$

$$= \mathbf{\Phi}(t)\mathbf{x}(0^-) + \text{convolution}[\mathbf{\Phi}(t), \mathbf{B}\mathbf{u}(t)]$$

where the state transition matrix is

$$\mathbf{\Phi}(t) = \exp(\mathbf{A}t) = \mathbf{I} + \mathbf{A}t + \frac{1}{2!}\mathbf{A}^2t^2 + \cdots + \frac{1}{i!}\mathbf{A}^it^i \cdots$$

$$= \mathcal{L}^{-1}[(s\mathbf{I} - \mathbf{A})^{-1}]$$

Two interesting example systems were then examined. A chamber for precision temperature control involves a simple but significant nonlinearity. Although the form of the equations describing this system are known from physical principles, it would be difficult to accurately predict the numerical values of some of its parameters. The parameters were instead identified by curve-fitting of experimental data. The resulting model was then linearized about an operating point. A monorail train provided an example of developing a state variable model of a translational mechanical system.

# REFERENCES

The references at the end of each chapter do not constitute a bibliography. They are intended to help the reader to quickly find additional, compatible material on the chapter's subjects.

Classical continuous-time control system design was taught to generations of engineers and scientists with such early texts as the following:

J. G. Truxal, *Control System Synthesis*. New York: McGraw-Hill, 1955;

C. J. Savant, Jr., *Basic Feedback Control System Design*. New York: McGraw-Hill, 1958;

R. N. Clark, *Introduction to Automatic Control Systems*. New York: Wiley, 1962.

In later years, other texts such as

R. C. Dorf, *Modern Control Systems*. Reading, MA: Addison-Wesley, 1967;

B. C. Kuo, *Automatic Control Systems*. Englewood Cliffs, NJ: Prentice-Hall, 1967;

J. J. D'Azzo and C. H. Houpis, *Linear Control System Analysis and Design*. New York: McGraw-Hill, 1975;

and their later editions were popular. One of the best *Schaum's Outlines* is

J. J. DiStefano III, A. R. Stubberud, and I. J. Williams, *Feedback and Control Systems (Schaum's Outline)*. New York: McGraw-Hill, 1967

and this remains an excellent presentation of the classical theory and results. We are a bit partial toward

G. H. Hostetter, C. J. Savant, Jr., and R. T. Stefani, *Design of Feedback Control Systems*. New York: Holt, Rinehart and Winston, 1982.

There are many fine texts on matrix methods. Among these are

L. Mirsky, *An Introduction to Linear Algebra*. New York: Dover, 1982. Originally, Oxford: Clarendon Press, 1955;

R. Bellman, *Introduction to Matrix Analysis*. New York: McGraw-Hill, 1960;

L. A. Pipes, *Matrix Methods for Engineering*. Englewood Cliffs, NJ: Prentice-Hall, 1963;

G. W. Stewart, *Introduction to Matrix Computations*. New York: Academic Press, 1973;

G. Strang, *Linear Algebra and Its Applications*, 2nd edition. New York: Academic Press, 1980.

An outstanding book on continuous-time state variable system models is

P. M. DeRusso, R. J. Roy, and C. M. Close, *State Variables for Engineers*. New York: Wiley, 1965.

Many other texts contain several chapters on continuous-time state variables. The paper by Kalman,

R. E. Kalman, "Mathematical Description of Linear Dynamical Systems," *SIAM J. Control series A*, 1, 1963, pp. 152–192

that did much to popularize state variable control system models is good and quite easy to read. The paper

I. C. Horowitz and U. Shaked, "Superiority of Transfer Function over State Variable Methods in Linear, Time-Invariant Feedback System Design," *IEEE Trans. Automatic Control*, Vol. AC-20, February, 1975, pp. 84–97

compares state variable transfer function design methods.

Physical system modeling is covered well and in detail in

R. H. Cannon, Jr., *Dynamics of Physical Systems*. New York: McGraw-Hill, 1967;

W. R. Perkins and J. B. Cruz, Jr., *Engineering of Dynamic Systems*. New York: Wiley, 1969;

and

C. M. Close and D. K. Frederick, *Modeling and Analysis of Dynamic Systems*. Boston: Houghton Mifflin, 1978.

## CHAPTER ONE PROBLEMS

**1-1.** For a single-input, single-output system described by the equation

$$\frac{d^2y}{dt^2} + 2\frac{dy}{dt} + 10y = 5\frac{dr}{dt} - 3r$$

find an input $r(t)$ that will, with zero initial conditions, produce the same output $y(t)$ as the nonzero initial conditions (with no input)

$$y'(0^-) = -4 \qquad y(0^-) = 1$$

**1-2.** The table below gives approximate measurements of the output of a system when the system input is a unit step.

**a.** Using the data, find an approximate first-order system model, specifying its transfer function.

**b.** Repeat (a), but find an approximate second-order system model. Specify the transfer function.

**c.** Carefully explain how higher-order models could be obtained from this data. What is the highest-order model that can be obtained in this way?

**d.** How might one determine a "best" model order and a "best" model?

**e.** For another system with a second-order model

$$T(s) = \frac{3}{s^2 + 4s + 3}$$

find an approximate *first*-order model for its step response. Compare the step responses of the two models.

| Time in Seconds, t | Value of Output, y(t) |
|---|---|
| 0.0 | 3.0 |
| 0.2 | 3.1 |
| 0.5 | 2.6 |
| 0.8 | 2.1 |
| 1.1 | 1.7 |
| 1.65 | 1.4 |
| 1.9 | 1.2 |
| 2.2 | 1.1 |
| 2.7 | 1.05 |
| 3.25 | 1.0 |

**1-3.** For the plant with transfer function

$$G_1(s) = \frac{4}{s + 3}$$

find a rational controller transfer function $G_2(s)$ such that the feedback system with transfer function

$$T(s) = \frac{G_1(s)G_2(s)}{1 + G_1(s)G_2(s)}$$

is second-order and critically damped. A solution to this problem is not unique.

**1-4.** A certain system has error to a unit step input given by

$$E(s) = \frac{s + 2K}{s^2 + 2s + 1}$$

where $K$ is an adjustable parameter. For what value of $K$, if any, is the performance measure

$$I = \int_{0^-}^{\infty} e^2(t)dt$$

minimum?

**1-5.** For unity feedback systems with transfer functions

$$T(s) = \frac{G_c(s)G_p(s)}{1 + G_c(s)G_p(s)}$$

design cascade compensators $G_c(s)$ such that, for the following plant transfer functions $G_p(s)$, the overall systems have large relative stability and small steady state error between the output and the input when the input is a step:

**a.** $G_p(s) = \dfrac{s + 5}{s^2 + 5s + 6}$ **b.** $G_p(s) = \dfrac{250}{(s + 2)(s^2 + 10s + 125)}$

**c.** $G_p(s) = \dfrac{s + 3}{s(s^2 + 2s + 50)}$ **d.** $G_p(s) = \dfrac{s + 2}{(s + 1)^2(s^2 + 2s + 10)}$

**1-6.** Show that for square matrices:

    **a.** $\mathbf{B} = \mathbf{A} + \mathbf{A}^t$ is symmetric.
    **b.** $\mathbf{D} = \mathbf{A}^t\mathbf{A}$ is symmetric.
    **c.** trace $(\mathbf{AB})$ = trace $(\mathbf{BA})$.

**1-7.** Show that:

$$\frac{d}{dt}(\mathbf{Ab}) = \frac{d\mathbf{A}}{dt}\mathbf{b} + \mathbf{A}\frac{d\mathbf{b}}{dt}$$

where $\mathbf{b}$ is a vector. From this result

$$\frac{d}{dt}(\mathbf{AB}) = \frac{d\mathbf{A}}{dt}\mathbf{B} + \mathbf{A}\frac{d\mathbf{B}}{dt}$$

follows easily because each column of the general relation is of the form of the vector relation. Using the above, find

$$\frac{d}{dt}(\mathbf{A}^3)$$

in terms of $\mathbf{A}$ and $d\mathbf{A}/dt$.

**1-8.** Indicate two different ways that the following matrices might be partitioned so that the submatrices are conformable for multiplication. Find the product using each of the partitionings.

$$
\begin{bmatrix}
1 & 0 & 3 & -2 \\
-5 & 1 & -1 & 4 \\
1 & -2 & 3 & 8 \\
-4 & -7 & 1 & -1
\end{bmatrix}
\begin{bmatrix}
-4 & -4 & 4 & 1 \\
-5 & -2 & 2 & -1 \\
7 & 0 & -3 & -5 \\
-1 & 3 & 3 & -4
\end{bmatrix}
$$

**1-9.** Find the ranks of the following matrices:

a.
$$
\begin{bmatrix}
0 & 0 & 0 & 0 & 0 & 0 \\
0 & 3 & 0 & 0 & 6 & -2 \\
0 & -2 & 0 & 0 & -4 & 1
\end{bmatrix}
$$

b.
$$
\begin{bmatrix}
1 & 2 & 3 & 4 \\
5 & 6 & 7 & 8 \\
9 & 10 & 11 & 12 \\
13 & 14 & 15 & 16
\end{bmatrix}
$$

**1-10.** Find the following:

a. Two square matrices $A$ and $B$ such that $AB \neq BA$.
b. Two *different* nonzero square matrices $A$ and $B$ such that $AB = BA$.
c. A set of nonzero matrices $A$, $B$, and $C$ such that $AB = AC$ but $B \neq C$.
d. Two nonzero matrices $A$ and $B$ such that $AB = 0$.
e. A nonzero $2 \times 2$ matrix $A$ such that $A^2 = 0$.
f. A $2 \times 2$ matrix $A$ such that $A^2 = -I$. This matrix is analogous to $\sqrt{-1}$.

**1-11.** Find the following:

a. Two equations in three variables with no solution.
b. Three equations in two variables with a unique solution.
c. Three equations in two variables with an underdetermined solution.

**1-12.** Find the inverses, if they exist, of the following matrices, using

$$
A^{-1} = \frac{\text{adj } (A)}{|A|}
$$

a. $A = \begin{bmatrix} 1 & 2 & 3 \\ 7 & 8 & 9 \\ 4 & 5 & 6 \end{bmatrix}$   b. $A = \begin{bmatrix} 0 & 1 & 0 \\ 0 & 0 & 1 \\ -1 & 0 & 0 \end{bmatrix}$

c. $A = \begin{bmatrix} 2 & 0 & -1 & 0 \\ 0 & 0 & 3 & 1 \\ 0 & -2 & 0 & 1 \\ 4 & 2 & 0 & 0 \end{bmatrix}$

**1-13.** Determine how many of the following vectors are linearly independent:

$$\begin{bmatrix} 1 \\ 2 \\ 1 \end{bmatrix}, \begin{bmatrix} 1 \\ 1 \\ 1 \end{bmatrix}, \begin{bmatrix} 0 \\ 1 \\ 1 \end{bmatrix}, \begin{bmatrix} 3 \\ 6 \\ 2 \end{bmatrix}, \begin{bmatrix} -1 \\ -2 \\ -1 \end{bmatrix}$$

Specify a subset of these vectors that contains the largest number of linearly independent vectors.

**1-14.** Find a linear transformation that transforms the vector

$$\begin{bmatrix} 1 \\ 0 \\ 0 \end{bmatrix} \text{ to } \begin{bmatrix} 0 \\ 0 \\ 1 \end{bmatrix}$$

the vector

$$\begin{bmatrix} 0 \\ 1 \\ 0 \end{bmatrix} \text{ to } \begin{bmatrix} 0 \\ 1 \\ 0 \end{bmatrix}$$

and the vector

$$\begin{bmatrix} 0 \\ 0 \\ 1 \end{bmatrix} \text{ to } \begin{bmatrix} 1 \\ 1 \\ 1 \end{bmatrix}$$

**1-15.** Find a basis for the range space and a basis for the null space for the following matrices:

$$\textbf{a.} \begin{bmatrix} 2 & -2 & 3 \\ 1 & -1 & 1 \\ 1 & -1 & 2 \end{bmatrix} \quad \textbf{b.} \begin{bmatrix} 1 & -2 & 3 \\ 2 & 2 & 0 \\ -1 & 1 & 0 \end{bmatrix} \quad \textbf{c.} \begin{bmatrix} 1 & -2 & 1 \\ -1 & 2 & -1 \\ 2 & -4 & 2 \end{bmatrix}$$

**1-16.** Find the state and output equations represented by each of the following integration diagrams.

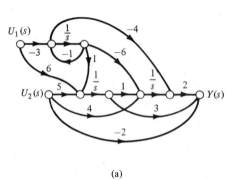

(a)

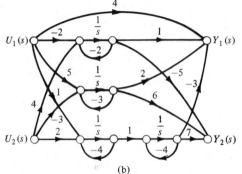

(b)

**1-17.** Draw integration diagrams to represent the following systems:

a.
$$\begin{bmatrix} \dot{x}_1(t) \\ \dot{x}_2(t) \end{bmatrix} = \begin{bmatrix} 2 & 1 \\ -2 & 3 \end{bmatrix} \begin{bmatrix} x_1(t) \\ x_2(t) \end{bmatrix} + \begin{bmatrix} 9 \\ -3 \end{bmatrix} u(t)$$

$$y(t) = \begin{bmatrix} 4 & 2 \end{bmatrix} \begin{bmatrix} x_1(t) \\ x_2(t) \end{bmatrix}$$

b.
$$\begin{bmatrix} \dot{x}_1(t) \\ \dot{x}_2(t) \\ \dot{x}_3(t) \end{bmatrix} = \begin{bmatrix} 3 & -1 & 2 \\ 1 & 8 & 3 \\ 5 & 0 & -1 \end{bmatrix} \begin{bmatrix} x_1(t) \\ x_2(t) \\ x_3(t) \end{bmatrix} + \begin{bmatrix} 2 & -1 \\ 3 & -3 \\ 0 & 2 \end{bmatrix} \begin{bmatrix} u_1(t) \\ u_2(t) \end{bmatrix}$$

$$\begin{bmatrix} y_1(t) \\ y_2(t) \end{bmatrix} = \begin{bmatrix} 6 & 3 & 1 \\ 0 & -2 & 1 \end{bmatrix} \begin{bmatrix} x_1(t) \\ x_2(t) \\ x_3(t) \end{bmatrix} + \begin{bmatrix} 1 & 0 \\ -1 & 4 \end{bmatrix} \begin{bmatrix} u_1(t) \\ u_2(t) \end{bmatrix}$$

c.
$$\dot{x}(t) = \begin{bmatrix} 6 & 1 & 3 & 0 \\ 3 & 0 & 8 & 1 \\ -1 & 2 & -2 & 1 \\ 2 & -2 & 0 & 4 \end{bmatrix} x(t) + \begin{bmatrix} 0 & 1 & 0 \\ -2 & 0 & 6 \\ 3 & 4 & 4 \\ 1 & 2 & -2 \end{bmatrix} u(t)$$

$$y(t) = \begin{bmatrix} 4 & 0 & 3 & 1 \\ -1 & 0 & -1 & 0 \end{bmatrix} x(t)$$

**1-18.** Find a set of state equations for the following system. A solution to this problem is not unique.

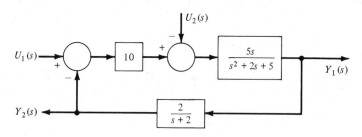

**1-19.** Use Laplace transformation to find the state $x(t)$ and the output $y(t)$ for $t \geq 0$:

a.
$$\begin{bmatrix} \dot{x}_1(t) \\ \dot{x}_2(t) \end{bmatrix} = \begin{bmatrix} 2 & -3 \\ -4 & 6 \end{bmatrix} \begin{bmatrix} x_1(t) \\ x_2(t) \end{bmatrix} + \begin{bmatrix} 1 \\ 1 \end{bmatrix} u(t)$$

$$y(t) = \begin{bmatrix} 3 & -2 \end{bmatrix} \begin{bmatrix} x_1(t) \\ x_2(t) \end{bmatrix} + 3u(t)$$

$$u(t) = 2e^{-4t}$$

$$\begin{bmatrix} x_1(0) \\ x_2(0) \end{bmatrix} = \begin{bmatrix} 6 \\ -3 \end{bmatrix}$$

**b.** $\begin{bmatrix} \dot{x}_1(t) \\ \dot{x}_2(t) \end{bmatrix} = \begin{bmatrix} 0 & 2 \\ -2 & 0 \end{bmatrix} \begin{bmatrix} x_1(t) \\ x_2(t) \end{bmatrix} + \begin{bmatrix} 1 & 1 \\ 0 & 1 \end{bmatrix} \begin{bmatrix} u_1(t) \\ u_2(t) \end{bmatrix}$

$\begin{bmatrix} y_1(t) \\ y_2(t) \end{bmatrix} = \begin{bmatrix} 1 & 0 \\ -1 & 1 \end{bmatrix} \begin{bmatrix} x_1(t) \\ x_2(t) \end{bmatrix} + \begin{bmatrix} 0 & 0 \\ 2 & 0 \end{bmatrix} \begin{bmatrix} u_1(t) \\ u_2(t) \end{bmatrix}$

$\begin{bmatrix} u_1(t) \\ u_2(t) \end{bmatrix} = \begin{bmatrix} \delta(t) \\ 7 \end{bmatrix}$

where $\delta(t)$ is the unit impulse, and $x(0^-) = 0$.

**c.** $\dot{x}(t) = \begin{bmatrix} -2 & 0 & 0 \\ 0 & -1 & 1 \\ 0 & 0 & -1 \end{bmatrix} x(t) + \begin{bmatrix} 4 \\ 0 \\ 5 \end{bmatrix} u(t)$

$y(t) = \begin{bmatrix} 3 & 1 & 0 \\ 0 & 0 & -1 \end{bmatrix} x(t) + \begin{bmatrix} 0 \\ 2 \end{bmatrix} u(t)$

$u(t) = 10e^{-3t}$

$x(0^-) = 0$

**1-20.** Find the transfer function matrices of the following systems, using

$$T(s) = C[sI - A]^{-1}B + D$$

**a.** $\begin{bmatrix} \dot{x}_1(t) \\ \dot{x}_2(t) \end{bmatrix} = \begin{bmatrix} 2 & -4 \\ -3 & 6 \end{bmatrix} \begin{bmatrix} x_1(t) \\ x_2(t) \end{bmatrix} + \begin{bmatrix} 2 & 0 \\ 1 & 1 \end{bmatrix} \begin{bmatrix} u_1(t) \\ u_2(t) \end{bmatrix}$

$y(t) = \begin{bmatrix} 1 & -2 \end{bmatrix} \begin{bmatrix} x_1(t) \\ x_2(t) \end{bmatrix}$

**b.** $\dot{x}(t) = \begin{bmatrix} 2 & 1 & 3 \\ 4 & -1 & 0 \\ -2 & 0 & 1 \end{bmatrix} x(t) + \begin{bmatrix} 0 & 0 \\ 1 & 3 \\ -1 & 2 \end{bmatrix} u(t)$

$y(t) = \begin{bmatrix} 0 & 1 & 2 \\ 0 & 1 & -2 \end{bmatrix} x(t) + \begin{bmatrix} 0 & 1 \\ 0 & 0 \end{bmatrix} u(t)$

**1-21.** Find the transfer function matrices of the following system by converting to an integration diagram and finding transfer functions from the diagram.

**a.** $\begin{bmatrix} \dot{x}_1(t) \\ \dot{x}_2(t) \end{bmatrix} = \begin{bmatrix} 2 & -1 \\ 3 & 4 \end{bmatrix} \begin{bmatrix} x_1(t) \\ x_2(t) \end{bmatrix} + \begin{bmatrix} 0 \\ 1 \end{bmatrix} u(t)$

$y(t) = \begin{bmatrix} 2 & 0 \end{bmatrix} \begin{bmatrix} x_1(t) \\ x_2(t) \end{bmatrix} + 2u(t)$

$$\textbf{b.} \begin{bmatrix} \dot{x}_1(t) \\ \dot{x}_2(t) \\ \dot{x}_3(t) \end{bmatrix} = \begin{bmatrix} 1 & 0 & 3 \\ 0 & 2 & -2 \\ 4 & 1 & 0 \end{bmatrix} \begin{bmatrix} x_1(t) \\ x_2(t) \\ x_3(t) \end{bmatrix} + \begin{bmatrix} 0 & 0 \\ 3 & -1 \\ 2 & 1 \end{bmatrix} \begin{bmatrix} u_1(t) \\ u_2(t) \end{bmatrix}$$

$$y(t) = \begin{bmatrix} 1 & 0 & 3 \end{bmatrix} \begin{bmatrix} x_1(t) \\ x_2(t) \\ x_3(t) \end{bmatrix}$$

**1-22.** Find the state transition matrices using $\Phi(t) = \mathcal{L}^{-1}\{[s\mathbf{I} - \mathbf{A}]^{-1}\}$ for systems with the following state coupling matrices, $\mathbf{A}$:

**a.** $\mathbf{A} = \begin{bmatrix} -3 & 1 \\ -2 & 0 \end{bmatrix}$

**b.** $\mathbf{A} = \begin{bmatrix} 0 & 1 \\ -3 & 2 \end{bmatrix}$

**c.** $\mathbf{A} = \begin{bmatrix} -1 & 1 & -2 \\ -2 & 2 & -1 \\ 0 & 0 & 3 \end{bmatrix}$

**1-23.** For the precision temperature system, find a linearized state model about the operating point where

$$\bar{\Theta}_{\text{outside}} = 35°C$$

$$\bar{\Theta}_{\text{inside}} = 47°C$$

if the oven temperature and steady state data are as given in the tables below:

## Oven Temperature Decay Data

| Time | Temperature ($°C$) |
|------|---------------------|
| 10:05:00 AM | 135 |
| 10:08:30 | 125 |
| 10:13:10 | 110 |
| 10:21:30 | 90 |
| 10:31:30 | 75 |
| 10:37:30 | 60 |
| 10:53:00 | 50 |
| 11:10:00 | 40 |

## Steady State Oven Temperature Data

| Heater Voltage $V_h$ (volts) | Steady State Oven Temperature (°C) |
|:---:|:---:|
| 10 | 35 |
| 15 | 47 |
| 20 | 65 |
| 25 | 88 |

1-24. The figure shows typical characteristic curves for a 2N2222A transistor. Characteristic curves for junction transistors with the same type number can differ by factors of two or more, so these curves are for a specific device, not all 2N2222A's.

  **a.** For this device, with a constant base current $I_B = 400$ microamperes ($\mu$A), find a linearized model of the relationship between the collector current $I_C$ and the collector-emitter voltage $V_{CE}$, about the operating point where $V_{CE} = 12$ volts.

  **b.** For this device, with a constant collector current $I_C = 20$ milliamperes (mA), find a linearized model of the relationship between the base current $I_B$ and the collector-emitter voltage $V_{CE}$, about the operating point where $I_B = 300$ $\mu$A.

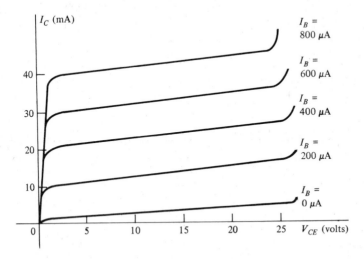

1-25. Find state equations for the simple monorail system having three cars instead of two. Let the cars and the couplings be identical, with

$$M_2 = M_3 = M_4 = 6{,}200 \text{ kg} \qquad B_{12} = B_{23} = B_{34} = 450 \text{ N·s/m}$$

$$B_2 = B_3 = B_4 = 1{,}300 \text{ N·s/m} \qquad K_{12} = K_{23} = K_{34} = 4{,}400 \text{ N/m}$$

and let

$$M_1 = 10,500 \text{ kg} \qquad B_1 = 8,000 \text{ N·s/m}$$

**1-26.** Write state equations for the following translational mechanical systems, using the positions of the masses as the state variables. All quantities are in SI units: Masses are in kg, the spring constants in N/m, viscous friction constants in N·s/m, and applied forces in N.

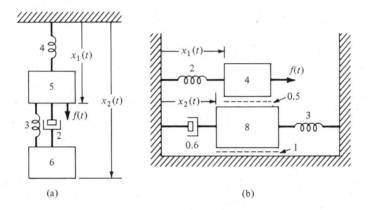

(a)    (b)

**1-27.** Write state equations for the following rotational mechanical systems, using the angles of rotation of the masses as the state variables. All quantities are in SI units: Moments of inertia are in kg·m², rotational spring constants are in N·m, rotational viscous friction constants are in N·m·s, and applied torques are in N·m.

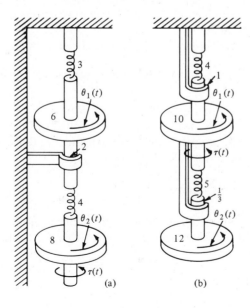

(a)    (b)

# Discrete-Time Systems and Z-Transformation

2

## 2.1 Preview

Digital control systems offer many advantages over their analog counterparts. Among these advantages are the following:

1. Low susceptibility to environmental conditions such as temperature, humidity, and component aging;
2. The cost reduction and interference rejection associated with digital signal transmission;
3. Zero "drift" of parameters;
4. High potential reliability;
5. The ability to perform highly complex tasks at low cost;
6. The potential flexibility of easily making changes in software;
7. Relatively simple interfaces with other digital systems such as those for accounting, forecasting, and data collection.

To be sure, there are possible disadvantages also:

1. The introduction of errors (or "noise") due to the finite precision of digital computation and the abrupt changes due to the discrete-time nature of digital control;
2. The need for more sophisticated engineering in order to take advantage of higher-performance control algorithms;
3. Greater limitations on speed of operation;
4. Greater potential for catastrophic failure.

This chapter covers fundamental concepts relating to digital control. We first introduce the idea of a discrete-time sequence and the z-transformation. Discrete-time systems are described in terms of difference equations and z-transfer functions. Then, the sampling of continuous-time signals and their reconstruction from samples is considered.

Digital controllers are sometimes designed by first designing an acceptable analog controller, then deriving a digital controller that closely approximates the analog controller's response. This approach is especially useful when a portion of an existing control system is to be replaced, but it usually results in poorer performance than can be obtained by designing a complete digital controller directly. This digitizing of analog controllers is discussed and several illustrative examples are given. Then, in the final section of the chapter, there is an overview of direct digital design methods paralleling those of classical continuous-time control. From today's perspective, the classical discrete-time design procedures have the same limitations as their classical counterparts in continuous-time control. Nonetheless, the concepts and tools are necessary and useful in understanding and applying the state variable methods to follow.

## 2.2 Discrete-Time Signals

A discrete-time signal $f(k)$ is a function of a discrete variable $k$. It is a sequence of numbers, called *samples*, indexed by the sample number $k$. We now examine common and important sequences, most of which consist of evenly spaced samples of familiar continuous-time functions. The z-transformation is introduced and is used to simplify sequence manipulation. Transforms of basic sequences and important z-transforms properties are shown, and transform inversion is discussed.

### 2.2.1 Representing Sequences

Some fundamental sequences, all having samples that are zero prior to $k = 0$, are shown in Figure 2-1. The unit pulse sequence, Figure 2-1(a), has a unit sample for $k = 0$, and all subsequent samples zero. The unit step sequence, Figure 2-1(b), has samples that are unity for $k = 0$ and thereafter. The unit ramp sequence, Figure 2-1(c), is defined by

$$f(k) = ku(k)$$

where $u(k)$ is the unit step sequence. The step and ramp sequences consist of samples that are values of the corresponding continuous-time function at evenly spaced points in time. The unit pulse sequence and the unit impulse function are not related in this way because the impulse is infinite at $t = 0$ and the pulse has a unit sample at $k = 0$.

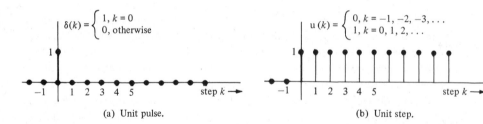

(a) Unit pulse.  (b) Unit step.

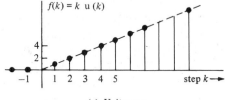

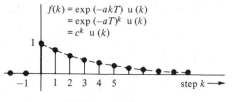

(c) Unit ramp.  (d) Geometric (or exponential).

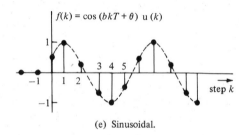

(e) Sinusoidal.

**FIGURE 2-1. Some fundamental sequences.**

Evenly spaced samples of an exponential function

$$f(k) = e^{-at}|_{t=kT} = e^{-akT} = (e^{-aT})^k = c^k$$

as in Figure 2-1(d), result in a geometric (or exponential) sequence. Geometric sequences have samples that are progressive powers of the number

$$c = e^{-aT}$$

Similarly, evenly spaced samples of a sinusoidal continuous-time function

$$f(k) = \cos(\omega t + \theta)|_{t=kT} = \cos(\omega kT + \theta)$$

as in Figure 2-1(e), constitute a sinusoidal sequence. When a sequence is derived by sampling a continuous-time function, the constant $T$, which is the time interval between samples, is termed the *sampling interval*. The use of the symbol $T$ for both transfer functions and sampling interval is common and should not be confusing.

An arbitrary sequence can be expressed as the sum of scaled and shifted pulses. The sequence

$$f(k) = \begin{cases} 4, & k = 0 \\ -3, & k = 1 \\ 2, & k = 2 \\ 1, & k = 3 \\ 0, & \text{otherwise} \end{cases}$$

for example, is, in terms of pulses:

$$f(k) = 4\delta(k) - 3\delta(k-1) + 2\delta(k-2) + \delta(k-3)$$

## 2.2.2 Z-Transformation

The $z$-transform of a sequence $f(k)$

$$\mathscr{Z}[f(k)] = F(z) = \sum_{k=0}^{\infty} f(k)z^{-k}$$

plays much the same role in the description of discrete-time signals as the Laplace transform does with continuous-time signals. When written out, the transform is

$$F(z) = f(0)z^{-0} + f(1)z^{-1} + f(2)z^{-2} + f(3)z^{-3} + \cdots$$

Each sample of the sequence, starting with step zero, is the coefficient of an inverse power of the variable $z$. Samples before step zero do not affect the transform. The utility of the transform is that simple expressions can be obtained for important sequences and that the transform converts linear, step-invariant difference equations to equivalent linear algebraic equations.

Table 2-1 lists some important sequences and their $z$-transforms. The $z$-transform of the unit pulse is

$$\mathscr{Z}[\delta(k)] = \sum_{k=0}^{\infty} \delta(k)z^{-k} = z^{-0} = 1$$

**TABLE 2-1   Z-Transform Pairs**

| f(k) | F(z) |
| --- | --- |
| $\delta(k)$, unit pulse | $1$ |
| $u(k)$, unit step | $\dfrac{z}{z-1}$ |
| $ku(k)$ | $\dfrac{z}{(z-1)^2}$ |
| $c^k u(k)$ | $\dfrac{z}{z-c}$ |
| $kc^k u(k)$ | $\dfrac{cz}{(z-c)^2}$ |
| $u(k)\sin \Omega k$ | $\dfrac{z \sin \Omega}{z^2 - 2z \cos \Omega + 1}$ |
| $u(k)\cos \Omega k$ | $\dfrac{z(z - \cos \Omega)}{z^2 - 2z \cos \Omega + 1}$ |
| $u(k)c^k \sin \Omega k$ | $\dfrac{z(c \sin \Omega)}{z^2 - (2c \cos \Omega)z + c^2}$ |
| $u(k)c^k \cos \Omega k$ | $\dfrac{z(z - c \cos \Omega)}{z^2 - (2c \cos \Omega)z + c^2}$ |

The unit step sequence has $z$-transform given by

$$\mathscr{Z}[u(k)] = \sum_{k=0}^{\infty} z^{-k}$$

Using the geometric series formula

$$\sum_{k=0}^{\infty} x^k = \frac{1}{1 - x}, \quad |x| < 1$$

this becomes

$$\mathscr{Z}[u(k)] = \sum_{k=0}^{\infty} z^{-k} = \sum_{k=0}^{\infty} \left(\frac{1}{z}\right)^k = \frac{1}{1 - \left(\dfrac{1}{z}\right)} = \frac{z}{z - 1}, \quad \left|\frac{1}{z}\right| < 1$$

The ability to recover a sequence uniquely from its $z$-transform rests upon there being at least one value of $z$ for which the infinite series converges. The unit step sequence converges for any complex value of $z$ with

$$|z| > 1$$

and there are similar regions of convergence on the $z$-plane for the $z$-transforms of other sequences.*

A geometric sequence

$$f(k) = c^k$$

has $z$-transform

$$\mathscr{L}[f(k)] = \sum_{k=0}^{\infty} c^k z^{-k} = \sum_{k=0}^{\infty} \left(\frac{c}{z}\right)^k = \frac{1}{1 - (c/z)} = \frac{z}{z - c}$$

The transform converges for any complex value of $z$ for which

$$|z| > |c|$$

A sampled exponential function

$$f(k) = e^{-akT} = (e^{-aT})^k$$

whether decaying or expanding, is of this form where the constant $c$ is chosen to be

$$c = e^{-aT}$$

The transforms of sampled sinusoids given in Table 2-1 can be found by expanding the sequence into complex exponential components. For the

---

*One can express the inverse $z$-transform as $f(k) = \dfrac{1}{2\pi j} \oint F(z)z^{k-1}dz$, a closed contour integration on the complex plane within the region of convergence of $F(z)$, similar to the situation with the inverse Laplace transformation. It is usually much easier to deal with the infinite series $F(z)$ directly, however. Like the Laplace transform, the *two-sided* $z$-transform, $F(z) = \sum\limits_{k=-\infty}^{\infty} f(k)z^{-k}$, which will not be used here, is not generally unique. That is, two different sequences can have the same two-sided $z$-transform, each with a different region of convergence. It is then necessary to additionally specify the region of convergence in order to specify the sequence.

sampled cosine

$$\mathscr{Z}[\cos \Omega k] = \frac{1}{2}\mathscr{Z}[e^{j\Omega k}] + \frac{1}{2}\mathscr{Z}[e^{-j\Omega k}] = \frac{1}{2}\frac{z}{z - e^{j\Omega}} + \frac{1}{2}\frac{z}{z - e^{-j\Omega}}$$

$$= \frac{\frac{1}{2}z(z - e^{-j\Omega}) + \frac{1}{2}z(z - e^{j\Omega})}{(z - e^{j\Omega})(z - e^{-j\Omega})} = \frac{z^2 - \frac{1}{2}(e^{j\Omega} + e^{-j\Omega})z}{z^2 - (e^{j\Omega} + e^{-j\Omega})z + 1}$$

$$= \frac{z^2 - z \cos \Omega}{z^2 - 2z \cos \Omega + 1}$$

## 2.2.3 Z-Transform Properties

Important properties of the z-transformation are listed in Table 2-2. A sequence weighted by the step index k has z-transform

$$\mathscr{Z}[kf(k)] = \sum_{k=0}^{\infty} kf(k)z^{-k} = \sum_{k=0}^{\infty} f(k)(kz^{-k})$$

$$= \sum_{k=0}^{\infty} \left\{ f(k)\left[-z\frac{d}{dz}z^{-k}\right] \right\} = -z\frac{d}{dz}\left[\sum_{k=0}^{\infty} f(k)z^{-k}\right]$$

$$= -z\frac{d}{dz}F(z)$$

Applying this result to the unit step sequence gives the transform of the unit ramp sequence

$$\mathscr{Z}[ku(k)] = -z\frac{d}{dz}\left(\frac{z}{z-1}\right) = -z\left[\frac{z - 1 - z}{(z - 1)^2}\right]$$

$$= \frac{z}{(z - 1)^2}$$

Applying the result to the geometric sequence gives

$$\mathscr{Z}[kc^k u(k)] = -z\frac{d}{dz}\left(\frac{z}{z-c}\right) = -z\left[\frac{z - c - z}{(z - c)^2}\right]$$

$$= \frac{cz}{(z - c)^2}$$

as listed in Table 2-1.

**TABLE 2-2   Z-Transform Properties**

$$\mathscr{L}[f(k)] = \sum_{k=0}^{\infty} f(k)z^{-k} = F(z)$$

$$\mathscr{L}[cf(k)] = cF(z), \quad c \text{ a constant}$$

$$\mathscr{L}[f(k) + g(k)] = F(z) + G(z)$$

$$\mathscr{L}[kf(k)] = -z\frac{dF(z)}{dz}$$

$$\mathscr{L}[c^k f(k)] = f\left(\frac{z}{c}\right), \quad c \text{ a constant}$$

$$\mathscr{L}[f(k-1)] = f(-1) + z^{-1}F(z)$$

$$\mathscr{L}[f(k-2)] = f(-2) + z^{-1}f(-1) + z^{-2}F(z)$$

$$\mathscr{L}[f(k-n)] = f(-n) + z^{-1}f(1-n) + z^{-2}f(2-n) + \cdots + z^{1-n}f(-1) + z^{-n}F(z)$$

$$\mathscr{L}[f(k+1)] = zF(z) - zf(0)$$

$$\mathscr{L}[f(k+2)] = z^2F(z) - z^2f(0) - zf(1)$$

$$\mathscr{L}[f(k+n)] = z^n F(z) - z^n f(0) - z^{n-1}f(1) - \cdots - z^2 f(n-2) - zf(n-1)$$

$$f(0) = \lim_{z \to \infty} F(z)$$

If $\lim_{k \to \infty} f(k)$ exists and is finite, $\displaystyle\lim_{k \to \infty} f(k) = \lim_{z \to 1} \left[\frac{z-1}{z} F(z)\right]$

$$\mathscr{L}\left[\sum_{i=0}^{k} f_1(k-i)f_2(i)\right] = F_1(z)F_2(z)$$

A sequence weighted by a geometric sequence $c^k$ has $z$-transform

$$\mathscr{L}[c^k f(k)] = \sum_{k=0}^{\infty} c^k f(k)z^{-k} = \sum_{k=0}^{\infty} f(k)\left(\frac{z}{c}\right)^{-k}$$

$$= F\left(\frac{z}{c}\right)$$

Applying this result to the unit ramp sequence gives

$$\mathscr{L}[c^k ku(k)] = \frac{z}{(z-1)^2}\Big|_{z=(z/c)} = \frac{cz}{(z-c)^2}$$

Applying it to the sampled cosine sequence gives

$$\mathscr{L}[c^k u(k)\cos \Omega k] = \frac{z(z-\cos \Omega)}{z^2 - 2z \cos \Omega + 1}\Big|_{z=(z/c)}$$

$$= \frac{z(z-c \cos \Omega)}{z^2 - (2c \cos \Omega)z + c^2}$$

as in Table 2-1.

A sequence that is delayed one step has $z$-transform

$$\mathscr{L}[f(k-1)] = \sum_{k=0}^{\infty} f(k-1)z^{-k} = \sum_{k=-1}^{\infty} f(k)z^{-(k+1)}$$

$$= f(-1) + z^{-1} \sum_{k=0}^{\infty} f(k)z^{-k} = f(-1) + z^{-1}F(z)$$

The initial condition term $f(-1)$ occurs because the $z$-transform of the shifted sequence is affected by an additional sample that has no effect on the $z$-transform of the original sequence. Applying this result repeatedly gives

$$\mathscr{L}[f(k-2)] = f(-2) + z^{-1}[f(-1) + z^{-1}F(z)]$$

$$= f(-2) + z^{-1}f(-1) + z^{-2}F(z)$$

$$\mathscr{L}[f(k-3)] = f(-3) + z^{-1}[f(-2) + z^{-1}f(-1) + z^{-2}F(z)]$$

$$= f(-3) + z^{-1}f(-2) + z^{-2}f(-1) + z^{-3}F(z)$$

and so on.

A one-step advance of a sequence has $z$-transform

$$\mathscr{L}[f(k+1)] = \sum_{k=0}^{\infty} f(k+1)z^{-k} = \sum_{k=1}^{\infty} f(k)z^{-k+1}$$

$$= z \sum_{k=1}^{\infty} f(k)z^{-k} = zF(z) - zf(0)$$

The advance of a sequence also involves an initial condition term, in this case

$f(0)$. Applying this result repeatedly

$$\mathscr{Z}[f(k+2)] = z[zF(z) - zf(0)] - f(1)$$
$$= z^2 F(z) - z^2 f(0) - zf(1)$$

$$\mathscr{Z}[f(k+3)] = z[z^2 F(z) - z^2 f(0) - zf(1)] - zf(2)$$
$$= z^3 F(z) - z^3 f(0) - z^2 f(1) - zf(2)$$

Analogous to the initial value theorem for the Laplace transform

$$f(0) = \lim_{z \to \infty} [f(0) + f(1)z^{-1} + f(2)z^{-2} + f(3)z^{-3} + \cdots]$$

$$= \lim_{z \to \infty} F(z)$$

Provided that the sequence $f(k)$ approaches a finite limit, the final value theorem for sequences is

$$\lim_{k \to \infty} f(k) = f_\infty = \lim_{z \to 1} \left[ \frac{z-1}{z} F(z) \right]$$

For the final value theorem to apply, the transform $F(z)$ must have all poles within the unit circle on the complex plane except possibly a single pole at $z = 1$. To show this result, consider the two finite summations

$$\sum_{k=0}^{n} f(k)z^{-k} = f(0) + f(1)z^{-1} + f(2)z^{-2} + \cdots + f(n)z^{-n}$$

and

$$\sum_{k=1}^{n} f(k-1)z^{-k} = f(0)z^{-1} + f(1)z^{-2} + \cdots + f(n-1)z^{-n}$$

$$= z^{-1} \sum_{k=0}^{n-1} f(k)z^{-k}$$

In the limit, as $z$ approaches unity, the difference between these two summations is

$$\lim_{z \to 1} \left[ \sum_{k=0}^{n} f(k)z^{-k} - z^{-1} \sum_{k=0}^{n-1} f(k)z^{-k} \right] = f(n)$$

The limit of this equality as $n$ becomes very large is

$$\lim_{n \to \infty} \left\{ \lim_{z \to 1} \left[ \sum_{k=0}^{n} f(k)z^{-k} - z^{-1} \sum_{k=0}^{n-1} f(k)z^{-k} \right] \right\} = f_{\infty}$$

when the limit exists. Interchanging the order of the limits

$$\lim_{z \to 1} \left\{ \lim_{n \to \infty} \left[ \sum_{k=0}^{n} f(k)z^{-k} - z^{-1} \sum_{k=0}^{n-1} f(k)z^{-k} \right] \right\} = f_{\infty}$$

or

$$\lim_{z \to 1} \left[ (1 - z^{-1})F(z) \right] = f_{\infty}$$

## 2.2.4 *Z-Transform Inversion*

The sequence of samples represented by a rational *z*-transform can be obtained by long division, expanding the transform into a power series in $z^{-1}$ with coefficients that are the samples:

$$F(z) = f(0)z^{-0} + f(1)z^{-1} + f(2)z^{-2} + f(3)z^{-3} + \cdots$$

For the *z*-transform

$$F(z) = \frac{2z^3 + 2z^2 + 3z - 4}{z^3 + 0.4z^2 - 0.6z + 0.3}$$

for example, long division gives

$$
\begin{array}{r}
2 + 1.2z^{-1} + 3.72z^{-2} - 5.368z^{-3} + \cdots \\
z^3 + 0.4z^2 - 0.6z + 0.3 \overline{\smash{\big)}\ 2z^3 + 2z^2 + 3z - 4} \\
\underline{2z^3 + 0.8z^2 - 1.2z + 0.6} \\
1.2z^2 + 4.2z - 4.6 \\
\underline{1.2z^2 + 0.48z - 0.72 + 0.36z^{-1}} \\
3.72z - 3.88 - 0.36z^{-1} \\
\underline{3.72z + 1.488 - 2.232z^{-1} + 1.116z^{-2}} \\
- 5.368 + 1.872z^{-1} - 1.116z^{-2}
\end{array}
$$

The first several samples of the sequences are given by

$$f(k) = 2\delta(k) + 1.2\delta(k-1) + 3.72\delta(k-2) - 5.368\delta(k-3) + \cdots$$

or

$$f(0) = 2$$
$$f(1) = 1.2$$
$$f(2) = 3.72$$
$$f(3) = -5.368$$
$$\vdots$$

In principle, as many terms in the sequence as desired can be found in this way, but a closed-form expression for the sequence does not generally result.

The inverse $z$-transform always yields a sequence with all samples zero prior to $k = 0$.

To find formulas for the sequences of samples represented by a rational $z$-transform, partial fraction expansion is used. Rather than expanding a $z$-transform $F(z)$ directly in partial fractions, the function $F(z)/z$ is expanded so that terms with a $z$ in the numerator result. For example, for the $z$-transform

$$F(z) = \frac{-2z^2 + 11z}{z^2 - z - 6}$$

$$\frac{F(z)}{z} = \frac{-2z + 11}{z^2 - z - 6} = \frac{-3}{z + 2} + \frac{1}{z - 3}$$

giving

$$F(z) = \frac{-3z}{z + 2} + \frac{z}{z - 3}$$

$$f(k) = -3(-2)^k + 3^k, \qquad k = 0, 1, 2, 3, \ldots$$

Another example is the following:

$$F(z) = \frac{2z - 3}{z(z - 0.5)(z + 0.3)}$$

$$\frac{F(z)}{z} = \frac{2z - 3}{z^2(z - 0.5)(z + 0.3)} = \frac{-40}{z} + \frac{20}{z^2} + \frac{-10}{z - 0.5} + \frac{50}{z + 0.3}$$

so that

$$F(z) = -40 + \frac{20}{z} + \frac{-10z}{z - 0.5} + \frac{50z}{z + 0.3}$$

$$f(k) = -40\delta(k) + 20\delta(k-1) - 10(0.5)^k + 50(-0.3)^k \qquad k = 0, 1, 2, 3, \ldots$$

When complex conjugate pairs of terms occur, they can be combined into a single term with a quadratic denominator, then separated into terms of the form of the last two entries in Table 2-1. For example, for the $z$-transform

$$F(z) = \frac{-6z^2 + z}{(z-1)(z - \frac{1}{2} + j\frac{1}{4})(z - \frac{1}{2} - j\frac{1}{4})}$$

$$\frac{F(z)}{z} = \frac{-6z + 1}{(z-1)(z - \frac{1}{2} + j\frac{1}{4})(z - \frac{1}{2} - j\frac{1}{4})}$$

$$= \frac{-16}{z-1} + \frac{8 + j4}{z - \frac{1}{2} + j\frac{1}{4}} + \frac{8 - j4}{z - \frac{1}{2} - j\frac{1}{4}} = \frac{-16}{z-1} + \frac{16z - 6}{z^2 - z + \frac{5}{16}}$$

$$F(z) = \frac{-16z}{z-1} + \frac{z(16z - 6)}{z^2 - z + \frac{5}{16}}$$

Equating

$$\frac{z(16z - 6)}{z^2 - z + \frac{5}{16}} = \frac{K_1 z(c \sin \Omega)}{z^2 - (2c \cos \Omega)z + c^2} + \frac{K_2 z(z - c \cos \Omega)}{z^2 - (2c \cos \Omega)z + c^2}$$

where $c$, $\Omega$, $K_1$ and $K_2$ are determined as follows,

$$c^2 = \frac{5}{16}; \qquad c = 0.56$$

$$2c \cos \Omega = 1; \qquad \cos \Omega = 0.893; \qquad \Omega = 0.468 \text{ rad.}$$

$$c \sin \Omega = 0.56 \sin (0.468) = 0.252$$

Then

$$F(z) = \frac{-16z}{z-1} + \frac{(23.81)z(0.252)}{z^2 - z + \frac{5}{16}} + \frac{(12)z(z - 0.5)}{z^2 - z + \frac{5}{16}}$$

$$f(k) = -16 + c^k \sin(\Omega k) + 12c^k \cos(\Omega k)$$

$$= -16 + (0.56)^k[23.81 \sin(0.468k) + 12 \cos(0.468k)], \qquad k = 0, 1, 2, \ldots$$

**TABLE 2-3   Sequences Corresponding to Various Z-Transform Partial Fraction Terms**

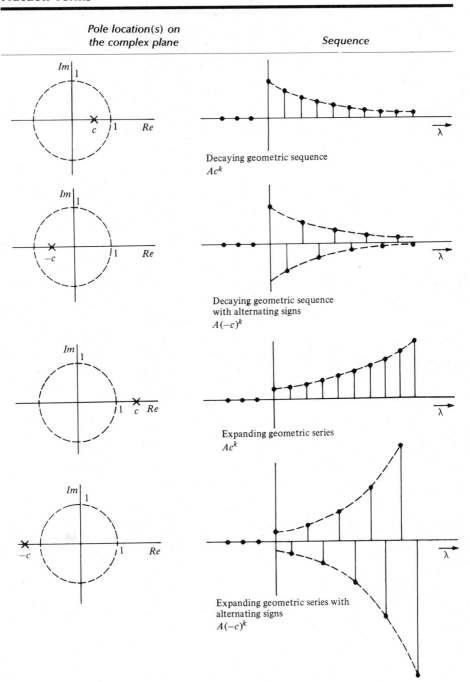

| Pole location(s) on the complex plane | Sequence |

Decaying geometric sequence
$Ac^k$

Decaying geometric sequence with alternating signs
$A(-c)^k$

Expanding geometric series
$Ac^k$

Expanding geometric series with alternating signs
$A(-c)^k$

**TABLE 2-3** (cont.)

| Pole location(s) on the complex plane | Sequence |
| --- | --- |
| 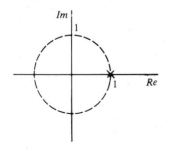 | 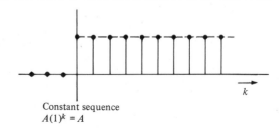<br>Constant sequence<br>$A(1)^k = A$ |
| 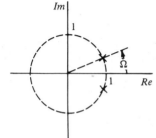 | 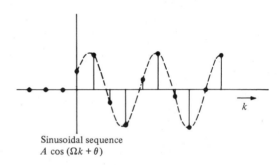<br>Sinusoidal sequence<br>$A \cos (\Omega k + \theta)$ |
| 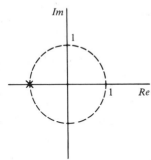 | 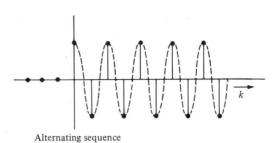<br>Alternating sequence<br>$A(-1)^k$ |
| 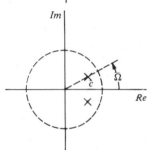 | 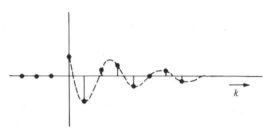<br>Damped sinusoidal sequence<br>$Ac^k \cos (\Omega k + \theta)$ |

**TABLE 2-3** (cont.)

| Pole location(s) on the complex plane | Sequence |
|---|---|

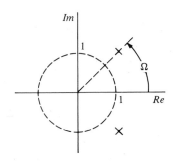

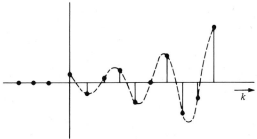

Exponentially expanding sinusoidal
sequence
$A^k \cos(\Omega k + \theta)$

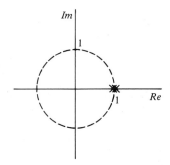

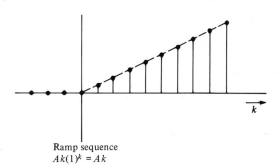

Ramp sequence
$Ak(1)^k = Ak$

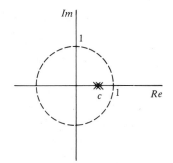

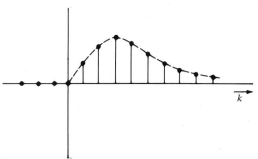

Ramp-weighted geometric sequence
$Akc^k$

Table 2-3 shows, for rational $z$-transforms, the types of sequences corresponding to various partial fraction term pole (denominator root) locations. For poles inside the unit circle on the complex plane, these sequences decay with step. For nonrepeated poles on the unit circle, the sequences neither expand nor decay with step. Poles outside the unit circle and repeated poles on the unit circle represent sequences that expand with step.

## 2.3 Discrete-Time Systems

The input-output behavior of discrete-time systems is described by difference equations, analogous to the differential equations that describe continuous-time systems. In this section, we examine the properties of difference equations and apply $z$-transform methods to find their solutions. Discrete frequency response, an important technique for experimentally finding $z$-transfer function models, is introduced, and bilinear transformation is shown to convert discrete-time stability determination to an equivalent continuous-time problem.

### 2.3.1 Difference Equations

Discrete-time systems are described by difference equations which in the linear, step-invariant case have the form

$$y(k + n) + a_{n-1} y(k + n - 1) + a_{n-2} y(k + n - 2) + \cdots$$
$$+ a_1 y(k + 1) + a_0 y(k)$$
$$= b_m r(k + m) + b_{m-1} r(k + m - 1) + \cdots + b_1 r(k + 1) + b_0 r(k) \quad (2\text{-}1)$$

where $y$ is the output and $r$ is an input. When expressed this way, the coefficient of $y(k + n)$ is made unity, $b_m$ is nonzero, and either $a_0$ or $b_0$, or both, are nonzero. The *order* of a difference equation is $n$, the number of past output steps that are involved in calculating the present output:

$$y(k + n) =$$

$$\underbrace{- a_{n-1} y(k + n - 1) - a_{n-2} y(k + n - 2) - \cdots - a_1 y(k + 1) - a_0 y(k)}_{n \text{ terms}}$$

$$\underbrace{+ b_m r(k + m) + b_{m-1} r(k + m - 1) + \cdots + b_1 r(k + 1) + b_0 r(k)}_{m \text{ terms}}$$

A discrete-time system is termed *causal* if $m \leqslant n$ so that only present and past inputs (not future ones) are involved in the calculation of the present output. If a system has more than a single output, there is a difference equation for each output. If a discrete-time system has more than a single input, there are terms in the equation(s) for each input.

Since a difference equation holds for each integer value of the index $k$, there are many equivalent forms for the equation. Replacing $k$ by $k - n$ in equation (2-1), for example, gives

$$y(k) + a_{n-1}y(k-1) + a_{n-2}y(k-2) + \cdots + a_1 y(k-n+1) + a_0 y(k-n)$$
$$= b_m r(k-n+m) + b_{m-1}r(k-n+m-1) + \cdots + b_1 r(k-n+1)$$
$$+ b_0 r(k-n)$$

Given the input $r(k)$ for $k = -n, -n + 1, \ldots, 0, 1, 2, \ldots$ and the initial conditions $y(-1), y(-2), y(-3), \ldots, y(-n)$ the solution $y(k)$ to an $n$th order causal difference equation. can be calculated for $k = 0, 1, 2, \ldots$ by repeatedly using the equation. Consider the difference equation

$$y(k + 2) = 2y(k + 1) - 3y(k) + 4r(k + 1) - r(k)$$

with input

$$r(k) = (-1)^k$$

and initial conditions

$$y(-1) = 5; \qquad y(-2) = -6$$

Using $k = -2$ and substituting

$$y(0) = 2y(-1) - 3y(-2) + 4r(-1) - r(-2)$$
$$= 10 + 18 - 4 - 1 = 23$$

Using $k = -1$ and substituting

$$y(1) = 2y(0) - 3y(-1) + 4r(0) - r(-1)$$
$$= 46 - 15 + 4 - 1 = 34$$

Similarly:

$$y(2) = 2y(1) - 3y(0) + 4r(1) - r(0) = 68 - 69 - 4 - 1 = -6$$

$$y(3) = 2y(2) - 3y(1) + 4r(2) - r(1)$$

$$= -12 - 102 + 4 + 1 = -109$$

and so on. This is known as a *recursive* solution of the equation, using the equation and solutions at past steps to calculate the solution at the next step.

One can construct a difference equation in computer software by programming its recursive solution. For example, the second order difference equation

$$y(k + 2) + \frac{1}{2}y(k + 1) - \frac{1}{3}y(k) = r(k + 2) - 4r(k)$$

or

$$y(k) = -\frac{1}{2}y(k - 1) + \frac{1}{3}y(k - 2) + r(k) - 4r(k - 2)$$

is realized by the digital computer program in Basic given in Table 2-4. The initial conditions incorporated were chosen arbitrarily. A digital hardware realization of this difference equation can also be constructed by coding the signals as binary words, storing present and past values of the input and output in registers, and using binary arithmetic devices to multiply the signals by the equation coefficients and add them to form the output.

### 2.3.2 Z-Transfer Function Methods

Formulas for the responses of step-invariant discrete-time systems can be found using $z$-transformation. For example, consider the single-input, single-output system

$$y(k + 2) + \frac{1}{4}y(k + 1) - \frac{1}{8}y(k) = 3r(k + 1) - r(k)$$

with input

$$r(k) = (-1)^k u(k)$$

and initial conditions

$$y(-1) = 5; \qquad y(-2) = -6$$

**TABLE 2-4  Digital Computer Program in Basic to Realize a Difference Equation**

```
100  REM DIFFERENCE EQUATION SOLUTION
110  REM
120  REM Y IS PRESENT OUTPUT
130  REM Y1 IS OUTPUT DELAYED ONE STEP
140  REM Y2 IS OUTPUT DELAYED TWO STEPS
150  REM R IS PRESENT INPUT
160  REM R1 IS INPUT DELAYED ONE STEP
170  REM R2 IS INPUT DELAYED TWO STEPS
180  REM K IS STEP NUMBER
190  REM
200  REM ASSIGN INITIAL CONDITIONS
210  Y2 = 3
220  Y1 = -1
230  R1 = -2
240  R2 = 4
250  REM START AT STEP ZERO
260  K = 0
270  REM ENTER INPUT R(K)
280  PRINT "ENTER STEP "; K;" INPUT: ";
290  INPUT R
300  REM COMPUTE AND PRINT Y(K)
310  Y = -(1/2)*Y1 + (1/3)*Y2 + R - 4*R2
320  PRINT "STEP "; K;" OUTPUT IS "; Y
330  REM INCREMENT STEP INDEX
350  K = K + 1
360  Y2 = Y1
370  Y1 = Y
380  R2 = R1
390  R1 = R
400  REM LOOP TO COMPUTE NEXT OUTPUT
410  GOTO 270
420  END
```

The difference equation is first converted to the equivalent form

$$y(k) + \frac{1}{4}y(k-1) - \frac{1}{8}y(k-2) = 3r(k-1) - r(k-2)$$

Then

$$Y(z) + \frac{1}{4}[z^{-1}Y(z) + y(-1)] - \frac{1}{8}[z^{-2}Y(z) + z^{-1}y(-1) + y(-2)]$$

$$= 3[z^{-1}R(z) + r(-1)] - [z^{-2}R(z) + z^{-1}r(-1) + r(-2)]$$

Since

$$r(-1) = r(-2) = 0$$

$$\left(1 + \frac{1}{4}z^{-1} - \frac{1}{8}z^{-2}\right)Y(z) = (3z^{-1} - z^{-2})R(z) + \frac{5}{8}z^{-1} - 2$$

$$\left(z^2 + \frac{1}{4}z - \frac{1}{8}\right)Y(z) = (3z - 1)R(z) + \frac{5}{8}z - 2z^2$$

$$Y(z) = \underbrace{\frac{3z - 1}{z^2 + \frac{1}{4}z - \frac{1}{8}}}_{\text{zero-state component}} R(z) + \underbrace{\frac{-2z^2 + \frac{5}{8}z}{z^2 + \frac{1}{4}z - \frac{1}{8}}}_{\text{zero-input component}}$$

For

$$R(z) = \mathscr{Z}[(-1)^k] = \frac{z}{z+1}$$

then

$$Y(z) = \frac{-2z^3 + \frac{13}{8}z^2 - \frac{3}{8}z}{(z + \frac{1}{2})(z - \frac{1}{4})(z + 1)}$$

and $Y(z)$ is inverted to obtain $y(k)$.
   Expanding $Y(z)/z$ into partial fractions

$$\frac{Y(z)}{z} = \frac{-2z^2 + \frac{13}{8}z - \frac{3}{8}}{(z + \frac{1}{2})(z - \frac{1}{4})(z + 1)} = \frac{\frac{9}{2}}{z + \frac{1}{2}} + \frac{-\frac{1}{10}}{z - \frac{1}{4}} + \frac{-\frac{32}{5}}{z + 1}$$

then

$$Y(z) = \frac{(\frac{9}{2})z}{z + \frac{1}{2}} + \frac{(-\frac{1}{10})z}{z - \frac{1}{4}} + \frac{-(\frac{32}{5})z}{z + 1}$$

so that

$$y(k) = \left[ \left( \frac{9}{2} \right) \left( -\frac{1}{2} \right)^k - \left( \frac{1}{10} \right) \left( \frac{1}{4} \right)^k - \left( \frac{32}{5} \right) (-1)^k \right] u(k)$$

In general, an $n$th order causal single-input system with input-output difference equation

$$y(k + n) + a_{n-1} y(k + n - 1) + \cdots + a_1 y(k + 1) + a_0 y(k)$$

$$= b_m r(k + m) + \cdots + b_1 r(k + 1) + b_0 r(k)$$

or

$$y(k) + a_{n-1} y(k - 1) + \cdots + a_1 y(k - n + 1) + a_0 y(k - n)$$

$$= b_m r(k + m - n) + \cdots + b_1 r(k - n + 1) + b_0 r(k - n)$$

has a $z$-transformed output given by

$$Y(z) + a_{n-1}[z^{-1} Y(z) + y(-1)] + \cdots$$

$$+ a_1[z^{-n+1} Y(z) + z^{-n+2} y(-1) + \cdots + y(-n + 1)]$$

$$+ a_0[z^{-n} Y(z) + z^{-n+1} y(-1) + \cdots + y(-n)]$$

$$= b_m[z^{-n+m} R(z) + z^{-n+m-1} r(-1) + \cdots + r(-n + m - 1)] + \cdots$$

$$+ b_0[z^{-n} R(z) + z^{-n+1} r(-1) + \cdots + r(-n)]$$

$$Y(z) = \underbrace{\frac{b_m z^m + b_{m-1} z^{m-1} + \cdots + b_1 z + b_0}{z^n + a_{n-1} z^{n-1} + \cdots + a_1 z + a_0} R(z)}_{\text{zero-state component}}$$

$$+ \underbrace{\frac{(\text{polynomial in } z \text{ of degree } n \text{ or less with coefficients dependent on initial conditions})}{z^n + a_{n-1} z^{n-1} + \cdots + a_1 z + a_0}}_{\text{zero-input component}}$$

The zero-input response component is zero if all the initial conditions are zero. The zero-state response component is the product of the system $z$-transfer function

$$T(z) = \frac{b_m z^m + b_{m-1} z^{m-1} + \cdots + b_1 z + b_0}{z^n + a_{n-1} z^{n-1} + \cdots + a_1 z + a_0}$$

and the $z$-transform of the input:

$$Y_{\text{zero state}}(z) = T(z)R(z)$$

The transfer function is the ratio of $z$-transformed output to $z$-transformed input when all initial conditions are zero.

It is also common practice to separate system response into two other components, *natural* (or *transient*) and *forced* (or *steady-state*). Both the zero-state and the zero-input response components share the system's characteristic polynomial

$$q(z) = z^n + a_{n-1}z^{n-1} + \cdots + a_1 z + a_0 = (z - z_1)(z - z_2)\ldots(z - z_n)$$

and each of these potentially contributes terms of the form

$$\frac{K_1 z}{z - z_1}, \quad \frac{K_2 z}{z - z_2}, \ldots, \quad \frac{K_n z}{z - z_n}$$

(or the equivalent if the characteristic equation has repeated roots) to the output transform. The sum of all these is the natural response component while the remainder of the response, which has form dependent on the specific input, is the forced response component.

As indicated in Figure 2-2, the unit pulse response of a linear, step-invariant system, the response when the input is the unit pulse $\delta(k)$ and all initial conditions are zero, is given by

$$Y_{\text{pulse}}(z) = R(z)T(z) = T(z)$$

Its $z$-transform is equal to the transfer function. A single-input, single-output system is said to be *input-output stable* if its unit pulse response decays asymptotically to zero. This occurs if and only if the denominator polynomial of the transfer function has all of its roots inside the unit circle on the complex plane.

When a system has more than one output, there is an input-output equation for each of the outputs. When there is more than a single input, each input-output equation can contain terms for each input. As with continuous-

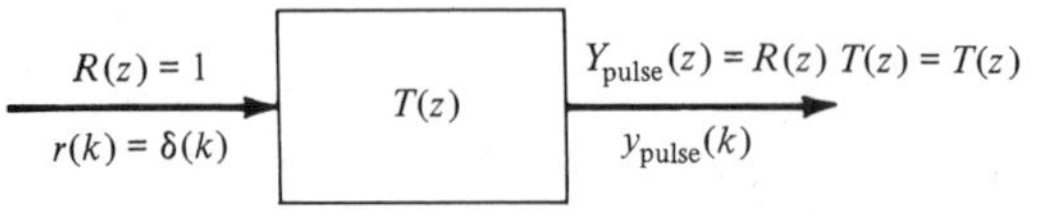

$$R(z) = 1 \quad \boxed{\quad T(z) \quad} \quad Y_{\text{pulse}}(z) = R(z)\,T(z) = T(z)$$
$$r(k) = \delta(k) \qquad\qquad\qquad y_{\text{pulse}}(k)$$

**FIGURE 2-2.   Unit pulse response of a discrete-time system.**

time systems, a multiple-input, multiple-output discrete-time system has a $z$-transfer function for each combination of input and output. Each $z$-transfer function is the ratio of the $z$-transform of one of the outputs to the $z$-transform of one of the inputs when all initial conditions and all other inputs are zero. Using the superposition property of linear systems, the zero-state component of each output is the sum of the contributions to that output of each input acting alone. A multiple-input, multiple-output system is input-output stable if and only if all of the poles of all of its $z$-transfer functions are inside the unit circle on the complex plane.

The last entry in the listing of $z$-transform properties, Table 2-2, is that the inverse $z$-transform of the product of two transforms, $F_1(z)$ and $F_2(z)$, is the discrete convolution of the two sequences, $f_1(k)$ and $f_2(k)$. Using

$$\mathscr{Z}\left[\sum_{i=0}^{k} f_1(k-i)f_2(i)\right] = F_1(z)F_2(z)$$

and inverse transforming both sides,

$$\mathscr{Z}^{-1}[F_1(z)F_2(z)] = \sum_{i=0}^{k} f_1(k-i)f_2(i) = \text{convolution}[f_1(k), f_2(k)]$$

$$= \text{convolution}[f_2(k), f_1(k)] = \sum_{i=0}^{k} f_2(k-i)f_1(i)$$

The convolution relation holds for values of $z$ for which both $F_1(z)$ and $F_2(z)$ converge. This is the form of the zero-state component of a single-input system's output

$$y_{\text{zero-state}}(k) = \mathscr{Z}^{-1}[T(z)R(z)] = \text{convolution}[h(k), r(k)]$$

where $T(z)$ is the transfer function and $R(z)$ is the input. Using the relation, the zero-state output is seen to be the convolution of the system's unit pulse response

$$h(k) = \mathscr{Z}^{-1}[T(z)]$$

with the input $r(k)$.

The convolution relation is derived as follows. For convergent transforms and sequences that are zero for negative step:

$$F_1(z)F_2(z) = \left[\sum_{i=0}^{\infty} f_2(i)z^{-i}\right]\left[\sum_{k=0}^{\infty} f_1(k)z^{-k}\right] = \left[\sum_{i=0}^{\infty} f_2(i)\left[z^{-i}\sum_{k=0}^{\infty} f_1(k)^{-k}\right]\right]$$

Using the delayed sequence property, with $f_2(k)$ zero prior to $k = 0$ so that the initial condition terms are all zero

$$z^{-i} \sum_{k=0}^{\infty} f_1(k)z^{-k} = \mathscr{Z}[f_1(k-i)] = \sum_{k=0}^{\infty} f_1(k-i)z^{-k}$$

and

$$F_1(z)F_2(z) = \sum_{i=0}^{\infty} f_2(i)\left[\sum_{k=0}^{\infty} f_1(k-i)z^{-k}\right] = \sum_{k=0}^{\infty}\left[\sum_{i=0}^{\infty} f_1(k-i)f_2(i)\right]z^{-k}$$

Now since $f_1$ is zero for negative arguments

$$F_1(z)F_2(z) = \sum_{k=0}^{\infty}\left[\sum_{i=0}^{k} f_1(k-i)f_2(i)\right]z^{-k} = \mathscr{Z}\left[\sum_{i=0}^{k} f_1(k-i)f_2(i)\right]$$

Figure 2-3 shows the process involved in discrete convolution. In Figure 2-3(a), two sequences, $f_1(k)$ and $f_2(k)$, are shown. They are plotted offset slightly for clarity. In Figure 2-3(b), the step index is changed to $i$ and $f_1(k - i)$ and $f_2(i)$ are plotted. Changing the argument of a sequence from $i$ to $k - i$ (versus step $i$) reverses the direction of the sequence and delays it $k$ steps, as shown. For a specific step $k$, the products $f_1(k - i)f_2(i)$ are plotted versus $i$ in Figure 2-3(c), and the sum of these is the convolution for that step $k$. The sum of products as a function of $k$, which is the convolution of the two sequences, is shown in Figure 2-3(d).

As a numerical example of convolution, let

$$f_1(k) = \left(\frac{1}{4}\right)^k; \qquad f_2(k) = \left(\frac{1}{2}\right)^k$$

Then

$$g(k) = \text{convolution}[f_1(k), f_2(k)] = \sum_{i=0}^{k} f_1(k-i)f_2(i) = \sum_{i=0}^{k}\left(\frac{1}{4}\right)^{k-i}\left(\frac{1}{2}\right)^i$$

The first several values of the convolution are as follows:

$$g(0) = \left(\frac{1}{4}\right)^0\left(\frac{1}{2}\right)^0 = 1$$

$$g(1) = \left(\frac{1}{4}\right)^1\left(\frac{1}{4}\right)^0 + \left(\frac{1}{4}\right)^0\left(\frac{1}{2}\right)^1 = \frac{1}{4} + \frac{1}{2} = \frac{3}{4}$$

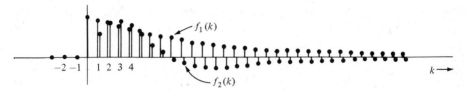

(a) Functions to be convolved set to zero prior to $k = 0$.

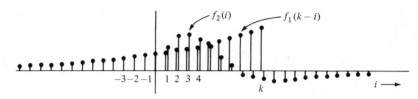

(b) Step index changed to $i$ and one function reversed in step.

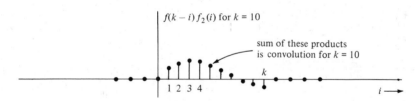

(c) Products of overlapping samples.

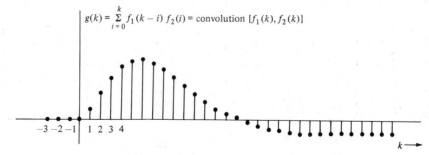

(d) Sums of products of overlapping samples as a function of the shift, $k$.

**FIGURE 2-3.   Discrete convolution of two sequences that are zero prior to $k = 0$.**

$$g(2) = \left(\frac{1}{4}\right)^2\left(\frac{1}{2}\right)^0 + \left(\frac{1}{4}\right)^1\left(\frac{1}{2}\right)^1 + \left(\frac{1}{4}\right)^0\left(\frac{1}{2}\right)^2 = \frac{1}{16} + \frac{1}{8} + \frac{1}{4} = \frac{7}{16}$$

$$g(3) = \left(\frac{1}{4}\right)^3\left(\frac{1}{2}\right)^0 + \left(\frac{1}{4}\right)^2\left(\frac{1}{2}\right)^1 + \left(\frac{1}{4}\right)^1\left(\frac{1}{2}\right)^2 + \left(\frac{1}{4}\right)^0\left(\frac{1}{2}\right)^3$$

$$= \frac{1}{64} + \frac{1}{32} + \frac{1}{16} + \frac{1}{8} = \frac{15}{64}$$

These values compare with the transform solution

$$G(z) = \left(\frac{z}{z - \frac{1}{4}}\right)\left(\frac{z}{z - \frac{1}{2}}\right) = \frac{-z}{z - \frac{1}{4}} + \frac{2z}{z - \frac{1}{2}}$$

$$g(k) = \left[ -\left(\frac{1}{4}\right)^k + 2\left(\frac{1}{2}\right)^k \right] u(k)$$

which gives

$$g(0) = -\left(\frac{1}{4}\right)^0 + 2\left(\frac{1}{2}\right)^0 = 1$$

$$g(1) = -\left(\frac{1}{4}\right)^1 + 2\left(\frac{1}{2}\right)^1 = -\frac{1}{4} + 1 = \frac{3}{4}$$

$$g(2) = -\left(\frac{1}{4}\right)^2 + 2\left(\frac{1}{2}\right)^2 = -\frac{1}{16} + \frac{2}{4} = \frac{7}{16}$$

$$g(3) = -\left(\frac{1}{4}\right)^3 + 2\left(\frac{1}{2}\right)^3 = -\frac{1}{64} + \frac{2}{8} = \frac{15}{64}$$

Z-transfer functions for discrete-time systems and system components are manipulated in the same way as are transfer functions for continuous-time systems. For example, a system block diagram is shown in Figure 2-4. Using the block diagram equivalences as for continuous-time systems, the overall z-transfer function is found to be

$$T(z) = \frac{\left(\frac{1}{z + \frac{1}{2}}\right)\left(\frac{1}{z^2 - \frac{1}{2}z + 2}\right)}{1 + \left(\frac{1}{z + \frac{1}{2}}\right)\left(\frac{1}{z^2 - \frac{1}{2}z + 2}\right)\left(z - \frac{1}{2}\right)} = \frac{1}{z^3 + \frac{11}{4}z + \frac{1}{2}}$$

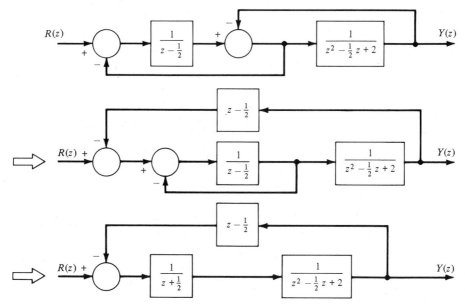

**FIGURE 2-4.  Manipulating z-transforms.**

Like its continuous-time counterpart, a pole-zero plot of a $z$-transfer function consists of X's denoting poles and O's denoting zeros on the complex plane. It is helpful to also place the multiplying constant of the function in a box at the right of the plot. The $z$-transfer function

$$T(z) = \frac{3z + 3z^3}{4z^4 + 6z^3 - 4z^2 + z + 2} = \left(\frac{3}{4}\right) \frac{z(z + j)(z - j)}{(z + 2)(z + \frac{1}{2})(z - \frac{1}{2} + j\frac{1}{2})(z - \frac{1}{2} - j\frac{1}{2})}$$

has the pole-zero plot given in Figure 2-5. It represents an unstable discrete-time system since there is a pole (at $z = -2$) outside the unit circle. The usual graphical evaluation and root locus techniques can also be applied without change in the discrete-time case, although it is the unit circle rather than the imaginary axis that is the stability boundary.

### 2.3.3  Discrete Frequency Response

When the input to a linear, step-invariant discrete-time system is a geometric (or sampled exponential) sequence

$$r(k) = Ac^k$$

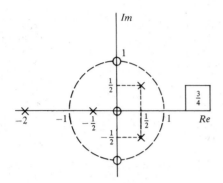

**FIGURE 2-5.    Poles and zeros of a z-transfer function.**

where $A$ and $c$ are constants, the corresponding forced output is also a geometric sequence:

$$y_{\text{forced}}(k) = Bc^k$$

with the same geometric constant $c$. This is similar to the result for forced exponential response of a continuous-time system.

If the discrete-time system's difference equation is

$$y(k + n) + a_{n-1}y(k + n - 1) + \cdots + a_1 y(k + 1) + a_0 y(k)$$
$$= b_m r(k + m) + b_{m-1}r(k + m - 1) + \cdots + b_0 r(k)$$

these signals satisfy

$$(c^n + a_{n-1}c^{n-1} + \cdots + a_1 c + a_0)Ac^k = (b_m c^m + b_{m-1}c^{m-1} + \cdots + b_0)Bc^k$$

The ratio of forced output to geometric input is

$$\frac{y_{\text{forced}}(k) = Bc^k}{r(k) = Ac^k} = \frac{b_m c^m + b_{m-1}c^{m-1} + \cdots + b_0}{c^n + a_{n-1}c^{n-1} + \cdots + a_1 c + a_0}$$

which is the z-transfer function relating the output and input, evaluated at $z = c$. As an example, if the input to a system with z-transfer function

$$T(z) = \frac{2z - 1}{z^2 + \frac{1}{2}z}$$

is

$$r(k) = 3 \left(\frac{1}{3}\right)^k$$

then the forced output is

$$y_{forced}(k) = T(z = \tfrac{1}{3})r(k) = -\tfrac{18}{5}(\tfrac{1}{3})^k$$

The forced output for a complex exponential input

$$\underline{r}(k) = A \cos(\Omega k + \theta) + jA \sin(\Omega k + \theta) = Ae^{j(\Omega k + \theta)} = (Ae^{j\theta})(e^{j\Omega})^k$$

where $A$, $\Omega$, and $\theta$ are constants is then

$$y_{forced}(k) = T(z = e^{j\Omega})r(k)$$

The sinusoidal sequence

$$r(k) = A \cos(\Omega k + \theta)$$

which is the real part of the complex exponential input, has forced response that is the real part of the complex exponential forced response:

$$y_{forced}(k) = Re[T(z = e^{j\Omega})Ae^{j\theta}(e^{j\Omega})^k] = B \cos(\Omega k + \phi)$$

where, for $A$ positive:

$$B = |T(z = e^{j\Omega})| A$$

$$\phi = \theta + \underline{/T(z = e^{j\Omega})}$$

Hence, when the input to a linear, step-invariant discrete-time system is a sinusoidal sequence, the system's forced output is another sinusoidal sequence with the same frequency $\Omega$, but generally with a different amplitude $B$ and phase shift $\phi$. Figure 2-6 illustrates the idea.
    Samples of the sinusoidal continuous-time function

$$r(t) = A \cos(\omega t + \theta)$$

at sampling interval $T$ are

$$r(k) = A \cos(\omega k T + \theta) = A \cos(\Omega k + \theta)$$

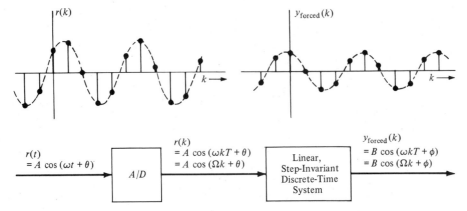

**FIGURE 2-6.   Discrete-time system with a sinusoidal input sequence and the sinusoidal forced output sequence.**

where

$$\omega\Omega = T$$

The discrete-time system's forced response

$$y_{forced}(k) = B \cos(\omega kT + \phi) = B \cos(\Omega k + \phi)$$

consists of samples of another sinusoidal function of the same frequency,

$$y(t) = B \cos(\omega t + \phi)$$

or of any frequency $\omega_i$ for which

$$\omega_i = \omega + i\frac{2\pi}{T}, \qquad i = \pm 1, \pm 2, \ldots$$

The magnitude of the z-transfer function, evaluated at $z = \exp(j\Omega)$, is the ratio of forced sinusoidal output sequence amplitude to sinusoidal input amplitude:

$$\frac{B}{A} = |T(z = e^{j\Omega})|$$

The angle of the z-transfer function, evaluated at $z = \exp(j\Omega)$, is the phase shift from input to output:

$$\phi - \theta = \underline{/T(z = e^{j\Omega})}$$

This result is similar to the counterpart for continuous-time systems, where the transfer function $T(s)$ is evaluated at $s = j\omega$.

Suppose that a system with $z$-transfer function

$$T(z) = \frac{2z}{z - \frac{1}{3}}$$

is driven with the sinusoidal input sequence

$$r(k) = 10 \cos\left(\frac{1}{2} k + \frac{\pi}{8}\right) = A \cos(\Omega k + \theta)$$

where arguments of all trigonometric functions are in radians. The $z$-transfer function, evaluated at $z = \exp(j\Omega)$ is

$$T(z = e^{j1/2}) = T(z = 0.877 + j0.48) = \frac{2(0.877 + j0.48)}{(0.877 + j0.48) - \frac{1}{3}}$$

$$= \frac{2e^{j1/2}}{0.544 + j0.48} = \frac{2e^{j1/2}}{0.725e^{j0.72}} = 2.76e^{-j0.22}$$

The amplitude of the forced sinusoidal output sequence is then

$$B = A|T(z = e^{j1/2})| = 10(2.76) = 27.6$$

and the output sequence phase is

$$\phi = \theta + \underline{/T(z = e^{j1/2})} = \frac{\pi}{8} - 0.22 = 0.173 \text{ rad}$$

so that

$$y_{\text{forced}}(k) = 27.6 \cos\left(\frac{1}{2} k + 0.173\right), \qquad k = 0, 1, 2, \ldots$$

Frequency response plots for a linear, step-invariant discrete-time system consist of plots of the magnitude and angle of the $z$-transfer function, evaluated at $z = \exp(j\Omega)$, versus $\Omega$. The magnitude plot is the ratio of forced

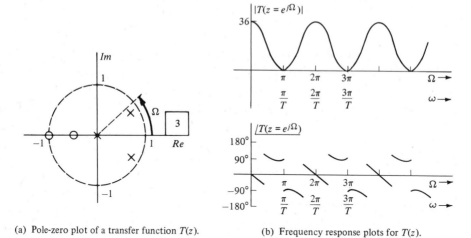

(a) Pole-zero plot of a transfer function $T(z)$.          (b) Frequency response plots for $T(z)$.

**FIGURE 2-7.   Periodicity of the frequency response of a discrete-time system.**

output amplitude to input amplitude as a function of frequency. The angle plot is the phase shift between the forced output and input as a function of frequency.

Evaluation of a transfer function at $z = \exp(j\Omega)$ is the evaluation at a point $z$ at angle $\Omega$ on the unit circle, as indicated on the pole-zero plot for a $z$-transfer function in Figure 2-7(a). As $\exp(j\Omega)$ is periodic in $\Omega$ with period $2\pi$, frequency response plots for discrete-time systems are periodic as in the example in Figure 2-7(b), which gives the frequency response for the $z$-transfer function in the accompanying pole-zero plot. The frequency response has been deliberately graphed over a wide range of $\Omega$ to emphasize this periodicity. Frequency response plots for discrete-time systems are also symmetric about $\Omega = \pi$, as shown. The amplitude ratio is even-symmetric about $\Omega = \pi$, and the phase shift is odd-symmetric. Consequently, the frequency range of $\Omega$ from 0 to $\pi$ is adequate to completely specify a discrete-time system's frequency response.

## 2.3.4  Bilinear Transformation

The bilinear transformation

$$z = \frac{1 + w}{1 - w}; \qquad w = \frac{z - 1}{z + 1}$$

maps the unit circle on the $z$-plane to the imaginary axis on the $w$-plane. The interior of the unit circle in $z$ maps to the left half-plane (LHP) in $w$ and the exterior of the unit circle on the $z$-plane maps to the right half-plane (RHP) on the $w$-plane. If this bilinear transformation is applied to the $z$-transfer function of a discrete-time system, the transfer function as a function of $w$ will have RHP poles if and only if the $z$-transfer function has poles outside the unit circle. The stability of a discrete-time system can thus be investigated by applying the bilinear transformation and testing the transfer function of a related continuous-time system.

For example, consider the $z$-transfer function

$$T(z) = \frac{3z^4 + 2z^3 - z^2 + 4z + 5}{z^4 + 0.5z^3 - 0.2z^2 + z + 0.4}$$

When the bilinear change of variables is made on the denominator polynomial,

$$q(z) = z^4 + 0.5z^3 - 0.2z^2 + z + 0.4$$

there results

$$q(w) = \left(\frac{1+w}{1-w}\right)^4 + 0.5\left(\frac{1+w}{1-w}\right)^3 - 0.2\left(\frac{1+w}{1-w}\right)^2 + \left(\frac{1+w}{1-w}\right) + 0.4$$

$$= \frac{-0.3w^4 + 3.4w^3 + 8.8w^2 + 1.4w + 2.7}{(1-w)^4}$$

A Routh-Hurwitz testing of the zeros of $q(w)$

| | | | |
|---|---|---|---|
| $w^4$ | $-0.3$ | 8.8 | 2.7 |
| $w^3$ | 3.4 | 1.4 | |
| $w^2$ | 8.92 | 2.7 | |
| $w^1$ | 0.37 | | |
| $w^0$ | 2.7 | | |

shows that $q(w)$ has one RHP root. Therefore, $T(z)$ has one pole outside the unit circle.

There exist tests analogous to the Routh-Hurwitz test, where the number of roots of a polynomial that lie outside the unit circle on the complex plane can be found directly, without transformation. One of these is called the *Jury test*, after E. I. Jury who developed it. The tests proposed so far, however, are quite involved compared to the Routh-Hurwitz test. Bilinear transformation followed by a Routh-Hurwitz test, particularly when each is so easily automated on a computer, appears to be the most efficient approach to step-invariant discrete-time system stability testing without factoring.

When the bilinear transformation is applied to discrete-time frequency response data, Bode plot methods can be applied to find an approximate system model.

# 2.4 Sampling and Reconstruction

Sampling is the process of deriving a discrete-time sequence from a continuous-time function. Usually, but not always, the samples are evenly spaced in time. *Reconstruction* is the reverse; it is the formation of a continuous-time function from a sequence of samples. Many different continuous-time functions can have the same set of samples, so a reconstruction is not unique.

In this section, we discuss sampling and determine how the $z$-transform of a sampled continuous-time function $f(t)$ is related to the Laplace transform $F(s)$. We then consider piecewise constant and other reconstructions of continuous-time functions from evenly-spaced samples. The sampling theorem, while it does not apply to most control system signals because they are not adequately bandlimited, is of some guidance in deciding how to process sensor signals before sampling. Finally, a simple procedure for finding the $z$-transfer functions of discrete-time systems or subsystems containing continuous-time components is developed and demonstrated.

## 2.4.1 *Sampling and A/D Conversion*

Samples of a continuous-time signal form a discrete-time sequence, as shown in Figure 2-8(a). Here, the samples will always be spaced evenly in time and, unless otherwise stated, the sampling will be synchronized so that a sample is taken at time $t = 0$, as shown. Devices for performing sampling are called *analog-to-digital* (A/D) *converters*. An electronic A/D converter produces a binary representation (typically using from 6 to 16 bits) of the applied input signal at each sample time.

The symbol for an A/D converter is given in Figure 2-8(b). An incoming continuous-time signal $f(t)$ is sampled to produce the discrete-time sequence $f(k)$. The sampling interval $T$ is generally known and is indicated on the diagram or elsewhere. As is common, the same symbol (in this case, $f$) will be used to represent both a continuous-time signal $f(t)$ and its related sequence of samples $f(k)$. Which is meant is inferred from the argument of the function.

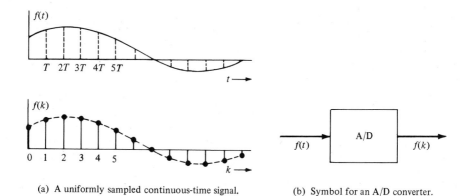

(a) A uniformly sampled continuous-time signal.   (b) Symbol for an A/D converter.

**FIGURE 2-8.   Analog-to-digital (A/D) conversion.**

Using a finite number of bits to represent a signal sample generally results in *quantization errors* in the A/D process. The maximum quantization error in 16-bit A/D conversion is $2^{-16} = 0.0015$ percent, which is quite low compared to typical errors in analog sensors. This error, if taken to be "noise," gives a signal-to-noise ratio of $20 \log_{10} (2^{-16}) = 96.3$ dB, which is much better than that of most high-fidelity audio systems. The designer must ensure that enough bits are used to give the desired system accuracy. Beyond this, the digital computations used must maintain adequate accuracy. Study of the effects of roundoff or truncation errors in digital computation is beyond our scope, but it is important to use adequate word lengths in fixed or floating-point computations. Years ago, digital hardware was very expensive, so minimizing word lengths was much more important than it is today.

When a continuous-time signal $f(t)$ is sampled to form the sequence $f(k)$, there is a close relationship between the Laplace transform of $f(t)$ and the $z$-transform of $f(k)$. If a rational Laplace transform is expanded into partial fraction terms, the corresponding continuous-time signal components in the time domain are powers of time, exponentials, sinusoids, and so on. Uniform samples of these elementary signal components have, in turn, simple $z$-transforms that can be summed to give the $z$-transform of the entire sampled signal. Table 2-5 lists Laplace transform terms and the resulting $z$-transforms when the corresponding time functions are sampled uniformly. The $z$-transform terms generally involve the length $T$ of the sampling interval.

As an example, consider the continuous-time function with Laplace transform

$$F(s) = \frac{3s^2 + 2s + 3}{s^3 + 4s^2 + 3s} = \frac{1}{s} + \frac{-2}{s+1} + \frac{4}{s+3}$$

**TABLE 2-5  Laplace and Z- Transform Pairs**

| $f(t)$ | $F(s)$ | $f(k)$ | $F(z)$ |
|---|---|---|---|
| $u(t)$, unit step | $\dfrac{1}{s}$ | $u(k)$, unit step | $\dfrac{z}{z-1}$ |
| $tu(t)$ | $\dfrac{1}{s^2}$ | $kTu(k)$ | $\dfrac{Tz}{(z-1)^2}$ |
| $e^{-at}u(t)$ | $\dfrac{1}{s+a}$ | $(e^{-at})^k u(k) = c^k u(k)$ where $c = e^{-aT}$ | $\dfrac{z}{z-e^{-aT}} = \dfrac{z}{z-c}$ |
| $te^{-at}u(t)$ | $\dfrac{1}{(s+a)^2}$ | $kT(e^{-aT})^k u(k) = kTc^k u(k)$ | $\dfrac{Tze^{-aT}}{(z-e^{-aT})^2} = \dfrac{Tcz}{(z-c)^2}$ |
| $(\sin\omega t)u(t)$ | $\dfrac{\omega}{s^2+\omega^2}$ | $(\sin k\omega T)u(k) = \sin\Omega k$ where $\Omega = \omega T$ | $\dfrac{z\sin\Omega}{z^2-2z\cos\Omega+1}$ |
| $(\cos\omega t)u(t)$ | $\dfrac{s}{s^2+\omega^2}$ | $(\cos k\omega T)u(k) = \cos\Omega k$ | $\dfrac{z(z-\cos\Omega)}{z^2-2z\cos\Omega+1}$ |
| $e^{-at}(\sin\omega t)u(t)$ | $\dfrac{\omega}{(s+a)^2+\omega^2}$ | $(e^{-aT})^k(\sin k\omega T)u(k) = c^k(\sin\Omega k)u(k)$ | $\dfrac{z(e^{(-a+j\omega)T})}{(z-e^{(-a+j\omega)T})(z-e^{(-a-j\omega)T})} = \dfrac{zc\sin\Omega}{z^2-(2c\cos\Omega)z+c^2}$ |
| $e^{-at}(\cos\omega t)u(t)$ | $\dfrac{s+a}{(s+a)^2+\omega^2}$ | $(e^{-aT})^k(\cos k\omega T)u(k) = c^k(\cos\Omega k)u(k)$ | $\dfrac{z(z-e^{-aT}\cos\Omega)}{(z-e^{(-a+j\omega)T})(z-e^{(-a-j\omega)T})} = \dfrac{z(z-c\cos\Omega)}{z^2-(2c\cos\Omega)z+c^2}$ |

The z-transform of the sampled signal with a sampling interval $T = 0.2$ is

$$F(z) = \frac{z}{z - 1} + \frac{-2z}{z - e^{-0.2}} + \frac{4z}{z - e^{-0.6}}$$

$$= \frac{3z^3 - 5.55z^2 + 2.63z}{(z - 1)(z - 0.82)(z - 0.55)}$$

If the continuous-time signal involves delays that are multiples of the sampling interval $T$, the delays are simply z-transformed, each Laplace transform term of the form $\exp(-sT)$ becoming a z-transform term $z^{-1}$. For example, when the continuous-time signal with Laplace transform

$$F(s) = \frac{3e^{-0.2s} + 3}{s(s + 3)} = (e^{-0.2s} + 1)\left(\frac{1}{s} + \frac{-1}{s + 3}\right)$$

is sampled with $T = 0.1$, it has z-transform

$$F(z) = (z^{-2} + 1)\left(\frac{z}{z - 1} + \frac{-z}{z - e^{-0.3}}\right) = \frac{0.26z(z^2 + 1)}{z^2(z - 1)(z - 0.74)}$$

We will denote this process of conversion of a continuous-time function's Laplace transform $F(s)$ to the z-transform $F(z)$ of its sequence of uniform samples at interval $T$ by

$$F(z) = \frac{\text{sample}}{\text{at } T}\left[F(s)\right]$$

If the above signal is, instead, sampled at an interval that is not a multiple of the 0.2 second delay, say at $T = 0.3$, then one cannot simply substitute inverse powers of $z$ for delays. With this sampling rate

$$F(s) = (e^{-0.2s} + 1)\left(\frac{1}{s} + \frac{-1}{s + 3}\right)$$

and

$$f(t) = u(t) + u(t - 0.2) - e^{-3t}u(t) - e^{-3(t - 0.2)}u(t - 0.2)$$

The two delayed step functions are zero at step 0 so that

$$f(0) = 1 + 0 - 1 - 0 = 0$$

At step 1 (at time $t = T = 0.3$) and thereafter, the step functions have value unity, and

$$f(k) = 2 - e^{-0.9k} - e^{-0.9k + 0.6} = 2 - (1 + e^{0.6})e^{-0.9k}$$
$$= 2 - 2.82e^{-0.9k} = 2 - 2.82(0.41)^k$$

Then

$$f(k) = 0.82\delta(k) + 2 - 2.82(0.41)^k, \qquad k = 0, 1, 2, \ldots$$

so that

$$F(z) = 0.82 + \frac{2z}{z - 1} - \frac{2.82z}{z - 0.41} = \frac{0.84z + 0.336}{(z - 1)(z - 0.41)}$$

### 2.4.2  *Reconstruction and D/A Conversion*

Reconstruction is the process of converting a discrete-time sequence into a continuous-time signal. Figure 2-9 shows a continuous-time signal $f(t)$, the sequence $f(k)$ resulting from uniform sampling, and a piecewise constant approximation to $f(t)$ constructed from the samples $f(k)$. This latter continuous-time waveform is termed the *step reconstruction of $f(t)$*. For a

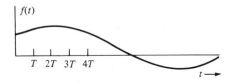

(a)  Continuous-time signal.

(b)  Sequence of samples of the continuous-time signal, $f(k) = f(t = kT)$.

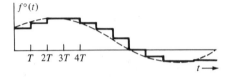

(c)  Step reconstruction of $f(t)$.

$$f^0(t) = \sum_{k=0}^{\infty} f(k) \left\{ u(t - kT) - u[t - (k + 1)T] \right\}$$

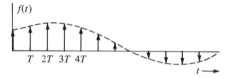

(d)  Impulse train for $f(t)$.

$$f^*(t) = \sum_{k=0}^{\infty} f(k)\, \delta(t - kT)$$

**FIGURE 2-9.    Continuous-time signal sampling and reconstruction.**

sampling interval $T$, the step reconstruction is related to the sample sequence $f(k)$ by

$$f^0(t) = \sum_{k=0}^{\infty} f(k)\{u(t - kT) - u[t - (k + 1)T]\}$$

Although very often the continuous-time signal reconstructed from a sequence is a sampled-and-held waveform, that is not always the case. A more fundamental continuous-time signal related to a sequence of samples is a series of impulses, timed at intervals $T$, with strengths equal to the corresponding samples, as in Figure 2-9(d). This *impulse train* corresponding to a sequence $f(k)$ and a sampling interval $T$ is denoted by $f^*(t)$ and is given by

$$f^*(t) = \sum_{k=0}^{\infty} f(k)\delta(t - kT)$$

Devices for performing reconstruction are called *digital-to-analog* (D/A) *converters*. Electronic D/A converters typically produce a step reconstruction from incoming signal samples by converting the binary-coded digital input to a voltage, transferring the voltage to the output and holding the output voltage constant until the next sample is available. The symbol for a D/A converter that generates the step reconstruction $f^0(t)$ from signal samples $f(k)$ is given in Figure 2-10(a). D/A refers to the process of converting digital codes to signal samples. *Sample-and-hold* (S/H) is the operation of holding

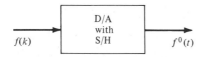

$f(k)$    D/A with S/H    $f^0(t)$

(a) Symbol for D/A conversion with S/H.

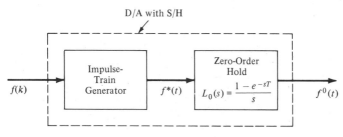

(b) Representation of a D/A converter with S/H as an impulse-train generator driving a zero-order hold.

**FIGURE 2-10.** **Digital-to-analog (D/A) conversion with sample-and-hold (S/H).**

each of these samples for a sampling interval $T$ to form the step reconstruction. The step reconstruction of a continuous-time signal from samples
can be represented as the conversion of the sequence $f(k)$ to its corresponding
impulse train $f^*(t)$, then conversion of the impulse train to the step
reconstruction, as in Figure 2-10(b). This viewpoint neatly separates conversion of the discrete sequence to a continuous-time waveform and the details
of the shape of the reconstructed waveform.

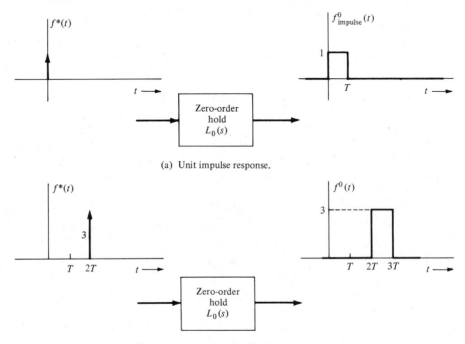

(a) Unit impulse response.

(b) Response to a scaled, shifted impulse.

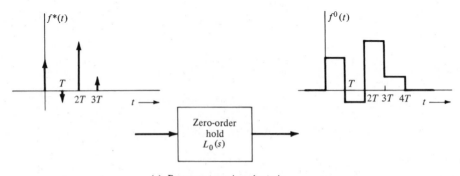

(c) Response to an impulse train

**FIGURE 2-11.   Responses of the zero-order hold.**

The continuous-time transfer function that converts an impulse train with sampling interval $T$ to a step reconstruction, termed the *zero-order hold*, has the impulse response pictured in Figure 2-11(a). Each incoming impulse produces a rectangular pulse of duration $T$ and of height equal to the impulse strength. An impulse train input produces a train of such pulses, which sum to give the step reconstruction, as in Figure 2-11(b) and (c). The zero-order hold has unit impulse response given by

$$f^0_{\text{impulse}}(t) = u(t) - u(t - T)$$

or

$$F^0_{\text{impulse}}(s) = \frac{1}{s}(1 - e^{-sT})$$

so that

$$L_0(s) = \frac{1}{s}(1 - e^{-st})$$

Other reconstructions can also be represented in a similar way. For example, practical D/A converters can exhibit substantial "rise time" when compared to perfect step reconstruction, as indicated in Figure 2-12(a). A

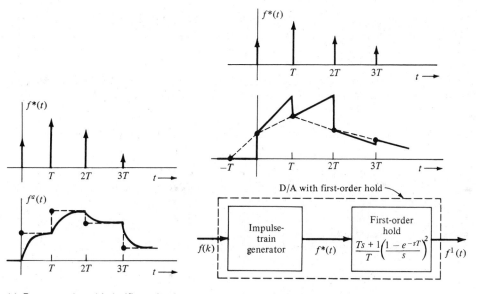

(a) Reconstruction with significant rise time.     (b) First-order hold reconstruction.

**FIGURE 2-12.   Using the impulse train in modeling other reconstructions.**

model that includes this imperfection (which, by the way, might not be detrimental to system performance at all) would simply have a different transfer function in place of that for the zero-order hold.

To improve upon the accuracy of the reconstruction, higher-order holds, using more than a single sample at a time for reconstruction, can be used. A _first-order hold_ uses the previous two samples to construct a straight line approximation during each sampling interval, as shown in Figure 2-12(b). Connecting the sample points with straight lines, what is called a _linear point connector_, is a possibility also but this requires that the future sample be known in advance of the time the reconstruction is begun.

### 2.4.3  The Sampling Theorem

Figure 2-13 shows two different continuous-time signals that have the same samples, illustrating how, except in highly restricted circumstances, a sampled function is not uniquely determined by its samples. One important situation for which samples of a continuous-time function are unique is when the function is _bandlimited_. A signal $g(t)$ and its Fourier transform $G(\omega)$ are generally related by

$$G(\omega) = \int_{-\infty}^{\infty} g(t)e^{-j\omega t}dt$$

$$g(t) = \frac{1}{2\pi} \int_{-\infty}^{\infty} G(\omega)e^{j\omega t}d\omega \tag{2-2}$$

This relationship is similar to Laplace transformation with $s = j\omega$, but the transform integral of equation (2-2) extends over all time rather than from

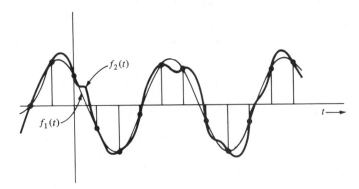

**FIGURE 2-13.   Two different continuous-time signals with the same samples.**

$t = 0^-$ on. The Fourier transform $G(\omega)$ is termed the *spectrum* of $g(t)$. A signal is bandlimited at (hertz) frequency $f_B$ if

$$G(\omega) = 0 \qquad \text{for} \qquad |\omega| > 2\pi f_B = \omega_B$$

so that equation (2-2) becomes

$$g(t) = \frac{1}{2\pi} \int_{-\omega_B}^{\omega_B} G(\omega)e^{j\omega t}d\omega$$

If a signal $g(t)$ is uniformly sampled with sampling interval $T$ to form the sequence

$$g(k) = g(t = kT)$$

then the corresponding impulse train that extends both ways in time

$$g^*(t) = \sum_{k=-\infty}^{\infty} g(k)\delta(t - kT)$$

has Fourier transform

$$G^*(\omega) = \frac{1}{T} \sum_{i=-\infty}^{\infty} G(\omega - i\omega_S) \tag{2-3}$$

where

$$\omega_S = 2\pi f_S = \frac{2\pi}{T}$$

If the sampling frequency $f_S$ is more than twice the bandlimit frequency $f_B$, the individual terms in equation (2-3) do not overlap, and $G(\omega)$ and thus $g(t)$ can be determined from $G^*(\omega)$ which, in turn, is determined from the samples $g(k)$.

A statement of the sampling theorem is:

> **The uniform samples of a signal $g(t)$ that is bandlimited above (hertz) frequency $f_B$ are unique if and only if the sampling frequency is higher than $2f_B$.**

The frequency $2f_B$ is termed the *Nyquist frequency* for a bandlimited signal. If the sampling frequency does not exceed the Nyquist frequency, the individual terms in equation (2-3) overlap, a phenomenon called *aliasing* (or *foldover*).

The sampling theorem is important to control system design because of the following: When A/D conversion is done on noisy signals that have significant frequency components above half the sampling frequency, the high frequencies produce errors in the sampling that are *indistinguishable* from the presence of lower-frequency errors. For this reason, low-pass filters, termed *prefilters* or *antialiasing filters*, are often used to reduce high frequencies present in sensor signals before their A/D conversion.

A constructive statement of how to recover a suitably bandlimited signal from its samples is:

> **To recover a signal $g(t)$ that is bandlimited above frequency $f_B$ from its samples $g(k)$, form the impulse train $g^*(t)$ with the sample frequency $f_S = 1/T > 2f_B$. Pass it through a low-pass filter that removes all frequencies in $g^*(t)$ above $\frac{1}{2}f_S$ and passes, unchanged, all frequencies below $f_B$.**

A great deal is implied here that is seldom evident at first. Perfect reconstruction requires that an infinite number of samples, dating from $t = -\infty$, be processed. If instead, we begin the processing at a finite time, $t = 0$, the bandlimited signal will *never* be perfectly reconstructed, although as time goes on the reconstruction can be increasingly accurate. After all, how much can one determine about the spectrum of a signal from only, say, the first three samples? Practical bandlimited signal reconstruction devices have response that consists of the desired perfect reconstruction plus a significant and usually long-lasting transient error.

In applications such as voice communications, where the signals of interest are inherently bandlimited and where highly inaccurate reconstruction (or delayed reconstruction) can be tolerated initially (perhaps for the first several hundred samples or more), this approach is sensible. For control systems, where the signals are not sharply bandlimited and where long transients are usually highly undesirable, a bandlimited reconstruction approach has little to offer.

## 2.4.4  Discrete-Time Equivalents

It often happens that we wish to find the transfer function of a system or subsystem with discrete-time input and discrete-time output but which contains continuous-time components. Figure 2-14(a) shows a general situation where a discrete-time system or subsystem has an intervening continuous-time transfer function $G(s)$. It is desired to find the overall $z$-transfer function $H(z)$ of the arrangement, and this can be done by finding its pulse response. For a unit pulse input

$$f(k) = \delta(k)$$

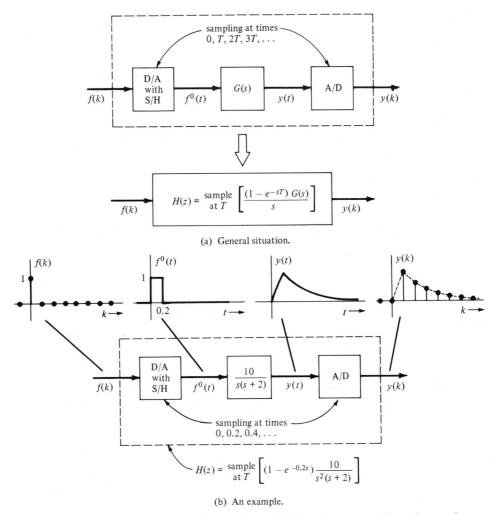

(a) General situation.

(b) An example.

**FIGURE 2-14.** Finding the discrete-time equivalent of a system with continuous-time components.

the sampled-and-held continuous-time signal that is the input to $G(s)$ is given by

$$f^0(t) = u(t) - u(t - T)$$

or

$$F^0(s) = \frac{1 - e^{-sT}}{s}$$

where $T$ is the sampling interval. Then

$$Y(s) = F^0(s)G(s) = \frac{1 - e^{-sT}}{s} G(s)$$

and

$$H(z) = \frac{\text{sample}}{\text{at } T}\left[ Y(s) \right] = \frac{\text{sample}}{\text{at } T}\left[ \frac{1 - e^{-sT}}{s} G(s) \right]$$

is found by the usual substitution for each delay and partial fraction expansion term of $Y(s)$.

For the numerical example of Figure 2-14(b) where

$$G(s) = \frac{10}{s(s + 2)}$$

and the sampling interval is $T = 0.2$, a unit pulse input produces a continuous-time signal to be converted that has Laplace transform

$$Y(s) = F^0(s)G(s) = \frac{1 - e^{-0.2s}}{s}\left[ \frac{10}{s(s + 2)} \right] = (1 - e^{-0.2s})\left[ \frac{10}{s^2(s + 2)} \right]$$

$$= (1 - e^{-0.2s})\left[ \frac{-\frac{5}{2}}{s} + \frac{5}{s^2} + \frac{\frac{5}{2}}{s + 2} \right] \tag{2-4}$$

Samples of $y(t)$, at the interval $T = 0.2$ have z-transform

$$Y(z) = H(z) = (1 - z^{-1})\left[ \frac{-(\frac{5}{2})z}{z - 1} + \frac{5(0.2)z}{(z - 1)^2} + \frac{(\frac{5}{2})z}{z - e^{-0.4}} \right]$$

$$= \frac{(z - 1)(0.175z + 0.155)}{(z - 1)^2(z - 0.67)} = \frac{0.175z + 0.155}{(z - 1)(z - 0.67)}$$

A similar solution process also applies to situations where the A/D and D/A converters are not synchronized. For the example with Laplace transform given by Equation (2-4), suppose that the A/D samples are taken at the times 0.1, 0.3, 0.5, . . . instead of the times 0, 0.2, 0.4, . . . when the D/A samples are taken. Then since

$$y(t) = \left( -\frac{5}{2} + 5t + \frac{5}{2}e^{-2t} \right)u(t) - \left[ -\frac{5}{2} + 5(t - 0.2) + \frac{5}{2}e^{-2(t - 0.2)} \right]u(t - 0.2)$$

the A/D samples are, as a function of step $k = 0, 1, \ldots$

$$y(t) = 0.1 + 0.2k) = \left[ -\frac{5}{2} + 5(0.1 + 0.2k) + \frac{5}{2} e^{-2(0.1 + 0.2k)} \right]$$

$$- \left[ -\frac{5}{2} + 5(0.2k - 0.1) + \frac{5}{2} e^{-2(0.2k - 0.1)} \right] u(0.2k - 0.1)$$

$$= (2.5 + 0.5 + k + 2.5e^{-0.2}e^{-0.4k})$$

$$- (-2.5 + k - 0.5 + 2.5e^{0.2}e^{-0.4k})u(0.2k - 0.1)$$

$$= (-2 + k + 2.05e^{-0.4k})$$

$$- (-3 + k + 3.05e^{-0.4k})u(0.2k - 0.1)$$

$$= \begin{cases} 0.05, & k = 0 \\ 1 - e^{-0.4k}, & k = 1, 2, 3, \ldots \end{cases}$$

The $z$-transform of these samples, which is the system's $z$-transfer function, is

$$H(z) = Y(z) = \frac{z}{z - 1} - \frac{z}{z - 0.67} - 0.95 = \frac{-0.95z^2 + 1.92z - 0.64}{(z - 1)(z - 0.67)}$$

## 2.5 Digitizing Analog Controllers

A simple method of designing digital controllers for continuous-time plants is to first design a continuous-time (or *analog*) controller for the plant, then approximate the behavior of the analog controller with a digital one. As indicated in Figure 2-15, a digital controller that might approximate the behavior of a single-input, single-output analog controller consists of an A/D converter driving a discrete-time system with $z$-transfer function $H(z)$, followed by D/A conversion with sample-and-hold. This configuration is also

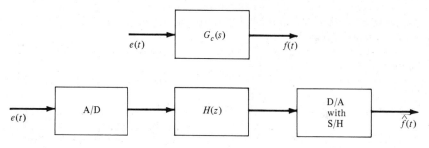

**FIGURE 2-15.   Digitizing an analog controller.**

called a *digital filter*. If the sample rate is sufficiently high and the approximation sufficiently good, the behavior of the digital controller will be nearly indistinguishable from that of the analog controller. The digital controller will have such advantages as high reliability, low drift with temperature, power supply and age, the ability to make changes in software, and so on.

### 2.5.1 Digital Approximations of Integrators

One way to approximate an analog controller is to simply approximate numerically each of the analog integration operations. The integrations are evident from an integration diagram for the analog controller. For example, consider the system of Figure 2-16(a), where a continuous-time plant with transfer function

$$G_p(s) = \frac{25}{s^2 + 9s + 40}$$

is controlled by an analog controller with transfer function

$$G_c(s) = \frac{(s + 10)}{s(s + 4)}$$

This feedback system has overall transfer function

$$T(s) = \frac{G_c(s)G_p(s)}{1 + G_c(s)G_p(s)} = \frac{25s + 250}{s^4 + 13s^3 + 76s^2 + 185s + 250}$$

which has all poles to the left of about $s = -1.5$ on the complex plane and zero steady state error to a step input. The controller can be described by the state equations (in controllable form)

$$\begin{bmatrix} \dot{x}_1(t) \\ \dot{x}_2(t) \end{bmatrix} = \begin{bmatrix} 0 & 1 \\ 0 & -4 \end{bmatrix} \begin{bmatrix} x_1(t) \\ x_2(t) \end{bmatrix} + \begin{bmatrix} 0 \\ 1 \end{bmatrix} e(t)$$

$$r(t) = [10 \quad 1] \begin{bmatrix} x_1(t) \\ x_2(t) \end{bmatrix}$$

which are represented by the integration diagram of Figure 2-16(b).

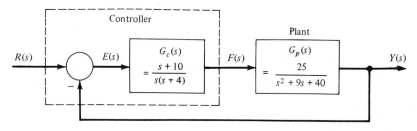

(a) Analog control system.

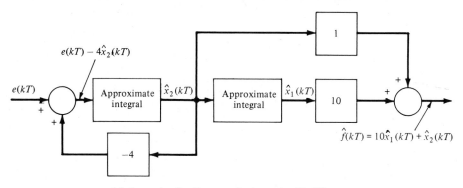

(b) State variable model of the controller transmittance $G_c(s)$.

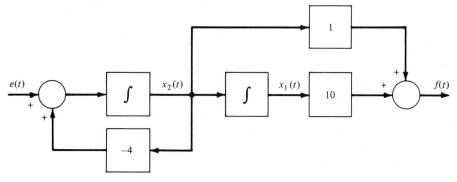

(c) Approximating the controller integrals with differences.

**FIGURE 2-16. First-order approximation of an analog controller.**

In Figure 2-16(c), the signals in the integration diagram of the controller have been expressed in terms of samples at times $t = kT, k = 0, 1, 2, \ldots$ and the integrations involved have been approximated in some way. A "hat" over a symbol here denotes an approximation of the quantity. The simplest approximation is to approximate the integral at step $k + 1$ by the integral at step $k$ plus the integrand at step $k$ times the sampling interval $T$. For this approximation, the controller signal samples are related by

$$\begin{cases} \hat{x}_1[(k+1)T] = \hat{x}_1(kT) + T\hat{x}_2(kT) \\ \hat{x}_2[(k+1)T] = \hat{x}_2(kT) + T[e(kT) - 4\hat{x}_2(kT)] \end{cases}$$

The $z$-transforms of these relations are

$$\begin{cases} z\hat{X}_1(z) - \hat{x}_1(0) = \hat{X}_1(z) + T\hat{X}_2(z) \\ z\hat{X}_2(z) - \hat{x}_2(0) = \hat{X}_2(z) + T[E(z) - 4\hat{X}_2(z)] \end{cases}$$

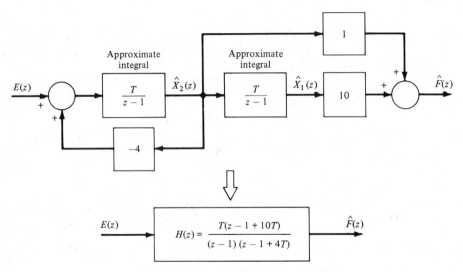

(a) Z-transformation of a difference approximation.

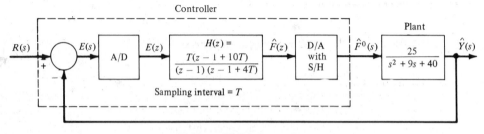

(b) Plant with digital controller.

**FIGURE 2-17. Obtaining the $z$-transfer function associated with a first-order approximation of an analog controller.**

so that each approximate integrator has $z$-transfer function

$$I(z) = \frac{T}{z - 1}$$

as shown in Figure 2-17. For this discrete-time controller, the overall approximating $z$-transfer function, using block diagram reduction, is

$$D(z) = \frac{T(z - 1 + 10T)}{(z - 1)(z - 1 + 4T)}$$

Figure 2-18 shows step response of this first-order digital approximation to the original analog controller. Since the analog controller has a pole at the origin of the complex plane representing pure integration, its step response has a ramp component. For a relatively large sampling interval $T$, the controller approximation deviates significantly from the analog controller. When $T$ is sufficiently small so that there are several steps during each time constant of the analog controller's fastest mode, $e^{-4t}$, the analog and

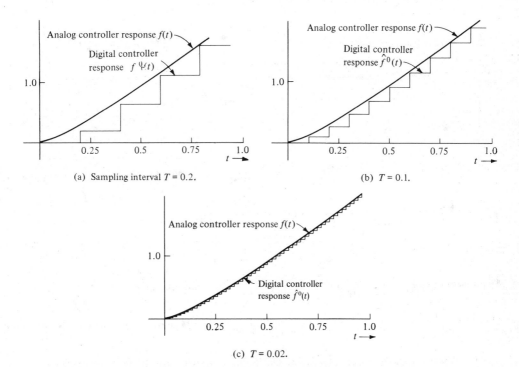

(a) Sampling interval $T = 0.2$.

(b) $T = 0.1$.

(c) $T = 0.02$.

**FIGURE 2-18.   Step response of the first-order approximation digital controller.**

the digital controller step responses are nearly the same. Step responses of the feedback system for various sampling intervals $T$ are compared in Figure 2-19.

When more than one sample at a time is used in updating the approximation of analog controller integrations, the performance of the digital controller can be improved over that of a simpler approximation. Table 2-6 gives some common difference approximations for integrals, together with the corresponding $z$-transfer function of each integral approximation.

For the previous plant and controller example, suppose we use instead, the two-sample difference approximation for each integral. Each approximate integral block in Figure 2-17(c) then has $z$-transfer function

$$\frac{T(z + 1)}{2(z - 1)}$$

which gives the controller $z$-transfer function

$$H(z) = \frac{T(z + 1)[(5T + 1)z + (5T - 1)]}{(z - 1)[(4T + 2)z + (4T - 2)]}$$

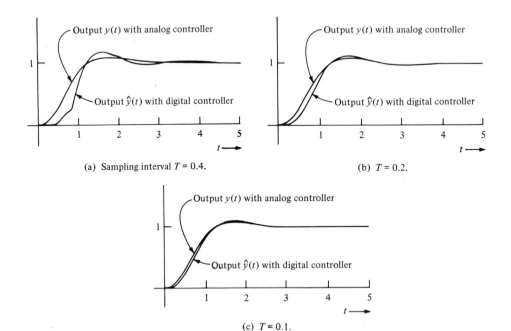

(a)  Sampling interval $T = 0.4$.

(b)  $T = 0.2$.

(c)  $T = 0.1$.

**FIGURE 2-19.   Step response of the feedback system with the first-order approximation digital controller.**

**TABLE 2-6  Some Integral Approximations Using Present and Past Integrand Samples**

| Approximation to the integral over one step | Difference equation for the approximate integral | Z-transmittance of the approximate integrator |
|---|---|---|

**One-Sample**

$$\int_{kT}^{kT+T} f(t)dt \cong Tf(kT)$$

$$\hat{x}[(k+1)T] = \hat{x}(kT) + Tf(kT)$$

$$\frac{T}{z-1}$$

**Two-Sample (Tustin approximation)**

$$\int_{kT}^{kT+T} f(t)dt \cong T\left\{\frac{1}{2}f[(k+1)T] + \frac{1}{2}f(kT)\right\}$$

$$\hat{x}[(k+1)T] = \hat{x}(kT) + \frac{T}{2}f[(k+1)T] + \frac{T}{2}f(kT)$$

$$\frac{T(z+1)}{2(z-1)}$$

**Three-Sample**

$$\int_{kT}^{kT+T} f(t)dt \cong T\left\{\frac{5}{12}f[(k+1)T] + \frac{8}{12}f(kT) - \frac{1}{12}f[(k-1)T]\right\}$$

$$\hat{x}[(k+1)T] = \hat{x}(kT) + \frac{5T}{12}f[(k+1)T] + \frac{8T}{12}f(kT) + \frac{T}{12}f[(k-1)T]$$

$$\frac{T\left(\frac{5}{12}z^2 + \frac{8}{12}z - \frac{1}{12}\right)}{z(z-1)}$$

The character of the response of this controller is similar to that of the first-order controller response shown in Figure 2-18. For the same sampling interval, the higher-order approximation controller will tend to track the analog controller output more accurately at the sample times because the approximations to the analog integrations are better. Because the one-sample and the two-sample approximations result in controllers of the same order, the designer usually opts for the two-sample approximation, which is, by the way, a form of bilinear transformation. This second-order approximation is also called *Tustin's approximation.*

Higher-order approximations result in digital controllers of progressively higher order. The higher the order of the approximation, the better the approximations to the analog integrations and the more accurately the digital controller output will tend to track samples of the analog controller output for any input. The digital controller will, however, probably have a sampled-and-held output between samples, so accurate tracking of samples is often of less concern to the designer than the sample rate.

## 2.5.2 *Matching Step and Other Response*

Another method of approximating an analog controller by a digital one is to require that, at the sample times, the digital controller step response be samples of the analog controller step response. Figure 2-20(a) shows the unit step response $f_{\text{step}}(t)$ of an analog controller with transmittance $G_c(s)$. If, as in Figure 2-20(b), the discrete-time portion $H(z)$ of the digital controller is chosen so that its response to a unit step sequence consists of samples of $f_{\text{step}}(t)$, then the digital controller of Figure 2-20(c) will have step response that equals the analog controller step response at the sample times. This is termed a *step-invariant approximation* of an analog system by a digital system.

For example, a continuous-time controller with transfer function

$$G_c(s) = \frac{4s^2 + 17s + 12}{s^2 + 5s + 6}$$

has unit step response

$$F_{\text{step}}(s) = \left(\frac{1}{s}\right) G_c(s) = \frac{4s^2 + 17s + 12}{s(s+2)(s+3)} = \frac{2}{s} + \frac{3}{s+2} + \frac{-1}{s+3}$$

For a sampling rate $T = 0.2$, the samples of $f_{\text{step}}(t)$ have z-transform

$$F_{\text{step}}(z) = \frac{2z}{z-1} + \frac{3z}{z - e^{-0.4}} - \frac{z}{z - e^{-0.6}}$$

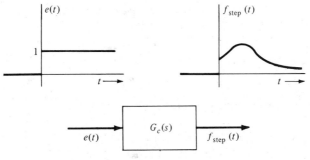

(a) Analog controller step response

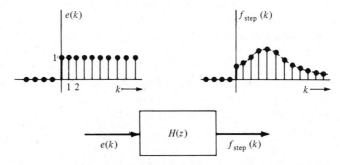

(b) Discrete step response consisting of samples of the analog
controller step response.

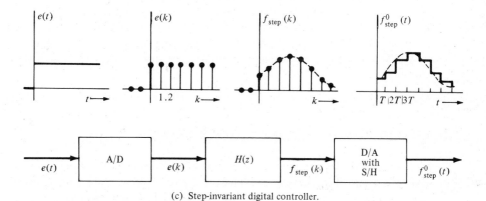

(c) Step-invariant digital controller.

**FIGURE 2-20. Finding a step-invariant approximation of a continuous-time
controller.**

Taking these samples to be the output of a discrete-time system $H(z)$ driven by a unit step sequence

$$F_{step}(z) = \left(\frac{z}{z-1}\right) H(z) = \frac{2z}{z-1} + \frac{3z}{z-0.67} - \frac{z}{z-0.54}$$

the step-invariant approximation is

$$H(z) = 2 + \frac{3(z-1)}{z-0.67} - \frac{(z-1)}{z-0.54} = \frac{4z^2 - 5.37z + 1.67}{(z-0.67)(z-0.54)}$$

It is occasionally desirable to design digital controllers so that their response to some input other than a step consists of a sampled-and-held version of an analog controller's response to that input. A *ramp-invariant approximation*, for example, has a discrete-time response to a unit ramp sequence that consists of samples of the unit ramp response of the continuous-time system.

Most every digital approximation to an analog controller, one-sample integration approximation, two-sample integration approximation, step-invariant approximation, etc., tends to perform well for a sufficiently short sampling interval $T$. For longer sampling intervals, which are often dictated by cost constraints, one approximation or another might perform the best in a given situation.

Digitizing an analog controller is not a very good general design technique, although it is very useful occasionally, as when the designer is *replacing* an existing analog controller or part of a controller with a digital one. The technique requires beginning with a good analog design, which is probably as difficult as directly doing a good digital design. And, it usually performs less well than the analog counterpart from which it was derived. The step-invariant and other approximations are not easily extended to systems with multiple inputs and outputs. When the resulting feedback system performance is inadequate, the designer may have few options besides raising the sampling rate.

## 2.6  Design of a Videotape Drive Control

In this section we present an overview of classical discrete-time control system design using an example. There are two basic ways of approaching classical discrete-time control. In the sampled-data approach, discrete-time signals are represented by continuous-time impulse trains so that all signals in a plant and controller model are continuous-time ones. This was appealing in the early days of digital control when digital concepts were new and most designers had backgrounds that were solidly in continuous-time control. There is little to recommend this complexity nowadays, though.* In the conventional approach, which will be used here, discrete-time signals are represented as sequences.

Similar to classical continuous-time control system design, acceptable discrete-time zero-input response is obtained by choosing a controller that results in acceptable feedback system pole locations in the $z$-plane. At the same time, requirements are placed on the overall system's zero-state response component for representative discrete-time input signals such as steps or ramps. Any resulting continuous-time signals of interest are then examined and if their between-sample response is not acceptable, the design is modified, perhaps by increasing the sampling rate.

## 2.6.1 *Plant Model and Controller Structure*

The configuration of a commercial broadcast videotape positioning system is shown in Figure 2-21(a). The relationship between applied drive motor armature voltage and tape speed at the recording and playback heads is approximated by the transfer function $G(s)$. The delay term involved accounts for the propagation of speed changes along the tape over the distance of physical separation of the tape drive mechanism and the recording and playback heads. The pole term in $G(s)$ represents the dynamics of the motor and tape drive capstan. Tape position is sensed by a recorded signal on the tape itself.

The digital controller that is to be designed should result in zero steady state error to any step change in desired tape position. It should have a zero-input (or transient) response that decays to no more than 10 percent of any initial value within a 1/30 second interval. One-thirtieth of a second is the video frame rate.

The sampling interval of the controller is chosen to be $T = 1/120$ based on the desirability of synchronizing the tape motion control with the 1/60 second field rate (each frame consists of two fields) of the recorded video. In Figure 2-21(b) the diagram of Fig. 2-21(a) has been rearranged to emphasize the discrete-time input $R(z)$ and the discrete-time samples $P(z)$ of the tape

---

*Among the difficulties is the possibility (indeed the likelihood) of having to deal with impulse trains derived from signals containing steps and impulses that occur at the sampling times. Offsetting sampler timing will give a "fix" of the problem, but the result is not very satisfying, particularly when feedback loops are involved.

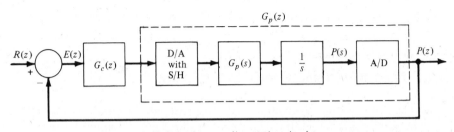

(a) Block diagram.

(b) Relation between discrete-time signals.

**FIGURE 2-21. Videotape positioning system.**

position. The indicated open-loop $z$-transfer function is

$$
G_p(z) = \begin{array}{c} \text{sample at} \\ T = 1/120 \end{array} \left[ \left( \frac{1 - e^{-(1/120)s}}{s} \right) \left( \frac{40e^{-(1/120)s}}{s + 40} \right) \left( \frac{1}{s} \right) \right]
$$

$$
= \begin{array}{c} \text{sample at} \\ T = 1/120 \end{array} \left\{ \left[ 1 - e^{-(1/120)s} \right] e^{-(1/120)s} \left[ \frac{-\frac{1}{40}}{s} + \frac{1}{s^2} + \frac{\frac{1}{40}}{s + 40} \right] \right\}
$$

$$
= (1 - z^{-1})z^{-1} \left[ \frac{-\frac{1}{40}z}{z - 1} + \frac{\frac{1}{120}z}{(z - 1)^2} + \frac{\frac{1}{40}z}{z - 0.72} \right] = \frac{0.00133(z + 0.75)}{z(z - 1)(z - 0.72)}
$$

$$(2\text{-}5)$$

In terms of the compensator's $z$-transfer function $G_c(z)$, the position error signal is given by

$$
E(z) = R(z) - Y(z) = \left[ 1 - \frac{G_c(z)G_p(z)}{1 + G_c(z)G_p(z)} \right] R(z) = \frac{1}{1 + G_c(z)G_p(z)} R(z)
$$

For a unit step input sequence

$$E(z) = \frac{1}{1 + G_c(z)G_p(z)} \left( \frac{z}{z - 1} \right)$$

assuming that the feedback system is stable:

$$\underset{k \to \infty}{\text{limit}}\ e(k) = \underset{z \to 1}{\text{limit}} \left[ \frac{z - 1}{z}\ E(z) \right] = \underset{z \to 1}{\text{limit}} \left[ \frac{1}{1 + G_c(z)G_p(z)} \right]$$

In view of the pole at $z = 1$ in $G_p(z)$, equation (2-5), the steady state error to a step input will be zero provided that the compensator does not have a zero at $z = 1$.

For the feedback system transient response to decay at least by a factor of $1/10$ within $1/30$ second, the closed-loop poles must be located such that a decay of at least this amount occurs every four $1/120$ second steps. This is to say that all closed-loop poles must be within a radius $c$ of the origin on the complex plane, where

$$c^4 = \frac{1}{10}; \qquad c = 0.56$$

### 2.6.2 Root Locus Compensator Design

A compensator consisting of only a gain $K$ is inadequate, as is shown in Figure 2-22. The feedback system is stable for

$$0 < K < 95$$

but, regardless of $K$, there are always poles at distances from the origin greater than the required $c = 0.56$. For negative $K$, the feedback system is unstable.

In Figure 2-23, the controller with $z$-transfer function

$$G_c(z) = \frac{K(z - 0.72)}{z}$$

which cancels the plant pole at $z = 0.72$, is shown. As before, the feedback system is unstable for negative values of the adjustable constant $K$. For positive $K$, the root locus is as shown in Figure 2-23(b). The closed-loop

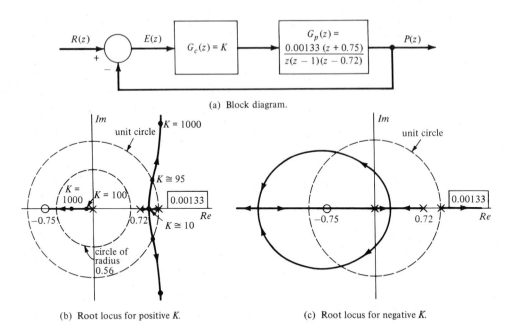

(a) Block diagram.

(b) Root locus for positive $K$.

(c) Root locus for negative $K$.

**FIGURE 2-22.   Constant-gain compensator.**

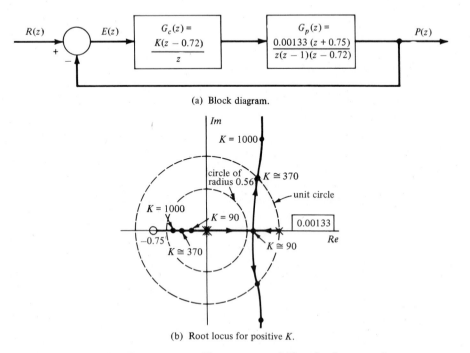

(a) Block diagram.

(b) Root locus for positive $K$.

**FIGURE 2-23.   Compensator with zero at $z = 0.72$ and pole at $z = 0$.**

system is stable for

$$0 < K < 370$$

but there is always a pole or two at radial distance greater than $c = 0.56$. For $K = 90$, this design is close to meeting the requirements, but it is not quite good enough.

When the compensator pole is moved from the origin to the left, as shown in Figure 2-24, the root locus is pulled to the left and the performance requirements can be met. For the compensator with $z$-transfer function

$$G_c(z) = \frac{150(z - 0.72)}{z + 0.4} \qquad (2\text{-}6)$$

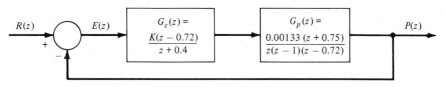

(a) Block diagram.

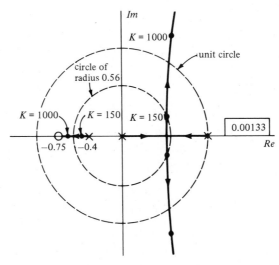

(b) Root locus for positive $K$.

**FIGURE 2-24.** Compensator with zero at $z = 0.72$ and pole at $z = -0.4$.

shown, the feedback system $z$-transfer function is

$$T(z) = \frac{G_c(z)G_p(z)}{1 + G_c(z)G_p(z)} = \frac{0.2(z + 0.75)}{z^3 - 0.6z^2 - 0.2z + 0.15}$$

$$= \frac{0.2(z + 0.75)}{(z - 0.539 - j0.155)(z - 0.539 + j0.155)(z + 0.477)}$$

As expected, the steady state error to a step input sequence is zero:

$$\lim_{z \to 1} \left\{ \left( \frac{z - 1}{z} \right)[1 - T(z)] \left( \frac{z}{z - 1} \right) \right\} = \lim_{z \to 1} \frac{z^3 - 0.6z^2 - 0.4z}{z^3 - 0.6z^2 - 0.2z + 0.15}$$

$$= 0$$

The steady state error to a unit ramp input sequence is

$$\lim_{z \to 1} \left\{ \left( \frac{z - 1}{z} \right)[1 - T(z)] \left[ \frac{z}{(z - 1)^2} \right] \right\} = \lim_{z \to 1} \frac{z^2 + 0.4z}{z^3 - 0.6z^2 - 0.2z + 0.15}$$

$$= \frac{1.4}{0.35} = 4$$

For a compensator with $z$-transfer function of the form

$$G_c(z) = \frac{150(z - 0.72)}{z + a}$$

the feedback system has $z$-transfer function

$$T(z) = \frac{G_c(z)G_p(z)}{1 + G_c(z)G_p(z)} = \frac{0.2(z + 0.75)}{(z + a)(z^2 - z) + 0.2(z + 0.75)}$$

$$= \frac{0.2(z + 0.75)}{z^3 - z^2 + 0.2z + 0.15 + a(z^2 - z)} = \frac{\dfrac{0.2(z + 0.75)}{z^3 - z^2 + 0.2z + 0.15}}{1 + a\,\dfrac{z(z - 1)}{z^3 - z^2 + 0.2z + 0.15}}$$

$$= \frac{\text{numerator}}{1 + a\,\dfrac{z(z - 1)}{(z - 0.637 - j0.378)(z - 0.637 + j0.378)(z + 0.274)}}$$

A pole-zero plot in terms of positive $a$ is shown in Figure 2-25, from which it

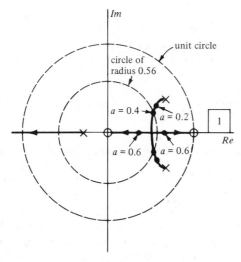

**FIGURE 2-25.** Root locus plot as a function of the compensator pole location.

is seen that choices of *a* between 0.4 and about 0.5 will give a controller that meets the performance requirements.

Classical pole-zero discrete-time control system design is much the same as its continuous-time counterpart. Increasingly complicated controllers are tried until both steady state error and transient performance requirements are met. In this iterative process, root locus is an important tool because it easily indicates qualitative closed-loop system pole locations as a function of a parameter. Once feasible controllers are selected, root locus plots are refined to show quantitative results.

## 2.6.3 Simulation Studies

Another important system design tool is *simulation*, computer modeling of the plant and controller to verify the properties of a preliminary design and to test its performance under conditions (e.g., noise, disturbances, parameter variations, and nonlinearities) that might be difficult or cumbersome to study analytically.

When a digital controller is used to control a continuous-time plant, proper discrete-time design will insure that *samples* of continuous-time plant response behave acceptably, as is the case with this example. However, it is often additionally important that continuous-time plant signals be well-behaved between the sampling times also. A simulation of the unit step response of the video tape positioning system with controller described by

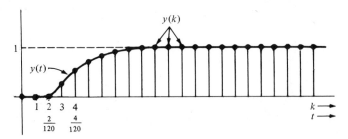

**FIGURE 2-26.    Continuous-time response of the videotape drive control.**

equation (2-6) is shown in Figure 2-26. The tape position $y(t)$ is seen to vary smoothly between sampling times, so the between-sample response of this design is probably quite acceptable. In Chapter 7, we will develop and apply methods for improving the between-sample response of digitally controlled continuous-time plants.

## 2.7 Summary

A discrete-time signal or sequence is a function of a discrete variable $k$, termed *the step index*. The z-transform of a sequence $f(k)$ is

$$\mathscr{Z}[f(k)] = F(z) = \sum_{k=0}^{\infty} f(k)z^{-k} = f(0)z^{-0} + f(1)z^{-1} + f(2)z^{-2} + \cdots$$

Important z-transform pairs are listed in Table 2-1 and properties of the z-transform are summarized in Table 2-2. For rational $F(z)$, sequence samples can be obtained from $F(z)$ by long division. The sequence as a function of step is found by expanding $F(z)/z$ in partial fractions and using Table 2-1. Rational z-transforms with denominator roots inside the unit circle on the complex plane represent sequences that decay with step. If there are non-repeated denominator roots on the unit circle, the corresponding sequence neither decays nor expands with step. If there is a repeated unit circle root or any root outside the unit circle, the sequence is an expanding one.

Linear discrete-time systems are described by linear difference equations. If the difference equation coefficients are constant, the system is step-invariant. Given the system initial conditions and inputs, a difference equation can be applied repeatedly to recursively calculate the system outputs. Any signal in a linear discrete-time system can be expressed as the sum of a zero-input component that is due to the initial conditions but not the inputs, plus a zero-state component that is due to the inputs but not the initial conditions. The part of the zero-state response due to each input is the discrete convolution of the input and the unit pulse response for that input.

The $z$-transfer function of a single-input, single-output system is the $z$-transform of its unit pulse response when the initial conditions are zero. If there are multiple inputs and outputs, the system has a $z$-transfer function for each combination of input and output, each calculated with all other inputs zero. Z-transfer functions for discrete-time systems are manipulated in the same way as are continuous-time system transfer functions. A linear, step-invariant discrete-time system is input-output stable if and only if its unit pulse responses decay asymptotically to zero, which occurs only when all denominator roots (poles) of all its $z$-transfer functions lie inside the unit circle on the complex plane.

The bilinear transformation

$$z = \frac{1 + w}{1 - w}; \qquad w = \frac{z - 1}{z + 1}$$

maps the inside of the unit circle on the complex plane to the left half-plane. When applied to a $z$-transfer function, it converts a discrete-time stability problem to an equivalent continuous-time one. Like its continuous-time counterpart, discrete frequency response is useful for the experimental determination of $z$-transfer functions.

Discrete-time sequences are often derived from continuous-time functions by sampling. Devices that perform sampling are called *analog-to-digital* (A/D) converters. For evenly spaced samples at sampling interval $T$

$$t = kT, \qquad k = 0, 1, 2, \ldots$$

the Laplace transform $F(s)$ of a continuous-time function and the $z$-transform $F(z)$ of its sequence of samples are related by

$$F(z) = \begin{array}{c} \text{sample} \\ \text{at } T \end{array} \left[ F(s) \right]$$

where the "sample at $T$" operation involves expanding $F(s)$ in partial fractions and replacing each term by the corresponding $z$-transform term of Table 2-5. Each time delay of interval $T$ is replaced by $z^{-1}$.

Reconstruction is the process of forming a continuous-time function from samples. Since many different continuous-time functions can have the same samples, reconstruction is not unique. The most common reconstruction device is the digital-to-analog (D/A) converter with sample-and-hold (S/H). It produces a stepwise constant reconstruction which can be considered to be the production of a train of impulses $f*(t)$ with strengths equal to the samples followed by a zero-order hold with transfer function

$$L_0(s) = \frac{1 - e^{-sT}}{s}$$

The sampling theorem states that when a bandlimited continuous-time signal is sampled at a rate higher than twice the bandlimit frequency, the samples can be used to uniquely reconstruct the original continuous-time signal. Although the sampling theorem is not applicable to most discrete-time control systems because the signals (e.g., steps and ramps) are not band-limited and because good reconstruction requires long time delays, it does provide some guidance in deciding how best to filter sensor signals before sampling them.

A system or subsystem with discrete-time input and output but with intervening D/A conversion with S/H, a transfer function $G(s)$, then A/D conversion has $z$-transfer function

$$H(z) = \frac{\text{sample}}{\text{at } T} \left[ \frac{1 - e^{-sT}}{s} G(s) \right]$$

This relationship is very useful for the simplification of system models involving both discrete-time and continuous-time elements.

Digital controllers for continuous-time plants can be designed by beginning with an analog controller design and approximating it with a digital filter. The filter design can approximate the integrations with discrete-time operations or it can be made to have step (or other) response samples that are equal to samples of the analog controller's step (or other) response. Usually, even for relatively high sample rates, the digital approximation will perform less well than the analog controller from which it was derived.

The classical approach to directly designing a digital controller, which has many variations, parallels the classical approach to analog controller design. One begins with simple discrete-time controllers, increasing their complexity until the performance requirements can be met. The controller poles, zeros, and multiplying constant are selected to give feedback system pole locations that will result in acceptable zero-input response. At the same time, the parameters are constrained so that the resulting system has adequate zero-state (or "steady state") response to important inputs such as steps and ramps. We illustrated the classical approach with the design of a commercial videotape drive unit.

## REFERENCES

The period from about 1955 to 1965 was an especially exciting and productive one for the advancement of control system theory. At Columbia University, John Ragazzini and his students, including Eli Jury, Gene Franklin, Jack Sklansky, John Bertram, Bernard Friedland, Lofti Zadeh, and Rudolf Kalman, led the development of digital control methods that paralleled those of classical continuous-time control. (Bertram and Kalman also contributed heavily to the application of state space concepts, and Kalman made fundamental advances in the design of systems for stochastic estimation and control.) Many others, at leading universities and in industry, were also highly involved of course. Much of the original theory of sampled-data control was given in the classical texts:

J. R. Ragazzini and G. F. Franklin, *Sampled–Data Control Systems*. New York: McGraw-Hill, 1958;

E. I. Jury, *Sampled–Data Control Systems*. New York: Wiley, 1958.

A comprehensive treatment of classical discrete-time control system design is also given in

B. C. Kuo, *Analysis and Synthesis of Sampled-Data Control Systems*. Englewood Cliffs, NJ: Prentice-Hall, 1963.

Conventional classical digital control is covered in depth in such texts as

B. C. Kuo, *Digital Control Systems*. New York: Holt, Rinehart and Winston, 1980;

and later editions, and

C. L. Phillips and H. T. Nagle, Jr., *Digital Control System Analysis and Design*. Englewood Cliffs, NJ: Prentice-Hall, 1984.

A delightful mixture of classical and some modern digital control system design is found in

G. F. Franklin and J. D. Powell, *Digital Control of Dynamic Systems*. Reading, MA: Addison-Wesley, 1980.

Much of the viewpoint of classical discrete-time control here was inspired by far-looking courses taught by Allen Stubberud at UCLA in the early 1960s.

## CHAPTER TWO PROBLEMS

**2-1.** Sketch the following sequences for $k = 0, 1, 2, \ldots$

    **a.** $f_1(k) = (0.9)^k$

    **b.** $f_2(k) = 2\delta(k - 2) + e^{-0.2k}[u(k - 3) - u(k - 7)]$

    **c.** $f_3(k) = 3 \cos 0.1k + 4 \sin 0.1k$

**2-2.** A bank account pays 6 percent annual interest, compounded monthly. Initially, a deposit of \$200 is made. Thereafter, \$50 is deposited into the account each month. Describe the monthly bank balance as a function of the month $k$ after the initial deposit.

**2-3.** Find more compact mathematical expressions for the following sequences for $k \geqslant 0$:

**a.** $f_1(k) = \begin{cases} e^{-k} \cos k, & k = 0, 1, 2, 3 \\ 0, & \text{otherwise} \end{cases}$

**b.** $f_2(k) = \begin{cases} -1, & k \text{ odd} \\ 0, & \text{otherwise} \end{cases}$

**c.** $f_3(k) = \begin{cases} 3k, & k \text{ odd} \\ -3k, & k \text{ even} \end{cases}$

**2-4.** Find the $z$-transforms of the following sequences:

**a.** $f_1(k) = (0.5)^k - 3(0.3)^k$

**b.** $f_2(k) = 4e^{-k} - 3e^{-2k}$

**c.** $f_3(k) = \begin{cases} (-1)^k, & k = 4, 5, 6, \ldots \\ 0, & \text{otherwise} \end{cases}$

**d.** $f_4(k) = \cos[4k + (\pi/4)]$

**e.** $f_5(k) = \begin{cases} 2, & k = 1 \\ -3, & k = 4 \\ 8, & k = 7 \\ 0, & \text{otherwise} \end{cases}$

**f.** $f_6(k) = k^3 - 2k^2 + 3k + 4$

**g.** $f_7(k) = \begin{cases} 3e^{-2k}, & k = 1, 2, 3, 4 \\ 0, & \text{otherwise} \end{cases}$

**h.** $f_8(k) = ke^{-0.1k} \sin 3k$

**2-5.** Use long division to show that

$$\mathscr{Z}^{-1}\left[\frac{8z}{(z-1)^2}\right] = 8k \qquad k = 0, 1, 2, \ldots$$

**2-6.** Find closed form expressions for $k \geqslant 0$ for the inverse $z$-transforms of the following:

**a.** $F_1(z) = \dfrac{2z^2 - 3}{z^2 - 9z + 20}$

**b.** $F_2(z) = \dfrac{10}{z^3 - 9z^2 + 20z}$

**c.** $F_3(z) = \dfrac{4z^2 - 3z}{z^2 + 2z + 1}$

**d.** $F_4(z) = \dfrac{4z^2 - 3z + 2}{z^2 + 2z + 1}$

e. $F_5(z) = \dfrac{z^2 - 4z}{z^2 + z + (5/4)}$

f. $F_6(z) = \dfrac{-6z + 1}{z^{50}(z^2 + 5z + 6)}$

g. $F_7(z) = \dfrac{z^3}{(z^2 + 1/4)(z - 1/2)}$

h. $F_8(z) = \dfrac{z^2 + 2z - 3}{(z - \frac{1}{2} + j\frac{1}{4})(z - \frac{1}{2} - j\frac{1}{4})(z - \frac{1}{2})}$

**2-7.** For the difference equation

$$y(k + 2) + 3y(k + 1) - y(k) = r(k + 1) - 2r(k)$$

if

$$y(-1) = -4 \text{ and } y(-2) = 5$$

and $r(k) = 2$, for all $k$,

use the equation to calculate $y(0)$, $y(1)$, $y(2)$ and $y(3)$.

**2-8.** Use $z$-transformation to find the solutions of the following difference equations with the given initial conditions and inputs:

a. $y(k + 2) = (1/2)y(k + 1) + (1/2)y(k) + r(k + 1) - r(k)$
$y(-1) = 3; \qquad y(-2) = -5$
$r(k) = [3 + 4(1/4)^k]u(k)$

b. $y(k + 3) - 4y(k + 2) - 4y(k + 1) = 6r(k + 2) - r(k)$
$y(-1) = 2; \qquad y(-2) = -3; \qquad y(-3) = 4$
$r(k) = 3\delta(k - 1)$

c. $y(k + 2) = -y(k + 1) - (1/2)y(k) + 3r(k + 2) - 2r(k + 1)$
$y(-1) = 1; \qquad y(-2) = -4$
$r(k) = 5(1/2)^k u(k)$

**2-9.** Use discrete convolution to find

$$\mathcal{Z}^{-1}[F_1(z)F_2(z)]$$

by convolving

$$f_1(k) = (\tfrac{1}{2})^k u(k) \text{ and } f_2(k) = 3[u(k) - u(k - 5)]$$

**2-10.** Find the z-transfer functions of the following discrete-time systems. Express as rational functions of z.

   **a.** $y(k + 2) + 3y(k + 1) - 2y(k) = 6r(k + 1) - 7r(k)$

   **b.** $y(k + 2) - y(k + 1) + y(k) = 2r(k + 3) - r(k + 2) + 3r(k + 1) + r(k)$

   **c.** $y(k + 3) = 2r(k + 3) - r(k + 2) + 3r(k + 1) - 4r(k)$

**2-11.** For discrete-time systems with the following z-transfer functions and input sequences, find the output sequences for $k \geqslant 0$ if the initial conditions are zero:

   **a.** $T(z) = \dfrac{10}{z^2 - (3/4)z + (1/8)}$

      $r(k) = 4u(k)$

   **b.** $T(z) = \dfrac{z^2 + 4}{(z - 1)^2}$

      $r(k) = (1/2)^k u(k)$

   **c.** $T(z) = \dfrac{z}{z - (1/2)}$

      $r(k) = \sin(0.1k)u(k)$

**2-12.** Find the sequences $y(k)$ if all initial conditions are zero:

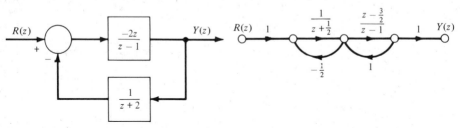

   **a.** $r(k) = \delta(k)$, the unit pulse.                 **b.** $r(k) = 6$.

**2-13.** For the discrete-time system with z-transfer function

   $T(z) = \dfrac{z^2 + 3}{z^2 - (1/4)}$

input sequence

$r(k) = (1/4)^k u(k)$

for all $k$ (including negative $k$), and initial conditions

$y(0) = 2$

$$y(1) = -6$$

find $y(k)$.

**2-14.** Find and carefully sketch the frequency response of the following systems:

**a.** $y(k + 1) + \dfrac{1}{2} y(k) = r(k + 1)$

**b.** $T(z) = \dfrac{3}{z(z - 1)}$

**c.**

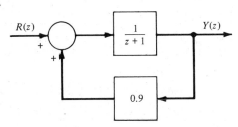

**2-15.** Determine whether each of the following discrete-time systems is stable:

**a.** $T(z) = \dfrac{z^3 + 3z^2 - 2z + 1}{z^3}$

**b.** $y(k + 2) = 2y(k + 1) - 5y(k) + 10r(k + 2) - 3r(k + 1) + 4r(k)$

**c.**

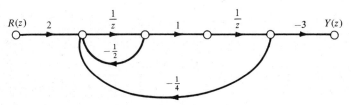

**2-16.** Use the bilinear transformation and a Routh-Hurwitz test to determine whether the systems with the following transfer functions are stable:

**a.** $T_1(z) = \dfrac{3z - 2}{z^2 + 0.5z + 0.9}$

**b.** $T_2(z) = \dfrac{1.2z^3 - 0.6z^2}{z^3 - 0.8z^2 + 1.2z - 1}$

**c.** $T_3(z) = \dfrac{2z^4 - 3z^3 + z^2 - 3z + 4}{z^4 + 0.6z^3 - 0.7z^2 + 0.8z - 0.9}$

**2-17.** For continuous-time signals with the following Laplace transforms, find the sequences of samples $f(kT)$, $k = 0, 1, 2, \ldots$ with the given sampling interval $T$.

**a.** $F_1(s) = \dfrac{3s - 2}{s^2 + 3s + 2};$  $T = 0.3$

**b.** $F_2(s) = \dfrac{16}{s^3 + 4s^2 + 4s};$  $T = 0.1$

**c.** $F_3(s) = \dfrac{2s - 6e^{-0.4s}}{(s + 1)(s^2 + 4)};$  $T = 0.2$

**d.** $F_4(s) = \dfrac{2 - e^{-0.2s}}{(s + 2)(s + 4)};$  $T = 0.3$

**e.** $F_5(s) = \dfrac{3 + se^{-0.3s}}{s(s + 3)};$  $T = 0.2$

**2-18.** Find the overall $z$-transfer functions. The sampling interval for each system is $T = 0.2$ second.

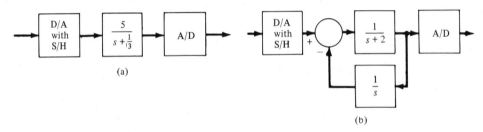

(a)

(b)

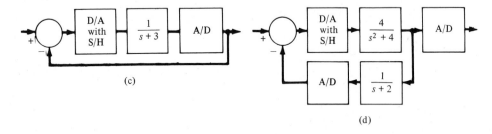

(c)

(d)

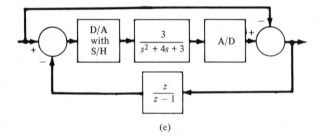

(e)

**2-19.** Draw integration diagrams for continuous-time systems with the following transfer functions. Approximate the integrations by two-sample difference equations with the indicated sampling interval $T$ and find the corresponding $z$-transfer function of the approximation.

    **a.** $G_1(s) = \dfrac{(1/3)s}{s + (1/3)};$     $T = 0.5$

    **b.** $G_2(s) = \dfrac{(1/3)s}{s + (1/3)};$     $T = 0.2$

    **c.** $G_3(s) = \dfrac{2s - 1}{s(s + 2)};$     $T = 0.1$

**2-20.** Find the $z$-transfer function for a three-sample digital approximation of a controller transfer function

$$G_c(s) = \frac{3s - 4}{s^2 + 5s + 6}$$

Use the sampling interval $T = 0.3$.

**2-21.** The discrete approximations to integrals in Table 2-6 are obtained by passing polynomial curves through the integrand samples, then approximating the integral between the most recent two samples by the area under the polynomial. For example, the three-sample approximation is the area between $t = kT$ and $t = (k + 1)T$ under a quadratic curve that passes through the three points $f[(k - 1)T]$, $f(kT)$, and $f[(k + 1)T]$.

    Derive this result, then find the corresponding result for the four-sample approximation. For this case, also find the difference equation for the approximate integral and the $z$-transfer function of the approximate integrator.

**2-22.** Find step-invariant digital approximations to continuous-time controllers with the following transfer functions using the indicated sampling intervals, $T$.

    **a.** $G_1(s) = \dfrac{2s}{s^2 + 3s + 2};$     $T = 0.2$

    **b.** $G_2(s) = \dfrac{4s - 6}{s^2 + (3/2)s + (1/2)};$     $T = 0.2$

    **c.** $G_3(s) = \dfrac{4s - 6}{s^2 + (3/2)s + (1/2)};$     $T = 0.4$

**2-23.** For a continuous-time controller with transfer function

$$G_c(s) = \frac{s + 4}{s^2 + 3s + 2}$$

and a sampling interval $T = 0.2$, find the ramp-invariant digital approximation.

# State Descriptions of Discrete-Time Systems

# 3

## 3.1 Preview

State variable models are now developed for discrete-time systems, paralleling then extending considerably the analogous topics for continuous-time systems in Chapter 1. The form of the equations is established, then system response is expressed in terms of discrete convolution and in terms of $z$-transforms. Z-transfer function matrices of multiple-input, multiple-output systems are found in terms of the state equations, and the controllable and observable forms for the equations are discussed.

   The characteristic value problem, which is considered in some detail and with a number of illustrative examples in this chapter, is fundamental to many topics to follow. A nonsingular change of state variables changes the internal description of a system but leaves its input-output relations unchanged. The change of variables involved in the characteristic value problem decouples the state equations from one another, simplifying their solution and giving important insight into system structure and behavior. Transformations to block real number representations in the case of complex eigenvalues, and transformations to block Jordan form in the case of repeated eigenvalues are also developed.

   There is the possibility that certain systems cannot be completely controlled from their inputs or that it may not be possible to completely determine their state from the available outputs. These topics, controllability and observability, which pertain to the question of whether or not a given system *can* be controlled, are developed in the final section of this chapter.

## 3.2 Discrete-Time State Equations

Discrete-time state variable models are now introduced. Like their continuous-time counterparts, discrete-time state variables are a convenient and powerful way of describing and dealing with systems, especially those with more than a single input and a single output. Two special forms for state equations, controllable form and observable form, are discussed in part in this section. Using them, it is especially easy to synthesize systems having desired $z$-transfer functions.

### 3.2.1 Delay Diagrams and State Equations

State variable descriptions of discrete-time systems are mathematical models consisting of coupled first-order difference equations. For linear, step-invariant discrete-time systems, state variable models involve the operations of summation, multiplication by a constant, and one-step delay. A block diagram or signal flow graph expressed in terms of these operations is called a *delay diagram* for the system. Delay diagrams relate the system inputs, the system outputs, and the internal state variables. The output of each delay is a state variable and the number of state variables, which is the number of delays, is the order of the system. Delay diagrams are arranged so that the input to each delay is a linear combination of the system inputs and the state variables, as is each system output.

An example of a delay diagram for a single-input, single-output system is the signal flow graph shown in Figure 3-1. In it, there are three delays, so the system represented is of third-order. The state variables are each of the delay outputs, and the inputs to the delays are each a linear combination of the system input and the state variables. From the diagram, the $z$-transformed state equations are

$$
\begin{cases}
X_1(z) = \dfrac{1}{z}\left[\dfrac{1}{2}X_1(z) + \dfrac{1}{4}X_2(z) + 2X_3(z) + U(z)\right] \\[2mm]
X_2(z) = \dfrac{1}{z}\left[-\dfrac{1}{2}X_2(z) - X_3(z) - U(z)\right] \\[2mm]
X_3(z) = \dfrac{1}{z}\left[3X_2(z) + \dfrac{1}{3}X_3(z) + 2U(z)\right]
\end{cases}
$$

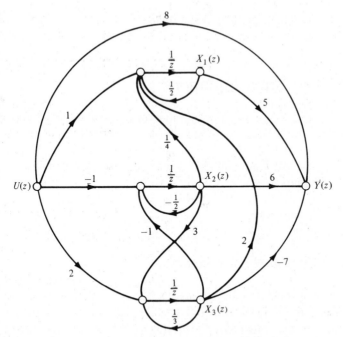

**FIGURE 3-1.   Delay diagram in terms of $z$-transforms.**

or

$$\begin{cases} zX_1(z) = \dfrac{1}{2}\,X_1(z) + \dfrac{1}{4}\,X_2(z) + 2X_3(z) + U(z) \\[2mm] zX_2(z) = -\dfrac{1}{2}\,X_2(z) - X_3(z) - U(z) \\[2mm] zX_3(z) = 3X_2(z) + \dfrac{1}{3}\,X_3(z) + 2U(z) \end{cases}$$

As functions of step, these state equations are

$$\begin{cases} x_1(k+1) = \dfrac{1}{2}\,x_1(k) + \dfrac{1}{4}\,x_2(k) + 2x_3(k) + u(k) \\[2mm] x_2(k+1) = -\dfrac{1}{2}\,x_2(k) - x_3(k) - u(k) \\[2mm] x_3(k+1) = 3x_2(k) + \dfrac{1}{3}\,x_3(k) + 2u(k) \end{cases}$$

which in matrix form is

$$\begin{bmatrix} x_1(k+1) \\ x_2(k+1) \\ x_3(k+1) \end{bmatrix} = \begin{bmatrix} \frac{1}{2} & \frac{1}{4} & 2 \\ 0 & -\frac{1}{2} & -1 \\ 0 & 3 & \frac{1}{3} \end{bmatrix} \begin{bmatrix} x_1(k) \\ x_2(k) \\ x_3(k) \end{bmatrix} + \begin{bmatrix} 1 \\ -1 \\ 2 \end{bmatrix} u(k)$$

The output of the system is a linear combination of the state variables and the system input

$$Y(z) = 5X_1(z) + 6X_2(z) - 7X_3(z) + 8U(z)$$

or

$$y(k) = \begin{bmatrix} 5 & 6 & -7 \end{bmatrix} \begin{bmatrix} x_1(k) \\ x_2(k) \\ x_3(k) \end{bmatrix} + 8u(k)$$

Delay diagrams show how a system can be constructed in hardware, with digital multipliers and adders, and with shift registers to provide the delays. It also shows how the system can be realized recursively in software, with the state and output for the next step produced during each program loop. Alternatively, a delay diagram can be expressed in terms of the signals themselves, rather than their $z$-transforms, as in the block diagram of Figure 3-2. The initial delay outputs are the initial system state. One can deal either in the step or the transform domain for step-invariant systems. For step-varying systems, however, $z$-transforms are no longer of much use.

Another delay diagram, one for a second-order system with multiple inputs and outputs, is shown in Figure 3-3. For this system, state equations are

$$\begin{bmatrix} x_1(k+1) \\ x_2(k+1) \end{bmatrix} = \begin{bmatrix} -1 & 2 \\ \frac{1}{4} & \frac{1}{2} \end{bmatrix} \begin{bmatrix} x_1(k) \\ x_2(k) \end{bmatrix} + \begin{bmatrix} 2 & 0 \\ -2 & 3 \end{bmatrix} \begin{bmatrix} u_1(k) \\ u_2(k) \end{bmatrix}$$

The output equations are

$$\begin{bmatrix} y_1(k) \\ y_2(k) \\ y_3(k) \end{bmatrix} = \begin{bmatrix} 6 & 5 \\ -3 & 0 \\ 1 & 7 \end{bmatrix} \begin{bmatrix} x_1(k) \\ x_2(k) \end{bmatrix} + \begin{bmatrix} 0 & 0 \\ 0 & 0 \\ 0 & 10 \end{bmatrix} \begin{bmatrix} u_1(k) \\ u_2(k) \end{bmatrix}$$

In general, $n$th order discrete-time state equations are of the form

$$\begin{bmatrix} x_1(k+1) \\ x_2(k+1) \\ \vdots \\ x_n(k+1) \end{bmatrix} = \begin{bmatrix} a_{11} & a_{12} & \cdots & a_{1n} \\ a_{21} & a_{22} & \cdots & a_{2n} \\ \vdots & & & \\ a_{n1} & a_{n2} & \cdots & a_{nn} \end{bmatrix} \begin{bmatrix} x_1(k) \\ x_2(k) \\ \vdots \\ x_n(k) \end{bmatrix} + \begin{bmatrix} b_{11} & b_{12} & \cdots & b_{1r} \\ b_{21} & b_{22} & \cdots & b_{2r} \\ \vdots & & & \\ b_{n1} & b_{n2} & \cdots & b_{nr} \end{bmatrix} \begin{bmatrix} u_1(k) \\ u_2(k) \\ \vdots \\ u_r(k) \end{bmatrix}$$

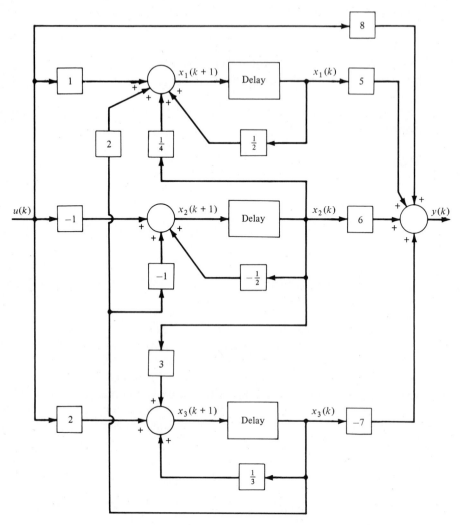

**FIGURE 3-2.  Delay diagram in terms of time-domain signals.**

or

$$\mathbf{x}(k + 1) = \mathbf{A}\mathbf{x}(k) + \mathbf{B}\mathbf{u}(k)$$

where the state vector $\mathbf{x}(k)$ is an $n$-vector, the state coupling matrix $\mathbf{A}$ is $n \times n$, the input vector $\mathbf{u}(k)$ is an $r$-vector of input signals, and the input coupling

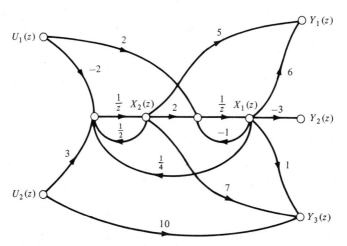

**FIGURE 3-3.** A delay diagram with multiple inputs and outputs.

matrix **B** is $n \times r$. The general form of the output equations is

$$
\begin{bmatrix} y_1(k) \\ y_2(k) \\ \vdots \\ y_m(k) \end{bmatrix} = \begin{bmatrix} c_{11} & c_{12} & \cdots & c_{1n} \\ c_{21} & c_{22} & \cdots & c_{2n} \\ \vdots & & & \\ c_{m1} & c_{m2} & \cdots & c_{mn} \end{bmatrix} \begin{bmatrix} x_1(k) \\ x_2(k) \\ \vdots \\ x_n(k) \end{bmatrix} + \begin{bmatrix} d_{11} & d_{12} & \cdots & d_{1r} \\ d_{21} & d_{22} & \cdots & d_{2r} \\ \vdots & & & \\ d_{m1} & d_{m2} & \cdots & d_{mr} \end{bmatrix} \begin{bmatrix} u_1(k) \\ u_2(k) \\ \vdots \\ u_r(k) \end{bmatrix}
$$

or

$$\mathbf{y}(k) = \mathbf{C}\mathbf{x}(k) + \mathbf{D}\mathbf{u}(k)$$

where the output vector $\mathbf{y}(k)$ is an $m$-vector of output signals, the output coupling matrix $\mathbf{C}$ is $m \times n$, and the input-to-output coupling matrix $\mathbf{D}$ is $m \times r$. A block diagram showing how the vectors $\mathbf{u}(k)$, $\mathbf{x}(k)$ and $\mathbf{y}(k)$ are related is given in Figure 3-4. In this diagram, the wide arrows represent vectors of signals.

As is common in practice, we have elected to use the same symbols, $\mathbf{x}$, $\mathbf{u}$, $\mathbf{y}$, **A**, **B**, **C**, **D**, to describe discrete-time state equations as were used earlier for continuous-time state equations. The quantities are not the same, of course, but real conflict only occurs when discrete-time and continuous-time systems are considered simultaneously. When that situation occurs, as it will later in connection with discrete-time models of continuous-time systems, script symbols will be used for the continuous-time state variable matrices.

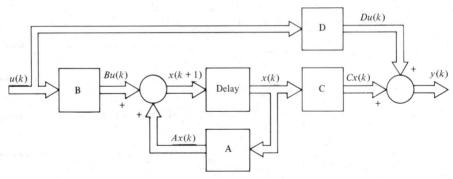

**FIGURE 3-4.**  **Block diagram showing the relations between signal vectors in a discrete-time state variable model.**

## 3.2.2 Controllable Form

A particularly convenient arrangement for obtaining state equations for a single-input system with specified transfer functions is the *controllable* (or *phase variable*) *form*, shown with a single output in Figure 3-5. Applying Mason's gain rule (see Table 3-1 for a summary), the system $z$-transfer

**TABLE 3-1    Signal Flow Graph Definitions and Mason's Gain Rule**

| | |
|---|---|
| *Path:* | A succession of branches, from input to output, in the direction of the arrows, which does not pass any node more than once. |
| *Path Gain:* | Product of the transmittances of the branches of the path. For the $i$th path, the path gain is denoted by $P_i$. |
| *Loop:* | A closed succession of branches, in the direction of the arrows, which does not pass any node more than once. |
| *Loop Gain:* | Product of the transmittances of the branches of the loop. |
| *Touching:* | Loops with one or more nodes in common are termed *touching*. A loop and a path are touching if they have a common node. |
| *Determinant:* | The determinant of a signal flow graph is $\Delta = 1 - $ (sum of all loop gains) + (sum of products of gains of all combinations of 2 nontouching loops) $-$ (sum of products of gains of all combinations of 3 nontouching loops) $+ \ldots$ |
| *Cofactor:* | The cofactor of the $i$th path, denoted by $\Delta_i$, is the determinant of the signal flow graph formed by deleting all loops touching path $i$. |
| *Mason's Gain Rule:* | $T(z) = \dfrac{P_1 \Delta_1 + P_2 \Delta_2 + \cdots}{\Delta}$ |

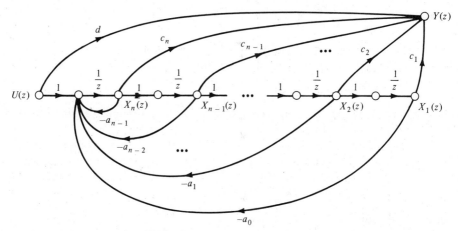

**FIGURE 3-5.** Controllable form for a single-input, single-output discrete-time system.

function is

$$T(z) = \frac{d\Delta + P_1\Delta_1 + P_2\Delta_2 + P_3\Delta_3 + \cdots}{\Delta} = d + \frac{P_1 + P_2 + P_3 + \cdots}{\Delta}$$

$$= d + \frac{\dfrac{c_n}{z} + \dfrac{c_{n-1}}{z^2} + \cdots + \dfrac{c_2}{z^{n-1}} + \dfrac{c_1}{z^n}}{1 + \dfrac{\alpha_{n-1}}{z} + \dfrac{\alpha_{n-2}}{z^2} + \cdots + \dfrac{\alpha_1}{z^{n-1}} + \dfrac{\alpha_0}{z^n}}$$

$$= d + \frac{c_n z^{n-1} + c_{n-1} z^{n-2} + \cdots + c_2 z + c_1}{z^n + \alpha_{n-1} z^{n-1} + \alpha_{n-2} z^{n-2} + \cdots + \alpha_1 z + \alpha_0}$$

Except for the path $d$, each path and each loop share the node at the input to the leftmost delay, so all of the path cofactors are unity and there are no product of loop gain terms in the determinant of the signal flow graph.

The state and output equations for the system are, from the delay diagram,

$$
\begin{bmatrix}
x_1(k+1) \\
x_2(k+1) \\
x_3(k+1) \\
\vdots \\
x_{n-1}(k+1) \\
x_n(k+1)
\end{bmatrix}
=
\begin{bmatrix}
0 & 1 & 0 & \cdots & 0 & 0 \\
0 & 0 & 1 & \cdots & 0 & 0 \\
0 & 0 & 0 & \cdots & 0 & 0 \\
\vdots & & & & & \\
0 & 0 & 0 & \cdots & 0 & 1 \\
-\alpha_0 & -\alpha_1 & -\alpha_2 & \cdots & -\alpha_{n-2} & -\alpha_{n-1}
\end{bmatrix}
\begin{bmatrix}
x_1(k) \\
x_2(k) \\
x_3(k) \\
\vdots \\
x_{n-1}(k) \\
x_n(k)
\end{bmatrix}
+
\begin{bmatrix}
0 \\
0 \\
0 \\
\vdots \\
0 \\
1
\end{bmatrix}
u(k)
$$

$$y(k) = [c_1 \quad c_2 \quad \cdots \quad c_{n-1} \quad c_n] \begin{bmatrix} x_1(k) \\ x_2(k) \\ \vdots \\ x_{n-1}(k) \\ x_n(k) \end{bmatrix} + du(k)$$

so it is a simple matter to find state and output equations of this form with a given $z$-transfer function.

Single-input multiple-output systems with specified $z$-transfer functions, provided that the transfer function numerator degrees are no higher than that of the denominator, can be synthesized by simply appending additional output equations to the state variable description. For example, a single-input, two-output system with $z$-transfer functions

$$T_1(z) = \frac{Y_1(z)}{U(z)}\bigg|_{\text{zero initial conditions}} = \frac{3z^2 - z - 3}{z^2 + \frac{1}{3}z - \frac{2}{3}} = 3 + \frac{-2z - 1}{z^2 + \frac{1}{3}z - \frac{2}{3}}$$

$$= 3 + \frac{-\dfrac{2}{z} - \dfrac{1}{z^2}}{1 + \dfrac{\frac{1}{3}}{z} - \dfrac{\frac{2}{3}}{z^2}}$$

$$T_2(z) = \frac{Y_2(z)}{U(z)}\bigg|_{\text{zero initial conditions}} = \frac{6}{z + 1} = \frac{6(z - \frac{2}{3})}{(z + 1)(z - \frac{2}{3})}$$

$$= \frac{6z - 4}{z^2 + \frac{1}{3}z - \frac{2}{3}} = \frac{\dfrac{6}{z} - \dfrac{4}{z^2}}{1 + \dfrac{\frac{1}{3}}{z} - \dfrac{\frac{2}{3}}{z^2}}$$

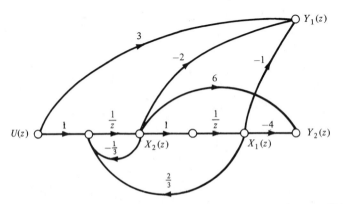

**FIGURE 3-6.   A multiple-output discrete-time system in controllable form.**

has the delay diagram given in Figure 3-6. Its controllable form state and output equations are

$$\begin{bmatrix} x_1(k+1) \\ x_2(k+1) \end{bmatrix} = \begin{bmatrix} 0 & 1 \\ \frac{2}{3} & -\frac{1}{3} \end{bmatrix} \begin{bmatrix} x_1(k) \\ x_2(k) \end{bmatrix} + \begin{bmatrix} 0 \\ 1 \end{bmatrix} u(k)$$

$$\begin{bmatrix} y_1(k) \\ y_2(k) \end{bmatrix} = \begin{bmatrix} -1 & -2 \\ -4 & 6 \end{bmatrix} \begin{bmatrix} x_1(k) \\ x_2(k) \end{bmatrix} + \begin{bmatrix} 3 \\ 0 \end{bmatrix} u(k)$$

## 3.2.3 Observable Form

The structure for the delay diagram of a single-input, single-output system in *observable form* is shown in Figure 3-7. In applying Mason's gain rule to find the system's transfer function, every path except the uppermost one, and every loop, passes through the $X_1$ node. Since every one of the loops touches each of these paths, their cofactors are all unity. Since each of the loops touch one another, the determinant of the signal flow graph is simply unity minus the sum of the loop transmittances. The cofactor of the upper path is the same as the signal flow graph determinant because none of the loops touch it. The transfer function is then

$$T(s) = \frac{d\Delta + P_1\Delta_1 + P_2\Delta_2 + P_3\Delta_3 + \cdots}{\Delta} = d + \frac{P_1 + P_2 + P_3 + \cdots}{\Delta}$$

$$= d + \frac{\dfrac{b_1}{z} + \dfrac{b_2}{z^2} + \cdots + \dfrac{b_{n-1}}{z^{n-1}} + \dfrac{b_n}{z^n}}{1 + \dfrac{\alpha_{n-1}}{z} + \dfrac{\alpha_{n-2}}{z^2} + \cdots + \dfrac{\alpha_1}{z^{n-1}} + \dfrac{\alpha_0}{z^n}}$$

$$= d + \frac{b_1 z^{n-1} + b_2 z^{n-2} + \cdots + b_{n-1} z + b_n}{z^n + \alpha_{n-1} z^{n-1} + \alpha_{n-2} z^{n-2} + \cdots + \alpha_1 z + \alpha_0}$$

which has coefficients that are the gains in the signal flow graph. State variable equations for this system in observable form are

$$\begin{bmatrix} x_1(k+1) \\ x_2(k+1) \\ x_3(k+1) \\ \vdots \\ x_{n-1}(k+1) \\ x_n(k+1) \end{bmatrix} = \begin{bmatrix} -\alpha_{n-1} & 1 & 0 & \cdots & 0 & 0 \\ -\alpha_{n-2} & 0 & 1 & \cdots & 0 & 0 \\ -\alpha_{n-3} & 0 & 0 & \cdots & 0 & 0 \\ \vdots & & & & & \\ -\alpha_1 & 0 & 0 & \cdots & 0 & 1 \\ -\alpha_0 & 0 & 0 & \cdots & 0 & 0 \end{bmatrix} \begin{bmatrix} x_1(k) \\ x_2(k) \\ x_3(k) \\ \vdots \\ x_{n-1}(k) \\ x_n(k) \end{bmatrix} + \begin{bmatrix} b_1 \\ b_2 \\ b_3 \\ \vdots \\ b_{n-1} \\ b_n \end{bmatrix} u(k)$$

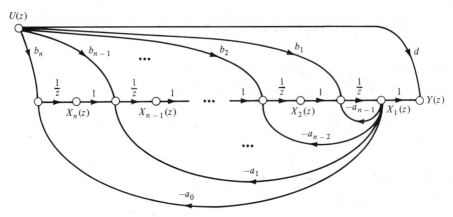

**FIGURE 3-7.    Observable form for a single-input, single-output discrete-time system.**

$$y(k) = [1 \quad 0 \quad 0 \quad \cdots \quad 0 \quad 0] \begin{bmatrix} x_1(k) \\ x_2(k) \\ x_3(k) \\ \vdots \\ x_{n-1}(k) \\ x_n(k) \end{bmatrix} + du(k)$$

To accommodate multiple inputs, the state variable equations are

$$\begin{bmatrix} x_1(k+1) \\ x_2(k+1) \\ \vdots \\ x_n(k+1) \end{bmatrix} = \begin{bmatrix} -\alpha_{n-1} & 1 & \cdots & 0 \\ -\alpha_{n-2} & 0 & \cdots & 0 \\ \vdots & & & \\ -\alpha_0 & 0 & \cdots & 0 \end{bmatrix} \begin{bmatrix} x_1(k) \\ x_2(k) \\ \vdots \\ x_n(k) \end{bmatrix} + \begin{bmatrix} b_{11} & b_{12} & \cdots & b_{1r} \\ b_{21} & b_{22} & \cdots & b_{2r} \\ \vdots & & & \\ b_{n1} & b_{n2} & \cdots & b_{nr} \end{bmatrix} \begin{bmatrix} u_1(k) \\ u_2(k) \\ \vdots \\ u_r(k) \end{bmatrix}$$

$$y(k) = [1 \quad 0 \quad \cdots \quad 0] \begin{bmatrix} x_1(k) \\ x_2(k) \\ \vdots \\ x_n(k) \end{bmatrix} + [d_1 \quad d_2 \quad \cdots \quad d_r] \begin{bmatrix} u_1(k) \\ u_2(k) \\ \vdots \\ u_r(k) \end{bmatrix}$$

and the $z$-transfer functions are

$$T_1(z) = \frac{Y(z)}{U_1(z)}\bigg|_{\substack{\text{zero initial} \\ \text{conditions}}} = d_1 + \frac{b_{11}z^{n-1} + b_{21}z^{n-2} + \cdots + b_{n1}}{z^n + \alpha_{n-1}z^{n-1} + \cdots + \alpha_1 z + \alpha_0}$$

$$T_2(z) = \left.\frac{Y(z)}{U_2(z)}\right|_{\substack{\text{zero initial}\\\text{conditions}}} = d_2 + \frac{b_{12}z^{n-1} + b_{22}z^{n-2} + \cdots + b_{n2}}{z^n + \alpha_{n-1}z^{n-1} + \cdots + \alpha_1 z + \alpha_0}$$

$$\vdots$$

$$T_r(z) = \left.\frac{Y(z)}{U_r(z)}\right|_{\substack{\text{zero initial}\\\text{conditions}}} = d_r + \frac{b_{1r}z^{n-1} + b_{2r}z^{n-2} + \cdots + b_{nr}}{z^n + \alpha_{n-1}z^{n-1} + \cdots + \alpha_1 z + \alpha_0}$$

For example, a single-input, single-output system with $z$-transfer function

$$T(z) = \frac{-2z^3 + 2z^2 - z + 2}{z^3 + z^2 - z - \frac{3}{4}} = -2 + \frac{4z^2 - 3z + \frac{1}{2}}{z^3 + z^2 - z - \frac{3}{4}}$$

in observable form has the delay diagram of Figure 3-8(a) and has state variable equations

$$\begin{bmatrix} x_1(k+1) \\ x_2(k+1) \\ x_3(k+1) \end{bmatrix} = \begin{bmatrix} -1 & 1 & 0 \\ 1 & 0 & 1 \\ \frac{3}{4} & 0 & 0 \end{bmatrix} \begin{bmatrix} x_1(k) \\ x_2(k) \\ x_3(k) \end{bmatrix} + \begin{bmatrix} 4 \\ -3 \\ \frac{1}{2} \end{bmatrix} u(k)$$

$$y(k) = \begin{bmatrix} 1 & 0 & 0 \end{bmatrix} \begin{bmatrix} x_1(k) \\ x_2(k) \\ x_3(k) \end{bmatrix} - 2u(k)$$

The three-input, single output system with $z$-transfer functions

$$T_1(z) = \left.\frac{Y(z)}{U_1(z)}\right|_{\substack{\text{zero initial}\\\text{conditions}}} = \frac{z^2 + 2z + 2}{z^2 + \frac{1}{2}z - \frac{1}{2}} = 1 + \frac{\frac{3}{2}z + \frac{5}{2}}{z^2 + \frac{1}{2}z - \frac{1}{2}}$$

$$T_2(z) = \left.\frac{Y(z)}{U_2(z)}\right|_{\substack{\text{zero initial}\\\text{conditions}}} = \frac{-z}{z - \frac{1}{2}} = \frac{-z(z+1)}{(z - \frac{1}{2})(z+1)} = -1 + \frac{-\frac{1}{2}z - \frac{1}{2}}{z^2 + \frac{1}{2}z - \frac{1}{2}}$$

$$T_3(z) = \left.\frac{Y(z)}{U_3(z)}\right|_{\substack{\text{zero initial}\\\text{conditions}}} = \frac{4}{z^2 + \frac{1}{2}z - \frac{1}{2}}$$

has the observable form delay diagram of Figure 3-8(b) and state variable equations

$$\begin{bmatrix} x_1(k+1) \\ x_2(k+1) \end{bmatrix} = \begin{bmatrix} -\frac{1}{2} & 1 \\ \frac{1}{2} & 0 \end{bmatrix} \begin{bmatrix} x_1(k) \\ x_2(k) \end{bmatrix} + \begin{bmatrix} \frac{3}{2} & -\frac{1}{2} & 0 \\ \frac{5}{2} & -\frac{1}{2} & 4 \end{bmatrix} \begin{bmatrix} u_1(k) \\ u_2(k) \\ u_3(k) \end{bmatrix}$$

$$y(k) = \begin{bmatrix} 1 & 0 \end{bmatrix} \begin{bmatrix} x_1(k) \\ x_2(k) \end{bmatrix} + \begin{bmatrix} 1 & -1 & 0 \end{bmatrix} \begin{bmatrix} u_1(k) \\ u_2(k) \\ u_3(k) \end{bmatrix}$$

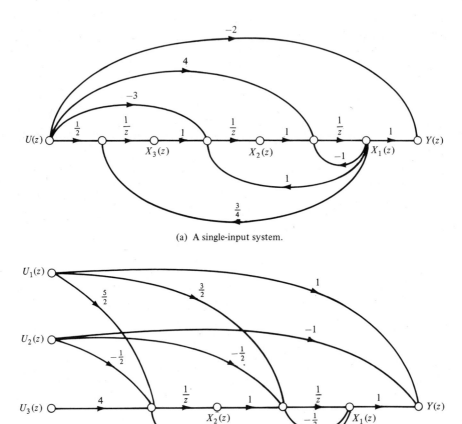

(a) A single-input system.

(b) A multiple-input system.

**FIGURE 3-8.    Examples of discrete-time systems in observable form.**

Observable form is especially convenient for synthesis of multiple-input, single-output systems, just as controllable form is convenient for single-input, multiple-output synthesis.

## 3.3 Discrete-Time System Response

The state and output signals of a discrete-time system are now found from the inputs and the initial state. Repeated application of the state variable equations is used to express the state and output signals in terms of a discrete convolution. Then, the $z$-transform is applied to find $z$-transfer functions and closed-form solutions for response. Any nonsingular change of state variables is shown to result in new state variable equations with no change in the $z$-transfer functions relating the system's outputs and inputs.

### 3.3.1 Response in Terms of Discrete Convolution

The response of a discrete-time system can be calculated recursively, starting with an initial state and repeatedly using the state equations

$$\mathbf{x}(k+1) = \mathbf{Ax}(k) + \mathbf{Bu}(k)$$

From $\mathbf{x}(0)$ and $\mathbf{u}(0)$, $\mathbf{x}(1)$ can be calculated:

$$\mathbf{x}(1) = \mathbf{Ax}(0) + \mathbf{Bu}(0)$$

Then, using $\mathbf{x}(1)$ and $\mathbf{u}(1)$:

$$\mathbf{x}(2) = \mathbf{Ax}(1) + \mathbf{Bu}(1) = \mathbf{A}^2\mathbf{x}(0) + \mathbf{ABu}(0) + \mathbf{Bu}(1)$$

From $\mathbf{x}(2)$ and $\mathbf{u}(2)$:

$$\mathbf{x}(3) = \mathbf{Ax}(2) + \mathbf{Bu}(2) = \mathbf{A}^3\mathbf{x}(0) + \mathbf{A}^2\mathbf{Bu}(0) + \mathbf{ABu}(1) + \mathbf{Bu}(2)$$

and in general:

$$\mathbf{x}(k) = \mathbf{A}^k\mathbf{x}(0) + \mathbf{A}^{k-1}\mathbf{Bu}(0) + \mathbf{A}^{k-2}\mathbf{Bu}(1) + \cdots + \mathbf{ABu}(k-2) + \mathbf{Bu}(k-1)$$

$$= \underbrace{\mathbf{A}^k\mathbf{x}(0)}_{\text{zero-input component}} + \underbrace{\sum_{i=0}^{k-1} \mathbf{A}^{k-1-i}\mathbf{Bu}(i)}_{\text{zero-state component}}$$

$$= \mathbf{A}^k\mathbf{x}(0) + \text{convolution}[\mathbf{F}(k), \mathbf{Bu}(k)] \tag{3-1}$$

The term that depends on the initial state, but not the inputs, is the *zero-input component*. The *zero-state component* does not depend on the initial conditions and is the discrete convolution of the function $\mathbf{Bu}(k)$ with the function

$$\mathbf{F}(k) = \begin{cases} \mathbf{A}^{k-1}, & k = 1, 2, 3, \ldots \\ \mathbf{0}, & k = 0, -1, -2, \ldots \end{cases}$$

Recall that the convolution summation has an upper limit $k$, not $k - 1$,

$$\text{convolution } [f_1(k), f_2(k)] = \sum_{i=0}^{k} f_2(k - i)f_1(i)$$

so $\mathbf{F}(k)$ must be zero for $k = 0$.

As a numerical example, consider the system

$$\begin{bmatrix} x_1(k+1) \\ x_2(k+1) \end{bmatrix} = \begin{bmatrix} \frac{1}{2} & 1 \\ -\frac{1}{2} & 0 \end{bmatrix} \begin{bmatrix} x_1(k) \\ x_2(k) \end{bmatrix} + \begin{bmatrix} 0 \\ 4 \end{bmatrix} u(k) = \mathbf{A}\mathbf{x}(k) + \mathbf{b}u(k)$$

$$y(k) = \begin{bmatrix} 2 & -3 \end{bmatrix} \begin{bmatrix} x_1(k) \\ x_2(k) \end{bmatrix} = \mathbf{c}^\dagger \mathbf{x}(k)$$

with

$$\begin{bmatrix} x_1(0) \\ x_2(0) \end{bmatrix} = \begin{bmatrix} -5 \\ 6 \end{bmatrix}$$

and

$$u(k) = 1 \quad \text{for all } k$$

At the zeroth step:

$$y(0) = \begin{bmatrix} 2 & -3 \end{bmatrix} \begin{bmatrix} -5 \\ 6 \end{bmatrix} = -28$$

At step one:

$$\begin{bmatrix} x_1(1) \\ x_2(1) \end{bmatrix} = \begin{bmatrix} \frac{1}{2} & 1 \\ -\frac{1}{2} & 0 \end{bmatrix} \begin{bmatrix} -5 \\ 6 \end{bmatrix} + \begin{bmatrix} 0 \\ 4 \end{bmatrix}(1) = \begin{bmatrix} \frac{7}{2} \\ \frac{13}{2} \end{bmatrix}$$

$$y(1) = \begin{bmatrix} 2 & -3 \end{bmatrix} \begin{bmatrix} \frac{7}{2} \\ \frac{13}{2} \end{bmatrix} = -\frac{25}{2}$$

At step two:

$$\begin{bmatrix} x_1(2) \\ x_2(2) \end{bmatrix} = \begin{bmatrix} \frac{1}{2} & 1 \\ -\frac{1}{2} & 0 \end{bmatrix} \begin{bmatrix} \frac{7}{2} \\ \frac{13}{2} \end{bmatrix} + \begin{bmatrix} 0 \\ 4 \end{bmatrix}(1) = \begin{bmatrix} \frac{33}{4} \\ \frac{9}{4} \end{bmatrix}$$

$$y(2) = \begin{bmatrix} 2 & -3 \end{bmatrix} \begin{bmatrix} \frac{33}{4} \\ \frac{9}{4} \end{bmatrix} = \frac{39}{4}$$

At step three,

$$\begin{bmatrix} x_1(3) \\ x_2(3) \end{bmatrix} = \begin{bmatrix} \frac{1}{2} & 1 \\ -\frac{1}{2} & 0 \end{bmatrix} \begin{bmatrix} \frac{33}{4} \\ \frac{9}{4} \end{bmatrix} + \begin{bmatrix} 0 \\ 4 \end{bmatrix}(1) = \begin{bmatrix} \frac{51}{8} \\ -\frac{1}{8} \end{bmatrix}$$

$$y(3) = \begin{bmatrix} 2 & -3 \end{bmatrix} \begin{bmatrix} \frac{51}{8} \\ -\frac{1}{8} \end{bmatrix} = \frac{105}{8}$$

and so on.

In terms of the convolution formula, the system state at step three is given by

$$\mathbf{x}(3) = \mathbf{A}^3\mathbf{x}(0) + \mathbf{A}^2\mathbf{b}u(0) + \mathbf{A}\mathbf{b}u(1) + \mathbf{b}u(2)$$

$$= \begin{bmatrix} -\frac{3}{8} & -\frac{1}{4} \\ \frac{1}{8} & -\frac{1}{4} \end{bmatrix} \begin{bmatrix} -5 \\ 6 \end{bmatrix} + \begin{bmatrix} -\frac{1}{4} & \frac{1}{2} \\ -\frac{1}{4} & -\frac{1}{2} \end{bmatrix} \begin{bmatrix} 0 \\ 4 \end{bmatrix}(1) + \begin{bmatrix} \frac{1}{2} & 1 \\ -\frac{1}{2} & 0 \end{bmatrix} \begin{bmatrix} 0 \\ 4 \end{bmatrix}(1) + \begin{bmatrix} 0 \\ 4 \end{bmatrix}(1)$$

$$= \underbrace{\begin{bmatrix} \frac{3}{8} \\ -\frac{17}{8} \end{bmatrix}}_{\text{zero-input component}} + \underbrace{\begin{bmatrix} 2 \\ -2 \end{bmatrix} + \begin{bmatrix} 4 \\ 0 \end{bmatrix} + \begin{bmatrix} 0 \\ 4 \end{bmatrix}}_{\text{zero-state component}} = \begin{bmatrix} \frac{51}{8} \\ -\frac{1}{8} \end{bmatrix}$$

## 3.3.2  Z-Transformed Signals

Closed-form expressions for the signals in a linear, step-invariant state variable model can be found by $z$-transforming the equations, solving for the transform of the signals of interest, then inverting the transforms to obtain the signals themselves. For the specific system of Figure 3-9(a) for example, the state variable equations are

$$\begin{bmatrix} x_1(k+1) \\ x_2(k+1) \end{bmatrix} = \begin{bmatrix} \frac{3}{2} & -1 \\ 1 & -1 \end{bmatrix} \begin{bmatrix} x_1(k) \\ x_2(k) \end{bmatrix} + \begin{bmatrix} 3 \\ 2 \end{bmatrix} u(k) = \mathbf{A}\mathbf{x}(k) + \mathbf{b}u(k)$$

$$\begin{bmatrix} y_1(k) \\ y_2(k) \end{bmatrix} = \begin{bmatrix} -3 & 4 \\ -1 & 1 \end{bmatrix} \begin{bmatrix} x_1(k) \\ x_2(k) \end{bmatrix} + \begin{bmatrix} -2 \\ 0 \end{bmatrix} u(k) = \mathbf{C}\mathbf{x}(k) + \mathbf{d}u(k)$$

Let the system input be

$$u(k) = \left(\frac{1}{2}\right)^k$$

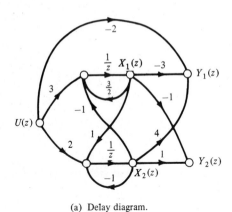 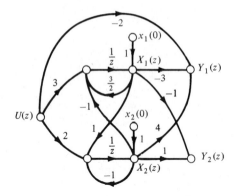

(a) Delay diagram.  (b) Delay diagram including initial conditions.

**FIGURE 3-9.** **Finding the response of a discrete-time system using z-transforms.**

and let the initial conditions be

$$\begin{bmatrix} x_1(0) \\ x_2(0) \end{bmatrix} = \begin{bmatrix} -5 \\ 1 \end{bmatrix}$$

The z-transformed state equations are

$$\begin{cases} zX_1(z) + 5z = \tfrac{3}{2}X_1(z) - X_2(z) + 3U(z) \\ zX_2(z) - \quad z = X_1(z) - X_2(z) + 2U(z) \end{cases}$$

or

$$\begin{cases} (z - \tfrac{3}{2})X_1(z) + X_2(z) = -5z + \dfrac{3z}{z - \tfrac{1}{2}} = \dfrac{-5z^2 + \tfrac{11}{2}z}{z - \tfrac{1}{2}} \\[4mm] -X_1(z) + (z + 1)X_2(z) = z + \dfrac{2z}{z - \tfrac{1}{2}} = \dfrac{z^2 + \tfrac{3}{2}z}{z - \tfrac{1}{2}} \end{cases}$$

These include the initial conditions for the state variables, which can be added to the delay diagram as in Figure 3-9(b), if desired.

Solving for $X_1(z)$ and $X_2(z)$ and expanding into partial fractions (in the form suitable for inverse z-transformation),

$$\begin{cases} X_1(z) = \dfrac{z(-5z^2 - \tfrac{1}{2}z + 4)}{(z - \tfrac{1}{2})(z^2 - \tfrac{1}{2}z - \tfrac{1}{2})} = \dfrac{-5z}{z - \tfrac{1}{2}} + \dfrac{2z}{z + \tfrac{1}{2}} + \dfrac{-2z}{z - 1} \\[4mm] X_2(z) = \dfrac{z(z^2 - 5z + \tfrac{13}{4})}{(z - \tfrac{1}{2})(z + \tfrac{1}{2})(z - 1)} = \dfrac{-2z}{z - \tfrac{1}{2}} + \dfrac{4z}{z + \tfrac{1}{2}} + \dfrac{-z}{z - 1} \end{cases}$$

there results:

$$\begin{cases} x_1(k) = -5(\tfrac{1}{2})^k + 2(-\tfrac{1}{2})^k - 2, \\ x_2(k) = -2(\tfrac{1}{2})^k + 4(-\tfrac{1}{2})^k - 1, \qquad k = 0, 1, 2, \dots \end{cases}$$

The system outputs are then

$$y_1(k) = -3x_1(k) + 4x_2(k) - 2u(k) = 5(\tfrac{1}{2})^k + 10(-\tfrac{1}{2})^k + 2, \qquad k = 0, 1, 2, \dots$$

$$y_2(k) = -x_1(k) + x_2(k) = 3(\tfrac{1}{2})^k + 2(-\tfrac{1}{2})^k + 1, \qquad k = 0, 1, 2, \dots$$

The $z$-transfer function matrix of a system is found by $z$-transforming the state equations with zero initial conditions. Solving for the state

$$z\mathbf{X}(z) = \mathbf{A}\mathbf{X}(z) + \mathbf{B}\mathbf{U}(z)$$

$$(z\mathbf{I} - \mathbf{A})\mathbf{X}(z) = \mathbf{B}\mathbf{U}(z)$$

$$\mathbf{X}(z) = (z\mathbf{I} - \mathbf{A})^{-1}\mathbf{B}\mathbf{U}(z)$$

and then finding the transform of the output vector in terms of the input vector transform:

$$\mathbf{Y}(z) = \mathbf{C}\mathbf{X}(z) + \mathbf{D}\mathbf{U}(z) = [\mathbf{C}(z\mathbf{I} - \mathbf{A})^{-1}\mathbf{B} + \mathbf{D}]\mathbf{U}(z)$$

The $m \times r$ transfer function matrix, where $m$ is the number of outputs and $r$ is the number of inputs, is

$$\mathbf{T}(z) = \mathbf{C}(z\mathbf{I} - \mathbf{A})^{-1}\mathbf{B} + \mathbf{D}$$

The element of $\mathbf{T}(z)$ in the $i$th row and $j$th column is the transfer function that relates the $i$th output to the $j$th input:

$$T_{ij}(z) = \left. \frac{Y_i(z)}{U_j(z)} \right|_{\substack{\text{zero initial conditions} \\ \text{and all other inputs zero}}}$$

The elements of a transfer function matrix are ratios of polynomials in the transform variable $z$. For an $n \times n$ matrix $\mathbf{A}$,

$$(z\mathbf{I} - \mathbf{A})^{-1} = \frac{\text{adj}(z\mathbf{I} - \mathbf{A})}{|z\mathbf{I} - \mathbf{A}|}$$

is composed of the $n \times n$ adjugate matrix with elements that are polynomials of maximum degree $n - 1$, each of which is divided by the determinant, which is an $n$th degree polynomial in $z$. Because each of the individual $z$-transfer functions shares the denominator polynomial

$$q(z) = |z\mathbf{I} - \mathbf{A}|$$

each $z$-transfer function has the same poles, although there may be pole-zero cancellations. The $z$-transfer function poles (or eigenvalues) are the solutions to the characteristic equation for the system

$$q(z) = |z\mathbf{I} - \mathbf{A}| = 0$$

Stability requires that the system poles (or eigenvalues) be with the unit circle on the complex plane.

The second-order three-input, two-output system within discrete-time state variable equations

$$\begin{bmatrix} x_1(k+1) \\ x_2(k+1) \end{bmatrix} = \begin{bmatrix} 2 & -5 \\ \frac{1}{2} & -1 \end{bmatrix} \begin{bmatrix} x_1(k) \\ x_2(k) \end{bmatrix} + \begin{bmatrix} 1 & -2 & 0 \\ 0 & 1 & 3 \end{bmatrix} \begin{bmatrix} u_1(k) \\ u_2(k) \\ u_3(k) \end{bmatrix}$$

$$= \mathbf{A}x(k) + \mathbf{B}u(k)$$

$$\begin{bmatrix} y_1(k) \\ y_2(k) \end{bmatrix} = \begin{bmatrix} 2 & 0 \\ 1 & -1 \end{bmatrix} \begin{bmatrix} x_1(k) \\ x_2(k) \end{bmatrix} + \begin{bmatrix} 0 & 4 & 0 \\ 0 & 0 & -2 \end{bmatrix} \begin{bmatrix} u_1(k) \\ u_2(k) \\ u_3(k) \end{bmatrix}$$

$$= \mathbf{C}x(k) + \mathbf{D}u(k)$$

for example, has characteristic equation

$$|z\mathbf{I} - \mathbf{A}| = \begin{vmatrix} (z-2) & 5 \\ -\frac{1}{2} & (z+1) \end{vmatrix} = z^2 - z + \frac{1}{2} = (z - \frac{1}{2} - j\frac{1}{2})(z - \frac{1}{2} + j\frac{1}{2}) = 0$$

Its six $z$-transfer functions all share the poles

$$z_1 = \tfrac{1}{2} + j\tfrac{1}{2}; \qquad z_2 = \tfrac{1}{2} - j\tfrac{1}{2}$$

The transfer function matrix for the system, which is stable, is given by

$$\mathbf{T}(z) = \mathbf{C}(z\mathbf{I} - \mathbf{A})^{-1}\mathbf{B} + \mathbf{D}$$

$$= \begin{bmatrix} 2 & 0 \\ 1 & -1 \end{bmatrix} \begin{bmatrix} (z-2) & 5 \\ -\frac{1}{2} & (z+1) \end{bmatrix}^{-1} \begin{bmatrix} 1 & -2 & 0 \\ 0 & 1 & 3 \end{bmatrix} + \begin{bmatrix} 0 & 4 & 0 \\ 0 & 0 & -2 \end{bmatrix}$$

$$= \frac{\begin{bmatrix} 2 & 0 \\ 1 & -1 \end{bmatrix} \begin{bmatrix} (z+1) & -5 \\ \frac{1}{2} & (z-2) \end{bmatrix} \begin{bmatrix} 1 & -2 & 0 \\ 0 & 1 & 3 \end{bmatrix}}{z^2 - z + \frac{1}{2}} + \begin{bmatrix} 0 & 4 & 0 \\ 0 & 0 & -2 \end{bmatrix}$$

$$= \begin{bmatrix} \dfrac{2z+2}{z^2 - z + \frac{1}{2}} & 4 + \dfrac{-4z - 14}{z^2 - z + \frac{1}{2}} & \dfrac{-30}{z^2 - z + \frac{1}{2}} \\[3mm] \dfrac{z + \frac{1}{2}}{z^2 - z + \frac{1}{2}} & \dfrac{-3z - 4}{z^2 - z + \frac{1}{2}} & -2 + \dfrac{-3z - 9}{z^2 - z + \frac{1}{2}} \end{bmatrix}$$

The transfer functions of a causal system described by rational functions of $z$ must have numerator polynomials of order less than or equal to that of the denominator polynomial. Only causal systems can be represented by the standard state variable model.

### 3.3.3 Change of State Variables

A nonsingular change of state variables

$$\mathbf{x}(k) = \mathbf{P}\mathbf{x}'(k); \qquad \mathbf{x}'(k) = \mathbf{P}^{-1}\mathbf{x}(k)$$

in discrete-time state variable equations

$$\mathbf{x}(k+1) = \mathbf{A}\mathbf{x}(k) + \mathbf{B}\mathbf{u}(k)$$

$$\mathbf{y}(k) = \mathbf{C}\mathbf{x}(k) + \mathbf{D}\mathbf{u}(k)$$

gives new equations of the same form:

$$\mathbf{x}'(k+1) = (\mathbf{P}^{-1}\mathbf{A}\mathbf{P})\mathbf{x}'(k) + (\mathbf{P}^{-1}\mathbf{B})\mathbf{u}(k) = \mathbf{A}'\mathbf{x}'(k) + \mathbf{B}'\mathbf{u}(k)$$

$$\mathbf{y}(k) = (\mathbf{C}\mathbf{P})\mathbf{x}'(k) + \mathbf{D}\mathbf{u}(k) = \mathbf{C}'\mathbf{x}'(k) + \mathbf{D}\mathbf{u}(k)$$

The system transfer function matrix is unchanged by a nonsingular change of state variables:

$$\mathbf{T}'(z) = \mathbf{C}'(z\mathbf{I} - \mathbf{A}')^{-1}\mathbf{B}' + \mathbf{D} = \mathbf{C}\mathbf{P}(z\mathbf{P}^{-1}\mathbf{P} - \mathbf{P}^{-1}\mathbf{A}\mathbf{P})^{-1}\mathbf{P}^{-1}\mathbf{B} + \mathbf{D}$$

$$= \mathbf{C}\mathbf{P}[\mathbf{P}^{-1}(z\mathbf{I} - \mathbf{A})\mathbf{P}]^{-1}\mathbf{P}^{-1}\mathbf{B} + \mathbf{D} = \mathbf{C}\mathbf{P}\mathbf{P}^{-1}(z\mathbf{I} - \mathbf{A})^{-1}\mathbf{P}\mathbf{P}^{-1}\mathbf{B} + \mathbf{D}$$

$$= \mathbf{C}(z\mathbf{I} - \mathbf{A})^{-1}\mathbf{B} + \mathbf{D} = \mathbf{T}(z)$$

Hence the input-output relations of such a system have many realizations, a different one for each different choice of state variables. The transformation of the state coupling matrix

$$\mathbf{A}' = \mathbf{P}^{-1}\mathbf{A}\mathbf{P}$$

is called a *similarity transformation*, to be discussed in detail in the next section.

## 3.4  The Characteristic Value Problem

One of the most useful changes of state variables is the one that results in a diagonal state coupling matrix. We now discuss the characteristic value problem, possibly as a review. It is the solution to the problem of transforming linear, step-invariant state equations to diagonal form. Because of its close relation to diagonalization and its importance to topics to be considered soon, the Cayley-Hamilton theorem is also covered in this section.

### 3.4.1  Eigenvalues and Eigenvectors

The characteristic value problem of linear algebra addresses the following question: For the set of linear equations

$$\mathbf{A}\mathbf{x} = \mathbf{y}$$

where $\mathbf{A}$ is square, is there a nonsingular transformation of the vectors $\mathbf{x}$ and $\mathbf{y}$

$$\mathbf{x} = \mathbf{P}\mathbf{x}'; \qquad \mathbf{x}' = \mathbf{P}^{-1}\mathbf{x}$$

$$\mathbf{y} = \mathbf{P}\mathbf{y}'; \qquad \mathbf{y}' = \mathbf{P}^{-1}\mathbf{y}$$

such that in terms of the new coordinates, the equations are

$$\mathbf{\Lambda}\mathbf{x}' = \mathbf{y}'$$

where $\mathbf{\Lambda}$ is a diagonal matrix? It is more convenient to define $\mathbf{P}$ as the transformation from $\mathbf{x}'$ to $\mathbf{x}$, as has been done here, rather than as the transformation from $\mathbf{x}$ to $\mathbf{x}'$. A transformation matrix $\mathbf{P}$ with this property is called a *modal matrix*. Substituting and premultiplying gives

$$\mathbf{Ax} = \mathbf{APx'} = \mathbf{Py'}$$

$$(\mathbf{P}^{-1}\mathbf{AP})\mathbf{x'} = \mathbf{y'}$$

so that the diagonal matrix, called a *spectral matrix*, is related to $\mathbf{A}$ by

$$\mathbf{\Lambda} = \mathbf{P}^{-1}\mathbf{AP}$$

In terms of the spectral matrix $\mathbf{\Lambda}$,

$$\mathbf{AP} = \mathbf{P\Lambda} = [\mathbf{p}^1 \mid \mathbf{p}^2 \mid \cdots \mid \mathbf{p}^n] \begin{bmatrix} \lambda_1 & 0 & 0 & \cdots & 0 \\ 0 & \lambda_2 & 0 & \cdots & 0 \\ & \vdots & & & \\ 0 & 0 & & \cdots & \lambda_n \end{bmatrix}$$

where the columns of the modal matrix $\mathbf{P}$ are denoted by the vectors $\mathbf{p}^1$, $\mathbf{p}^2, \ldots, \mathbf{p}^n$ and the elements along the diagonal of the spectral matrix $\mathbf{\Lambda}$ (which is a diagonal matrix) are $\lambda_1, \lambda_2, \ldots, \lambda_n$. Each column of $\mathbf{P}$ satisfies an equation of the form

$$\mathbf{Ap} = \lambda\mathbf{p}$$

or

$$(\lambda\mathbf{I} - \mathbf{A})\mathbf{p} = \mathbf{0} \tag{3-2}$$

Of course, the trivial solution $\mathbf{p} = \mathbf{0}$ will be of no help, since a column of zeros would make $\mathbf{P}$ singular.

The set of $n$ individual homogeneous equations (3-2) in the $n$ elements of $\mathbf{p}$ has a nontrivial solution only if their determinant is zero:

$$|\lambda\mathbf{I} - \mathbf{A}| = 0$$

This is an $n$th degree polynomial equation in $\lambda$, termed the *characteristic equation* of the matrix $\mathbf{A}$:

$$\lambda^n + \alpha_{n-1}\lambda^{n-1} + \cdots + \alpha_1\lambda + \alpha_0 = 0$$

The $n$ roots of the characteristic equation, $\lambda_1, \lambda_2, \ldots, \lambda_n$ are the *eigenvalues* of the matrix $\mathbf{A}$. A simple example of finding the three eigenvalues of the $3 \times 3$

matrix

$$\mathbf{A} = \begin{bmatrix} -1 & -2 & 0 \\ 1 & 2 & 0 \\ -2 & -1 & -3 \end{bmatrix}$$

is as follows:

$$\lambda\mathbf{I} - \mathbf{A} = \begin{bmatrix} (\lambda + 1) & 2 & 0 \\ -1 & (\lambda - 2) & 0 \\ 2 & 1 & (\lambda + 3) \end{bmatrix}$$

$$|\lambda\mathbf{I} - \mathbf{A}| = \lambda^3 + 2\lambda^2 - 3\lambda = \lambda(\lambda - 1)(\lambda + 3) = 0$$

$$\lambda_1 = 0; \qquad \lambda_2 = 1; \qquad \lambda_3 = -3$$

An $n \times n$ matrix always has an $n$th degree characteristic equation and thus $n$ eigenvalues. If the elements of $\mathbf{A}$ are real numbers, the coefficients of the characteristic equation are real numbers, and complex roots always occur in conjugate pairs. Table 3-2 lists some other important properties of the eigenvalues of a matrix.

Corresponding to each of the $n$ eigenvalues $\lambda_i$ of a matrix $\mathbf{A}$ is an *eigenvector* $\mathbf{p}^i$, satisfying

$$\mathbf{A}\mathbf{p}^i = \lambda_i\mathbf{p}^i$$

The eigenvectors form the columns of the desired transformation matrix $\mathbf{P}$. If the eigenvalues $\lambda_i$ are distinct, the eigenvectors can be found by determining nontrivial solutions $\mathbf{p}^i$ to the n homogeneous equations of the form

$$(\lambda_i\mathbf{I} - \mathbf{A})\mathbf{p}^i = \mathbf{0}$$

each involving a different eigenvalue $\lambda_i$. The sets of homogeneous equations will each have a nontrivial solution, because the $\lambda_i$ are precisely the numbers necessary to make $(\lambda_i\mathbf{I} - \mathbf{A})$ singular. As with any solution of a set of homogeneous equations, a nonzero constant times an eigenvector is also an eigenvector. For example, for the matrix

$$\mathbf{A} = \begin{bmatrix} -1 & -2 & 0 \\ 1 & 2 & 0 \\ -2 & -1 & -3 \end{bmatrix}$$

---

**TABLE 3-2   Properties of the Eigenvalues of a Matrix**

---

### *Defining Property*

    **A.** $|\lambda \mathbf{I} - \mathbf{A}| = 0$

### *Further Properties*

These properties follow from the defining property:

    **B.** *$\lambda = 0$ is an eigenvalue of $\mathbf{A}$ if and only if $\mathbf{A}$ is singular. Since for $\lambda = 0$,*

$$|\lambda \mathbf{I} - \mathbf{A}| = |-\mathbf{A}| = -|\mathbf{A}| = 0$$

    **C.** *The eigenvalues of the matrix $(k\,\mathbf{A})$ are $k$ times the eigenvalues of $\mathbf{A}$, for any scalar $k$ because*

$$|k\lambda \mathbf{I} - k\mathbf{A}| = 0$$

*for each value of $\lambda$ for which*

$$|\lambda \mathbf{I} - \mathbf{A}| = 0$$

    **D.** *The eigenvalues of $\mathbf{A}^{\dagger}$ are the same as the eigenvalues of $\mathbf{A}$.*

    **E.** *The eigenvalues of $\mathbf{A}^{-1}$, provided $\mathbf{A}^{-1}$ exists, are the inverses of the eigenvalues of $\mathbf{A}$:*

$$|\lambda \mathbf{I} - \mathbf{A}| = |\lambda \mathbf{A}\mathbf{A}^{-1} - \mathbf{A}| = |\mathbf{A}(\lambda \mathbf{A}^{-1} - \mathbf{I})| = -|\mathbf{A}|\left|\left(\frac{1}{\lambda}\right)\mathbf{I} - \mathbf{A}^{-1}\right|$$

    **F.** *The eigenvalues of $\mathbf{A}^{k}$ ($k$ an integer) are the eigenvalues of $\mathbf{A}$ raised to the kth power:*

$$0 = |\lambda \mathbf{I} - \mathbf{A}| = |\lambda \mathbf{I} - \mathbf{A}||\lambda \mathbf{I} + \mathbf{A}|$$
$$= |(\lambda \mathbf{I} - \mathbf{A})(\lambda \mathbf{I} + \mathbf{A})| = |\lambda^{2}\mathbf{I} - \mathbf{A}^{2}|$$

    **G.** *The eigenvalues of a diagonal matrix are the diagonal elements*

    **H.** *The sum of the eigenvalues of an $n \times n$ matrix $\mathbf{A}$ with characteristic equation*

$$\lambda^{n} + \alpha_{n-1}\lambda^{n-1} + \cdots + \alpha_{1}\lambda + \alpha_{0} = 0$$

*is*

$$\lambda_{1} + \lambda_{2} + \cdots + \lambda_{n} = -\alpha_{n-1} = \text{trace }(\mathbf{A})$$

**TABLE 3-2  (cont.)**

## Further Properties

I.  *The product of the eigenvalues of an n × n matrix* **A** *with characteristic equation*

$$\lambda^n + \alpha_{n-1}\lambda^{n-1} + \cdots + \alpha_1\lambda + \alpha_0 = (\lambda - \lambda_1)(\lambda - \lambda_2)\cdots(\lambda - \lambda_n) = 0$$

*is*

$$\lambda_1\lambda_2\cdots\lambda_n = (-1)^n\alpha_0 = |\mathbf{A}|$$

it was previously found that the eigenvalues were

$$\lambda_1 = 0; \qquad \lambda_2 = 1; \qquad \lambda_3 = -3$$

The eigenvector $\mathbf{p}^1$ corresponding to $\lambda_1$ has components that satisfy

$$(\lambda_1\mathbf{I} - \mathbf{A})\mathbf{p}^1 = \begin{bmatrix} 1 & 2 & 0 \\ -1 & -2 & 0 \\ 2 & 1 & 3 \end{bmatrix}\begin{bmatrix} p_{11} \\ p_{21} \\ p_{31} \end{bmatrix} = \mathbf{0}$$

or

$$\begin{cases} p_{11} + 2p_{21} & = 0 \\ -p_{11} - 2p_{21} & = 0 \\ 2p_{11} + p_{21} + 3p_{31} = 0 \end{cases}$$

Deleting the first of these equations, since it is obviously linearly dependent, there results

$$\begin{cases} -p_{11} - 2p_{21} & = 0 \\ 2p_{11} + p_{21} + 3p_{31} = 0 \end{cases}$$

Choosing $p_{11} = 2$ for convenience

$$\mathbf{p}^1 = \begin{bmatrix} 2 \\ -1 \\ -1 \end{bmatrix}$$

The eigenvector $\mathbf{p}^2$ satisfies

$$(\lambda_2 I - A)\mathbf{p}^2 = \begin{bmatrix} 2 & 2 & 0 \\ -1 & -1 & 0 \\ 2 & 1 & 4 \end{bmatrix} \begin{bmatrix} p_{12} \\ p_{22} \\ p_{32} \end{bmatrix} = 0$$

or

$$\begin{cases} 2p_{12} + 2p_{22} & = 0 \\ -p_{12} - p_{22} & = 0 \\ 2p_{12} + p_{22} + 4p_{32} = 0 \end{cases}$$

Deleting the first equation as being linearly dependent:

$$\begin{cases} p_{12} + p_{22} & = 0 \\ 2p_{12} + p_{22} + 4p_{32} = 0 \end{cases}$$

Choosing $p_{12} = 4$,

$$\mathbf{p}^2 = \begin{bmatrix} 4 \\ -4 \\ -1 \end{bmatrix}$$

The eigenvector $\mathbf{p}^3$ satisfies

$$(\lambda_3 I - A)\mathbf{p}^3 = \begin{bmatrix} -2 & 2 & 0 \\ -1 & -5 & 0 \\ 2 & 1 & 0 \end{bmatrix} \begin{bmatrix} p_{13} \\ p_{23} \\ p_{33} \end{bmatrix} = 0$$

or

$$\begin{cases} -2p_{13} + 2p_{23} = 0 \\ -p_{13} - 5p_{23} = 0 \\ 2p_{13} + p_{23} = 0 \end{cases}$$

The only solution for $p_{13}$ and $p_{23}$ is

$$\begin{cases} p_{13} = 0 \\ p_{23} = 0 \end{cases}$$

but $p_{33}$ can be anything. Choosing $p_{33} = 1$,

$$\mathbf{p}^3 = \begin{bmatrix} 0 \\ 0 \\ 1 \end{bmatrix}$$

Important properties of the eigenvectors of a matrix are summarized in Table 3-3. That the eigenvectors corresponding to distinct eigenvalues are linearly independent can be shown in the following way. Suppose that two eigenvectors, $\mathbf{p}^i$ and $\mathbf{p}^j$, corresponding to two distinct eigenvalues, $\lambda_i$ and $\lambda_j$, are linearly dependent. This is equivalent to supposing $\mathbf{p}^i = \mathbf{p}^j$ because the

**TABLE 3-3   Properties of the Eigenvectors of a Matrix**

*Defining Property*

A. $\mathbf{Ap} = \lambda\mathbf{p}$

*Further Properties*

These properties follow from the defining property and the properties of eigenvalues:

B. *If two eigenvalues of a matrix are distinct, the corresponding eigenvectors are linearly independent.*

C. *For a matrix* $\mathbf{A}$ *with real elements, the eigenvectors, if complex, can be expressed as complex conjugate pairs.*

D. *The eigenvectors of a matrix* $(k\mathbf{A})$ *are identical to the eigenvectors of* $\mathbf{A}$, *for any scalar* $k$. Since the eigenvalues of $(k\mathbf{A})$ are $k$ times the eigenvalues of $\mathbf{A}$, if

$$\mathbf{Ap} = \lambda\mathbf{p}$$

then

$$(k\mathbf{A})\mathbf{p} = (k\lambda)\mathbf{p}$$

E. *The eigenvectors of* $\mathbf{A}^{-1}$ *are the same as the eigenvectors of* $\mathbf{A}$. Eigenvalues of $\mathbf{A}^{-1}$ are the inverses of the eigenvalues of $\mathbf{A}$ and if

$$\mathbf{Ap} = \lambda\mathbf{p}$$

$$\left(\frac{1}{\lambda}\right)\mathbf{A}^{-1}\mathbf{Ap} = \mathbf{A}^{-1}\mathbf{p}$$

or

$$\mathbf{A}^{-1}\mathbf{p} = \left(\frac{1}{\lambda}\right)\mathbf{p}$$

scaling of an eigenvector is arbitrary. Then

$$(\lambda_i \mathbf{I} - \mathbf{A})\mathbf{p}^i = (\lambda_j \mathbf{I} - \mathbf{A})\mathbf{p}^j = (\lambda_j \mathbf{I} - \mathbf{A})\mathbf{p}^i = \mathbf{0}$$

Subtracting:

$$(\lambda_i - \lambda_j)\mathbf{p}^i = \mathbf{0}$$

which can only be true for $\mathbf{p}^i = \mathbf{0}$ or $\lambda_i = \lambda_j$. Thus $\mathbf{p}^i$ and $\mathbf{p}^j$ must be linearly independent. In a similar way, every pair of the eigenvectors can be shown to be independent of one another, hence the eigenvectors are mutually independent.

## 3.4.2 Diagonalizing Transformations

When a matrix $\mathbf{A}$ has distinct eigenvalues, the eigenvectors are linearly independent and so the modal matrix

$$\mathbf{P} = [\mathbf{p}^1 \mid \mathbf{p}^2 \mid \cdots \mid \mathbf{p}^n]$$

is nonsingular. The transformation

$$\mathbf{x} = \mathbf{P}\mathbf{x}'; \qquad \mathbf{x}' = \mathbf{P}^{-1}\mathbf{x}$$
$$\mathbf{y} = \mathbf{P}\mathbf{y}'; \qquad \mathbf{y}' = \mathbf{P}^{-1}\mathbf{y}$$

substituted into the equations

$$\mathbf{A}\mathbf{x} = \mathbf{y}$$

gives

$$\mathbf{A}\mathbf{P}\mathbf{x}' = \mathbf{P}\mathbf{y}'$$
$$(\mathbf{P}^{-1}\mathbf{A}\mathbf{P})\mathbf{x}' = \Lambda\mathbf{x}' = \mathbf{y}'$$

where the spectral matrix $\Lambda$ is diagonal:

$$\Lambda = \begin{bmatrix} \lambda_1 & 0 & \cdots & 0 \\ 0 & \lambda_2 & \cdots & 0 \\ \vdots & & & \\ 0 & 0 & \cdots & \lambda_n \end{bmatrix}$$

The order in which the eigenvalues appear along the diagonal of the spectral matrix is the order that the eigenvectors are placed as columns of the modal matrix **P**. Thus there are a number of different modal matrices, each yielding a different but closely related spectral matrix. Any column of a modal matrix can be multiplied by a nonzero constant, giving a new modal matrix, because the eigenvectors, being solutions of homogeneous equations, are of arbitrary norm. Eigenvector scaling changes in the modal matrix do not affect the spectral matrix.

Continuing the example, with

$$\mathbf{A} = \begin{bmatrix} -1 & -2 & 0 \\ 1 & 2 & 0 \\ -2 & -1 & -3 \end{bmatrix}$$

and

$$\mathbf{p}^1 = \begin{bmatrix} 2 \\ -1 \\ -1 \end{bmatrix} \quad \mathbf{p}^2 = \begin{bmatrix} 4 \\ -4 \\ -1 \end{bmatrix} \quad \mathbf{p}^3 = \begin{bmatrix} 0 \\ 0 \\ 1 \end{bmatrix}$$

a modal matrix is

$$\mathbf{P} = \begin{bmatrix} 2 & 4 & 0 \\ -1 & -4 & 0 \\ -1 & -1 & 1 \end{bmatrix}$$

The inverse of this modal matrix is

$$\mathbf{P}^{-1} = \begin{bmatrix} 1 & 1 & 0 \\ -\frac{1}{4} & -\frac{1}{2} & 0 \\ \frac{3}{4} & \frac{1}{2} & 1 \end{bmatrix}$$

and

$$\mathbf{P}^{-1}\mathbf{A}\mathbf{P} = \begin{bmatrix} 0 & 0 & 0 \\ 0 & 1 & 0 \\ 0 & 0 & -3 \end{bmatrix} = \mathbf{\Lambda}$$

As another numerical example of characteristic value problem solution, this one having a matrix with complex eigenvalues, consider

$$\mathbf{A} = \begin{bmatrix} -2 & 1 \\ -5 & 0 \end{bmatrix}$$

Its characteristic equation is

$$|\lambda \mathbf{I} - \mathbf{A}| = \begin{vmatrix} (\lambda + 2) & -1 \\ 5 & \lambda \end{vmatrix} = \lambda^2 + 2\lambda + 5 = 0$$

and the eigenvalues are

$$\lambda_1, \lambda_2 = -1 \pm j2$$

The eigenvector $\mathbf{p}^1$ corresponding to the root $\lambda_1 = -1 + j2$ satisfies

$$(\lambda_1 \mathbf{I} - \mathbf{A})\mathbf{p}^1 = \begin{bmatrix} 1 + j2 & -1 \\ 5 & -1 + j2 \end{bmatrix} \begin{bmatrix} p_{11} \\ p_{21} \end{bmatrix} = \mathbf{0}$$

or

$$\begin{cases} (1 + j2)p_{11} & -p_{21} = 0 \\ 5p_{11} + (-1 + j2)p_{21} = 0 \end{cases}$$

As the determinant of these two equations is zero, the two equations are linearly dependent. The first equation multiplied by $(1 - j2)$ equals the second. Deleting the second equation, and choosing $p_{11} = 1$ gives

$$p_{21} = 1 + j2$$

and

$$\mathbf{p}^1 = \begin{bmatrix} 1 \\ 1 + j2 \end{bmatrix}$$

The eigenvector corresponding to the complex conjugate root $\lambda_2 = \lambda_1^*$ is $\mathbf{p}^2 = \mathbf{p}^{1*}$ so

$$\mathbf{P} = [\mathbf{p}^1 \mid \mathbf{p}^2] = \begin{bmatrix} 1 & 1 \\ 1 + j2 & 1 - j2 \end{bmatrix}$$

and

$$\mathbf{P}^{-1} = \begin{bmatrix} (\tfrac{1}{2} + j\tfrac{1}{4}) & -j\tfrac{1}{4} \\ (\tfrac{1}{2} - j\tfrac{1}{4}) & j\tfrac{1}{4} \end{bmatrix}$$

giving

$$\mathbf{P}^{-1}\mathbf{AP} = \begin{bmatrix} (-1+j2) & 0 \\ 0 & (-1-j2) \end{bmatrix} = \begin{bmatrix} \lambda_1 & 0 \\ 0 & \lambda_2 \end{bmatrix}$$

Any nonsingular transformation that diagonalizes a matrix $\mathbf{A}$ also diagonalizes $\mathbf{A}^2, \mathbf{A}^3, \ldots$ . If

$$\mathbf{P}^{-1}\mathbf{AP} = \Lambda$$

then

$$\mathbf{P}^{-1}(\mathbf{A}^2)\mathbf{P} = \mathbf{P}^{-1}\mathbf{AIAP} = \mathbf{P}^{-1}\mathbf{APP}^{-1}\mathbf{AP} = (\mathbf{P}^{-1}\mathbf{AP})(\mathbf{P}^{-1}\mathbf{AP}) = \Lambda^2$$

Similarly,

$$\mathbf{P}^{-1}\mathbf{A}^3\mathbf{P} = \Lambda^3$$

and so on. A transformation that diagonalizes $\mathbf{A}$ also diagonalizes $\mathbf{A}^{-1}$:

$$(\mathbf{P}^{-1}\mathbf{AP})^{-1} = \mathbf{P}^{-1}\mathbf{A}^{-1}\mathbf{P} = \Lambda^{-1}$$

Since $\Lambda$ is diagonal, $\Lambda^{-1}$ is diagonal, with diagonal elements that are the reciprocals of the diagonal elements of $\Lambda$.

If the matrix $\mathbf{A}$ has repeated eigenvalues, linearly independent eigenvectors corresponding to the same root must be found for each eigenvalue repetition, or else a nonsingular modal matrix $\mathbf{P}$ will not exist. There must be an additional linearly independent solution of

$$(\lambda_i\mathbf{I} - \mathbf{A})\mathbf{p}^i = \mathbf{0}$$

for each repetition of $\lambda_i$. This occurs only if

$$\text{rank}(\lambda_i\mathbf{I} - \mathbf{A}) = n - r$$

where $r$ is the number of repetitions of the root $\lambda_i$, which is not likely to be the case.

Any nonsingular transformation $\mathbf{P}$ of a matrix $\mathbf{A}$, of the form

$$\mathbf{A}' = \mathbf{P}^{-1}\mathbf{AP}$$

is termed a *similarity transformation*. The diagonalizing transformation by a modal matrix is a special kind of similarity transformation. Important properties of similarity transformation are listed in Table 3-4. To show that a similarity transformation does not change the eigenvalues of a matrix, consider

$$|\lambda \mathbf{I} - \mathbf{A}'| = |\lambda \mathbf{P}^{-1}\mathbf{P} - \mathbf{P}^{-1}\mathbf{A}\mathbf{P}| = |\mathbf{P}^{-1}(\lambda \mathbf{I} - \mathbf{A})\mathbf{P}|$$
$$= |\mathbf{P}^{-1}||\lambda \mathbf{I} - \mathbf{A}||\mathbf{P}| = |\lambda \mathbf{I} - \mathbf{A}|$$

The determinant

$$|\lambda \mathbf{I} - \mathbf{A}'| = 0$$

if and only if

$$|\lambda \mathbf{I} - \mathbf{A}| = 0$$

## TABLE 3-4 Properties of Similarity Transformations

A nonsingular transformation $\mathbf{P}$ of a matrix $\mathbf{A}$, of the form

$$\mathbf{B} = \mathbf{P}^{-1}\mathbf{A}\mathbf{P}$$

has the following properties:

A. $\mathbf{P}^{-1}(\mathbf{A}^2)\mathbf{P} = \mathbf{B}^2$

   $\mathbf{P}^{-1}(\mathbf{A}^3)\mathbf{P} = \mathbf{B}^3$

   and so on.

B. Provided $\mathbf{A}^{-1}$ exists,

   $\mathbf{P}^{-1}(\mathbf{A}^{-1})\mathbf{P} = \mathbf{B}^{-1}$

C. trace $(\mathbf{B})$ = trace $(\mathbf{A})$

D. $|\mathbf{B}| = |\mathbf{A}|$

E. The eigenvalues of $\mathbf{B}$ are identical to those of $\mathbf{A}$; they are unchanged by a similarity transformation.

### 3.4.3 The Cayley-Hamilton Theorem

The Cayley-Hamilton theorem describes a remarkable property of every square matrix $\mathbf{A}$. If the characteristic equation of $\mathbf{A}$ is

$$\lambda^n + \alpha_{n-1}\lambda^{n-1} + \cdots + \alpha_1\lambda + \alpha_0 = 0$$

the matrix itself satisfies the same equation, namely

$$\mathbf{A}^n + \alpha_{n-1}\mathbf{A}^{n-1} + \cdots + \alpha_1\mathbf{A} + \alpha_0\mathbf{I} = \mathbf{0}$$

The result holds in general, but it will be shown now for matrices that can be diagonalized, that is, matrices with distinct eigenvalues. For a matrix with distinct eigenvalues,

$$\mathbf{A} = \mathbf{P}\boldsymbol{\Lambda}\mathbf{P}^{-1}$$

where $\mathbf{P}$ is a modal matrix and

$$\boldsymbol{\Lambda} = \begin{bmatrix} \lambda_1 & 0 & \cdots & 0 \\ 0 & \lambda_2 & \cdots & 0 \\ \vdots & & & \\ 0 & 0 & \cdots & \lambda_n \end{bmatrix}$$

is a spectral matrix for $\mathbf{A}$. And,

$$\mathbf{A}^2 = \mathbf{P}\boldsymbol{\Lambda}\mathbf{P}^{-1}\mathbf{P}\boldsymbol{\Lambda}\mathbf{P}^{-1} = \mathbf{P}\boldsymbol{\Lambda}^2\mathbf{P}^{-1}$$

where

$$\boldsymbol{\Lambda}^2 = \begin{bmatrix} \lambda_1^2 & 0 & \cdots & 0 \\ 0 & \lambda_2^2 & \cdots & 0 \\ \vdots & & & \\ 0 & 0 & \cdots & \lambda_n^2 \end{bmatrix}$$

Similarly,

$$\mathbf{A}^m = \mathbf{P}\boldsymbol{\Lambda}^m\mathbf{P}^{-1}$$

Then

$$\mathbf{A}^n + \alpha_{n-1}\mathbf{A}^{n-1} + \cdots + \alpha_1\mathbf{A} + \alpha_0\mathbf{I}$$

$$= \mathbf{P}\{\boldsymbol{\Lambda}^n + \alpha_{n-1}\boldsymbol{\Lambda}^{n-1} + \cdots + \alpha_1\boldsymbol{\Lambda} + \alpha_0\mathbf{I}\}\mathbf{P}^{-1}$$

$$= \mathbf{P} \begin{bmatrix} (\lambda_1^n + \alpha_{n-1}\lambda_1^{n-1} + \cdots + \alpha_1\lambda_1 + \alpha_0) & 0 & \cdots \\ 0 & (\lambda_2^n + \alpha_{n-1}\lambda_2^{n-1} + \cdots + \alpha_1\lambda_2 + \alpha_0) & \cdots \\ \vdots & & \\ 0 & 0 & \cdots \end{bmatrix} \mathbf{P}^{-1}$$

$$= \mathbf{0}$$

Using the Cayley-Hamilton theorem, the $n$th power of $\mathbf{A}$ can be expressed in terms of lesser powers of $\mathbf{A}$:

$$\mathbf{A}^n = -\alpha_{n-1}\mathbf{A}^{n-1} - \cdots - \alpha_1\mathbf{A} - \alpha_0\mathbf{I}$$

In fact, by repeatedly substituting for $\mathbf{A}^n$, any power of $\mathbf{A}$ can be expressed in terms of the $(n-1)$th power of $\mathbf{A}$ and lower powers, down to and including the zeroth power of $\mathbf{A}$, the identity matrix.

# 3.5 Uncoupling State Equations

In this section, the solution of the characteristic value problem is applied to the problem of determining changes of state variables that take a system to a realization where its state coupling matrix is diagonal. Before doing so, the existence and structure of diagonal forms, found by expanding $z$-transfer functions into partial fractions, are examined.

## 3.5.1 Transformation to Diagonal Form

A single-input, single-output system with $z$-transfer function

$$T(z) = \frac{2z^2 - \frac{1}{3}z + \frac{1}{6}}{(z - \frac{1}{2})(z + \frac{1}{2})(z - \frac{1}{3})} = \frac{3}{z - \frac{1}{2}} + \frac{1}{z + \frac{1}{2}} + \frac{-2}{z - \frac{1}{3}}$$

can be considered to be three tandem first-order subsystems, as shown in Figure 3-10(a). Expressing each of the subsystems in terms of a delay diagram as in Figure 3-10(b) results in state equations that have a diagonal state coupling matrix:

$$\begin{bmatrix} x_1(k+1) \\ x_2(k+1) \\ x_3(k+1) \end{bmatrix} = \begin{bmatrix} \frac{1}{2} & 0 & 0 \\ 0 & -\frac{1}{2} & 0 \\ 0 & 0 & \frac{1}{3} \end{bmatrix} \begin{bmatrix} x_1(k) \\ x_2(k) \\ x_3(k) \end{bmatrix} + \begin{bmatrix} 3 \\ 1 \\ -2 \end{bmatrix} u(k)$$

$$y(k) = \begin{bmatrix} 1 & 1 & 1 \end{bmatrix} \begin{bmatrix} x_1(k) \\ x_2(k) \\ x_3(k) \end{bmatrix} \tag{3-3}$$

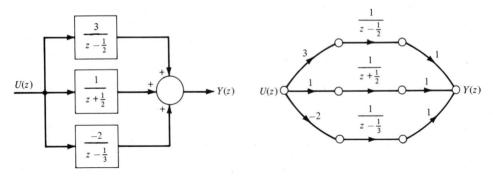

(a)  Block diagram and signal flow graph of tandem first-order subsystems.

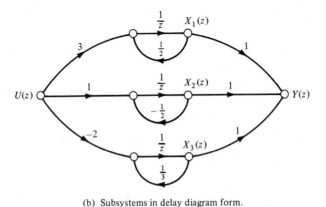

(b)  Subsystems in delay diagram form.

**FIGURE 3-10.    A diagonal single-input, single-output discrete-time system.**

When the state coupling matrix of a system is diagonal, the individual state equations are decoupled from one another. The third-order difference equation represented by the system (3-3) is in the form of three equivalent first-order equations:

$$\begin{cases} x_1(k + 1) = \tfrac{1}{2}x_1(k) + 3u(k) \\ x_2(k + 1) = -\tfrac{1}{2}x_2(k) + u(k) \\ x_3(k + 1) = \tfrac{1}{3}x_3(k) - 2u(k) \end{cases}$$

For a system

$$\mathbf{x}(k + 1) = \mathbf{A}\mathbf{x}(k) + \mathbf{B}\mathbf{u}(k)$$

$$\mathbf{y}(k) = \mathbf{C}\mathbf{x}(k) + \mathbf{D}\mathbf{u}(k)$$

with distinct eigenvalues, finding the change of state variables

$$\mathbf{x}(k) = \mathbf{P}\mathbf{x}'(k); \qquad \mathbf{x}'(k) = \mathbf{P}^{-1}\mathbf{x}(k)$$

$$\mathbf{x}'(k + 1) = (\mathbf{P}^{-1}\mathbf{A}\mathbf{P})\mathbf{x}(k) + (\mathbf{P}^{-1}\mathbf{B})\mathbf{u}(k)$$

$$\mathbf{y}(k) = (\mathbf{C}\mathbf{P})\mathbf{x}(k) + \mathbf{D}\mathbf{u}(k)$$

that diagonalizes the state coupling matrix

$$\mathbf{P}^{-1}\mathbf{A}\mathbf{P} = \mathbf{\Lambda}$$

is the characteristic value problem. As a numerical example, the system

$$
\begin{bmatrix} x_1(k + 1) \\ x_2(k + 1) \\ x_3(k + 1) \end{bmatrix} =
\begin{bmatrix} -5 & 1 & 0 \\ -6 & 0 & 1 \\ 0 & 0 & 0 \end{bmatrix}
\begin{bmatrix} x_1(k) \\ x_2(k) \\ x_3(k) \end{bmatrix} +
\begin{bmatrix} 3 & 0 \\ 0 & 0 \\ 1 & -1 \end{bmatrix}
\begin{bmatrix} u_1(k) \\ u_2(k) \end{bmatrix}
$$

$$= \mathbf{A}\mathbf{x}(k) + \mathbf{B}\mathbf{u}(k)$$

$$
\begin{bmatrix} y_1(k) \\ y_2(k) \end{bmatrix} =
\begin{bmatrix} 1 & 2 & 0 \\ 0 & -1 & 0 \end{bmatrix}
\begin{bmatrix} x_1(k) \\ x_2(k) \\ x_3(k) \end{bmatrix} +
\begin{bmatrix} 2 & -1 \\ 0 & 0 \end{bmatrix}
\begin{bmatrix} u_1(k) \\ u_2(k) \end{bmatrix}
$$

$$= \mathbf{C}\mathbf{x}(k) + \mathbf{D}\mathbf{u}(k)$$

has real and distinct eigenvalues given by

$$|\lambda\mathbf{I} - \mathbf{A}| =
\begin{vmatrix} (\lambda + 5) & -1 & 0 \\ 6 & \lambda & -1 \\ 0 & 0 & \lambda \end{vmatrix}
= \lambda^3 + 5\lambda^2 + 6\lambda = \lambda(\lambda + 2)(\lambda + 3) = 0$$

$$\lambda_1 = 0; \qquad \lambda_2 = -2; \qquad \lambda_3 = -3$$

The transformation $\mathbf{P}$ in

$$\mathbf{x} = \mathbf{P}\mathbf{x}'; \qquad \mathbf{x}' = \mathbf{P}^{-1}\mathbf{x}$$

has columns that are the eigenvectors of $\mathbf{A}$.
    The eigenvector corresponding to $\lambda_1$ satisfies

$$
\begin{bmatrix} 5 & -1 & 0 \\ 6 & 0 & -1 \\ 0 & 0 & 0 \end{bmatrix}
\begin{bmatrix} p_{11} \\ p_{21} \\ p_{31} \end{bmatrix} =
\begin{bmatrix} 0 \\ 0 \\ 0 \end{bmatrix}
$$

a nontrivial solution to which is

$$\begin{bmatrix} p_{11} \\ p_{21} \\ p_{31} \end{bmatrix} = \begin{bmatrix} 1 \\ 5 \\ 6 \end{bmatrix}$$

For $\lambda_2$:

$$\begin{bmatrix} 3 & -1 & 0 \\ 6 & -2 & -1 \\ 0 & 0 & -2 \end{bmatrix}\begin{bmatrix} p_{12} \\ p_{22} \\ p_{32} \end{bmatrix} = \begin{bmatrix} 0 \\ 0 \\ 0 \end{bmatrix}; \qquad \begin{bmatrix} p_{12} \\ p_{22} \\ p_{32} \end{bmatrix} = \begin{bmatrix} 1 \\ 3 \\ 0 \end{bmatrix}$$

For $\lambda_3$:

$$\begin{bmatrix} 2 & -1 & 0 \\ 6 & -3 & -1 \\ 0 & 0 & -3 \end{bmatrix}\begin{bmatrix} p_{13} \\ p_{23} \\ p_{33} \end{bmatrix} = \begin{bmatrix} 0 \\ 0 \\ 0 \end{bmatrix}; \qquad \begin{bmatrix} p_{13} \\ p_{23} \\ p_{33} \end{bmatrix} = \begin{bmatrix} 1 \\ 2 \\ 0 \end{bmatrix}$$

Then

$$\mathbf{P} = \begin{bmatrix} 1 & 1 & 1 \\ 5 & 3 & 2 \\ 6 & 0 & 0 \end{bmatrix}; \qquad \mathbf{P}^{-1} = \frac{1}{6}\begin{bmatrix} 0 & 0 & 1 \\ -12 & 6 & -3 \\ 18 & -6 & 2 \end{bmatrix}$$

$$\mathbf{A}' = \mathbf{P}^{-1}\mathbf{AP} = \frac{1}{6}\begin{bmatrix} 0 & 0 & 1 \\ -12 & 6 & -3 \\ 18 & -6 & 2 \end{bmatrix}\begin{bmatrix} -5 & 1 & 0 \\ -6 & 0 & 1 \\ 0 & 0 & 0 \end{bmatrix}\begin{bmatrix} 1 & 1 & 1 \\ 5 & 3 & 2 \\ 6 & 0 & 0 \end{bmatrix}$$

$$= \begin{bmatrix} 0 & 0 & 0 \\ 0 & -2 & 0 \\ 0 & 0 & -3 \end{bmatrix}$$

$$\mathbf{B}' = \mathbf{P}^{-1}\mathbf{B} = \frac{1}{6}\begin{bmatrix} 0 & 0 & 1 \\ -12 & 6 & -3 \\ 18 & -6 & 2 \end{bmatrix}\begin{bmatrix} 3 & 0 \\ 0 & 0 \\ 1 & -1 \end{bmatrix} = \frac{1}{6}\begin{bmatrix} 1 & -1 \\ -39 & 3 \\ 56 & -2 \end{bmatrix}$$

$$\mathbf{C}' = \mathbf{CP} = \begin{bmatrix} 1 & 2 & 0 \\ 0 & -1 & 0 \end{bmatrix}\begin{bmatrix} 1 & 1 & 1 \\ 5 & 3 & 2 \\ 6 & 0 & 0 \end{bmatrix} = \begin{bmatrix} 11 & 7 & 5 \\ -5 & -3 & -2 \end{bmatrix}$$

$$\mathbf{D}' = \mathbf{D} = \begin{bmatrix} 2 & -1 \\ 0 & 0 \end{bmatrix}$$

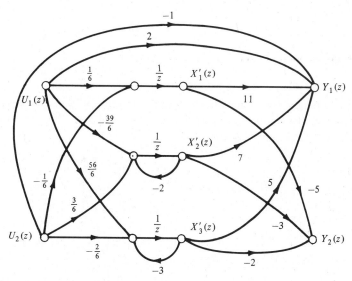

**FIGURE 3-11.** **Delay diagram in diagonal form of a system with real, distinct eigenvalues.**

so that the system description in terms of the new state variables is

$$\begin{bmatrix} x_1'(k+1) \\ x_2'(k+1) \\ x_3'(k+1) \end{bmatrix} = \begin{bmatrix} 0 & 0 & 0 \\ 0 & -2 & 0 \\ 0 & 0 & -3 \end{bmatrix} \begin{bmatrix} x_1'(k) \\ x_2'(k) \\ x_3'(k) \end{bmatrix} + \begin{bmatrix} \frac{1}{6} & -\frac{1}{6} \\ -\frac{39}{6} & \frac{3}{6} \\ \frac{56}{6} & -\frac{2}{6} \end{bmatrix} \begin{bmatrix} u_1(k) \\ u_2(k) \end{bmatrix}$$

$$\begin{bmatrix} y_1(k) \\ y_2(k) \end{bmatrix} = \begin{bmatrix} 11 & 7 & 5 \\ -5 & -3 & -2 \end{bmatrix} \begin{bmatrix} x_1'(k) \\ x_2'(k) \\ x_3'(k) \end{bmatrix} + \begin{bmatrix} 2 & -1 \\ 0 & 0 \end{bmatrix} \begin{bmatrix} u_1(k) \\ u_2(k) \end{bmatrix}$$

and the state equations are decoupled from one another. A delay diagram for this system is shown in Figure 3-11.

### 3.5.2 Complex Eigenvalues

When the system eigenvalues are complex, diagonal state equations involve complex coefficients. It is often more convenient to combine each pair of nonrepeated first-order complex conjugate subsystems into an equivalent second-order subsystem. The result is a state coupling matrix with $2 \times 2$ blocks along the diagonal for each complex eigenvalue pair.

For example, the single-input, single-output system with $z$-transfer function

$$T(z) = \frac{4z^2 + 3z - \frac{3}{8}}{z^3 + \frac{1}{2}z^2 - \frac{3}{16}z - \frac{5}{32}} = \frac{2}{z - \frac{1}{2}} + \frac{1 + j2}{z + \frac{1}{2} + j\frac{1}{4}} + \frac{1 - j2}{z + \frac{1}{2} - j\frac{1}{4}}$$

involves complex eigenvalues. A delay diagram of a diagonal system having this $z$-transfer function is shown in Figure 3-12(a). The corresponding state and output equations are

$$\begin{bmatrix} x_1(k+1) \\ x_2(k+1) \\ x_3(k+1) \end{bmatrix} = \begin{bmatrix} \frac{1}{2} & 0 & 0 \\ 0 & (-\frac{1}{2} - j\frac{1}{4}) & 0 \\ 0 & 0 & (-\frac{1}{2} + j\frac{1}{4}) \end{bmatrix} \begin{bmatrix} x_1(k) \\ x_2(k) \\ x_3(k) \end{bmatrix} + \begin{bmatrix} 1 \\ 1 \\ 1 \end{bmatrix} u(k)$$

$$y(k) = \begin{bmatrix} 2 & (1 + j2) & (1 - j2) \end{bmatrix} \begin{bmatrix} x_1(k) \\ x_2(k) \\ x_3(k) \end{bmatrix}$$

If the complex conjugate terms in the $z$-transfer function are combined, the individual terms each involve only real numbers:

$$T(z) = \frac{2}{z - \frac{1}{2}} + \frac{2z + 2}{z^2 + z + \frac{5}{16}}$$

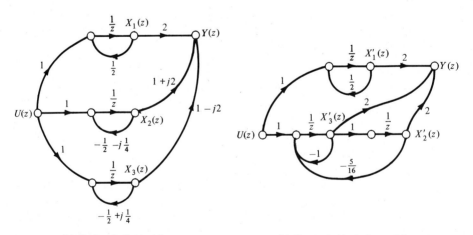

(a)  System in diagonal form.          (b)  System in block diagonal form.

**FIGURE 3-12.  Diagonal and block diagonal realizations of a discrete-time system with complex eigenvalues.**

The second-order subsystem can be realized with real number coefficients in a variety of ways with a resulting $2 \times 2$ block along the diagonal of the system's state coupling matrix. Expanding this second-order subsystem in controllable form

$$\frac{2z + 2}{z^2 + z + \frac{5}{16}} = \frac{\frac{2}{z} + \frac{2}{z^2}}{1 + \frac{1}{z} + \frac{5}{16}{z^2}}$$

gives the realization of Figure 3-12(b) for which the state and output equations are

$$\begin{bmatrix} x_1'(k + 1) \\ x_2'(k + 1) \\ x_3'(k + 1) \end{bmatrix} = \begin{bmatrix} \frac{1}{2} & 0 & 0 \\ 0 & 0 & 1 \\ 0 & -\frac{5}{16} & -1 \end{bmatrix} \begin{bmatrix} x_1'(k) \\ x_2'(k) \\ x_3'(k) \end{bmatrix} + \begin{bmatrix} 1 \\ 0 \\ 1 \end{bmatrix} u(k)$$

$$y(k) = \begin{bmatrix} 2 & 2 & 2 \end{bmatrix} \begin{bmatrix} x_1'(k) \\ x_2'(k) \\ x_3'(k) \end{bmatrix}$$

### 3.5.3 Block Jordan Forms

A $z$-transfer function with repeated poles generally cannot be realized by a diagonal system because its partial fraction expansion is not the sum of first-order subsystems. For example, a single-input, single-output system with $z$-transfer function

$$T(z) = \frac{3z^2 - 4z + 6}{(z - \frac{1}{3})^3} = \frac{3}{z - \frac{1}{3}} + \frac{-2}{(z - \frac{1}{3})^2} + \frac{5}{(z - \frac{1}{3})^3}$$

can be considered as the tandem (parallel) connection of subsystems shown in Figure 3-13(a). The system shown, however, is of sixth order. By interleaving the three identical first order subsystems as in Figure 3-13(b), a third-order realization results. Expanding this into a delay diagram, Figure 3-13(c) gives the state and output equations

$$\begin{bmatrix} x_1(k + 1) \\ x_2(k + 1) \\ x_3(k + 1) \end{bmatrix} = \begin{bmatrix} \frac{1}{3} & 1 & 0 \\ 0 & \frac{1}{3} & 1 \\ 0 & 0 & \frac{1}{3} \end{bmatrix} \begin{bmatrix} x_1(k) \\ x_2(k) \\ x_3(k) \end{bmatrix} + \begin{bmatrix} 0 \\ 0 \\ 1 \end{bmatrix} u(k)$$

$$y(k) = \begin{bmatrix} 5 & -2 & 3 \end{bmatrix} \begin{bmatrix} x_1(k) \\ x_2(k) \\ x_3(k) \end{bmatrix}$$

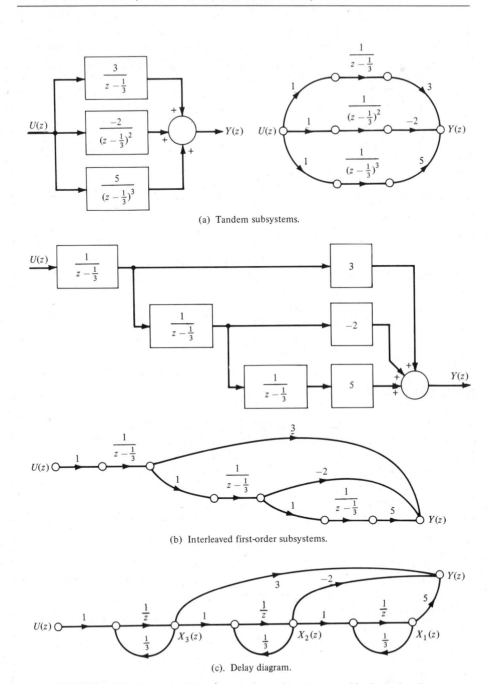

(a) Tandem subsystems.

(b) Interleaved first-order subsystems.

(c). Delay diagram.

**FIGURE 3-13.   System with repeated eigenvalues in upper block Jordan form.**

These have a state coupling matrix with the repeated eigenvalue along the diagonal and ones just above the diagonal. When repeated eigenvalues are represented in this way, the equations are in *upper block Jordan* form. One can also arrange things so that the ones are just below the diagonal, obtaining a *lower block Jordan* form, if desired.

To transform a matrix $\mathbf{A}_0$ with all eigenvalues $\lambda = \lambda_0$ repeated to the upper block Jordan form

$$
\boldsymbol{\Lambda}_0 = \begin{bmatrix} \lambda_0 & 1 & 0 & 0 & \cdots & 0 & 0 \\ 0 & \lambda_0 & 1 & 0 & \cdots & & \\ \vdots & & & & & & \\ 0 & 0 & 0 & 0 & \cdots & \lambda_0 & 1 \\ 0 & 0 & 0 & 0 & \cdots & 0 & \lambda_0 \end{bmatrix}
$$

the transformation matrix $\mathbf{P}$ must satisfy

$$\mathbf{P}^{-1}\mathbf{A}_0\mathbf{P} = \boldsymbol{\Lambda}_0$$

or

$$\mathbf{A}_0\mathbf{P} = \mathbf{P}\boldsymbol{\Lambda}_0$$

Partitioning $\mathbf{P}$ into columns,

$$\mathbf{A}_0[\mathbf{p}^1 \mid \mathbf{p}^2 \mid \cdots \mid \mathbf{p}^n]$$

$$
= [\mathbf{p}^1 \mid \mathbf{p}^2 \mid \cdots \mid \mathbf{p}^n] \begin{bmatrix} \lambda_0 & 1 & 0 & \cdots & 0 & 0 \\ 0 & \lambda_0 & 1 & \cdots & 0 & 0 \\ \vdots & & & & & \\ 0 & 0 & 0 & \cdots & \lambda_0 & 1 \\ 0 & 0 & 0 & \cdots & 0 & \lambda_0 \end{bmatrix}
$$

and equating the columns, there results

$$
\begin{cases}
\mathbf{A}_0\mathbf{p}^1 = \lambda_0\mathbf{p}^1 \\
\mathbf{A}_0\mathbf{p}^2 = \lambda_0\mathbf{p}^2 + \mathbf{p}^1 \\
\mathbf{A}_0\mathbf{p}^3 = \lambda_0\mathbf{p}^3 + \mathbf{p}^2 \\
\quad\vdots \\
\mathbf{A}_0\mathbf{p}^n = \lambda_0\mathbf{p}^n + \mathbf{p}^{n-1}
\end{cases}
$$

or

$$
\begin{cases}
(\lambda_0 I - A_0)p^1 = 0 \\
(\lambda_0 I - A_0)p^2 = -p^1 \\
(\lambda_0 I - A_0)p^3 = -p^2 \\
\quad \vdots \\
(\lambda_0 I - A_0)p^n = -p^{n-1}
\end{cases}
$$

When an $n \times n$ matrix $A$ contains a mixture of eigenvalues, the eigenvectors satisfying

$$(\lambda_i I - A)p^i = 0$$

are found until an eigenvalue repetition is encountered. If, as is usually the case, no additional linearly independent eigenvectors exist, then the relations

$$
\begin{cases}
(\lambda_i I - A)p^{i+1} = -p^i \\
(\lambda_i I - A)p^{i+2} = -p^{i+1} \\
\quad \vdots
\end{cases}
$$

are used to form columns of the transformation matrix for the eigenvalue repetitions. The resulting matrix $\Lambda$ will have any nonrepeated eigenvalues along its diagonal and an upper Jordan block along the diagonal for the repeated eigenvalues.

The system

$$
\begin{bmatrix} x_1(k+1) \\ x_2(k+1) \\ x_3(k+1) \end{bmatrix} =
\begin{bmatrix} 0 & 1 & 0 \\ 0 & 0 & 1 \\ -3 & 5 & -1 \end{bmatrix}
\begin{bmatrix} x_1(k) \\ x_2(k) \\ x_3(k) \end{bmatrix} +
\begin{bmatrix} 0 \\ 0 \\ 1 \end{bmatrix} u(k) = Ax(k) + bu(k)
$$

$$
\begin{bmatrix} y_1(k) \\ y_2(k) \end{bmatrix} =
\begin{bmatrix} 0 & 3 & 0 \\ 1 & 0 & -2 \end{bmatrix}
\begin{bmatrix} x_1(k) \\ x_2(k) \\ x_3(k) \end{bmatrix} +
\begin{bmatrix} 2 \\ 0 \end{bmatrix} u(k) = Cx(k) + du(k)
$$

for example, has eigenvalues given by

$$
|\lambda I - A| =
\begin{vmatrix} \lambda & -1 & 0 \\ 0 & \lambda & -1 \\ 3 & -5 & (\lambda+1) \end{vmatrix}
= \lambda^3 + \lambda^2 - 5\lambda + 3 = (\lambda + 3)(\lambda - 1)^2 = 0
$$

$$\lambda_1 = -3; \qquad \lambda_2 = 1; \qquad \lambda_3 = 1$$

which involves a repeated eigenvalue. For $\lambda_1$:

$$(\lambda_1 I - A)p^1 = 0$$

$$\begin{bmatrix} -3 & -1 & 0 \\ 0 & -3 & -1 \\ 3 & -5 & -2 \end{bmatrix} \begin{bmatrix} p_{11} \\ p_{21} \\ p_{31} \end{bmatrix} = \begin{bmatrix} 0 \\ 0 \\ 0 \end{bmatrix}; \qquad p^1 = \begin{bmatrix} -1 \\ 3 \\ -9 \end{bmatrix}$$

For $\lambda_2$:

$$(\lambda_2 I - A)p^2 = 0$$

$$\begin{bmatrix} 1 & -1 & 0 \\ 0 & 1 & -1 \\ 3 & -5 & 2 \end{bmatrix} \begin{bmatrix} p_{12} \\ p_{22} \\ p_{32} \end{bmatrix} = \begin{bmatrix} 0 \\ 0 \\ 0 \end{bmatrix}; \qquad p^2 = \begin{bmatrix} 1 \\ 1 \\ 1 \end{bmatrix}$$

For the repetition of the root at $\lambda = 1$, since there is not another linearly independent solution of the equations for $p^2$, we solve

$$(\lambda_2 I - A)p^3 = -p^2$$

$$\begin{bmatrix} 1 & -1 & 0 \\ 0 & 1 & -1 \\ 3 & -5 & 2 \end{bmatrix} \begin{bmatrix} p_{13} \\ p_{23} \\ p_{33} \end{bmatrix} = - \begin{bmatrix} 1 \\ 1 \\ 1 \end{bmatrix}$$

which has solution

$$p^3 = \begin{bmatrix} 0 \\ 1 \\ 2 \end{bmatrix}$$

A transformation to upper block Jordan form then has

$$P = \begin{bmatrix} -1 & 1 & 0 \\ 3 & 1 & 1 \\ -9 & 1 & 2 \end{bmatrix}; \qquad P^{-1} = \frac{1}{16} \begin{bmatrix} -1 & 2 & -1 \\ 15 & 2 & -1 \\ -12 & 8 & 4 \end{bmatrix}$$

giving

$$A' = P^{-1}AP$$

$$= \frac{1}{16} \begin{bmatrix} -1 & 2 & -1 \\ 15 & 2 & -1 \\ -12 & 8 & 4 \end{bmatrix} \begin{bmatrix} 0 & 1 & 0 \\ 0 & 0 & 1 \\ -3 & 5 & -1 \end{bmatrix} \begin{bmatrix} -1 & 1 & 0 \\ 3 & 1 & 1 \\ -9 & 1 & 2 \end{bmatrix} = \begin{bmatrix} -3 & 0 & 0 \\ 0 & 1 & 1 \\ 0 & 0 & 1 \end{bmatrix}$$

$$\mathbf{b'} = \mathbf{P}^{-1}\mathbf{b} = \frac{1}{16}\begin{bmatrix} -1 & 2 & -1 \\ 15 & 2 & -1 \\ -12 & 8 & 4 \end{bmatrix}\begin{bmatrix} 0 \\ 0 \\ 1 \end{bmatrix} = \frac{1}{16}\begin{bmatrix} -1 \\ -1 \\ 4 \end{bmatrix}$$

$$\mathbf{C'} = \mathbf{CP} = \begin{bmatrix} 0 & 3 & 0 \\ 1 & 0 & -2 \end{bmatrix}\begin{bmatrix} -1 & 1 & 0 \\ 3 & 1 & 1 \\ -9 & 1 & 2 \end{bmatrix} = \begin{bmatrix} 9 & 3 & 3 \\ 17 & -1 & -4 \end{bmatrix}$$

so that the system description in terms of the new state variables is

$$\begin{bmatrix} x_1'(k+1) \\ x_2'(k+1) \\ x_3'(k+1) \end{bmatrix} = \begin{bmatrix} -3 & 0 & 0 \\ 0 & 1 & 1 \\ 0 & 0 & 1 \end{bmatrix}\begin{bmatrix} x_1'(k) \\ x_2'(k) \\ x_3'(k) \end{bmatrix} + \begin{bmatrix} -\frac{1}{16} \\ -\frac{1}{16} \\ \frac{1}{4} \end{bmatrix}u(k)$$

$$\begin{bmatrix} y_1(k) \\ y_2(k) \end{bmatrix} = \begin{bmatrix} 9 & 3 & 3 \\ 17 & -1 & -4 \end{bmatrix}\begin{bmatrix} x_1'(k) \\ x_2'(k) \\ x_3'(k) \end{bmatrix} + \begin{bmatrix} 2 \\ 0 \end{bmatrix}u(k)$$

The state coupling matrix of the system in terms of the state variables $\mathbf{x'}$ is in upper block Jordan form.

## 3.6 Observability and Controllability

When state variable equations for a system are placed in diagonal form or, in the case of repeated eigenvalues, block Jordan form, fundamental structural aspects of the system are apparent. We now examine that structure and find whether it is possible to control a system's state from its inputs and whether it is possible to determine a system's state from its outputs.

### 3.6.1 Unobservable and Uncontrollable Modes

When state equations are in diagonal form, each state variable appears in only one equation so the equations are all of first-order and are decoupled from one another. The form of the zero-input response of each of these first-order subsystems is termed its *mode*, or the mode associated with the corresponding state variable, and each output of the system has a zero-input response consisting of a linear combination of the individual modes.

If, when in diagonal form, any column of the output coupling matrix is zero, the corresponding state variable does not couple to any output, and the mode associated with that diagonal form state variable is termed *unobservable*. Otherwise, a mode is observable. If, in diagonal form, any row of the input coupling matrix is zero, no input can affect the corresponding first-order equation, and that equation's mode is termed *uncontrollable;* otherwise it is controllable. Each mode of a system is either observable or unobservable. And, each mode of a system is either controllable or uncontrollable. If all the modes of a system are observable, the system is *completely observable.* Similarly, if all system modes are controllable, the system is *completely controllable.*

For the diagonal system

$$\begin{bmatrix} x_1'(k+1) \\ x_2'(k+1) \\ x_3'(k+1) \\ x_4'(k+1) \end{bmatrix} = \begin{bmatrix} 1 & 0 & 0 & 0 \\ 0 & 0 & 0 & 0 \\ 0 & 0 & -2 & 0 \\ 0 & 0 & 0 & \frac{1}{3} \end{bmatrix} \begin{bmatrix} x_1'(k) \\ x_2'(k) \\ x_3'(k) \\ x_4'(k) \end{bmatrix} + \begin{bmatrix} -2 \\ 4 \\ 0 \\ 3 \end{bmatrix} u(k)$$

$$\begin{bmatrix} y_1(k) \\ y_2(k) \end{bmatrix} = \begin{bmatrix} -1 & 1 & 0 & 0 \\ 0 & -2 & 0 & 0 \end{bmatrix} \begin{bmatrix} x_1'(k) \\ x_2'(k) \\ x_3'(k) \\ x_4'(k) \end{bmatrix} + \begin{bmatrix} 5 \\ 0 \end{bmatrix} u(k)$$

the individual decoupled first-order equations are

$$\begin{cases} x_1'(k+1) = x_1'(k) - 2u(k) \\ x_2'(k+1) = 4u(k) \\ x_3'(k+1) = -2x_3'(k) \\ x_4'(k+1) = \frac{1}{3}x_4'(k) + 3u(k) \end{cases}$$

and the corresponding modes are $1^k$, $0^k$, $(-2)^k$ and $(1/3)^k$. The input does not couple to the $(-2)^k$ mode, so that mode is uncontrollable. The $(-2)^k$ and $(1/3)^k$ modes do not couple to either output, so both these modes are unobservable. The $1^k$ and $0^k$ modes are each controllable and observable.

A delay diagram for this system is shown in Figure 3-14. The two system transfer functions are

$$T_1(z) = \frac{Y_1(z)}{U(z)}\bigg|_{\substack{\text{zero initial} \\ \text{conditions}}} = \frac{(-1)(-2)}{z-1} + \frac{(1)(4)}{z} + 5 = \frac{5z^2 + z - 4}{z(z-1)}$$

$$T_2(z) = \frac{Y_2(z)}{U(z)}\bigg|_{\substack{\text{zero initial} \\ \text{conditions}}} = \frac{(-2)(4)}{z} = -\frac{8}{z}$$

Whenever, in diagonal form, there is no coupling to a mode from an input or no coupling from a mode to an output, the transfer function relating that

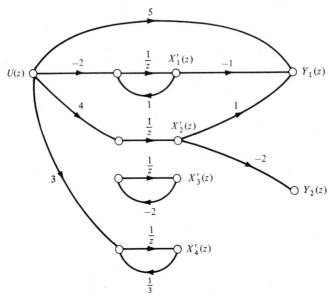

**FIGURE 3-14.    Diagonal system with unobservable and uncontrollable modes.**

output and input does not have a pole (eigenvalue) corresponding to that mode. In calculating the system transfer function matrix according to

$$T(z) = C(zI - A)^{-1}B + D$$

where every element of $T(z)$ shares the denominator polynomial $|zI - A|$, a $z$-transfer function without one of these poles must have a pole-zero cancellation. If any mode is unobservable or uncontrollable, every element of the transfer function matrix will have a pole-zero cancellation. In general, a system can be decomposed into four parts, one each in which the modes are

> **controllable and observable**
> **controllable but not observable**
> **not controllable but observable**
> **not controllable and not observable**

as indicated in Figure 3-15. The transfer function matrix characterizes only the controllable and observable subsystem.

The modes associated with a Jordan block in the state coupling matrix representing repeated eigenvalues $a$ are $a^k$, $ka^k$, $k^2a^k$, and so on. As an example, the delay diagrm for the portion of a system represented by a $4 \times 4$

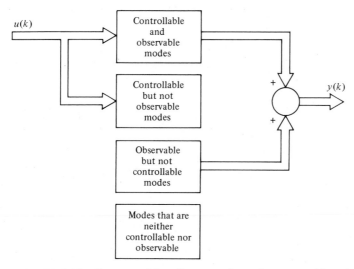

**FIGURE 3-15.   Decomposition of a system into subsystems with various combinations of mode observability and controllability.**

Jordan block

$$
\begin{bmatrix} x_i(k+1) \\ x_{i+1}(k+1) \\ x_{i+2}(k+1) \\ x_{i+3}(k+1) \end{bmatrix} = \begin{bmatrix} a & 1 & 0 & 0 \\ 0 & a & 1 & 0 \\ 0 & 0 & a & 1 \\ 0 & 0 & 0 & a \end{bmatrix} \begin{bmatrix} x_i(k) \\ x_{i+1}(k) \\ x_{i+2}(k) \\ x_{i+3}(k) \end{bmatrix} + (\text{input terms})
$$

is shown in Figure 3-16. Input coupling to the last state variable, in this case to the $x_{i+3}(k)$ equation, affects all the block's state variables. If no input couples to the last equation of the block, the highest degree mode, $k^3 a^k$ in the example, cannot be controlled. In general, controllability of all the modes associated with a Jordan block rests on whether there is input coupling to the last state variable in the block. If there is not, the highest degree mode is not controllable. Controllability of the rest of the modes depends on whether there is input coupling to the next-to-last state variable, and so on.

If the first state variable in the Jordan block couples to an output, all of the state variables of the block can affect the output, and all of the block's modes are observable. If the first state variable in the block does not couple to any output, the highest degree mode, $k^3 a^k$ in the example, cannot be observed. Observability of the $k^2 a^k$, $k a^k$ and $a^k$ modes requires coupling to an output from the second state variable, and so on.

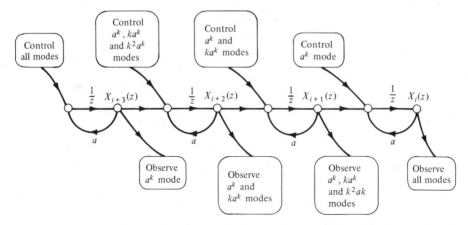

**FIGURE 3-16.** **Illustration of controllability and observability of modes associated with repeated system eigenvalues.**

Most of the fine points connected with observability and controllability have to do with systems with repeated eigenvalues, where the repeated eigenvalue has more than one Jordan block. For example, a system with block diagonal state coupling matrix

$$\mathbf{A} = \begin{bmatrix} -\frac{1}{4} & 0 & 0 \\ 0 & \frac{1}{2} & 1 \\ 0 & 0 & \frac{1}{2} \end{bmatrix}$$

has the eigenvalue 1/2 repeated in a single Jordan block, while a system with the same eigenvalues but with diagonal state coupling matrix

$$\mathbf{A} = \begin{bmatrix} -\frac{1}{4} & 0 & 0 \\ 0 & \frac{1}{2} & 0 \\ 0 & 0 & \frac{1}{2} \end{bmatrix}$$

has two Jordan "blocks" with the same eigenvalue. For the latter system to be completely controllable, there must be two inputs, each of which couple in different ways to the repeated mode. For example,

$$\begin{bmatrix} x_1(k+1) \\ x_2(k+1) \\ x_3(k+1) \end{bmatrix} = \begin{bmatrix} -\frac{1}{4} & 0 & 0 \\ 0 & \frac{1}{2} & 0 \\ 0 & 0 & \frac{1}{2} \end{bmatrix} \begin{bmatrix} x_1(k) \\ x_2(k) \\ x_3(k) \end{bmatrix} + \begin{bmatrix} 2 & 3 \\ 1 & 0 \\ 0 & 1 \end{bmatrix} \begin{bmatrix} u_1(k) \\ u_2(k) \end{bmatrix}$$

is completely controllable, while

$$\begin{bmatrix} x_1(k+1) \\ x_2(k+1) \\ x_3(k+1) \end{bmatrix} = \begin{bmatrix} -\frac{1}{4} & 0 & 0 \\ 0 & \frac{1}{2} & 0 \\ 0 & 0 & \frac{1}{2} \end{bmatrix} \begin{bmatrix} x_1(k) \\ x_2(k) \\ x_3(k) \end{bmatrix} + \begin{bmatrix} 3 \\ 1 \\ 2 \end{bmatrix} u(k) \qquad (3\text{-}4)$$

is not. In (3-4) the change of state variable

$$x_3'(k) = -2x_2(k) + x_3(k)$$

gives the realization

$$\begin{bmatrix} x_1(k+1) \\ x_2(k+1) \\ x_3'(k+1) \end{bmatrix} = \begin{bmatrix} -\frac{1}{4} & 0 & 0 \\ 0 & \frac{1}{2} & 0 \\ 0 & 0 & \frac{1}{2} \end{bmatrix} \begin{bmatrix} x_1(k) \\ x_2(k) \\ x_3'(k) \end{bmatrix} + \begin{bmatrix} 3 \\ 1 \\ 0 \end{bmatrix} u(k)$$

from which it is seen that there is a part of the state, the state variable $x_3'(k)$, that is unaffected by any input. In general, controllability of a repeated mode requires that there be a number of system inputs equal to the maximum number of Jordan blocks having the same eigenvalue. Each must couple differently to Jordan blocks having the same eigenvalue.

Similarly, observability of a repeated mode having more than one Jordan block requires that the system have independent outputs from each such block. For example, the system

$$\begin{bmatrix} x_1(k+1) \\ x_2(k+1) \\ x_3(k+1) \end{bmatrix} = \begin{bmatrix} -\frac{1}{3} & 0 & 0 \\ 0 & \frac{1}{2} & 0 \\ 0 & 0 & \frac{1}{2} \end{bmatrix} \begin{bmatrix} x_1(k) \\ x_2(k) \\ x_3(k) \end{bmatrix} + \begin{bmatrix} 2 & 3 \\ 1 & 0 \\ 0 & 1 \end{bmatrix} \begin{bmatrix} u_1(k) \\ u_2(k) \end{bmatrix}$$

$$\begin{bmatrix} y_1(k) \\ y_2(k) \end{bmatrix} = \begin{bmatrix} 4 & 1 & 0 \\ -1 & 0 & 1 \end{bmatrix} \begin{bmatrix} x_1(k) \\ x_2(k) \\ x_3(k) \end{bmatrix}$$

is completely observable, but

$$\begin{bmatrix} x_1(k+1) \\ x_2(k+1) \\ x_3(k+1) \end{bmatrix} = \begin{bmatrix} -\frac{1}{4} & 0 & 0 \\ 0 & \frac{1}{2} & 0 \\ 0 & 0 & \frac{1}{2} \end{bmatrix} \begin{bmatrix} x_1(k) \\ x_2(k) \\ x_3(k) \end{bmatrix} + \begin{bmatrix} 2 & 3 \\ 1 & 0 \\ 0 & 1 \end{bmatrix} \begin{bmatrix} u_1(k) \\ u_2(k) \end{bmatrix}$$

$$y(k) = \begin{bmatrix} 4 & 3 & 2 \end{bmatrix} \begin{bmatrix} x_1(k) \\ x_2(k) \\ x_3(k) \end{bmatrix} \qquad (3\text{-}5)$$

is not. In (3-5), the change of state variables where

$$x_2(k) = x'_2 + 2x'_3(k); \qquad x'_2(k) = x_2(k) + \tfrac{2}{3}x_3(k)$$

$$x_3(k) = -3x'_3(k); \qquad x'_3(k) = -\tfrac{1}{3}x_3(k)$$

gives the realization

$$\begin{bmatrix} x_1(k+1) \\ x'_2(k+1) \\ x'_3(k+1) \end{bmatrix} = \begin{bmatrix} -\tfrac{1}{4} & 0 & 0 \\ 0 & \tfrac{1}{2} & 0 \\ 0 & 0 & \tfrac{1}{2} \end{bmatrix} \begin{bmatrix} x_1(k) \\ x'_2(k) \\ x'_3(k) \end{bmatrix} + \begin{bmatrix} 2 & 3 \\ 1 & \tfrac{2}{3} \\ 0 & -\tfrac{1}{3} \end{bmatrix} \begin{bmatrix} u_1(k) \\ u_2(k) \end{bmatrix}$$

$$y(k) = \begin{bmatrix} 4 & 3 & 0 \end{bmatrix} \begin{bmatrix} x_1(k) \\ x'_2(k) \\ x'_3(k) \end{bmatrix}$$

which shows that part of the state, the variable $x'_3(k)$, does not affect the output.

### 3.6.2 Transformation to Controllable Form

Any completely controllable single-input system can be realized in controllable form. The needed change of state variables, which will be used again early in the next chapter, is now derived. Let the transformation matrix **P** in

$$\mathbf{x} = \mathbf{P}\mathbf{x}'; \qquad \mathbf{x}' = \mathbf{P}^{-1}\mathbf{x}$$

take a completely controllable single-input system into the controllable form. Partition **P** into columns and let the characteristic equation of **A** be

$$\lambda^n + \alpha_{n-1}\lambda^{n-1} + \cdots + \alpha_1\lambda + \alpha_0 = 0$$

where the coefficients $\alpha_i$ have been found. Then

$$\mathbf{P}^{-1}\mathbf{b} = \mathbf{b}_c; \qquad \mathbf{b} = \mathbf{P}\mathbf{b}_c$$

or

$$\mathbf{b} = \begin{bmatrix} \mathbf{p}^1 & \vdots & \mathbf{p}^2 & \vdots & \cdots & \vdots & \mathbf{p}^n \end{bmatrix} \begin{bmatrix} 0 \\ 0 \\ \vdots \\ 0 \\ 1 \end{bmatrix}$$

which gives

$$\mathbf{p}^n = \mathbf{b} \tag{3-6}$$

Using

$$\mathbf{P}^{-1}\mathbf{A}\mathbf{P} = \mathbf{A}_c; \qquad \mathbf{A}\mathbf{P} = \mathbf{P}\mathbf{A}_c$$

then

$$\mathbf{A}[\mathbf{p}^1 \mid \mathbf{p}^2 \mid \cdots \mid \mathbf{p}^{n-1} \mid \mathbf{p}^n]$$

$$= [\mathbf{p}^1 \mid \mathbf{p}^2 \mid \cdots \mid \mathbf{p}^{n-1} \mid \mathbf{p}^n] \begin{bmatrix} 0 & 1 & 0 & \cdots & 0 & 0 \\ 0 & 0 & 1 & \cdots & 0 & 0 \\ \vdots & & & & & \\ 0 & 0 & 0 & \cdots & 0 & 1 \\ -\alpha_0 & -\alpha_1 & -\alpha_2 & \cdots & -\alpha_{n-2} & -\alpha_{n-1} \end{bmatrix}$$

Equating columns, from right to left

$$\begin{cases} \mathbf{A}\mathbf{p}^n = \mathbf{p}^{n-1} - \alpha_{n-1}\mathbf{p}^n \\ \mathbf{A}\mathbf{p}^{n-1} = \mathbf{p}^{n-2} - \alpha_{n-2}\mathbf{p}^n \\ \vdots \\ \mathbf{A}\mathbf{p}^2 = \mathbf{p}^1 - \alpha_1\mathbf{p}^n \\ \mathbf{A}\mathbf{p}^1 = -\alpha_0\mathbf{p}^n \end{cases} \tag{3-7}$$

(3-6) and (3-7) form the recursive algorithm

$$\begin{cases} \mathbf{p}^n = \mathbf{b} \\ \mathbf{p}^{n-1} = \mathbf{A}\mathbf{p}^n + \alpha_{n-1}\mathbf{b} \\ \vdots \\ \mathbf{p}^2 = \mathbf{A}\mathbf{p}^3 + \alpha_2\mathbf{b} \\ \mathbf{p}^1 = \mathbf{A}\mathbf{p}^2 + \alpha_1\mathbf{b} \end{cases} \tag{3-8}$$

where the relation

$$\mathbf{A}\mathbf{p}^1 = -\alpha_0\mathbf{p}^n$$

is not used because, using the Cayley-Hamilton theorem, it can be shown to be redundant. It is, however, a good check on the calculations.

As a numerical example, for the system

$$\begin{bmatrix} x_1(k+1) \\ x_2(k+1) \\ x_3(k+1) \end{bmatrix} = \begin{bmatrix} -2 & 1 & 1 \\ 0 & 2 & -1 \\ 0 & 1 & 3 \end{bmatrix} \begin{bmatrix} x_1(k) \\ x_2(k) \\ x_3(k) \end{bmatrix} + \begin{bmatrix} 1 \\ 0 \\ -1 \end{bmatrix} u(k)$$

$$\begin{bmatrix} y_1(k) \\ y_2(k) \end{bmatrix} = \begin{bmatrix} 2 & 0 & 1 \\ 0 & -2 & 4 \end{bmatrix} \begin{bmatrix} x_1(k) \\ x_2(k) \\ x_3(k) \end{bmatrix} + \begin{bmatrix} -3 \\ 5 \end{bmatrix} u(k)$$

the characteristic equation is

$$|\lambda \mathbf{I} - \mathbf{A}| = \begin{vmatrix} \lambda+2 & -1 & -1 \\ 0 & (\lambda-2) & 1 \\ 0 & -1 & (\lambda-3) \end{vmatrix} = (\lambda+2)(\lambda^2 - 5\lambda + 7)$$

$$= \lambda^3 - 3\lambda^2 - 3\lambda + 14 = 0$$

The columns of the transformation matrix $\mathbf{P}$ are given by

$$\mathbf{p}^3 = \mathbf{b} = \begin{bmatrix} 1 \\ 0 \\ -1 \end{bmatrix}$$

$$\mathbf{p}^2 = \mathbf{A}\mathbf{p}^3 - 3\mathbf{b} = \begin{bmatrix} -2 & 1 & 1 \\ 0 & 2 & -1 \\ 0 & 1 & 3 \end{bmatrix} \begin{bmatrix} 1 \\ 0 \\ -1 \end{bmatrix} - 3 \begin{bmatrix} 1 \\ 0 \\ -1 \end{bmatrix} = \begin{bmatrix} -6 \\ 1 \\ 0 \end{bmatrix}$$

$$\mathbf{p}^1 = \mathbf{A}\mathbf{p}^2 - 3\mathbf{b} = \begin{bmatrix} -2 & 1 & 1 \\ 0 & 2 & -1 \\ 0 & 1 & 3 \end{bmatrix} \begin{bmatrix} -6 \\ 1 \\ 0 \end{bmatrix} - 3 \begin{bmatrix} 1 \\ 0 \\ -1 \end{bmatrix} = \begin{bmatrix} 10 \\ 2 \\ 4 \end{bmatrix}$$

so that

$$\mathbf{P} = \begin{bmatrix} 10 & -6 & 1 \\ 2 & 1 & 0 \\ 4 & 0 & -1 \end{bmatrix}$$

A controllable form representation of a single-input system exists if and only if the system is completely controllable. This can be shown as follows: Using the recursive transformation relations of equation (3-8) the transformation can be expressed in the form

$$\mathbf{P} = [\mathbf{p}^1 \;\vdots\; \mathbf{p}^2 \;\vdots\; \cdots \;\vdots\; \mathbf{p}^n]$$

$$= \underbrace{[\mathbf{b} \;\vdots\; \mathbf{Ab} \;\vdots\; \mathbf{A}^2\mathbf{b} \;\vdots\; \cdots \;\vdots\; \mathbf{A}^{n-1}\mathbf{b}]}_{\mathbf{M}_c} \begin{bmatrix} \alpha_1 & \alpha_2 & \cdots & \alpha_{n-2} & \alpha_{n-1} & 1 \\ \alpha_2 & \alpha_3 & \cdots & \alpha_{n-1} & 1 & 0 \\ \alpha_3 & \alpha_4 & \cdots & 1 & 0 & 0 \\ \vdots & \vdots & & & & \\ \alpha_{n-2} & \alpha_{n-1} & \cdots & 0 & 0 & 0 \\ \alpha_{n-1} & 1 & \cdots & 0 & 0 & 0 \\ 1 & 0 & \cdots & 0 & 0 & 0 \end{bmatrix}$$

where the matrix $\mathbf{M}_c$ is termed the *controllability matrix* of the system. The matrix at the right is nonsingular for any $\alpha_i$'s since each column, right to left, is linearly independent of the previous columns. Thus the transformation to controllable form is nonsingular if and only if the single-input system's controllability matrix $\mathbf{M}_c$ is nonsingular. As will be demonstrated in the next chapter, a single-input system is completely controllable if and only if $\mathbf{M}_c$ is nonsingular.

## 3.6.3 *Transformation to Observable Form*

The transformation matrix $\mathbf{Q} = \mathbf{P}^{-1}$ in

$$\mathbf{x} = \mathbf{P}\mathbf{x}' = \mathbf{Q}^{-1}\mathbf{x}'; \qquad \mathbf{x}' = \mathbf{P}^{-1}\mathbf{x} = \mathbf{Q}\mathbf{x}$$

that takes a completely observable single-output system into the observable form can be found as follows. Partition the rows of $\mathbf{Q}$ and let the characteristic equation of $\mathbf{A}$ be

$$\lambda^n + \alpha_{n-1}\lambda^{n-1} + \cdots + \alpha_1\lambda + \alpha_0 = 0$$

Then

$$\mathbf{c}_0^\dagger = \mathbf{c}^\dagger\mathbf{P} = \mathbf{c}^\dagger\mathbf{Q}^{-1}; \qquad \mathbf{c}_0^\dagger\mathbf{Q} = \mathbf{c}^\dagger$$

or

$$[1 \quad 0 \quad \cdots \quad 0] \begin{bmatrix} \mathbf{q}_1^\dagger \\ \hline \mathbf{q}_2^\dagger \\ \hline \vdots \\ \hline \mathbf{q}_n^\dagger \end{bmatrix} = \mathbf{c}^\dagger$$

which gives

$$\mathbf{q}_1^\dagger = \mathbf{c}^\dagger \tag{3-9}$$

and

$$\mathbf{P}^{-1}\mathbf{AP} = \mathbf{QAQ}^{-1} = \mathbf{A}_0; \qquad \mathbf{QA} = \mathbf{A}_0\mathbf{Q}$$

or

$$
\begin{bmatrix} \mathbf{q}_1^\dagger \\ \hline \mathbf{q}_2^\dagger \\ \hline \vdots \\ \hline \mathbf{q}_{n-1}^\dagger \\ \hline \mathbf{q}_n^\dagger \end{bmatrix}
\mathbf{A} =
\begin{bmatrix}
-\alpha_{n-1} & 1 & 0 & \cdots & 0 & 0 \\
-\alpha_{n-2} & 0 & 1 & \cdots & 0 & 0 \\
\vdots & & & & & \\
-\alpha_1 & 0 & 0 & \cdots & 0 & 1 \\
-\alpha_0 & 0 & 0 & \cdots & 0 & 0
\end{bmatrix}
\begin{bmatrix} \mathbf{q}_1^\dagger \\ \hline \mathbf{q}_2^\dagger \\ \hline \vdots \\ \hline \mathbf{q}_{n-1}^\dagger \\ \hline \mathbf{q}_n^\dagger \end{bmatrix}
\tag{3-10}
$$

Equating rows from top to bottom and using equation (3-9) gives the recursive algorithm

$$
\begin{cases}
\mathbf{q}_1^\dagger = \mathbf{c}^\dagger \\
\mathbf{q}_2^\dagger = \mathbf{q}_1^\dagger \mathbf{A} + \alpha_{n-1}\mathbf{c}^\dagger \\
\vdots \\
\mathbf{q}_{n-1}^\dagger = \mathbf{q}_{n-2}^\dagger \mathbf{A} + \alpha_2\mathbf{c}^\dagger \\
\mathbf{q}_n^\dagger = \mathbf{q}_{n-1}^\dagger \mathbf{A} + \alpha_1\mathbf{c}^\dagger
\end{cases}
$$

where the last equation from (3-10) is redundant and is not used.

For example, for the system

$$
\begin{bmatrix} x_1(k+1) \\ x_2(k+1) \\ x_3(k+1) \end{bmatrix} =
\begin{bmatrix} -2 & 2 & 0 \\ -1 & -3 & 0 \\ 1 & 0 & 1 \end{bmatrix}
\begin{bmatrix} x_1(k) \\ x_2(k) \\ x_3(k) \end{bmatrix} +
\begin{bmatrix} 3 & 1 \\ 4 & 1 \\ -2 & 0 \end{bmatrix}
\begin{bmatrix} u_1(k) \\ u_2(k) \end{bmatrix}
$$

$$= \mathbf{Ax}(k) + \mathbf{Bu}(k)$$

$$
y(k) = \begin{bmatrix} 0 & -2 & 1 \end{bmatrix}
\begin{bmatrix} x_1(k) \\ x_2(k) \\ x_3(k) \end{bmatrix} +
\begin{bmatrix} 1 & 0 \end{bmatrix}
\begin{bmatrix} u_1(k) \\ u_2(k) \end{bmatrix}
$$

$$= \mathbf{c}^\dagger \mathbf{x}(k) + \mathbf{d}^\dagger \mathbf{u}(k)$$

the characteristic equation is

$$|\lambda I - A| = \begin{bmatrix} (\lambda + 2) & -2 & 0 \\ 1 & (\lambda + 3) & 0 \\ -1 & 0 & (\lambda - 1) \end{bmatrix} = (\lambda - 1)(\lambda^2 + 5\lambda + 8)$$

$$= \lambda^3 + 4\lambda^2 + 3\lambda - 8 = 0$$

The rows of the inverse transformation matrix $\mathbf{Q}$ are given by

$$\mathbf{q}_1^\dagger = \mathbf{c}^\dagger = \begin{bmatrix} 0 & -2 & 1 \end{bmatrix}$$

$$\mathbf{q}_2^\dagger = \mathbf{q}_1^\dagger \mathbf{A} + \alpha_2 \mathbf{c}^\dagger = \begin{bmatrix} 0 & -2 & 1 \end{bmatrix} \begin{bmatrix} -2 & 2 & 0 \\ -1 & -3 & 0 \\ 1 & 0 & 1 \end{bmatrix} + 4\begin{bmatrix} 0 & -2 & 1 \end{bmatrix}$$

$$= \begin{bmatrix} 3 & -2 & 5 \end{bmatrix}$$

$$\mathbf{q}_3^\dagger = \mathbf{q}_2^\dagger \mathbf{A} + \alpha_1 \mathbf{c}^\dagger = \begin{bmatrix} 3 & -2 & 5 \end{bmatrix} \begin{bmatrix} -2 & 2 & 0 \\ -1 & -3 & 0 \\ 1 & 0 & 1 \end{bmatrix} + 3\begin{bmatrix} 0 & -2 & 1 \end{bmatrix}$$

$$= \begin{bmatrix} 1 & 6 & 8 \end{bmatrix}$$

so that

$$\mathbf{Q} = \begin{bmatrix} 0 & -2 & 1 \\ 3 & -2 & 5 \\ 1 & 6 & 8 \end{bmatrix}$$

Similar to the situation with controllable form, the transformation matrix $\mathbf{Q}$ for the observable canonical form of a single-output system is nonsingular if and only if the system is completely observable.

## 3.7 Summary

Linear, step-invariant discrete-time system models have the form

$$\mathbf{x}(k + 1) = \mathbf{A}\mathbf{x}(k) + \mathbf{B}\mathbf{u}(k)$$

$$\mathbf{y}(k) = \mathbf{C}\mathbf{x}(k) + \mathbf{D}\mathbf{u}(k)$$

where $\mathbf{u}(k)$ is the $r$-vector of inputs, $\mathbf{y}(k)$ is the $m$-vector of outputs, and $\mathbf{x}(k)$ is the $n$-vector state. A delay diagram is an easy way to visualize discrete-time systems graphically, in terms of delays, multiplications by constants and additions. For a single-input system, when the $n \times n$ state coupling matrix and the $n \times 1$ input coupling matrix have the forms

$$
A = \begin{bmatrix}
0 & 1 & 0 & \cdots & 0 & 0 \\
0 & 0 & 1 & \cdots & 0 & 0 \\
0 & 0 & 0 & \cdots & 0 & 0 \\
\vdots & & & & & \\
0 & 0 & 0 & \cdots & 0 & 1 \\
-\alpha_0 & -\alpha_1 & -\alpha_2 & \cdots & -\alpha_{n-2} & -\alpha_{n-1}
\end{bmatrix}; \quad
b = \begin{bmatrix} 0 \\ 0 \\ 0 \\ \vdots \\ 0 \\ 1 \end{bmatrix}
$$

the system is said to be in controllable form. Its $z$-transfer function numerator polynomials are easily related to the elements of the $C$ and $d$ matrices, and all $z$-transfer functions share the denominator polynomial

$$z^n + \alpha_{n-1} z^{n-1} + \alpha_{n-2} z^{n-2} + \cdots + \alpha_1 z + \alpha_0$$

which is the characteristic polynomial of the system. When a single-output system has

$$
A = \begin{bmatrix}
-\alpha_{n-1} & 1 & 0 & \cdots & 0 & 0 \\
-\alpha_{n-2} & 0 & 1 & \cdots & 0 & 0 \\
-\alpha_{n-3} & 0 & 0 & \cdots & 0 & 0 \\
\vdots & & & & & \\
-\alpha_1 & 0 & 0 & \cdots & 0 & 1 \\
-\alpha_0 & 0 & 0 & \cdots & 0 & 0
\end{bmatrix}; \quad
c^\dagger = \begin{bmatrix} 1 & 0 & 0 & \cdots & 0 & 0 \end{bmatrix}
$$

it is in observable form. Its $z$-transfer functions share the denominator polynomial

$$z^n + \alpha_{n-1} z^{n-1} + \alpha_{n-2} z^{n-2} + \cdots + \alpha_1 z + \alpha_0$$

and have numerator polynomials that are easily related to the elements of the $B$ and $d$ matrices.

In terms of the initial state and the inputs

$$x(k) = \underbrace{A^k x(0)}_{\substack{\text{zero-input} \\ \text{component}}} + \underbrace{\sum_{i=0}^{k-1} A^{k-1-i} Bu(i)}_{\substack{\text{zero-state} \\ \text{component}}}$$

$$y(k) = Cx(k) + Du(k)$$

The matrix of system $z$-transfer functions is given by

$$\mathbf{T}(z) = \mathbf{C}(z\mathbf{I} - \mathbf{A})^{-1}\mathbf{B} + \mathbf{D}$$

Each element of $\mathbf{T}(z)$ is a ratio of polynomials in $z$ that shares the denominator polynomial

$$|z\mathbf{I} - \mathbf{A}| = z^n + \alpha_{n-1}z^{n-1} + \alpha_{n-2}z^{n-2} + \cdots + \alpha_1 z + \alpha_0$$

which is the characteristic polynomial of the state coupling matrix $\mathbf{A}$. The roots of

$$|z\mathbf{I} = \mathbf{A}| = 0$$

the eigenvalues of $\mathbf{A}$ are the poles of each of the $z$-transfer function elements. A state variable system is stable if and only if all the eigenvalues of $\mathbf{A}$ are within the unit circle on the complex plane.

A nonsingular change of state variables,

$$\mathbf{x}(k) = \mathbf{P}\mathbf{x}'(k); \qquad \mathbf{x}'(k) = \mathbf{P}^{-1}\mathbf{x}(k)$$

results in new state variable equations of the same form:

$$\mathbf{x}'(k + 1) = (\mathbf{P}^{-1}\mathbf{A}\mathbf{P})\mathbf{x}'(k) + (\mathbf{P}^{-1}\mathbf{B})\mathbf{u}(k) = \mathbf{A}'\mathbf{x}'(k) + \mathbf{B}'\mathbf{u}(k)$$

$$\mathbf{y}(k) = (\mathbf{C}\mathbf{P})\mathbf{x}'(k) + \mathbf{D}\mathbf{u}(k) = \mathbf{C}'\mathbf{x}'(k) + \mathbf{D}\mathbf{u}(k)$$

but no change in the $z$-transfer function matrix. Each different set of state variable equations having the same $z$-transfer function matrix is termed a realization of the $z$-transfer functions.

If the eigenvalues of $\mathbf{A}$ are distinct, there are changes of state variables for which

$$\Lambda = \mathbf{P}^{-1}\mathbf{A}\mathbf{P}$$

is diagonal, with the eigenvalues of $\mathbf{A}$ along the diagonal. The state equations are then decoupled from one another. Each equation involves only one state variable. Each equation's zero-input response is a geometric sequence that is termed a mode of the system. The zero-input part of every system output is a linear combination of the modes.

Finding a diagonalizing transformation is the characteristic value problem of linear algebra, which was developed in Section 3.4. Also discussed in that section was the related Cayley-Hamilton theorem: an $n \times n$ matrix $\mathbf{A}$ satisfies its own characteristic equation. This means that $\mathbf{A}^n$ and any higher powers of $\mathbf{A}$ can be expressed as a linear combination of $\mathbf{A}^{n-1}, \mathbf{A}^{n-2}, \ldots, \mathbf{A}^0 = \mathbf{I}$.

When a system's state coupling matrix $\mathbf{A}$ has repeated eigenvalues, a change of state variables will place it in upper block Jordan form where, for a repeated eigenvalue $\lambda_i$, a block of the following form occurs:

$$
\mathbf{A} = \begin{bmatrix} \ddots & & & & \\ & \lambda_i & 1 & 0 & \cdots \\ & 0 & \lambda_i & 1 & \\ & 0 & 0 & \lambda_i & \\ & & \vdots & & \\ & & & & \ddots \end{bmatrix}
$$

The corresponding modes are $(\lambda_i)^k$, $k(\lambda_i)^k$, $k^2(\lambda_i)^k, \ldots$ and so on.

Structural properties are especially apparent when a system is in diagonal or block diagonal form. If, in diagonal form, there is no coupling to one of the state equations from any input, the mode associated with that equation cannot be affected by any input and is said to be uncontrollable. Similarly, modes are unobservable if they do not couple to any output. For repeated eigenvalues, if all repetitions of an eigenvalue are in the same upper Jordan block, there must be coupling of an input to the last state variable of the block for controllability of all the block's modes. There must be coupling to an output of the first state variable of the block for observability of all the block's modes. As discussed, if the same eigenvalue occurs in more than one block, the situation can be more complicated.

In the concluding sections of the chapter, the change of state variables that take a completely controllable single-input system to controllable form was derived. Then the change of variables that transforms a completely observable single-output system to observable form was found.

# REFERENCES

Discrete-time state equations are discussed in many other books, including

J. A. Cadzow, *Discrete-Time Systems*. Englewood Cliffs, NJ: Prentice-Hall, 1973;

D. G. Luenberger, *Introduction to Dynamic Systems*. New York: Wiley, 1979;

and as part of texts on control system design such as

H. F. VanLandingham, *Introduction to Digital Control Systems*. New York: Macmillan, 1985.

The characteristic value problem is discussed in greater detail in

E. A. Guillemin, *The Mathematics of Circuit Analysis*. New York: McGraw-Hill, 1949;

R. Bellman, *Introduction to Matrix Analysis*. New York: McGraw-Hill, 1960;

G. Strang, *Linear Algebra and It's Applications*, 2nd edition, New York: Academic Press, 1980.

Key papers on observability and controllability include

R. E. Kalman, "Canonical Structure of Linear Dynamical Systems," *Proc. Nat. Acad. Sci.*, Vol. 48, no. 4, April 1962, pp. 596–600;

and

E. G. Gilbert, "Controllability and Observability in Multivariable Control Systems," *J. Soc. Ind. Appl. Math.*, ser. A, Vol. 1 1963, pp. 128–51;

Extensive discussions of the concepts, particularly in connection with continuous-time systems, can be found in

T. Kailath, *Linear Systems*. Englewood Cliffs, NJ: Prentice-Hall, 1980.

The transformations to controllable and observable forms used here are based on those proposed by

W. G. Tuel, Jr., "On the Transformation to (Phase-Variable) Canonical Form," *IEEE Trans. Automatic Control*, Vol. AC-11, April 1966, pp. 300–303

and

D. S. Rane, "A Simplified Transformation to (Phase-Variable) Canonical Form," *IEEE Trans. Automatic Control*, Vol. AC-11, July 1966, p. 608.

## CHAPTER THREE PROBLEMS

**3-1.**  Sketch a delay diagram for the system with state equations

$$
\begin{bmatrix} x_1(k+1) \\ x_2(k+1) \\ x_3(k+1) \end{bmatrix} = \begin{bmatrix} 2 & 0 & 1 \\ 0 & -3 & 4 \\ 1 & 1 & 0 \end{bmatrix} \begin{bmatrix} x_1(k) \\ x_2(k) \\ x_3(k) \end{bmatrix} + \begin{bmatrix} -2 \\ 0 \\ 5 \end{bmatrix} u(k)
$$

$$
y(k) = \begin{bmatrix} 3 & -3 & 0 \end{bmatrix} \begin{bmatrix} x_1(k) \\ x_2(k) \\ x_3(k) \end{bmatrix} - 2u(k)
$$

Use Mason's gain rule to find the system's $z$-transfer function.

**3-2.** Draw a delay diagram for a one-input, two-output system, in controllable form, with z-transfer functions

$$T_1(z) = \frac{2z^2 + 3z - 4}{z^3 + z^2 - z + 4}$$

$$T_2(z) = \frac{-3z^3}{z^3 + z^2 - z + 4}$$

Find state variable equations for this system.

**3-3.** Draw a delay diagram for a two-input, one-output system, in observable form, with z-transfer functions

$$T_1(z) = \frac{-2z^2 + 5z - 1}{z^3 - 2z^2 + z - 3}$$

$$T_2(z) = \frac{4z^3 + 3}{z^3 - 2z^2 + z - 3}$$

Find state variable equations for this system.

**3-4.** Given the following block diagram for a discrete-time system, find a state variable representation for the system.

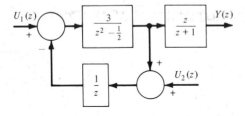

**3-5.** For the system

$$\begin{bmatrix} x_1(k+1) \\ x_2(k+1) \\ x_3(k+1) \end{bmatrix} = \begin{bmatrix} -1 & 0 & 0 \\ 4 & 1 & 2 \\ 1 & -5 & 3 \end{bmatrix} \begin{bmatrix} x_1(k) \\ x_2(k) \\ x_3(k) \end{bmatrix} + \begin{bmatrix} 2 \\ -1 \\ 0 \end{bmatrix} u(k)$$

$$y(k) = \begin{bmatrix} 1 & 1 & 3 \end{bmatrix} \begin{bmatrix} x_1(k) \\ x_2(k) \\ x_3(k) \end{bmatrix}$$

find the state vectors and outputs, $x(1)$, $x(2)$, $x(3)$, $y(1)$, $y(2)$, $y(3)$ if

$$x(0) = \begin{bmatrix} -1 \\ 2 \\ 4 \end{bmatrix}$$

and

$$u(k) = 2 - 3\delta(k)$$

**3-6.**   Find the z-transform of the state and output of the system of Problem 3-5.

**3-7.**   Find the z-transfer function matrix of the following system:

$$\begin{bmatrix} x_1(k+1) \\ x_2(k+1) \\ x_3(k+1) \end{bmatrix} = \begin{bmatrix} 3 & 0 & 0 \\ 0 & 2 & 1 \\ 0 & -1 & 0 \end{bmatrix} \begin{bmatrix} x_1(k) \\ x_2(k) \\ x_3(k) \end{bmatrix} + \begin{bmatrix} -3 & 0 \\ 0 & -1 \\ 4 & 0 \end{bmatrix} \begin{bmatrix} u_1(k) \\ u_2(k) \end{bmatrix}$$

$$\begin{bmatrix} y_1(k) \\ y_2(k) \end{bmatrix} = \begin{bmatrix} 0 & 0 & -2 \\ 1 & 0 & 0 \end{bmatrix} \begin{bmatrix} x_1(k) \\ x_2(k) \\ x_3(k) \end{bmatrix} + \begin{bmatrix} 2 & 3 \\ 0 & 0 \end{bmatrix} \begin{bmatrix} u_1(k) \\ u_2(k) \end{bmatrix}$$

**3-8.**   For the system of Problem 3-7, make the change of state variables

$$\mathbf{x}' = \begin{bmatrix} 3 & -1 & 0 \\ -2 & 1 & 0 \\ 0 & 0 & 2 \end{bmatrix} \mathbf{x}$$

and find the state and output equations in terms of $\mathbf{x}'$.

**3-9.**   Find the eigenvalues of the following matrices. For which of these matrices does an inverse exist?

a. $\begin{bmatrix} -3 & 1 \\ -2 & 0 \end{bmatrix}$

b. $\begin{bmatrix} -3 & 1 & 0 \\ -3 & 0 & 1 \\ -1 & 0 & 0 \end{bmatrix}$

c. $\begin{bmatrix} 4 & -3 & 2 \\ 1 & 0 & -1 \\ 3 & -2 & 3 \end{bmatrix}$

**3-10.**  Find the characteristic equation, eigenvalues, eigenvectors and a modal matrix for each of the following matrices:

a. $\begin{bmatrix} 0 & -2 \\ 2 & 5 \end{bmatrix}$

b. $\begin{bmatrix} -3 & 1 & 0 \\ -2 & 0 & 1 \\ 0 & 0 & 0 \end{bmatrix}$

c. $\begin{bmatrix} 2 & 0 & -1 \\ 0 & -3 & 2 \\ 0 & 0 & 1 \end{bmatrix}$

d. $\begin{bmatrix} -2 & 3 \\ 1 & 4 \end{bmatrix}$

e. $\begin{bmatrix} -4 & -3 & 0 \\ 1 & 0 & 0 \\ 0 & 1 & 0 \end{bmatrix}$

**3-11.** For the following matrices, find a modal matrix **P** and the corresponding spectral matrix $\Lambda$. Verify that $\mathbf{P}^{-1}\mathbf{AP} = \Lambda$.

a. $\begin{bmatrix} 0 & 0 \\ 0 & -2 \end{bmatrix}$

b. $\begin{bmatrix} 1 & 2 \\ -1 & 4 \end{bmatrix}$

c. $\begin{bmatrix} 4 & -3 & 0 \\ 1 & 0 & 0 \\ 0 & 0 & 0 \end{bmatrix}$

d. $\begin{bmatrix} 0 & 1 & 4 \\ 1 & 0 & -1 \\ 0 & 0 & -6 \end{bmatrix}$

e. $\begin{bmatrix} 1 & 2 \\ -2 & 1 \end{bmatrix}$

**3-12.** For the matrix

$$\mathbf{A} = \begin{bmatrix} 0 & 1 & 0 \\ 0 & 0 & 1 \\ 2 & -1 & 4 \end{bmatrix}$$

express the matrix polynomial

$$\mathbf{A}^4 + 2\mathbf{A}^3 + \mathbf{A}^2 - \mathbf{A} + 3\mathbf{I}$$

in terms of $\mathbf{A}^2$, $\mathbf{A}$ and $\mathbf{I}$.

**3-13.** For any nonsingular matrix **A** with distinct eigenvalues, one can find $\mathbf{A}^{-1}$ by diagonalizing **A**

$$\mathbf{P}^{-1}\mathbf{AP} = \begin{bmatrix} \lambda_1 & 0 & \cdots \\ 0 & \lambda_2 & \\ \vdots & & \ddots \end{bmatrix}$$

using

$$P^{-1}(A^{-1})P = R = \begin{bmatrix} \left(\dfrac{1}{\lambda_1}\right) & 0 & \cdots \\ 0 & \left(\dfrac{1}{\lambda_2}\right) & \\ \vdots & & \ddots \end{bmatrix}$$

and forming

$$A^{-1} = PRP^{-1}$$

Use this method to find the inverse of

$$A = \begin{bmatrix} -2 & 1 & 0 \\ 1 & 0 & 1 \\ 2 & 0 & 0 \end{bmatrix}$$

**3-14.** Find diagonal state equations for a two-input, one output system with $z$-transfer functions

$$T_1(z) = \frac{z^2 + z + 2}{z^3 - \frac{1}{4}z}$$

$$T_2(z) = \frac{4z - 3}{z^3 - \frac{1}{4}z}$$

**3-15.** Find a transformation matrix $P$ in

$$x = Px'; \qquad x' = P^{-1}x$$

that takes the system

$$\begin{bmatrix} x_1(k+1) \\ x_2(k+1) \\ x_3(k+1) \end{bmatrix} = \begin{bmatrix} -5 & 1 & 0 \\ -6 & 0 & 1 \\ 0 & 0 & 0 \end{bmatrix} \begin{bmatrix} x_1(k) \\ x_2(k) \\ x_3(k) \end{bmatrix} + \begin{bmatrix} 3 & 0 \\ 0 & 0 \\ 1 & -1 \end{bmatrix} \begin{bmatrix} u_1(k) \\ u_2(k) \end{bmatrix}$$

$$\begin{bmatrix} y_1(k) \\ y_2(k) \end{bmatrix} = \begin{bmatrix} 1 & 2 & 0 \\ 0 & -1 & 0 \end{bmatrix} \begin{bmatrix} x_1(k) \\ x_2(k) \\ x_3(k) \end{bmatrix} + \begin{bmatrix} 2 & -1 \\ 0 & 0 \end{bmatrix} \begin{bmatrix} u_1(k) \\ u_2(k) \end{bmatrix}$$

into a diagonal form. Find the new state equations in terms of $x'$.

**3-16.** Find a set of diagonal state equations for a single-input, single-output system with $z$-transfer function

$$T(z) = \frac{-3z^2 - 2z + 1}{z^3 + z^2 + \frac{1}{2}z}$$

Then find an alternative block diagonal representation that does not involve complex numbers.

**3-17.** Find a transformation matrix **P** in

$$\mathbf{x} = \mathbf{P}\mathbf{x}'; \qquad \mathbf{x}' = \mathbf{P}^{-1}\mathbf{x}$$

that takes the system with complex eigenvalues

$$\begin{bmatrix} x_1(k+1) \\ x_2(k+1) \end{bmatrix} = \begin{bmatrix} -2 & -1 \\ 1 & -2 \end{bmatrix} \begin{bmatrix} x_1(k) \\ x_2(k) \end{bmatrix} + \begin{bmatrix} 1 \\ -3 \end{bmatrix} u(k)$$

$$y(k) = \begin{bmatrix} 3 & 0 \end{bmatrix} \begin{bmatrix} x_1(k) \\ x_2(k) \end{bmatrix} + u(k)$$

into diagonal form. Find the new state equations in terms of $\mathbf{x}'$.

**3-18.** Find a set of block Jordan state equations for a single-input, two-output system with $z$-transfer functions

$$T_1(z) = \frac{z^2 + 4z - 3}{z^3 - z^2 + \frac{1}{4}z}$$

$$T_2(z) = \frac{6z^3 - 3z^2 + 4}{z^3 - z^2 + \frac{1}{4}z}$$

**3-19.** Find a transformation matrix **P** in

$$\mathbf{x} = \mathbf{P}\mathbf{x}'; \qquad \mathbf{x}' = \mathbf{P}^{-1}\mathbf{x}$$

that takes the system with repeated eigenvalues

$$\begin{bmatrix} x_1(k+1) \\ x_2(k+1) \\ x_3(k+1) \end{bmatrix} = \begin{bmatrix} 0 & 1 & 0 \\ 0 & 0 & 1 \\ \frac{1}{8} & -\frac{3}{4} & \frac{3}{2} \end{bmatrix} \begin{bmatrix} x_1(k) \\ x_2(k) \\ x_3(k) \end{bmatrix} + \begin{bmatrix} 1 \\ 0 \\ -1 \end{bmatrix} u(k)$$

$$y(k) = \begin{bmatrix} 2 & 2 & 1 \end{bmatrix} \begin{bmatrix} x_1(k) \\ x_2(k) \\ x_3(k) \end{bmatrix} - 2u(k)$$

into a block Jordan form.

3-20. Show that for a system with distinct eigenvalues, the eigenvectors of the state coupling matrix are the initial states for which the amplitudes of all but one of the modes in the zero-input response are zero. That is, initial conditions equal to an eigenvector excite only a single zero-input mode, the one associated with the corresponding eigenvalue. Then, for the system

$$\begin{bmatrix} x_1(k+1) \\ x_2(k+1) \\ x_3(k+1) \end{bmatrix} = \begin{bmatrix} -\frac{1}{2} & 1 & 0 \\ \frac{1}{2} & 0 & 1 \\ 0 & 0 & 0 \end{bmatrix} \begin{bmatrix} x_1(k) \\ x_2(k) \\ x_3(k) \end{bmatrix} = \mathbf{A}\mathbf{x}(k)$$

determine nonzero initial conditions $\mathbf{x}(0)$ such that only the $(\frac{1}{2})^k$ mode is excited.

3-21. Determine whether the following system is completely controllable and whether it is completely observable by transforming it into a diagonal form:

$$\begin{bmatrix} x_1(k+1) \\ x_2(k+1) \\ x_3(k+1) \end{bmatrix} = \begin{bmatrix} 4 & -6 & 0 \\ 3 & -5 & 0 \\ 0 & 0 & -1 \end{bmatrix} \begin{bmatrix} x_1(k) \\ x_2(k) \\ x_3(k) \end{bmatrix} + \begin{bmatrix} 2 & -2 \\ 1 & -1 \\ 2 & 0 \end{bmatrix} \begin{bmatrix} u_1(k) \\ u_2(k) \end{bmatrix}$$

$$y(k) = \begin{bmatrix} -3 & 6 & 1 \end{bmatrix} \begin{bmatrix} x_1(k) \\ x_2(k) \\ x_3(k) \end{bmatrix} + \begin{bmatrix} 3 & 0 \end{bmatrix} \begin{bmatrix} u_1(k) \\ u_2(k) \end{bmatrix}$$

Identify any uncontrollable and/or unobservable modes.

3-22. For each of the following systems, find the transformation matrix $\mathbf{P}$ in

$$\mathbf{x} = \mathbf{P}\mathbf{x}'; \qquad \mathbf{x}' = \mathbf{P}^{-1}\mathbf{x}$$

that takes the system into the controllable form. Find the new state equations in terms of $\mathbf{x}'$.

a.  $$\begin{bmatrix} x_1(k+1) \\ x_2(k+1) \end{bmatrix} = \begin{bmatrix} 3 & -1 \\ 2 & -1 \end{bmatrix} \begin{bmatrix} x_1(k) \\ x_2(k) \end{bmatrix} + \begin{bmatrix} 0 \\ 3 \end{bmatrix} u(k)$$

$$y(k) = \begin{bmatrix} -2 & 1 \end{bmatrix} \begin{bmatrix} x_1(k) \\ x_2(k) \end{bmatrix} - u(k)$$

b.  $$\begin{bmatrix} x_1(k+1) \\ x_2(k+1) \\ x_3(k+1) \end{bmatrix} = \begin{bmatrix} -2 & 1 & 1 \\ 0 & 2 & -1 \\ 0 & 1 & 3 \end{bmatrix} \begin{bmatrix} x_1(k) \\ x_2(k) \\ x_3(k) \end{bmatrix} + \begin{bmatrix} 1 \\ 0 \\ -1 \end{bmatrix} u(k)$$

$$\begin{bmatrix} y_1(k) \\ y_2(k) \end{bmatrix} = \begin{bmatrix} 2 & 0 & 1 \\ 0 & -2 & 4 \end{bmatrix} \begin{bmatrix} x_1(k) \\ x_2(k) \\ x_3(k) \end{bmatrix} + \begin{bmatrix} -3 \\ 5 \end{bmatrix} u(k)$$

**3-23.** For each of the following systems, find the transformation matrix $\mathbf{P}$ in

$$\mathbf{x} = \mathbf{Px'}; \qquad \mathbf{x'} = \mathbf{P}^{-1}\mathbf{x}$$

that takes the system into the observable form. Find the new state equations in terms of $\mathbf{x'}$.

**a.**
$$\begin{bmatrix} x_1(k+1) \\ x_2(k+1) \end{bmatrix} = \begin{bmatrix} 1 & 1 \\ -2 & -3 \end{bmatrix} \begin{bmatrix} x_1(k) \\ x_2(k) \end{bmatrix} + \begin{bmatrix} 2 & -1 \\ 0 & 1 \end{bmatrix} \begin{bmatrix} u_1(k) \\ u_2(k) \end{bmatrix}$$

$$y(k) = \begin{bmatrix} 3 & 2 \end{bmatrix} \begin{bmatrix} x_1(k) \\ x_2(k) \end{bmatrix} + \begin{bmatrix} 4 & 0 \end{bmatrix} \begin{bmatrix} u_1(k) \\ u_2(k) \end{bmatrix}$$

**b.**
$$\begin{bmatrix} x_1(k+1) \\ x_2(k+1) \\ x_3(k+1) \end{bmatrix} = \begin{bmatrix} -2 & 2 & 0 \\ -1 & 3 & 0 \\ 1 & 0 & 1 \end{bmatrix} \begin{bmatrix} x_1(k) \\ x_2(k) \\ x_3(k) \end{bmatrix} + \begin{bmatrix} 3 \\ 4 \\ -2 \end{bmatrix} u(k)$$

$$y(k) = \begin{bmatrix} 0 & -2 & 1 \end{bmatrix} \begin{bmatrix} x_1(k) \\ x_2(k) \\ x_3(k) \end{bmatrix} + u(k)$$

# Discrete-Time Observation, Control and Feedback

4

## 4.1 Preview

Feedback control involves determining something about the plant state from plant outputs and using this information to generate control inputs that force the plant to behave in a desired way. It is the use of plant outputs that forms a *feedback* system. For a plant with a known model, the plant state summarizes everything there is presently to know about the plant, so the most information that can be derived from the outputs is the state of the plant. This is not to say that it is necessary to determine the plant state in order to do good feedback control, but if we are able to do so, all possible relevant information about the plant is available for generating the control. Similarly, one can do no more than to control a plant's state. We may or may not need to control the entire state of a plant, but if we are able to do so, then we are able to control the plant to any lesser degree also.

In this chapter, methods are developed for the determination of the state of a completely observable plant from its outputs and inputs for a finite number of steps. This leads naturally to the use of least squares methods when more than the minimum amount of measurement data is available. A brief introduction is given to plant parameter identification, for which least squares is also very useful. Similar methods are then developed for driving a completely controllable plant through its inputs to a given desired state in a finite number of steps. Optimal control, when more than the minimal number of input steps are available for the control, is then introduced.

When a completely controllable plant's state is available for feedback, it is always possible to place the feedback system eigenvalues at any locations selected by the designer. This important result is derived and a number of illustrative design examples are given. When the plant state is not available for feedback, arbitrary feedback system eigenvalue placement using output feedback alone might not be possible. This situation is discussed in the last section of this chapter and is to be considered further in the next chapter.

# 4.2 Observability and State Observation

Observability was defined in Chapter 3 in terms of the coupling of modes to plant outputs. Complete observability also means that the state of a plant can be determined from a finite number of its most recent inputs and outputs. That is the subject of this section. Determining the state of a plant from its inputs and outputs is an important capability in control system design because in some situations it is necessary (or at least convenient) to know the actual state in order to effectively control that state. In the process of learning how to calculate the state of a plant from input and output measurements, we develop the observability matrix rank test.

### 4.2.1 Observability and the Rank Test

If a discrete-time system is completely observable, its state $x(k)$, at any specific step $k$ can be determined from the system model and a finite number of steps of its inputs and outputs, starting at step $k$. For a step-invariant system, if it is possible to determine the state at any step, say $x(0)$, then with a shift of step, the state at any other step can be determined in the same way.

For a system

$$x(k + 1) = Ax(k) + Bu(k)$$

$$y(k) = Cx(k) + Du(k)$$

the initial state $x(0)$ is, in terms of the outputs and inputs, given by

$$
\begin{cases}
y(0) = Cx(0) + Du(0) \\
y(1) = Cx(1) + Du(1) = CAx(0) + CBu(0) + Du(1) \\
y(2) = Cx(2) + Du(2) = CA^2x(0) + CABu(0) + CBu(1) + Du(2) \\
\quad \vdots \\
y(n - 1) = Cx(n - 1) + Du(n - 1) \\
\qquad = CA^{n-1}x(0) + CA^{n-2}Bu(0) + CA^{n-3}Bu(1) + \cdots + CBu(n - 2) \\
\qquad + Du(n - 1)
\end{cases}
$$

Collecting the $\mathbf{x}(0)$ terms on the left:

$$
\begin{cases}
\mathbf{Cx}(0) = \mathbf{y}(0) - \mathbf{Du}(0) \\
\mathbf{CAx}(0) = \mathbf{y}(1) - \mathbf{CBu}(0) - \mathbf{Du}(1) \\
\mathbf{CA}^2\mathbf{x}(0) = \mathbf{y}(2) - \mathbf{CABu}(0) - \mathbf{CBu}(1) - \mathbf{Du}(2) \\
\quad\vdots \\
\mathbf{CA}^{n-1}\mathbf{x}(0) = \mathbf{y}(n-1) - \mathbf{CA}^{n-2}\mathbf{Bu}(0) - \cdots - \mathbf{CBu}(n-2) - \mathbf{Du}(n-1)
\end{cases}
$$

This set of linear algebraic equations can be solved for $\mathbf{x}(0)$ only if the array of coefficients

$$
\mathbf{M}_0 = \begin{bmatrix}
\mathbf{C} \\
\hline
\mathbf{CA} \\
\hline
\mathbf{CA}^2 \\
\hline
\vdots \\
\hline
\mathbf{CA}^{n-1}
\end{bmatrix}
$$

is of full rank. Additional outputs are of no help, since they yield additional equations with coefficients $\mathbf{CA}^n$, $\mathbf{CA}^{n+1}, \ldots$, which by the Cayley-Hamilton theorem can be expressed in terms of a linear combination of $\mathbf{A}^{n-1}$ and lower powers of $\mathbf{A}$. Additional equations are thus linear combinations of those already considered.*

For a multiple-output system, the smallest integer $v$ for which

$$
\mathbf{M}_0(v) = \begin{bmatrix}
\mathbf{C} \\
\hline
\mathbf{CA} \\
\hline
\mathbf{CA}^2 \\
\hline
\vdots \\
\hline
\mathbf{CA}^{v-1}
\end{bmatrix}
$$

has full rank is termed the *observability index* of the system. It is the minimum number of steps required to determine the system state.

---

*There are special cases for which the state of a system *after the initial step $k$* can be determined from system inputs and outputs even when $\mathbf{M}_0$ is singular. For example, if $\mathbf{A} = \mathbf{0}$ then $\mathbf{x}(k)$ might not be determinable from the plant inputs and outputs beginning with step $k$, but $\mathbf{x}(k+1) = \mathbf{Bu}(k)$. That is, it might be possible to find $\mathbf{x}(k+1)$ or the state at some later step using *previous* inputs and outputs. Because of this possibility, some authors use the term *observability* more loosely, allowing the use of input and output data from before step $k$ to find $\mathbf{x}(k)$. The term *constructability* is then used for the more stringent definition. System modes should then probably be classified as "constructable" and "unconstructable" instead of "observable" and "unobservable." There is no distinction between the two definitions when $\mathbf{A}$ is nonsingular.

## 4.2.2 Observing Single-Output Systems

The state of a completely observable $n$th order single-output system

$$\mathbf{x}(k + 1) = \mathbf{A}\mathbf{x}(k) + \mathbf{B}\mathbf{u}(k)$$

$$y(k) = \mathbf{c}^\dagger\mathbf{x}(k) + \mathbf{d}^\dagger\mathbf{u}(k) \tag{4-1}$$

can always be found at any step $i$ from its outputs and inputs at steps $i$ through $i + n - 1$. The resulting $n$ simultaneous equations in the $n$ unknown components of the state $\mathbf{x}(i)$

$$\begin{cases} y(i) = \mathbf{c}^\dagger\mathbf{x}(i) + \mathbf{d}^\dagger\mathbf{u}(i) \\ y(i + 1) = \mathbf{c}^\dagger[\mathbf{A}\mathbf{x}(i) + \mathbf{B}\mathbf{u}(i)] + \mathbf{d}^\dagger\mathbf{u}(i + 1) \\ \vdots \\ y(i + n - 1) = \mathbf{c}^\dagger[\mathbf{A}^{n-1}\mathbf{x}(i) + \mathbf{A}\mathbf{B}\mathbf{u}(i) + \mathbf{A}^2\mathbf{B}\mathbf{u}(i - 1) + \cdots \\ \qquad\qquad\qquad + \mathbf{B}\mathbf{u}(i + n - 2)] + \mathbf{d}^\dagger\mathbf{u}(i + n - 1) \end{cases} \tag{4-2}$$

have a unique solution whenever the system's observability matrix (which is $n \times n$ for a single-output system) is nonsingular.

Once $\mathbf{x}(i)$ is known, the state equation 4-1 can be used to find $\mathbf{x}(i + 1)$, $\mathbf{x}(i + 2), \ldots, \mathbf{x}(i + n)$. If the input is also known at step $i + n$ and perhaps beyond, the state equation can also be used to find $\mathbf{x}(i + n + 1)$ and so on. If the input is known at step $i - 1$ and perhaps further backward in step, the state equation can be used as

$$\mathbf{x}(k) = \mathbf{A}^{-1}[\mathbf{x}(k + 1) - \mathbf{B}\mathbf{u}(k)]$$

to solve for the state at steps prior to step $i$ if $\mathbf{A}$ is nonsingular.

As a numerical example, consider the single-output system

$$\begin{bmatrix} x_1(k + 1) \\ x_2(k + 1) \\ x_3(k + 1) \end{bmatrix} = \begin{bmatrix} 2 & -1 & 1 \\ 0 & 1 & 3 \\ -2 & 0 & 1 \end{bmatrix} \begin{bmatrix} x_1(k) \\ x_2(k) \\ x_3(k) \end{bmatrix} + \begin{bmatrix} 3 \\ 1 \\ 0 \end{bmatrix} u(k) = \mathbf{A}\mathbf{x}(k) + \mathbf{b}u(k)$$

$$y(k) = \begin{bmatrix} 0 & 2 & -1 \end{bmatrix} \begin{bmatrix} x_1(k) \\ x_2(k) \\ x_3(k) \end{bmatrix} + 2u(k) = \mathbf{c}^\dagger\mathbf{x}(k) + 2u(k)$$

Suppose that

$$y(0) = 8; \quad y(1) = 5; \quad y(2) = -4;$$

$$u(0) = 3; \quad u(1) = 0; \quad u(2) = -2$$

and that it is desired to find $\mathbf{x}(0)$ from these. Then

$$y(0) = 8 = \mathbf{c}^t\mathbf{x}(0) + 2u(0) = [0 \quad 2 \quad -1]\begin{bmatrix} x_1(0) \\ x_2(0) \\ x_3(0) \end{bmatrix} + 2(3)$$

$$= 2x_2(0) - x_3(0) + 6$$

$$y(1) = 5 = \mathbf{c}^t\mathbf{A}\mathbf{x}(0) + \mathbf{c}^t\mathbf{b}u(0) + du(1)$$

$$= [0 \quad 2 \quad -1]\begin{bmatrix} 2 & -1 & 1 \\ 0 & 1 & 3 \\ -2 & 0 & 1 \end{bmatrix}\begin{bmatrix} x_1(0) \\ x_2(0) \\ x_3(0) \end{bmatrix}$$

$$+ [0 \quad 2 \quad -1]\begin{bmatrix} 3 \\ 1 \\ 0 \end{bmatrix}(3) + 2(0)$$

$$= 2x_1(0) + 2x_2(0) + 5x_3(0) + 6$$

$$y(2) = -4 = \mathbf{c}^t\mathbf{A}^2\mathbf{x}(0) + \mathbf{c}^t\mathbf{A}\mathbf{b}u(0) + \mathbf{c}^t\mathbf{b}u(1) + du(2)$$

$$= [2 \quad 2 \quad 5]\begin{bmatrix} 2 & -1 & 1 \\ 0 & 1 & 3 \\ -2 & 0 & 1 \end{bmatrix}\begin{bmatrix} x_1(0) \\ x_2(0) \\ x_3(0) \end{bmatrix}$$

$$+ [2 \quad 2 \quad 5]\begin{bmatrix} 3 \\ 1 \\ 0 \end{bmatrix}(3) + 2(0) + 2(-2)$$

$$= -6x_1(0) + 13x_3(0) + 20$$

Solving these equations for $\mathbf{x}(0)$

$$\begin{cases} 2x_2(0) - x_3(0) = 2 \\ 2x_1(0) + 2x_2(0) + 5x_3(0) = -1 \\ 6x_1(0) + 13x_3(0) = -24 \end{cases}$$

$$\begin{bmatrix} x_1(0) \\ x_2(0) \\ x_3(0) \end{bmatrix} = \begin{bmatrix} \frac{105}{62} \\ \frac{29}{62} \\ -\frac{66}{62} \end{bmatrix}$$

From $\mathbf{x}(0)$ and the inputs, $\mathbf{x}(1)$, $\mathbf{x}(2)$, and $\mathbf{x}(3)$ can now be found also, if desired:

$$\mathbf{x}(1) = \mathbf{A}\mathbf{x}(0) + \mathbf{b}u(0) = \begin{bmatrix} \frac{673}{62} \\ \frac{17}{62} \\ -\frac{276}{62} \end{bmatrix}$$

$$\mathbf{x}(2) = \mathbf{A}\mathbf{x}(1) + \mathbf{b}u(1) = \begin{bmatrix} \frac{1053}{62} \\ -\frac{811}{62} \\ -\frac{1622}{62} \end{bmatrix}$$

$$\mathbf{x}(3) = \mathbf{A}\mathbf{x}(2) + \mathbf{b}u(2) = \begin{bmatrix} \frac{923}{62} \\ -\frac{5801}{62} \\ -\frac{3728}{62} \end{bmatrix}$$

If, instead, this system's outputs and inputs for steps 4, 5, and 6 were known, then the state at the first of these steps, $\mathbf{x}(4)$, would be found from

$$\begin{cases} y(4) = 8 = \mathbf{c}^\dagger\mathbf{x}(4) + du(4) \\ y(5) = 5 = \mathbf{c}^\dagger\mathbf{A}\mathbf{x}(4) + \mathbf{c}^\dagger\mathbf{b}u(4) + du(5) \\ y(6) = -4 = \mathbf{c}^\dagger\mathbf{A}^2\mathbf{x}(4) + \mathbf{c}^\dagger\mathbf{A}\mathbf{b}u(4) + \mathbf{c}^\dagger\mathbf{b}u(5) + du(6) \end{cases}$$

From $\mathbf{x}(4)$ and the inputs, $\mathbf{x}(5)$, $\mathbf{x}(6)$, and $\mathbf{x}(7)$ can be determined.

### 4.2.3 Observing Multiple-Output Systems

The outputs of a system are *linearly independent* if the rows of the output coupling matrix $\mathbf{C}$ are linearly independent of one another. Linearly dependent outputs are combinations of the other outputs and inputs, and so are of no help in observing a system's state because they do not contribute any linearly independent rows to the system's observability matrix. In practice there may be other reasons, such as improved reliability, for using linearly dependent outputs. However, for the present, we will assume that all outputs are linearly independent.

When multiple linearly independent outputs are available from an $n$th order system, the system's initial state can be determined from its inputs and outputs in less than $n$ steps, since each step yields more than one equation involving the $n$ components of the initial state. For example, in the two-output system

$$\begin{bmatrix} x_1(k+1) \\ x_2(k+1) \\ x_3(k+1) \end{bmatrix} = \begin{bmatrix} 0 & 0 & 2 \\ 1 & -1 & 0 \\ -2 & 0 & 1 \end{bmatrix} \begin{bmatrix} x_1(k) \\ x_2(k) \\ x_3(k) \end{bmatrix} + \begin{bmatrix} 1 \\ 0 \\ 4 \end{bmatrix} u(k) = \mathbf{A}\mathbf{x}(k) + \mathbf{b}u(k)$$

$$\begin{bmatrix} y_1(k) \\ y_2(k) \end{bmatrix} = \begin{bmatrix} 1 & 0 & 2 \\ -1 & 3 & 0 \end{bmatrix} \begin{bmatrix} x_1(k) \\ x_2(k) \\ x_3(k) \end{bmatrix} = \mathbf{C}\mathbf{x}(k) \qquad (4\text{-}3)$$

suppose that

$$y(0) = \begin{bmatrix} 4 \\ 5 \end{bmatrix}; \qquad y(1) = \begin{bmatrix} -7 \\ 2 \end{bmatrix}$$

and

$$u(k) = 1, \qquad k = 0, 1, 2, \ldots$$

Then

$$\begin{cases} y(0) = Cx(0) \\ y(1) = Cx(1) = C[Ax(0) + bu(0)] \end{cases}$$

or

$$\begin{cases} \begin{bmatrix} 4 \\ 5 \end{bmatrix} = \begin{bmatrix} 1 & 0 & 2 \\ -1 & 3 & 0 \end{bmatrix} \begin{bmatrix} x_1(0) \\ x_2(0) \\ x_3(0) \end{bmatrix} \\ \\ \begin{bmatrix} -7 \\ 2 \end{bmatrix} = \begin{bmatrix} -4 & 0 & 4 \\ 3 & -3 & -2 \end{bmatrix} \begin{bmatrix} x_1(0) \\ x_2(0) \\ x_3(0) \end{bmatrix} + \begin{bmatrix} 9 \\ -1 \end{bmatrix} \end{cases}$$

The two vector outputs then yield these four linear equations:

$$\begin{bmatrix} C \\ \hline CA \end{bmatrix} x(0) = \begin{bmatrix} 1 & 0 & 2 \\ -1 & 3 & 0 \\ -4 & 0 & 4 \\ 3 & -3 & -2 \end{bmatrix} \begin{bmatrix} x_1(0) \\ x_2(0) \\ x_3(0) \end{bmatrix} = \begin{bmatrix} 4 \\ 5 \\ -16 \\ 3 \end{bmatrix} \qquad (4\text{-}4)$$

The first three equations represented by (4-4)

$$\begin{bmatrix} 1 & 0 & 2 \\ -1 & 3 & 0 \\ -4 & 0 & 4 \end{bmatrix} \begin{bmatrix} x_1(0) \\ x_2(0) \\ x_3(0) \end{bmatrix} = \begin{bmatrix} 4 \\ 5 \\ -16 \end{bmatrix}$$

have the solution

$$x_1(0) = 4; \qquad x_2(0) = 3; \qquad x_3(0) = 0$$

The fourth equation of (4-4) is automatically satisfied.

### 4.2.4 Observability in Diagonal Form

When the concept of complete observability was first introduced in Chapter 3, our concern was with whether every system mode could be detected at the system's outputs. If not, the system state could not be determined from its inputs and outputs because an unobservable mode affects the state but not the outputs. The observability of each mode of a system is most apparent when the system is in diagonal form or, if its eigenvalues have repetitions, when it is in block Jordan form. Now we have another test for a system's complete observability, that of the rank of the observability matrix $\mathbf{M}_0$. The rank test is simpler than diagonalization, but it does not indicate which of the modes are unobservable. We now outline the relation between the two tests.

A nonsingular change of state variables

$$\mathbf{x} = \mathbf{P}\mathbf{x}'; \qquad \mathbf{x}' = \mathbf{P}^{-1}\mathbf{x}$$

$$\mathbf{A}' = \mathbf{P}^{-1}\mathbf{A}\mathbf{P}; \qquad \mathbf{C}' = \mathbf{C}\mathbf{P}$$

does not affect the rank of the observability matrix, since

$$\mathbf{M}_0' = \begin{bmatrix} \mathbf{C}' \\ \mathbf{C}'\mathbf{A}' \\ \mathbf{C}'\mathbf{A}'^2 \\ \vdots \\ \mathbf{C}'\mathbf{A}'^{m-1} \end{bmatrix} = \begin{bmatrix} \mathbf{C}\mathbf{P} \\ \mathbf{C}\mathbf{P}\mathbf{P}^{-1}\mathbf{A}\mathbf{P} \\ \mathbf{C}\mathbf{P}\mathbf{P}^{-1}\mathbf{A}^2\mathbf{P} \\ \vdots \\ \mathbf{C}\mathbf{P}\mathbf{P}^{-1}\mathbf{A}^{n-1}\mathbf{P} \end{bmatrix} = \begin{bmatrix} \mathbf{C} \\ \mathbf{C}\mathbf{A} \\ \mathbf{C}\mathbf{A}^2 \\ \vdots \\ \mathbf{C}\mathbf{A}^{n-1} \end{bmatrix} \mathbf{P} = \mathbf{M}_0\mathbf{P}$$

When a system with distinct eigenvalues is placed in a diagonal form, the state equations are decoupled from one another, each having the form

$$x_i'(k + 1) = \lambda_i x_i'(k) + \mathbf{b}_i'^\dagger \mathbf{u}(k)$$

where $\mathbf{b}_i'^\dagger$ is the $i$th row of the input coupling matrix $\mathbf{B}'$. The state signals have solutions of the form

$$x_i'(k) = (\lambda_i)^k x_i'(0) + \sum_{p=0}^{k-1} (\lambda_i)^{k-1-p}\mathbf{b}_i'^\dagger \mathbf{u}(p)$$

If there is no coupling of $x_i'$ to any of the system outputs, the initial condition $x_i'(0)$ cannot be determined from the system outputs and inputs. If, in diagonal form, the $i$th column of the output coupling matrix $\mathbf{C}'$ is zero, the $i$th column of the diagonal system's observability matrix

$$
\mathbf{M}_0' = \begin{bmatrix} \mathbf{C}' \\ \hline \mathbf{C}'\boldsymbol{\Lambda} \\ \hline \mathbf{C}'\boldsymbol{\Lambda}^2 \\ \hline \vdots \\ \hline \mathbf{C}'\boldsymbol{\Lambda}^{n-1} \end{bmatrix}
$$

will be zero, indicating that the system is not completely observable. If, in diagonal form, the output coupling matrix does not have any columns of zeros, the system is completely observable and the observability matrix will necessarily be of full rank. Whatever collection of decoupled state variables connect to some output $y_i$, the initial states of those signals can be determined from the inputs and that single output, since (because of the decoupling) that output could as well be the output of a system with only the connected modes present.

This analysis is extended to the case of repeated eigenvalues by considering the system to be in upper block Jordan form. It is straightforward but tedious to show that the observability matrix is of full rank only if all plant modes are observable.

Observability is an algebraic property of the matrices $\mathbf{A}$ and $\mathbf{C}$, independent of any state space interpretations. Thus it applies to the same algebraic problem for continuous-time systems: all modes of a continuous-time system are observable if and only if the observability matrix is of full rank.

## 4.3   Estimation and Identification

It often happens that more equations than the minimum number necessary to uniquely characterize a system are available to the designer. Slight errors in measurements generally result in an overdetermined set of equations that is (slightly) inconsistent. For a set of linear algebraic equations with $n$ unknowns, one solution method is to simply solve the first $n$ linearly independent and consistent equations and to ignore any additional equations. A better method is to make use of all the available equations and find an estimate $\hat{\mathbf{x}}$ that is a "best fit" to all the equations.

In this section, the least squares estimate is derived and is applied to state estimation. We also investigate parameter estimation, to which least squares methods also apply. Later, in Chapter 8 (concerning linear step-varying systems), recursive least squares algorithms are developed and applied.

## 4.3.1 Least Squares Solution

The basic least squares problem involves an overdetermined set of linear algebraic equations

$$\mathbf{Hx} = \mathbf{z}$$

where the matrix $\mathbf{H}$ is $m \times n$ and $m > n$. The equations are inconsistent and so have no solution, so we seek an approximate solution vector $\hat{\mathbf{x}}$ such that the sum of the squares of the errors between the actual knowns $\mathbf{z}$ and the knowns $\mathbf{H}\hat{\mathbf{x}}$ necessary for the equations to be consistent,

$$J(\hat{\mathbf{x}}) = (\mathbf{z} - \mathbf{H}\hat{\mathbf{x}})^{\dagger}(\mathbf{z} - \mathbf{H}\hat{\mathbf{x}}) = \mathbf{v}^{\dagger}\mathbf{v} = v_1^2 + v_2^2 + \cdots$$

is minimized. That is, an estimate $\hat{\mathbf{x}}$ is to be found such that in

$$\mathbf{H}\hat{\mathbf{x}} + \mathbf{v} = \mathbf{z}$$

the sum of squares of the elements of $\mathbf{v}$ is minimum. To find the minimum, the partial derivatives of $J$ with respect to each of the elements of $\hat{\mathbf{x}}$ are equated to zero:

$$\left(\frac{\partial J}{\partial \hat{\mathbf{x}}}\right)^{\dagger} = \begin{bmatrix} \dfrac{\partial J}{\partial \hat{x}_1} \\[2mm] \dfrac{\partial J}{\partial \hat{x}_2} \\[2mm] \vdots \\[2mm] \dfrac{\partial J}{\partial \hat{x}_n} \end{bmatrix} = -\mathbf{H}^{\dagger}(\mathbf{z} - \mathbf{H}\hat{\mathbf{x}}) = \mathbf{0}$$

Then

$$\mathbf{H}^{\dagger}\mathbf{H}\hat{\mathbf{x}} = \mathbf{H}^{\dagger}\mathbf{z}$$

$$\hat{\mathbf{x}} = (\mathbf{H}^{\dagger}\mathbf{H})^{-1}\mathbf{H}^{\dagger}\mathbf{z} \tag{4-5}$$

It can be shown that if $\mathbf{H}$ is of full rank, $(\mathbf{H}^{\dagger}\mathbf{H})^{-1}$ exists, and the estimate given by equation (4-5) is unique and a minimum. The least squares solution $\hat{\mathbf{x}}$ is a linear transformation of the known $\mathbf{z}$, which is to be expected because derivatives of quadratic functions are linear functions.

As a first-order example of a least-squares estimate, consider the three linear algebraic equations

$$\begin{cases} 3x = & 4.2 \\ -2x = & -3.3 \\ x = & 1.4 \end{cases}$$

which are of the form

$$\begin{bmatrix} 3 \\ -2 \\ 1 \end{bmatrix} x = \begin{bmatrix} 4.2 \\ -3.3 \\ 1.4 \end{bmatrix}$$

or

$$\mathbf{h}x = \mathbf{z}$$

These might represent three different measurements of the altitude of an aircraft, each possibly slightly in error. The least squares estimate of $x$ is

$$\hat{x} = (\mathbf{h^\dagger h})^{-1}\mathbf{h^\dagger z} = \left( \begin{bmatrix} 3 & -2 & 1 \end{bmatrix} \begin{bmatrix} 3 \\ -2 \\ 1 \end{bmatrix} \right)^{-1} \begin{bmatrix} 3 & -2 & 1 \end{bmatrix} \begin{bmatrix} 4.2 \\ -3.3 \\ 1.4 \end{bmatrix}$$

$$= (14)^{-1}(20.6) = 1.47$$

For the overdetermined equations

$$\begin{cases} 3x_1 - x_2 = -4 \\ 2x_1 + x_2 = 1 \\ x_1 - 2x_2 = -5 \\ 2x_1 + 2x_2 = 1 \end{cases}$$

which are of the form

$$\mathbf{Hx} = \begin{bmatrix} 3 & -1 \\ 2 & 1 \\ 1 & -2 \\ 2 & 2 \end{bmatrix} \begin{bmatrix} x_1 \\ x_2 \end{bmatrix} = \mathbf{z} = \begin{bmatrix} -4 \\ 1 \\ -5 \\ 1 \end{bmatrix}$$

the least squares estimate $\hat{\mathbf{x}}$ of the vector $\mathbf{x}$ is

$$\hat{\mathbf{x}} = (\mathbf{H}^{\dagger}\mathbf{H})^{-1}\mathbf{H}^{\dagger}\mathbf{z}$$

$$= \left( \begin{bmatrix} 3 & 2 & 1 & 2 \\ -1 & 1 & -2 & 2 \end{bmatrix} \begin{bmatrix} 3 & -1 \\ 2 & 1 \\ 1 & -2 \\ 2 & 2 \end{bmatrix} \right)^{-1} \begin{bmatrix} 3 & 2 & 1 & 2 \\ -1 & 1 & -2 & 2 \end{bmatrix} \begin{bmatrix} -4 \\ 1 \\ -5 \\ 1 \end{bmatrix}$$

$$= \begin{bmatrix} 18 & 1 \\ 1 & 10 \end{bmatrix}^{-1} \begin{bmatrix} -13 \\ 17 \end{bmatrix} = \frac{1}{179} \begin{bmatrix} 10 & -1 \\ -1 & 18 \end{bmatrix} \begin{bmatrix} -13 \\ 17 \end{bmatrix}$$

$$= \begin{bmatrix} -\frac{147}{179} \\ \frac{319}{179} \end{bmatrix} = \begin{bmatrix} -0.821 \\ 1.782 \end{bmatrix}$$

The estimate $\hat{\mathbf{x}}$ might be interpreted as the "most likely" value of the vector $\mathbf{x}$ to have produced a set of measurements, $\mathbf{z}$.

Karl Friedrich Gauss (1777–1855) invented the method of least squares estimation in 1795 and applied it to the calculation of planetary and comet orbits from telescopic measurement data. Six precise measurements would suffice to determine the six parameters of each orbit, but the individual measurements available were likely to be quite inaccurate. More than the minimum number of measurements were used, and the "best fit" to an orbit was found by minimizing the sum of squares of the parameter measurement errors. Adrien Marie Legendre (1707–1783) independently developed least squares estimation and was first to publish the method, in 1806.

### 4.3.2 State Estimation

In practice, one expects that measured plant outputs will contain slight errors, so that estimates of the plant state can likely be improved by using more than the minimum number of output measurements. If there are errors, however slight, in the outputs, the resulting overdetermined set of linear equations for the initial state will be inconsistent and will not have a solution. We can, however, seek the least squares estimate of the plant state.

Suppose that for the example state variable system of (4-3), the system outputs, which should be

$$\mathbf{y}(0) = \begin{bmatrix} 4 \\ 5 \end{bmatrix}; \quad \mathbf{y}(1) = \begin{bmatrix} -7 \\ 2 \end{bmatrix}$$

are measured with error as

$$\bar{\mathbf{y}}(0) = \begin{bmatrix} 4.5 \\ 4.8 \end{bmatrix}; \qquad \bar{\mathbf{y}}(1) = \begin{bmatrix} -6 \\ 2 \end{bmatrix}$$

The equations giving the system initial state from the measured outputs are, instead of (4-4):

$$\begin{bmatrix} 1 & 0 & 2 \\ -1 & 3 & 0 \\ -4 & 0 & 4 \\ 3 & -3 & -2 \end{bmatrix} \begin{bmatrix} x_1(0) \\ x_2(0) \\ x_3(0) \end{bmatrix} = \mathbf{Hx} = \begin{bmatrix} 4.5 \\ 4.8 \\ -15 \\ 3 \end{bmatrix} = \mathbf{z}$$

These are inconsistent and have no solution $\mathbf{x}(0)$. Their least squares estimate is

$$\hat{\mathbf{x}}(0) = (\mathbf{H}^\dagger \mathbf{H})^{-1} \mathbf{H}^\dagger \mathbf{z}$$

$$= \left( \begin{bmatrix} 1 & -1 & -4 & 3 \\ 0 & 3 & 0 & -3 \\ 2 & 0 & 4 & -2 \end{bmatrix} \begin{bmatrix} 1 & 0 & 2 \\ -1 & 3 & 0 \\ -4 & 0 & 4 \\ 3 & -3 & -2 \end{bmatrix} \right)^{-1} \times$$

$$\begin{bmatrix} 1 & -1 & -4 & 3 \\ 0 & 3 & 0 & -3 \\ 2 & 0 & 4 & -2 \end{bmatrix} \begin{bmatrix} 4.5 \\ 4.8 \\ -15 \\ 3 \end{bmatrix} = \begin{bmatrix} 27 & -12 & -20 \\ -12 & 18 & 6 \\ -20 & 6 & 24 \end{bmatrix}^{-1} \begin{bmatrix} 68.7 \\ 5.4 \\ -57 \end{bmatrix}$$

$$= \begin{bmatrix} 0.136 & 0.058 & 0.099 \\ 0.058 & 0.085 & 0.027 \\ 0.099 & 0.027 & 0.117 \end{bmatrix} \begin{bmatrix} 68.7 \\ 5.4 \\ -57.0 \end{bmatrix} = \begin{bmatrix} 4.011 \\ 2.893 \\ 0.244 \end{bmatrix}$$

### 4.3.3 Parameter Identification

Measurements of the input and the output of a system can also be used to determine the coefficients of the system's input-output equation(s) or, equivalently, the coefficients of the system transfer function(s). This is called *system identification*. It can be done to all or part of an existing plant to aid in developing a plant model before controller design is done. Or, it can be done as part of the control strategy in what is called *adaptive control*. In adaptive control, the plant is repetitively identified and the controller is changed if the measurements indicate that the plant has changed.

The input-output relations of a system are unchanged by any nonsingular change of state variables, so there are many state variable models that could account for the same data. Only the transfer functions or some equivalent set of unique parameters can be found from the system inputs and outputs. To convey the ideas involved without getting bogged down in notation for general equations, we will consider a specific system of relatively low order. It is straightforward to extend these results to higher-order systems, systems with multiple inputs and multiple outputs, and situations where some of the parameters are known.

A causal second-order single-input, single-output system has an input-output difference equation of the form

$$y(k + 2) + a_1 y(k + 1) + a_0 y(k) = b_2 u(k + 2) + b_1 u(k + 1) + b_0 u(k) \qquad (4-6)$$

If the initial conditions are zero so that the initial inputs $u(-1)$, $u(-2)$ and the initial outputs $y(-1)$, $y(-2)$ are zero, then

$$\begin{cases} y(0) = b_2 u(0) \\ y(1) = -a_1 y(0) + b_2 u(1) + b_1 u(0) \\ y(2) = -a_1 y(1) - a_0 y(0) + b_2 u(2) + b_1 u(1) + b_0 u(0) \\ y(3) = -a_1 y(2) - a_0 y(1) + b_2 u(3) + b_1 u(2) + b_0 u(1) \\ \vdots \end{cases}$$

Given the outputs $y$ and the inputs $u$, the first five of these equations can be solved for the five unknown system parameters $a_1$, $a_0$, $b_2$, $b_1$, and $b_0$. Any additional equations will then be automatically satisfied if the data and calculations are without error. For example, suppose that the initial conditions for the system described by equation (4-6) are zero and that the first five outputs and inputs are

$$\begin{aligned} y(0) &= \phantom{-}1; & u(0) &= \phantom{-}1 \\ y(1) &= \phantom{-}0; & u(1) &= -1 \\ y(2) &= \phantom{-}1; & u(2) &= \phantom{-}0 \\ y(3) &= \phantom{-}3; & u(3) &= \phantom{-}5 \\ y(4) &= -2; & u(4) &= -3 \end{aligned} \qquad (4-7)$$

Then

$$\begin{cases} y(0) = b_2 u(0) \\ y(1) = -a_1 y(0) + b_2 u(1) + b_1 u(0) \\ y(2) = -a_1 y(1) - a_0 y(0) + b_2 u(2) + b_1 u(1) + b_0 u(0) \\ y(3) = -a_1 y(2) - a_0 y(1) + b_2 u(3) + b_1 u(2) + b_0 u(1) \\ y(4) = -a_1 y(3) - a_0 y(2) + b_2 u(4) + b_1 u(3) + b_0 u(2) \end{cases}$$

or

$$
\begin{cases}
\phantom{-a_1} \quad\quad\quad b_2 \phantom{-b_1 +b_1} = 1 \\
-a_1 \phantom{aaaa} -b_2 +b_1 \phantom{aaaa} = 0 \\
\phantom{-a_1} -a_0 \phantom{aa} -b_1 +b_0 = 1 \\
-a_1 \phantom{aaa} +5b_2 \phantom{aa} -b_0 = 3 \\
-3a_1 -a_0 -3b_2 +5b_1 \phantom{aa} = -2
\end{cases}
$$

which has solution

$$a_1 = -1; \quad a_0 = 2$$

$$b_2 = 1; \quad\quad b_1 = 0; \quad\quad b_0 = 3$$

If the system initial conditions are not known, one must begin at a step where all the $y$'s and $u$'s are known. For the second-order example system (4-6), if the inputs and outputs are known beginning at step zero, those equations are

$$
\begin{cases}
y(2) = -a_1 y(1) - a_0 y(0) + b_2 u(2) + b_1 u(1) + b_0 u(0) \\
y(3) = -a_1 y(2) - a_0 y(1) + b_2 u(3) + b_1 u(2) + b_0 u(1) \\
y(4) = -a_1 y(3) - a_0 y(2) + b_2 u(4) + b_1 u(3) + b_0 u(2) \\
\quad \vdots
\end{cases}
$$

$$(4\text{-}8)$$

Five such equations are enough to find the five unknown parameters, but seven successive inputs and outputs are required. Suppose that for the example system, the initial conditions are not known, but the sixth and seventh outputs and inputs

$$y(5) = -1; \quad u(5) = 3$$

$$y(6) = -2; \quad u(6) = 4$$

are known in addition to the other five outputs and inputs listed in equations (4-7). Then the first five equations of (4-8) are

$$
\begin{cases}
y(2) = -a_1 y(1) - a_0 y(0) + b_2 u(2) + b_1 u(1) + b_0 u(0) \\
y(3) = -a_1 y(2) - a_0 y(1) + b_2 u(3) + b_1 u(2) + b_0 u(1) \\
y(4) = -a_1 y(3) - a_0 y(2) + b_2 u(4) + b_1 u(3) + b_0 u(2) \\
y(5) = -a_1 y(4) - a_0 y(3) + b_2 u(5) + b_1 u(4) + b_0 u(3) \\
y(6) = -a_1 y(5) - a_0 y(4) + b_2 u(6) + b_1 u(5) + b_0 u(4)
\end{cases}
$$

or

$$
\begin{bmatrix}
0 & -1 & 0 & -1 & 1 \\
-1 & 0 & 5 & 0 & -1 \\
-3 & -1 & -3 & 5 & 0 \\
2 & -3 & 3 & -3 & 5 \\
1 & 2 & 4 & 3 & -3
\end{bmatrix}
\begin{bmatrix}
a_1 \\ a_0 \\ b_2 \\ b_1 \\ b_0
\end{bmatrix}
=
\begin{bmatrix}
1 \\ 3 \\ -2 \\ -1 \\ -2
\end{bmatrix}
$$

which can be solved for $a_1$, $a_0$, $b_2$, $b_1$, and $b_0$.

It is possible that, for some input sequences, the equations for the system parameters are such that one or more parameters cannot be identified. The simplest examples of such sequences are ones that are identically zero or a constant, but there are usually other possible pathological sequences that can frustrate identification too. The common terminology is that identification is hampered if the input is not *persistently exciting*. Similarly, if a transfer function to be identified has a pole-zero cancellation, the coefficients associated with the cancellation can be found only if the initial conditions are such that the associated mode appears in the zero-input response component of the system output. Because of the cancellation, the mode does not appear in the zero-state response component.

If, as is often the case, the available system output and input data has small (but significant) errors, it is appropriate to use more than the minimum number of measurements necessary for parameter identification. Least squares estimates of the parameters from overdetermined equations is an especially simple and generally useful method.

### 4.3.4 Combined Parameter Identification and State Estimation

Once the independent parameters of a system have been identified, input and output measurements can also be used to determine the system's state. The parameters, once found, determine the unknown part of the state variable model, then the usual methods are applied to determine the state from input and output measurements. The same data can be used for both parameter identification and state estimation, if desired, and each can employ least squares estimation.

As a simple numerical example, consider a causal single-input, single-output second-order system with measured outputs and inputs as follows:

$$
\begin{aligned}
y(0) &= 2; & u(0) &= 1 \\
y(1) &= 1; & u(1) &= 2 \\
y(2) &= 5; & u(2) &= -1
\end{aligned}
$$

$$y(3) = -2; \quad u(3) = \quad 0$$
$$y(4) = \quad 0; \quad u(4) = -2$$
$$y(5) = -6; \quad u(5) = \quad 3$$
$$y(6) = \quad 7; \quad u(6) = \quad 4 \tag{4-9}$$

The input-output equation coefficients in

$$y(k + 2) = -a_1 y(k + 1) - a_0 y(k) + b_2 u(k + 2) + b_1 u(k + 1) + b_0 u(k)$$

satisfy

$$\begin{cases} -a_1 & -2a_0 & -b_2 & +2b_1 & +b_0 & = & 5 \\ -5a_1 & -a_0 & & -b_1 & +2b_0 & = & -2 \\ 2a_1 & -5a_0 & -2b_2 & & -b_0 & = & 0 \\ & 2a_0 & +3b_2 & -2b_1 & & = & -6 \\ 6a_1 & & +4b_2 & +3b_1 & -2b_0 & = & 7 \end{cases}$$

which has solution

$$a_1 = -1; \quad a_0 = 0;$$
$$b_2 = 0; \quad b_1 = 3; \quad b_0 = -2$$

The system's $z$-transfer function has thus been identified to be

$$T(z) = \frac{b_2 z^2 + b_1 z + b_0}{z^2 + a_1 z + a_0} = \frac{3z - 2}{z^2 - z}$$

If the state variable description of this system is in observable form, it must then be

$$\begin{bmatrix} x_1(k + 1) \\ x_2(k + 1) \end{bmatrix} = \begin{bmatrix} 1 & 1 \\ 0 & 0 \end{bmatrix} \begin{bmatrix} x_1(k) \\ x_2(k) \end{bmatrix} + \begin{bmatrix} 3 \\ -2 \end{bmatrix} u(k) = \mathbf{A}\mathbf{x}(k) + \mathbf{b}u(k)$$

$$y(k) = \begin{bmatrix} 1 & 0 \end{bmatrix} \begin{bmatrix} x_1(k) \\ x_2(k) \end{bmatrix} = \mathbf{c}^\dagger \mathbf{x}(k)$$

Using some of the same data of (4-9) again:

$$y(0) = \mathbf{c}^\dagger \mathbf{x}(0)$$

$$y(1) = \mathbf{c}^\dagger \mathbf{x}(1) = \mathbf{c}^\dagger \mathbf{A}\mathbf{x}(0) + \mathbf{c}^\dagger \mathbf{b}u(0)$$

so

$$\mathbf{x}(0) = \begin{bmatrix} \mathbf{c}^\dagger \\ \hdashline \mathbf{c}^\dagger \mathbf{A} \end{bmatrix}^{-1} \begin{bmatrix} y(0) \\ \hdashline y(1) - \mathbf{c}^\dagger \mathbf{b} u(0) \end{bmatrix} = \begin{bmatrix} 1 & 0 \\ -1 & 1 \end{bmatrix} \begin{bmatrix} 2 \\ -2 \end{bmatrix} = \begin{bmatrix} 2 \\ -4 \end{bmatrix}$$

Then

$$\mathbf{x}(1) = \mathbf{A}\mathbf{x}(0) + \mathbf{b}u(0) = \begin{bmatrix} 1 & 1 \\ 0 & 0 \end{bmatrix} \begin{bmatrix} 2 \\ -4 \end{bmatrix} + \begin{bmatrix} 3 \\ -2 \end{bmatrix} (1) = \begin{bmatrix} 1 \\ -2 \end{bmatrix}$$

and so on, through

$$\mathbf{x}(7) = \mathbf{A}\mathbf{x}(6) + \mathbf{b}u(6) = \begin{bmatrix} 7 \\ -6 \end{bmatrix}$$

## 4.4 Controllability and State Control

Controllability was defined in Chapter 3 in terms of input access to each plant mode. Complete controllability also means that there are plant inputs that will bring a plant from any arbitrary initial state to any desired later state in a finite number of steps. This is the subject of this section. Occasionally, this is what one wants to do for control. For example, moving a space vehicle from one orbit to another involves changing the vehicle's state from one three-dimensional position, velocity, orientation, and motion about its center of mass to another.

In tracking systems, a more demanding result is desired: one or more plant tracking output signals are to be nearly equal to available external reference signals. For tracking, controllability is one of several concerns.

In the course of learning how to control a system's state at a later step, the controllability rank test will be derived.

### 4.4.1 Controllability and the Rank Test

If a discrete-time system is completely controllable, then knowing the system model and its state $\mathbf{x}(k)$ at any initial step $k$, an input sequence $\mathbf{u}(k)$, $\mathbf{u}(k + 1), \ldots, \mathbf{u}(k + i - 1)$ can be determined that will take the system to any desired later state $\mathbf{x}(k + i)$ in a finite number of steps. For a step-invariant system, if it is possible to move the state at any step, say $\mathbf{x}(0)$, to an arbitrary state at a later step, then it is possible to move to an arbitrary desired state starting with any beginning step.

For a system

$$\mathbf{x}(k+1) = \mathbf{A}\mathbf{x}(k) + \mathbf{B}\mathbf{u}(k)$$

$$\mathbf{y}(k) = \mathbf{C}\mathbf{x}(k) + \mathbf{D}\mathbf{u}(k)$$

and a desired state $\delta$, the system state at step $n$, in terms of the initial state $\mathbf{x}(0)$ and the inputs, is

$$\delta = \mathbf{x}(n) = \mathbf{A}^n\mathbf{x}(0) + \sum_{i=0}^{n-1} \mathbf{A}^{n-1-i}\mathbf{B}\mathbf{u}(i)$$

or

$$\mathbf{B}\mathbf{u}(n-1) + \mathbf{A}\mathbf{B}\mathbf{u}(n-2) + \cdots + \mathbf{A}^{n-2}\mathbf{B}\mathbf{u}(1) + \mathbf{A}^{n-1}\mathbf{B}\mathbf{u}(0) = \underbrace{\delta - \mathbf{A}^n\mathbf{x}(0)}_{\text{known}}$$

For a nonzero known vector, these equations have a solution for the inputs $\mathbf{u}(0), \mathbf{u}(1), \ldots, \mathbf{u}(n-1)$ if and only if the array of coefficients, which is the system's controllability matrix

$$\mathbf{M}_c = [\mathbf{B} \mid \mathbf{A}\mathbf{B} \mid \cdots \mid \mathbf{A}^{n-2}\mathbf{B} \mid \mathbf{A}^{n-1}\mathbf{B}]$$

is of full rank. Additional steps, giving additional equations with coefficients $\mathbf{A}^n\mathbf{B}, \mathbf{A}^{n+1}\mathbf{B}$, and so on, do not affect this result since, by the Cayley-Hamilton theorem, the higher powers of $\mathbf{A}$ can be expressed as a linear combination of $\mathbf{A}^{n-1}$ and lower powers of $\mathbf{A}$. The resulting additional equations are linearly dependent on those already considered.

For a multiple-input system, the smallest integer $\eta$ for which

$$\mathbf{M}_c(\eta) = [\mathbf{B} \mid \mathbf{A}\mathbf{B} \mid \mathbf{A}^2\mathbf{B} \mid \cdots \mid \mathbf{A}^{\eta-1}\mathbf{B}]$$

has full rank is called the *controllability index* of the system. It is the minimum number of input steps required to control the system state.

The replacements

$$\begin{cases} \mathbf{A} \to \mathbf{A}^\dagger \\ \mathbf{B} \to \mathbf{C}^\dagger \\ \mathbf{C} \to \mathbf{B}^\dagger \end{cases}$$

create a system with a controllability matrix which is the observability matrix of the original system and an observability matrix that is the controllability matrix of the original system. Every controllability result thus has a corresponding observability result and vice versa, a concept termed *duality*. This concept generalizes to step-varying discrete-time and time-varying continuous-time systems as well.

Similar to the situation with observability, a nonsingular change of state variables does not affect the rank of the controllability matrix, since if

$$\mathbf{x} = \mathbf{P}\mathbf{x}'; \qquad \mathbf{x}' = \mathbf{P}^{-1}\mathbf{x}$$

then

$$\mathbf{M}'_c = [\mathbf{P}^{-1}\mathbf{B} \mid \mathbf{P}^{-1}\mathbf{A}\mathbf{P}\mathbf{P}^{-1}\mathbf{B} \mid \mathbf{P}^{-1}\mathbf{A}^2\mathbf{P}\mathbf{P}^{-1}\mathbf{B} \mid \cdots \mid \mathbf{P}^{-1}\mathbf{A}^{n-1}\mathbf{P}\mathbf{P}^{-1}\mathbf{B}]$$

$$= \mathbf{P}^{-1}\mathbf{M}_c$$

The dual result to the rank test for complete observability is that a system is completely controllable if and only if its controllability matrix is of full rank.* The controllability matrix rank test, being an algebraic test of the structure of two matrices, $\mathbf{A}$ and $\mathbf{B}$, also applies to continuous-time systems.

## 4.4.2 Controlling Single-Input Systems

As an example of finding the control inputs needed to bring a completely controllable system to a desired state, consider the single-input system with state equations

$$\begin{bmatrix} x_1(k+1) \\ x_2(k+1) \\ x_3(k+1) \end{bmatrix} = \begin{bmatrix} 1 & 2 & 0 \\ 4 & -1 & 0 \\ 0 & 1 & 3 \end{bmatrix} \begin{bmatrix} x_1(k) \\ x_2(k) \\ x_3(k) \end{bmatrix} + \begin{bmatrix} -1 \\ 1 \\ 0 \end{bmatrix} u(k) = \mathbf{A}\mathbf{x}(k) + \mathbf{b}u(k)$$

Suppose that it is desired to take the state from

$$\begin{bmatrix} x_1(0) \\ x_2(0) \\ x_3(0) \end{bmatrix} = \begin{bmatrix} 0 \\ -1 \\ 3 \end{bmatrix} \quad \text{to} \quad \begin{bmatrix} x_1(i) \\ x_2(i) \\ x_3(i) \end{bmatrix} = \begin{bmatrix} 6 \\ -8 \\ 2 \end{bmatrix}$$

*The definition of controllability involves beginning with an arbitrary known initial state and moving to an *arbitrary* desired final state. If the desired final state is the origin, $\mathbf{x}(k+i) = \mathbf{0}$, then "controllability to the origin" might be achieved even if $\mathbf{M}_c$ is not of full rank. It could be that the system state coupling matrix has the property $\mathbf{A}^i = \mathbf{0}$ for example, so that the state decays to zero without any input at all.

*Reachability* is control of the state from an initial zero state to an arbitrary final state. A completely controllable system (not just "controllable to the origin") is reachable and vice versa. There are a variety of viewpoints in the literature, where "controllable to the origin" has sometimes been substituted for controllability. Because of this, some authors prefer the term *reachability*. However, one should probably then speak of reachable and unreachable system modes instead of "controllable" and "uncontrollable" ones.

If the input sequence is begun at step 0, this can be done by step $i = n = 3$ if the system is completely controllable. The desired state at step three is related to the system initial state and inputs by

$$\mathbf{x}(3) = \begin{bmatrix} 6 \\ -8 \\ 2 \end{bmatrix} = \mathbf{A}^3\mathbf{x}(0) + \mathbf{A}^2\mathbf{b}u(0) + \mathbf{A}\mathbf{b}u(1) + \mathbf{b}u(2)$$

or

$$\begin{bmatrix} 24 \\ -17 \\ -64 \end{bmatrix} = \begin{bmatrix} -9 \\ 9 \\ -2 \end{bmatrix} u(0) + \begin{bmatrix} 1 \\ -5 \\ 1 \end{bmatrix} u(1) + \begin{bmatrix} -1 \\ 1 \\ 0 \end{bmatrix} u(2)$$

These three simultaneous linear algebraic equations

$$\underbrace{\begin{bmatrix} -1 & 1 & -9 \\ 1 & -5 & 9 \\ 0 & 1 & -2 \end{bmatrix}}_{\mathbf{M}_c} \underbrace{\begin{bmatrix} u(2) \\ u(1) \\ u(0) \end{bmatrix}}_{\substack{\text{inputs in} \\ \text{reverse order}}} = \begin{bmatrix} 24 \\ -17 \\ -64 \end{bmatrix}$$

have solution

$$u(0) = \frac{249}{8}; \qquad u(1) = -\frac{7}{4}; \qquad u(2) = -\frac{2447}{8}$$

The state trajectory with these inputs is as follows:

$$\begin{bmatrix} x_1(2) \\ x_2(2) \\ x_3(2) \end{bmatrix} = \begin{bmatrix} 1 & 2 & 0 \\ 4 & -1 & 0 \\ 0 & 1 & 3 \end{bmatrix}\begin{bmatrix} 0 \\ -1 \\ 3 \end{bmatrix} + \begin{bmatrix} -1 \\ 1 \\ 0 \end{bmatrix}\frac{249}{8} = \begin{bmatrix} -\frac{265}{8} \\ \frac{257}{8} \\ 8 \end{bmatrix}$$

$$\begin{bmatrix} x_1(2) \\ x_2(2) \\ x_3(2) \end{bmatrix} = \begin{bmatrix} 1 & 2 & 0 \\ 4 & -1 & 0 \\ 0 & 1 & 3 \end{bmatrix}\begin{bmatrix} -\frac{265}{8} \\ \frac{257}{8} \\ 8 \end{bmatrix} + \begin{bmatrix} -1 \\ 1 \\ 0 \end{bmatrix}\left(-\frac{7}{4}\right) = \begin{bmatrix} \frac{263}{8} \\ -\frac{1331}{8} \\ \frac{449}{8} \end{bmatrix}$$

$$\begin{bmatrix} x_1(3) \\ x_2(3) \\ x_3(3) \end{bmatrix} = \begin{bmatrix} 1 & 2 & 0 \\ 4 & -1 & 0 \\ 0 & 1 & 3 \end{bmatrix}\begin{bmatrix} \frac{263}{8} \\ -\frac{1331}{8} \\ \frac{449}{8} \end{bmatrix} + \begin{bmatrix} -1 \\ 1 \\ 0 \end{bmatrix}\left(-\frac{2447}{8}\right) = \begin{bmatrix} 6 \\ -8 \\ 2 \end{bmatrix}$$

If, instead, it were desired to move this system's state from

$$\mathbf{x}(5) = \begin{bmatrix} 0 \\ -1 \\ 3 \end{bmatrix} \quad \text{to} \quad \mathbf{x}(8) = \begin{bmatrix} 6 \\ -8 \\ 2 \end{bmatrix}$$

then

$$\mathbf{x}(8) = \mathbf{A}^3\mathbf{x}(5) + \mathbf{A}^2\mathbf{b}u(5) + \mathbf{A}\mathbf{b}u(6) + \mathbf{b}u(7)$$

and the inputs required would be

$$u(5) = \frac{249}{8}; \quad u(6) = -\frac{7}{4}; \quad u(7) = \frac{-2447}{8}$$

When it is desired to control a system's state at a step later than the minimum number of steps necessary to achieve control, some of the inputs can be chosen arbitrarily. For example, for the system with state equations

$$\begin{bmatrix} x_1(k+1) \\ x_2(k+1) \end{bmatrix} = \begin{bmatrix} 1 & 1 \\ 2 & 0 \end{bmatrix} \begin{bmatrix} x_1(k) \\ x_2(k) \end{bmatrix} + \begin{bmatrix} 2 \\ -1 \end{bmatrix} u(k) \tag{4-10}$$

if it is desired to apply inputs to bring the state from

$$\mathbf{x}(0) = \begin{bmatrix} x_1(0) \\ x_2(0) \end{bmatrix} = \begin{bmatrix} 0 \\ -4 \end{bmatrix} \quad \text{to} \quad \mathbf{x}(k) = \begin{bmatrix} x_1(k) \\ x_2(k) \end{bmatrix} = \begin{bmatrix} 6 \\ 1 \end{bmatrix}$$

this can be done in two steps. That is, one can solve

$$\mathbf{x}(2) = \mathbf{A}^2\mathbf{x}(0) + \mathbf{A}\mathbf{b}u(0) + \mathbf{b}u(1)$$

for the inputs $u(0)$ and $u(1)$ that will achieve the desired state at step two. Suppose though, that it is desired to achieve the given state instead at step *three*. Then there are three input steps available to the designer, since

$$\mathbf{x}(3) = \mathbf{A}^3\mathbf{x}(0) + \mathbf{A}^2\mathbf{b}u(0) + \mathbf{A}\mathbf{b}u(1) + \mathbf{b}u(2)$$

One solution is to apply any input at the first step. This will result in some state $\mathbf{x}(1)$ at step one. With this as an initial state, the system can then be brought to the desired state in the remaining two steps. Another method is to impose additional requirements on the input sequence and/or the state sequence.

## 4.4.2 Controlling Multiple-Input Systems

The inputs to a system are said to be *linearly independent* if the columns of the input coupling matrix **B** are linearly independent of one another. A linearly dependent input is of no additional help in controlling a system because it does not contribute any linearly independent columns to the system's controllability matrix. There may be other reasons, such as increased reliability, for including linearly dependent inputs in practice, but for the present we will assume that all system inputs are linearly independent unless otherwise stated.

When multiple linearly independent inputs are available for control of an $n$th order system, the system state can be moved to a desired state in less than $n$ steps, since each step involves more than a single control variable. For example, in the two-input system with state equations

$$\begin{bmatrix} x_1(k+1) \\ x_2(k+1) \\ x_3(k+1) \end{bmatrix} = \begin{bmatrix} 0 & 1 & 1 \\ -1 & 0 & 2 \\ 0 & 3 & 0 \end{bmatrix} \begin{bmatrix} x_1(k) \\ x_2(k) \\ x_3(k) \end{bmatrix} + \begin{bmatrix} 1 & 0 \\ 0 & 0 \\ 1 & -1 \end{bmatrix} \begin{bmatrix} u_1(k) \\ u_2(k) \end{bmatrix}$$

$$= \mathbf{A}\mathbf{x}(k) + \mathbf{B}\mathbf{u}(k)$$

suppose that it is desired to take the state from

$$\begin{bmatrix} x_1(0) \\ x_2(0) \\ x_3(0) \end{bmatrix} = \begin{bmatrix} -1 \\ 3 \\ -2 \end{bmatrix} \quad \text{to} \quad \begin{bmatrix} x_1(i) \\ x_2(i) \\ x_3(i) \end{bmatrix} = \begin{bmatrix} 1 \\ 2 \\ 3 \end{bmatrix}$$

at the earliest later step $i$. In terms of the inputs, the system state at step two is

$$\mathbf{x}(2) = \mathbf{A}\mathbf{x}(1) + \mathbf{B}\mathbf{u}(1) = \mathbf{A}[\mathbf{A}\mathbf{x}(0) + \mathbf{B}\mathbf{u}(0)] + \mathbf{B}\mathbf{u}(1)$$

$$= \mathbf{A}^2\mathbf{x}(0) + \mathbf{A}\mathbf{B}\mathbf{u}(0) + \mathbf{B}\mathbf{u}(1)$$

Equating to the desired state

$$\begin{bmatrix} 1 \\ 2 \\ 3 \end{bmatrix} = \begin{bmatrix} 0 & 1 & 1 \\ -1 & 0 & 2 \\ 0 & 3 & 0 \end{bmatrix} \begin{bmatrix} 0 & 1 & 1 \\ -1 & 0 & 2 \\ 0 & 3 & 0 \end{bmatrix} \begin{bmatrix} -1 \\ 3 \\ -2 \end{bmatrix}$$

$$+ \begin{bmatrix} 0 & 1 & 1 \\ -1 & 0 & 2 \\ 0 & 3 & 0 \end{bmatrix} \begin{bmatrix} 1 & 0 \\ 0 & 0 \\ 1 & -1 \end{bmatrix} \begin{bmatrix} u_1(0) \\ u_2(0) \end{bmatrix} + \begin{bmatrix} 1 & 0 \\ 0 & 0 \\ 1 & -1 \end{bmatrix} \begin{bmatrix} u_1(1) \\ u_2(1) \end{bmatrix}$$

results in the following three simultaneous linear algebraic equations in four unknowns:

$$\begin{cases} u_1(0) - u_2(0) + u_1(1) & = -5 \\ u_1(0) - 2u_2(0) & = -15 \\ u_1(1) - u_2(1) = 12 \end{cases}$$

Arbitrarily choosing

$$u_1(0) = 0$$

then

$$u_2(0) = \frac{15}{2}; \quad u_1(1) = \frac{5}{2}; \quad u_2(1) = -\frac{19}{2}$$

With these inputs, the state trajectory is

$$\begin{bmatrix} x_1(1) \\ x_2(1) \\ x_3(1) \end{bmatrix} = \begin{bmatrix} 0 & 1 & 1 \\ -1 & 0 & 2 \\ 0 & 3 & 0 \end{bmatrix} \begin{bmatrix} -1 \\ 3 \\ -2 \end{bmatrix} + \begin{bmatrix} 1 & 0 \\ 0 & 0 \\ 1 & -1 \end{bmatrix} \begin{bmatrix} 0 \\ \frac{15}{2} \end{bmatrix} = \begin{bmatrix} 1 \\ -3 \\ \frac{3}{2} \end{bmatrix}$$

$$\begin{bmatrix} x_1(2) \\ x_2(2) \\ x_3(2) \end{bmatrix} = \begin{bmatrix} 0 & 1 & 1 \\ -1 & 0 & 2 \\ 0 & 3 & 0 \end{bmatrix} \begin{bmatrix} 1 \\ -3 \\ \frac{3}{2} \end{bmatrix} + \begin{bmatrix} 1 & 0 \\ 0 & 0 \\ 1 & -1 \end{bmatrix} \begin{bmatrix} \frac{5}{2} \\ -\frac{19}{2} \end{bmatrix} = \begin{bmatrix} 1 \\ 2 \\ 3 \end{bmatrix}$$

Each different choice of $u_1(0)$ (or any other of the input components, for that matter) will result in a different set of inputs that will bring this third-order system to the desired state at step two.

Control, in the sense of controllability, is fundamentally different from observation. Once enough linearly independent equations have been collected, one can continue to observe a known system's state at every step. The state can be controlled, however, only every $\eta$ steps or so. And, the state to be reached must be known $\eta$ steps in advance. Actually one can do a little better than this if the equations for control in $\eta$ steps are underdetermined, because their solution can be chosen to aid in control at one or more later steps.

### 4.4.3 Optimal Control

When the equations for control of a system are underdetermined, the designer can choose to formulate and solve an optimization problem. For a space satellite, for example, the state **x** might represent the satellite's orbital position and velocity and the inputs **u** might be thrusts from positioning rockets. While any number of **u** sequences would bring the satellite to a desired orbital state, one that does so with a minimum expenditure of energy or fuel is clearly desirable.

As a simple numerical example, consider the system (4-10) again, with

$$\mathbf{x}(0) = \begin{bmatrix} 0 \\ -4 \end{bmatrix}$$

and with the state at step three required to be

$$\mathbf{x}(3) = \begin{bmatrix} 6 \\ 1 \end{bmatrix}$$

The inputs $u(0)$, $u(1)$, and $u(2)$ in

$$\mathbf{x}(3) = \mathbf{A}^3\mathbf{x}(0) + \mathbf{A}^2\mathbf{b}u(0) + \mathbf{A}\mathbf{b}u(1) + \mathbf{b}u(2)$$

or

$$\begin{bmatrix} 6 \\ 1 \end{bmatrix} = \begin{bmatrix} -12 \\ -8 \end{bmatrix} + \begin{bmatrix} 5 \\ 2 \end{bmatrix} u(0) + \begin{bmatrix} 1 \\ 4 \end{bmatrix} u(1) + \begin{bmatrix} 2 \\ -1 \end{bmatrix} u(2)$$

are to be selected. Rather than arbitrarily choosing $u(0)$ and then solving for the resulting necessary $u(1)$ and $u(2)$, suppose that we seek the solution for which

$$J = u^2(0) + u^2(1) + u^2(2)$$

is minimum. The solution in terms of $u(0)$ is

$$\begin{cases} u(1) + 2u(2) = 18 - 5u(0) \\ 4u(1) - u(2) = 9 - 2u(0) \end{cases}$$

or

$$u(1) = \frac{\begin{vmatrix} 18 - 5u(0) & 2 \\ 9 - 2u(0) & -1 \end{vmatrix}}{\begin{vmatrix} 1 & -2 \\ 4 & -1 \end{vmatrix}} = \frac{-36 + 9u(0)}{-9} = 4 - u(0)$$

$$u(2) = \frac{\begin{vmatrix} 1 & 18 - 5u(0) \\ 4 & 9 - 2u(0) \end{vmatrix}}{-9} = \frac{-63 + 18u(0)}{-9} = 7 - 2u(0)$$

In terms of $u(0)$, the performance index is

$$J = u^2(0) + u^2(1) + u^2(2) = u^2(0) + [4 - u(0)]^2 + [7 - 2u(0)]^2$$
$$= 6u^2(0) - 36u(0) + 65$$

and its minimum with respect to $u(0)$ is given by

$$\frac{\partial J}{\partial u(0)} = 12u(0) - 36 = 0; \qquad u(0) = 3$$

Then

$$u(1) = 4 - u(0) = 1$$
$$u(2) = 7 - 2u(0) = 1$$

There are many variations on this theme of *optimal control*, including problems where the performance measure $J$ includes terms involving the error between desired and actual states and where the final step number is not fixed. We will derive and discuss the solution to a highly useful general optimal control problem in Chapter 8.

## 4.5 State Feedback

We now examine the situation when the plant input, instead of being some sequence dictated in part by a known initial and desired later state, is a linear transformation of the plant state at each step. For a plant with state equations

$$\mathbf{x}(k + 1) = \mathbf{A}\mathbf{x}(k) + \mathbf{B}\mathbf{u}(k)$$

we consider the state feedback

$$\mathbf{u}(k) = \mathbf{E}\mathbf{x}(k) = \boldsymbol{\rho}(k)$$

where $\boldsymbol{\rho}(k)$ is a vector of external inputs, as shown in Figure 4-1. Provided that the plant is completely controllable, a feedback gain matrix $\mathbf{E}$ can always be chosen so that each of the eigenvalues of the feedback system

$$\mathbf{x}(k + 1) = (\mathbf{A} + \mathbf{B}\mathbf{E})\mathbf{x}(k) + \mathbf{B}\boldsymbol{\rho}(k)$$

are at arbitrary desired locations selected by the designer. Methods for performing feedback system eigenvalue placement will now be developed.

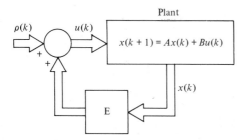

**FIGURE 4-1. State feedback.**

Eigenvalue placement will ultimately provide a solution to controlling the zero-input component of a plant's response. By selecting the feedback system eigenvalues, the designer specifies the zero-input response modes and thus the character of that response, the plant's transient response. As the plant initial conditions are not generally known, this is usually the best that can be done; whatever the initial conditions, the zero-input response is made to decay in a desired manner. For now, it is supposed that the plant state is available for feedback. Normally it is not, and subsequently we will extend these results to the usual case where only the plant inputs and outputs are accessible.

### 4.5.1 Eigenvalue Placement in Controllable Form

If a single-input plant is in controllable form, finding the feedback gains for arbitrary eigenvalue placement is especially simple. For example, consider the single-input system with state equations

$$\begin{bmatrix} x_1(k+1) \\ x_2(k+1) \\ x_3(k+1) \end{bmatrix} = \begin{bmatrix} 0 & 1 & 0 \\ 0 & 0 & 1 \\ -4 & -2 & -1 \end{bmatrix} \begin{bmatrix} x_1(k) \\ x_2(k) \\ x_3(k) \end{bmatrix} + \begin{bmatrix} 0 \\ 0 \\ 1 \end{bmatrix} u(k) = \mathbf{A}\mathbf{x}(k) + \mathbf{b}u(k)$$

which has characteristic equation with coefficients given by the last row of the state coupling matrix:

$$\lambda^3 + \lambda^2 + 2\lambda + 4 = 0$$

Suppose that it is desired to have the three eigenvalues of the state feedback system at

$$\lambda_1 = 0; \qquad \lambda_2 = -\tfrac{1}{2} + j\tfrac{1}{2}; \qquad \lambda_3 = -\tfrac{1}{2} - j\tfrac{1}{2}$$

Then the desired characteristic equation is

$$\lambda(\lambda + \tfrac{1}{2} + j\tfrac{1}{2})(\lambda + \tfrac{1}{2} - j\tfrac{1}{2}) = \lambda^3 + \lambda^2 + \tfrac{1}{2}\lambda = 0$$

The feedback

$$u(k) = \mathbf{e}^\dagger \mathbf{x}(k) + \rho(k) = [e_1 \quad e_2 \quad e_3] \begin{bmatrix} x_1(k) \\ x_2(k) \\ x_3(k) \end{bmatrix} + \rho(k)$$

$$= e_1 x_1(k) + e_2 x_2(k) + e_3 x_3(k) + \rho(k)$$

as indicated in Figure 4-2, results in a feedback system governed by

$$\begin{bmatrix} x_1(k+1) \\ x_2(k+1) \\ x_3(k+1) \end{bmatrix} = \begin{bmatrix} 0 & 1 & 0 \\ 0 & 0 & 1 \\ -4 & -2 & -1 \end{bmatrix} \begin{bmatrix} x_1(k) \\ x_2(k) \\ x_3(k) \end{bmatrix}$$

$$+ \begin{bmatrix} 0 \\ 0 \\ 1 \end{bmatrix} [e_1 \quad e_2 \quad e_3] \begin{bmatrix} x_1(k) \\ x_2(k) \\ x_3(k) \end{bmatrix} + \begin{bmatrix} 0 \\ 0 \\ 1 \end{bmatrix} \rho(k)$$

$$= \begin{bmatrix} 0 & 1 & 0 \\ 0 & 0 & 1 \\ (e_1 - 4) & (e_2 - 2) & (e_3 - 1) \end{bmatrix} \begin{bmatrix} x_1(k) \\ x_2(k) \\ x_3(k) \end{bmatrix} + \begin{bmatrix} 0 \\ 0 \\ 1 \end{bmatrix} \rho(k)$$

The state feedback system has characteristic equation

$$\lambda^3 + (1 - e_3)\lambda^2 + (2 - e_2)\lambda + (4 - e_1) = 0$$

and the feedback gains

$$\mathbf{e}^\dagger = [4 \quad \tfrac{3}{2} \quad 0]$$

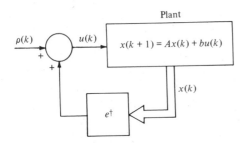

**FIGURE 4-2.   A single-input plant with state feedback.**

result in the desired characteristic equation

$$\lambda^3 + \lambda^2 + \tfrac{1}{2}\lambda = 0$$

## 4.5.2 *General Eigenvalue Placement for Single-Input Systems*

If the plant is single-input and completely controllable, it is helpful to transform to controllable form to calculate the state feedback gain for eigenvalue placement. For example, the completely controllable single-input system with state equations

$$\begin{bmatrix} x_1(k+1) \\ x_2(k+1) \\ x_3(k+1) \end{bmatrix} = \begin{bmatrix} 0 & 3 & -1 \\ -2 & 0 & 2 \\ 2 & 0 & -3 \end{bmatrix} \begin{bmatrix} x_1(k) \\ x_2(k) \\ x_3(k) \end{bmatrix} + \begin{bmatrix} 4 \\ 0 \\ 0 \end{bmatrix} u(k) = \mathbf{A}\mathbf{x}(k) + \mathbf{b}u(k) \tag{4-11}$$

has characteristic equation

$$|\lambda\mathbf{I} - \mathbf{A}| = \begin{vmatrix} \lambda & -3 & 1 \\ 2 & \lambda & -2 \\ -2 & 0 & (\lambda+3) \end{vmatrix} = \lambda^3 + 3\lambda^2 + 8\lambda + 6$$

$$= \lambda^3 + \alpha_2\lambda^2 + \alpha_1\lambda + \alpha_0 = 0$$

The transformation

$$\mathbf{x} = \mathbf{P}\mathbf{x}'; \qquad \mathbf{x}' = \mathbf{P}^{-1}\mathbf{x}$$

that takes this system to controllable form

$$\mathbf{P} = [\mathbf{p}^1 \mid \mathbf{p}^2 \mid \mathbf{p}^3]$$

is given (as shown in Section 3.6) by

$$\mathbf{p}^3 = \mathbf{b} = \begin{bmatrix} 4 \\ 0 \\ 0 \end{bmatrix}$$

$$\mathbf{p}^2 = \mathbf{A}\mathbf{p}^3 + \alpha_2\mathbf{b} = \begin{bmatrix} 12 \\ -8 \\ 8 \end{bmatrix}$$

$$\mathbf{p}^1 = \mathbf{A}\mathbf{p}^2 + \alpha_1\mathbf{b} = \begin{bmatrix} 0 \\ -8 \\ 0 \end{bmatrix}$$

so that

$$
\mathbf{P} = \begin{bmatrix} 0 & 12 & 4 \\ -8 & -8 & 0 \\ 0 & 8 & 0 \end{bmatrix}; \qquad \mathbf{P}^{-1} = \frac{1}{8}\begin{bmatrix} 0 & -1 & -1 \\ 0 & 0 & 1 \\ 2 & 0 & -3 \end{bmatrix}
$$

In terms of the new state variables, the plant is described by the state equations

$$
\begin{bmatrix} x'_1(k+1) \\ x'_2(k+1) \\ x'_3(k+1) \end{bmatrix} = \begin{bmatrix} 0 & 1 & 0 \\ 0 & 0 & 1 \\ -6 & -8 & -3 \end{bmatrix}\begin{bmatrix} x'_1(k) \\ x'_2(k) \\ x'_3(k) \end{bmatrix} + \begin{bmatrix} 0 \\ 0 \\ 1 \end{bmatrix} u(k) = \mathbf{A}'\mathbf{x}'(k) + \mathbf{b}'u(k)
$$

For the desired feedback system eigenvalues

$$\lambda = \tfrac{1}{2},\ -\tfrac{1}{4},\ -1$$

the desired characteristic equation is

$$(\lambda - \tfrac{1}{2})(\lambda + \tfrac{1}{4})(\lambda + 1) = \lambda^3 + \tfrac{3}{4}\lambda^2 - \tfrac{3}{8}\lambda - \tfrac{1}{8} = 0$$

If the *primed* state were fed back according to

$$u(k) = \mathbf{e}'^{\mathsf{t}}\mathbf{x}'(k) + \rho(k) = e'_1 x'_1(k) + e'_2 x'_2(k) + e'_3 x'_3(k) + \rho(k)$$

the composite system would be described by

$$\mathbf{x}'(k+1) = \mathbf{A}'\mathbf{x}'(k) + \mathbf{b}'\mathbf{e}'^{\mathsf{t}}\mathbf{x}'(k) + \mathbf{b}'\rho(k) = (\mathbf{A}' + \mathbf{b}'\mathbf{e}'^{\mathsf{t}})\mathbf{x}'(k) + \mathbf{b}'\rho(k)$$

$$
= \begin{bmatrix} 0 & 1 & 0 \\ 0 & 0 & 1 \\ (e'_1 - 6) & (e'_2 - 8) & (e'_3 - 3) \end{bmatrix}\begin{bmatrix} x'_1(k) \\ x'_2(k) \\ x'_3(k) \end{bmatrix} + \begin{bmatrix} 0 \\ 0 \\ 1 \end{bmatrix}\rho(k)
$$

which has characteristic equation

$$\lambda^3 + (3 - e'_3)\lambda^2 + (8 - e'_2)\lambda + (6 - e'_1) = 0$$

Choosing

$$\mathbf{e}'^{\mathsf{t}} = \begin{bmatrix} \tfrac{49}{8} & \tfrac{67}{8} & \tfrac{9}{4} \end{bmatrix}$$

gives the desired characteristic equation.

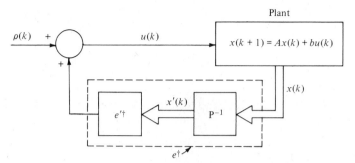

**FIGURE 4-3.** Use of controllable form to calculate state feedback gains.

But it is the original state $\mathbf{x}(k)$, not $\mathbf{x}'(k)$, that is assumed available for feedback. The two are related by

$$\mathbf{x}'(k) = \mathbf{P}^{-1}\mathbf{x}(k)$$

so that the feedback

$$\mathbf{e}'^{\dagger}\mathbf{P}^{-1}\mathbf{x}(k) = \mathbf{e}^{\dagger}\mathbf{x}(k)$$

where

$$\mathbf{e}^{\dagger} = \mathbf{e}'^{\dagger}\mathbf{P}^{-1} = [\tfrac{9}{16} \quad \tfrac{-49}{64} \quad \tfrac{-9}{16}] \tag{4-12}$$

will result in the desired eigenvalue placement, as indicated in Figure 4-3. The original system will have these same eigenvalues, since the eigenvalues of a system are unchanged by a change in state variables.

### 4.5.3 Eigenvalue Placement with Multiple Inputs

If the plant for eigenvalue placement has multiple inputs and if it is completely controllable from one of the inputs, then that one input alone could be used for the feedback. For example, consider the system with state equations

$$\begin{bmatrix} x_1(k+1) \\ x_2(k+1) \\ x_3(k+1) \end{bmatrix} = \begin{bmatrix} 0 & 3 & -1 \\ -2 & 0 & 2 \\ 2 & 0 & -3 \end{bmatrix} \begin{bmatrix} x_1(k) \\ x_2(k) \\ x_3(k) \end{bmatrix} + \begin{bmatrix} 4 & 3 \\ 0 & -1 \\ 0 & 1 \end{bmatrix} \begin{bmatrix} u_1(k) \\ u_2(k) \end{bmatrix}$$

This is the previous system (4-11) with an additional input. To place the eigenvalues so that the characteristic equation of this system is, as in the earlier example

$$\lambda^3 + \tfrac{3}{4}\lambda^2 - \tfrac{3}{8}\lambda - \tfrac{1}{8} = 0$$

the second input can be ignored so far as feedback is concerned, with the state fed back through the gain of equation (4-12) found earlier

$$\mathbf{e}^\dagger = [\tfrac{9}{16} \quad \tfrac{-49}{64} \quad \tfrac{-9}{16}]$$

to the first input. Adding additional external inputs $\rho_1(k)$ and $\rho_2(k)$,

$$u_1(k) = \mathbf{e}^\dagger\mathbf{x}(k) + \rho_1(k)$$
$$u_2(k) = \rho_2(k)$$

This arrangement is shown in Figure 4-4.

If the plant is not completely controllable from a single input, a single input can usually be distributed to the multiple ones in such a way that the plant is completely controllable from the single input. For example, the two-input system with diagonal state equations

$$\begin{bmatrix} x_1(k+1) \\ x_2(k+1) \\ x_3(k+1) \end{bmatrix} = \begin{bmatrix} -\tfrac{1}{2} & 0 & 0 \\ 0 & \tfrac{1}{2} & 0 \\ 0 & 0 & 0 \end{bmatrix} \begin{bmatrix} x_1(k) \\ x_2(k) \\ x_3(k) \end{bmatrix} + \begin{bmatrix} 1 & 0 \\ 0 & -2 \\ -1 & 1 \end{bmatrix} \begin{bmatrix} u_1(k) \\ u_2(k) \end{bmatrix}$$

$$= \mathbf{A}\mathbf{x}(k) + \mathbf{B}\mathbf{u}(k)$$

is obviously not completely controllable from either input $u_1(k)$ or input $u_2(k)$ alone. Distributing the single input $\mu(k)$ to $u_1(k)$ and $u_2(k)$ in almost any way,

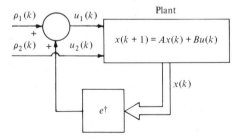

**FIGURE 4-4.   Use of a single plant input for state feedback.**

for example as

$$u_1(k) = 3\mu(k)$$

$$u_2(k) = \mu(k)$$

will result in a single-input system that is completely controllable from $\mu(k)$:

$$\begin{bmatrix} x_1(k+1) \\ x_2(k+1) \\ x_3(k+1) \end{bmatrix} = \begin{bmatrix} -\frac{1}{2} & 0 & 0 \\ 0 & \frac{1}{2} & 0 \\ 0 & 0 & 0 \end{bmatrix} \begin{bmatrix} x_1(k) \\ x_2(k) \\ x_3(k) \end{bmatrix} + \begin{bmatrix} 3 \\ -2 \\ -2 \end{bmatrix} \mu(k) = \mathbf{A}\mathbf{x}(k) + \mathbf{h}\mu(k)$$

This distribution of a single input to multiple plant inputs is shown in Figure 4-5.

With state feedback to the single input $\mu(k)$, the feedback system eigenvalues can be placed at any desired locations. The characteristic equation of the plant is

$$(\lambda + \tfrac{1}{2})(\lambda - \tfrac{1}{2})(\lambda) = \lambda^3 - \tfrac{1}{4}\lambda = 0$$

The change of state variables

$$\mathbf{x} = \mathbf{P}\mathbf{x}'; \qquad \mathbf{x}' = \mathbf{P}^{-1}\mathbf{x}$$

that takes the system with input $\mu(k)$ into the controllable form is

$$\mathbf{P} = \begin{bmatrix} 0 & -\frac{3}{2} & 3 \\ 0 & -1 & -2 \\ \frac{1}{2} & 0 & -2 \end{bmatrix}; \qquad \mathbf{P}^{-1} = \frac{1}{12}\begin{bmatrix} 8 & -12 & 24 \\ -4 & -6 & 0 \\ 2 & -3 & 0 \end{bmatrix}$$

and feedback of the primed state variables, of the form

$$\mu(k) = \mathbf{e}'^{\mathsf{t}}\mathbf{x}'(k)$$

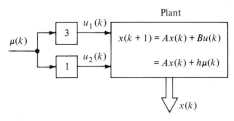

FIGURE 4-5.    Distribution of a single input to multiple plant inputs for state feedback.

results in the composite system equations

$$
\begin{bmatrix} x_1'(k+1) \\ x_2'(k+1) \\ x_3'(k+1) \end{bmatrix} = \left\{ \begin{bmatrix} 0 & 1 & 0 \\ 0 & 0 & 1 \\ 0 & \frac{1}{4} & 0 \end{bmatrix} + \begin{bmatrix} 0 \\ 0 \\ 1 \end{bmatrix} [e_1' \quad e_2' \quad e_3'] \right\} \begin{bmatrix} x_1'(k) \\ x_2'(k) \\ x_3'(k) \end{bmatrix}
$$

$$
= \begin{bmatrix} 0 & 1 & 0 \\ 0 & 0 & 1 \\ e_1' & \frac{1}{4}+e_2' & e_3' \end{bmatrix} \begin{bmatrix} x_1'(k) \\ x_2'(k) \\ x_3'(k) \end{bmatrix}
$$

If it is desired that all three eigenvalues of the feedback system be at $\lambda = 0$, so that the desired characteristic equation is

$$\lambda^3 = 0$$

then

$$\mathbf{e}'^\dagger = [0 \quad -\tfrac{1}{4} \quad 0]$$

In terms of the original state variables:

$$
\mathbf{e}^\dagger = \mathbf{e}'^\dagger \mathbf{P}^{-1} = [0 \quad -\tfrac{1}{4} \quad 0] \begin{bmatrix} 8 & -12 & 24 \\ -4 & -6 & 0 \\ 2 & -3 & 0 \end{bmatrix} (\tfrac{1}{12}) = [\tfrac{1}{12} \quad \tfrac{1}{8} \quad 0]
$$

Adding external inputs to each of the original two plant inputs, the resulting feedback system design is

$$
\begin{bmatrix} x_1(k+1) \\ x_2(k+1) \\ x_3(k+1) \end{bmatrix} = \begin{bmatrix} -\frac{1}{2} & 0 & 0 \\ 0 & \frac{1}{2} & 0 \\ 0 & 0 & 0 \end{bmatrix} \begin{bmatrix} x_1(k) \\ x_2(k) \\ x_3(k) \end{bmatrix} + \begin{bmatrix} 1 & 0 \\ 0 & -2 \\ -1 & 1 \end{bmatrix} \begin{bmatrix} u_1(k) \\ u_2(k) \end{bmatrix}
$$

where

$$u_1(k) = 3\mu(k) + \rho_1(k) = 3\mathbf{e}^\dagger \mathbf{x}(k) + \rho_1(k)$$

$$u_2(k) = \mu(k) + \rho_2(k) = \mathbf{e}^\dagger \mathbf{x}(k) + \rho_2(k)$$

or

$$
\begin{bmatrix} u_1(k) \\ u_2(k) \end{bmatrix} = \begin{bmatrix} 3\mathbf{e}^\dagger \\ \mathbf{e}^\dagger \end{bmatrix} \begin{bmatrix} x_1(k) \\ x_2(k) \\ x_3(k) \end{bmatrix} + \begin{bmatrix} \rho_1(k) \\ \rho_2(k) \end{bmatrix} = \begin{bmatrix} \frac{1}{4} & \frac{3}{8} & 0 \\ \frac{1}{12} & \frac{1}{8} & 0 \end{bmatrix} \begin{bmatrix} x_1(k) \\ x_2(k) \\ x_3(k) \end{bmatrix} + \begin{bmatrix} \rho_1(k) \\ \rho_2(k) \end{bmatrix}
$$

$$= \mathbf{E}\mathbf{x}(k) + \rho(k)$$

The structure of this system is shown in Figure 4-6.

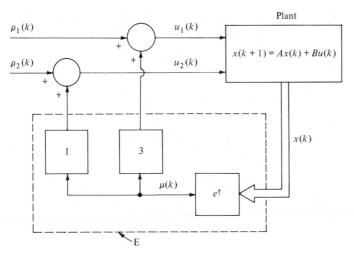

**FIGURE 4-6.** State feedback to a plant with multiple inputs.

When a feedback system is designed in this way, the feedback gain matrix **E** is of rank one and is not unique because the single input $\mu(k)$ can be distributed to the original plant inputs in many different ways. The feedback need not be designed in this way at all; distribution of a single input is simply a convenient design option since we already know how to place eigenvalues in a single-input system. This option is not always available, though, because it is not always possible to distribute a single input to a completely controllable multiple-input plant in such a way that the plant is completely controllable from the single input. If, in a block diagonal plant realization, there is more than one Jordan block involving the same eigenvalue and if each of two such blocks couple to different inputs (as they must for complete controllability), then making those inputs proportional will destroy controllability of the individual modes.

One may wish to feed the state back to more than one input even when the plant is completely controllable from a single input. Using more than one input can be more reliable in that all feedback is not lost if one input is damaged and becomes inactive. Also, the use of more than one input might make the overall system less susceptible to noise.

## 4.6 Output Feedback

It is the measurement output vector of a plant, not the state vector, that is available for feedback. In this section, we consider what eigenvalue placement can be done with output feedback alone. With enough linearly independent outputs, the plant state can be formed from the outputs and inputs and the state feedback results applied. With a single plant input and only a few outputs, the designer's options for placing feedback system eigenvalues could be (and often are) severely limited. Multiple plant inputs can also be used to advantage for eigenvalue placement with output feedback, but it still may not be possible to achieve an acceptable design.

## 4.6.1 State Feedback Derived From Outputs

If an $n$th order plant has $n$ linearly independent outputs, then the plant state can be recovered from the outputs and (if there is direct input-to-output coupling) the plant inputs. For example, for the system with state equations (4-11)

$$\begin{bmatrix} x_1(k+1) \\ x_2(k+1) \\ x_3(k+1) \end{bmatrix} = \begin{bmatrix} 0 & 3 & -1 \\ -2 & 0 & 2 \\ 2 & 0 & -3 \end{bmatrix} \begin{bmatrix} x_1(k) \\ x_2(k) \\ x_3(k) \end{bmatrix} + \begin{bmatrix} 4 \\ 0 \\ 0 \end{bmatrix} u(k)$$

where it was found that the state feedback gain (4-12)

$$\mathbf{e}^\dagger = \begin{bmatrix} \frac{9}{16} & \frac{-49}{64} & \frac{-9}{16} \end{bmatrix}$$

resulted in the desired eigenvalue placement, suppose that the state is not directly available for feedback but that the three linearly independent outputs

$$\begin{bmatrix} y_1(k) \\ y_2(k) \\ y_3(k) \end{bmatrix} = \begin{bmatrix} 2 & 0 & 1 \\ -1 & 3 & 1 \\ 0 & -2 & 4 \end{bmatrix} \begin{bmatrix} x_1(k) \\ x_2(k) \\ x_3(k) \end{bmatrix} + \begin{bmatrix} 3 \\ 0 \\ -1 \end{bmatrix} u(k) = \mathbf{C}\mathbf{x}(k) + \mathbf{d}u(k)$$

are available. Then the state is related to the outputs and input by

$$\mathbf{x}(k) = \mathbf{C}^{-1}[\mathbf{y}(k) - \mathbf{d}u(k)] = \mathbf{C}^{-1}\mathbf{y}(k) - \mathbf{C}^{-1}\mathbf{d}u(k)$$

so that

$$u(k) = \mathbf{e}^\dagger\mathbf{x}(k) + \rho(k) = \mathbf{e}^\dagger\mathbf{C}^{-1}\mathbf{y}(k) - \mathbf{e}^\dagger\mathbf{C}^{-1}\mathbf{d}u(k) + \rho(k)$$

as shown in Figure 4-7(a), where

$$\mathbf{e}^\dagger\mathbf{C}^{-1} = \begin{bmatrix} \frac{9}{16} & \frac{-49}{64} & \frac{-9}{16} \end{bmatrix} \frac{1}{30} \begin{bmatrix} 14 & -2 & -3 \\ 4 & 8 & -3 \\ 2 & 4 & 6 \end{bmatrix} = \begin{bmatrix} \frac{59}{480} & \frac{-152}{480} & \frac{-177}{1920} \end{bmatrix}$$

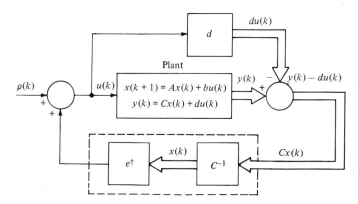

(a) Recovering the plant state from the input and output, then feeding it back.

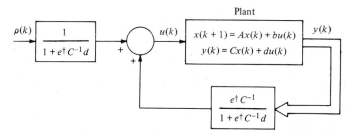

(b) State feedback expressed directly as output feedback.

**FIGURE 4-7. Use of output feedback for eigenvalue placement.**

and

$$\mathbf{e^\dagger C^{-1} d} = \frac{177}{384}$$

Feedback to the plant input can be expressed simply as a linear combination of plant outputs and external input, as in Figure 4-7(b), if desired, according to

$$u(k) = \mathbf{e^\dagger C^{-1}} y(k) - \mathbf{e^\dagger C^{-1}} du(k) + \rho(k)$$

$$= \frac{\mathbf{e^\dagger C^{-1}}}{1 + \mathbf{e^\dagger C^{-1} d}} y(k) + \frac{1}{1 + \mathbf{e^\dagger C^{-1} d}} \rho(k)$$

The external input $\rho(k)$ could be added directly to $u(k)$ instead of being scaled by the factor $1/(1 + \mathbf{e^\dagger C^{-1} d})$, of course.

The special case where

$$\mathbf{e}^\dagger \mathbf{C}^{-1}\mathbf{d} = -1$$

occurs when the state $\mathbf{x}(k)$ cannot be determined directly from the system outputs when there is feedback. Under these conditions, the feedback has caused the feedback system outputs to no longer be linearly independent of one another so that the state cannot be determined directly from the output, as was originally assumed. A small change in the feedback gains $\mathbf{e}^\dagger$, corresponding to small changes in the desired feedback system eigenvalue locations will eliminate the singularity.

If an $n$th order system has more than $n$ outputs, only $n$ of these can be linearly independent, so excess linearly dependent output equations can simply be ignored when recovering a system's state from its output. For example, if a third-order system has outputs

$$\begin{bmatrix} y_1(k) \\ y_2(k) \\ y_3(k) \\ y_4(k) \\ y_5(k) \end{bmatrix} = \begin{bmatrix} 0 & 1 & 0 \\ 2 & -1 & 3 \\ -2 & 0 & -3 \\ 1 & 1 & 0 \\ -1 & 4 & 2 \end{bmatrix} \begin{bmatrix} x_1(k) \\ x_2(k) \\ x_3(k) \end{bmatrix} + \begin{bmatrix} 3 \\ -1 \\ 0 \\ 4 \\ -5 \end{bmatrix} u(k) = \mathbf{C}\mathbf{x}(k) + \mathbf{d}u(k)$$

deleting the third equation (it is linearly dependent on the first two) and the fifth equation leaves

$$\begin{bmatrix} y_1(k) \\ y_2(k) \\ y_4(k) \end{bmatrix} = \begin{bmatrix} 0 & 1 & 0 \\ 2 & -1 & 3 \\ 1 & 1 & 0 \end{bmatrix} \begin{bmatrix} x_1(k) \\ x_2(k) \\ x_3(k) \end{bmatrix} + \begin{bmatrix} 3 \\ -1 \\ 4 \end{bmatrix} u(k) = \tilde{\mathbf{C}}\mathbf{x}(k) + \tilde{\mathbf{d}}u(k)$$

The state can be recovered directly from these outputs via

$$\mathbf{x}(k) = \tilde{\mathbf{C}}^{-1}\left( \begin{bmatrix} y_1(k) \\ y_2(k) \\ y_4(k) \end{bmatrix} - \begin{bmatrix} 3 \\ -1 \\ 4 \end{bmatrix} u(k) \right)$$

so

$$\begin{bmatrix} x_1(k) \\ x_2(k) \\ x_3(k) \end{bmatrix} = \begin{bmatrix} -1 & 0 & 0 & 1 & 0 \\ 1 & 0 & 0 & 0 & 0 \\ 1 & \frac{1}{3} & 0 & -\frac{2}{3} & 0 \end{bmatrix} \begin{bmatrix} y_1(k) \\ y_2(k) \\ y_3(k) \\ y_4(k) \\ y_5(k) \end{bmatrix} - \begin{bmatrix} 1 \\ 3 \\ 0 \end{bmatrix} u(k)$$

As a practical matter, one may wish instead to combine linearly dependent outputs with other of the outputs rather than to ignore them, to improve feedback system reliability and its performance in the presence of noise.

### 4.6.2 Output Feedback with a Single-Input Plant

When a single-input plant does not have enough linearly independent outputs for the state to be recovered directly from it, output feedback will not allow arbitrary feedback system eigenvalue placement. For example, consider the system with state equations

$$\begin{bmatrix} x_1(k+1) \\ x_2(k+1) \\ x_3(k+1) \end{bmatrix} = \begin{bmatrix} 0 & 1 & 0 \\ 0 & 0 & 1 \\ 0 & 2 & -1 \end{bmatrix} \begin{bmatrix} x_1(k) \\ x_2(k) \\ x_3(k) \end{bmatrix} + \begin{bmatrix} 0 \\ 0 \\ 1 \end{bmatrix} u(k) = \mathbf{A}\mathbf{x}(k) + \mathbf{b}u(k)$$

For convenience, these state equations are in controllable form. If there is a single output

$$y(k) = [4 \quad 0 \quad 1] \begin{bmatrix} x_1(k) \\ x_2(k) \\ x_3(k) \end{bmatrix} + 4u(k) = \mathbf{c}^\dagger\mathbf{x}(k) + du(k)$$

output feedback of the form

$$u(k) = f[y(k) - 4u(k)] + \rho(k) = [4f \quad 0 \quad f] \begin{bmatrix} x_1(k) \\ x_2(k) \\ x_3(k) \end{bmatrix} + \rho(k)$$

where $f$ is a scalar, gives the following feedback system state equations:

$$\begin{bmatrix} x_1(k+1) \\ x_2(k+1) \\ x_3(k+1) \end{bmatrix} = \begin{bmatrix} 0 & 1 & 0 \\ 0 & 0 & 1 \\ 4f & 2 & f-1 \end{bmatrix} \begin{bmatrix} x_1(k) \\ x_2(k) \\ x_3(k) \end{bmatrix} + \begin{bmatrix} 0 \\ 0 \\ 1 \end{bmatrix} \rho(k)$$

This feedback system, shown in Figure 4-8(a), has characteristic equation, in terms of $f$

$$\lambda^3 + (1 - f)\lambda^2 - 2\lambda - 4f = 0 \tag{4-13}$$

The characteristic equations that can be achieved with output feedback are of this form, for some value of $f$.

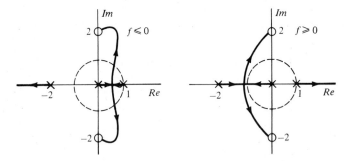

(a) System block diagram.

(b) Root locus for the system, as a function of the output feedback gain $f$.

**FIGURE 4-8.** **A third-order single-output system with output feedback.**

Collecting terms and arranging equation (4-13) as a root locus problem, there results

$$\lambda^3 + \lambda^2 - 2\lambda - f(\lambda^2 + 4) = 0$$

$$1 - f \frac{(\lambda + j2)(\lambda - j2)}{\lambda(\lambda - 1)(\lambda + 2)} = 0$$

Root locus plots for negative and for positive values of the adjustable constant $f$ are shown in Figure 4-8(b). In this case, no value of $f$ will result in even a stable system. Of course, this system could also be examined using $z$-transfer functions and classical root locus methods, where the same plots would result.

If there are instead two outputs, say

$$\begin{bmatrix} y_1(k) \\ y_2(k) \end{bmatrix} = \begin{bmatrix} 1 & 0 & -1 \\ -2 & 1 & 1 \end{bmatrix} \begin{bmatrix} x_1(k) \\ x_2(k) \\ x_3(k) \end{bmatrix} + \begin{bmatrix} 0 \\ 2 \end{bmatrix} u(k) = \mathbf{C}\mathbf{x}(k) + \mathbf{d}u(k)$$

then output feedback of the form

$$u(k) = \mathbf{f}^\dagger[\mathbf{y}(k) - \mathbf{d}u(k)] + \rho(k) = [f_1 \quad f_2] \begin{bmatrix} 1 & 0 & -1 \\ -2 & 1 & 1 \end{bmatrix} \begin{bmatrix} x_1(k) \\ x_2(k) \\ x_3(k) \end{bmatrix} + \rho(k)$$

$$= [(f_1 - 2f_2) \quad f_2 \quad (-f_1 + f_2)] \begin{bmatrix} x_1(k) \\ x_2(k) \\ x_3(k) \end{bmatrix} + \rho(k)$$

gives a feedback system governed by

$$\begin{bmatrix} x_1(k + 1) \\ x_2(k + 1) \\ x_3(k + 1) \end{bmatrix} = \begin{bmatrix} 0 & 1 & 0 \\ 0 & 0 & 1 \\ (f_1 - 2f_2) & (2 + f_2) & (-1 - f_1 + f_2) \end{bmatrix} \begin{bmatrix} x_1(k) \\ x_2(k) \\ x_3(k) \end{bmatrix} + \begin{bmatrix} 0 \\ 0 \\ 1 \end{bmatrix} \rho(k)$$

Characteristic polynomials of the form

$$\lambda^3 + (1 + f_1 - f_2)\lambda^2 + (-2 - f_2)\lambda + (-f_1 + 2f_2) = 0 \tag{4-14}$$

for any $f_1$ and $f_2$ can be achieved with output feedback in this system. As the three roots of equation (4-14) are constrained, it may or may not be possible to choose the constants $f_1$ and $f_2$ to achieve acceptable feedback system eigenvalue locations.

## 4.6.3 General Output Feedback

The dual result to that of single-output system eigenvalue placement with state feedback is this: the eigenvalues of a completely observable single-output system having independent inputs to each state equation

$$\mathbf{x}(k + 1) = \mathbf{A}\mathbf{x}(k) + \mathbf{u}(k)$$
$$\mathbf{y}(k) = \mathbf{c}^\dagger \mathbf{x}(k) \tag{4-15}$$

can be placed arbitrarily by appropriate choice of the feedback gains $\mathbf{f}$ in

$$\mathbf{u}(k) = \mathbf{f}y(k) \tag{4-16}$$

In (4-15), a separate component of the $n$-vector input $\mathbf{u}(k)$ couples to each of the $n$ state equations. This result also applies for a system

$$\mathbf{x}(k + 1) = \mathbf{A}\mathbf{x}(k) + \mathbf{B}\mathbf{u}(k)$$
$$y(k) = \mathbf{c}^\dagger\mathbf{x}(k) \tag{4-17}$$

where $\mathbf{B}$ is of rank $n$. If the input coupling matrix is square and nonsingular, for example, the choice

$$\mathbf{u}(k) = \mathbf{B}^{-1}\mathbf{f}y(k) = \mathbf{f}'y(k)$$

gives the same feedback system

$$\mathbf{x}(k + 1) = (\mathbf{A} + \mathbf{f}\mathbf{c}^\dagger)\mathbf{x}(k)$$

for (4-17) as for (4-16).

When such a system is in observable form, the feedback gains are especially easy to determine. For example, the system

$$\begin{bmatrix} x_1(k + 1) \\ x_2(k + 1) \\ x_3(k + 1) \end{bmatrix} = \begin{bmatrix} 2 & 1 & 0 \\ 1 & 0 & 1 \\ 3 & 0 & 0 \end{bmatrix}\begin{bmatrix} x_1(k) \\ x_2(k) \\ x_3(k) \end{bmatrix} + \begin{bmatrix} 2 & -1 & 0 \\ -1 & 1 & 0 \\ 0 & 0 & 1 \end{bmatrix}\begin{bmatrix} u_1(k) \\ u_2(k) \\ u_3(k) \end{bmatrix}$$

$$= \mathbf{A}\mathbf{x}(k) + \mathbf{B}\mathbf{u}(k)$$

$$y(k) = \begin{bmatrix} 1 & 0 & 0 \end{bmatrix}\begin{bmatrix} x_1(k) \\ x_2(k) \\ x_3(k) \end{bmatrix} = \mathbf{c}^\dagger\mathbf{x}(k)$$

with feedback

$$\begin{bmatrix} u_1(k) \\ u_2(k) \\ u_3(k) \end{bmatrix} = \begin{bmatrix} f_1 \\ f_2 \\ f_3 \end{bmatrix}y(k) = \mathbf{B}^{-1}\begin{bmatrix} f'_1 \\ f'_2 \\ f'_3 \end{bmatrix}y(k)$$

is described by

$$\begin{bmatrix} x_1(k + 1) \\ x_2(k + 1) \\ x_3(k + 1) \end{bmatrix} = \begin{bmatrix} (2 + f'_1) & 1 & 0 \\ (1 + f'_2) & 0 & 1 \\ (3 + f'_3) & 0 & 0 \end{bmatrix}\begin{bmatrix} x_1(k) \\ x_2(k) \\ x_3(k) \end{bmatrix} = (\mathbf{A} + \mathbf{f}'\mathbf{c}^\dagger)\mathbf{x}(k)$$

which has characteristic equation

$$\lambda^3 - (2 + f'_1)\lambda^2 - (1 + f'_2)\lambda - (3 + f'_3) = 0$$

Choosing

$$\mathbf{f}' = \begin{bmatrix} -2 \\ -\frac{3}{4} \\ -3 \end{bmatrix}; \quad \mathbf{f} = \mathbf{B}^{-1}\mathbf{f}' = \begin{bmatrix} -\frac{11}{4} \\ -\frac{7}{2} \\ -3 \end{bmatrix}$$

gives the characteristic equation

$$\lambda(\lambda + \tfrac{1}{2})(\lambda - \tfrac{1}{2}) = 0$$

If an $n$th order single-output plant has multiple inputs, but not $n$ linearly independent ones, the characteristic equations that can be achieved are constrained, as they are in the case of a multiple-output, single-input plant.

When a completely observable and completely controllable plant has both multiple outputs and multiple inputs, but not $n$ of either, it may or may not be possible to arbitrarily place the feedback system eigenvalues. Certainly, the number of gains to be chosen must be at least as large as the system (and characteristic equation) order. Except in the single-input and the single-output cases, the feedback system characteristic equation coefficients are nonlinear functions of the feedback gains.

## 4.7 Summary

If an $n$th order linear, step-invariant plant

$$\mathbf{x}(k + 1) = \mathbf{A}\mathbf{x}(k) + \mathbf{B}\mathbf{u}(k)$$

$$\mathbf{y}(k) = \mathbf{C}\mathbf{x}(k) + \mathbf{D}\mathbf{u}(k)$$

is completely observable, its state at any step can be calculated from a finite number of its most recent inputs and outputs. The linear algebraic equations for the state $\mathbf{x}(k)$ at any step $k$ in terms of known plant inputs and outputs from step $k$ onward have the plant's observability matrix,

$$\mathbf{M}_0 = \begin{bmatrix} \mathbf{C} \\ \hline \mathbf{CA} \\ \hline \mathbf{CA}^2 \\ \vdots \\ \hline \mathbf{CA}^{n-1} \end{bmatrix}$$

as the coefficient matrix. Hence the plant is completely observable and $x(k)$ can be found from measurements of $y(k)$, $y(k + 1)$, ..., $y(k + n − 1)$ and $u(k)$, $u(k + 1)$, ..., $u(k + n − 1)$ if and only if $M_0$ is of full rank. From $x(k)$ and the inputs, $x(k + 1)$, $x(k + 2)$,... can also be computed. The rank test of $M_0$ for complete observability also applies to continuous-time systems.

A set of overdetermined, inconsistent linear algebraic equations,

$$Hx = z$$

occurs in plant state estimation when more than the minimum number of measurements are available and when there are measurement errors. The least squares estimate of $x$ is the solution $\hat{x}$ of the consistent equations

$$H\hat{x} + v = z$$

such that the sum of squares of measurement errors

$$J = v_1^2 + v_2^2 + \cdots = v^\dagger v$$

is minimum. That solution is

$$\hat{x} = (H^\dagger H)^{-1} H^\dagger z$$

which is a linear transformation of the measurements, $z$.

Plant input and output measurements can also be used to identify plant parameters. If the parameters to be found are $z$-transfer function coefficients (which are also the input-output equation coefficients), the solution involves solving linear algebraic equations. When more than the minimal number of measurements are available, least squares estimation can be applied. Once the parameters are identified, the same input and output data can be used to determine or to estimate the plant state.

If an $n$th order linear, step-invariant plant is completely controllable, there are plant inputs that will bring the plant state from an initial state at any initial step to any desired later state in a finite number of steps. The linear algebraic equations for the required input sequence have the system's controllability matrix

$$M_c = [B \mid AB \mid A^2B \mid \cdots \mid A^{n-1}B]$$

as the coefficient matrix. There is a solution for an input sequence and the plant is therefore completely controllable if and only if $M_c$ is of full rank. The controllability matrix rank test also applies to continuous-time plants.

If the equations for control of a plant have a unique solution, there are no choices to be made; only one sequence of inputs will bring the plant to the desired state at the required step. If, instead, the equations are underdetermined, there are a family of solutions and the designer can select the "best" one according to some criterion. When this is done, the solution is optimal with respect to the criterion used. The simplest optimization involves minimizing a quadratic function of the state variables and inputs because the minimum is then described by linear equations.

When the state of a plant is available and is used for feedback

$$\mathbf{u}(k) = \mathbf{E}\mathbf{x}(k) + \boldsymbol{\rho}(k)$$

where $\boldsymbol{\rho}(k)$ is an external input, the state equation for the plant with feedback is

$$\mathbf{x}(k + 1) = (\mathbf{A} + \mathbf{BE})\mathbf{x}(k) + \mathbf{B}\boldsymbol{\rho}(k)$$

If the plant is completely controllable, the eigenvalues of the feedback system, those of $(\mathbf{A} + \mathbf{BE})$, can be placed at any locations selected by the designer by appropriately choosing the feedback gain matrix $\mathbf{E}$. Eigenvalue placement with state feedback for a single-input plant in controllable form is especially simple because, in that form, each element of the feedback gain vector determines one coefficient of the feedback system's characteristic equation. Transformation to and from controllable form can be used for feedback system eigenvalue placement design for any completely controllable single-input plant.

If an $n$th order plant has $n$ linearly independent outputs, its state is just a nonsingular linear transformation of the outputs minus any direct plant input-to-output coupling. The state is then obtainable from the output and output feedback can be used to place all the eigenvalues of the plant with feedback. When the plant has fewer than $n$ linearly independent outputs, its state cannot be obtained from an output transformation. If the plant has a single input, it will not be possible to arbitrarily place all the output feedback system eigenvalues. If the plant has multiple inputs, arbitrarily output feedback eigenvalue placement may or may not be possible.

# REFERENCES

Key references on observability and controllability were listed in Chapter 3. Least squares methods are discussed in detail in

T. C. Hsia, *System Identification.* Lexington, MA: D. C. Heath, 1977;

C. L. Lawson and R. J. Hanson, *Solving Least Squares Problems*, Englewood Cliffs, NJ: Prentice-Hall, 1974;

H. W. Sorenson, *Parameter Estimation.* New York: Marcel Dekker, 1980;

and in the article

H. W. Sorenson, "Least-Squares Estimation: from Gauss to Kalman," *IEEE Spectrum*, Vol. 7, no. 7, July 1970, pp. 63–68.

Results for eigenvalue placement with state feedback were developed by a number of researchers at about the same time:

W. M. Wonham, "On Pole Assignment in Multi-Input Controllable Linear Systems," *IEEE Trans. Automatic Control*, Vol. AC-12, Dec. 1967, pp. 660–665;

C.-T. Chen, "A Note on Pole Assignment," *IEEE Trans. Automatic Control*, Vol. AC-13, Oct. 1968, pp. 597–598;

E. J. Davison, "On Pole Assignment in Multivariable Linear Systems," *IEEE Trans. Automatic Control*, vol. AC-13, Dec. 1968, pp. 747–748;

M. Heymann, "Comments on Pole Assignment in Multi-Input Controllable Linear Systems," *IEEE Trans. Automatic Control*, Vol. AC-13, Dec. 1968, pp. 748–749.

## CHAPTER FOUR PROBLEMS

**4-1.** Use observability matrix rank tests to determine whether the following systems are completely observable:

**a.**
$$\begin{bmatrix} x_1(k+1) \\ x_2(k+1) \end{bmatrix} = \begin{bmatrix} 3 & 1 \\ -1 & 2 \end{bmatrix} \begin{bmatrix} x_1(k) \\ x_2(k) \end{bmatrix} + \begin{bmatrix} 6 \\ -4 \end{bmatrix} u(k)$$

$$y(k) = \begin{bmatrix} 0 & 1 \end{bmatrix} \begin{bmatrix} x_1(k) \\ x_2(k) \end{bmatrix} + 4u(k)$$

**b.**
$$\begin{bmatrix} x_1(k+1) \\ x_2(k+1) \\ x_3(k+1) \end{bmatrix} = \begin{bmatrix} 0 & -1 & -1 \\ 0 & -1 & 1 \\ 3 & 5 & -1 \end{bmatrix} \begin{bmatrix} x_1(k) \\ x_2(k) \\ x_3(k) \end{bmatrix} + \begin{bmatrix} -1 & 2 \\ 0 & 0 \\ 3 & 0 \end{bmatrix} \begin{bmatrix} u_1(k) \\ u_2(k) \end{bmatrix}$$

$$\begin{bmatrix} y_1(k) \\ y_2(k) \end{bmatrix} = \begin{bmatrix} 3 & 1 & 0 \\ 0 & 2 & 1 \end{bmatrix} \begin{bmatrix} x_1(k) \\ x_2(k) \\ x_3(k) \end{bmatrix} + \begin{bmatrix} 4 & -1 \\ -1 & \frac{1}{2} \end{bmatrix} \begin{bmatrix} u_1(k) \\ u_2(k) \end{bmatrix}$$

**4-2.** For the system

$$\begin{bmatrix} x_1(k+1) \\ x_2(k+1) \end{bmatrix} = \begin{bmatrix} 1 & 1 \\ -2 & -3 \end{bmatrix} \begin{bmatrix} x_1(k) \\ x_2(k) \end{bmatrix} + \begin{bmatrix} 2 \\ 3 \end{bmatrix} u(k)$$

$$y(k) = [2 \quad -1]\begin{bmatrix} x_1(k) \\ x_2(k) \end{bmatrix} + 2u(k)$$

find $\mathbf{x}(0)$ if $u(0) = 0$, $u(1) = 2$, $y(0) = -3$, and $y(1) = 4$. Then find $\mathbf{x}(1)$.

**4-3.**   For the system of Problem 4-2, find $\mathbf{x}(5)$ if $u(4) = -1$, $u(5) = 2$, $y(4) = 0$, and $y(5) = 3$.

**4-4.**   For the system

$$\begin{bmatrix} x_1(k+1) \\ x_2(k+1) \\ x_3(k+1) \end{bmatrix} = \begin{bmatrix} 2 & -1 & -1 \\ 0 & 1 & 3 \\ -2 & 0 & 1 \end{bmatrix} \begin{bmatrix} x_1(k) \\ x_2(k) \\ x_3(k) \end{bmatrix} + \begin{bmatrix} 3 \\ 1 \\ 0 \end{bmatrix} u(k)$$

$$y(k) = [0 \quad 2 \quad -1] \begin{bmatrix} x_1(k) \\ x_2(k) \\ x_3(k) \end{bmatrix} + 2u(k)$$

find $\mathbf{x}(0)$ if

$$y(0) = 3; \quad y(1) = 4; \quad y(2) = -2;$$
$$u(0) = 1; \quad u(1) = -2; \quad u(2) = 2$$

**4-5.**   For the system

$$\begin{bmatrix} x_1(k+1) \\ x_2(k+1) \end{bmatrix} = \begin{bmatrix} 3 & -1 \\ -2 & 1 \end{bmatrix} \begin{bmatrix} x_1(k) \\ x_2(k) \end{bmatrix} + \begin{bmatrix} 1 \\ -4 \end{bmatrix} u(k)$$

$$y(k) = [-1 \quad 2] \begin{bmatrix} x_1(k) \\ x_2(k) \end{bmatrix} + 2u(k)$$

find $\mathbf{x}(4)$ if $u(0) = 1$, $u(1) = 0$, $u(2) = -1$, $u(3) = 2$, $y(1) = 3$ and $y(2) = 0$.

**4-6.**   Find least squares estimates for the following sets of equations:

$$\mathbf{a.} \begin{cases} 2x = -3 \\ 3x = -10 \\ -x = 1 \end{cases}$$

$$\mathbf{b.} \begin{bmatrix} 1 & -2 \\ 2 & 2 \\ 3 & -1 \\ -1 & 1 \end{bmatrix} \begin{bmatrix} x_1 \\ x_2 \end{bmatrix} = \begin{bmatrix} 5 \\ 0 \\ 10 \\ -4 \end{bmatrix}$$

**4-7.**   The system

$$\begin{bmatrix} x_1(k+1) \\ x_2(k+1) \end{bmatrix} = \begin{bmatrix} 2 & 1 \\ -1 & 1 \end{bmatrix} \begin{bmatrix} x_1(k) \\ x_2(k) \end{bmatrix} + \begin{bmatrix} 1 \\ -1 \end{bmatrix} u(k)$$

$$y(k) = \begin{bmatrix} 1 & 1 \end{bmatrix} \begin{bmatrix} x_1(k) \\ x_2(k) \end{bmatrix}$$

has the following approximate input and output data:

$y(0) = -2;$    $u(0) = -2;$
$y(1) = -6;$    $u(1) = 1;$
$y(2) = -10;$   $u(2) = -1;$
$y(3) = -13;$   $u(3) = 1$

    **a.** Find the least squares estimate of the initial state, $\mathbf{x}(0)$.
    **b.** Using all the data, find the least squares estimate of $\mathbf{x}(1)$.

**4-8.**  A causal second-order single-input, single-output system has inputs and outputs as follows:

$y(0) = 1;$    $u(0) = 1;$
$y(1) = 0;$    $u(1) = 0;$
$y(2) = -1;$   $u(2) = 3;$
$y(3) = 2;$    $u(3) = 0;$
$y(4) = 0;$    $u(4) = -2;$
$y(5) = -1;$   $u(5) = -1;$
$y(6) = 1;$    $u(6) = 0$

    **a.** Find the system's input-output equation.
    **b.** If the system's state variable equations are in controllable form, find its state at steps 0, 1, and 2.

**4-9.**  A single-input, two-output, system has $z$-transfer functions of the form

$$T_1(z) = \frac{b}{z + a_0}$$

$$T_2(z) = \frac{b_1 z + b_0}{z + a_0}$$

Find the coefficients $a_0$, $b$, $b_1$, and $b_0$ if the system has the following outputs and inputs:

$y_1(3) = 3;$    $y_2(3) = 0;$    $u(3) = 1;$
$y_1(4) = -2;$   $y_2(4) = 1;$    $u(4) = -1;$
$y_1(5) = 1;$    $y_2(5) = 3;$    $u(5) = 0;$

**4-10.** A two-input, one-output system has $z$-transfer functions of the form

$$T_1(z) = \frac{b_1 z + b_0}{z + a_0}$$

$$T_2(z) = \frac{b}{z + a_0}$$

Find the coefficients $a_0$, $b_1$, $b_0$, and $b$ if the system has the following outputs and inputs:

| | | |
|---|---|---|
| $y(0) = 0;$ | $u_1(0) = 3;$ | $u_2(0) = -2;$ |
| $y(1) = -1;$ | $u_1(1) = -3;$ | $u_2(1) = -1;$ |
| $y(2) = 0;$ | $u_1(2) = 1;$ | $u_2(2) = 1;$ |
| $y(3) = 2;$ | $u_1(3) = 1;$ | $u_2(3) = 0;$ |
| $y(4) = 1;$ | $u_1(4) = 2$ | |

**4-11.** A system with $z$-transfer function

$$T(z) = \frac{b_1 z + b_0}{z + a_0} = \frac{3z + 6}{z + 2} = 3$$

has a pole-zero cancellation. Show that if the initial conditions are zero the parameters $a_0$ and $b_0$ cannot be separately identified from subsequent input and output data, but that the data will show that $b_0 = 3a_0$. Then let the initial conditions be $y(-1) = 4$, $u(-1) = 0$ and show that $a_0$, $b_1$, and $b_0$ can be identified from the outputs and inputs at steps 0, 1, and 2.

**4-12.** If the parameters of a system vary slowly enough with step, they can be identified accurately, as they vary, by simply using the minimum amount of most recent data to solve for them at each step. For a system with slowly step-varying input-output equation

$$y(k + 2) + a_1(k)y(k + 1) + a_0(k)y(k) = b_0(k)u(k)$$

generate (with computer aid) input and output data for steps $k = 0$ through $k = 99$. Then use the most recent data available to compute $a_1(k)$, $a_0(k)$, and $b_0(k)$ at each step from $k = 4$ on. Use the following parameters and inputs, and compare the actual and the computed parameters.

**a.** $a_1(k) = 0.5 + 0.01k,$ $\quad a_0(k) = 0.2,$
  $b_0(k) = 4 - 0.2k,$ $\quad u(k) = 0.95^k - 0.8^k$
**b.** $a_1(k) = 0.5 + 0.1k,$ $\quad a_0(k) = 0.2,$
  $b_0(k) = 4 - 0.5k,$ $\quad u(k) = 0.98^k$

**4-13.** Suppose the data of Problem 4-8 is for a causal *first*-order single-input, single-output system. Find the least squares solution for the parameters in the system's input-output equation.

**4-14.** Describe how the parameters of a *continuous-time* system can be found from samples of its outputs. Apply the method to a second-order example system.

**4-15.** Use controllability matrix rank tests to determine whether the systems with the following state equations are completely controllable:

a.
$$\begin{bmatrix} x_1(k+1) \\ x_2(k+1) \\ x_3(k+1) \end{bmatrix} = \begin{bmatrix} 1 & 1 & 2 \\ -1 & 2 & 0 \\ 0 & 3 & -3 \end{bmatrix} \begin{bmatrix} x_1(k) \\ x_2(k) \\ x_3(k) \end{bmatrix} + \begin{bmatrix} 2 \\ 0 \\ -2 \end{bmatrix} u(k)$$

b.
$$\begin{bmatrix} x_1(k+1) \\ x_2(k+1) \\ x_3(k+1) \end{bmatrix} = \begin{bmatrix} 0 & 0 & 3 \\ -1 & -1 & 5 \\ -1 & 1 & -1 \end{bmatrix} \begin{bmatrix} x_1(k) \\ x_2(k) \\ x_3(k) \end{bmatrix} + \begin{bmatrix} 0 & 3 \\ 2 & 1 \\ 1 & 0 \end{bmatrix} \begin{bmatrix} u_1(k) \\ u_2(k) \end{bmatrix}$$

**4-16.** For the system with state equations

$$\begin{bmatrix} x_1(k+1) \\ x_2(k+1) \end{bmatrix} = \begin{bmatrix} -1 & 3 \\ -1 & 2 \end{bmatrix} \begin{bmatrix} x_1(k) \\ x_2(k) \end{bmatrix} + \begin{bmatrix} 1 \\ -2 \end{bmatrix} u(k)$$

find the inputs $u(0)$ and $u(1)$ that will bring the state from

$$\mathbf{x}(0) = \begin{bmatrix} 4 \\ 6 \end{bmatrix} \quad \text{to} \quad \mathbf{x}(2) = \begin{bmatrix} -1 \\ 0 \end{bmatrix}$$

**4-17.** For the system of Problem 4-16, find the inputs $u(4)$ and $u(5)$ that will bring the state from

$$\mathbf{x}(4) = \begin{bmatrix} 1 \\ 0 \end{bmatrix} \quad \text{to} \quad \mathbf{x}(6) = \begin{bmatrix} 0 \\ 1 \end{bmatrix}$$

**4-18.** For the system with state equations

$$\begin{bmatrix} x_1(k+1) \\ x_2(k+1) \\ x_3(k+1) \end{bmatrix} = \begin{bmatrix} 1 & 2 & 0 \\ 4 & -1 & 0 \\ 0 & 1 & 3 \end{bmatrix} \begin{bmatrix} x_1(k) \\ x_2(k) \\ x_3(k) \end{bmatrix} + \begin{bmatrix} -1 \\ 1 \\ 0 \end{bmatrix} u(k)$$

find the inputs $u(0)$, $u(1)$ and $u(2)$ that will bring the state from

$$\begin{bmatrix} x_1(0) \\ x_2(0) \\ x_3(0) \end{bmatrix} = \begin{bmatrix} 6 \\ -3 \\ 1 \end{bmatrix} \quad \text{to} \quad \begin{bmatrix} x_1(3) \\ x_2(3) \\ x_3(3) \end{bmatrix} = \begin{bmatrix} 2 \\ 0 \\ -2 \end{bmatrix}$$

**4.19.** Find another set of inputs in Problem 4-18 that will bring the system from the given $\mathbf{x}(0)$ to a state where the *output*

$$\begin{bmatrix} y_1(k) \\ y_2(k) \end{bmatrix} = \begin{bmatrix} 3 & 0 & -2 \\ 1 & 1 & 0 \end{bmatrix} \begin{bmatrix} x_1(k) \\ x_2(k) \\ x_3(k) \end{bmatrix}$$

is

$$\begin{bmatrix} y_1 \\ y_2 \end{bmatrix} = \begin{bmatrix} 3 \\ 4 \end{bmatrix}$$

Can this be done in two steps?

**4-20.** For the system with state equations

$$\begin{bmatrix} x_1(k+1) \\ x_2(k+1) \end{bmatrix} = \begin{bmatrix} 3 & 1 \\ 2 & -1 \end{bmatrix} \begin{bmatrix} x_1(k) \\ x_2(k) \end{bmatrix} + \begin{bmatrix} 1 & 2 \\ -1 & 0 \end{bmatrix} \begin{bmatrix} u_1(k) \\ u_2(k) \end{bmatrix}$$

find inputs $\mathbf{u}(1)$, $\mathbf{u}(2)$, and $\mathbf{u}(3)$ that will bring the state $\mathbf{x}$ from

$$\mathbf{x}(1) = \begin{bmatrix} 2 \\ -1 \end{bmatrix} \quad \text{to} \quad \mathbf{x}(4) = \begin{bmatrix} 0 \\ 3 \end{bmatrix}$$

**4-21.** For the discrete-time system with state equations

$$\begin{bmatrix} x_1(k+1) \\ x_2(k+1) \\ x_3(k+1) \end{bmatrix} = \begin{bmatrix} 0 & 1 & 0 \\ 0 & 0 & 1 \\ -2 & 1 & -1 \end{bmatrix} \begin{bmatrix} x_1(k) \\ x_2(k) \\ x_3(k) \end{bmatrix} + \begin{bmatrix} 0 \\ 0 \\ 1 \end{bmatrix} u(k)$$

find the state feedback gains $\mathbf{e}$ in

$$u(k) = \mathbf{e}^\dagger \mathbf{x}(k) + \rho(k)$$

such that the feedback system has eigenvalues at $\lambda = \frac{1}{2}$ and at $\lambda = (\frac{1}{2}) \pm j(\frac{1}{4})$

**4-22.** For the discrete-time system with state equations

$$\begin{bmatrix} x_1(k+1) \\ x_2(k+1) \\ x_3(k+1) \end{bmatrix} = \begin{bmatrix} 0 & -2 & 2 \\ 3 & 2 & 0 \\ -1 & 0 & -3 \end{bmatrix} \begin{bmatrix} x_1(k) \\ x_2(k) \\ x_3(k) \end{bmatrix} + \begin{bmatrix} 0 \\ 4 \\ 0 \end{bmatrix} u(k)$$

find the state feedback gains $\mathbf{e}$ in

$$u(k) = \mathbf{e}^\dagger \mathbf{x}(k) + \rho(k)$$

such that the feedback system has eigenvalues at $\lambda = 0$ and at $\lambda = \pm j$.

**4-23.** For the discrete-time system with state equations

$$\begin{bmatrix} x_1(k+1) \\ x_2(k+1) \\ x_3(k+1) \end{bmatrix} = \begin{bmatrix} 1 & 0 & 0 \\ 0 & \frac{1}{2} & 0 \\ 0 & 0 & -1 \end{bmatrix} \begin{bmatrix} x_1(k) \\ x_2(k) \\ x_3(k) \end{bmatrix} + \begin{bmatrix} 2 & 0 \\ -1 & 1 \\ 0 & 3 \end{bmatrix} \begin{bmatrix} u_1(k) \\ u_2(k) \end{bmatrix}$$

find the state feedback gains $\mathbf{E}$ in

$$
\begin{bmatrix} u_1(k) \\ u_2(k) \end{bmatrix} = \begin{bmatrix} e_{11} & e_{12} & e_{13} \\ e_{21} & e_{22} & e_{23} \end{bmatrix} \begin{bmatrix} x_1(k) \\ x_2(k) \\ x_3(k) \end{bmatrix} + \begin{bmatrix} \rho_1(k) \\ \rho_2(k) \end{bmatrix} = \mathbf{E}\mathbf{x}(k) + \mathbf{\rho}(k)
$$

such that the feedback system has all eigenvalues at $\lambda = 0$.

**4-24.** Find a *different* set of feedback gains $\mathbf{E}$ for Problem 4-23.

**4-25.** For the system

$$
\begin{bmatrix} x_1(k+1) \\ x_2(k+1) \\ x_3(k+1) \end{bmatrix} = \begin{bmatrix} 0 & 1 & 0 \\ 0 & 0 & 1 \\ -2 & 1 & -1 \end{bmatrix} \begin{bmatrix} x_1(k) \\ x_2(k) \\ x_3(k) \end{bmatrix} + \begin{bmatrix} 0 \\ 0 \\ 1 \end{bmatrix} u(k)
$$

$$
\begin{bmatrix} y_1(k) \\ y_2(k) \\ y_3(k) \end{bmatrix} = \begin{bmatrix} 1 & -1 & 0 \\ 2 & 0 & 1 \\ 0 & 2 & -1 \end{bmatrix} \begin{bmatrix} x_1(k) \\ x_2(k) \\ x_3(k) \end{bmatrix} + \begin{bmatrix} 3 \\ -2 \\ 4 \end{bmatrix} u(k)
$$

find the output feedback gains $\mathbf{f}$ in

$$
u(k) = \mathbf{f}^{\dagger}[\mathbf{y}(k) - \mathbf{d}u(k)] + \rho(k)
$$

such that the feedback system has eigenvalues at $\lambda = 0$ and at $\lambda = \pm j\frac{1}{2}$.

**4-26.** For the system of Problem 4-25, suppose instead that the outputs

$$
\begin{bmatrix} y_1(k) \\ y_2(k) \\ y_3(k) \\ y_4(k) \end{bmatrix} = \begin{bmatrix} 1 & 2 & 3 \\ 4 & 5 & 6 \\ 3 & 1 & -2 \\ -1 & 3 & 7 \end{bmatrix} \begin{bmatrix} x_1(k) \\ x_2(k) \\ x_3(k) \end{bmatrix} + \begin{bmatrix} 6 \\ -3 \\ 0 \\ 4 \end{bmatrix} u(k)
$$

are available. Design an output feedback system such that the overall system's characteristic equation is

$$
\lambda^3 = 0
$$

Verify that the system you have designed has this property.

**4-27.** Repeat Problem 4-26 designing a different feedback system for which the characteristic equation of the overall system is

$$
\lambda^3 - \lambda^2 + \lambda + \tfrac{1}{2} = 0
$$

In this design, have *all four* outputs couple to the input $u(k)$ with nonzero coefficients.

4-28. For the system

$$\begin{bmatrix} x_1(k+1) \\ x_2(k+1) \\ x_3(k+1) \end{bmatrix} = \begin{bmatrix} 3 & 1 & 0 \\ 1 & 0 & 1 \\ -2 & 0 & 0 \end{bmatrix} \begin{bmatrix} x_1(k) \\ x_2(k) \\ x_3(k) \end{bmatrix} + \begin{bmatrix} 1 & 0 & -1 \\ -4 & 1 & 2 \\ 2 & 0 & 1 \end{bmatrix} \begin{bmatrix} u_1(k) \\ u_2(k) \\ u_3(k) \end{bmatrix}$$

$$y(k) = \begin{bmatrix} 1 & 0 & 0 \end{bmatrix} \begin{bmatrix} x_1(k) \\ x_2(k) \\ x_3(k) \end{bmatrix}$$

find the output feedback gains $\mathbf{f}$ in

$$\mathbf{u}(k) = \mathbf{f} y(k)$$

such that the feedback system has eigenvalues at $\lambda = \frac{1}{2}$ and at $\lambda = \pm j$.

# Digital Regulator Design

5

## 5.1 Preview

In 1964, David Luenberger of Stanford University put forth the idea of *observers*, systems that recursively estimate the state of other systems. It was soon realized that observers offer a powerful, unified framework for feedback control system design.

This chapter addresses the first of two concerns of digital tracking system design, that of obtaining acceptable feedback system zero-input response. The systems that result are *regulators*. When the plant state is not entirely accessible, as is usually the case, the state is estimated with an observer and the estimated state is used in place of the actual state for feedback. Basic observer theory is now developed and a simple, complete observer design procedure, yielding observers of minimal order if desired, is applied. It is then shown that by using the plant state estimate for feedback in place of the measured plant state itself, the designer has complete freedom to place all of the feedback system eigenvalues.

## 5.2 Full-Order State Observers

When a plant's state is not available for feedback, a suitably formed estimate of the state, from the plant outputs and inputs, can be used in place of the state itself. An *observer* of a plant is another system with inputs that are the plant inputs and the plant outputs. The observer produces an estimate of the plant state or of a transformation of that state.

### 5.2.1 Basic Theory

For an $n$th order plant

$$\mathbf{x}(k + 1) = \mathbf{Ax}(k) + \mathbf{Bu}(k)$$

$$\mathbf{y}(k) = \mathbf{Cx}(k) + \mathbf{Du}(k) \tag{5-1}$$

another $n$th order system, driven by the inputs and outputs of the plant as in Figure 5-1,

$$\xi(k + 1) = \mathbf{F}\xi(k) + \mathbf{Gy}(k) + \mathbf{Hu}(k) \tag{5-2}$$

is termed *a full order state observer* of the plant, provided that the error between the plant and observer states

$$\mathbf{x}(k + 1) - \xi(k + 1) = \mathbf{Ax}(k) + \mathbf{Bu}(k) - \mathbf{F}\xi(k) - \mathbf{Gy}(k) - \mathbf{Hu}(k)$$

$$= \mathbf{Ax}(k) + \mathbf{Bu}(k) - \mathbf{F}\xi(k) - \mathbf{GCx}(k) - \mathbf{GDu}(k) - \mathbf{Hu}(k)$$

$$= (\mathbf{A} - \mathbf{GC})\mathbf{x}(k) - \mathbf{F}\xi(k) + (\mathbf{B} - \mathbf{GD} - \mathbf{H})\mathbf{u}(k)$$

is governed by an autonomous (zero-input) equation. When $\mathbf{F}$ and $\mathbf{H}$ are chosen as

$$\mathbf{F} = \mathbf{A} - \mathbf{GC}$$

$$\mathbf{H} = \mathbf{B} - \mathbf{GD}$$

so that the error signal satisfies

$$\mathbf{x}(k + 1) - \xi(k + 1) = (\mathbf{A} - \mathbf{GC})[\mathbf{x}(k) - \xi(k)]$$

then the system (5-2) is a full-order state observer of the plant (5-1). If the matrix $\mathbf{G}$ can be chosen so that all the eigenvalues of $\mathbf{F} = \mathbf{A} - \mathbf{GC}$ are inside the unit circle in the complex plane, the error will approach zero with step. *Full-order* means that the observer is of the same order as the plant; *state*

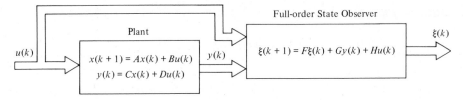

**FIGURE 5-1. A full-order state observer of a plant.**

*observer* means that the output (which is here the observer state) approaches the plant state rather than some transformation of the plant state. The full-order state observer relations are summarized in Table 5-1.

## 5.2.2 Observers of Systems in Observable Form

For a single-output plant, Figure 5-2

$$x(k + 1) = \mathbf{A}x(k) + \mathbf{B}u(k)$$

$$y(k) = c^\dagger x(k) + \mathbf{d}^\dagger u(k)$$

the full-order state observer relations are

$$\xi(k + 1) = \mathbf{F}\xi(k) + \mathbf{g}y(k) + \mathbf{H}u(k)$$
$$= (\mathbf{A} - \mathbf{g}c^\dagger)\xi(k) + \mathbf{g}y(k) + (\mathbf{B} - \mathbf{g}d^\dagger)u(k)$$

**TABLE 5-1   Full-Order State Observer Relations**

### *Plant Model*

$$x(k + 1) = \mathbf{A}x(k) + \mathbf{B}u(k)$$

$$y(k) = \mathbf{C}x(k) + \mathbf{D}u(k)$$

### *Observer*

$$\xi(k + 1) = \mathbf{F}\xi(k) + \mathbf{G}y(k) + \mathbf{H}u(k)$$

where

$$\mathbf{F} = \mathbf{A} - \mathbf{GC}$$

$$\mathbf{H} = \mathbf{B} - \mathbf{GD}$$

### *Observer Error*

$$x(k + 1) - \xi(k + 1) = \mathbf{F}[x(k) - \xi(k)]$$

$$x(k) - \xi(k) = \mathbf{F}^k[x(0) - \xi(0)]$$

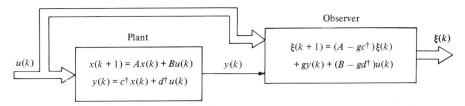

**FIGURE 5-2.   Full-order state observer of a single-output plant.**

and the error between the plant state and the observer state is governed by

$$\mathbf{x}(k + 1) - \xi(k + 1) = (\mathbf{A} - \mathbf{gc^t})[\mathbf{x}(k) - \xi(k)]$$

The eigenvalues of $\mathbf{F} = \mathbf{A} - \mathbf{gc^t}$ can be placed arbitrarily by choice of $\mathbf{g}$ provided that $(\mathbf{A}, \mathbf{c})$ is completely observable. This is similar to the situation with state feedback, where the eigenvalues of $\mathbf{A} + \mathbf{be^t}$ can be placed arbitrarily by choice of $\mathbf{e}$ providing that the system $(\mathbf{A}, \mathbf{b})$ is completely controllable.

For example, consider the plant

$$\begin{bmatrix} x_1(k + 1) \\ x_2(k + 1) \\ x_3(k + 1) \end{bmatrix} = \begin{bmatrix} \frac{1}{2} & 1 & 0 \\ -1 & 0 & 1 \\ 0 & 0 & 0 \end{bmatrix} \begin{bmatrix} x_1(k) \\ x_2(k) \\ x_3(k) \end{bmatrix} + \begin{bmatrix} 1 & 4 \\ 0 & 0 \\ -3 & 2 \end{bmatrix} \begin{bmatrix} u_1(k) \\ u_2(k) \end{bmatrix} = \mathbf{A}\mathbf{x}(k) + \mathbf{B}\mathbf{u}(k)$$

$$y(k) = \begin{bmatrix} 1 & 0 & 0 \end{bmatrix} \begin{bmatrix} x_1(k) \\ x_2(k) \\ x_3(k) \end{bmatrix} + \begin{bmatrix} 0 & 4 \end{bmatrix} \begin{bmatrix} u_1(k) \\ u_2(k) \end{bmatrix} = \mathbf{c^t}\mathbf{x}(k) + \mathbf{d^t}\mathbf{u}(k) \qquad (5\text{-}3)$$

which is in observable form. A full-order state observer of this plant is another third-order system. If the observer output is the observer state, then

$$\xi(k + 1) = \mathbf{F}\xi(k) + \mathbf{g}y(k) + \mathbf{H}\mathbf{u}(k) = (\mathbf{A} - \mathbf{gc^t})\xi(k) + \mathbf{g}y(k) + (\mathbf{B} - \mathbf{gd^t})\mathbf{u}(k)$$

or

$$\begin{bmatrix} \xi_1(k + 1) \\ \xi_2(k + 1) \\ \xi_3(k + 1) \end{bmatrix} = \left( \begin{bmatrix} \frac{1}{2} & 1 & 0 \\ -1 & 0 & 1 \\ 0 & 0 & 0 \end{bmatrix} - \begin{bmatrix} g_1 \\ g_2 \\ g_3 \end{bmatrix} \begin{bmatrix} 1 & 0 & 0 \end{bmatrix} \right) \begin{bmatrix} \xi_1(k) \\ \xi_2(k) \\ \xi_3(k) \end{bmatrix}$$

$$+ \begin{bmatrix} g_1 \\ g_2 \\ g_3 \end{bmatrix} y(k) + \left( \begin{bmatrix} 1 & 4 \\ 0 & 0 \\ -3 & 2 \end{bmatrix} - \begin{bmatrix} g_1 \\ g_2 \\ g_3 \end{bmatrix} \begin{bmatrix} 0 & 4 \end{bmatrix} \right) \begin{bmatrix} u_1(k) \\ u_2(k) \end{bmatrix}$$

$$
= \begin{bmatrix} (\frac{1}{2} - g_1) & 1 & 0 \\ (-1 - g_2) & 0 & 1 \\ -g_3 & 0 & 0 \end{bmatrix} \begin{bmatrix} \xi_1(k) \\ \xi_2(k) \\ \xi_3(k) \end{bmatrix} + \begin{bmatrix} g_1 \\ g_2 \\ g_3 \end{bmatrix} y(k)
$$

$$
+ \begin{bmatrix} 1 & (4 - 4g_1) \\ 0 & -4g_2 \\ -3 & (2 - 4g_3) \end{bmatrix} \begin{bmatrix} u_1(k) \\ u_2(k) \end{bmatrix}
$$

The characteristic equation of the observer is, in terms of the gains $g_1, g_2$, and $g_3$:

$$
\lambda^3 + (-\tfrac{1}{2} + g_1)\lambda^2 + (1 + g_2)\lambda + g_3 = 0
$$

If it is desired that the observer have eigenvalues of 0 and $-\tfrac{1}{2} \pm j\tfrac{1}{4}$ then the desired characteristic equation is

$$
\lambda(\lambda + \tfrac{1}{2} + j\tfrac{1}{4})(\lambda + \tfrac{1}{2} - j\tfrac{1}{4}) = \lambda^3 + \lambda^2 + \tfrac{5}{16}\lambda = 0
$$

which is achieved for

$$
\mathbf{g} = \begin{bmatrix} g_1 \\ g_2 \\ g_3 \end{bmatrix} = \begin{bmatrix} \frac{3}{2} \\ -\frac{11}{16} \\ 0 \end{bmatrix}
$$

The observer with these eigenvalues is

$$
\begin{bmatrix} \xi_1(k+1) \\ \xi_2(k+1) \\ \xi_3(k+1) \end{bmatrix} = \begin{bmatrix} -1 & 1 & 0 \\ -\frac{5}{16} & 0 & 1 \\ 0 & 0 & 0 \end{bmatrix} \begin{bmatrix} \xi_1(k) \\ \xi_2(k) \\ \xi_3(k) \end{bmatrix} + \begin{bmatrix} \frac{3}{2} \\ -\frac{11}{16} \\ 0 \end{bmatrix} y(k)
$$

$$
+ \begin{bmatrix} 1 & -2 \\ 0 & \frac{11}{4} \\ -3 & 2 \end{bmatrix} \begin{bmatrix} u_1(k) \\ u_2(k) \end{bmatrix} \tag{5-4}
$$

In Figure 5-3, the state of the plant (5-3) and of the observer (5-4) are shown for arbitrarily chosen plant inputs and initial conditions. The error between the state of the plant and the observer state is described by

$$
\mathbf{x}(k+1) - \xi(k+1) = \mathbf{F}[\mathbf{x}(k) - \xi(k)]
$$

and decays as $\mathbf{F}^k$.

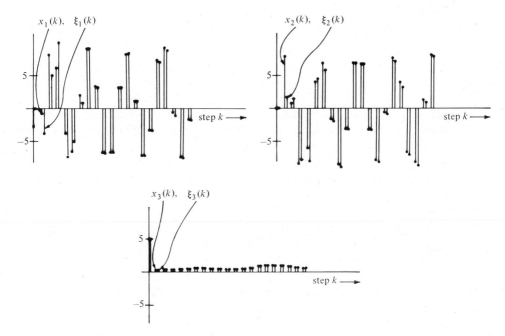

**FIGURE 5-3.** Comparison of plant and observer states.

## 5.2.3 Deadbeat Observation

If the characteristic equation of an $n$th order observer is chosen to be

$$\lambda^n = 0$$

that is, with all eigenvalues at $\lambda = 0$, then applying the Cayley-Hamilton theorem:

$$\mathbf{F}^n = \mathbf{0}$$

At the $n$th step, the error between the plant state and the observer state is given by

$$\mathbf{x}(n) - \xi(n) = \mathbf{F}^n[\mathbf{x}(0) - \xi(0)] = \mathbf{0}$$

so

$$\xi(n) = \mathbf{x}(n)$$

and the observer state equals the plant state. Such an observer is termed *deadbeat*. In subsequent steps, the observer state continues to equal the plant state.

By placing all observer eigenvalues at $\lambda = 0$, the observer state is made to converge to that of the plant in $n$ steps. The same can be done with conventional calculation; the state of a completely observable single-output plant can be determined from its inputs and outputs over the preceding $n$ steps by solving the $n$ simultaneous linear algebraic equations involving the observability matrix, as was done earlier. A deadbeat observer is thus a recursive way to solve a set of linear algebraic equations.

A full-order state observer of the plant (5-3), when designed to be deadbeat, is governed by

$$\begin{bmatrix} \xi_1(k+1) \\ \xi_2(k+1) \\ \xi_3(k+1) \end{bmatrix} = \begin{bmatrix} 0 & 1 & 0 \\ 0 & 0 & 1 \\ 0 & 0 & 0 \end{bmatrix} \begin{bmatrix} \xi_1(k) \\ \xi_2(k) \\ \xi_3(k) \end{bmatrix} + \begin{bmatrix} \frac{1}{2} \\ -1 \\ 0 \end{bmatrix} y(k) + \begin{bmatrix} 1 & -2 \\ 0 & 4 \\ -3 & 2 \end{bmatrix} \begin{bmatrix} u_1(k) \\ u_2(k) \end{bmatrix}$$

and has the typical response shown in Figure 5-4. The observer state converges to that of the plant in three steps, regardless of inputs and initial conditions.

The control system designer may or may not wish to design an observer to be deadbeat. A more gradual approach to the plant state by the state of the

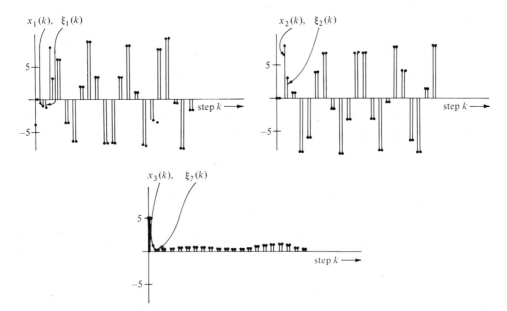

**FIGURE 5-4.  Typical response of a deadbeat observer of a third order plant.**

observer might be preferred. Conventional step-invariant deadbeat observers can exhibit very large errors during the steps before convergence occurs and can be overly susceptible to errors due to noise affecting the plant state and measurements.

### 5.2.4 Observers of General Single-Output Systems

For a completely observable single-output plant that is not in observable form, one method of design is to change state variables to the observable form, design the observer in that form, then convert back to the original system realization. The state variables of a completely observable single-output plant of the form

$$\mathbf{x}(k + 1) = \mathbf{A}\mathbf{x}(k) + \mathbf{B}\mathbf{u}(k)$$
$$y(k) = \mathbf{c}^\dagger\mathbf{x}(k) + \mathbf{d}^\dagger\mathbf{u}(k)$$

are changed via

$$\mathbf{x}(k) = \mathbf{P}\mathbf{x}'(k) = \mathbf{Q}^{-1}\mathbf{x}'(k); \qquad \mathbf{x}'(k) = \mathbf{P}^{-1}\mathbf{x}(k) = \mathbf{Q}\mathbf{x}(k)$$

to place it in observable form

$$\mathbf{x}'(k + 1) = \mathbf{A}'\mathbf{x}'(k) + \mathbf{B}'\mathbf{u}(k)$$
$$y(k) = \mathbf{c}'^\dagger\mathbf{x}'(k) + \mathbf{d}^\dagger\mathbf{u}(k)$$

where

$$\mathbf{A}' = \mathbf{Q}\mathbf{A}\mathbf{Q}^{-1}$$
$$\mathbf{B}' = \mathbf{Q}\mathbf{B}$$
$$\mathbf{c}'^\dagger = \mathbf{c}^\dagger\mathbf{Q}^{-1}$$

A full-order observer of $\mathbf{x}'(k)$, with eigenvalues selected by the designer, is formed

$$\boldsymbol{\xi}'(k + 1) = \mathbf{F}'\boldsymbol{\xi}(k) + \mathbf{g}'y(k) + \mathbf{H}'\mathbf{u}(k)$$

where

$$\mathbf{F}' = \mathbf{A}' - \mathbf{g}'\mathbf{c}'^\dagger$$
$$\mathbf{H}' = \mathbf{B}' - \mathbf{g}'\mathbf{d}^\dagger$$

Using the observer output equation

$$\mathbf{w}(k) = \mathbf{P}\xi'(k) = \mathbf{Q}^{-1}\xi'(k)$$

transforms the observer state $\xi'(k)$ that observes $\mathbf{x}'(k)$ to $\mathbf{w}(k)$ that observes $\mathbf{x}(k)$, as shown in Figure 5-5(a). Or, transforming the observer state according to

$$\xi(k) = \mathbf{P}\xi'(k) = \mathbf{Q}^{-1}\xi'(k); \qquad \xi'(k) = \mathbf{P}^{-1}\xi(k) = \mathbf{Q}\xi(k)$$

to give

$$\xi(k + 1) = \mathbf{F}\xi(k) + \mathbf{g}y(k) + \mathbf{H}u(k)$$

where

$$\mathbf{g} = \mathbf{Q}^{-1}\mathbf{g}'$$
$$\mathbf{F} = \mathbf{Q}^{-1}\mathbf{F}'\mathbf{Q} = \mathbf{Q}^{-1}\mathbf{A}'\mathbf{Q} - \mathbf{Q}^{-1}\mathbf{g}'\mathbf{c}'^{\dagger}\mathbf{Q} = \mathbf{A} - \mathbf{g}\mathbf{c}^{\dagger}$$
$$\mathbf{H} = \mathbf{Q}^{-1}\mathbf{H}' = \mathbf{Q}^{-1}\mathbf{B}' - \mathbf{Q}^{-1}\mathbf{g}'\mathbf{d}^{\dagger} = \mathbf{B} - \mathbf{g}\mathbf{d}^{\dagger}$$

results in a full-order state observer of $\mathbf{x}(k)$. This arrangement is shown in Figure 5-5(b).

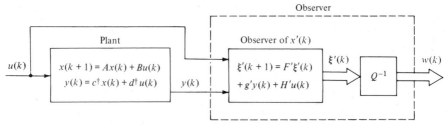

(a) State observer with output that converges to the plant state.

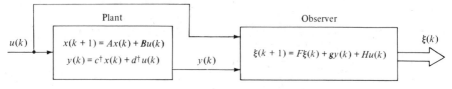

(b) Alternative where the observer state converges to the plant state.

**FIGURE 5-5.    Full-order observers of a single-output system.**

For example, the plant

$$\begin{bmatrix} x_1(k+1) \\ x_2(k+1) \\ x_3(k+1) \end{bmatrix} = \begin{bmatrix} 0 & 3 & 0 \\ 0 & 2 & 1 \\ 1 & 1 & 0 \end{bmatrix} \begin{bmatrix} x_1(k) \\ x_2(k) \\ x_3(k) \end{bmatrix} + \begin{bmatrix} 2 \\ 1 \\ -1 \end{bmatrix} u(k) = \mathbf{A}\mathbf{x}(k) + \mathbf{b}u(k)$$

$$y(k) = \begin{bmatrix} 0 & 2 & 1 \end{bmatrix} \begin{bmatrix} x_1(k) \\ x_2(k) \\ x_3(k) \end{bmatrix} + u(k) = \mathbf{c}^\dagger\mathbf{x}(k) + du(k)$$

has characteristic equation

$$\begin{vmatrix} \lambda & -3 & 0 \\ 0 & (\lambda - 2) & -1 \\ -1 & -1 & \lambda \end{vmatrix} = \lambda^3 - 2\lambda^2 - \lambda - 3 = \lambda^3 + \alpha_2\lambda^2 + \alpha_1\lambda + \alpha_0 = 0$$

The transformation that takes this plant to observable form is given by

$$\mathbf{Q} = \begin{bmatrix} \mathbf{q}_1^\dagger \\ \hline \mathbf{q}_2^\dagger \\ \hline \mathbf{q}_3^\dagger \end{bmatrix}$$

where

$$\mathbf{q}_1^\dagger = \mathbf{c}^\dagger = \begin{bmatrix} 0 & 2 & 1 \end{bmatrix}$$

$$\mathbf{q}_2^\dagger = \mathbf{q}_1^\dagger\mathbf{A} + \alpha_2\mathbf{c}^\dagger = \begin{bmatrix} 0 & 2 & 1 \end{bmatrix} \begin{bmatrix} 0 & 3 & 0 \\ 0 & 2 & 1 \\ 1 & 1 & 0 \end{bmatrix} + (-2)\begin{bmatrix} 0 & 2 & 1 \end{bmatrix}$$

$$= \begin{bmatrix} 1 & 1 & 0 \end{bmatrix}$$

$$\mathbf{q}_3^\dagger = \mathbf{q}_2^\dagger\mathbf{A} + \alpha_1\mathbf{c}^\dagger = \begin{bmatrix} 1 & 1 & 0 \end{bmatrix} \begin{bmatrix} 0 & 3 & 0 \\ 0 & 2 & 1 \\ 1 & 1 & 0 \end{bmatrix} + (-1)\begin{bmatrix} 0 & 2 & 1 \end{bmatrix}$$

$$= \begin{bmatrix} 0 & 3 & 0 \end{bmatrix}$$

So

$$\mathbf{Q} = \mathbf{P}^{-1} = \begin{bmatrix} 0 & 2 & 1 \\ 1 & 1 & 0 \\ 0 & 3 & 0 \end{bmatrix}; \qquad \mathbf{Q}^{-1} = \mathbf{P} = \begin{bmatrix} 0 & 1 & -\frac{1}{3} \\ 0 & 0 & \frac{1}{3} \\ 1 & 0 & -\frac{2}{3} \end{bmatrix}$$

The transformed plant is

$$
\begin{bmatrix} x_1'(k+1) \\ x_2'(k+1) \\ x_3'(k+1) \end{bmatrix} = \begin{bmatrix} 2 & 1 & 0 \\ 1 & 0 & 1 \\ 3 & 0 & 0 \end{bmatrix} \begin{bmatrix} x_1'(k) \\ x_2'(k) \\ x_3'(k) \end{bmatrix} + \begin{bmatrix} 1 \\ 3 \\ 3 \end{bmatrix} u(k) = \mathbf{A}'\mathbf{x}'(k) + \mathbf{b}'u(k)
$$

$$
y(k) = \begin{bmatrix} 1 & 0 & 0 \end{bmatrix} \begin{bmatrix} x_1'(k) \\ x_2'(k) \\ x_3'(k) \end{bmatrix} + u(k) = \mathbf{c}'^{\mathsf{t}}\mathbf{x}(k) + du(k)
$$

and, since it is in observable form, a full-order state observer of $\mathbf{x}'(k)$ is easy to design.

Suppose that it is desired that all three observer eigenvalues be at $\lambda = 0$, so that the desired observer is deadbeat, with characteristic equation

$$
\lambda^3 = 0
$$

Then an observer of the $\mathbf{x}'$ state has state coupling matrix

$$
\mathbf{F}' = \mathbf{A}' - \mathbf{g}'\mathbf{c}'^{\mathsf{t}} = \begin{bmatrix} 2 & 1 & 0 \\ 1 & 0 & 1 \\ 3 & 0 & 0 \end{bmatrix} - \begin{bmatrix} g_1' \\ g_2' \\ g_3' \end{bmatrix} \begin{bmatrix} 1 & 0 & 0 \end{bmatrix} = \begin{bmatrix} 2 - g_1' & 1 & 0 \\ 1 - g_2' & 0 & 1 \\ 3 - g_3' & 0 & 0 \end{bmatrix}
$$

The observer's characteristic equation, in terms of $g_1'$, $g_2'$, and $g_3'$, is

$$
\lambda^3 + (g_1' - 2)\lambda^2 + (g_2' - 1)\lambda + (g_3' - 3) = 0
$$

and becomes the desired

$$
\lambda^3 = 0
$$

for

$$
\mathbf{g}' = \begin{bmatrix} g_1' \\ g_2' \\ g_3' \end{bmatrix} = \begin{bmatrix} 2 \\ 1 \\ 3 \end{bmatrix}
$$

with this choice of $\mathbf{g}'$, the coupling of the input $u(k)$ into the observer is

$$
\mathbf{h}' = \mathbf{b}' - \mathbf{g}'d = \begin{bmatrix} 1 \\ 3 \\ 3 \end{bmatrix} - \begin{bmatrix} 2 \\ 1 \\ 3 \end{bmatrix}(1) = \begin{bmatrix} -1 \\ 2 \\ 0 \end{bmatrix}
$$

so that the observer of the $\mathbf{x}'$ state has equations

$$\begin{bmatrix} \xi_1'(k+1) \\ \xi_2'(k+1) \\ \xi_3'(k+1) \end{bmatrix} = \begin{bmatrix} 0 & 1 & 0 \\ 0 & 0 & 1 \\ 0 & 0 & 0 \end{bmatrix} \begin{bmatrix} \xi_1'(k) \\ \xi_2'(k) \\ \xi_3'(k) \end{bmatrix} + \begin{bmatrix} 2 \\ 1 \\ 3 \end{bmatrix} y(k) + \begin{bmatrix} -1 \\ 2 \\ 0 \end{bmatrix} u(k)$$

$$= \mathbf{F}'\xi'(k) + \mathbf{g}'y(k) + \mathbf{h}'u(k)$$

To observe the original state $\mathbf{x}$ rather than $\mathbf{x}'$, this observer's state can be transformed with an output equation

$$\mathbf{w}(k) = \mathbf{P}\xi'(k) = \mathbf{Q}^{-1}\xi'(k)$$

or

$$\begin{bmatrix} w_1(k) \\ w_2(k) \\ w_3(k) \end{bmatrix} = \begin{bmatrix} 0 & 1 & -\frac{1}{3} \\ 0 & 0 & \frac{1}{3} \\ 1 & 0 & -\frac{2}{3} \end{bmatrix} \begin{bmatrix} \xi_1'(k) \\ \xi_2'(k) \\ \xi_3'(k) \end{bmatrix}$$

This observer then has output that converges to the plant state. Or, the change of variables

$$\xi = \mathbf{P}\xi' = \mathbf{Q}^{-1}\xi'; \qquad \xi' = \mathbf{P}^{-1}\xi = \mathbf{Q}\xi$$

can be made in the observer state:

$$\mathbf{Q}\xi(k+1) = \mathbf{F}'\mathbf{Q}\xi(k) + \mathbf{g}'y(k) + \mathbf{h}'u(k)$$

$$\xi(k+1) = (\mathbf{Q}^{-1}\mathbf{F}'\mathbf{Q})\xi(k) + (\mathbf{Q}^{-1}\mathbf{g}')y(k) + (\mathbf{Q}^{-1}\mathbf{h}')u(k)$$

$$= \mathbf{F}\xi(k) + \mathbf{g}y(k) + \mathbf{h}u(k)$$

where

$$\mathbf{F} = \mathbf{Q}^{-1}\mathbf{F}'\mathbf{Q} = \begin{bmatrix} 0 & 3 & 0 \\ 0 & 0 & 0 \\ 1 & 1 & 0 \end{bmatrix}$$

$$\mathbf{g} = \mathbf{Q}^{-1}\mathbf{g}' = \begin{bmatrix} 0 & 1 & -\frac{1}{3} \\ 0 & 0 & \frac{1}{3} \\ 1 & 0 & -\frac{2}{3} \end{bmatrix} \begin{bmatrix} 2 \\ 1 \\ 3 \end{bmatrix} = \begin{bmatrix} 0 \\ 1 \\ 0 \end{bmatrix}$$

$$\mathbf{h} = \mathbf{Q}^{-1}\mathbf{h}' = \begin{bmatrix} 0 & 1 & -\frac{1}{3} \\ 0 & 0 & \frac{1}{3} \\ 1 & 0 & -\frac{2}{3} \end{bmatrix} \begin{bmatrix} -1 \\ 2 \\ 0 \end{bmatrix} = \begin{bmatrix} 2 \\ 0 \\ -1 \end{bmatrix}$$

This results in an observer where the observer state approaches the plant state

$$
\begin{bmatrix} \xi_1(k+1) \\ \xi_2(k+1) \\ \xi_3(k+1) \end{bmatrix} = \begin{bmatrix} 0 & 3 & 0 \\ 0 & 0 & 0 \\ 1 & 1 & 0 \end{bmatrix} \begin{bmatrix} \xi_1(k) \\ \xi_2(k) \\ \xi_3(k) \end{bmatrix} + \begin{bmatrix} 0 \\ 1 \\ 0 \end{bmatrix} y(k) + \begin{bmatrix} 2 \\ 0 \\ -1 \end{bmatrix} u(k)
$$

As this is a deadbeat observer, it will converge to the plant state in three steps.

## 5.3 More About Observers

We now extend the basic ideas about observers. Using observable form to design a full-order observer requires that the plant have a single output. One way to accommodate multiple-output plants is to arrange them as equivalent single-output plants when possible. However, some of the available design freedom is used in combining multiple outputs before observation, so doing so may not result in the best possible design.

An observer's state and output can be made to converge to a linear transformation of the plant state instead of the state itself. Relations and properties for this more general kind of observer are developed in this section. These are used in the following sections as the basis for simple but powerful general observer design methods.

### 5.3.1 Observers for Multiple-Output Systems

If a multiple-output plant is completely observable from one of its outputs, then that single output can be used to drive an observer of the plant state. For example, the plant

$$
\begin{bmatrix} x_1(k+1) \\ x_2(k+1) \\ x_3(k+1) \end{bmatrix} = \begin{bmatrix} -1 & 1 & 0 \\ 0 & 0 & 1 \\ 1 & 0 & 0 \end{bmatrix} \begin{bmatrix} x_1(k) \\ x_2(k) \\ x_3(k) \end{bmatrix} + \begin{bmatrix} 3 \\ -1 \\ 0 \end{bmatrix} u(k) = \mathbf{A}\mathbf{x}(k) + \mathbf{b}u(k)
$$

$$
\begin{bmatrix} y_1(k) \\ y_2(k) \end{bmatrix} = \begin{bmatrix} 1 & -1 & 2 \\ 1 & 0 & 0 \end{bmatrix} \begin{bmatrix} x_1(k) \\ x_2(k) \\ x_3(k) \end{bmatrix} + \begin{bmatrix} 2 \\ -2 \end{bmatrix} u(k) = \mathbf{C}\mathbf{x}(k) + \mathbf{d}u(k)
$$

is completely observable from the output $y_2(k)$. For convenience, the plant with single output $y_2$ is in observable form; if it were not originally in that form, the transformation to observable form, as in the previous section, is straightforward. A full-order state observer, of the form

$$\xi(k + 1) = F\xi(k) + gy_2(k) + hu(k)$$

can be designed with the usual methods. Suppose that the desired observer characteristic equation is

$$\lambda^3 - \tfrac{1}{4}\lambda^2 + \tfrac{1}{4}\lambda + \tfrac{1}{16} = 0$$

Then

$$F = A - gc_2^\dagger = \begin{bmatrix} (-1 - g_1) & 1 & 0 \\ -g_2 & 0 & 1 \\ (1 - g_3) & 0 & 0 \end{bmatrix}$$

has characteristic equation

$$\lambda^3 + (g_1 + 1)\lambda^2 + (g_2)\lambda + (g_3 - 1) = 0$$

so that

$$g = \begin{bmatrix} g_1 \\ g_2 \\ g_3 \end{bmatrix} = \begin{bmatrix} -\tfrac{5}{4} \\ \tfrac{1}{4} \\ \tfrac{17}{16} \end{bmatrix}$$

and

$$h = b - gd_2 = \begin{bmatrix} 3 \\ -1 \\ 0 \end{bmatrix} - \begin{bmatrix} -\tfrac{5}{4} \\ \tfrac{1}{4} \\ \tfrac{17}{16} \end{bmatrix}(-2) = \begin{bmatrix} \tfrac{1}{2} \\ -\tfrac{1}{2} \\ \tfrac{17}{8} \end{bmatrix}$$

The observed plant is temporarily imagined to have only the output $y_2$, as illustrated in Figure 5-6, so only the second rows of C and d are used in these computations. The observer is then described by

$$\begin{bmatrix} \xi_1(k + 1) \\ \xi_2(k + 1) \\ \xi_3(k + 1) \end{bmatrix} = \begin{bmatrix} \tfrac{1}{4} & 1 & 0 \\ -\tfrac{1}{4} & 0 & 1 \\ -\tfrac{1}{16} & 0 & 0 \end{bmatrix} \begin{bmatrix} \xi_1(k) \\ \xi_2(k) \\ \xi_2(k) \end{bmatrix} + \begin{bmatrix} 0 & -\tfrac{5}{4} \\ 0 & \tfrac{1}{4} \\ 0 & \tfrac{17}{16} \end{bmatrix} \begin{bmatrix} y_1(k) \\ y_2(k) \end{bmatrix} + \begin{bmatrix} \tfrac{1}{2} \\ -\tfrac{1}{2} \\ \tfrac{17}{8} \end{bmatrix} u(k)$$

$$= F\xi(k) + Gy(k) + hu(k)$$

where a column of zeros has been included in the matrix G to represent not using the output $y_1$.

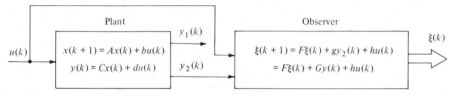

**FIGURE 5-6.  Use of a single plant output for observation.**

If the plant to be observed is completely observable, but not completely observable from an single output, then a single output that is a linear combination of the individual multiple outputs might be formed, from which the plant is completely observable. For example, the plant

$$\begin{bmatrix} x_1(k+1) \\ x_2(k+1) \\ x_3(k+1) \end{bmatrix} = \begin{bmatrix} \frac{1}{2} & 0 & 0 \\ 0 & -\frac{1}{2} & 0 \\ 0 & 0 & 1 \end{bmatrix} \begin{bmatrix} x_1(k) \\ x_2(k) \\ x_3(k) \end{bmatrix} + \begin{bmatrix} 2 \\ 1 \\ -3 \end{bmatrix} u(k) = \mathbf{A}\mathbf{x}(k) + \mathbf{b}u(k)$$

$$\begin{bmatrix} y_1(k) \\ y_2(k) \end{bmatrix} = \begin{bmatrix} 1 & 0 & 3 \\ -1 & 2 & 0 \end{bmatrix} \begin{bmatrix} x_1(k) \\ x_2(k) \\ x_3(k) \end{bmatrix} + \begin{bmatrix} -4 \\ -5 \end{bmatrix} u(k) = \mathbf{C}\mathbf{x}(k) + \mathbf{d}u(k)$$

which is in diagonal form, is not completely observable from either of its two outputs. Any linear combination of these two outputs except one proportional to $y_1 + y_2$ will produce a new output from which the plant is completely observable. Choosing

$$\tilde{y}(k) = y_1(k) - y_2(k) = \begin{bmatrix} 2 & -2 & 3 \end{bmatrix} \begin{bmatrix} x_1(k) \\ x_2(k) \\ x_3(k) \end{bmatrix} + u(k)$$

$$= \tilde{\mathbf{c}}^\dagger \mathbf{x}(k) + \tilde{d}u(k)$$

as indicated in Figure 5-7, and temporarily taking the plant to have the single output $\tilde{y}(k)$, an observer is designed in the usual way.

The transformation

$$\mathbf{x} = \mathbf{P}\mathbf{x}' = \mathbf{Q}^{-1}\mathbf{x}'; \qquad \mathbf{x}' = \mathbf{P}^{-1}\mathbf{x} = \mathbf{Q}\mathbf{x}$$

that takes the plant with output $\tilde{y}(k)$ to observable canonical form is given by

$$\mathbf{Q} = \mathbf{P}^{-1} = \begin{bmatrix} 2 & -2 & 3 \\ -1 & 3 & 0 \\ -1 & -1 & -\frac{3}{4} \end{bmatrix}$$

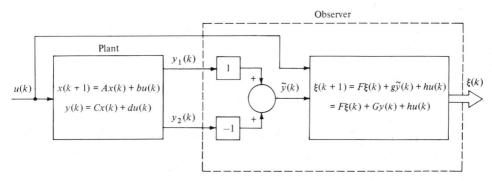

**FIGURE 5-7.   State observation using multiple plant outputs.**

The transformed plant is

$$\begin{bmatrix} x_1'(k+1) \\ x_2'(k+1) \\ x_3'(k+1) \end{bmatrix} = \begin{bmatrix} 1 & 1 & 0 \\ \frac{1}{4} & 0 & 1 \\ -\frac{1}{4} & 0 & 0 \end{bmatrix} \begin{bmatrix} x_1'(k) \\ x_2'(k) \\ x_3'(k) \end{bmatrix} + \begin{bmatrix} 7 \\ 1 \\ -\frac{3}{4} \end{bmatrix} u(k) = \mathbf{A}'\mathbf{x}'(k) + \mathbf{b}'u(k)$$

$$\tilde{y}(k) = [1 \quad 0 \quad 0] \begin{bmatrix} x_1'(k) \\ x_2'(k) \\ x_3'(k) \end{bmatrix} + u(k) = \tilde{\mathbf{c}}'^{\mathsf{t}}\mathbf{x}'(k) + \tilde{d}u(k) \tag{5-5}$$

and, being in observable form, makes the observer design simple. Let the desired observer characteristic equation be

$$\lambda^3 - \tfrac{1}{4}\lambda^2 = 0$$

Then the observer of the state $\mathbf{x}'$ from the output $\tilde{y}$ has state coupling matrix

$$\mathbf{F}' = \mathbf{A}' - \mathbf{g}'\tilde{\mathbf{c}}'^{\mathsf{t}} = \begin{bmatrix} 1 & 1 & 0 \\ \frac{1}{4} & 0 & 1 \\ -\frac{1}{4} & 0 & 0 \end{bmatrix} - \begin{bmatrix} g_1' \\ g_2' \\ g_3' \end{bmatrix} [1 \quad 0 \quad 0] = \begin{bmatrix} (1 - g_1') & 1 & 0 \\ (\frac{1}{4} - g_2') & 0 & 1 \\ (-\frac{1}{4} - g_3') & 0 & 0 \end{bmatrix}$$

The observer's characteristic equation is

$$\lambda^3 + (g_1' - 1)\lambda^2 + (g_2' - \tfrac{1}{4})\lambda + (g_3' + \tfrac{1}{4}) = 0$$

from which

$$\mathbf{g}' = \begin{bmatrix} g_1' \\ g_2' \\ g_3' \end{bmatrix} = \begin{bmatrix} \frac{3}{4} \\ \frac{1}{4} \\ -\frac{1}{4} \end{bmatrix}; \quad \mathbf{h}' = \mathbf{b}' - \mathbf{g}'\tilde{d} = \begin{bmatrix} 7 \\ 1 \\ -\frac{3}{4} \end{bmatrix} - \begin{bmatrix} \frac{3}{4} \\ \frac{1}{4} \\ -\frac{1}{4} \end{bmatrix} = \begin{bmatrix} \frac{25}{4} \\ \frac{3}{4} \\ -\frac{1}{2} \end{bmatrix}$$

and

$$
\begin{bmatrix} \xi_1'(k+1) \\ \xi_2'(k+1) \\ \xi_3'(k+1) \end{bmatrix} = \begin{bmatrix} \frac{1}{4} & 1 & 0 \\ 0 & 0 & 1 \\ 0 & 0 & 0 \end{bmatrix} \begin{bmatrix} \xi_1'(k) \\ \xi_2'(k) \\ \xi_3'(k) \end{bmatrix} + \begin{bmatrix} \frac{3}{4} \\ \frac{1}{4} \\ -\frac{1}{4} \end{bmatrix} \tilde{y}(k) + \begin{bmatrix} \frac{25}{4} \\ \frac{3}{4} \\ -\frac{1}{2} \end{bmatrix} u(k)
$$

Expressing $\tilde{y}(k)$ in terms of the original system outputs (5-5), the observer is

$$
\begin{bmatrix} \xi_1'(k+1) \\ \xi_2'(k+1) \\ \xi_3'(k+1) \end{bmatrix} = \begin{bmatrix} \frac{1}{4} & 1 & 0 \\ 0 & 0 & 1 \\ 0 & 0 & 0 \end{bmatrix} \begin{bmatrix} \xi_1'(k) \\ \xi_2'(k) \\ \xi_3'(k) \end{bmatrix}
$$

$$
+ \begin{bmatrix} \frac{3}{4} & -\frac{3}{4} \\ \frac{1}{4} & -\frac{1}{4} \\ -\frac{1}{4} & \frac{1}{4} \end{bmatrix} \begin{bmatrix} y_1(k) \\ y_2(k) \end{bmatrix} + \begin{bmatrix} \frac{25}{4} \\ \frac{3}{4} \\ -\frac{1}{2} \end{bmatrix} u(k)
$$

To converge to the original plant's state $\mathbf{x}$ rather than $\mathbf{x}'$, an output equation

$$
\mathbf{w}(k) = \mathbf{Q}^{-1}\xi'(k)
$$

$$
\begin{bmatrix} w_1(k) \\ w_2(k) \\ w_3(k) \end{bmatrix} = \frac{1}{9} \begin{bmatrix} -\frac{9}{4} & -\frac{9}{2} & -9 \\ -\frac{3}{4} & \frac{3}{2} & -3 \\ 4 & 4 & 4 \end{bmatrix} \begin{bmatrix} \xi_1'(k) \\ \xi_2'(k) \\ \xi_3'(k) \end{bmatrix}
$$

can be added to the observer, or the change of variables

$$
\xi(k) = \mathbf{Q}^{-1}\xi'(k)
$$

can be made so that the observer state converges to $\mathbf{x}$ instead of $\mathbf{x}'$.

Observers designed in this way have proportional columns in the **G** matrix. An observer of a multiple-output system need not have such a restricted kind of **G** matrix; this is simply a convenient design method. Even when a multiple-output system is completely observable from a single output, one might choose to use more than the single output to drive an observer to achieve such benefits as greater reliability and improved performance in the presence of noise.

Not all completely observable plants can be made observable from a single linear combination of their outputs. If, in a block diagonal plant realization, there is more than one Jordan block involving the same eigenvalue and if two such blocks couple to different outputs (as they must for observability), then any linear combination of the outputs will destroy observability of the repeated mode.

### 5.3.2 Observers as Error Feedback Systems

For a plant

$$\mathbf{x}(k + 1) = \mathbf{A}\mathbf{x}(k) + \mathbf{B}\mathbf{u}(k)$$

$$\mathbf{y}(k) = \mathbf{C}\mathbf{x}(k) + \mathbf{D}\mathbf{u}(k)$$

it is enlightening to express the full-order state observer equations

$$\boldsymbol{\xi}(k + 1) = \mathbf{F}\boldsymbol{\xi}(k) + \mathbf{G}\mathbf{y}(k) + \mathbf{H}\mathbf{u}(k)$$

where

$$\mathbf{F} = \mathbf{A} - \mathbf{GC}$$

$$\mathbf{H} = \mathbf{B} - \mathbf{GD}$$

in the form

$$\boldsymbol{\xi}(k + 1) = (\mathbf{A} - \mathbf{GC})\boldsymbol{\xi}(k) + \mathbf{G}\mathbf{y}(k) + (\mathbf{B} - \mathbf{GD})\mathbf{u}(k)$$

$$= \mathbf{A}\boldsymbol{\xi}(k) + \mathbf{B}\mathbf{u}(k) + \mathbf{G}[\mathbf{y}(k) - \mathbf{w}(k)]$$

where

$$\mathbf{w}(k) = \mathbf{C}\boldsymbol{\xi}(k) + \mathbf{D}\mathbf{u}(k)$$

As illustrated in Figure 5-8, the observer consists of a model of the plant driven, as the plant is, by the input $\mathbf{u}(k)$ and additionally by the error between the plant output $\mathbf{y}(k)$ and the plant output that is estimated by that model, $\mathbf{w}(k)$.

### 5.3.3 Observing Linear State Transformations

When an observer's state

$$\boldsymbol{\xi}(k + 1) = \mathbf{F}\boldsymbol{\xi}(k) + \mathbf{G}\mathbf{y}(k) + \mathbf{H}\mathbf{u}(k)$$

estimates a linear transformation $\mathbf{M}\mathbf{x}(k)$ of the plant state rather than the plant state itself, the error between the observer state and the plant state

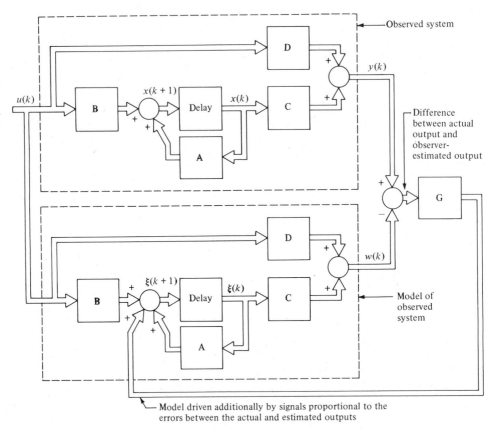

**FIGURE 5-8. Full-order state observer arranged as an error feedback system.**

transformation is given by

$$\mathbf{M}x(k+1) - \xi(k+1) = \mathbf{MA}x(k) + \mathbf{MB}u(k) - \mathbf{F}\xi(k) - \mathbf{G}y(k) - \mathbf{H}u(k)$$
$$= (\mathbf{MA} - \mathbf{GC})x(k) - \mathbf{F}\xi(k) + (\mathbf{MB} - \mathbf{GD} - \mathbf{H})u(k)$$

Requiring that the error satisfy an autonomous equation

$$\mathbf{M}x(k+1) - \xi(k+1) = \mathbf{F}[\mathbf{M}x(k) - \xi(k)]$$

gives

$$\mathbf{FM} = \mathbf{MA} - \mathbf{GC}$$

$$\mathbf{H} = \mathbf{MB} - \mathbf{GD}$$

which are generalizations of the results for full-order state observers, where the *observation matrix* **M** is the identity matrix. These relations are summarized in Table 5-2.

The notation

$$\xi(k) \rightarrow \mathbf{M}\mathbf{x}(k)$$

is used to indicate that the observer state signals *observe* the state transformation **Mx**(*k*). That is, the error between **Mx**(*k*) and $\xi(k)$ is governed by the observer state coupling matrix **F**, the eigenvalues of which are selectable by the designer. In general, the observation matrix **M** need not be square.

**TABLE 5-2   Relations for Observers of Linear State Transformations**

### *Plant Model*

$$\mathbf{x}(k + 1) = \mathbf{A}\mathbf{x}(k) + \mathbf{B}\mathbf{u}(k)$$

$$\mathbf{y}(k) = \mathbf{C}\mathbf{x}(k) + \mathbf{D}\mathbf{u}(k)$$

### *Observer*

$$\xi(k + 1) = \mathbf{F}\xi(k) + \mathbf{G}\mathbf{y}(k) + \mathbf{H}\mathbf{u}(k)$$

$$\mathbf{w}(k) = \mathbf{L}\xi(k) + \mathbf{N}\mathbf{x}(k)$$

where

$$\mathbf{FM} = \mathbf{MA} - \mathbf{GC}$$

$$\mathbf{H} = \mathbf{MB} - \mathbf{GD}$$

### *Observer Error*

$$\mathbf{M}\mathbf{x}(k + 1) - \xi(k + 1) = \mathbf{F}[\mathbf{M}\mathbf{x}(k) - \xi(k)]$$

$$\mathbf{M}\mathbf{x}(k) - \xi(k) = \mathbf{F}^k[\mathbf{M}\mathbf{x}(0) - \xi(0)]$$

or

$$\xi(k) \rightarrow \mathbf{M}\mathbf{x}(k)$$

$$\mathbf{w}(k) \rightarrow (\mathbf{LM} + \mathbf{N})\mathbf{x}(k) = \mathbf{E}\mathbf{x}(k)$$

If the observer has an output equation of the form

$$\mathbf{w}(k) = \mathbf{L}\boldsymbol{\xi}(k) + \mathbf{N}\mathbf{x}(k)$$

then the observer output observes

$$\mathbf{w}(k) \rightarrow (\mathbf{LM} + \mathbf{N})\mathbf{x}(k)$$

as indicated in Table 5-2.

# 5.4 Observer Design

For observers with distinct eigenvalues, a very convenient method of observer design is to consider a collection of first-order observers, each with one of the desired observer eigenvalues. From the individual plant state transformation observed by each first-order observer, observer gains and a transformation of the observer state is found to achieve the observation desired.

## 5.4.1 First-Order Observers

For a discrete-time plant

$$\mathbf{x}(k + 1) = \mathbf{A}\mathbf{x}(k) + \mathbf{B}\mathbf{u}(k)$$

$$\mathbf{y}(k) = \mathbf{C}\mathbf{x}(k) + \mathbf{D}\mathbf{u}(k)$$

a first-order observer

$$\xi(k + 1) = f\xi(k) + \mathbf{g}^\dagger \mathbf{y}(k) + \mathbf{h}^\dagger \mathbf{u}(k)$$

where $\xi(k)$ is a scalar, observes the linear state transformation

$$\xi \rightarrow \mathbf{m}^\dagger \mathbf{x}$$

given by (applying the results summarized in Table 5-2)

$$\mathbf{m}^\dagger \mathbf{A} - \mathbf{g}^\dagger \mathbf{C} = f\mathbf{m}^\dagger$$

$$\mathbf{m}^\dagger = \mathbf{g}^\dagger \mathbf{C}(\mathbf{A} - f\mathbf{I})^{-1}$$

The observer coupling of the plant input **h** is given by

$$\mathbf{h}^\dagger = \mathbf{m}^\dagger \mathbf{B} - \mathbf{g}^\dagger \mathbf{D}$$

These *first-order* observer relations are collected in Table 5-3.

The matrix inverse involved exists whenever the observer eigenvalue does not equal a plant eigenvalue. If an observer and the plant have an eigenvalue in common, it means that the corresponding mode in the observer error will occur even if the observer is not connected to the plant. The part of the observer with the common eigenvalue is thus redundant.

For example, for the plant

$$\begin{bmatrix} x_1(k+1) \\ x_2(k+1) \end{bmatrix} = \begin{bmatrix} 1 & 0 \\ 2 & -1 \end{bmatrix} \begin{bmatrix} x_1(k) \\ x_2(k) \end{bmatrix} + \begin{bmatrix} 0 \\ 3 \end{bmatrix} u(k) = \mathbf{A}\mathbf{x}(k) + \mathbf{b}u(k)$$

$$y(k) = \begin{bmatrix} -1 & 2 \end{bmatrix} \begin{bmatrix} x_1(k) \\ x_2(k) \end{bmatrix} + 4u(k) = \mathbf{c}^\dagger \mathbf{x}(k) + du(k)$$

a first-order observer with eigenvalue $\lambda = \frac{1}{4}$, of the form

$$\xi(k+1) = \tfrac{1}{4}\xi(k) + gy(k) + hu(k)$$

observes the linear state transformation $\mathbf{m}^\dagger \mathbf{x}$, where the observation matrix is

$$\mathbf{m}^\dagger = g\mathbf{c}^\dagger(\mathbf{A} - f\mathbf{I})^{-1} = g\begin{bmatrix} -1 & 2 \end{bmatrix}\begin{bmatrix} \frac{3}{4} & 0 \\ 2 & -\frac{5}{4} \end{bmatrix}^{-1}$$

$$= g\begin{bmatrix} -1 & 2 \end{bmatrix}\begin{bmatrix} \frac{4}{3} & 0 \\ \frac{32}{15} & -\frac{4}{5} \end{bmatrix} = g\begin{bmatrix} \frac{44}{15} & -\frac{8}{5} \end{bmatrix}$$

The coupling of the plant input to the observer is

$$h = \mathbf{m}^\dagger \mathbf{b} - gd = g\begin{bmatrix} \frac{4}{5} & -\frac{8}{5} \end{bmatrix}\begin{bmatrix} 0 \\ 3 \end{bmatrix} - 4g = -\frac{44}{5}g$$

This observer will observe any linear transformation of the state that is proportional to

$$\left(\frac{1}{g}\right)\mathbf{m}^\dagger = \begin{bmatrix} \frac{44}{15} & -\frac{8}{5} \end{bmatrix}$$

## TABLE 5-3   First-Order Observer Relations

### *Plant Model*

$\mathbf{x}(k + 1) = \mathbf{A}\mathbf{x}(k) + \mathbf{B}\mathbf{u}(k)$

$\mathbf{y}(k) = \mathbf{C}\mathbf{x}(k) + \mathbf{D}\mathbf{u}(k)$

### *Observer*

$\xi(k + 1) = f\xi(k) + \mathbf{g}^\dagger\mathbf{y}(k) + \mathbf{h}^\dagger\mathbf{u}(k)$

where

$\mathbf{m}^\dagger = \mathbf{g}^\dagger\mathbf{C}(\mathbf{A} - f\mathbf{I})^{-1}$

$\mathbf{h}^\dagger = \mathbf{m}^\dagger\mathbf{B} - \mathbf{g}^\dagger\mathbf{D}$

### *Observer Error*

$\mathbf{m}^\dagger\mathbf{x}(k + 1) - \xi(k + 1) = f[\mathbf{m}^\dagger\mathbf{x}(k) - \xi(k)]$

$\mathbf{m}^\dagger\mathbf{x}(k) - \xi(k) = f^k[\mathbf{m}^\dagger\mathbf{x}(0) - \xi(0)]$

or

$\xi(k) \rightarrow \mathbf{m}^\dagger\mathbf{x}(k)$

## *5.4.2 Collections of First-Order Observers*

We now form full-order state observers with distinct eigenvalues by designing $n$ first-order observers for an $n$th order plant. The collection of these first-order component observers constitutes an $n$th order observer in diagonal form. It has the selected eigenvalues and it observes a transformation of the plant state which is always nonsingular if the plant is completely observable and the observer eigenvalues are different from those of the plant. Forming an observer output equation involving the inverse of this transformation or changing observer state variables produces an observer of the plant state.

As an example, consider the plant

$$\begin{bmatrix} x_1(k + 1) \\ x_2(k + 1) \end{bmatrix} = \begin{bmatrix} 0 & 2 \\ 1 & -1 \end{bmatrix}\begin{bmatrix} x_1(k) \\ x_2(k) \end{bmatrix} + \begin{bmatrix} 0 & 0 \\ 2 & -1 \end{bmatrix}\begin{bmatrix} u_1(k) \\ u_2(k) \end{bmatrix} = \mathbf{A}\mathbf{x}(k) + \mathbf{B}\mathbf{u}(k)$$

$$y(k) = [0 \quad -2]\begin{bmatrix} x_1(k) \\ x_2(k) \end{bmatrix} + [0 \quad 1]\begin{bmatrix} u_1(k) \\ u_2(k) \end{bmatrix} = \mathbf{c}^\dagger \mathbf{x}(k) + \mathbf{d}^\dagger \mathbf{u}(k)$$

and suppose that it is desired to design a full-order state observer of this plant with eigenvalues $\lambda = \pm\frac{1}{2}$. A first-order observer with eigenvalue $\frac{1}{2}$ has the form

$$\xi_1(k+1) = \tfrac{1}{2}\xi_1(k) + g_1\,y(k) + \mathbf{h}_1^\dagger\mathbf{u}(k) \tag{5-6}$$

and observes the scalar linear state transformation proportional to $g_1$ that is given by

$$\mathbf{m}_1^\dagger = g_1\mathbf{c}^\dagger(\mathbf{A} - \tfrac{1}{2}\mathbf{I})^{-1} = g_1[0 \quad -2]\begin{bmatrix} -\frac{1}{2} & 2 \\ 1 & -\frac{3}{2} \end{bmatrix}^{-1} = g_1[-\tfrac{8}{5} \quad -\tfrac{4}{5}]$$

The input coupling to this observer is

$$\mathbf{h}_1^\dagger = \mathbf{m}_1^\dagger\mathbf{B} - g_1\mathbf{d}^\dagger = g_1[-\tfrac{8}{5} \quad -\tfrac{1}{5}]$$

giving

$$\mathbf{m}_2^\dagger = g_2\mathbf{c}^\dagger(\mathbf{A} + \tfrac{1}{2}\mathbf{I})^{-1} = g_2[0 \quad -2]\begin{bmatrix} \frac{1}{2} & 2 \\ 1 & -\frac{1}{2} \end{bmatrix}^{-1} = g_2[-\tfrac{8}{9} \quad \tfrac{4}{9}]$$

This observer has coupling of the plant input

$$\mathbf{h}_2^\dagger = \mathbf{m}_2^\dagger\mathbf{B} - g_2\mathbf{d}^\dagger = g_2[\tfrac{8}{9} \quad -\tfrac{13}{9}]$$

giving

$$\xi_2(k+1) = -\tfrac{1}{2}\xi_2(k) + g_2\,y(k) + g_2[\tfrac{8}{9} \quad -\tfrac{13}{9}]\begin{bmatrix} u_1(k) \\ u_2(k) \end{bmatrix}$$

Since the vectors $[-\tfrac{8}{5} \quad -\tfrac{4}{5}]$ and $[-\tfrac{8}{9} \quad \tfrac{4}{9}]$ are linearly independent, any plant state transformation can be obtained with a linear combination $\xi_1(k)$

and $\xi_2(k)$. The observer gains $g_1$ and $g_2$ only serve to scale the observer state signals, so they can each be chosen to be unity. Then the observer combining the first-order subsystems (5-6) and (5-7)

$$\begin{bmatrix} \xi_1(k+1) \\ \xi_2(k+1) \end{bmatrix} = \begin{bmatrix} \frac{1}{2} & 0 \\ 0 & -\frac{1}{2} \end{bmatrix} \begin{bmatrix} \xi_1(k) \\ \xi_2(k) \end{bmatrix} + \begin{bmatrix} 1 \\ 1 \end{bmatrix} y(k) + \begin{bmatrix} -\frac{8}{5} & -\frac{1}{5} \\ \frac{8}{9} & -\frac{13}{9} \end{bmatrix} \begin{bmatrix} u_1(k) \\ u_2(k) \end{bmatrix}$$

$$= \mathbf{F}\boldsymbol{\xi}(k) + \mathbf{g}y(k) + \mathbf{H}\mathbf{u}(k)$$

observes

$$\boldsymbol{\xi}(k) = \begin{bmatrix} \xi_1(k) \\ \xi_2(k) \end{bmatrix} \rightarrow \begin{bmatrix} -\frac{8}{5} & -\frac{4}{5} \\ -\frac{8}{9} & \frac{4}{9} \end{bmatrix} \begin{bmatrix} x_1(k) \\ x_2(k) \end{bmatrix} = \mathbf{M}\mathbf{x}(k)$$

To observe the state $\mathbf{x}(k)$ rather than $\mathbf{M}\mathbf{x}(k)$, one only need form the observer output signals

$$\begin{bmatrix} w_1(k) \\ w_2(k) \end{bmatrix} = \begin{bmatrix} -\frac{8}{5} & -\frac{4}{5} \\ -\frac{8}{9} & \frac{4}{9} \end{bmatrix}^{-1} \begin{bmatrix} \xi_1(k) \\ \xi_2(k) \end{bmatrix} = \frac{1}{64} \begin{bmatrix} -20 & -36 \\ -40 & 72 \end{bmatrix} \begin{bmatrix} \xi_1(k) \\ \xi_2(k) \end{bmatrix} = \mathbf{M}^{-1}\boldsymbol{\xi}(k)$$

This arrangement is indicated in Figure 5-9(a). Or, the change of state

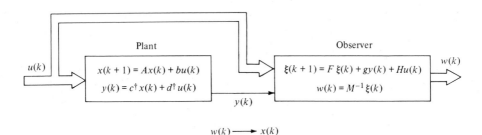

(a) Diagonalized observer with an output equation.

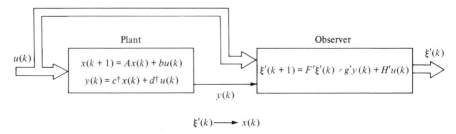

(b) Change of observer state variables so that the observer state observes the plant state.

**FIGURE 5-9.    Observing a plant state with a collection of first-order observers.**

variables

$$\begin{bmatrix} \xi_1'(k) \\ \xi_2'(k) \end{bmatrix} = \frac{1}{64} \begin{bmatrix} -20 & -36 \\ -40 & 72 \end{bmatrix} \begin{bmatrix} \xi_1(k) \\ \xi_2(k) \end{bmatrix} = \mathbf{M}^{-1}\boldsymbol{\xi}(k)$$

can be made so that the observer output is its state $\boldsymbol{\xi}'(k)$ and the observer state observes the state $\mathbf{x}(k)$:

$$\mathbf{M}\boldsymbol{\xi}'(k+1) = \mathbf{FM}\boldsymbol{\xi}'(k) + \mathbf{g}y(k) + \mathbf{H}u(k)$$

$$\begin{aligned} \boldsymbol{\xi}'(k+1) &= (\mathbf{M}^{-1}\mathbf{FM})\boldsymbol{\xi}'(k) + (\mathbf{M}^{-1}\mathbf{g})y(k) + (\mathbf{M}^{-1}\mathbf{H})u(k) \\ &= \mathbf{F}'\boldsymbol{\xi}'(k) + \mathbf{g}'(y(k) + \mathbf{H}'u(k) \end{aligned}$$

as shown in Figure 5-9(b).

When complex conjugate pairs of observer eigenvalues are desired, the observer, being in diagonal form, has matrices with complex elements. Transformation to a block diagonal form or to an observer with state that observes $\mathbf{x}(k)$ results in an observer with real matrices.

### 5.4.3 Repeated Observer Eigenvalues

When it is desired that an observer have repeated eigenvalues, these methods must be modified slightly. An observer of $i$th order, with all eigenvalues equal to $f$, with state coupling matrix in upper block Jordan form, has the structure

$$\begin{bmatrix} \xi_1(k+1) \\ \xi_2(k+1) \\ \vdots \\ \xi_{i-1}(k+1) \\ \xi_i(k+1) \end{bmatrix} = \begin{bmatrix} f & 1 & 0 & \cdots & 0 & 0 \\ 0 & f & 1 & \cdots & 0 & 0 \\ \vdots & & & & & \\ 0 & 0 & 0 & \cdots & f & 1 \\ 0 & 0 & 0 & \cdots & 0 & f \end{bmatrix} \begin{bmatrix} \xi_1(k) \\ \xi_2(k) \\ \vdots \\ \xi_{i-1}(k) \\ \xi_i(k) \end{bmatrix} + \begin{bmatrix} \mathbf{g}_1^\dagger \\ \mathbf{g}_2^\dagger \\ \vdots \\ \mathbf{g}_{i-1}^\dagger \\ \mathbf{g}_i^\dagger \end{bmatrix} y(k)$$

$$ + \begin{bmatrix} \mathbf{h}_1^\dagger \\ \mathbf{h}_2^\dagger \\ \vdots \\ \mathbf{h}_{i-1}^\dagger \\ \mathbf{h}_i^\dagger \end{bmatrix} u(k) = \mathbf{F}\boldsymbol{\xi}(k) + \mathbf{G}y(k) + \mathbf{H}u(k)$$

where $\mathbf{G}$ and $\mathbf{H}$ have been partitioned into rows. This observer observes some plant state transformation $\mathbf{Mx}(k)$ where the observation matrix $\mathbf{M}$ satisfies

$$\mathbf{MA} - \mathbf{GC} = \mathbf{FM}$$

Partitioning **M** into rows

$$
\begin{bmatrix} \mathbf{m}_1^\dagger \\ \hdashline \mathbf{m}_2^\dagger \\ \hdashline \vdots \\ \hdashline \mathbf{m}_{i-1}^\dagger \\ \hdashline \mathbf{m}_i^\dagger \end{bmatrix} \left\{ \mathbf{A} - \begin{bmatrix} \mathbf{g}_1^\dagger \\ \hdashline \mathbf{g}_2^\dagger \\ \hdashline \vdots \\ \hdashline \mathbf{g}_{i-1}^\dagger \\ \hdashline \mathbf{g}_i^\dagger \end{bmatrix} \mathbf{C} \right\} = \begin{bmatrix} f & 1 & 0 & \cdots & 0 & 0 \\ 0 & f & 1 & \cdots & 0 & 0 \\ \vdots & & & & & \\ 0 & 0 & 0 & \cdots & f & 1 \\ 0 & 0 & 0 & \cdots & 0 & f \end{bmatrix} \begin{bmatrix} \mathbf{m}_1^\dagger \\ \hdashline \mathbf{m}_2^\dagger \\ \hdashline \vdots \\ \hdashline \mathbf{m}_{i-1}^\dagger \\ \hdashline \mathbf{m}_i^\dagger \end{bmatrix}
$$

there result the relations

$$
\begin{cases}
\mathbf{m}_i^\dagger = \mathbf{g}_i^\dagger \mathbf{C}(\mathbf{A} - f\mathbf{I})^{-1} \\
\mathbf{m}_{i-1}^\dagger = (\mathbf{g}_{i-1}^\dagger \mathbf{C} + \mathbf{m}_i^\dagger)(\mathbf{A} - f\mathbf{I})^{-1} \\
\vdots \\
\mathbf{m}_2^\dagger = (\mathbf{g}_2^\dagger \mathbf{C} + \mathbf{m}_3^\dagger)(\mathbf{A} - f\mathbf{I})^{-1} \\
\mathbf{m}_1^\dagger = (\mathbf{g}_1^\dagger \mathbf{C} + \mathbf{m}_2^\dagger)(\mathbf{A} - f\mathbf{I})^{-1}
\end{cases}
$$

The first of these is the relation for an ordinary first-order observer; the remaining ones are for repetitions of the observer eigenvalue.

The observer plant input gains are given by

$$\mathbf{H} = \mathbf{MB} - \mathbf{GD}$$

$$
\begin{bmatrix} \mathbf{h}_1^\dagger \\ \hdashline \mathbf{h}_2^\dagger \\ \hdashline \vdots \\ \hdashline \mathbf{h}_{i-1}^\dagger \\ \hdashline \mathbf{h}_i^\dagger \end{bmatrix} = \begin{bmatrix} \mathbf{m}_1^\dagger \\ \hdashline \mathbf{m}_2^\dagger \\ \hdashline \vdots \\ \hdashline \mathbf{m}_{i-1}^\dagger \\ \hdashline \mathbf{m}_i^\dagger \end{bmatrix} \mathbf{B} - \begin{bmatrix} \mathbf{g}_1^\dagger \\ \hdashline \mathbf{g}_2^\dagger \\ \hdashline \vdots \\ \hdashline \mathbf{g}_{i-1}^\dagger \\ \hdashline \mathbf{g}_i^\dagger \end{bmatrix} \mathbf{D}
$$

or

$$
\begin{cases}
\mathbf{h}_i^\dagger = \mathbf{m}_i^\dagger \mathbf{B} - \mathbf{g}_i^\dagger \mathbf{D} \\
\mathbf{h}_{i-1}^\dagger = \mathbf{m}_{i-1}^\dagger \mathbf{B} - \mathbf{g}_{i-1}^\dagger \mathbf{D} \\
\vdots \\
\mathbf{h}_2^\dagger = \mathbf{m}_2^\dagger \mathbf{B} - \mathbf{g}_2^\dagger \mathbf{D} \\
\mathbf{h}_1^\dagger = \mathbf{m}_1^\dagger \mathbf{B} - \mathbf{g}_1^\dagger \mathbf{D}
\end{cases}
$$

The equations for observer design with repeated observer eigenvalues are summarized in Table 5-4.

**TABLE 5-4   Relations for an Observer with All Eigenvalues Identical**

### *Plant Model*

$$\mathbf{x}(k + 1) = \mathbf{A}\mathbf{x}(k) + \mathbf{B}\mathbf{u}(k)$$

$$\mathbf{y}(k) = \mathbf{C}\mathbf{x}(k) + \mathbf{D}\mathbf{u}(k)$$

### *Observer*

$$\xi(k + 1) = \mathbf{F}\xi(k) + \mathbf{G}\mathbf{y}(k) + \mathbf{H}\mathbf{u}(k)$$

where

$$\mathbf{F} = \begin{bmatrix} f & 1 & 0 & \cdots & 0 & 0 \\ 0 & f & 1 & \cdots & 0 & 0 \\ \vdots & & & & & \\ 0 & 0 & 0 & \cdots & f & 1 \\ 0 & 0 & 0 & \cdots & 0 & f \end{bmatrix}; \quad \mathbf{G} = \begin{bmatrix} \mathbf{g}_1^\dagger \\ \mathbf{g}_2^\dagger \\ \vdots \\ \mathbf{g}_{i-1}^\dagger \\ \mathbf{g}_i^\dagger \end{bmatrix}; \quad \mathbf{H} = \begin{bmatrix} \mathbf{h}_1^\dagger \\ \mathbf{h}_2^\dagger \\ \vdots \\ \mathbf{h}_{i-1}^\dagger \\ \mathbf{h}_i^\dagger \end{bmatrix}$$

### *Observer Error*

$$\mathbf{M}\mathbf{x}(k + 1) - \xi(k + 1) = \mathbf{F}[\mathbf{M}\mathbf{x}(k) - \xi(k)]$$

$$\mathbf{M}\mathbf{x}(k) - \xi(k) = \mathbf{F}^k[\mathbf{M}\mathbf{x}(0) - \xi(0)]$$

or

$$\xi(k) \rightarrow \mathbf{M}\mathbf{x}(k)$$

where

$$\mathbf{M} = \begin{bmatrix} \mathbf{m}_1^\dagger \\ \mathbf{m}_2^\dagger \\ \vdots \\ \mathbf{m}_{i-1}^\dagger \\ \mathbf{m}_i^\dagger \end{bmatrix}$$

**TABLE 5-4** (cont.)

### Recursive Relations for Observer Parameters

$$
\begin{cases}
\mathbf{m}_i^\dagger = \mathbf{g}_i^\dagger \mathbf{C}(\mathbf{A} - f\mathbf{I})^{-1} \\
\mathbf{m}_{i-1}^\dagger = (\mathbf{g}_{i-1}^\dagger \mathbf{C} + \mathbf{m}_i^\dagger)(\mathbf{A} - f\mathbf{I})^{-1} \\
\vdots \\
\mathbf{m}_2^\dagger = (\mathbf{g}_2^\dagger \mathbf{C} + \mathbf{m}_3^\dagger)(\mathbf{A} - f\mathbf{I})^{-1} \\
\mathbf{m}_1^\dagger = (\mathbf{g}_1^\dagger \mathbf{C} + \mathbf{m}_2^\dagger)(\mathbf{A} - f\mathbf{I})^{-1}
\end{cases}
$$

$$
\mathbf{h}_j^\dagger = \mathbf{m}_j^\dagger \mathbf{B} - \mathbf{g}_j^\dagger \mathbf{D}, \qquad j = 1, 2, \ldots, i
$$

As a numerical example, consider the plant

$$
\begin{bmatrix} x_1(k+1) \\ x_2(k+1) \end{bmatrix} = \begin{bmatrix} \frac{1}{2} & 0 \\ 1 & -\frac{1}{2} \end{bmatrix} \begin{bmatrix} x_1(k) \\ x_2(k) \end{bmatrix} + \begin{bmatrix} 1 \\ -2 \end{bmatrix} u(k) = \mathbf{A}\mathbf{x}(k) + \mathbf{b}u(k)
$$

$$
y(k) = [2 \quad 1] \begin{bmatrix} x_1(k) \\ x_2(k) \end{bmatrix} + 2u(k) = \mathbf{c}^\dagger \mathbf{x}(k) + du(k)
$$

for which it is desired to design a full-order state observer with both eigenvalues at $\lambda = \frac{1}{4}$. An observer of the form

$$
\begin{bmatrix} \xi_1(k+1) \\ \xi_2(k+1) \end{bmatrix} = \begin{bmatrix} \frac{1}{4} & 1 \\ 0 & \frac{1}{4} \end{bmatrix} \begin{bmatrix} \xi_1(k) \\ \xi_2(k) \end{bmatrix} + \begin{bmatrix} g_1 \\ g_2 \end{bmatrix} y(k) + \begin{bmatrix} h_1 \\ h_2 \end{bmatrix} u(k)
$$

will observe the linear plant state transformation

$$
\begin{bmatrix} \xi_1(k) \\ \xi_2(k) \end{bmatrix} \rightarrow \begin{bmatrix} \mathbf{m}_1^\dagger \\ \hline \mathbf{m}_2^\dagger \end{bmatrix} \begin{bmatrix} x_1(k) \\ x_2(k) \end{bmatrix} = \mathbf{M}\mathbf{x}(k)
$$

where the observation matrix has rows

$$
\mathbf{m}_2^\dagger = g_2 \mathbf{c}^\dagger (\mathbf{A} - f\mathbf{I})^{-1} = g_2 [\tfrac{40}{3} \quad -\tfrac{4}{3}]
$$

and

$$
\mathbf{m}_1^\dagger = (g_1 \mathbf{c}^\dagger + \mathbf{m}_2^\dagger)(\mathbf{A} - f\mathbf{I})^{-1} = g_1 [\tfrac{40}{3} \quad -\tfrac{4}{3}] + g_2 [\tfrac{416}{9} \quad \tfrac{16}{9}]
$$

The corresponding plant input gains to the observer are

$$h_2^\dagger = m_2^\dagger b - g_2^\dagger d = 14g_2$$

$$h_1^\dagger = m_1^\dagger b - g_1^\dagger d = 14g_1 + \tfrac{128}{3}g_2$$

Choosing

$$g_1 = 3; \qquad g_2 = 9$$

for convenience, the observer

$$\begin{bmatrix} \xi_1(k+1) \\ \xi_2(k+1) \end{bmatrix} = \begin{bmatrix} \tfrac{1}{4} & 1 \\ 0 & \tfrac{1}{4} \end{bmatrix} \begin{bmatrix} \xi_1(k) \\ \xi_2(k) \end{bmatrix} + \begin{bmatrix} 3 \\ 9 \end{bmatrix} y(k) + \begin{bmatrix} 426 \\ 126 \end{bmatrix} u(k) \qquad (5\text{-}8)$$

observes the linear plant state transformation

$$\begin{bmatrix} \xi_1(k) \\ \xi_2(k) \end{bmatrix} \rightarrow \begin{bmatrix} 456 & 12 \\ 120 & -12 \end{bmatrix} \begin{bmatrix} x_1(k) \\ x_2(k) \end{bmatrix} = \mathbf{M}x(k)$$

so that the observer with state variables

$$\xi'(k) = \mathbf{M}^{-1}\xi(k)$$

or

$$\begin{bmatrix} \xi_1'(k) \\ \xi_2'(k) \end{bmatrix} = \frac{1}{576} \begin{bmatrix} 1 & 1 \\ 10 & -38 \end{bmatrix} \begin{bmatrix} \xi_1(k) \\ \xi_2(k) \end{bmatrix}$$

has state that observes $\mathbf{x}(k)$:

$$\xi'(k) \rightarrow \mathbf{x}(k)$$

Typical response of this observer for arbitrarily chosen plant initial conditions and input is shown in Figure 5-10. Alternatively, the observer of equation (5-8) with output equation

$$\mathbf{w}(k) = \mathbf{M}^{-1}\xi(k)$$

could be used and the observer output would observe the plant state:

$$\mathbf{w}(k) \rightarrow \mathbf{x}(k)$$

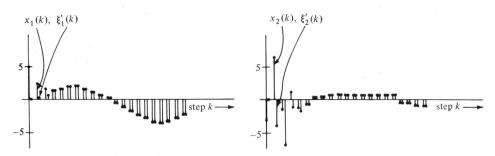

**FIGURE 5-10.   Response of an observer with repeated eigenvalues.**

For the plant

$$\begin{bmatrix} x_1(k+1) \\ x_2(k+1) \\ x_3(k+1) \end{bmatrix} = \begin{bmatrix} -1 & 2 & 0 \\ 0 & 1 & 0 \\ -1 & 1 & 1 \end{bmatrix} \begin{bmatrix} x_1(k) \\ x_2(k) \\ x_3(k) \end{bmatrix} + \begin{bmatrix} 2 & 0 \\ -1 & 3 \\ 0 & -2 \end{bmatrix} \begin{bmatrix} u_1(k) \\ u_2(k) \end{bmatrix}$$

$$\begin{bmatrix} y_1(k) \\ y_2(k) \end{bmatrix} = \begin{bmatrix} 0 & 1 & -1 \\ 1 & 2 & 0 \end{bmatrix} \begin{bmatrix} x_1(k) \\ x_2(k) \\ x_3(k) \end{bmatrix} + \begin{bmatrix} 1 & 3 \\ 0 & 0 \end{bmatrix} \begin{bmatrix} u_1(k) \\ u_2(k) \end{bmatrix}$$

suppose that it is desired to design a full-order state observer with eigenvalues 0, 0, and $\frac{1}{2}$. A second-order observer with both eigenvalues at $\lambda = 0$,

$$\begin{bmatrix} \xi_1(k+1) \\ \xi_2(k+1) \end{bmatrix} = \begin{bmatrix} 0 & 1 \\ 0 & 0 \end{bmatrix} \begin{bmatrix} \xi_1(k) \\ \xi_2(k) \end{bmatrix} + \begin{bmatrix} \mathbf{g}_1^\dagger \\ \mathbf{g}_2^\dagger \end{bmatrix} \begin{bmatrix} y_1(k) \\ y_2(k) \end{bmatrix} + \begin{bmatrix} \mathbf{h}_1^\dagger \\ \mathbf{h}_2^\dagger \end{bmatrix} \begin{bmatrix} u_1(k) \\ u_2(k) \end{bmatrix}$$

observing the linear plant state transformation

$$\begin{bmatrix} \xi_1(k) \\ \xi_2(k) \end{bmatrix} \rightarrow \begin{bmatrix} \mathbf{m}_1^\dagger \\ \mathbf{m}_2^\dagger \end{bmatrix} \begin{bmatrix} x_1(k) \\ x_2(k) \\ x_3(k) \end{bmatrix}$$

is designed, as in the previous example. For this observer subsystem:

$$\mathbf{m}_2^\dagger = \mathbf{g}_2^\dagger \mathbf{C} \mathbf{A}^{-1} = [g_{21} \quad g_{22}] \begin{bmatrix} 0 & 1 & -1 \\ 1 & 2 & 0 \end{bmatrix} \begin{bmatrix} -1 & 2 & 0 \\ 0 & 1 & 0 \\ -1 & 1 & 1 \end{bmatrix}^{-1}$$

$$= [(g_{21} - g_{22}) \quad 4g_{22} \quad -g_{21}]$$

$$\mathbf{m}_1^\dagger = (\mathbf{g}_1^\dagger \mathbf{C} + \mathbf{m}_2^\dagger)\mathbf{A}^{-1} = \left( \begin{bmatrix} g_{11} & g_{12} \end{bmatrix} \begin{bmatrix} 0 & 1 & -1 \\ 1 & 2 & 0 \end{bmatrix} \right.$$

$$\left. + \begin{bmatrix} (g_{21} - g_{22}) & 4g_{12} & -g_{21} \end{bmatrix} \right) \begin{bmatrix} -1 & 2 & 0 \\ 0 & 1 & 0 \\ -1 & 1 & 1 \end{bmatrix}^{-1}$$

$$= \begin{bmatrix} (g_{11} - g_{12} + g_{22}) & (4g_{12} + g_{21} + g_{22}) & (-g_{12} - g_{21}) \end{bmatrix}$$

The corresponding plant input gains are

$$\mathbf{h}_2^\dagger = \mathbf{m}_2^\dagger \mathbf{B} - \mathbf{g}_2^\dagger \mathbf{D}; \qquad \mathbf{h}_1^\dagger = \mathbf{m}_1^\dagger \mathbf{B} - \mathbf{g}_1^\dagger \mathbf{D}$$

Next, a first-order observer subsystem with eigenvalue $\lambda = \frac{1}{2}$,

$$\xi_3(k + 1) = \tfrac{1}{2}\xi_3(k) + \mathbf{g}_3^\dagger \mathbf{y}(k) + \mathbf{h}_3^\dagger \mathbf{u}(k)$$

observing

$$\xi_3(k) \to \mathbf{m}_3^\dagger \mathbf{x}(k)$$

is designed. For this observer,

$$\mathbf{m}_3^\dagger = \mathbf{g}_3^\dagger \mathbf{C}(\mathbf{A} - f\mathbf{I})^{-1} = \begin{bmatrix} g_{31} & g_{32} \end{bmatrix} \begin{bmatrix} 0 & 1 & -1 \\ 1 & 2 & 0 \end{bmatrix} \begin{bmatrix} -\frac{3}{2} & 2 & 0 \\ 0 & \frac{1}{2} & 0 \\ -1 & 1 & \frac{1}{2} \end{bmatrix}^{-1}$$

$$= \begin{bmatrix} \left( \dfrac{4}{3}g_{31} - \dfrac{2}{3}g_{32} \right) & \left( \dfrac{2}{3}g_{31} + \dfrac{20}{3}g_{32} \right) & -2g_{31} \end{bmatrix}$$

and

$$\mathbf{h}_3^\dagger = \mathbf{m}_3^\dagger \mathbf{B} - \mathbf{g}_3 \mathbf{D}$$

The gain vectors $g_1$, $g_2$, $g_3$ are next chosen so that the collection of observers observe a nonsingular transformation of the plant state. Arbitrarily choosing

$$g_{11} = 1; \qquad g_{12} = 1;$$

$$g_{21} = 1; \qquad g_{22} = 1;$$

$$g_{31} = 3; \qquad g_{32} = 0$$

the observer having these gains

$$
\begin{bmatrix} \xi_1(k+1) \\ \xi_2(k+1) \\ \xi_3(k+1) \end{bmatrix} = \begin{bmatrix} 0 & 1 & 0 \\ 0 & 0 & 0 \\ 0 & 0 & \frac{1}{2} \end{bmatrix} \begin{bmatrix} \xi_1(k) \\ \xi_2(k) \\ \xi_3(k) \end{bmatrix} + \begin{bmatrix} 1 & 1 \\ 1 & 1 \\ 1 & 1 \end{bmatrix} \begin{bmatrix} y_1(k) \\ y_2(k) \end{bmatrix} + \begin{bmatrix} -6 & 22 \\ -5 & 11 \\ 3 & 9 \end{bmatrix} \begin{bmatrix} u_1(k) \\ u_2(k) \end{bmatrix}
$$

$$(5\text{-}9)$$

observes

$$
\begin{bmatrix} \xi_1(k) \\ \xi_2(k) \\ \xi_3(k) \end{bmatrix} \rightarrow \begin{bmatrix} \mathbf{m}_1^\dagger \\ \mathbf{m}_2^\dagger \\ \mathbf{m}_3^\dagger \end{bmatrix} \begin{bmatrix} x_1(k) \\ x_2(k) \\ x_3(k) \end{bmatrix} = \begin{bmatrix} 1 & 7 & -2 \\ 0 & 4 & -1 \\ 4 & 2 & -6 \end{bmatrix} \begin{bmatrix} x_1(k) \\ x_2(k) \\ x_3(k) \end{bmatrix} = \mathbf{M}x(k)
$$

Finally, an observer output equation

$$\mathbf{w}(k) = \mathbf{M}^{-1}\boldsymbol{\xi}(k)$$

$$
\begin{bmatrix} w_1(k) \\ w_2(k) \\ w_3(k) \end{bmatrix} = \begin{bmatrix} 1.22 & -2.11 & -0.056 \\ 0.222 & -0.111 & -0.056 \\ 0.889 & -1.44 & 0.222 \end{bmatrix} \begin{bmatrix} \xi_1(k) \\ \xi_2(k) \\ \xi_3(k) \end{bmatrix}
$$

is added so that

$$\mathbf{w}(k) \rightarrow \mathbf{x}(k)$$

Alternatively, the change of variables

$$\boldsymbol{\xi}'(k) = \mathbf{M}^{-1}\boldsymbol{\xi}(k)$$

can be used on the equations (5-9) so that the observer state observes the plant state:

$$\boldsymbol{\xi}'(k) \rightarrow \mathbf{x}(k)$$

## 5.5　Lower-Order Observers

Plant outputs, themselves, involve linear transformations of the plant state. If these are coupled directly to the observer output, the observer's order can be reduced. In this section, we first consider reduction in the order of state observers. Then we develop methods for further lowering the order of an observer used for feedback system eigenvalue placement by estimating only the linear state transformation to be fed back rather than the entire plant state. There is a simple solution for the minimal-order observer when the plant is single-input so that the needed observer output is a scalar. When there are multiple plant inputs, there is the possibility of lowering the necessary observer order still further.

### 5.5.1  Reduced-Order State Observers

If a completely observable plant has $m$ linearly independent outputs, a *reduced order* observer, of order $n - m$, can be constructed having an output that observes the plant state. Reduced-order means that the state observer order (which without using the plant outputs directly is $n$) is reduced by the number of linearly independent plant outputs, to order $n - m$. The $n - m$ observer eigenvalues can be placed arbitrarily by the designer so long as none equal plant eigenvalues. The order reduction occurs because the observer uses the $m$ linearly independent scalar state transformations involved in the plant outputs. These are coupled to the observer output through direct input-to-output coupling, which is not present in a full-order state observer.

For the plant

$$\mathbf{x}(k + 1) = \mathbf{Ax}(k) + \mathbf{Bu}(k)$$

$$\mathbf{y}(k) = \mathbf{Cx}(k) + \mathbf{Du}(k)$$

and an $(n - m)$th order observer with state equation of the form

$$\xi(k + 1) = \mathbf{F}\xi(k) + \mathbf{Gy}(k) + \mathbf{Hu}(k)$$

having designer-selected eigenvalues, the combination of plant outputs and observer state observes

$$\mathbf{w}(k) = \begin{bmatrix} \mathbf{y}(k) - \mathbf{Du}(k) \\ \hline \xi(k) \end{bmatrix} \rightarrow \mathbf{Ex}(k) = \begin{bmatrix} \mathbf{C} \\ \hline \mathbf{M} \end{bmatrix} \mathbf{x}(k)$$

where the observer state observes

$$\xi(k) \rightarrow \mathbf{Mx}(k)$$

The symbol $\mathbf{E}$ is used for the observation of the $n$-vector observer output, while $\mathbf{M}$ is the observation matrix of the observer state.

If the plant is completely observable, it is always possible to choose

## TABLE 5-5  General State Observer Design Method

**1.** To construct a state observer for the $n$th-order plant

$$\mathbf{x}(k + 1) = \mathbf{A}\mathbf{x}(k) + \mathbf{B}\mathbf{u}(k)$$

$$\mathbf{y}(k) = \mathbf{C}\mathbf{x}(k) + \mathbf{D}\mathbf{u}(k) = \begin{bmatrix} \mathbf{c}_1^\dagger \\ \vdots \\ \mathbf{c}_m^\dagger \end{bmatrix} \mathbf{x}(k) + \begin{bmatrix} \mathbf{d}_1^\dagger \\ \vdots \\ \mathbf{d}_m^\dagger \end{bmatrix} \mathbf{u}(k)$$

with $m$ linearly independent outputs, first form a nonsingular observation matrix $\mathbf{E}$ and the associated first-order observer state and observer output equations as follows:

**A.** If the observer is to be of *reduced-order*, the linearly independent rows of $\mathbf{C}$ are included in $\mathbf{E}$. For each, an observer output signal

$$w_i(k) = y_i(k) - \mathbf{d}_i^\dagger \mathbf{u}(k)$$

is formed. If the observer is to be of full-order, rows of $\mathbf{C}$ are not included in $\mathbf{E}$.

**B.** For each distinct observer eigenvalue, a first-order observer, of the form

$$\xi_i(k + 1) = f_i \xi_i(k) + \mathbf{g}_i^\dagger \mathbf{y}(k) + \mathbf{h}_i^\dagger \mathbf{u}(k)$$

is designed. The individual observer observation matrix

$$\mathbf{m}_i^\dagger = \mathbf{g}_i^\dagger \mathbf{C}(\mathbf{A} - f_i\mathbf{I})^{-1}$$

which depends on $\mathbf{g}_i$, is included as a row of the overall observation matrix $\mathbf{E}$. The observer state becomes another observer output:

$$w_i(k) = \xi_i(k)$$

**C.** If observer eigenvalue repetitions are desired, the observer design is governed by the recursive relations of Table 5-4. Each of the individual observed state transformations is included in $\mathbf{E}$, and the observer state variables are each added to the collection of observer outputs.

**2.** For a reduced-order state observer, the observer order is $n - m$. For a full-order state observer, the observer order is $n$. In either case, $\mathbf{E}$ is $n \times n$. Make convenient but arbitrary choices for all the observer gains $\mathbf{g}_i$ so that $\mathbf{E}$ is nonsingular.

**3.** The observer output equation is

$$\mathbf{w}'(k) = \mathbf{E}^{-1}\mathbf{w}(k)$$

and

$$\mathbf{w}'(k) \to \mathbf{x}(k)$$

Or, the change of variables

$$\boldsymbol{\xi}'(k) = \mathbf{E}^{-1}\boldsymbol{\xi}(k)$$

can be made so that

$$\boldsymbol{\xi}'(k) \to \mathbf{x}(k)$$

---

observer gains so that $\mathbf{E}$ is nonsingular. With such a choice

$$\mathbf{w}'(k) = \mathbf{E}^{-1}\mathbf{w}(k) \to \mathbf{x}(k)$$

A summary of this general method of state observer design is given in Table 5-5.
For the system

$$\begin{bmatrix} x_1(k+1) \\ x_2(k+1) \end{bmatrix} = \begin{bmatrix} 1 & 0 \\ -2 & 3 \end{bmatrix}\begin{bmatrix} x_1(k) \\ x_2(k) \end{bmatrix} + \begin{bmatrix} -1 \\ 2 \end{bmatrix} u(k) = \mathbf{A}x(k) + \mathbf{b}u(k)$$

$$y(k) = \begin{bmatrix} 1 & 2 \end{bmatrix}\begin{bmatrix} x_1(k) \\ x_2(k) \end{bmatrix} - 3u(k) = \mathbf{c}^\dagger x(k) + du(k)$$

a first-order observer with eigenvalue $\lambda = 1/2$, of the form

$$\xi(k+1) = \tfrac{1}{2}\xi(k) + gy(k) + hu(k)$$

observes

$$\xi(k) \to \mathbf{m}^\dagger \mathbf{x}(k)$$

where

$$\mathbf{m}^\dagger = g\mathbf{c}^\dagger(\mathbf{A} - \tfrac{1}{2}\mathbf{I})^{-1} = g\begin{bmatrix} 1 & 2 \end{bmatrix}\begin{bmatrix} \tfrac{1}{2} & 0 \\ -2 & \tfrac{5}{2} \end{bmatrix}^{-1} = g\begin{bmatrix} \tfrac{26}{5} & \tfrac{4}{5} \end{bmatrix}$$

As the observer gain $g$ only serves to scale the observed functional, it will be set to unity so that

$$\mathbf{m}^\dagger = [\tfrac{26}{5} \quad \tfrac{4}{5}]$$

For this observer

$$h = \mathbf{m}^\dagger \mathbf{b} - d = [\tfrac{26}{5} \quad \tfrac{4}{5}] \begin{bmatrix} -1 \\ 2 \end{bmatrix} + 3 = -\frac{3}{5}$$

The two signals observe

$$\begin{bmatrix} y(k) + 3u(k) \\ \xi(k) \end{bmatrix} \rightarrow \begin{bmatrix} \mathbf{c}^\dagger \\ \hline \mathbf{m}^\dagger \end{bmatrix} \mathbf{x}(k) = \begin{bmatrix} 1 & 2 \\ \tfrac{26}{5} & \tfrac{4}{5} \end{bmatrix} \begin{bmatrix} x_1(k) \\ x_2(k) \end{bmatrix} = \mathbf{E}\mathbf{x}(k)$$

hence the two-output first-order observer

$$\xi(k + 1) = \tfrac{1}{2}\xi(k) + y(k) - \tfrac{3}{5}u(k)$$

$$\begin{bmatrix} w_1(k) \\ w_2(k) \end{bmatrix} = \begin{bmatrix} 0 \\ 1 \end{bmatrix} \xi(k) + \begin{bmatrix} 1 \\ 0 \end{bmatrix} y(k) + \begin{bmatrix} 3 \\ 0 \end{bmatrix} u(k)$$

has output that observes

$$\mathbf{w}(k) \rightarrow \begin{bmatrix} 1 & 2 \\ \tfrac{26}{5} & \tfrac{4}{5} \end{bmatrix} \mathbf{x}(k) = \mathbf{E}\mathbf{x}(k)$$

Transforming the output to form

$$\mathbf{w}'(k) = \mathbf{E}^{-1}\mathbf{w}(k) = \frac{1}{48} \begin{bmatrix} -4 & 10 \\ 26 & -5 \end{bmatrix} \mathbf{w}(k)$$

$$\begin{bmatrix} w_1'(k) \\ w_2'(k) \end{bmatrix} = \frac{1}{48} \begin{bmatrix} -4 & 10 \\ 26 & -5 \end{bmatrix} \begin{bmatrix} 0 \\ 1 \end{bmatrix} \xi(k) + \frac{1}{48} \begin{bmatrix} -4 & 10 \\ 26 & -5 \end{bmatrix} \begin{bmatrix} 1 \\ 0 \end{bmatrix} y(k)$$

$$+ \frac{1}{48} \begin{bmatrix} -4 & 10 \\ 26 & -5 \end{bmatrix} \begin{bmatrix} 3 \\ 0 \end{bmatrix} u(k)$$

$$= \begin{bmatrix} \tfrac{10}{48} \\ -\tfrac{5}{48} \end{bmatrix} \xi(k) + \begin{bmatrix} -\tfrac{4}{48} \\ \tfrac{26}{48} \end{bmatrix} y(k) + \begin{bmatrix} -\tfrac{12}{48} \\ \tfrac{78}{48} \end{bmatrix} u(k)$$

results in an observer with output that observes the state $\mathbf{x}(k)$.

For the third-order two-output plant

$$\begin{bmatrix} x_1(k+1) \\ x_2(k+1) \\ x_3(k+1) \end{bmatrix} = \begin{bmatrix} 2 & 0 & 3 \\ 1 & 0 & 1 \\ 0 & -2 & 0 \end{bmatrix} \begin{bmatrix} x_1(k) \\ x_2(k) \\ x_3(k) \end{bmatrix} + \begin{bmatrix} 1 \\ 0 \\ 0 \end{bmatrix} u(k) = \mathbf{A}\mathbf{x}(k) + \mathbf{b}u(k)$$

$$\begin{bmatrix} y_1(k) \\ y_2(k) \end{bmatrix} = \begin{bmatrix} 0 & 2 & 1 \\ 1 & -1 & 2 \end{bmatrix} \begin{bmatrix} x_1(k) \\ x_2(k) \\ x_3(k) \end{bmatrix} + \begin{bmatrix} 3 \\ 0 \end{bmatrix} u(k) = \mathbf{C}\mathbf{x}(k) + \mathbf{d}u(k)$$

a first-order observer with eigenvalue $\lambda = 0$, of the form

$$\xi(k+1) = (0)\xi(k) + \mathbf{g}^\dagger \mathbf{y}(k) + hu(k)$$

observes the scalar state transformation

$$\mathbf{m}^\dagger = \mathbf{g}^\dagger \mathbf{C}(\mathbf{A} - 0 \cdot \mathbf{I})^{-1} = [g_1 \quad g_2] \begin{bmatrix} 0 & 2 & 1 \\ 1 & -1 & 2 \end{bmatrix} \begin{bmatrix} 2 & 0 & 3 \\ 1 & 0 & 1 \\ 0 & -2 & 0 \end{bmatrix}^{-1}$$

$$= g_1[1 \quad -2 \quad -1] + g_2[1 \quad -1 \quad \tfrac{1}{2}]$$

For this observer:

$$h = \mathbf{m}^\dagger \mathbf{b} - \mathbf{g}^\dagger \mathbf{d} = -2g_1 + g_2$$

The three signals

$$\begin{bmatrix} w_1(k) \\ w_2(k) \\ w_3(k) \end{bmatrix} = \begin{bmatrix} y_1(k) - 3u(k) \\ y_2(k) \\ \xi(k) \end{bmatrix} = \begin{bmatrix} 0 \\ 0 \\ 1 \end{bmatrix} \xi(k) + \begin{bmatrix} 1 & 0 \\ 0 & 1 \\ 0 & 0 \end{bmatrix} \begin{bmatrix} y_1(k) \\ y_2(k) \end{bmatrix} + \begin{bmatrix} -3 \\ 0 \\ 0 \end{bmatrix} u(k)$$

observe

$$\mathbf{w}(k) \rightarrow \begin{bmatrix} \mathbf{C} \\ \hline \mathbf{m}^\dagger \end{bmatrix} \mathbf{x}(k) = \begin{bmatrix} 0 & 2 & 1 \\ 1 & -1 & 2 \\ (g_1 + g_2) & (-2g_1 - g_2) & (-g_1 + \tfrac{1}{2}g_2) \end{bmatrix} \begin{bmatrix} x_1(k) \\ x_2(k) \\ x_3(k) \end{bmatrix}$$

$$= \mathbf{E}\mathbf{x}(k)$$

Arbitrarily choosing

$$g_1 = -1; \qquad g_2 = 0$$

which is one choice of observer gains for which $\mathbf{E}$ is nonsingular

$$\mathbf{E} = \begin{bmatrix} 0 & 2 & 1 \\ 1 & -1 & 2 \\ -1 & 2 & 1 \end{bmatrix}; \quad \mathbf{E}^{-1} = \begin{bmatrix} 1 & 0 & -1 \\ \frac{3}{5} & -\frac{1}{5} & -\frac{1}{5} \\ -\frac{1}{5} & \frac{2}{5} & \frac{2}{5} \end{bmatrix}$$

the observer

$$\xi(k+1) = \begin{bmatrix} -1 & 0 \end{bmatrix}\begin{bmatrix} y_1(k) \\ y_2(k) \end{bmatrix} + 3u(k)$$

$$\mathbf{w}'(k) = \mathbf{E}^{-1}\mathbf{w}(k) = \begin{bmatrix} 1 & 0 & -1 \\ \frac{3}{5} & -\frac{1}{5} & -\frac{1}{5} \\ -\frac{1}{5} & \frac{2}{5} & \frac{2}{5} \end{bmatrix}\begin{bmatrix} 0 \\ 0 \\ 1 \end{bmatrix}\xi(k)$$

$$+ \begin{bmatrix} 1 & 0 & -1 \\ \frac{3}{5} & -\frac{1}{5} & -\frac{1}{5} \\ -\frac{1}{5} & \frac{2}{5} & \frac{2}{5} \end{bmatrix}\begin{bmatrix} 1 & 0 \\ 0 & 1 \\ 0 & 0 \end{bmatrix}\begin{bmatrix} y_1(k) \\ y_2(k) \end{bmatrix} + \begin{bmatrix} 1 & 0 & -1 \\ \frac{3}{5} & -\frac{1}{5} & -\frac{1}{5} \\ -\frac{1}{5} & \frac{2}{5} & \frac{2}{5} \end{bmatrix}\begin{bmatrix} -3 \\ 0 \\ 0 \end{bmatrix}u(k)$$

$$= \begin{bmatrix} -1 \\ -\frac{1}{5} \\ \frac{2}{5} \end{bmatrix}\xi(k) + \begin{bmatrix} 1 & 0 \\ \frac{3}{5} & -\frac{1}{5} \\ -\frac{1}{5} & \frac{2}{5} \end{bmatrix}\begin{bmatrix} y_1(k) \\ y_2(k) \end{bmatrix} + \begin{bmatrix} -3 \\ -\frac{9}{5} \\ \frac{3}{5} \end{bmatrix}u(k)$$

observes $\mathbf{x}(k)$.

## 5.5.2 Minimal-Order Observers of a Scalar State Transformation

For feedback eigenvalue placement for a single-input plant, only a single scalar linear transformation of the plant state is needed for feedback. We now develop observer design methods similar to the previous ones to design observers of a given scalar linear transformation of the plant state.

If an $n$th-order plant has a single output, then obtaining observation of an arbitrary scalar linear plant state transformation will generally require $n$ first-order observers if the plant output is not used directly, or $n - 1$ first-order observers if it is. It would be a lucky circumstance if the desired scalar state transformation were a linear combination of the individual scalar state transformations observed by a lesser number of component first-order observers. Thus one may as well construct a state observer, then form the desired scalar transformation from the observed plant state. When the plant has more than one output, however, each first-order observer observes a linear combination of $m$ scalar state transformations, where $m$ is the number of plant outputs. The specific linear combination is determined by the choice of observer gains, so each first-order observer contributes an arbitrary linear combination of $m$ scalar transformations to a single output from a collection of observers.

This procedure for design of a minimum-order observer of a scalar linear plant state transformation is summarized in Table 5-6.

As an example, consider the system

$$
\begin{bmatrix} x_1(k+1) \\ x_2(k+1) \\ x_3(k+1) \end{bmatrix} = \begin{bmatrix} 0 & 1 & 0 \\ 0 & 0 & 1 \\ 0 & 0 & 0 \end{bmatrix} \begin{bmatrix} x_1(k) \\ x_2(k) \\ x_3(k) \end{bmatrix} + \begin{bmatrix} 2 \\ 0 \\ -2 \end{bmatrix} u(k) = \mathbf{A}\mathbf{x}(k) + \mathbf{b}u(k)
$$

$$
\begin{bmatrix} y_1(k) \\ y_2(k) \end{bmatrix} = \begin{bmatrix} 0 & 1 & -1 \\ 1 & 2 & 0 \end{bmatrix} \begin{bmatrix} x_1(k) \\ x_2(k) \\ x_3(k) \end{bmatrix} + \begin{bmatrix} 0 \\ 3 \end{bmatrix} u(k) = \mathbf{C}\mathbf{x}(k) + \mathbf{d}u(k) \qquad (5\text{-}11)
$$

where two outputs are available to the observer.

A zeroth-order observer (one with no state equation) of the form

$$
w(k) = \gamma_1 y_1(k) + \gamma_2 [y_2(k) - 3u(k)]
$$

where $\gamma_1$ and $\gamma_2$ are arbitrary constants, will equal (and thus observe) any scalar linear transformation of the plant state $\mathbf{e}^\dagger \mathbf{x}$ of the form

$$
\mathbf{e}^\dagger = \gamma_1 [0 \quad 1 \quad -1] + \gamma_2 [1 \quad 2 \quad 0] \qquad (5\text{-}12)
$$

If the plant state transformation to be observed, $\mathbf{e}^\dagger$, can be expressed in this form, equation (5-12) is solved for $\gamma_1$ and $\gamma_2$ and the resulting observer will have no dynamics; the state transformation can be derived from the two plant outputs alone.

If, as is likely, equation (5-12) does not have a solution, a first-order observer is added. If it is desired that the observer eigenvalue be $\lambda = -1/4$, then this observer has the form

$$
\xi_1(k+1) = -\tfrac{1}{4}\xi_1(k) + [g_{11} \quad g_{12}] \begin{bmatrix} y_1(k) \\ y_2(k) \end{bmatrix} + h_1 u(k)
$$

and has the observation matrix

$$
\mathbf{m}_1^\dagger = \mathbf{g}_1^\dagger \mathbf{C}(\mathbf{A} + \tfrac{1}{4}\mathbf{I})^{-1} = [g_{11} \quad g_{12}] \begin{bmatrix} 0 & 1 & -1 \\ 1 & 2 & 0 \end{bmatrix} \begin{bmatrix} \tfrac{1}{4} & 1 & 0 \\ 0 & \tfrac{1}{4} & 1 \\ 0 & 0 & \tfrac{1}{4} \end{bmatrix}^{-1}
$$

$$
= g_{11}[0 \quad 4 \quad -20] + g_{12}[4 \quad -8 \quad 32]
$$

## TABLE 5-6    Design of Minimal-Order Observers of a Scalar Linear State Transformation

To construct a minimal-order observer of a scalar linear state transformation

$$w(k) \rightarrow \mathbf{e}^\dagger \mathbf{x}(k)$$

for the plant

$$\mathbf{x}(k + 1) = \mathbf{A}\mathbf{x}(k) + \mathbf{B}\mathbf{u}(k)$$

$$\mathbf{y}(k) = \mathbf{C}\mathbf{x}(k) + \mathbf{D}\mathbf{u}(k) = \begin{bmatrix} \mathbf{c}_1^\dagger \\ \vdots \\ \mathbf{c}_m^\dagger \end{bmatrix} \mathbf{x}(k) + \begin{bmatrix} \mathbf{d}_1^\dagger \\ \vdots \\ \mathbf{d}_m^\dagger \end{bmatrix} \mathbf{u}(k)$$

collect terms in the equation

$$\gamma_1 \mathbf{c}_1^\dagger + \gamma_2 \mathbf{c}_2^\dagger + \cdots + \gamma_m \mathbf{c}_m^\dagger + \mathbf{m}_1^\dagger + \mathbf{m}_2^\dagger + \cdots + \mathbf{m}_i^\dagger = \mathbf{e}^\dagger \tag{5-10}$$

until a solution exists for the $\gamma$'s and the observer gains. A solution to equation (5-10) defines a specific linear combination of the plant output state transformations and a choice of observer gains for which the observer output observes the scalar state transformation $\mathbf{e}^\dagger \mathbf{x}(k)$.

If the plant outputs are to be used by the observer, each row of $\mathbf{C}$ is included in equation (5-10) and, for each, a term

$$w(k) = \cdots + \gamma_i [y_i(k) - \mathbf{d}_i^\dagger \mathbf{u}(k)] + \cdots$$

is added to the single observer output, where $\gamma_i$ is a constant to be determined. Otherwise, these terms are not used. For each distinct observer eigenvalue, a first-order observer of the form

$$\xi_i(k + 1) = f_i \xi_i(k) + \mathbf{g}_i^\dagger \mathbf{y}(k) + \mathbf{h}_i^\dagger \mathbf{u}(k)$$

is designed. The observation matrix

$$\mathbf{m}_i^\dagger = \mathbf{g}_i^\dagger \mathbf{C}(\mathbf{A} - f_i \mathbf{I})^{-1}$$

involves a linear combination of the elements of the observer gain vector $\mathbf{g}_i$ to be determined. Each observation matrix $\mathbf{m}_i$ is added to equation (5-10), and the observer state is added to the single observer output:

$$w(k) = \cdots + \xi_i(k) + \cdots$$

When enough terms are added to equation (5-10), a solution for the variables $\gamma_1$, $\gamma_2, \ldots$, and the elements of $\mathbf{g}_1, \mathbf{g}_2, \ldots$ exists and is found.

If observer eigenvalue repetitions are desired, the observer design is governed by the recursive relations of Table 5-4. Each of the observed scalar state transformations is added to equation (5-10) and each of the observer states is added to the observer output $w(k)$.

The plant input coupling to this observer is

$$h_1 = \mathbf{m}_1^\dagger \mathbf{b} - \mathbf{g}_1^\dagger \mathbf{d} = 40g_{11} - 59g_{12}$$

giving

$$\xi_1(k+1) = -\tfrac{1}{4}\xi_1(k) + [g_{11} \quad g_{12}]\begin{bmatrix} y_1(k) \\ y_2(k) \end{bmatrix} + (40g_{11} - 59g_{12})u(k) \tag{5-13}$$

The observer output

$$w(k) = \gamma_1 y_1(k) + \gamma_2[y_2(k) - 3u(k)] + \xi_1(k)$$

observes a linear transformation of the plant state $\mathbf{e}^\dagger \mathbf{x}$ of the form

$$\begin{aligned} \mathbf{e}^\dagger = \gamma_1[0 \quad & 1 \quad -1] + \gamma_2[1 \quad 2 \quad 0] \\ + g_{11}[0 \quad & 4 \quad -20] + g_{12}[4 \quad -8 \quad 32] \end{aligned} \tag{5-14}$$

which, with appropriate choice of $\gamma_1, \gamma_2, g_{11}$, and $g_{12}$, can observe any scalar linear plant state transformation. If it is desired that

$$w(k) \rightarrow [1 \quad 0 \quad 0]\mathbf{x}(k) = \mathbf{e}^\dagger \mathbf{x}(k)$$

the $\gamma$'s and $g$'s must satisfy

$$\begin{cases} \gamma_2 & + \ 4g_{12} = 1 \\ \gamma_1 + 2\gamma_2 + \ 4g_{11} - \ 8g_{12} = 0 \\ -\gamma_2 & - \ 20g_{11} + 32g_{12} = 0 \end{cases} \tag{5-15}$$

one solution to which is

$$\gamma_1 = -\tfrac{5}{2}; \qquad \gamma_2 = 1$$
$$g_{11} = \tfrac{1}{8}; \qquad g_{12} = 0$$

This solution defines the observer

$$\xi_1(k + 1) = -\tfrac{1}{4}\xi(k) + [\tfrac{1}{8} \quad 0]y(k) + u(k)$$

$$w(k) = \xi_1(k) + [-\tfrac{5}{2} \quad 1]y(k) - 3u(k)$$

There are many other solutions to equations (5-15), of course.

For the plant (5-11), suppose instead that a solution is desired that does not use the plant outputs directly. That is, there is to be no direct coupling of $y(k)$ to the observer output. We may wish to have this property because it tends to reduce the effects of plant output noise. Beginning with the first-order observer (5-13), the observer output

$$w(k) = \xi_1(k)$$

will observe any scalar linear plant state transformation $\mathbf{e}^t\mathbf{x}$ of the form (setting $\gamma_i = \gamma_2 = 0$ in equation (5-14))

$$\mathbf{e}^t = g_{11}[0 \quad 4 \quad -20] + g_{12}[4 \quad -8 \quad 32]$$

If the state transformation to be observed is of this form, then $g_{11}$ and $g_{22}$ are found. If not, as is likely because $\mathbf{e}$ has three components and there are only two variables, another first-order observer is added to the design.

Another first-order observer, with eigenvalue chosen to be $\lambda = 1/2$, has the form

$$\xi_2(k + 1) = \tfrac{1}{2}\xi_2(k) + [g_{21} \quad g_{22}]\begin{bmatrix} y_1(k) \\ y_2(k) \end{bmatrix} + h_2 u(k)$$

and has observation matrix

$$\mathbf{m}_2^t = \mathbf{g}_2^t \mathbf{C}(\mathbf{A} - \tfrac{1}{2}\mathbf{I})^{-1} = [g_{21} \quad g_{22}]\begin{bmatrix} 0 & 1 & -1 \\ 1 & 2 & 0 \end{bmatrix}\begin{bmatrix} -\tfrac{1}{2} & 1 & 0 \\ 0 & -\tfrac{1}{2} & 1 \\ 0 & 0 & -\tfrac{1}{2} \end{bmatrix}^{-1}$$

$$= g_{21}[0 \quad -2 \quad -2] + g_{22}[-2 \quad -8 \quad -16]$$

The plant input coupling to this observer is

$$h_2 = \mathbf{m}_2^t \mathbf{b} - \mathbf{g}_2^t \mathbf{d} = 4g_{21} + 25g_{22}$$

giving

$$\xi_2(k + 1) = \tfrac{1}{2}\xi_2(k) + [g_{21} \quad g_{22}]\begin{bmatrix} y_1(k) \\ y_2(k) \end{bmatrix} + (4g_{21} + 25g_{22})u(k)$$

The observer output

$$w(k) = \xi_1(k) + \xi_2(k)$$

observes any scalar linear plant state transformation $\mathbf{e}^\dagger \mathbf{x}$ of the form

$$\mathbf{e}^\dagger = g_{11}[0 \quad 4 \quad -20] + g_{12}[4 \quad -8 \quad 32]$$
$$+ g_{21}[0 \quad -2 \quad -2] + g_{22}[-2 \quad -8 \quad -16]$$

For

$$\mathbf{e}^\dagger = [1 \quad 0 \quad 0]$$

the **g**'s must satisfy

$$\begin{cases} 4g_{12} \quad - \quad 2g_{22} = 1 \\ 4g_{11} - 8g_{12} - 2g_{21} - 8g_{22} = 0 \\ -20g_{11} + 32g_{12} - 2g_{21} - 16g_{22} = 0 \end{cases}$$

one solution to which is

$$g_{11} = \tfrac{5}{12}; \qquad g_{12} = \tfrac{1}{4}; \qquad g_{21} = -\tfrac{1}{6}; \qquad g_{22} = 0$$

The observer

$$\begin{bmatrix} \xi_1(k+1) \\ \xi_2(k+1) \end{bmatrix} = \begin{bmatrix} -\tfrac{1}{4} & 0 \\ 0 & \tfrac{1}{2} \end{bmatrix} \begin{bmatrix} \xi_1(k) \\ \xi_2(k) \end{bmatrix} + \begin{bmatrix} \tfrac{5}{12} & \tfrac{1}{4} \\ -\tfrac{1}{6} & 0 \end{bmatrix} \begin{bmatrix} y_1(k) \\ y_2(k) \end{bmatrix} + \begin{bmatrix} \tfrac{23}{12} \\ -\tfrac{1}{6} \end{bmatrix} u(k)$$

$$w(k) = [1 \quad 1] \begin{bmatrix} \xi_1(k) \\ \xi_2(k) \end{bmatrix}$$

then has output $w(k)$ that observes $\mathbf{e}^\dagger \mathbf{x}$.

For a completely observable plant of order $n$, with $m$ outputs and no observer eigenvalue equaling a plant eigenvalue, the order $j$ of a minimal-order observer of an arbitrary scalar plant state transformation is given by

$$m + jm \geq n; \qquad j \geq \frac{n}{m} - 1 = \frac{n - m}{m}$$

If the observer is to have no direct coupling of plant signals to its output, then

$$jm \geq n; \qquad j \geq \frac{n}{m}$$

**TABLE 5-7    Observer Orders for Feedback Eigenvalue Placement for a Tenth-Order Plant**

| Number of plant outputs | Order of the full-order state observer | Order of the reduced-order state observer | Order of the minimal-order observer of a scalar transformation of the plant state: | |
| --- | --- | --- | --- | --- |
| | | | without direct plant coupling to its output | with direct plant coupling to its output |
| 1 | 10 | 9 | 10 | 9 |
| 2 | 10 | 8 | 5 | 4 |
| 3 | 10 | 7 | 4 | 3 |
| 4 | 10 | 6 | 3 | 2 |
| 5 | 10 | 5 | 2 | 1 |
| 6 | 10 | 4 | 2 | 1 |
| 7 | 10 | 3 | 2 | 1 |
| 8 | 10 | 2 | 2 | 1 |
| 9 | 10 | 1 | 2 | 1 |
| 10 | 10 | 0 | 1 | 0 |

Table 5-7 lists observer orders for a tenth-order plant with various numbers of outputs, as a representative comparison.

### 5.5.3 Observers of Multiple Scalar State Transformations

If an observer is used for feedback system eigenvalue placement for a multiple-input plant, it may be desirable to observe more than a single scalar linear plant state transformation, but not $n$ of them, which would amount to observing the entire plant state. For feedback eigenvalue placement, the additional freedom in the choice of individual state feedback vectors $e_i$, one for each plant input, can also be exploited in reducing the required observer order. A minimal-order feedback observer solution for eigenvalue placement does exist, but it is fairly involved. We will not pursue the topic of minimal-order observers further here because most often, as we will see, the higher-order solutions give better overall tracking system performance.

# 5.6 Eigenvalue Placement with Observer Feedback

The eigenvalues of a plant, or of a plant with feedback, determine the character of the system's zero-input response. Normally, the initial conditions of the plant are not entirely known, and since the amplitudes of each zero-input response mode depends on these, the best one can usually do is to select the modes themselves. If the plant state is available for feedback, the designer can place all of the feedback system eigenvalues as desired and thus completely design the form of a controlled system's zero-input response. When, as is usual, the plant state is not accessible for feedback, an observer's estimate of the plant state can be fed back in place of the actual state.

It should be noted that we normally avoid choosing observer eigenvalues equal to any of the original plant eigenvalues. There is no reason to avoid having observer eigenvalues equal to those of the plant-with-feedback.

## 5.6.1 The Separation Theorem

We now prove the separation theorem: when observer feedback is used in place of plant state feedback, the eigenvalues of the feedback system are those the plant would have if state feedback were used and those of the observer. The arrangement of the plant and the observer is shown in Figure 5-11. To easily see the principle involved, the result is first shown for feedback by a full-order state observer.

Consider the $n$th order plant

$$\mathbf{x}(k + 1) = \mathbf{A}\mathbf{x}(k) + \mathbf{B}\mathbf{u}(k)$$
$$\mathbf{y}(k) = \mathbf{C}\mathbf{x}(k) + \mathbf{D}\mathbf{u}(k)$$

with feedback

$$\mathbf{u}(k) = \mathbf{E}\boldsymbol{\xi}(k) + \boldsymbol{\rho}(k)$$

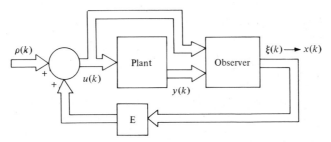

**FIGURE 5-11.**   An observer estimate of the plant state, fed back in place of the state.

from a full-order state observer

$$\xi(k + 1) = \mathbf{F}\xi(k) + \mathbf{G}y(k) + \mathbf{H}u(k)$$

where

$$\mathbf{F} = \mathbf{A} - \mathbf{GC}$$

$$\mathbf{H} = \mathbf{B} - \mathbf{GD}$$

Rather than dealing with the $2n$ state variables $\mathbf{x}$ and $\xi$, we use $\mathbf{x}$ and the $n$ observer error variables

$$\varepsilon(k) = \mathbf{x}(k) - \xi(k)$$

to describe the feedback system. Either set of variables can be used, but using the latter results in simplified equations. One can view this as a choice of new state variables, $\mathbf{x}$ and $\varepsilon$, that are related to the old ones, $\mathbf{x}$ and $\xi$, by a nonsingular transformation. Substituting for $\mathbf{u}(k)$ in the plant state equations in terms of $\varepsilon(k)$, there results

$$\mathbf{x}(k + 1) = \mathbf{A}\mathbf{x}(k) + \mathbf{BE}\xi(k) + \mathbf{B}\rho(k)$$

$$= (\mathbf{A} + \mathbf{BE})\mathbf{x}(k) - \mathbf{BE}\varepsilon(k) + \mathbf{B}\rho(k)$$

The observer error is governed by

$$\varepsilon(k + 1) = \mathbf{F}\varepsilon(k)$$

so that equations for the feedback system are

$$\begin{bmatrix} \mathbf{x}(k + 1) \\ \varepsilon(k + 1) \end{bmatrix} = \begin{bmatrix} \mathbf{A} + \mathbf{BE} & -\mathbf{BE} \\ \mathbf{0} & \mathbf{F} \end{bmatrix} \begin{bmatrix} \mathbf{x}(k) \\ \varepsilon(k) \end{bmatrix} + \begin{bmatrix} \mathbf{B} \\ \mathbf{0} \end{bmatrix} \rho(k) \qquad (5\text{-}17)$$

The characteristic equation for (5-17) is given by

$$\begin{vmatrix} \lambda\mathbf{I} - (\mathbf{A} + \mathbf{BE}) & \mathbf{BE} \\ \mathbf{0} & \lambda\mathbf{I} - \mathbf{F} \end{vmatrix} = |\lambda\mathbf{I} - (\mathbf{A} + \mathbf{BE})||\lambda\mathbf{I} - \mathbf{F}| = 0$$

which demonstrates that the eigenvalues of the plant with full-order state observer feedback are those of the state feedback system

$$|\lambda\mathbf{I} - (\mathbf{A} + \mathbf{BE})| = 0$$

and those of the observer

$$|\lambda \mathbf{I} - \mathbf{F}| = 0$$

We next consider observer feedback when the observer is possibly of different order than that of the plant and involves an output equation:

$$\xi(k + 1) = \mathbf{F}\xi(k) + \mathbf{G}\mathbf{y}(k) + \mathbf{H}\mathbf{u}(k)$$

$$\mathbf{w}(k) = \mathbf{L}\xi(k) + \mathbf{N}\mathbf{x}(k)$$

Here, the observer output equation is expressed in a form emphasizing that the fed back state estimate $\mathbf{w}(k)$ is a combination of observer state and plant state feedback. The observer state observes a linear transformation of the plant state

$$\xi(k) \rightarrow \mathbf{M}\mathbf{x}(k)$$

and the error in this observation is governed by

$$\varepsilon(k + 1) = \mathbf{M}\mathbf{x}(k + 1) - \xi(k + 1) = \mathbf{F}[\mathbf{M}\mathbf{x}(k) - \xi(k)] = \mathbf{F}\varepsilon(k)$$

The observer output equation is formed so that

$$\mathbf{w}(k) \rightarrow \mathbf{x}(k)$$

That is, since

$$\xi(k) \rightarrow \mathbf{M}\mathbf{x}(k)$$

then

$$\mathbf{L}\mathbf{M} + \mathbf{N} = \mathbf{I}$$

Substituting

$$\mathbf{u}(k) = \mathbf{E}\mathbf{w}(k) + \rho(k)$$

in the plant state equations in terms of $\varepsilon(k)$,

$$\mathbf{x}(k + 1) = \mathbf{A}\mathbf{x}(k) + \mathbf{B}\mathbf{E}\mathbf{w}(k) + \mathbf{B}\rho(k)$$

$$= \mathbf{A}\mathbf{x}(k) + \mathbf{B}\mathbf{E}\mathbf{L}\xi(k) + \mathbf{B}\mathbf{E}\mathbf{N}\mathbf{x}(k) + \mathbf{B}\rho(k)$$

$$= \mathbf{A}\mathbf{x}(k) + \mathbf{BEL}[\mathbf{M}\mathbf{x}(k) - \varepsilon(k)] + \mathbf{BEN}\mathbf{x}(k) + \mathbf{B}\rho(k)$$

$$= [\mathbf{A} + \mathbf{BE}(\mathbf{LM} + \mathbf{N})]\mathbf{x}(k) - \mathbf{BEL}\varepsilon(k) + \mathbf{B}\rho(k)$$

$$= (\mathbf{A} + \mathbf{BE})\mathbf{x}(k) - \mathbf{BEL}\varepsilon(k) + \mathbf{B}\rho(k)$$

The feedback system equations are then

$$
\begin{bmatrix} \mathbf{x}(k+1) \\ \varepsilon(k+1) \end{bmatrix} = \begin{bmatrix} \mathbf{A} + \mathbf{BE} & -\mathbf{BEL} \\ \mathbf{0} & \mathbf{F} \end{bmatrix} \begin{bmatrix} \mathbf{x}(k) \\ \varepsilon(k) \end{bmatrix} + \begin{bmatrix} \mathbf{B} \\ \mathbf{0} \end{bmatrix} \rho(k)
$$

and, as in the case of the full-order state observer, have eigenvalues that are those of the state feedback system and those of the observer.

## 5.6.2 Full-Order State Observer Feedback Example

Even though a lower-order observer might suffice, full-order state observers are often used for feedback in practice because of the close relationship that can be arranged between the plant state variables and the state variables of the observer. If $x_1$ is a temperature, it can be arranged so that $\xi_1$ is the observer estimate of that temperature, and so on. Full-order observers also need not have direct input-to-output coupling, so they can give more smoothing of noisy signals.

As an example of full-order state observer feedback, consider the plant

$$
\begin{bmatrix} x_1(k+1) \\ x_2(k+1) \end{bmatrix} = \begin{bmatrix} 2 & -1 \\ -1 & 1 \end{bmatrix} \begin{bmatrix} x_1(k) \\ x_2(k) \end{bmatrix} + \begin{bmatrix} 4 \\ 3 \end{bmatrix} u(k) = \mathbf{A}\mathbf{x}(k) + \mathbf{b}u(k)
$$

$$
y(k) = \begin{bmatrix} 1 & 1 \end{bmatrix} \begin{bmatrix} x_1(k) \\ x_2(k) \end{bmatrix} + 7u(k) = \mathbf{c}^\dagger\mathbf{x}(k) + du(k) \tag{5-18}
$$

which is completely controllable and completely observable. The plant's characteristic equation is

$$
|\lambda\mathbf{I} - \mathbf{A}| = \begin{vmatrix} (\lambda - 2) & 1 \\ 1 & (\lambda - 1) \end{vmatrix} = \lambda^2 - 3\lambda + 1 = \lambda^2 + \alpha_1\lambda + \alpha_0 = 0
$$

In this example, transformations to controllable and observable form will be used to design the plant feedback and the observer. The transformation to controllable form is

$$\mathbf{x} = \mathbf{P}\mathbf{x}'; \qquad \mathbf{x}' = \mathbf{P}^{-1}\mathbf{x}$$

$$\mathbf{P} = \begin{bmatrix} -7 & 4 \\ -10 & 3 \end{bmatrix}; \qquad \mathbf{P}^{-1} = \frac{1}{19} \begin{bmatrix} 3 & -4 \\ 10 & -7 \end{bmatrix}$$

The plant state equations in controllable form are

$$\mathbf{x}'(k + 1) = \mathbf{P}^{-1}\mathbf{APx}'(k) + \mathbf{P}^{-1}\mathbf{b}u(k) = \mathbf{A}'\mathbf{x}'(k) + \mathbf{b}'u(k)$$

or

$$\begin{bmatrix} x_1'(k + 1) \\ x_2'(k + 1) \end{bmatrix} = \begin{bmatrix} 0 & 1 \\ -1 & 3 \end{bmatrix} \begin{bmatrix} x_1'(k) \\ x_2'(k) \end{bmatrix} + \begin{bmatrix} 0 \\ 1 \end{bmatrix} u(k)$$

Feedback of the primed plant state

$$u(k) = \mathbf{e}'^\dagger \mathbf{x}'(k) + \rho(k)$$

results in the feedback system

$$\mathbf{x}'(k + 1) = (\mathbf{A}' + \mathbf{b}'\mathbf{e}'^\dagger)\mathbf{x}'(k) + \mathbf{b}'\rho(k) = \begin{bmatrix} 0 & 1 \\ (e_1' - 1) & (e_2' + 3) \end{bmatrix} \mathbf{x}'(k) + \mathbf{b}'\rho(k)$$

which has characteristic equation, in terms of the feedback gains $e_1'$ and $e_2'$,

$$\lambda^2 + (-3 - e_2')\lambda + (1 - e_1') = 0$$

If the desired eigenvalues are $\pm j\frac{1}{2}$, the desired characteristic equation is

$$(\lambda + j\tfrac{1}{2})(\lambda - j\tfrac{1}{2}) = \lambda^2 + \tfrac{1}{4} = 0$$

and the feedback gains for the $\mathbf{x}'$ state are

$$\begin{bmatrix} e_1' \\ e_2' \end{bmatrix} = \begin{bmatrix} \frac{3}{4} \\ -3 \end{bmatrix}$$

If, instead, the $\mathbf{x}$ state is fed back, the gains required are given by

$$\mathbf{e}'^\dagger \mathbf{x}'(k) = \mathbf{e}'^\dagger \mathbf{P}^{-1}\mathbf{x}(k) = \mathbf{e}^\dagger \mathbf{x}(k)$$

$$\mathbf{e}^\dagger = \mathbf{e}'^\dagger \mathbf{P}^{-1} = \begin{bmatrix} \frac{3}{4} & -3 \end{bmatrix} \begin{bmatrix} 3 & -4 \\ 10 & -7 \end{bmatrix} \left( \frac{1}{19} \right) = \begin{bmatrix} -\frac{111}{76} & \frac{18}{19} \end{bmatrix}$$

To design an observer for the plant (5-18), we transform to the observable form using

$$\mathbf{x}'' = \mathbf{Qx}; \qquad \mathbf{x} = \mathbf{Q}^{-1}\mathbf{x}''$$

where

$$\mathbf{Q} = \begin{bmatrix} 1 & 1 \\ -2 & -3 \end{bmatrix}; \qquad \mathbf{Q}^{-1} = \begin{bmatrix} 3 & 1 \\ -2 & -1 \end{bmatrix}$$

The plant equations in observable form are thus

$$\mathbf{x}''(k+1) = \mathbf{QAQ}^{-1}\mathbf{x}''(k) + \mathbf{QB}u(k) = \mathbf{A}''\mathbf{x}''(k) + \mathbf{b}''u(k)$$

$$y(k) = \mathbf{c}^{\mathsf{t}}\mathbf{Q}^{-1}\mathbf{x}''(k) + du(k) = \mathbf{c}''^{\mathsf{t}}\mathbf{x}''(k) + du(k)$$

or

$$\begin{bmatrix} x_1''(k+1) \\ x_2''(k+1) \end{bmatrix} = \begin{bmatrix} 3 & 1 \\ -1 & 0 \end{bmatrix}\begin{bmatrix} x_1''(k) \\ x_2''(k) \end{bmatrix} + \begin{bmatrix} 7 \\ -17 \end{bmatrix}u(k) = \mathbf{A}''\mathbf{x}''(k) + \mathbf{b}''u(k)$$

$$y(k) = \begin{bmatrix} 1 & 0 \end{bmatrix}\begin{bmatrix} x_1''(k) \\ x_2''(k) \end{bmatrix} + 7u(k) = \mathbf{c}''^{\mathsf{t}}\mathbf{x}''(k) + du(k)$$

An observer of the $\mathbf{x}''$ plant state has the form

$$\xi''(k+1) = \mathbf{F}''\xi''(k) + \mathbf{g}''y(k) + \mathbf{h}''u(k)$$

where

$$\mathbf{F}'' = \mathbf{A}'' - \mathbf{g}''\mathbf{c}''^{\mathsf{t}} = \begin{bmatrix} 3 & 1 \\ -1 & 0 \end{bmatrix} - \begin{bmatrix} g_1'' \\ g_2'' \end{bmatrix}\begin{bmatrix} 1 & 0 \end{bmatrix} = \begin{bmatrix} (3 - g_1'') & 1 \\ (-1 - g_2'') & 0 \end{bmatrix}$$

The characteristic equation of the observer is, in terms of $g_1''$ and $g_2''$

$$\lambda^2 + (g_1'' - 3)\lambda + (g_2'' + 1) = 0$$

If the desired observer characteristic equation is

$$(\lambda - \tfrac{1}{2})(\lambda - \tfrac{1}{4}) = \lambda^2 - \tfrac{3}{4}\lambda + \tfrac{1}{8} = 0$$

then the observer gains are

$$\mathbf{g}'' = \begin{bmatrix} g_1'' \\ g_2'' \end{bmatrix} = \begin{bmatrix} \tfrac{9}{4} \\ -\tfrac{7}{8} \end{bmatrix}$$

$$\mathbf{h}'' = \mathbf{b}'' - \mathbf{g}''d = \begin{bmatrix} 7 \\ -17 \end{bmatrix} - \begin{bmatrix} \frac{9}{4} \\ -\frac{7}{8} \end{bmatrix} (7) = \begin{bmatrix} -\frac{35}{4} \\ -\frac{87}{8} \end{bmatrix}$$

so that the observer equations are

$$\begin{bmatrix} \xi_1''(k+1) \\ \xi_2''(k+1) \end{bmatrix} = \begin{bmatrix} \frac{3}{4} & 1 \\ -\frac{1}{8} & 0 \end{bmatrix} \begin{bmatrix} \xi_1''(k) \\ \xi_2''(k) \end{bmatrix} + \begin{bmatrix} \frac{9}{4} \\ -\frac{7}{8} \end{bmatrix} y(k) + \begin{bmatrix} -\frac{35}{4} \\ -\frac{87}{8} \end{bmatrix} u(k)$$

$$= \mathbf{F}''\boldsymbol{\xi}''(k) + \mathbf{g}''y(k) + \mathbf{h}''u(k)$$

The variables

$$\boldsymbol{\xi}(k) = \mathbf{Q}^{-1}\boldsymbol{\xi}''(k)$$

observe the $\mathbf{x}$ plant state, and in terms of them, the observer equations are

$$\mathbf{Q}\boldsymbol{\xi}(k+1) = \mathbf{F}''\mathbf{Q}\boldsymbol{\xi}(k) + \mathbf{g}''y(k) + \mathbf{h}''u(k)$$

$$\boldsymbol{\xi}(k+1) = (\mathbf{Q}^{-1}\mathbf{F}''\mathbf{Q})\boldsymbol{\xi}(k) + (\mathbf{Q}^{-1}\mathbf{g}'')y(k) + (\mathbf{Q}^{-1}\mathbf{h}'')u(k)$$

$$= \mathbf{F}\boldsymbol{\xi}(k) + \mathbf{g}y(k) + \mathbf{h}u(k)$$

where

$$\mathbf{F} = \mathbf{Q}^{-1}\mathbf{F}''\mathbf{Q} = \begin{bmatrix} -\frac{31}{8} & -\frac{55}{8} \\ \frac{21}{8} & \frac{37}{8} \end{bmatrix}$$

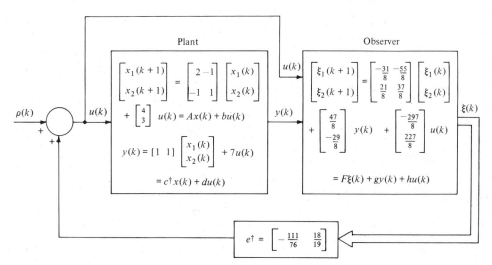

**FIGURE 5-12.   A full order state observer used for feedback.**

$$\mathbf{g} = \mathbf{Q}^{-1}\mathbf{g}'' = \begin{bmatrix} \frac{47}{8} \\ -\frac{29}{8} \end{bmatrix}; \qquad \mathbf{h} = \mathbf{Q}^{-1}\mathbf{h}'' = \begin{bmatrix} -\frac{297}{8} \\ \frac{227}{8} \end{bmatrix}$$

The plant, observer, and feedback relationships are summarized in Figure 5-12, where plant state feedback is replaced by feedback of the observer estimate of the plant state.

### 5.6.3 *Reduced Order Observer Feedback Example*

The separation theorem applies to feedback by any observer, including feedback by reduced order state observers and observers of linear plant state transformations. As another numerical example of observer feedback, consider the plant

$$\begin{bmatrix} x_1(k+1) \\ x_2(k+1) \\ x_3(k+1) \end{bmatrix} = \begin{bmatrix} 0 & 1 & 0 \\ 0 & 0 & 1 \\ 3 & -1 & 2 \end{bmatrix} \begin{bmatrix} x_1(k) \\ x_2(k) \\ x_3(k) \end{bmatrix} + \begin{bmatrix} 0 \\ 0 \\ 1 \end{bmatrix} u(k) = \mathbf{A}\mathbf{x}(k) + \mathbf{b}u(k)$$

$$\begin{bmatrix} y_1(k) \\ y_2(k) \end{bmatrix} = \begin{bmatrix} 2 & -1 & 0 \\ 1 & 0 & 0 \end{bmatrix} \begin{bmatrix} x_1(k) \\ x_2(k) \\ x_3(k) \end{bmatrix} + \begin{bmatrix} -2 \\ 0 \end{bmatrix} u(k) = \mathbf{C}\mathbf{x}(k) + \mathbf{d}u(k)$$

which is conveniently in controllable form. State feedback, of the form

$$u(k) = \mathbf{e}^\dagger \mathbf{x}(k) + \rho(k)$$

gives

$$\begin{bmatrix} x_1(k+1) \\ x_2(k+1) \\ x_3(k+1) \end{bmatrix} = \begin{bmatrix} 0 & 1 & 0 \\ 0 & 0 & 0 \\ (3+e_1) & (-1+e_2) & (2+e_3) \end{bmatrix} \begin{bmatrix} x_1(k) \\ x_2(k) \\ x_3(k) \end{bmatrix} + \begin{bmatrix} 0 \\ 0 \\ 1 \end{bmatrix} u(k)$$

which has the characteristic equation

$$\lambda^3 + (-2 - e_3)\lambda^2 + (1 - e_2)\lambda + (-3 - e_1) = 0$$

If it is desired that all feedback system eigenvalues be at $\lambda = 0$, the desired characteristic equation is

$$\lambda^3 = 0$$

and the state feedback gains needed are

$$\mathbf{e}^\dagger = [-3 \quad 1 \quad -2]$$

A first-order observer with eigenvalue $\lambda = 0$, of the form

$$\xi(k + 1) = 0 \cdot \xi(k) + [g_1 \quad g_2]\begin{bmatrix} y_1(k) \\ y_2(k) \end{bmatrix} + hu(k) = \mathbf{g}^\dagger \mathbf{y}(k) + hu(k)$$

observes the scalar linear state transformation $\mathbf{m}^\dagger \mathbf{x}(k)$, where

$$\mathbf{m}^\dagger = \mathbf{g}^\dagger \mathbf{C}(\mathbf{A} - 0 \cdot \mathbf{I})^{-1} = [g_1 \quad g_2]\begin{bmatrix} 2 & -1 & 0 \\ 1 & 0 & 0 \end{bmatrix}\begin{bmatrix} 0 & 1 & 0 \\ 0 & 0 & 1 \\ 3 & -1 & 2 \end{bmatrix}^{-1}$$

$$= g_1[-\tfrac{1}{3} \quad -\tfrac{4}{3} \quad \tfrac{2}{3}] + g_2[\tfrac{1}{3} \quad -\tfrac{2}{3} \quad \tfrac{1}{3}]$$

For this observer

$$h = \mathbf{m}^\dagger \mathbf{b} - gd = \tfrac{8}{3}g_1 + \tfrac{1}{3}g_2$$

The collection of signals

$$\begin{bmatrix} w_1(k) \\ w_2(k) \\ w_3(k) \end{bmatrix} = \begin{bmatrix} y_1(k) + 2u(k) \\ y_2(k) \\ \xi(k) \end{bmatrix} = \begin{bmatrix} 0 \\ 0 \\ 1 \end{bmatrix}\xi(k) + \begin{bmatrix} 1 & 0 \\ 0 & 1 \\ 0 & 0 \end{bmatrix}\begin{bmatrix} y_1(k) \\ y_2(k) \end{bmatrix} + \begin{bmatrix} 2 \\ 0 \\ 0 \end{bmatrix}u(k)$$

observes

$$\begin{bmatrix} w_1(k) \\ w_2(k) \\ w_3(k) \end{bmatrix} \rightarrow \begin{bmatrix} \mathbf{C} \\ \hline \mathbf{m}^\dagger \end{bmatrix}\mathbf{x}(k)$$

$$= \begin{bmatrix} 2 & -1 & 0 \\ 1 & 0 & 0 \\ (-\tfrac{1}{3}g_1 + \tfrac{1}{3}g_2) & (-\tfrac{4}{3}g_1 - \tfrac{2}{3}g_2) & (\tfrac{2}{3}g_1 + \tfrac{1}{3}g_2) \end{bmatrix}\mathbf{x}(k)$$

$$= \mathbf{M}\mathbf{x}(k)$$

Choosing one set of gains $g_1$ and $g_2$ for which $\mathbf{M}$ is nonsingular

$$g_1 = 1; \quad g_2 = 1$$

gives the observer

$$\xi(k+1) = \begin{bmatrix} 1 & 1 \end{bmatrix}\begin{bmatrix} y_1(k) \\ y_2(k) \end{bmatrix} + 3u(k)$$

$$\begin{bmatrix} w_1(k) \\ w_2(k) \\ w_3(k) \end{bmatrix} = \begin{bmatrix} 0 \\ 0 \\ 1 \end{bmatrix}\xi(k) + \begin{bmatrix} 1 & 0 \\ 0 & 1 \\ 0 & 0 \end{bmatrix}\begin{bmatrix} y_1(k) \\ y_2(k) \end{bmatrix} + \begin{bmatrix} 2 \\ 0 \\ 0 \end{bmatrix}u(k)$$

which observes

$$\mathbf{w}(k) \to \mathbf{M}\mathbf{x}(k) = \begin{bmatrix} 2 & -1 & 0 \\ 1 & 0 & 0 \\ 0 & -2 & 1 \end{bmatrix}\begin{bmatrix} x_1(k) \\ x_2(k) \\ x_3(k) \end{bmatrix}$$

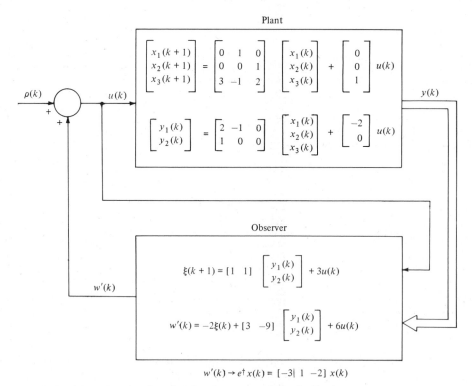

FIGURE 5-13. A reduced-order observer used for feedback.

An observer output

$$w'(k) = \mathbf{e}^{\dagger}\mathbf{M}^{-1}\mathbf{w}(k) = \begin{bmatrix} -3 & 1 & -2 \end{bmatrix} \begin{bmatrix} 0 & 1 & 0 \\ -1 & 2 & 0 \\ -2 & 4 & 1 \end{bmatrix} \mathbf{w}(k)$$

observes

$$w'(k) \rightarrow \mathbf{e}^{\dagger}\mathbf{x}(k)$$

This output is

$$w'(k) = -2\xi(k) + \begin{bmatrix} 3 & -9 \end{bmatrix} \begin{bmatrix} y_1(k) \\ y_2(k) \end{bmatrix} + 6u(k)$$

and the completed observer design is shown in Figure 5-13. The feedback system, which is of fourth-order, has all eigenvalues placed at $\lambda = 0$.

As in the case of eigenvalue placement with state feedback, the feedback system eigenvalues are usually chosen as a compromise between speed of response (that is, rate of decay of the zero-input response component) and susceptibility to errors or "noise."

# 5.7 Summary

Digital tracking system design for linear systems can be divided into two parts:

1. Obtaining acceptable zero-input response of the tracking outputs;
2. Obtaining acceptable zero-state response of the tracking outputs.

The first of these two parts is addressed for step-invariant plants and controllers in this chapter. In the final chapter, the methods are extended to step-varying plants and controllers. When the plant initial conditions are unknown, the best one can do is to shape the zero-input response by selecting the eigenvalues of the combination of the plant and controller. The zero-input response is thereby made to decay to zero in an acceptable manner.

In the previous chapter, it was shown that for a completely controllable plant, state feedback will place the feedback system eigenvalues at any locations desired. When, as is usual, the state is not available for feedback, an observer's estimate of the state can be fed back in place of the state. For a completely observable, completely controllable plant, this feedback system has the observer eigenvalues and the eigenvalues that would have resulted from the corresponding plant feedback, a property known as the separation theorem. Eigenvalue placement with observer feedback can thus be done in two parts:

1. Plant eigenvalue placement with state feedback:
2. Replacement of the state feedback with an observer's estimate of the state feedback.

For an $n$th order plant

$$\mathbf{x}(k + 1) = \mathbf{Ax}(k) + \mathbf{Bu}(k)$$

$$\mathbf{y}(k) = \mathbf{Cx}(k) + \mathbf{Du}(k)$$

a full-order state observer is another $n$th order system, driven by the plant inputs and outputs

$$\xi(k + 1) = \mathbf{F}\xi(k) + \mathbf{Gy}(k) + \mathbf{Hu}(k)$$

for which the error between the observer state and the plant state is autonomous. For arbitrary $\mathbf{G}$ and

$$\mathbf{F} = \mathbf{A} - \mathbf{GC}$$

$$\mathbf{H} = \mathbf{B} - \mathbf{GD}$$

the error is autonomous, being governed by

$$\mathbf{x}(k + 1) - \xi(k + 1) = \mathbf{F}[\mathbf{x}(k) - \xi(k)]$$

The observer consists of a model of the plant, driven by the error between the plant output and the observer estimate of that output

$$\xi(k + 1) = \mathbf{A}\xi(k) + \mathbf{Bu}(k) + \mathbf{G}[\mathbf{y(k)} - \mathbf{w}(k)]$$

where

$$\mathbf{w}(k) = \mathbf{C}\xi(k) + \mathbf{Du}(k)$$

If the plant is completely observable, the observer gain matrix $\mathbf{G}$ can always be chosen to place the observer eigenvalues, the eigenvalues of $\mathbf{F}$, at any locations selected by the designer. When all observer eigenvalues are placed at $\lambda = 0$, the observer is deadbeat

$$\mathbf{F}^n = \mathbf{0}$$

and the observer state equals the plant state after $n$ steps. If desired, a full-order state observer can have an output equation

$$\mathbf{w}(k) = \mathbf{P}\boldsymbol{\xi}(k)$$

and it can be arranged so that its $n$-vector output, rather than its state, converges to the plant state.

When the plant has a single output and its state variable equations are in observable form, it is simple to design a full-order state observer because, in that form, each observer gain vector element determines one coefficient of the observer's characteristic equation. Transformation to and from observable form can be used to design a full-order state observer of any completely observable single-output plant. Either the observer state or a nonsingular transformation of that state, given by an observer output equation, can be made to observe the plant state.

Observers of linear transformations of the plant state

$$\boldsymbol{\xi}(k + 1) = \mathbf{F}\boldsymbol{\xi}(k) + \mathbf{G}\mathbf{y}(k) + \mathbf{H}\mathbf{u}(k)$$

where the observer is not necessarily of the same order as the plant, have

$$\mathbf{FM} = \mathbf{MA} - \mathbf{GC}$$

$$\mathbf{H} = \mathbf{MB} - \mathbf{GD}$$

so that the error between the observer state and the transformation $\mathbf{Mx}(k)$ of the plant state is governed by

$$\mathbf{Mx}(k + 1) - \boldsymbol{\xi}(k + 1) = \mathbf{F}[\mathbf{Mx}(k) - \boldsymbol{\xi}(k)]$$

Observation of a transformation of the plant state is denoted by

$$\boldsymbol{\xi}(k) \rightarrow \mathbf{Mx}(k)$$

A first-order observer with eigenvalue $f$, distinct from the plant eigenvalues,

$$\xi(k + 1) = f\xi(k) + \mathbf{g}^\dagger \mathbf{y}(k) + \mathbf{h}^\dagger \mathbf{u}(k)$$

observes $\mathbf{m}^\dagger \mathbf{x}(k)$, where

$$\mathbf{m}^\dagger = \mathbf{g}^\dagger \mathbf{C}(\mathbf{A} - f\mathbf{I})^{-1}$$

providing that

$$\mathbf{h}^\dagger = \mathbf{m}^\dagger \mathbf{B} - \mathbf{g}^\dagger \mathbf{D}$$

A powerful general method of observer design is to form a collection of first-order observers, each having one desired eigenvalue. For repeated observer eigenvalues, the relations of Table 5-4 are applied. The collection of observer states observes

$$\xi(k) \to \mathbf{M}\mathbf{x}(k)$$

where the rows of $\mathbf{M}$ are the individual first-order observers' observation matrices. With $n$ such first-order observers having eigenvalues different from those of the plant, the gains $\mathbf{g}$ can always be chosen so that $\mathbf{M}$ is nonsingular. Then the observer output

$$\mathbf{w}(k) = \mathbf{M}^{-1}\xi(k) \to \mathbf{x}(k)$$

observes the plant state. If the state transformation associated with the $m$-vector of linearly independent plant outputs

$$\mathbf{y}(k) - \mathbf{D}\mathbf{u}(k) = \mathbf{C}\mathbf{x}(k)$$

is included in $\mathbf{M}$ and is supplied to the observer output, a reduced order state observer, of order $n - m$, can be constructed.

To observe a scalar transformation of the plant state, a sum of first-order observer states is formed and the observer gains are selected to form the desired observed transformation. A linear combination of the scalar plant state transformations derived from the plant outputs can also be included, if desired. When the first-order component observers are included one at a time until the desired observation is achieved, the resulting design is of minimal order.

The chapter concluded with proofs of the separation theorem and two numerical examples of eigenvalue placement with observer feedback.

# REFERENCES

The theory of observers is summarized in

D. G. Luenberger, "Observers for Multivariable Systems," *IEEE Trans. Automatic Control*, Vol. AC-11, April 1966, pp. 190–197;

D. G. Luenberger, "An Introduction to Observers," *IEEE Trans. Automatic Control*, Vol. AC-16, Dec. 1971, pp. 596–602,

and in the text

J. O'Reilly, *Observers for Linear Systems*. New York: Academic Press, 1983.

The application of observers to feedback system eigenvalue placement is discussed in

J. D. Ferguson and Z. V. Rekasius, "Optimal Linear Control Systems with Incomplete State Measurements," *IEEE Trans. Automatic Control*, Vol. AC-14, April 1969, pp. 135–140;

E. J. Davison, "On Pole Assignment in Linear Systems with Incomplete State Feedback," *IEEE Trans. Automatic Control*, Vol. AC-15, June 1970, pp. 348–351;

B. Gopinath, "On the Control of Linear Multiple Input-Output Systems," *Bell System Tech. J.*, Mar. 1971, pp. 1101–1113;

T. E. Fortmann and D. Williamson, "Design of Low-Order Observers for Linear Feedback Control Laws," *IEEE Trans. Automatic Control*, Vol. AC-17, April 1972, pp. 255–256,

and in the text

B. D. O. Anderson and J. B. Moore, *Linear Optimal Control*. Englewood Cliffs, NJ: Prentice-Hall, 1971, pp. 149–169, 190–224,

and in many later texts.
    An early observer design procedure used a special canonical form for multiple-output systems described in

D. G. Luenberger, "Canonical Forms for Linear Multivariable Systems," *IEEE Trans. Automatic Control*, Vol. AC-12, June 1967, pp. 290–293.

The design method used here was first described in

G. H. Hostetter and R. T. Stefani, "Observer and Controller Design Methods and Examples," *ASEE CoEd Trans.*, Vol. 8, no. 5, May 1976, pp. 53–60.

## CHAPTER FIVE PROBLEMS

**5-1.**   Design a full-order state observer of the plant

$$\begin{bmatrix} x_1(k+1) \\ x_2(k+1) \end{bmatrix} = \begin{bmatrix} \frac{1}{2} & 1 \\ -\frac{1}{4} & 0 \end{bmatrix} \begin{bmatrix} x_1(k) \\ x_2(k) \end{bmatrix} + \begin{bmatrix} 2 \\ -2 \end{bmatrix} u(k)$$

$$y(k) = \begin{bmatrix} 1 & 0 \end{bmatrix} \begin{bmatrix} x_1(k) \\ x_2(k) \end{bmatrix} + u(k)$$

Choose the observer eigenvalues to be $\lambda = \frac{1}{2} + j\frac{1}{4}$.

**5-2.**   Design a full-order deadbeat state observer of the plant

$$\begin{bmatrix} x_1(k+1) \\ x_2(k+1) \\ x_3(k+1) \end{bmatrix} = \begin{bmatrix} 3 & 1 & 0 \\ -2 & 0 & 1 \\ 1 & 0 & 0 \end{bmatrix} \begin{bmatrix} x_1(k) \\ x_2(k) \\ x_3(k) \end{bmatrix} + \begin{bmatrix} 1 \\ 2 \\ -2 \end{bmatrix} u(k)$$

$$y(k) = \begin{bmatrix} 1 & 0 & 0 \end{bmatrix} \begin{bmatrix} x_1(k) \\ x_2(k) \\ x_3(k) \end{bmatrix} - 3u(k)$$

**5-3.**   Design a full-order state observer of the plant

$$\begin{bmatrix} x_1(k+1) \\ x_2(k+1) \end{bmatrix} = \begin{bmatrix} -1 & 1 \\ 2 & -1 \end{bmatrix} \begin{bmatrix} x_1(k) \\ x_2(k) \end{bmatrix} + \begin{bmatrix} 0 \\ 4 \end{bmatrix} u(k)$$

$$y(k) = \begin{bmatrix} 2 & 1 \end{bmatrix} \begin{bmatrix} x_1(k) \\ x_2(k) \end{bmatrix} - 3u(k)$$

**5-4.**   Design a full-order state observer of the plant

$$\begin{bmatrix} x_1(k+1) \\ x_2(k+1) \\ x_3(k+1) \end{bmatrix} = \begin{bmatrix} -2 & 1 & 0 \\ -1 & 0 & 1 \\ 1 & 0 & 0 \end{bmatrix} \begin{bmatrix} x_1(k) \\ x_2(k) \\ x_3(k) \end{bmatrix} + \begin{bmatrix} 1 & -2 \\ 1 & 1 \\ 1 & -1 \end{bmatrix} \begin{bmatrix} u_1(k) \\ u_2(k) \end{bmatrix}$$

$$y(k) = \begin{bmatrix} 1 & 0 & 0 \end{bmatrix} \begin{bmatrix} x_1(k) \\ x_2(k) \\ x_3(k) \end{bmatrix} + \begin{bmatrix} 0 & -3 \end{bmatrix} \begin{bmatrix} u_1(k) \\ u_2(k) \end{bmatrix}$$

Choose the observer eigenvalues to all be $\lambda = \frac{1}{2}$.

**5-5.**   For the matrices

$$\mathbf{B} = \begin{bmatrix} 2 & -3 \\ -1 & 2 \end{bmatrix}; \quad \mathbf{c} = \begin{bmatrix} 1 \\ -1 \end{bmatrix}$$

find a vector $\mathbf{d}$ such that the eigenvalues of $\mathbf{A}$ are $-2 \pm j$, where

    **a.** $\mathbf{A} = \mathbf{B} + \mathbf{c}\mathbf{d}^\dagger$
    **b.** $\mathbf{A} = \mathbf{B} + \mathbf{d}\mathbf{c}^\dagger$

**5-6.**   A finite impulse response (FIR) system has the property that a unit pulse at any input produces a response at every output that is nonzero only for a finite number of steps. Show, using $z$-transfer functions, that linear, step-invariant *deadbeat* systems are FIR.

**5-7.**   Design a full-order state observer of the plant

$$\begin{bmatrix} x_1(k+1) \\ x_2(k+1) \\ x_3(k+1) \end{bmatrix} = \begin{bmatrix} 0 & 1 & 3 \\ -2 & 0 & 1 \\ 2 & 0 & 1 \end{bmatrix} \begin{bmatrix} x_1(k) \\ x_2(k) \\ x_3(k) \end{bmatrix} + \begin{bmatrix} 3 \\ 0 \\ 4 \end{bmatrix} u(k)$$

$$\begin{bmatrix} y_1(k) \\ y_2(k) \end{bmatrix} = \begin{bmatrix} 1 & 1 & 0 \\ 0 & -1 & 1 \end{bmatrix} \begin{bmatrix} x_1(k) \\ x_2(k) \\ x_3(k) \end{bmatrix} + \begin{bmatrix} 1 \\ 1 \end{bmatrix} u(k)$$

with all eigenvalues at $\lambda = 0$.

**5-8.**   Find another, *different* solution to Problem 5-7 that uses both outputs to drive the observer with nonzero gains.

**5-9.**   Design a full-order state observer of the plant

$$\begin{bmatrix} x_1(k+1) \\ x_2(k+1) \\ x_3(k+1) \end{bmatrix} = \begin{bmatrix} -1 & 0 & 1 \\ 0 & 0 & -1 \\ 1 & 2 & 0 \end{bmatrix} \begin{bmatrix} x_1(k) \\ x_2(k) \\ x_3(k) \end{bmatrix} + \begin{bmatrix} 3 & -1 \\ 1 & 2 \\ 0 & 0 \end{bmatrix} \begin{bmatrix} u_1(k) \\ u_2(k) \end{bmatrix}$$

$$\begin{bmatrix} y_1(k) \\ y_2(k) \end{bmatrix} = \begin{bmatrix} -1 & 0 & 1 \\ 2 & -1 & 1 \end{bmatrix} \begin{bmatrix} x_1(k) \\ x_2(k) \\ x_3(k) \end{bmatrix} + \begin{bmatrix} 0 & 2 \\ 1 & -1 \end{bmatrix} \begin{bmatrix} u_1(k) \\ u_2(k) \end{bmatrix}$$

with eigenvalues at $\lambda = \frac{1}{2}, \pm j\frac{1}{2}$.

**5-10.**  An observer of the plant

$$\begin{bmatrix} x_1(k+1) \\ x_2(k+1) \\ x_3(k+1) \end{bmatrix} = \begin{bmatrix} 2 & 1 & 3 \\ 0 & -1 & 0 \\ 1 & 0 & -1 \end{bmatrix} \begin{bmatrix} x_1(k) \\ x_2(k) \\ x_3(k) \end{bmatrix} + \begin{bmatrix} 3 \\ -2 \\ 1 \end{bmatrix} u(k)$$

$$y(k) = \begin{bmatrix} 1 & 1 & -2 \end{bmatrix} \begin{bmatrix} x_1(k) \\ x_2(k) \\ x_3(k) \end{bmatrix} - 2u(k)$$

has the form

$$\begin{bmatrix} \xi_1(k+1) \\ \xi_2(k+1) \end{bmatrix} = \begin{bmatrix} \frac{1}{2} & 0 \\ 0 & \frac{1}{4} \end{bmatrix} \begin{bmatrix} \xi_1(k) \\ \xi_2(k) \end{bmatrix} + \mathbf{g}y(k) + \mathbf{h}u(k)$$

Find the observation matrix $\mathbf{M}$ in the linear state transformation

$$\xi(k) \to \mathbf{M}\mathbf{x}(k)$$

for this observer, and find the required input coupling matrix $\mathbf{h}$ in terms of $\mathbf{g}$.

**5-11.** For the plant

$$\begin{bmatrix} x_1(k+1) \\ x_2(k+1) \\ x_3(k+1) \end{bmatrix} = \begin{bmatrix} 2 & 0 & -1 \\ 1 & 2 & 1 \\ 0 & 0 & -1 \end{bmatrix} \begin{bmatrix} x_1(k) \\ x_2(k) \\ x_3(k) \end{bmatrix} + \begin{bmatrix} 1 & 0 \\ -1 & 0 \\ 2 & 1 \end{bmatrix} \begin{bmatrix} u_1(k) \\ u_2(k) \end{bmatrix}$$

$$y(k) = \begin{bmatrix} 1 & -1 & 2 \end{bmatrix} \begin{bmatrix} x_1(k) \\ x_2(k) \\ x_3(k) \end{bmatrix} + \begin{bmatrix} 3 & -2 \end{bmatrix} \begin{bmatrix} u_1(k) \\ u_2(k) \end{bmatrix}$$

find the observation matrix $\mathbf{m}$ in

$$\xi(k) \to \mathbf{m}^\dagger \mathbf{x}(k)$$

where $\xi(k)$ is the state of a first-order observer of the form

$$\xi(k+1) = \tfrac{1}{4}\xi(k) + y(k) + \mathbf{h}^\dagger \mathbf{u}(k)$$

Also find the required observer input coupling, $\mathbf{h}$.

**5-12.** Use a collection of first-order observers to design a full-order state observer of the plant

$$\begin{bmatrix} x_1(k+1) \\ x_2(k+1) \end{bmatrix} = \begin{bmatrix} 1 & 2 \\ -1 & 1 \end{bmatrix} \begin{bmatrix} x_1(k) \\ x_2(k) \end{bmatrix} + \begin{bmatrix} 2 \\ 0 \end{bmatrix} u(k)$$

$$y(k) = \begin{bmatrix} 1 & 3 \end{bmatrix} \begin{bmatrix} x_1(k) \\ x_2(k) \end{bmatrix} + u(k)$$

Choose the observer eigenvalues to be $\lambda = \pm j\frac{1}{2}$.

**5-13.** Use a collection of first-order observers to design a full-order state observer of the plant

$$\begin{bmatrix} x_1(k+1) \\ x_2(k+1) \\ x_3(k+1) \end{bmatrix} = \begin{bmatrix} 1 & 1 & 0 \\ -1 & 0 & 1 \\ 2 & 0 & 0 \end{bmatrix} \begin{bmatrix} x_1(k) \\ x_2(k) \\ x_3(k) \end{bmatrix} + \begin{bmatrix} 0 \\ 3 \\ 0 \end{bmatrix} u(k)$$

$$\begin{bmatrix} y_1(k) \\ y_2(k) \end{bmatrix} = \begin{bmatrix} 2 & -1 & 0 \\ 0 & 0 & 1 \end{bmatrix} \begin{bmatrix} x_1(k) \\ x_2(k) \\ x_3(k) \end{bmatrix} + \begin{bmatrix} 1 \\ -2 \end{bmatrix} u(k)$$

Choose the observer eigenvalues to be $\lambda = 0, \pm \frac{2}{3}$.

**5-14.** Design a full-order deadbeat state observer of the plant

$$\begin{bmatrix} x_1(k+1) \\ x_2(k+1) \end{bmatrix} = \begin{bmatrix} \frac{1}{2} & -1 \\ \frac{1}{2} & 1 \end{bmatrix} \begin{bmatrix} x_1(k) \\ x_2(k) \end{bmatrix} + \begin{bmatrix} 0 & -1 \\ 3 & -1 \end{bmatrix} \begin{bmatrix} u_1(k) \\ u_2(k) \end{bmatrix}$$

$$y(k) = \begin{bmatrix} 1 & 1 \end{bmatrix} \begin{bmatrix} x_1(k) \\ x_2(k) \end{bmatrix} + \begin{bmatrix} 0 & 2 \end{bmatrix} \begin{bmatrix} u_1(k) \\ u_2(k) \end{bmatrix}$$

using the methods of this chapter.

**5-15.** Design a full-order state observer of the plant

$$\begin{bmatrix} x_1(k+1) \\ x_2(k+1) \\ x_3(k+1) \end{bmatrix} = \begin{bmatrix} 0 & 1 & -1 \\ 0 & 0 & 2 \\ 2 & 1 & -1 \end{bmatrix} \begin{bmatrix} x_1(k) \\ x_2(k) \\ x_3(k) \end{bmatrix} + \begin{bmatrix} 2 \\ 1 \\ 0 \end{bmatrix} u(k)$$

$$y(k) = \begin{bmatrix} 1 & 0 & 1 \end{bmatrix} \begin{bmatrix} x_1(k) \\ x_2(k) \\ x_3(k) \end{bmatrix} + u(k)$$

using the methods of this chapter. Choose the observer eigenvalues to be $\lambda = 0, 0, -\frac{1}{2}$.

**5-16.** Design a reduced-order state observer of the plant

$$\begin{bmatrix} x_1(k+1) \\ x_2(k+1) \end{bmatrix} = \begin{bmatrix} 1 & 2 \\ 0 & -1 \end{bmatrix} \begin{bmatrix} x_1(k) \\ x_2(k) \end{bmatrix} + \begin{bmatrix} 4 \\ 4 \end{bmatrix} u(k)$$

$$y(k) = \begin{bmatrix} 2 & 3 \end{bmatrix} \begin{bmatrix} x_1(k) \\ x_2(k) \end{bmatrix}$$

Let the observer have eigenvalue $\lambda = \frac{1}{4}$.

**5-17.** Design a reduced-order state observer of the plant

$$\begin{bmatrix} x_1(k+1) \\ x_2(k+1) \\ x_3(k+1) \end{bmatrix} = \begin{bmatrix} 3 & 0 & 1 \\ 2 & -1 & 0 \\ 0 & 1 & 1 \end{bmatrix} \begin{bmatrix} x_1(k) \\ x_2(k) \\ x_3(k) \end{bmatrix} + \begin{bmatrix} 3 & -1 \\ 0 & 0 \\ 2 & -2 \end{bmatrix} \begin{bmatrix} u_1(k) \\ u_2(k) \end{bmatrix}$$

$$y(k) = \begin{bmatrix} 0 & 1 & 1 \end{bmatrix} \begin{bmatrix} x_1(k) \\ x_2(k) \\ x_3(k) \end{bmatrix} + \begin{bmatrix} 2 & 0 \end{bmatrix} \begin{bmatrix} u_1(k) \\ u_2(k) \end{bmatrix}$$

Let the observer eigenvalues be $\pm j\frac{1}{4}$.

**5-18.** Design a minimal-order state observer of the plant

$$\begin{bmatrix} x_1(k+1) \\ x_2(k+1) \\ x_3(k+1) \end{bmatrix} = \begin{bmatrix} 3 & 0 & 1 \\ 2 & 0 & -1 \\ 0 & -2 & 0 \end{bmatrix} \begin{bmatrix} x_1(k) \\ x_2(k) \\ x_3(k) \end{bmatrix} + \begin{bmatrix} 4 \\ 0 \\ -2 \end{bmatrix} u(k)$$

$$\begin{bmatrix} y_1(k) \\ y_2(k) \end{bmatrix} = \begin{bmatrix} -1 & 1 & -1 \\ 0 & 2 & 1 \end{bmatrix} \begin{bmatrix} x_1(k) \\ x_2(k) \\ x_3(k) \end{bmatrix} + \begin{bmatrix} 2 \\ 3 \end{bmatrix} u(k)$$

Let the observer eigenvalue(s) be from the set $(0, \pm\frac{1}{2}, \pm\frac{1}{4})$.

**5-19.** For the plant of Problem 5-18, and using eigenvalues from those listed for that problem, design a minimal-order observer of the state transformation $e^t x(k)$ where

$$e^t = \begin{bmatrix} -1 & 0 & 2 \end{bmatrix}.$$

**5-20.** For the plant

$$\begin{bmatrix} x_1(k+1) \\ x_2(k+1) \end{bmatrix} = \begin{bmatrix} -1 & 0 \\ 1 & 2 \end{bmatrix} \begin{bmatrix} x_1(k) \\ x_2(k) \end{bmatrix} + \begin{bmatrix} 1 \\ 1 \end{bmatrix} u(k)$$

$$y(k) = \begin{bmatrix} 1 & 1 \end{bmatrix} \begin{bmatrix} x_1(k) \\ x_2(k) \end{bmatrix} + 4u(k)$$

design a full-order state feedback observer arrangement so that the feedback system has the following eigenvalues:

$$\lambda = 0, 0, \tfrac{1}{2}, \tfrac{1}{4}$$

**5-21.** Modify the solution to Problem 5-20 so that the first state variable of the observer, $\xi_1(k)$ is the feedback signal to the plant input:

$$u(k) = \xi_1(k) + \rho(k)$$

**5-22.** Design a reduced-order observer for the plant of Problem 5-20 so that the feedback system has eigenvalues

$$\lambda = 0, 0, \tfrac{1}{2}$$

**5-23.** For the plant

$$\begin{bmatrix} x_1(k+1) \\ x_2(k+1) \\ x_3(k+1) \end{bmatrix} = \begin{bmatrix} 1 & 0 & 2 \\ -1 & 1 & 0 \\ 0 & 0 & 2 \end{bmatrix} \begin{bmatrix} x_1(k) \\ x_2(k) \\ x_3(k) \end{bmatrix} + \begin{bmatrix} 1 \\ 0 \\ 1 \end{bmatrix} u(k)$$

$$y(k) = \begin{bmatrix} 3 & 1 & 1 \end{bmatrix} \begin{bmatrix} x_1(k) \\ x_2(k) \\ x_3(k) \end{bmatrix} + 4u(k)$$

design a full-order state observer feedback arrangement so that the composite system has the following eigenvalues:

$$\lambda = 0, 0, \tfrac{1}{2}, \tfrac{1}{2}, \pm j\tfrac{1}{2}$$

**5-24.** Design a second-order observer for the plant of Problem 5-23 so that the feedback system has eigenvalues

$$\lambda = 0, 0, \tfrac{1}{2}, \pm j\tfrac{1}{2}$$

# Digital Tracking System Design

6

## 6.1 Preview

In what follows, it is assumed that the first concern of tracking system design, satisfactory zero-input response by feedback system eigenvalue placement, has been achieved. The second concern, the zero-state tracking response, is the subject of this chapter. The three basic tracking system design methods are explored in detail:

1. Ideal tracking system design
2. Response model design
3. Reference model design.

The first of these, when a solution exists, achieves exact zero-state tracking of any reference input. It involves constructing an inverse filter for the plant. This may require an unstable or noncausal solution. An ideal tracking solution can also have other undesirable properties such as unreasonably large gains, highly oscillatory plant control inputs, and the necessity of cancelling plant poles and zeros when the plant model is not known accurately.

In response model design, the entire tracking system is made to have the same $z$-transfer functions as an acceptable model system. The added design freedom over ideal tracking system design allows solutions when the ideal system is unstable, noncausal, or otherwise undesirable. Higher-order solutions can achieve improved performance. Given the plant and the model, design feasibility is governed by simultaneous linear algebraic equations. The difficulty with this method is in choosing suitable model systems.

Reference model design concentrates on the class of representative reference input signals that are to be tracked exactly by the plant's zero-state response. A state variable model is made for the class of inputs of interest, then the plant system is, itself, considered to be an observer of the reference input signal model. Thus the powerful methods of observer theory are used twice in the design process. First, observer feedback is used to place the feedback system eigenvalues at locations chosen by the designer. The character of the feedback system's zero-input response is thereby selected. Then that feedback system, with the original plant inputs and additional inputs to each of the observer states, is made an observer of the input signal model by selecting plant and observer input gains. If the order of the reference model is high, the order of the controller is raised until the reference model can be observed as desired. All design options are expressed as solutions of linear algebraic equations.

Plant disturbances are undesired, inaccessible plant input signals that the plant should *not* track. When they are modeled, disturbance effects on the plant state can be observed and reduced. A phase-locked loop system design provides an interesting disturbance model application example.

A great deal of creativity and engineering judgement is involved in modern control system design, perhaps more now than ever. These sections on tracking system design are intended to convey not only the methods, but some of the flavor of the design process.

## 6.2 Ideal Tracking System Design

A tracking system has one or more output signals that are controlled so that they become and remain nearly equal to externally applied *reference* signals $r(k)$. These outputs are said to "track" or "follow" the reference inputs. As a plant signal that is to track an external input is not necessarily one of the accessible plant outputs, we distinguish between the *measurement outputs* $y(k)$ that are available for processing and feedback and the *tracking outputs* $\bar{y}(k)$ that are to do the tracking. It is generally a good idea to measure the tracking outputs and to feed them back, but it is not necessary to do so.

In the feedback design of the previous chapter, it was important to distinguish between the plant inputs $u$ and the feedback system inputs $\rho$. When observer feedback was employed, the plant state vector was $x$ and the observer state was $\xi$. Now, we assume that any feedback has already been designed. The "plant" with state $x$ and input $u$ will now mean the original plant and its feedback, if used.

The response of the tracking outputs of a plant

$$\mathbf{x}(k + 1) = \mathbf{A}\mathbf{x}(k) + \mathbf{B}\mathbf{u}(k)$$

$$\bar{\mathbf{y}}(k) = \bar{\mathbf{C}}\mathbf{x}(k) + \bar{\mathbf{D}}\mathbf{u}(k)$$

is of the form

$$\bar{\mathbf{y}}(k) = \bar{\mathbf{y}}_{\text{zero-input}}(k) + \bar{\mathbf{y}}_{\text{zero-state}}(k)$$

Usually, the plant initial conditions are unknown and there is little one can do about the zero-input response term beyond selecting its modes through placing the feedback system eigenvalues in the regulator portion of the design. *Ideal tracking* is obtained if we can arrange things so that

$$\bar{\mathbf{y}}_{\text{zero-state}}(k) = \mathbf{r}(k)$$

The tracking outputs $\bar{\mathbf{y}}(k)$ will have an initial transient error due to any nonzero plant initial conditions, after which they will be equal to the reference inputs $\mathbf{r}(k)$, no matter what those inputs are.

Suppose that a plant with feedback has $z$-transfer function matrix $\mathbf{T}(z)$ relating the tracking outputs to the plant inputs:

$$\bar{\mathbf{Y}}(z) = \mathbf{T}(z)\mathbf{U}(z)$$

A *reference input filter* as in Figure 6-1 with $z$-transfer function matrix $\mathbf{G}(z)$, for which

$$\mathbf{U}(z) = \mathbf{G}(z)\mathbf{R}(z)$$

gives

$$\bar{\mathbf{Y}}(z) = \mathbf{T}(z)\mathbf{G}(z)\mathbf{R}(z)$$

The reference input filter does not change the plant eigenvalues, which are assumed to have been previously placed with output or observer feedback. Ideal tracking will be achieved if

$$\mathbf{T}(z)\mathbf{G}(z) = \mathbf{I}$$

where $\mathbf{I}$ is the identity matrix of dimension equal to the number of reference inputs and tracking outputs. That is, ideal tracking is obtained if the reference input filter is an *inverse filter* for the plant.

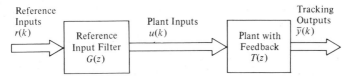

**FIGURE 6-1.** Using a reference input filter for tracking.

In this section, we first consider the case of a single-input plant with a single tracking output. Then, multiple-input plants with a single tracking output are shown to offer additional design freedom. In subsequent sections, it will be shown that observers used for plant feedback provide additional plant inputs and how arrangements other than the reference input filter can be used.

## 6.2.1 Ideal Single-Input, Single-Output Tracking

For a single-input plant with a single tracking output, if the $z$-transfer function that relates the tracking output to the plant input is

$$T(z) = \frac{\bar{Y}(z)}{U(z)}\bigg|_{\substack{\text{zero initial} \\ \text{conditions}}}$$

then

$$\bar{Y}_{\text{zero-state}}(z) = T(z)U(z)$$

For ideal tracking, the inverse filter has $z$-transfer function

$$G(z) = \frac{U(z)}{R(z)}\bigg|_{\substack{\text{zero initial} \\ \text{conditions}}} = \frac{1}{T(z)}$$

so that

$$\bar{Y}_{\text{zero-state}}(z) = T(z)G(z)R(z) = R(z)$$

For example, consider the second-order, single-input plant

$$\begin{bmatrix} x_1(k+1) \\ x_2(k+1) \end{bmatrix} = \begin{bmatrix} 0 & 1 \\ \frac{1}{4} & 0 \end{bmatrix} \begin{bmatrix} x_1(k) \\ x_2(k) \end{bmatrix} + \begin{bmatrix} 0 \\ 1 \end{bmatrix} u(k)$$

$$\bar{y}(k) = \begin{bmatrix} \frac{7}{18} & -\frac{1}{3} \end{bmatrix} \begin{bmatrix} x_1(k) \\ x_2(k) \end{bmatrix} + 2u(k)$$

where it is desired that the single tracking output $\bar{y}(k)$ track a reference input signal $r(k)$. The system description is in controllable form, which is convenient for finding the transfer function, but the use of special forms is not necessary for this design process. The $z$-transfer function of the plant is

$$T(z) = \frac{-\frac{1}{3}z + \frac{7}{18}}{z^2 - \frac{1}{4}} + 2 = \frac{2(z - \frac{1}{3})(z + \frac{1}{6})}{(z + \frac{1}{2})(z - \frac{1}{2})}$$

The inverse filter has $z$-transfer function

$$G(z) = \frac{1}{T(z)} = \frac{\frac{1}{2}(z + \frac{1}{2})(z - \frac{1}{2})}{(z - \frac{1}{3})(z + \frac{1}{6})} = \frac{1}{2} + \frac{\frac{1}{12}z - \frac{7}{12}}{z^2 - \frac{1}{6}z - \frac{1}{18}}$$

It is realized by the filter (also chosen to be in controllable form, for convenience)

$$\begin{bmatrix} \mu_1(k+1) \\ \mu_2(k+1) \end{bmatrix} = \begin{bmatrix} 0 & 1 \\ \frac{1}{18} & \frac{1}{6} \end{bmatrix} \begin{bmatrix} \mu_1(k) \\ \mu_2(k) \end{bmatrix} + \begin{bmatrix} 0 \\ 1 \end{bmatrix} r(k)$$

$$u(k) = \begin{bmatrix} \frac{1}{12} & -\frac{7}{72} \end{bmatrix} \begin{bmatrix} \mu_1(k) \\ \mu_2(k) \end{bmatrix} + \frac{1}{2}r(k)$$

The inverse filter gives ideal tracking

$$\bar{y}_{\text{zero-state}}(k) = r(k)$$

as is demonstrated in the typical response plot of Figure 6-2. For this plot and others later, the inverse filter initial conditions $\mu(0)$ were chosen to be zero, as is easily arranged in practice. The plant initial conditions were chosen arbitrarily and are not zero.

If there are any plant $z$-transfer function zeros outside the unit circle on the complex plane, the inverse reference input filter will be unstable, since the filter has poles where the plant transfer function has zeros. For example, the plant with tracking output

$$\begin{bmatrix} x_1(k+1) \\ x_2(k+1) \end{bmatrix} = \begin{bmatrix} 0 & 1 \\ \frac{1}{4} & 0 \end{bmatrix} \begin{bmatrix} x_1(k) \\ x_2(k) \end{bmatrix} + \begin{bmatrix} 0 \\ 1 \end{bmatrix} u(k)$$

$$\bar{y}(k) = \begin{bmatrix} -\frac{5}{12} & -\frac{5}{3} \end{bmatrix} \begin{bmatrix} x_1(k) \\ x_2(k) \end{bmatrix} + u(k)$$

does not have all of its $z$-transfer function zeros inside the unit circle on the

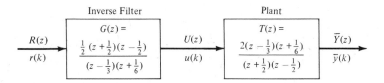

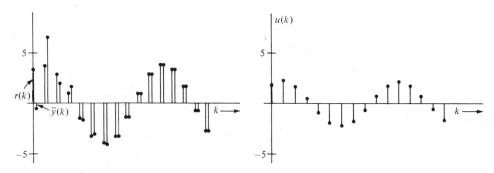

**FIGURE 6-2.**   **Response of a tracking system that uses an inverse filter.**

complex plane:

$$T(z) = 1 + \frac{-\frac{5}{3}z - \frac{5}{12}}{z^2 - \frac{1}{4}} = \frac{(z - 2)(z + \frac{1}{3})}{(z + \frac{1}{2})(z - \frac{1}{2})}$$

In consequence, the inverse filter, which has $z$-transfer function

$$G(z) = \frac{1}{T(z)} = \frac{(z + \frac{1}{2})(z - \frac{1}{2})}{(z - 2)(z + \frac{1}{3})}$$

is unstable. The plant input signal $u(k)$ generated by this filter will grow without bound, as in the typical response shown in Figure 6-3. While the entire system may work for a while, eventually the plant inputs will be too large for the plant to accommodate.

If the plant $z$-transfer function has a lower-order numerator than denominator polynomial, the resulting inverse reference input filter has a lower-order denominator than numerator, making the filter noncausal. The reference input must then be available to the filter one or more steps in advance. In some applications, the necessity of having advance samples of the reference input $r(k)$ available is a disadvantage; in others, it is not.

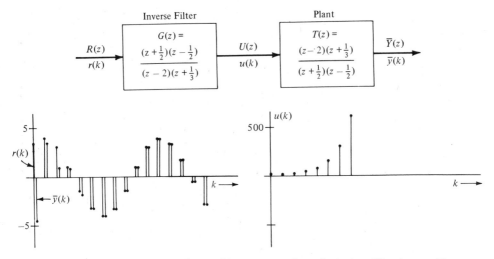

**FIGURE 6-3.** Response of a tracking system where the inverse filter is unstable.

For example, the plant and tracking output

$$\begin{bmatrix} x_1(k+1) \\ x_2(k+1) \end{bmatrix} = \begin{bmatrix} 0 & 1 \\ \frac{1}{4} & 0 \end{bmatrix} \begin{bmatrix} x_1(k) \\ x_2(k) \end{bmatrix} + \begin{bmatrix} 0 \\ 1 \end{bmatrix} u(k)$$

$$\bar{y}(k) = \begin{bmatrix} -\frac{1}{3} & 1 \end{bmatrix} \begin{bmatrix} x_1(k) \\ x_2(k) \end{bmatrix}$$

has $z$-transfer function

$$T(z) = \frac{z - \frac{1}{3}}{z^2 - \frac{1}{4}} = \frac{z - \frac{1}{3}}{(z + \frac{1}{2})(z - \frac{1}{2})}$$

Fortunately, the plant zero is inside the unit circle on the complex plane; but the inverse of $T(z)$ has a numerator polynomial of higher degree than its denominator polynomial:

$$G(z) = \frac{1}{T(z)} = \frac{(z + \frac{1}{2})(z - \frac{1}{2})}{z - \frac{1}{3}}$$

Rather than dealing with a noncausal reference input filter, the causal filter

$$\tilde{G}(z) = \frac{1}{zT(z)} = \frac{(z + \frac{1}{2})(z - \frac{1}{2})}{z(z - \frac{1}{3})}$$

is used, but then $r(k + 1)$ is needed as the filter input. In terms of $z$-transforms:

$$U(z) = zR(z)\tilde{G}(z) = \frac{1}{T(z)}\,R(z)$$

Typical response of this system is shown in Figure 6-4.

Suppose an $n$th order plant is deadbeat (all of its eigenvalues at $\lambda = 0$) and has an inverse reference input filter that is started with zero initial conditions. Then since the filter's zero-state response is zero and the plant's zero-state response dies to zero after $n$ steps, exact tracking is achieved after $n$ steps.

As an example of a tracking system with a deadbeat plant, consider the plant and accessible outputs

$$\begin{bmatrix} x_1(k + 1) \\ x_2(k + 1) \end{bmatrix} = \begin{bmatrix} 0 & 1 \\ \frac{1}{3} & \frac{2}{3} \end{bmatrix} \begin{bmatrix} x_1(k) \\ x_2(k) \end{bmatrix} + \begin{bmatrix} 0 \\ 1 \end{bmatrix} u(k) = \mathbf{A}\mathbf{x}(k) + \mathbf{b}u(k)$$

$$\begin{bmatrix} y_1(k) \\ y_2(k) \end{bmatrix} = \begin{bmatrix} 3 & 5 \\ 1 & 2 \end{bmatrix} \begin{bmatrix} x_1(k) \\ x_2(k) \end{bmatrix} = \mathbf{C}\mathbf{x}(k)$$

which is in controllable form, for convenience. The state feedback

$$u(k) = -\tfrac{1}{3}x_1(k) - \tfrac{2}{3}x_2(k) + \rho(k) = \mathbf{e}^{\dagger}\mathbf{x}(k) + \rho(k)$$

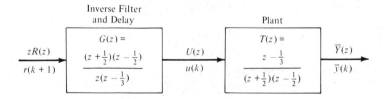

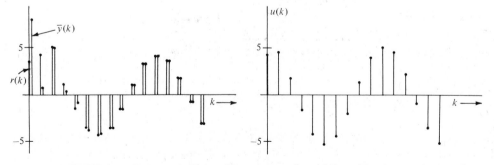

**FIGURE 6-4.** Response of a tracking system where the tracking input $r(k)$ must be supplied one step in advance if the inverse filter is to be causal.

where $\rho(k)$ is an external input, will place both plant eigenvalues at $\lambda = 0$ since, then:

$$\begin{bmatrix} x_1(k+1) \\ x_2(k+1) \end{bmatrix} = \left\{ \begin{bmatrix} 0 & 1 \\ \frac{1}{3} & \frac{2}{3} \end{bmatrix} + \begin{bmatrix} 0 \\ 1 \end{bmatrix} [-\frac{1}{3} \quad -\frac{2}{3}] \right\} \begin{bmatrix} x_1(k) \\ x_2(k) \end{bmatrix} + \begin{bmatrix} 0 \\ 1 \end{bmatrix} \rho(k)$$

The plant state can be obtained from the outputs according to

$$\mathbf{x}(k) = \mathbf{C}^{-1}\mathbf{y}(k) = \begin{bmatrix} 2 & -5 \\ -1 & 3 \end{bmatrix} \mathbf{y}(k)$$

so the output feedback

$$u(k) = \mathbf{e}^\dagger \mathbf{C}^{-1}\mathbf{y}(k) + \rho(k) = [-\frac{1}{3} \quad -\frac{9}{2}]\mathbf{y}(k) + \rho(k)$$

makes the plant deadbeat. With feedback:

$$\begin{bmatrix} x_1(k+1) \\ x_2(k+1) \end{bmatrix} = \begin{bmatrix} 0 & 1 \\ 0 & 0 \end{bmatrix} \begin{bmatrix} x_1(k) \\ x_2(k) \end{bmatrix} + \begin{bmatrix} 0 \\ 1 \end{bmatrix} \rho(k)$$

The output that is to track the input $r(k)$ in a tracking system may or may not be accessible for feedback. For this example, suppose that it is the signal

$$\bar{y}(k) = [\frac{1}{2} \quad \frac{2}{3}] \begin{bmatrix} x_1(k) \\ x_2(k) \end{bmatrix} + u(k) = \bar{\mathbf{c}}^\dagger \mathbf{x}(k) + \mathbf{e}^\dagger \mathbf{x}(k) + \rho(k)$$

$$= [\frac{1}{6} \quad \frac{5}{6}] \begin{bmatrix} x_1(k) \\ x_2(k) \end{bmatrix} + \rho(k)$$

that is to track $r(k)$. The $z$-transfer function relating $\bar{y}(k)$ and $\rho(k)$ is

$$T(z) = \frac{z^2 + \frac{5}{6}z + \frac{1}{6}}{z^2} = \frac{(z + \frac{1}{2})(z + \frac{1}{3})}{z^2}$$

so that the inverse reference input filter has $z$-transfer function

$$G(z) = \frac{1}{T(z)} = \frac{z^2}{(z + \frac{1}{2})(z + \frac{1}{3})}$$

which is both stable and causal. Typical response of this system is shown in Figure 6-5. Since the reference input filter is begun with zero initial conditions and the second-order plant is deadbeat, after two steps the tracking output $\bar{y}(k)$ equals the reference input $r(k)$.

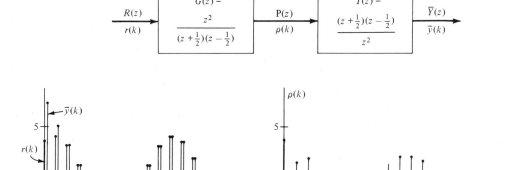

**FIGURE 6-5.** Response of a tracking system consisting of an inverse filter and a deadbeat plant.

## 6.2.2 Ideal Tracking with Multiple Plant Inputs

When more than one plant input can be used to achieve tracking of a single reference input, there is freedom in the choice of an inverse filter and it may be possible to obtain an acceptable design when the use of a single plant input alone would not yield a useable solution. For example, consider the following two-input plant, where it is desired that the tracking output $\bar{y}(k)$ track a reference input $r(k)$:

$$\begin{bmatrix} x_1(k+1) \\ x_2(k+1) \end{bmatrix} = \begin{bmatrix} 0 & 1 \\ \frac{1}{4} & 0 \end{bmatrix} \begin{bmatrix} x_1(k) \\ x_2(k) \end{bmatrix} + \begin{bmatrix} 1 & 2 \\ -1 & 0 \end{bmatrix} \begin{bmatrix} u_1(k) \\ u_2(k) \end{bmatrix} = \mathbf{A}\mathbf{x}(k) + \mathbf{B}\mathbf{u}(k)$$

$$\bar{y}(k) = \begin{bmatrix} 1 & -1 \end{bmatrix} \begin{bmatrix} x_1(k) \\ x_2(k) \end{bmatrix} + \begin{bmatrix} 0 & 1 \end{bmatrix} \begin{bmatrix} u_1(k) \\ u_2(k) \end{bmatrix} = \bar{\mathbf{c}}^\dagger \mathbf{x}(k) + \bar{\mathbf{d}}^\dagger \mathbf{u}(k)$$

The plant $z$-transfer functions are

$$\mathbf{T}(z) = \bar{\mathbf{c}}^\dagger (z\mathbf{I} - \mathbf{A})^{-1}\mathbf{B} + \bar{\mathbf{d}}^\dagger = \begin{bmatrix} \dfrac{2z - \frac{5}{4}}{z^2 - \frac{1}{4}} & \dfrac{z^2 + 2z - \frac{3}{4}}{z^2 - \frac{1}{4}} \end{bmatrix} = \begin{bmatrix} T_1(z) & T_2(z) \end{bmatrix}$$

The first $z$-transfer function, $T_1(z)$, has a numerator polynomial with order one less than the denominator polynomial order. If the plant input $u_1(k)$ alone were used to obtain tracking, the reference input $r(k)$ would have to be provided to the filter one step in advance of the step at which the plant is to track it. The second $z$-transfer function, $T_2(z)$, has a zero outside the unit circle on the complex plane. If the plant input $u_2$ alone was used for tracking, the inverse filter would be unstable.

If both inputs to this plant are used to obtain tracking, the single-input, two-output inverse filter has $z$-transfer functions $G_1(z)$ and $G_2(z)$ as in Figure 6-6 that must satisfy

$$\bar{Y}(z) = [T_1(z)G_1(z) + T_2(z)G_2(z)]R(z) = R(z)$$

or

$$T_1(z)G_1(z) + T_2(z)G_2(z) = 1$$

or

$$G_1(z)\left(\frac{2z - \frac{5}{4}}{z^2 - \frac{1}{4}}\right) + G_2(z)\left(\frac{z^2 + 2z - \frac{3}{4}}{z^2 - \frac{1}{4}}\right) = 1$$

In terms of the numerator and denominator polynomials of the inverse filter $z$-transfer functions

$$G_1(z) = \frac{n_1(z)}{d(z)}; \qquad G_2(z) = \frac{n_2(z)}{d(z)}$$

where each shares the denominator polynomial $d(z)$, ideal tracking requires that

$$n_1(z)(2z - \tfrac{5}{4}) + n_2(z)(z^2 + 2z - \tfrac{3}{4}) = d(z)(z^2 - \tfrac{1}{4}) \tag{6-1}$$

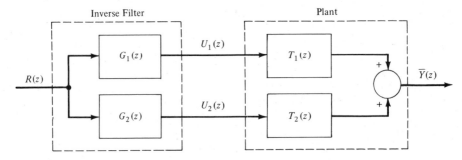

**FIGURE 6-6.** **Inverse filter and plant $z$-transfer functions for a two-input plant with one tracking output.**

To design an inverse filter of the lowest possible order, we begin by attempting to satisfy equation (6-1) with a zeroth-order filter with "polynomials" that are constants:

$$\begin{cases} n_1(z) = \alpha_1 \\ n_2(z) = \alpha_2 \\ d(z) = 1 \end{cases}$$

In terms of these, (6-1) becomes

$$\alpha_1(2z - \tfrac{5}{4}) + \alpha_2(z^2 + 2z - \tfrac{3}{4}) = z^2 - \tfrac{1}{4}$$

Equating coefficients of like powers of $z$, the following simultaneous linear algebraic equations result:

$$\begin{cases} \alpha_2 = 1 \\ 2\alpha_1 + 2\alpha_2 = 0 \\ -\tfrac{5}{4}\alpha_1 - \tfrac{3}{4}\alpha_2 = -\tfrac{1}{4} \end{cases}$$

These equations do not have a solution, so we try a first-order filter, with

$$\begin{cases} n_1(z) = \alpha_1 z + \alpha_2 \\ n_2(z) = \alpha_3 z + \alpha_4 \\ d(z) = z + \alpha_5 \end{cases}$$

instead. The requirement of (6-1) is now

$$(\alpha_1 z + \alpha_2)(2z - \tfrac{5}{4}) + (\alpha_3 z + \alpha_4)(z^2 + 2z - \tfrac{3}{4}) = (z + \alpha_5)(z^2 - \tfrac{1}{4})$$

and equating coefficients

$$\begin{cases} \alpha_3 = 1 \\ 2\alpha_1 + 2\alpha_3 + \alpha_4 = \alpha_5 \\ -\tfrac{5}{4}\alpha_1 + 2\alpha_2 - \tfrac{3}{4}\alpha_3 + 2\alpha_4 = -\tfrac{1}{4} \\ \tfrac{5}{4}\alpha_2 + \tfrac{3}{4}\alpha_4 = \tfrac{1}{4}\alpha_5 \end{cases}$$

These are four simultaneous linear algebraic equations in five unknowns. For the choice $\alpha_5 = 0$ so that

$$d(z) = z$$

the equations have solution

$$\alpha_1 = -\tfrac{14}{19}; \qquad \alpha_2 = \tfrac{6}{19}; \qquad \alpha_3 = 1;$$
$$\alpha_4 = -\tfrac{10}{19}; \qquad \alpha_5 = 0$$

which specify the inverse filter transfer functions

$$G_1(z) = \frac{\alpha_1 z + \alpha_2}{z + \alpha_5} = \frac{-\tfrac{14}{19}z + \tfrac{6}{19}}{z} = -\tfrac{14}{19} + \frac{\tfrac{6}{19}}{z}$$

$$G_2(z) = \frac{\alpha_3 z + \alpha_4}{z + \alpha_5} = \frac{z - \tfrac{10}{19}}{z} = 1 + \frac{-\tfrac{10}{19}}{z}$$

These can be realized by the controllable form state variable equations

$$\mu(k + 1) = r(k)$$

$$\begin{bmatrix} u_1(k) \\ u_2(k) \end{bmatrix} = \begin{bmatrix} \tfrac{6}{19} \\ -\tfrac{10}{19} \end{bmatrix} \mu(k) + \begin{bmatrix} -\tfrac{14}{19} \\ 1 \end{bmatrix} r(k)$$

Typical response of the plant with this inverse reference input filter is shown in Figure 6-7. By making use of the added design freedom of the additional input, it was possible in this case to give tracking with a stable inverse filter that does not require knowing the reference input $r(k)$ in advance.

### 6.2.3 *Ideal Tracking of Multiple Reference Signals*

It is sometimes possible to achieve simultaneous ideal tracking of two or more different reference inputs by an equal number of different plant tracking outputs. Figure 6-8(a) shows the interconnection of a two-input, two-tracking output plant and a two-input, two-output filter. To achieve simultaneous tracking of two reference inputs with this arrangement, the inverse reference input filter $z$-transfer functions $G_{11}, G_{21}, G_{12}$, and $G_{22}$ must be chosen so that

$$\begin{cases} \bar{Y}_1(z) = T_{11}(z)U_1(z) + T_{12}(z)U_2(z) \\ \qquad = T_{11}(G_{11}R_1 + G_{12}R_2) + T_{12}(G_{21}R_1 + G_{22}R_2) \\ \qquad = (T_{11}G_{11} + T_{12}G_{12})R_1 + (T_{11}G_{12} + T_{12}G_{22})R_2 = R_1 \\ \bar{Y}_2(z) = T_{21}(z)U_1(z) + T_{22}(z)U_2(z) \\ \qquad = T_{21}(G_{11}R_1 + G_{12}R_2) + T_{22}(G_{21}R_1 + G_{22}R_2) \\ \qquad = (T_{21}G_{11} + T_{22}G_{21})R_1 + (T_{21}G_{12} + T_{22}G_{22})R_2 = R_2 \end{cases}$$

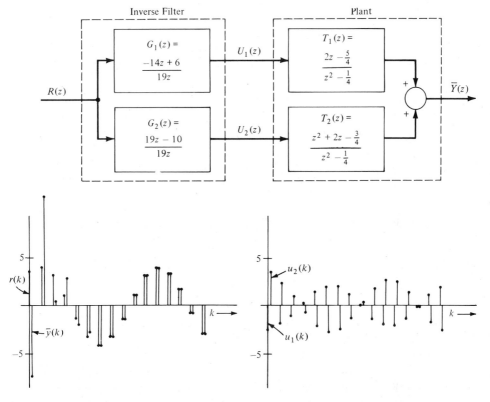

**FIGURE 6-7.** Response of an ideal tracking system for a two-input plant with a single tracking output.

or

$$\begin{cases} T_{11}(z)G_{11}(z) + T_{12}(z)G_{21}(z) = 1 \\ T_{11}(z)G_{12}(z) + T_{12}(z)G_{22}(z) = 0 \\ T_{21}(z)G_{11}(z) + T_{22}(z)G_{21}(z) = 0 \\ T_{21}(z)G_{12}(z) + T_{22}(z)G_{22}(z) = 1 \end{cases} \tag{6-2}$$

Should a noncausal filter result, the actual filter used would incorporate additional $z = 0$ poles as necessary and a corresponding advance of the reference input $r(k)$. Expressing each of these transfer functions as ratios of polynomials

$$T_{11}(z) = \frac{p_{11}(z)}{q(z)}; \quad T_{21}(z) = \frac{p_{21}(z)}{q(z)}; \quad T_{12}(z) = \frac{p_{12}(z)}{q(z)}; \quad T_{22}(z) = \frac{p_{22}(z)}{q(z)}$$

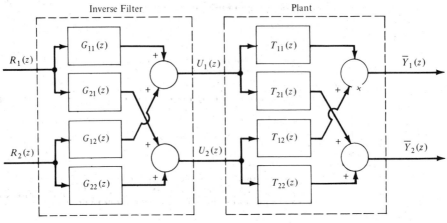

(a)  System with two plant inputs.

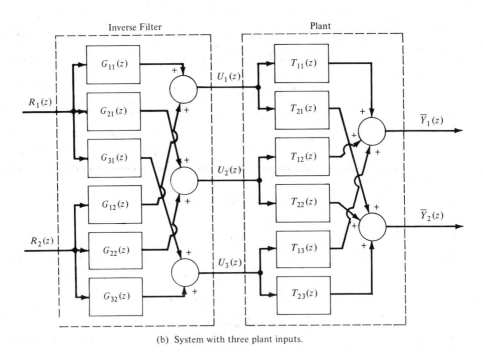

(b)  System with three plant inputs.

**FIGURE 6-8.    Simultaneous tracking of two reference signals.**

$$G_{11}(z) = \frac{g_{11}(z)}{d(z)}; \quad G_{21}(z) = \frac{g_{21}(z)}{d(z)}; \quad G_{12}(z) = \frac{g_{12}(z)}{d(z)}; \quad G_{22}(z) = \frac{g_{22}(z)}{d(z)}$$

the requirements of (6-2) are

$$\begin{cases} g_{11}(z)p_{11}(z) + g_{21}(z)p_{12}(z) = d(z)q(z) \\ g_{12}(z)p_{11}(z) + g_{22}(z)p_{12}(z) = 0 \\ g_{11}(z)p_{21}(z) + g_{21}(z)p_{22}(z) = 0 \\ g_{12}(z)p_{21}(z) + g_{22}(z)p_{22}(z) = d(z)q(z) \end{cases}$$

These requirements often do not have acceptable solutions in practice because of the likelihood that any solution will result in an unstable or noncausal filter.

When two reference signals are to be tracked with a three-input plant as in Figure 6-8(b), the inverse reference input filter requirements are

$$\begin{cases} T_{11}G_{11} + T_{12}G_{21} + T_{13}G_{31} = 1 \\ T_{11}G_{12} + T_{12}G_{22} + T_{13}G_{32} = 0 \\ T_{21}G_{11} + T_{22}G_{21} + T_{23}G_{31} = 0 \\ T_{21}G_{12} + T_{22}G_{22} + T_{23}G_{32} = 1 \end{cases} \tag{6-3}$$

In terms of the numerator and denominator polynomials of each $z$-transfer function

$$T_{ij}(z) = \frac{p_{ij}(z)}{q(z)}; \quad G_{ij}(z) = \frac{g_{ij}(z)}{d(z)}$$

the requirements of (6-3) are

$$\begin{cases} g_{11}p_{11} + g_{21}p_{12} + g_{31}p_{13} = dq \\ g_{12}p_{11} + g_{22}p_{12} + g_{32}p_{13} = 0 \\ g_{11}p_{21} + g_{21}p_{22} + g_{31}p_{23} = 0 \\ g_{12}p_{21} + g_{22}p_{22} + g_{32}p_{23} = dq \end{cases}$$

These are more likely to have an acceptable solution.

One should certainly have digital computer aid for the computations needed for design of all but the most simple tracking systems, especially those that are to track two or more reference signals. Design is straightforward, though, being governed by linear algebraic equations.

# 6.3  Response Model Tracking System Design

Inverse filters are useful in some situations but unfortunately a solution can be unstable and can be noncausal. Even when a stable, causal inverse reference input filter exists, the design might not be satisfactory if the filter is required to have poles within but near the unit circle on the complex plane, resulting in the filter having lightly damped zero-input response. A stable, causal filter design might be unsatisfactory also because a plant $z$-transfer function is not known accurately so that important pole-zero cancellations cannot be assured.

When ideal tracking is not possible or desirable, the designer can elect to design *response model tracking*, for which

$$\bar{\mathbf{Y}}_{\text{zero-state}}(z) = \mathbf{\Omega}(z)\mathbf{R}(z)$$

where the response model $z$-transfer function matrix $\mathbf{\Omega}(z)$ characterizes an acceptable relation between the zero-state components of the plant's tracking outputs and the reference inputs. The combination of a reference input filter and the plant does not have the ideal identity $z$-transfer function matrix that the inverse filter has. Instead, the filter and plant together behave as the response model. The reference input filter is designed so that it is stable and (if needed) causal and so that the response model, of which it is part, has acceptable response to important reference inputs such as powers-of-time. In this respect, response model design is a generalization of the classical design technique of imposing requirements for a controller's steady state response to power-of-time inputs.

In this section, we first design reference input filters for response model tracking system design. We then consider the use of additional control inputs to a feedback observer's states.

## 6.3.1  Reference Input Filters for Model Response

For a single-input plant with a single tracking input, response model tracking system design involves relaxing the reference input filter requirement from that of the inverse filter

$$T(z)G(z) = 1$$

to

$$T(z)G(z) = \Omega(z)$$

where $\Omega(z)$ is an acceptable *response model* $z$-transfer function relating the tracking output to the reference input:

$$\bar{Y}(z) = \Omega(z)R(z)$$

For example, consider again the single-input plant with single tracking output and $z$-transfer function

$$T(z) = \frac{(z - 2)(z + \frac{1}{3})}{(z + \frac{1}{2})(z - \frac{1}{2})}$$

Requiring that a reference input filter $G(z)$ result in an acceptable response model allows the designer to avoid an unstable filter due to the zero of $T(z)$ that is outside the unit circle on the complex plane. Choosing $G(z)$ to have the factors

$$G(z) = \frac{a(z + \frac{1}{2})(z - \frac{1}{2})}{(z - b)(z + \frac{1}{3})}$$

where $a$ and $b$ are constants to be chosen and where the $(z - b)$ factor in the denominator has been added to make $G(z)$ causal, then the response model $z$-transfer function is of the form

$$T(z)G(z) = \Omega(z) = \frac{a(z - 2)}{z - b}$$

This is the $z$-transfer function that will relate the plant tracking output to the reference input.

There are many other possibilities for $G(z)$, including not cancelling one or both of the $T(z)$ poles, not cancelling the $T(z)$ zero at $z = \frac{1}{2}$, and for which $G(z)$ has additional poles and zeros. This choice, however, results in the lowest-order response model for which $G(z)$ can be both stable and causal. The "best" choice of the constants $a$ and $b$ will depend on the design objective for the system. Certainly a choice with

$$|b| < 1$$

will be made so that the reference input filter is stable. Suppose the choice $b = 0$ is made, giving a pole at $z = 0$. Then $G(z)$ is of the form

$$G(z) = \frac{a(z + \frac{1}{2})(z - \frac{1}{2})}{z(z + \frac{1}{3})}$$

and $\Omega(z)$ has the form

$$\Omega(z) = \frac{a(z-2)}{z}$$

If it is desired that any constant input sequence

$$r(k) = \beta u(k); \qquad R(z) = \frac{\beta z}{z-1}$$

where $\beta$ is a constant, produce the same steady state system output, then using

$$\bar{Y}(z) = \Omega(z)R(z) = \left[\frac{a(z-2)}{z}\right]\left(\frac{\beta z}{z-1}\right)$$

$$\lim_{k \to \infty} \bar{y}(k) = \lim_{z \to 1} \left[\left(\frac{z-1}{z}\right)\bar{Y}(z)\right] = -a\beta = \beta$$

it is required that

$$a = -1$$

With these considerations, the response model chosen is

$$\Omega(z) = \frac{-(z-2)}{z}$$

and the corresponding reference input filter has $z$-transfer function

$$G(z) = \frac{-(z+\frac{1}{2})(z-\frac{1}{2})}{z(z+\frac{1}{3})}$$

Figure 6-9(a) shows the step response of this tracking system. In Figure 6-9(b), the response to an arbitrary tracking input is shown. The input used is the same one as was used in the examples in the previous section, including one with this same plant, in Figure 6-3. Tracking of the input is not good because the input varies so rapidly. In Figure 6-9(c) the response of this system to a more slowly varying reference input is shown. Clearly, the price one pays for the added design freedom of a response model can be poorer tracking performance. Performance can be improved, however, by increasing the order of the reference input filter.

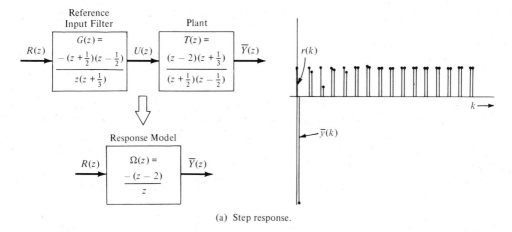

(a) Step response.

(b) Response to an arbitrary tracking input.

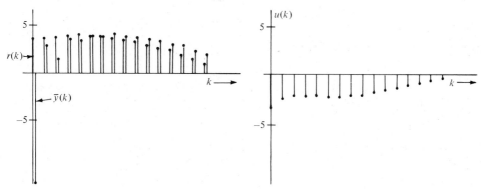

(c) Response to a more slowly varying tracking input.

**FIGURE 6-9.   Response model tracking system where the inverse filter for the plant is unstable.**

For a plant where an inverse filter is noncausal, as it is for the plant with $z$-transfer function

$$T(z) = \frac{z - \frac{1}{3}}{(z + \frac{1}{2})(z - \frac{1}{2})}$$

considered earlier, a response model design

$$T(z)G(z) = \Omega(z)$$

can result in a causal reference input filter. Choosing

$$G(z) = \frac{\frac{3}{2}(z - \frac{1}{2})}{z - \frac{1}{3}}$$

so that

$$T(z)G(z) = \Omega(z) = \frac{\frac{3}{2}}{z + \frac{1}{2}}$$

gives a causal first-order plant input filter and a tracking system with zero steady state error to a constant reference input. For

$$R(z) = \frac{\beta z}{z - 1}$$

$$R(z) - \bar{Y}(z) = [1 - \Omega(z)]R(z) = \left(\frac{z - 1}{z + \frac{1}{2}}\right)\left(\frac{\beta z}{z - 1}\right)$$

$$\lim_{k \to \infty} [r(k) - \bar{y}(k)] = \lim_{z \to 1} \left[\left(\frac{z - 1}{z}\right)\left(\frac{z - 1}{z + \frac{1}{2}}\right)\left(\frac{\beta z}{z - 1}\right)\right] = 0$$

Figure 6-10 shows typical response for this design.

One can add one or more additional pairs of poles and zeros to the response model $\Omega(z)$ to obtain improved performance. For the previous example, choosing instead

$$G(z) = \frac{(\frac{5}{2})(z - \frac{2}{5})(z - \frac{1}{2})}{z(z - \frac{1}{3})}$$

so that

$$T(z)G(z) = \Omega(z) = \frac{\frac{5}{2}(z - \frac{2}{5})}{z(z + \frac{1}{2})}$$

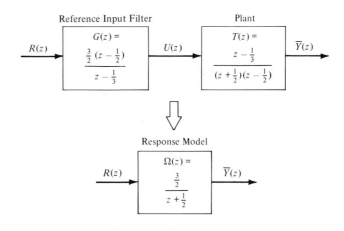

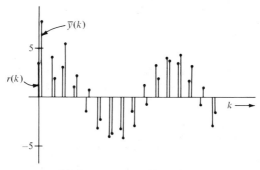

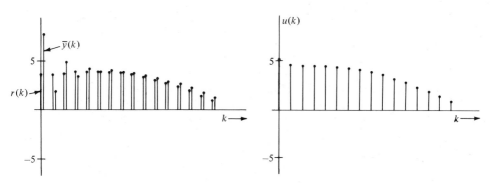

(a) Response to an arbitrary input.

(b) Response to a more slowly varying tracking input.

**FIGURE 6-10.  Another response model tracking system. The inverse filter for the plant is non-causal.**

results in a tracking system with zero steady state error to any constant-plus-ramp reference sequence. For

$$R(z) = \frac{\beta_1 z^2 + \beta_2 z}{(z-1)^2}$$

$$R(z) - \bar{Y}(z) = [1 - \Omega(z)]R(z) = \left[\frac{z^2 - 2z + 1}{z(z + \frac{1}{2})}\right]\left[\frac{\beta_1 z^2 + \beta_2 z}{(z-1)^2}\right]$$

$$\lim_{k \to \infty} [r(k) - \bar{y}(k)] = \lim_{z \to 1} \left\{\left(\frac{z-1}{z}\right)\left[\frac{\beta_1 z^2 + \beta_2 z}{z(z + \frac{1}{2})}\right]\right\} = 0$$

Typical response of this improved tracking system is shown in Figure 6-11.

These methods are easily generalized to systems with more than a single plant input and where simultaneous tracking of two or more reference signals is desired. For the case of a two-input plant that is to track a single reference input as in Figure 6-12(a),

$$T_1(z)G_1(z) + T_2(z)G_2(z) = \Omega(z)$$

where $\Omega(z)$ is the response model. For a two-input, two-output plant as in Figure 6-12(b) the reference input filter $z$-transfer functions satisfy

$$\begin{cases} T_{11}(z)G_{11}(z) + T_{12}(z)G_{21}(z) = \Omega_{11}(z) \\ T_{11}(z)G_{12}(z) + T_{12}(z)G_{22}(z) = \Omega_{12}(z) \\ T_{21}(z)G_{11}(z) + T_{22}(z)G_{21}(z) = \Omega_{21}(z) \\ T_{21}(z)G_{12}(z) + T_{22}(z)G_{22}(z) = \Omega_{22}(z) \end{cases}$$

when using a response model, rather than the inverse filter conditions where $\Omega_{11} = \Omega_{22} = 1$ and $\Omega_{12} = \Omega_{21} = 0$. The response model relates the two reference inputs to the two plant outputs as

$$\bar{Y}_1(z) = \Omega_{11}(z)R_1(z) + \Omega_{12}(z)R_2(z)$$

$$\bar{Y}_2(z) = \Omega_{21}(z)R_1(z) + \Omega_{22}(z)R_2(z)$$

For a three-input, two-output plant, the reference input filter $z$-transfer functions satisfy

$$\begin{cases} T_{11}G_{11} + T_{12}G_{21} + T_{13}G_{31} = \Omega_{11} \\ T_{11}G_{12} + T_{12}G_{22} + T_{13}G_{32} = \Omega_{12} \\ T_{21}G_{11} + T_{22}G_{21} + T_{23}G_{31} = \Omega_{21} \\ T_{21}G_{12} + T_{22}G_{22} + T_{23}G_{32} = \Omega_{22} \end{cases}$$

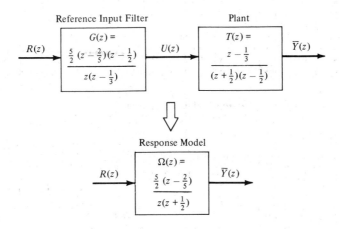

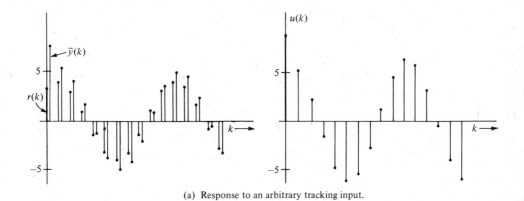

(a) Response to an arbitrary tracking input.

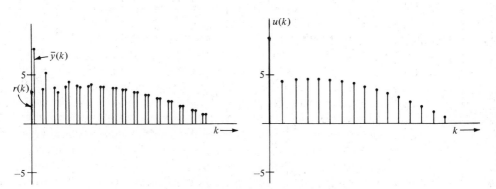

(b) Response to a more slowly varying tracking input.

**FIGURE 6-11.** **Response model tracking system for the previous plant with a higher-order reference input filter.**

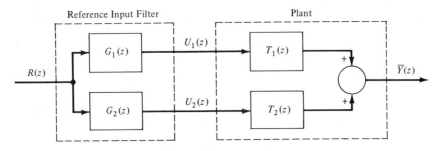

(a)  Two-input, one-output plant.

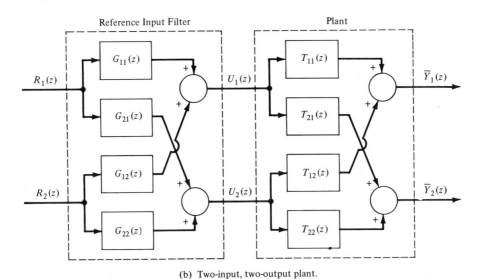

(b)  Two-input, two-output plant.

**FIGURE 6-12.   Use of a response model for more complicated design problems.**

Equating coefficients of like powers of $z$ in the transfer function conditions, the resulting design options are governed by linear algebraic equations. For the more complicated response model designs, however, it may be difficult to select the best solution when the model is incompletely specified.

There is, too, the problem of determining acceptable models. For the case of a single reference input, filter pole location and steady state performance requirements can be imposed, as in the examples here. Or, some other criteria can be used. When more than one reference input signal is to be tracked simultaneously, the response model $z$-transfer functions to be selected include not only those relating plant tracking outputs and the reference inputs they are to track, but also those relating unwanted couplings between each tracking output and the other reference inputs.

## 6.3.2 Using Feedback Observer Inputs

When there are multiple plant inputs available for a response model tracking system design, there is more design freedom for the filter, just as there is in the case of ideal reference input filter design. If an observer is used for feedback for plant eigenvalue placement, an additional independent external input can be added to each individual observer state equation, increasing the number of inputs available to be driven by a reference input filter.

As a simple numerical example of using both plant and feedback observer inputs in reference input filter design, consider the plant with identical measurement and tracking outputs

$$
\begin{bmatrix} x_1(k+1) \\ x_2(k+1) \end{bmatrix} = \begin{bmatrix} 0 & 1 \\ -\frac{1}{4} & -1 \end{bmatrix} \begin{bmatrix} x_1(k) \\ x_2(k) \end{bmatrix} + \begin{bmatrix} 0 \\ 1 \end{bmatrix} u(k) = \mathbf{A}\mathbf{x}(k) + \mathbf{b}u(k)
$$

$$
\bar{y}(k) = y(k) = \begin{bmatrix} 3 & -1 \end{bmatrix} \begin{bmatrix} x_1(k) \\ x_2(k) \end{bmatrix} + u(k) = \mathbf{c}^\dagger \mathbf{x}(k) + du(k) \tag{6-4}
$$

Suppose that it is desired that all system eigenvalues be at $\lambda = \frac{1}{4}$. If the plant state were available for feedback, the state feedback

$$
u(k) = \begin{bmatrix} \frac{3}{16} & \frac{3}{2} \end{bmatrix} \begin{bmatrix} x_1(k) \\ x_2(k) \end{bmatrix}
$$

places both plant eigenvalues at $\lambda = \frac{1}{4}$:

$$
\begin{bmatrix} x_1(k+1) \\ x_2(k+1) \end{bmatrix} = \left\{ \begin{bmatrix} 0 & 1 \\ -\frac{1}{4} & -1 \end{bmatrix} + \begin{bmatrix} 0 \\ 1 \end{bmatrix} \begin{bmatrix} \frac{3}{16} & \frac{3}{2} \end{bmatrix} \right\} \begin{bmatrix} x_1(k) \\ x_2(k) \end{bmatrix}
$$

A first-order observer with eigenvalue $\lambda = \frac{1}{4}$ and unit gain $g = 1$

$$
\xi(k+1) = \tfrac{1}{4}\xi(k) + y(k) + hu(k)
$$

observes the single linear plant state transformation

$$
\xi(k) \to \mathbf{m}^\dagger \mathbf{x}(k)
$$

given by

$$
\mathbf{m}^\dagger = \mathbf{c}^\dagger (\mathbf{A} - \tfrac{1}{4}\mathbf{I})^{-1} = \begin{bmatrix} \frac{-64}{9} & \frac{-44}{9} \end{bmatrix}
$$

where

$$h = \mathbf{m}^{\dagger}\mathbf{b} - gd = \frac{-53}{9}$$

A linear combination of this observer state and the signal $y(k) - u(k)$ observes the desired plant state feedback transformation:

$$-0.215\xi(k) - 0.448[y(k) - u(k)] \rightarrow [\tfrac{3}{16} \quad \tfrac{3}{2}]\mathbf{x}(k)$$

Adding external inputs $\rho_1(k)$ to the plant input and $\rho_2(k)$ to the observer, the plant with observer feedback is described by the plant equations (6-4) and

$$\xi(k + 1) = \tfrac{1}{4}\xi(k) + y(k) - \tfrac{53}{9}u(k) + \rho_2(k)$$

$$u(k) = -0.215\xi(k) - 0.448[y(k) - u(k)] + \rho_1(k) \tag{6-5}$$

as shown in Figure 6-13(a). Eliminating $u(k)$ on the right side of both equations (6-5), this controller is alternatively described by

$$\xi(k + 1) = 2.55\xi(k) + 5.77y(k) - 10.66\rho_1(k) + \rho_2(k)$$

$$u(k) = -0.39\xi(k) - 0.81\,y(k) + 1.81\rho_1(k)$$

as shown in Figure 6-13(b).

The $z$-transfer functions of this system, consisting of the plant with observer feedback, are

$$\begin{cases} T_1(z) = \dfrac{\bar{Y}(z)}{\rho_1(z)}\bigg|_{\substack{\text{zero initial conditions} \\ \text{and } P_2 = 0}} = \dfrac{z^3 - 0.25z^2 + 3.25z - 0.816}{z^3 - 0.75z^2 + 0.188z - 0.0156} \\[4mm] T_2(z) = \dfrac{\bar{Y}(z)}{\rho_2(z)}\bigg|_{\substack{\text{zero initial conditions} \\ \text{and } P_1 = 0}} = \dfrac{-0.215z^2 - 0.700}{z^3 - 0.75z^2 + 0.188z - 0.0156} \end{cases}$$

For a reference input filter with the structure of Figure 6-13(c), ideal tracking requires that

$$T_1(z)G_1(z) + T_2(z)G_2(z) = 1$$

or, in terms of the individual $z$-transfer function numerator and denominator

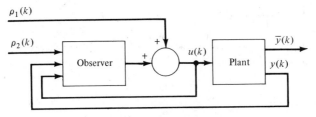

(a) Plant with observer feedback.

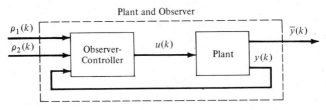

(b) The observer rearranged.

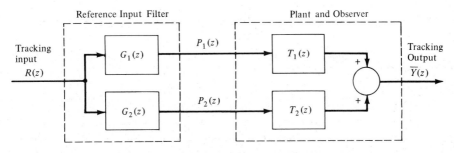

(c) Reference input filter for the plant with observer feedback

**FIGURE 6-13.** **Use of both observer and plant inputs for tracking.**

polynomials

$$T_1(z) = \frac{p_1(z)}{q(z)}; \qquad T_2(z) = \frac{p_2(z)}{q(z)}$$

$$G_1(z) = \frac{g_1(z)}{d(z)}; \qquad G_2(z) = \frac{g_2(z)}{d(z)}$$

then

$$g_1(z)p_1(z) + g_2(z)p_2(z) = d(z)q(z) \qquad (6-6)$$

A zeroth-order reference input filter will not satisfy (6-6). A first-order filter will satisfy (6-6) only if it has a pole at $z = 2.6$, which is unstable.

Choosing a second-order filter with both poles at $z = 0$, of the form

$$G_1(z) = \frac{\alpha_1 z^2 + \alpha_2 z + \alpha_3}{z^2}; \qquad G_2(z) = \frac{\alpha_4 z^2 + \alpha_5 z + \alpha_6}{z^2}$$

the requirement (6-6) for ideal tracking becomes

$$(\alpha_1 z^2 + \alpha_2 z + \alpha_3)(z^3 - 0.25 z^2 + 3.25 z - 0.816)$$
$$+ (\alpha_4 z^2 + \alpha_5 z + \alpha_6)(-0.215 z^2 - 0.7)$$
$$= z^2(z^3 - 0.75 z^2 + 0.188 z - 0.0156)$$

Equating coefficients and solving:

$$\alpha_1 = 1; \qquad \alpha_2 = -581; \qquad \alpha_3 = -1510;$$
$$\alpha_4 = -2700; \qquad \alpha_5 = -6335; \qquad \alpha_6 = 1760$$

the filter $z$-transfer functions are

$$G_1(z) = \frac{z^2 - 581 z - 1510}{z^2}; \qquad G_2(z) = \frac{-2700 z^2 - 6335 z + 1760}{z^2}$$

This solution is probably not acceptable because of the large gain coefficients involved. The unit pulse response of the filter has huge output samples and large changes from sample to sample. Not only might these signals overload the plant inputs for typical reference inputs, but the precision required of the plant model and the filter is likely to be unacceptably high because differences of large numbers must be involved in the plant to produce relatively small outputs from such large inputs.

We now attempt to find a lower-order reference input filter for an acceptable response model design rather than the previous ideal tracking system design. Requiring that

$$T_1(z)G_1(z) + T_2(z)G_2(z) = \Omega(z) = \frac{\gamma(z)}{\delta(z)}$$

gives the polynomial equation

$$[g_1(z)p_1(z) + g_2(z)p_2(z)]\delta(z) = d(z)q(z)\gamma(z)$$

Choosing a zeroth-order filter and

$$\delta(z) = q(z) = (z - \tfrac{1}{4})^3 = z^3 - 0.75z^2 + 0.188z - 0.0156$$

this becomes

$$\alpha_1 p_1(z) + \alpha_2 p_2(z) = \gamma(z) \tag{6-7}$$

where $\gamma(z)$ is the numerator polynomial of the response model $z$-transfer function:

$$\Omega(z) = \frac{\gamma(z)}{(z - \tfrac{1}{4})^3} = \frac{z^3 + \alpha_3 z^2 + \alpha_4 z + \alpha_5}{(z - \tfrac{1}{4})^3}$$

For the response model to have zero steady state error to a constant input,

$$\lim_{z \to 1} \left\{ \left( \frac{z-1}{z} \right) \left( \frac{z}{z-1} \right) [1 - \Omega(z)] \right\} = 0$$

or

$$\alpha_3 + \alpha_4 + \alpha_5 = -0.578 \tag{6-8}$$

In terms of the $\alpha$'s the design equation (6-7) is

$$\alpha_1(z^3 - 0.25z^2 + 3.25z - 0.816) + \alpha_2(-0.215z^2 - 0.700)$$
$$= z^3 + \alpha_3 z^2 + \alpha_4 z + \alpha_5$$

Equating coefficients and appending the steady state error requirement (6-8), these simultaneous linear algebraic equations result:

$$\begin{cases} \alpha_1 & & & & = 1 \\ -0.025\alpha_1 & -0.215\alpha_2 & -\alpha_3 & & = 0 \\ 3.25\,\alpha_1 & & & -\alpha_4 & = 0 \\ -0.816\alpha_1 & -0.700\alpha_2 & & & -\alpha_5 & = 0 \\ & & \alpha_3 & +\alpha_4 & +\alpha_5 & = -0.578 \end{cases}$$

The solution is

$$\alpha_1 = 1; \qquad \alpha_2 = 3.02; \qquad \alpha_3 = -0.899;$$
$$\alpha_4 = 3.25; \qquad \alpha_5 = -2.93$$

corresponding to the reference input filter with

$$G_1(z) = \alpha_1 = 1; \qquad G_2(z) = \alpha_2 = 3.02$$

### 6.3.3  Tracking Error Feedback

If the tracking output of a plant is available for feedback, its steady state error to a constant reference input can be made to be zero, even when the plant parameters are not known accurately. The tracking system of Figure 6-14(a), for example, has overall $z$-transfer function

$$T(z) = \frac{\left(\dfrac{\alpha}{z-1}\right)\left[\dfrac{p(z)}{q(z)}\right]}{1 + \left(\dfrac{\alpha}{z-1}\right)\left[\dfrac{p(z)}{q(z)}\right]} = \frac{\alpha p(z)}{(z-1)q(z) + \alpha p(z)}$$

where the plant $z$-transfer function is the ratio of polynomials

$$G_p(z) = \frac{p(z)}{q(z)}$$

The tracking error of this system is given by

$$E(z) = \bar{Y}(z) - R(z) = [1 - T(z)]R(z) = \frac{(z-1)q(z)}{(z-1)q(z) + \alpha p(z)} R(z)$$

For a constant reference input:

$$R(z) = \frac{z}{z-1}$$

the steady state tracking error is

$$\lim_{k \to \infty} e(k) = \lim_{z \to 1} \left(\frac{z-1}{z}\right) \frac{(z-1)q(z)}{(z-1)q(z) + \alpha p(z)} \left(\frac{z}{z-1}\right) = 0$$

provided that the feedback system is stable. The character of the feedback system's zero-input response is determined by its pole locations (eigenvalues), so the designer is usually interested in achieving more than just stability.

In classical tracking system design, one attempts to adjust the gain $\alpha$ to give acceptable feedback system pole locations. More generally, the orders and parameters of the compensators $G_c(z)$ and $H(z)$ in Figure 6-14(b), where

$$\lim_{z \to 1} H(z) = 1$$

can be chosen to give desirable feedback system poles. If the plant parameters

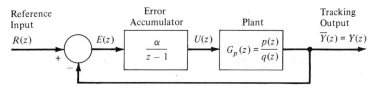

(a) Driving a plant with accumulated tracking error.

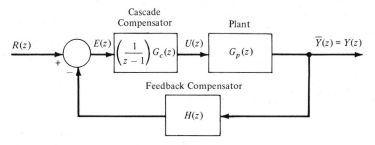

(b) Error accumulation and compensation.

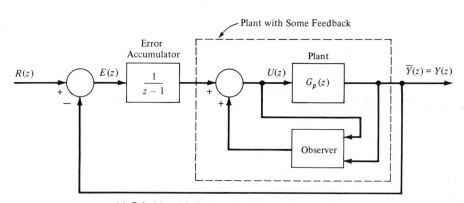

(c) Pole (eigenvalue) placement and error accumulation.

**FIGURE 6-14.    Tracking error feedback.**

differ from those used for design, the overall poles will be different, but there will be a range of plant parameters for which the feedback system has acceptable pole locations. Regardless of the plant parameters, so long as the feedback system is stable, there will be zero steady state error to any constant reference input. Such a design is said to be *robust* with regard to the plant parameters.

An equivalent way of achieving acceptable feedback system pole locations is shown in Figure 6-14(c). Feedback is placed around the original plant in such a way that the additional tracking error feedback results in desired overall pole locations. Again, different plant parameters will result in different overall feedback system poles, but there will be a range of plant parameters for which the feedback system pole locations are acceptable. For any plant parameters for which the feedback system poles are acceptable, there will be zero steady state error to any constant reference input. The tracking output is fed back to the plant both through the observer in the feedback subsystem and in the error signal difference with $r(k)$. The reference input $r(k)$, however, only occurs in the error signal, never alone.

To relate this kind of robustness to the observer feedback and plant input filter design of Figure 6-15(a), let the overall single-input, single-output tracking system have $z$-transfer function $T(z)$ and let the tracking error $z$-transfer function be of the form

$$\frac{R(z) - \bar{Y}(z)}{R(z)}\bigg|_{\substack{\text{zero initial}\\\text{conditions}}} = 1 - T(z) = \frac{(z-1)n(z)}{d(z)}$$

The zero at $z = 1$ gives zero steady state error to any constant reference input, and $n(z)$ and $d(z)$ are polynomials. Then

$$T(z) = \frac{\bar{Y}(z)}{R(z)}\bigg|_{\substack{\text{zero initial}\\\text{conditions}}} = \frac{d(z) - (z-1)n(z)}{d(z)}$$

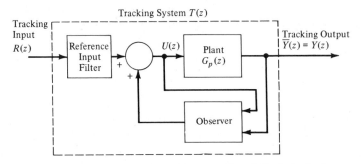

(a) Tracking system where the tracking output is available for feedback.

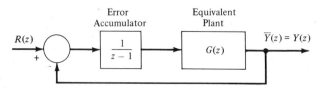

(b) Rearranged system.

**FIGURE 6-15.  Arranging a tracking system to have tracking error feedback and accumulation.**

Expressing $T(z)$ as a unity feedback system with an accumulator in the forward loop as in Figure 6-15(b), then

$$G(z) = \frac{d(z) - (z-1)n(z)}{n(z)}$$

Such a tracking system can thus be rearranged into the error feedback form, if desired.

In view of the inaccuracies and drift common with analog elements, for continuous-time control it can be important to actually form a tracking error signal and process it as a whole, rather than processing the reference input and the tracking output separately. Accuracy and freedom from drift are routinely obtained with digital control, however.

# 6.4 Reference Model Tracking System Design

The awkwardness of practical response model design is because of the difficulty in relating performance criteria to the $z$-transfer functions of response models. An alternate design method models the reference input signals $\mathbf{r}(k)$ instead of the system response. This method allows the designer to specify the class of representative reference inputs that are to be tracked perfectly, rather than having to specify acceptable response models for all possible inputs. Linear algebraic design equations result, so determining the feasibility of design options is straightforward.

## 6.4.1 Reference Signal Models

A scalar reference input signal can be modeled as the response of an autonomous (zero-input) system of the form

$$\boldsymbol{\sigma}(k + 1) = \boldsymbol{\psi}\boldsymbol{\sigma}(k)$$

$$r(k) = \boldsymbol{\theta}^{\dagger}\boldsymbol{\sigma}(k) \tag{6-9}$$

The model response is of the form

$$r(k) = \boldsymbol{\theta}^{\dagger}\boldsymbol{\psi}^{k}\boldsymbol{\sigma}(0)$$

which, for distinct eigenvalues $\lambda_1, \lambda_2, \ldots, \lambda_i$ is of the form

$$r(k) = \beta_1\lambda_1^k + \beta_2\lambda_2^k + \cdots + \beta_i\lambda_i^k$$

where the $\beta$'s are arbitrary constants dependent on the initial conditions $\sigma(0)$. When eigenvalues of the model are complex, a damped sinusoidal form for the corresponding response term is usually preferred. For repeated eigenvalues, response terms are as listed in Table 6-1. For example, a tracking input signal model with response of the form

$$r(k) = \beta_1 + \beta_2 k + \beta_3 (\tfrac{1}{2})^k + \beta_4 k (\tfrac{1}{2})^k$$

where $\beta_1$, $\beta_2$, $\beta_3$, and $\beta_4$ are any constants, is an autonomous system (6-9) with characteristic equation

$$(\lambda - 1)^2 (\lambda - \tfrac{1}{2})^2 = \lambda^4 - 3\lambda^3 + \tfrac{13}{2}\lambda^2 - \tfrac{3}{2}\lambda + \tfrac{1}{4} = 0$$

A convenient state variable model is the observable form:

$$\begin{bmatrix} \sigma_1(k+1) \\ \sigma_2(k+1) \\ \sigma_3(k+1) \\ \sigma_4(k+1) \end{bmatrix} = \begin{bmatrix} 3 & 1 & 0 & 0 \\ -\tfrac{13}{2} & 0 & 1 & 0 \\ \tfrac{3}{2} & 0 & 0 & 1 \\ -\tfrac{1}{4} & 0 & 0 & 0 \end{bmatrix} \begin{bmatrix} \sigma_1(k) \\ \sigma_2(k) \\ \sigma_3(k) \\ \sigma_4(k) \end{bmatrix}$$

$$r(k) = \begin{bmatrix} 1 & 0 & 0 & 0 \end{bmatrix} \begin{bmatrix} \sigma_1(k) \\ \sigma_2(k) \\ \sigma_3(k) \\ \sigma_4(k) \end{bmatrix}$$

## 6.4.2 Reference Input Model-Following

In reference model tracking system design, an autonomous model for the reference input is selected by the designer. If the tracking system is to track constant signals well, a model with response of the form

$$r(k) = \beta$$

is chosen. If the tracking system is to track arbitrary constant and arbitrary ramp signals well, then a model with response of the form

$$r(k) = \beta_1 + \beta_2 k$$

is used, and so on. Once the plant's zero-input response has been improved as necessary by measurement or observer feedback, the feedback system external input gains are selected so that the plant is an observer of the

**TABLE 6-1 Relations Between Eigenvalues and Zero-Input System Response**

| Eigenvalues | Characteristic Equation Factor(s) | Form of the Response |
|---|---|---|
| $1$ | $z - 1$ | $\beta_1$ |
| $1, 1$ | $(z - 1)^2$ | $\beta_1 + \beta_2 k$ |
| $1, 1, 1$ | $(z - 1)^3$ | $\beta_1 + \beta_2 k + \beta_3 k^2$ |
| $c$ | $(z - c)$ | $\beta_1 c^k$ |
| $c, c$ | $(z - c)^2$ | $\beta_1 c^k + \beta_2 k c^k$ |
| $c, c, c$ | $(z - c)^3$ | $\beta_1 c^k + \beta_2 k c^k + \beta_3 k^2 c^k$ |
| $e^{j\omega}, e^{-j\omega}$ | $(z - \cos \omega + j \sin \omega)(z - \cos \omega - j \sin \omega)$ $= (z^2 - 2z \cos \omega + 1)$ | $\beta_1 \cos \omega k + \beta_2 \sin \omega k$ $= \beta_1' \cos(\omega k + \beta_2')$ |
| $ce^{j\omega}, ce^{-j\omega}$ | $[z^2 - (2c \cos \omega)z + c^2]$ | $c^k(\beta_1 \cos \omega k + \beta_2 \sin \omega k)$ |
| $e^{j\omega}, e^{j\omega},$ $e^{-j\omega}, e^{-j\omega}$ | $(z^2 - 2z \cos \omega + 1)^2$ | $\beta_1 \cos \omega k + \beta_2 \sin \omega k$ $+ \beta_3 k \cos \omega k + \beta_4 k \sin \omega k$ |
| $ce^{j\omega}, ce^{j\omega},$ $ce^{-j\omega}, ce^{-j\omega}$ | $[z^2 - (2c \cos \omega)z + c^2]^2$ | $c^k(\beta_1 \cos \omega k + \beta_2 \sin \omega k$ $+ \beta_3 k \cos \omega k + \beta_4 k \sin \omega k)$ |

reference signal model, as indicated in Figure 6-16. After its zero-input response has died out, the plant will then exactly track any signal in the class of modeled signals.

The autonomous reference input model has no physical existence; the actual reference input $r(k)$ will likely deviate somewhat from the predictions of the model. The designer deals with representative reference inputs such as constants and ramps and by designing for exact tracking of these, obtains acceptable tracking performance for other reference inputs.

As an example, consider the plant and tracking output

$$
\begin{bmatrix} x_1(k+1) \\ x_2(k+1) \\ x_3(k+1) \end{bmatrix} = \begin{bmatrix} \frac{5}{6} & 1 & 0 \\ -\frac{1}{6} & 0 & 1 \\ 0 & 0 & 0 \end{bmatrix} \begin{bmatrix} x_1(k) \\ x_2(k) \\ x_3(k) \end{bmatrix} + \begin{bmatrix} 1 & -1 \\ 1 & 0 \\ 0 & 1 \end{bmatrix} \begin{bmatrix} u_1(k) \\ u_2(k) \end{bmatrix}
$$

$$
\bar{y}(k) = \begin{bmatrix} 1 & -2 & 0 \end{bmatrix} \begin{bmatrix} x_1(k) \\ x_2(k) \\ x_3(k) \end{bmatrix} + \begin{bmatrix} 2 & 0 \end{bmatrix} \begin{bmatrix} u_1(k) \\ u_2(k) \end{bmatrix}
$$

where it is assumed that any feedback, with or without an observer, is included in this model. When the reference input $r(k)$ is supplied to the plant

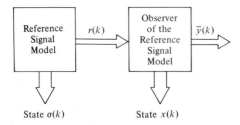

State $\sigma(k)$          State $x(k)$

**FIGURE 6-16.   Observing a reference signal model.**

through gains $\alpha_1$ and $\alpha_2$, to be determined,

$$u_1(k) = \alpha_1 r(k); \qquad u_2(k) = \alpha_2 r(k)$$

the state and tracking output equations are, in terms of $r(k)$:

$$\begin{bmatrix} x_1(k+1) \\ x_2(k+1) \\ x_3(k+1) \end{bmatrix} = \begin{bmatrix} \frac{5}{6} & 1 & 0 \\ -\frac{1}{6} & 0 & 1 \\ 0 & 0 & 0 \end{bmatrix} \begin{bmatrix} x_1(k) \\ x_2(k) \\ x_3(k) \end{bmatrix} + \begin{bmatrix} \alpha_1 - \alpha_2 \\ \alpha_1 \\ \alpha_2 \end{bmatrix} r(k)$$

$$= \mathbf{A}\mathbf{x}(k) + \mathbf{b}r(k)$$

$$\bar{y}(k) = \begin{bmatrix} 1 & -2 & 0 \end{bmatrix} \begin{bmatrix} x_1(k) \\ x_2(k) \\ x_3(k) \end{bmatrix} + 2\alpha_1 r(k) = \bar{\mathbf{c}}^{\mathsf{t}}\mathbf{x}(k) + \bar{d}r(k) \qquad (6\text{-}10)$$

It will now be required that this system be an observer of a suitable reference signal model. The first-order model

$$\sigma(k+1) = \sigma(k) = \psi\sigma(k)$$

$$r(k) = \sigma(k) = \theta\sigma(k)$$

is of an arbitrary constant reference input. When driven by $r(k)$, the plant state observes

$$\mathbf{x}(k) \rightarrow \mathbf{m}\sigma(k) = \mathbf{m}r(k)$$

where

$$\mathbf{m}\psi - \mathbf{A}\mathbf{m} = \mathbf{b}\theta$$

or

$$
\begin{bmatrix} m_1 \\ m_2 \\ m_3 \end{bmatrix} - \begin{bmatrix} \frac{5}{6} & 1 & 0 \\ -\frac{1}{6} & 0 & 1 \\ 0 & 0 & 0 \end{bmatrix} \begin{bmatrix} m_1 \\ m_2 \\ m_3 \end{bmatrix} = \begin{bmatrix} \alpha_1 - \alpha_2 \\ \alpha_1 \\ \alpha_2 \end{bmatrix} \tag{6-11}
$$

The plant tracking output observes

$$\bar{y}(k) = \bar{c}^\dagger x(k) + \bar{d}r(k) \rightarrow (\bar{c}^\dagger m + \bar{d})r(k)$$

so it is necessary that

$$\bar{c}^\dagger m + \bar{d} = 1$$

or

$$
\begin{bmatrix} 1 & -2 & 0 \end{bmatrix} \begin{bmatrix} m_1 \\ m_2 \\ m_3 \end{bmatrix} + 2\alpha_1 = 1 \tag{6-12}
$$

for

$$\bar{y}(k) \rightarrow r(k)$$

Collecting the design equations from (6-11) and (6-12), there results

$$
\begin{cases}
\frac{1}{6}m_1 - m_2 \phantom{+ m_3} - \alpha_1 \phantom{- \alpha_2} = 0 \\
\frac{1}{6}m_1 + m_2 + m_3 - \alpha_1 \phantom{- \alpha_2} = 0 \\
\phantom{\frac{1}{6}m_1 + m_2 +{}} m_3 \phantom{- \alpha_1} - \alpha_2 = 0 \\
m_1 - 2m_2 \phantom{+ m_3} + 2\alpha_1 \phantom{- \alpha_2} = 1
\end{cases} \tag{6-13}
$$

one solution to which is

$$m_1 = \tfrac{3}{4}; \qquad m_2 = 0; \qquad m_3 = 0;$$

$$\alpha_1 = \tfrac{1}{8}; \qquad \alpha_2 = 0$$

Figure 6-17 shows this controller and its typical response. It responds to an arbitrary constant signal as expected. Its response to other reference inputs is poor if the input varies too quickly.

As the design equations (6-13) were underdetermined, we now attempt to improve the design by using a higher-order reference signal model. The

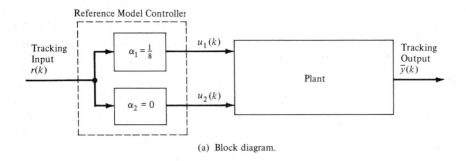

(a)  Block diagram.

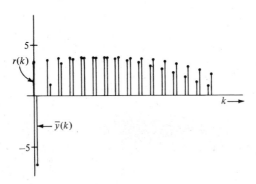

(b)  Step response.                    (c)  Response to an arbitrary reference input.

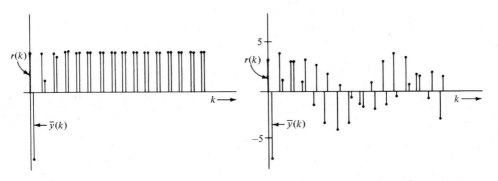

(d)  Response to a more slowly varying reference input.

**FIGURE 6-17.   A reference model tracking system where the reference signal model is of an arbitrary constant.**

second-order model

$$\begin{bmatrix} \sigma_1(k+1) \\ \sigma_2(k+1) \end{bmatrix} = \begin{bmatrix} 2 & 1 \\ -1 & 0 \end{bmatrix} \begin{bmatrix} \sigma_1(k) \\ \sigma_2(k) \end{bmatrix} = \boldsymbol{\psi}\boldsymbol{\sigma}(k)$$

$$r(k) = \begin{bmatrix} 1 & 0 \end{bmatrix} \begin{bmatrix} \sigma_1(k) \\ \sigma_2(k) \end{bmatrix} = \boldsymbol{\theta}^\dagger \boldsymbol{\sigma}(k)$$

is of an arbitrary constant plus an arbitrary ramp tracking input signal. When driven by $r(k)$ the plant state (6-10) observes

$$\mathbf{x}(k) \to \mathbf{M}\boldsymbol{\sigma}(k)$$

where $\mathbf{M}$ is $3 \times 2$ and where

$$\mathbf{M}\boldsymbol{\psi} - \mathbf{A}\mathbf{M} = \mathbf{b}\boldsymbol{\theta}^\dagger$$

or

$$\begin{bmatrix} m_{11} & m_{12} \\ m_{21} & m_{22} \\ m_{31} & m_{32} \end{bmatrix} \begin{bmatrix} 2 & 1 \\ -1 & 0 \end{bmatrix} - \begin{bmatrix} \frac{5}{6} & 1 & 0 \\ -\frac{1}{6} & 0 & 1 \\ 0 & 0 & 0 \end{bmatrix} \begin{bmatrix} m_{11} & m_{12} \\ m_{21} & m_{22} \\ m_{31} & m_{32} \end{bmatrix} = \begin{bmatrix} \alpha_1 - \alpha_2 \\ \alpha_1 \\ \alpha_2 \end{bmatrix} \begin{bmatrix} 1 & 0 \end{bmatrix}$$
(6-14)

The plant tracking output observes

$$\bar{y}(k) = \bar{\mathbf{c}}^\dagger \mathbf{x}(k) + \bar{d}r(k) \to \bar{\mathbf{c}}^\dagger \mathbf{M}\boldsymbol{\sigma}(k) + \bar{d}r(k)$$

and for

$$\bar{y}(k) \to r(k)$$

it is necessary that

$$\bar{\mathbf{c}}^\dagger \mathbf{M}\boldsymbol{\sigma}(k) + \bar{d}r(k) = r(k)$$

Since

$$\sigma_1(k) = r(k)$$

then

$$\begin{bmatrix} 1 & -2 & 0 \end{bmatrix} \begin{bmatrix} m_{11} & m_{12} \\ m_{21} & m_{22} \\ m_{31} & m_{32} \end{bmatrix} \begin{bmatrix} r(k) \\ \sigma_2(k) \end{bmatrix} + 2\alpha_1 r(k) = r(k)$$

or

$$\begin{cases} m_{11} - 2m_{12} + 2\alpha_1 = 1 \\ m_{12} - 2m_{22} \quad\quad = 0 \end{cases}$$

(6-15)

Collecting the design equations (6-14) and (6-15)

$$\begin{cases} \frac{7}{6}m_{11} - m_{12} - m_{21} & - \alpha_1 + \alpha_2 = 0 \\ \frac{1}{6}m_{11} \quad\quad +2m_{21} - m_{22} - m_{31} & - \alpha_1 \quad = 0 \\ \quad\quad 2m_{31} - m_{32} & - \alpha_2 = 0 \\ m_{11} - \frac{5}{6}m_{12} \quad - m_{22} & = 0 \\ \frac{1}{6}m_{12} \quad m_{21} \quad\quad -m_{32} & = 0 \\ \quad\quad m_{31} & = 0 \\ m_{11} \quad\quad - 2m_{21} \quad\quad + 2\alpha_1 & = 1 \\ m_{12} \quad - 2m_{22} & = 0 \end{cases}$$

which has the unique solution

$$m_{11} = 1.20; \quad m_{12} = 0.90; \quad m_{21} = 0.15;$$

$$m_{22} = 0.45; \quad m_{31} = 0; \quad m_{32} = 0.3;$$

$$\alpha_1 = 0.05; \quad \alpha_2 = -0.3$$

Figure 6-18 shows this controller and its typical response, which is clearly improved over that of the previous design. A still higher-order reference signal model cannot be used (without modifying the plant) because it would result in overdetermined design equations.

In reference model tracking system design, the concept of an observer is used in a new way; it is the *plant* or the plant with feedback that is the observer now. If the available plant inputs are sufficient to allow it, the plant becomes an observer of a fictitious reference input model system.

The basic reference model tracking system design process consists of these two steps:

1. Design plant measurement or observer feedback to place the feedback system eigenvalues as desired for the system zero-input response:
2. Choose observer and plant external input gains so that the feedback system observes a suitable reference input signal model. The model represents the class of reference input signals that will be tracked exactly, after the plant's zero-input response dies out.

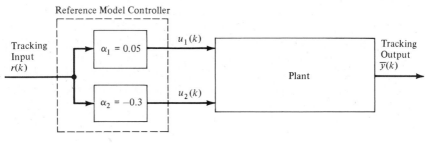

(a) Block diagram.

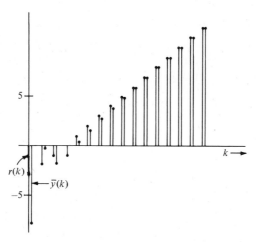

(b) Response to an arbitrary constant plus and arbitrary ramp reference input.

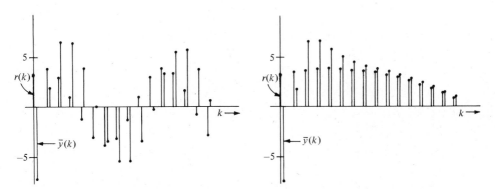

(c) Response to an arbitrary reference input.    (d) Response to a more slowly varying reference input.

**FIGURE 6-18.   A reference model tracking system for the previous plant, where the signal model is of a constant plus a ramp.**

These two steps are a state space multiple-input, multiple-output generalization of the classical approach (usually tractable only for low-order single-input, single-output plants) of seeking a controller that simultaneously meets feedback system eigenvalue (or pole) location and zero-state (or steady state) performance requirements. The design methods here result in simultaneous linear algebraic equations so that it is straightforward to determine design options.

### 6.4.3  Higher-Order Controllers

When, with a given plant and feedback, a reference model of sufficiently high order is not possible, the order of the observer used for feedback can be raised, which generally raises the highest feasible order of the reference signal model. As a simple example, consider the first-order plant

$$x(k + 1) = x(k) + u(k)$$

$$y(k) = x(k)$$

$$\bar{y}(k) = x(k) + 3u(k) \qquad\qquad (6\text{-}16)$$

and feedback of the accessible output according to

$$u(k) = -\tfrac{4}{5}y(k) + \alpha r(k)$$

where the gain $\alpha$ of the external input is to be determined, gives a feedback system described by

$$x(k + 1) = \tfrac{1}{5}x(k) + \alpha r(k) = ax(k) + br(k)$$

$$\bar{y}(k) = -\tfrac{7}{5}x(k) + 3\alpha r(k) = \bar{c}x(k) + \bar{d}r(k)$$

A first-order reference model

$$\sigma(k + 1) = \sigma(k) = \psi\sigma(k)$$

$$r(k) = \sigma(k) = \theta\sigma(k)$$

models an arbitrary constant reference input $r(k)$. The feedback system observes the model state according to

$$x(k) \rightarrow m\sigma(k)$$

where

$$m\psi - am = b\theta$$

or

$$(1 - \tfrac{1}{5})m = \alpha \tag{6-17}$$

The tracking output observes

$$\bar{y}(k) = -\tfrac{7}{5}x(k) + 3\alpha r(k) \rightarrow -\tfrac{7}{5}mr(k) + 3\alpha r(k)$$

and

$$\bar{y}(k) \rightarrow r(k)$$

requires that

$$-\tfrac{7}{5}m + 3\alpha = 1 \tag{6-18}$$

Solving the two simultaneous linear algebraic design equations (6-17) and (6-18) gives the unique solution

$$m = 1; \qquad \alpha = \tfrac{4}{5}$$

Figure 6-19 shows this tracking system and its typical response.

The feedback system cannot observe a reference input model of order greater than one. However, replacing the output feedback by a combination of output and observer feedback will raise the order of the resulting feedback system to two and allow observation of a higher-order model.

A first-order observer of the plant state (6-16) with eigenvalue $\lambda = 0$ is

$$\xi(k + 1) = y(k) + u(k) + \alpha_1 r(k)$$

where $\alpha_1$ is an external input gain to be determined. For this observer,

$$\xi(k) \rightarrow x(k)$$

The plant (6-16) with the observer feedback,

$$u(k) = -\tfrac{4}{5}\xi(k) + \alpha_2 r(k)$$

where $\alpha_2$ is an external input gain, places the eigenvalues of the second-order

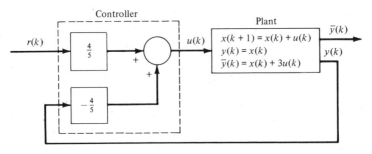

(a) Block diagram.

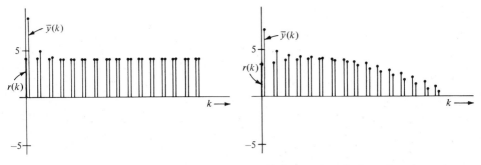

(b) Step response.                    (c) Response to a slowly varying reference input.

**FIGURE 6-19.   A reference model tracking system using a first-order reference input model.**

system consisting of the first-order plant and the first-order observer at $\lambda = \frac{1}{5}$ and $\lambda = 0$. This observer feedback system is described by

$$\begin{bmatrix} x(k+1) \\ \xi(k+1) \end{bmatrix} = \begin{bmatrix} 1 & -\frac{4}{5} \\ 1 & -\frac{4}{5} \end{bmatrix} \begin{bmatrix} x(k) \\ \xi(k) \end{bmatrix} + \begin{bmatrix} \alpha_2 \\ \alpha_1 + \alpha_2 \end{bmatrix} r(k)$$

$$= \mathbf{A}\mathbf{x}(k) + \mathbf{b}r(k)$$

$$\bar{y}(k) = \begin{bmatrix} 1 & -\frac{12}{5} \end{bmatrix} \begin{bmatrix} x(k) \\ \xi(k) \end{bmatrix} + 3\alpha_2 r(k) = \bar{\mathbf{c}}^\dagger \mathbf{x}(k) + \bar{d}r(k) \tag{6-19}$$

The vector state $\mathbf{x}(k)$ now includes the original scalar plant state $x(k)$ as one of its two components.

The second-order reference input model

$$\begin{bmatrix} \sigma_1(k+1) \\ \sigma_2(k+1) \end{bmatrix} = \begin{bmatrix} 2 & 1 \\ -1 & 0 \end{bmatrix} \begin{bmatrix} \sigma_1(k) \\ \sigma_2(k) \end{bmatrix} = \boldsymbol{\psi}\boldsymbol{\sigma}(k)$$

$$r(k) = \begin{bmatrix} 1 & 0 \end{bmatrix} \begin{bmatrix} \sigma_1(k) \\ \sigma_2(k) \end{bmatrix} = \theta^\dagger \sigma(k)$$

is of an arbitrary constant plus an arbitrary ramp input. When driven by $r(k)$, the observer feedback system (6-19) state observes

$$x(k) \rightarrow M\sigma(k)$$

where the $2 \times 2$ matrix $M$ satisfies

$$M\psi - AM = b\theta^\dagger$$

or

$$\begin{bmatrix} m_{11} & m_{12} \\ m_{21} & m_{22} \end{bmatrix} \begin{bmatrix} 2 & 1 \\ -1 & 0 \end{bmatrix} - \begin{bmatrix} 1 & -\frac{4}{5} \\ 1 & -\frac{4}{5} \end{bmatrix} \begin{bmatrix} m_{11} & m_{12} \\ m_{21} & m_{22} \end{bmatrix}$$

$$= \begin{bmatrix} \alpha_2 \\ \alpha_1 + \alpha_2 \end{bmatrix} \begin{bmatrix} 1 & 0 \end{bmatrix} \tag{6-20}$$

The plant tracking output $\bar{y}(k)$ observes

$$\bar{y}(k) = \bar{c}^\dagger x(k) + \bar{d}r(k) \rightarrow \bar{c}^\dagger M\sigma(k) + \bar{d}r(k)$$

and for

$$\bar{y}(k) \rightarrow r(k)$$

it is necessary that

$$\begin{bmatrix} 1 & -\frac{12}{5} \end{bmatrix} \begin{bmatrix} m_{11} & m_{12} \\ m_{21} & m_{22} \end{bmatrix} \begin{bmatrix} r(k) \\ \sigma_2(k) \end{bmatrix} + 3\alpha_2 r(k) = r(k) \tag{6-21}$$

Collecting the design equations (6-20) and (6-21), there results

$$\begin{cases} m_{11} - m_{12} + \frac{4}{5}m_{21} & - \alpha_2 = 0 \\ -m_{11} & + \frac{14}{5}m_{21} - m_{22} - \alpha_1 - \alpha_2 = 0 \\ m_{11} - m_{12} & + \frac{4}{5}m_{22} & = 0 \\ -m_{12} + m_{21} + \frac{4}{5}m_{22} & = 0 \\ m_{11} & - \frac{12}{5}m_{21} & + 3\alpha_2 = 1 \\ m_{12} & - \frac{12}{5}m_{22} & = 0 \end{cases}$$

which has the unique solution

$$m_{11} = -2; \qquad m_{12} = -3; \qquad m_{21} = -2;$$

$$m_{22} = -1.25; \qquad \alpha_1 = -1.75; \qquad \alpha_2 = -0.6$$

Figure 6-20 shows typical response of this higher-order observer-controller, which is improved over that of the previous lower-order design.

### 6.4.4 Tracking Multiple Inputs

The simultaneous tracking of multiple reference input signals can also be accommodated with the framework of reference model tracking system design. There occur situations in practice where two or more reference signals are related to one another, for example, when they are position and velocity of a single mass. Then, one simply models both the reference inputs and their relation to one another with state equations of the form

$$\sigma(k + 1) = \psi\sigma(k)$$

$$r(k) = \Theta\sigma(k) \tag{6-22}$$

where $r(k)$ is now a vector. When two reference inputs are not related to one another, they can be modeled separately as

$$\sigma^1(k + 1) = \psi_1\sigma^1(k)$$

$$r_1(k) = \Theta_1^\dagger\sigma^1(k)$$

and

$$\sigma^2(k + 1) = \psi_2\sigma^2(k)$$

$$r_2(k) = \Theta_2^\dagger\sigma^2(k)$$

then the uncoupled models combined in the form (6-22).

For example, consider two-input, third-order plant with two tracking outputs:

$$\begin{bmatrix} x_1(k + 1) \\ x_2(k + 1) \\ x_3(k + 1) \end{bmatrix} = \begin{bmatrix} \frac{1}{4} & 1 & 0 \\ 0 & 0 & 1 \\ 0 & 0 & 0 \end{bmatrix} \begin{bmatrix} x_1(k) \\ x_2(k) \\ x_3(k) \end{bmatrix} + \begin{bmatrix} 1 & -1 \\ 0 & 1 \\ 2 & 0 \end{bmatrix} \begin{bmatrix} u_1(k) \\ u_2(k) \end{bmatrix}$$

$$\begin{bmatrix} \bar{y}_1(k) \\ \bar{y}_2(k) \end{bmatrix} = \begin{bmatrix} 1 & 0 & 0 \\ -2 & -1 & 1 \end{bmatrix} \begin{bmatrix} x_1(k) \\ x_2(k) \\ x_3(k) \end{bmatrix}$$

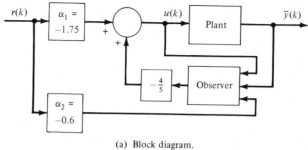

(a) Block diagram.

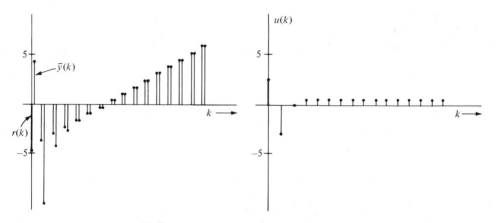

(b) Response to a constant plus ramp reference input.

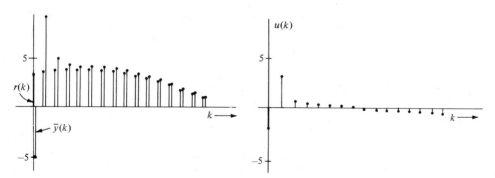

(c) Response to a slowly varying reference input.

**FIGURE 6-20.   A reference model tracking system using a second-order signal model. The plant is the same as for the previous system.**

If two reference inputs, $r_1(k)$ and $r_2(k)$, are coupled to this plant according to

$$u_1(k) = \alpha_1 r_1(k) + \alpha_2 r_2(k)$$
$$u_2(k) = \alpha_3 r_1(k) + \alpha_4 r_2(k) \tag{6-23}$$

the plant and the controller (6-23) are described by

$$\begin{bmatrix} x_1(k+1) \\ x_2(k+1) \\ x_3(k+1) \end{bmatrix} = \begin{bmatrix} \frac{1}{4} & 1 & 0 \\ 0 & 0 & 1 \\ 0 & 0 & 0 \end{bmatrix} \begin{bmatrix} x_1(k) \\ x_2(k) \\ x_3(k) \end{bmatrix} + \begin{bmatrix} (\alpha_1 - \alpha_3) & (\alpha_2 - \alpha_4) \\ \alpha_3 & \alpha_4 \\ 2\alpha_1 & 2\alpha_2 \end{bmatrix} \begin{bmatrix} r_1(k) \\ r_2(k) \end{bmatrix}$$
$$= \mathbf{A}\mathbf{x}(k) + \mathbf{B}\mathbf{r}(k)$$

$$\begin{bmatrix} \bar{y}_1(k) \\ \bar{y}_2(k) \end{bmatrix} = \begin{bmatrix} 1 & 0 & 0 \\ -2 & -1 & 1 \end{bmatrix} \begin{bmatrix} x_1(k) \\ x_2(k) \\ x_3(k) \end{bmatrix} = \bar{\mathbf{C}}\mathbf{x}(k)$$

Let the reference model be

$$\begin{bmatrix} \sigma_1(k+1) \\ \sigma_2(k+1) \end{bmatrix} = \begin{bmatrix} 1 & 0 \\ 0 & 1 \end{bmatrix} \begin{bmatrix} \sigma_1(k) \\ \sigma_2(k) \end{bmatrix} = \boldsymbol{\psi}\boldsymbol{\sigma}(k)$$

$$\begin{bmatrix} r_1(k) \\ r_2(k) \end{bmatrix} = \begin{bmatrix} 1 & 0 \\ 0 & 1 \end{bmatrix} \begin{bmatrix} \sigma_1(k) \\ \sigma_2(k) \end{bmatrix} = \boldsymbol{\Theta}\boldsymbol{\sigma}(k)$$

which models each of the two reference inputs as an independent arbitrary constant.

The plant with controller observes

$$\mathbf{x}(k) \rightarrow \mathbf{M}\mathbf{r}(k)$$

where the $3 \times 2$ matrix $\mathbf{M}$ satisfies

$$\mathbf{M}\boldsymbol{\psi} - \mathbf{A}\mathbf{M} = \mathbf{B}\boldsymbol{\Theta}$$

or

$$\begin{bmatrix} m_{11} & m_{12} \\ m_{21} & m_{22} \\ m_{31} & m_{32} \end{bmatrix} \begin{bmatrix} 1 & 0 \\ 0 & 1 \end{bmatrix} - \begin{bmatrix} \frac{1}{4} & 1 & 0 \\ 0 & 0 & 0 \\ 0 & 0 & 0 \end{bmatrix} \begin{bmatrix} m_{11} & m_{12} \\ m_{21} & m_{22} \\ m_{31} & m_{32} \end{bmatrix}$$
$$= \begin{bmatrix} (\alpha_1 - \alpha_3) & (\alpha_2 - \alpha_4) \\ \alpha_3 & \alpha_4 \\ 2\alpha_1 & 2\alpha_2 \end{bmatrix} \begin{bmatrix} 1 & 0 \\ 0 & 1 \end{bmatrix} \tag{6-24}$$

The plant tracking outputs observe

$$\bar{\mathbf{C}}\mathbf{x}(k) \rightarrow \bar{\mathbf{C}}\mathbf{M}\boldsymbol{\sigma}(k) = \bar{\mathbf{C}}\mathbf{M}\mathbf{r}(k)$$

so

$$\bar{\mathbf{y}}(k) \rightarrow \mathbf{r}(k)$$

requires that

$$\bar{\mathbf{C}}\mathbf{M} = \mathbf{I}$$

or

$$\begin{bmatrix} 1 & 0 & 0 \\ -2 & -1 & 1 \end{bmatrix} \begin{bmatrix} m_{11} & m_{12} \\ m_{21} & m_{22} \\ m_{31} & m_{32} \end{bmatrix} = \begin{bmatrix} 1 & 0 \\ 0 & 1 \end{bmatrix} \tag{6-25}$$

Collecting the design equations (6-24) and (6-25), there results the following 10 linear algebraic equations in 10 unknowns:

$$
\begin{cases}
\tfrac{3}{4}m_{11} & -m_{21} & & & -\alpha_1 & +\alpha_3 & = 0 \\
& m_{21} & -m_{31} & & & -\alpha_3 & = 0 \\
& & m_{31} & -2\alpha_1 & & & = 0 \\
\tfrac{3}{4}m_{12} & -m_{22} & & & -\alpha_2 & +\alpha_4 & = 0 \\
& m_{22} & m_{32} & & & -\alpha_4 & = 0 \\
& & m_{32} & -2\alpha_2 & & & = 0 \\
m_{11} & & & & & & = 1 \\
-2m_{11} & -m_{21} & +m_{31} & & & & = 0 \\
m_{12} & & & & & & = 0 \\
-2m_{12} & -m_{22} & +m_{32} & & & & = 1
\end{cases}
$$

The unique solution to these equations is

$$m_{11} = 1; \quad m_{12} = 0; \quad m_{21} = -\tfrac{3}{2};$$

$$m_{22} = -1; \quad m_{31} = \tfrac{1}{2}; \quad m_{32} = 0;$$

$$\alpha_1 = 0.25; \quad \alpha_2 = 0;$$

$$\alpha_3 = -2; \quad \alpha_4 = -1$$

and specifies the reference model controller of Figure 6-21.

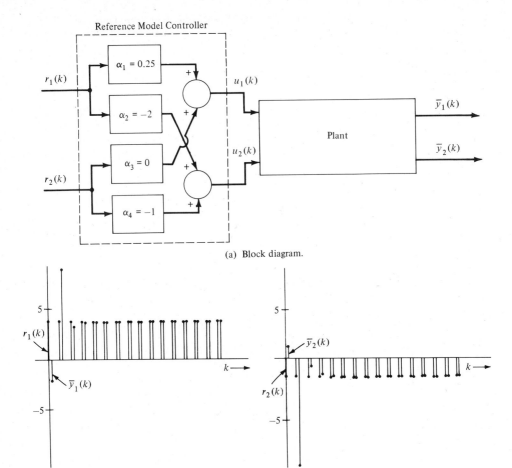

(a) Block diagram.

(b) Response to two constant reference inputs.

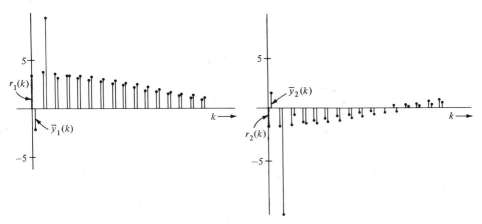

(c) Response to two slowly varying reference inputs.

**FIGURE 6-21.** **A reference model controller for the simultaneous tracking of two reference inputs.**

# 6.5 Disturbance Rejection

*Disturbances* are inputs to the plant that are not accessible for control. Examples of disturbances are wind gusts buffeting a microwave antenna positioning system, "noise" in electronic amplifiers, unknown offset calibration errors in sensors, and digital computation inaccuracies such as numerical roundoff and truncation. Disturbances are inputs that we *do not* want the plant to track. Like initial conditions, the specific disturbance signals are normally unknown, although something is probably known about their character and/or their statistics.

There are four basic ways to deal with plant disturbances:

1. *Ignore them* in the hope that their effects on system performance will be slight. Simulation studies can be used to evaluate the wisdom of this choice.
2. *Structure the control system* so that the effects of disturbances on those plant signals of concern are smaller. For example, negative feedback around a disturbance will often reduce its effects. Unfortunately, little can be said in general about selecting control structures because practical design problems typically have many specific structural constraints. One usually must rely on common sense and experience for the exploitation of those circumstances where it is possible and useful to vary the control structure. This is most often done with simple subsystems, before overall plant control design is begun.
3. *Model the disturbances as stochastic processes* and choose controller parameters (including the feedback system eigenvalues) to minimize disturbance effects in a statistical sense. This is very effective for disturbances like amplifier noise that are adequately described by known short-term means and variances. It is not very effective for disturbances like wind gusts and crosstalk that have unknown and widely-varying short-term statistics.
4. *Model the disturbances as plant modes with unknown amplitudes.* The possibilities include constant, ramp, exponential, and sinusoidal sequences and sums of these. The disturbance model then becomes part of the plant model. This is effective for disturbances that are highly correlated from step to step, and not so effective otherwise.

A combination of these approaches may be needed. Some disturbance sources are neglected, some are reduced by local feedback, some are smoothed by the choice of controller parameters, and some are partially or completely cancelled through modeling them as additional plant modes.

The theory and applications associated with (3), stochastic disturbance modeling, is the subject of another course of study, one typically called

"Kalman filtering" or "Stochastic estimation." One of the results is of interest in our present study. For zero-mean white noise sequence disturbances ("white" means that the signal has no sample-to-sample correlation) with constant variances, the linear step-invariant estimator that gives minimum state estimate error variance is a full-order state observer with eigenvalue locations that depend on the disturbance variances. That is, for disturbances of this type, the "best" observer to use (best in the sense of minimum state estimate variance) is a full-order one with certain specific eigenvalues. If the state estimator is allowed to be step-varying, the estimates can be further improved. Step-varying plants and disturbance variances that change with step can then be accommodated, too, More about this topic will appear in Chapter 8, in connection with recursive least squares estimation.

The remainder of this section concerns (4), deterministic disturbance modeling.

## 6.5.1 State Disturbance Models

Disturbances $v(k)$ can be modeled as the response of a $j$th order autonomous system of the form

$$\varepsilon(k + 1) = \mathbf{T}\varepsilon(k)$$
$$\mathbf{v}(k) = \mathbf{\Pi}\varepsilon(k) \tag{6-26}$$

The response of this model is, for distinct eigenvalues $\lambda_1, \lambda_2, \ldots, \lambda_j$,

$$\mathbf{v}(k) = \boldsymbol{\beta}_1 \lambda_1^k + \boldsymbol{\beta}_1 \lambda_2^k + \cdots + \boldsymbol{\beta}_j \lambda_j^k$$

where the $\boldsymbol{\beta}$'s are arbitrary vector constants dependent on the model initial conditions $\varepsilon(0)$. For repeated eigenvalues, the corresponding response terms are as listed in Table 6-1. This model, shown in Figure 6-22, is similar to that used for reference model tracking system design in Section 6.4, but its purpose is somewhat different; we model disturbances to account for their effects on the state of a plant and so that their effects on plant tracking outputs can be wholly or partially cancelled.

For a plant

$$\mathbf{x}(k + 1) = \mathbf{A}\mathbf{x}(k) + \mathbf{B}\mathbf{u}(k) + \mathbf{B}^v\mathbf{v}(k)$$
$$\mathbf{y}(k) = \mathbf{C}\mathbf{x}(k) + \mathbf{D}\mathbf{u}(k) + \mathbf{D}^v\mathbf{v}(k) \tag{6-27}$$

with disturbance inputs $\mathbf{v}(k)$ modeled in this way, one can combine (6-26) and

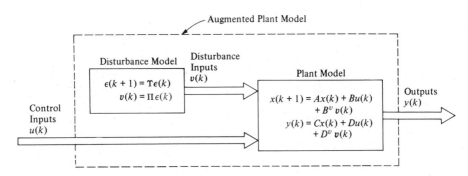

**FIGURE 6-22.** Modeling disturbances as the response of an autonomous disturbance model.

(6-27) into an *augmented* plant model

$$\begin{bmatrix} \mathbf{x}(k+1) \\ \hline \varepsilon(k+1) \end{bmatrix} = \begin{bmatrix} \mathbf{A} & \mathbf{B}^v \mathbf{\Pi} \\ \hline \mathbf{0} & \mathbf{T} \end{bmatrix} \begin{bmatrix} \mathbf{x}(k) \\ \hline \varepsilon(k) \end{bmatrix} + \begin{bmatrix} \mathbf{B} \\ \hline \mathbf{0} \end{bmatrix} \mathbf{u}(k)$$

$$\mathbf{y}(k) = [\mathbf{C} \mid \mathbf{D}^v \mathbf{\Pi}] \begin{bmatrix} \mathbf{x}(k) \\ \hline \varepsilon(k) \end{bmatrix} + \mathbf{D}\mathbf{u}(k) \qquad (6\text{-}28)$$

that can be handled in much the same way as the original plant model. If the disturbances are modeled accurately by (6-26), then they are fully accounted for in the augmented plant model. The disturbance modes are not controllable, however. If the disturbances are given only approximately by their model, then using the augmented plant model will only partially account for them. Better approximations will give better results.

## 6.5.2 Disturbance Rejection with Observer Feedback

Improved state estimates are obtained by modeling disturbances according to (6-26) and observing the augmented plant model consisting of the combination of the original plant model and the disturbance model. More accurate state estimates generally result in feedback systems that are less susceptible to the modeled disturbances.

Consider the plant

$$\begin{bmatrix} x_1(k+1) \\ x_2(k+1) \end{bmatrix} = \begin{bmatrix} 1 & 1 \\ -\frac{1}{4} & 0 \end{bmatrix} \begin{bmatrix} x_1(k) \\ x_2(k) \end{bmatrix} + \begin{bmatrix} 1 \\ 0 \end{bmatrix} u(k) + \begin{bmatrix} 2 \\ -1 \end{bmatrix} v(k)$$

$$y(k) = [1 \quad 0] \begin{bmatrix} x_1(k) \\ x_2(k) \end{bmatrix} + v(k) \qquad (6\text{-}29)$$

where $v(k)$ is a disturbance input. A full-order state observer of (6-29), with both eigenvalues $1/4$, that ignores the inaccessible disturbance input $v(k)$ is

$$\begin{bmatrix} \xi_1(k+1) \\ \xi_2(k+1) \end{bmatrix} = \begin{bmatrix} \frac{1}{2} & 1 \\ -\frac{1}{16} & 0 \end{bmatrix} \begin{bmatrix} \xi_1(k) \\ \xi_2(k) \end{bmatrix} + \begin{bmatrix} \frac{1}{2} \\ -\frac{3}{16} \end{bmatrix} y(k) + \begin{bmatrix} 1 \\ 0 \end{bmatrix} u(k)$$

Response of this observer for squarewave and triangular wave disturbances is shown in Figure 6-23. The plant control input $u(k)$ is temporarily set to zero so that the disturbance effects can be seen clearly. Hopefully, the amplitude of

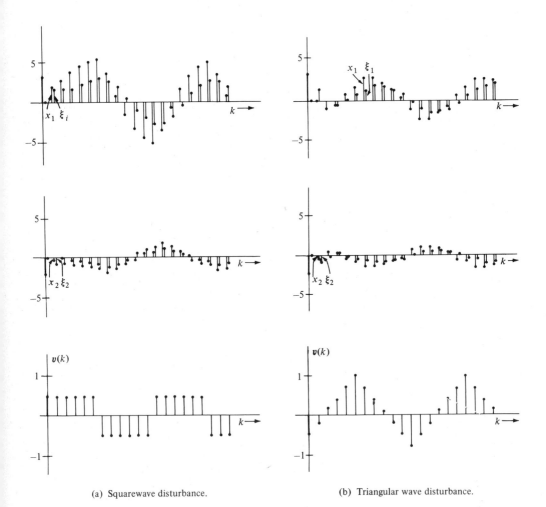

(a)  Squarewave disturbance.            (b)  Triangular wave disturbance.

**FIGURE 6-23.   Response of a plant and observer when the plant has a disturbance input. The control input is zero.**

any actual disturbance will be small so that errors in the observer estimate of the plant state will be small.

When the plant (6-29) has the state feedback

$$u(k) = [-1 \quad -1]\begin{bmatrix} x_1(k) \\ x_2(k) \end{bmatrix}$$

the feedback plant eigenvalues are both at $\lambda = 0$. So when the observer's state estimate is fed back in place of the state (which is not accessible),

$$u(k) = [-1 \quad -1]\begin{bmatrix} \xi_1(k) \\ \xi_2(k) \end{bmatrix}$$

the feedback system eigenvalues are 0, 0, 1/4, and 1/4. Response of this observer feedback system with the squarewave disturbance $v(k)$ is shown in Figure 6-24.

If instead, the disturbance is modeled as an unknown constant,

$$\varepsilon(k + 1) = \varepsilon(k)$$

$$v(k) = \varepsilon(k)$$

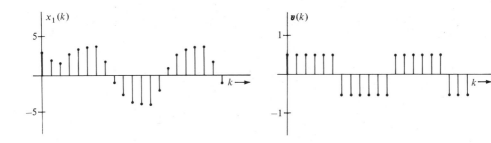

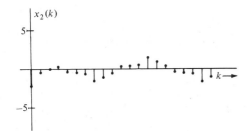

**FIGURE 6-24.** Response of the observer feedback system to a squarewave when the disturbance is not modeled.

the augmented plant model is

$$
\begin{bmatrix} x_1(k+1) \\ x_2(k+1) \\ \varepsilon(k+1) \end{bmatrix} = \begin{bmatrix} 1 & 1 & 2 \\ -\frac{1}{4} & 0 & -1 \\ 0 & 0 & 1 \end{bmatrix} \begin{bmatrix} x_1(k) \\ x_2(k) \\ \varepsilon(k) \end{bmatrix} + \begin{bmatrix} 1 \\ 0 \\ 0 \end{bmatrix} u(k)
$$

$$
= \mathbf{A}\mathbf{x}'(k) + \mathbf{b}u(k)
$$

$$
y(k) = \begin{bmatrix} 1 & 0 & 1 \end{bmatrix} \begin{bmatrix} x_1(k) \\ x_2(k) \\ \varepsilon(k) \end{bmatrix} = \mathbf{c}^\dagger \mathbf{x}'(k)
$$

The disturbance state $\varepsilon(k)$ is uncontrollable, as one would expect, but it is observable.

A full-order state observer of this augmented plant, with all three eigenvalues 1/4, is

$$
\begin{bmatrix} \xi_1(k+1) \\ \xi_2(k+1) \\ \xi_3(k+1) \end{bmatrix} = \begin{bmatrix} \frac{7}{80} & 1 & \frac{87}{80} \\ \frac{19}{80} & 0 & -\frac{41}{80} \\ -\frac{27}{80} & 0 & \frac{53}{80} \end{bmatrix} \begin{bmatrix} \xi_1(k) \\ \xi_2(k) \\ \xi_3(k) \end{bmatrix} + \begin{bmatrix} \frac{73}{80} \\ -\frac{39}{80} \\ \frac{27}{80} \end{bmatrix} y(k) + \begin{bmatrix} 1 \\ 0 \\ 0 \end{bmatrix} u(k) \qquad (6\text{-}30)
$$

If the disturbance $v$ is indeed a constant, the observer estimate converges to the plant state and to the constant disturbance, as shown in Figure 6-25(a). If the disturbance is not a constant, the estimate exhibits errors, but these can be much reduced from the error when the disturbance is simply ignored. Figure 6-25(b) shows the response of this observer with the same plant initial conditions and squarewave disturbance.

If state feedback were available for the augmented plant, a control input of the form

$$
u(k) = \begin{bmatrix} e_1 & e_2 & e_3 \end{bmatrix} \begin{bmatrix} x_1(k) \\ x_2(k) \\ \varepsilon(k) \end{bmatrix} = \mathbf{e}^\dagger \mathbf{x}'(k)
$$

would only place the two eigenvalues associated with the plant (6-29), which is the controllable part of the augmented plant:

$$
|\lambda\mathbf{I} - (\mathbf{A} + \mathbf{b}\mathbf{e}^\dagger)| = \begin{vmatrix} (\lambda - 1 - e_1) & -(1 + e_2) & -(2 + e_3) \\ \frac{1}{4} & \lambda & 1 \\ 0 & 0 & (\lambda - 1) \end{vmatrix}
$$

$$
= (\lambda - 1)[\lambda^2 - (1 + e_1)\lambda + (\tfrac{1}{4} + \tfrac{1}{4}e_2)]
$$

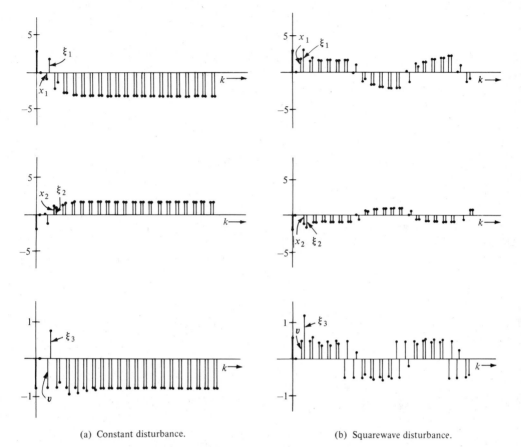

(a) Constant disturbance.                                      (b) Squarewave disturbance.

**FIGURE 6-25.** Response of the plant and an observer augmented by a disturbance model for an unknown constant disturbance.

Any feedback of the form

$$u(k) = \begin{bmatrix} -1 & -1 & e_3 \end{bmatrix} \begin{bmatrix} x_1(k) \\ x_2(k) \\ \varepsilon(k) \end{bmatrix}$$

will place both plant eigenvalues at $\lambda = 0$, as before; hence, any feedback from the observer (6-30) of the form

$$u(k) = \begin{bmatrix} -1 & -1 & e_3 \end{bmatrix} \begin{bmatrix} \xi_1(k) \\ \xi_2(k) \\ \xi_3(k) \end{bmatrix} \tag{6-31}$$

will result in an observer feedback system having the three $\lambda = 1/4$ observer eigenvalues and two $\lambda = 0$ plant eigenvalues.

Figure 6-26 shows the squarewave response of the plant and this observer for

$$u(k) = \begin{bmatrix} -1 & -1 & 0 \end{bmatrix} \begin{bmatrix} \xi_1(k) \\ \xi_2(k) \\ \xi_3(k) \end{bmatrix}$$

If instead, the disturbance is modeled as an arbitrary constant plus an arbitrary ramp sequence

$$\begin{bmatrix} \varepsilon_1(k+1) \\ \varepsilon_2(k+1) \end{bmatrix} = \begin{bmatrix} 2 & 1 \\ -1 & 0 \end{bmatrix} \begin{bmatrix} \varepsilon_1(k) \\ \varepsilon_2(k) \end{bmatrix}$$

$$v(k) = \begin{bmatrix} 1 & 0 \end{bmatrix} \begin{bmatrix} \varepsilon_1(k) \\ \varepsilon_2(k) \end{bmatrix}$$

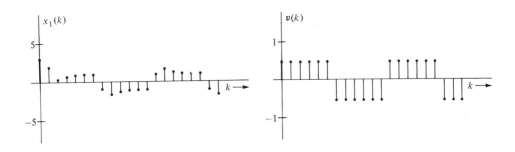

**FIGURE 6-26.** Response of the observer feedback system to a squarewave disturbance when the disturbance is modeled as an unknown constant.

the augmented plant model is

$$
\begin{bmatrix} x_1(k+1) \\ x_2(k+1) \\ \varepsilon_1(k+1) \\ \varepsilon_2(k+1) \end{bmatrix} = \begin{bmatrix} 1 & 1 & 2 & 0 \\ -\frac{1}{4} & 0 & -1 & 0 \\ 0 & 0 & 2 & 1 \\ 0 & 0 & -1 & 0 \end{bmatrix} \begin{bmatrix} x_1(k) \\ x_2(k) \\ \varepsilon_1(k) \\ \varepsilon_2(k) \end{bmatrix} + \begin{bmatrix} 1 \\ 0 \\ 0 \\ 0 \end{bmatrix} u(k)
$$

$$
y(k) = \begin{bmatrix} 1 & 0 & 1 & 0 \end{bmatrix} \begin{bmatrix} x_1(k) \\ x_2(k) \\ \varepsilon_1(k) \\ \varepsilon_2(k) \end{bmatrix}
$$

and an observer of this model will give still better disturbance rejection performance when used for feedback.

### 6.5.3 Disturbance Cancellation

To the extent that a disturbance is correctly modeled as in (6-26), its effect on the plant state is correctly calculated. Although the disturbance model modes cannot be changed by feedback because these modes are uncontrollable, feedback of observer estimates of disturbances can be used to reduce the effects of the disturbances on plant tracking outputs. Disturbance estimates can be used much as reference inputs, but where the objective is cancellation of their effects on the tracking outputs.

When disturbance estimates are fed back, the eigenvalue placement obtained through feedback of plant state estimates is not changed. For the general augmented plant (6-28), plant and disturbance model state feedback

$$
\mathbf{u}(k) = \mathbf{E}_x \mathbf{x}(k) + \mathbf{E}_\varepsilon \boldsymbol{\varepsilon}(k) + \boldsymbol{\rho}(k)
$$

gives the feedback system

$$
\begin{bmatrix} \mathbf{x}(k+1) \\ \hline \boldsymbol{\varepsilon}(k+1) \end{bmatrix} = \begin{bmatrix} \mathbf{A} + \mathbf{BE}_x & \mathbf{B}^v \boldsymbol{\Pi} + \mathbf{BE}_\varepsilon \\ \hline \mathbf{0} & \boldsymbol{\gamma} \end{bmatrix} \begin{bmatrix} \mathbf{x}(k) \\ \hline \boldsymbol{\varepsilon}(k) \end{bmatrix} + \begin{bmatrix} \mathbf{B} \\ \hline \mathbf{0} \end{bmatrix} \boldsymbol{\rho}(k)
$$

which has eigenvalues that are those of the plant with state feedback, $\mathbf{A} + \mathbf{BE}_x$ (independent of the disturbance feedback) and of the disturbance model, $\boldsymbol{\gamma}$.

Consider again the plant (6-29) augmented by a constant disturbance model and the full-order state observer (6-30) of the augmented plant. The observer variable $\xi_3(k)$ estimates any unknown constant disturbance input $v$.

By observing $v$ as well as the plant state, the effect of any arbitrary constant disturbance $v$ on the plant state is accounted for, and the observer will generate correct state estimates for feedback. The observer estimates of $v$ can be fed back, too, though the gain $e_3$ in (6-31), with affecting the feedback system eigenvalues. This estimate, $\xi_3(k)$ can be used to cancel a constant disturbance's effect on some plant signal of interest, as the observer estimate converges. For example, for the choice

$$e_3 = -2$$

the steady state effect of any constant disturbance $v$ on the state variable $x_1(k)$ is zero. Response of the feedback system consisting of the plant, the observer of the augmented plant, and observer feedback

$$u(k) = [-1 \quad -1 \quad -2] \begin{bmatrix} \xi_1(k) \\ \xi_2(k) \\ \xi_3(k) \end{bmatrix}$$

to a squarewave disturbance $v(k)$ is shown in Figure 6-27. The effect of this disturbance is much reduced from that with the same plant initial conditions and disturbance in Figure 6-26.

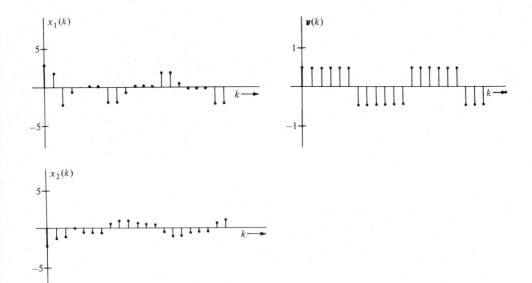

**FIGURE 6-27.** Response of the plant with observer feedback when the observer estimate of the disturbance is used for cancellation in the $x_1(k)$ signal.

## 6.6 A Digital Phase-Locked Loop

A digital phase-locked loop (PLL) produces a time-varying binary output signal in response to a nearly periodic time-varying binary input signal. The intervals between switching times of the input waveform are to change relatively slowly, but there may be small but rapid fluctuations from the ideal. The PLL produces an output waveform with switching times that are approximately at the same times as the input switchings but with any fluctuations in the switching times smoothed. Phase-locked loops are used to demodulate the stereo subcarrier in FM broadcast receivers, to detect the color information in TV receivers, to aid in synchronizing alternating current power distribution, to recover the master clock in digital data transmission and recording, and in many other applications.

Figure 6-28(a) is a block diagram of a digital phase-locked loop. The PLL input waveform switches at nearly constant intervals that are given by the input sequence $v(k)$. The running sum (accumulation) of the input switching intervals is the sequence of input switching times, which is nearly a ramp. Similarly, the accumulation of output intervals is the sequence of output

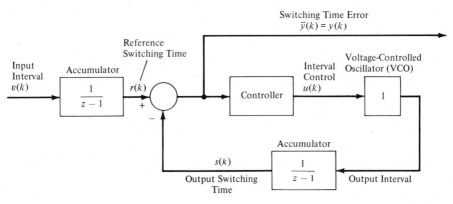

(a) A digital phase-locked loop.

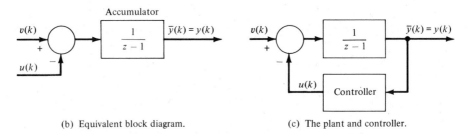

(b) Equivalent block diagram.

(c) The plant and controller.

**FIGURE 6-28. Phase-locked loop block diagrams.**

switching times. The differences between the input and output switching times is the switching time error, $\bar{y}(k) - y(k)$. The switching time error sequence is both accessible for feedback and is the system's output to be regulated. The controller controls the period of a voltage-controlled oscillator (VCO) that produces the output waveform.

It is desired that the switching time error $\bar{y}(k)$ decay to zero whenever $v(k)$ is constant. When the input interval $v(k)$ changes, perhaps erratically, the corresponding changes in the output interval $w(k)$ should be smoothed. One does not want simply to let $w(k)$ be a copy of $v(k)$ because, then, there is no smoothing action by the PLL. Every little fluctuation in $v(k)$ would also appear in $w(k)$. Instead, the controller is to allow only relatively slow changes in the VCO output interval.

In Figure 6-28(b), the plant portion of the digital phase-locked loop has been redrawn with the two separate accumulations combined. State variable equations for the plant are

$$x(k + 1) = x(k) + v(k) - u(k)$$

$$\bar{y}(k) = y(k) = x(k) \tag{6-32}$$

The plant equations are unusual in that the step index $k$ is the oscillation interval number, not a time step. When the interval lengths differ, each step $k$ represents a different length step in time. Figure 6-28(c) shows this plant with a controller that is to be designed. Although any of the other tracking system design methods could be applied to this problem, we will choose to consider the design to be that of a regulator with output $\bar{y}(k)$ and disturbance input $v(k)$. The regulator output $\bar{y}(k)$ should decay to zero for any constant disturbance $v(k)$. The modes of the overall system should be such that for rapid fluctuations in the input interval $v(k)$, the output interval $w(k)$ changes relatively slowly.

### 6.6.1 A First-Order Observer-Controller

If the disturbance $v(k)$ is modeled as an unknown constant

$$v(k + 1) = v(k)$$

the augmented plant model is

$$\begin{bmatrix} x(k + 1) \\ v(k + 1) \end{bmatrix} = \begin{bmatrix} 1 & 1 \\ 0 & 1 \end{bmatrix} \begin{bmatrix} x(k) \\ v(k) \end{bmatrix} + \begin{bmatrix} -1 \\ 0 \end{bmatrix} u(k) = \mathbf{A}\mathbf{x}(k) + \mathbf{b}u(k)$$

$$\bar{y}(k) = y(k) = \begin{bmatrix} 1 & 0 \end{bmatrix}\begin{bmatrix} x(k) \\ v(k) \end{bmatrix} = \mathbf{c}^\dagger \mathbf{x}(k)$$

This augmented plant is not completely controllable, as expected, because the disturbance input model is autonomous. It is completely observable, however.

If the augmented plant's state were available for feedback, state feedback of the form

$$u(k) = \begin{bmatrix} e_1 & e_2 \end{bmatrix}\begin{bmatrix} x(k) \\ v(k) \end{bmatrix} = \mathbf{e}^\dagger \mathbf{x}(k)$$

would result in the feedback system state coupling matrix

$$\mathbf{A} + \mathbf{be}^\dagger = \begin{bmatrix} (1 - e_1) & (1 - e_2) \\ 0 & 1 \end{bmatrix}$$

which has characteristic equation

$$(\lambda - 1)(\lambda - 1 + e_1) = 0$$

The $\lambda = 1$ eigenvalue of the uncontrollable disturbance model part of the augmented plant is not affected by any feedback. The original plant eigenvalue can be placed by feedback of the original plant state. It is not affected by feedback of the disturbance model state. Any state feedback with $e_1 = 1/2$ will result in the augmented plant eigenvalues $\lambda = 1$ and $\lambda = 1/2$.

For $e_1 = 1/2$, the augmented plant with feedback is

$$\begin{bmatrix} x(k + 1) \\ v(k + 1) \end{bmatrix} = \begin{bmatrix} \frac{1}{2} & (1 - e_2) \\ 0 & 1 \end{bmatrix}\begin{bmatrix} x(k) \\ v(k) \end{bmatrix}$$

$$\bar{y}(k) = \begin{bmatrix} 1 & 0 \end{bmatrix}\begin{bmatrix} x(k) \\ v(k) \end{bmatrix}$$

and its tracking output is related to the initial conditions by

$$\bar{y}(k) = (\tfrac{1}{2})^k x(0) + 2(1 - e_2)[1 - (\tfrac{1}{2})^k]v(0)$$

Choosing $e_2 = 1$ gives zero steady state error to any constant disturbance $v$.

The augmented plant state is not available for feedback, though, so we will design an observer of the state and feed back the observer's state estimate in place of the actual state. A first-order observer with eigenvalue $\lambda = 1/2$ and gain $g = 1$ is of the form

$$\xi(k + 1) = \tfrac{1}{2}\xi(k) + y(k) + hu(k)$$

It observes

$$\xi(k) \to \mathbf{m}^\dagger\mathbf{x}(k)$$

where

$$\mathbf{m}^\dagger = \mathbf{c}^\dagger(\mathbf{A} - \tfrac{1}{2}\mathbf{I})^{-1} = [2 \quad -4]$$

and

$$h = \mathbf{m}^\dagger\mathbf{b} = -2$$

The collection of signals

$$\begin{bmatrix} w_1(k) \\ w_2(k) \end{bmatrix} = \begin{bmatrix} 0 \\ -\tfrac{1}{4} \end{bmatrix} \xi(k) + \begin{bmatrix} 1 \\ \tfrac{1}{2} \end{bmatrix} y(k)$$

observes the augmented plant state

$$\mathbf{w}(k) \to \mathbf{x}(k)$$

The observer feedback

$$u(k) = \mathbf{e}^\dagger\mathbf{w}(k) = [\tfrac{1}{2} \quad 1]\mathbf{w}(k) = -\tfrac{1}{4}\xi(k) + y(k)$$

places the plant eigenvalue at $\lambda = 1/2$ and gives a tracking output signal $\bar{y}(t)$ that decays to zero for any constant disturbance input $v(k)$.
The observer-controller is described by

$$\xi(k + 1) = \tfrac{1}{2}\xi(k) + y(k) - 2u(k)$$

$$u(k) = -\tfrac{1}{4}\xi(k) + y(k)$$

Eliminating $u(k)$ from the first of these equations results in the controller state variable equations

$$\xi(k + 1) = \xi(k) - y(k)$$

$$u(k) = -\tfrac{1}{4}\xi(k) + y(k)$$

Using these and the plant equations (6-32), the zero-state tracking output and the disturbance input are related by

$$\bar{Y}(z) = \left[ \frac{z-1}{(z-\frac{1}{2})^2} \right] V(z) = T(z)V(z)$$

For any constant disturbance

$$V(z) = \frac{\beta z}{z-1}$$

then

$$\lim_{k \to \infty} \bar{y}(k) = \lim_{z \to 1} \left[ \frac{z-1}{z} V(z)T(z) \right] = 0$$

as expected.

Figure 6-29(a) shows the plant with this controller. Response of the system to a constant input is shown in Figure 6-29(b). As expected, the switching time error, which is the system's tracking output, decays to zero. Figure 6-29(c) shows the response of the system to a slowly-varying input.

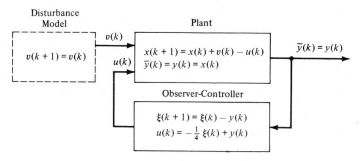

(a) Block diagram.

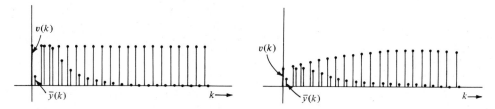

(b) Response when the input interval is constant.   (c) Response when the input interval varies slowly.

FIGURE 6-29.   The digital phase-locked loop with a controller based on a first-order disturbance signal model. Ideally, $\bar{y}(k)$ is zero.

## 6.6.2 A Higher-Order Controller

If, instead, the order of the disturbance signal model is raised so that $v(k)$ is modeled as an unknown constant plus an unknown ramp sequence, a disturbance model is

$$\begin{bmatrix} \sigma_1(k+1) \\ \sigma_2(k+1) \end{bmatrix} = \begin{bmatrix} 0 & 1 \\ -1 & 2 \end{bmatrix} \begin{bmatrix} \sigma_1(k) \\ \sigma_2(k) \end{bmatrix}$$

$$v(k) = \sigma_1(k)$$

The augmented plant model is

$$\begin{bmatrix} x(k+1) \\ \sigma_1(k+1) \\ \sigma_2(k+1) \end{bmatrix} = \begin{bmatrix} 1 & 1 & 0 \\ 0 & 0 & 1 \\ 0 & -1 & 2 \end{bmatrix} \begin{bmatrix} x(k) \\ \sigma_1(k) \\ \sigma_2(k) \end{bmatrix} + \begin{bmatrix} -1 \\ 0 \\ 0 \end{bmatrix} u(k) = \mathbf{A}\mathbf{x}(k) + \mathbf{b}u(k)$$

$$y(k) = \begin{bmatrix} 1 & 0 & 0 \end{bmatrix} \begin{bmatrix} x(k) \\ \sigma_1(k) \\ \sigma_2(k) \end{bmatrix} = \mathbf{c}^\dagger \mathbf{x}(k)$$

State feedback of the form

$$u(k) = \begin{bmatrix} e_1 & e_2 & e_3 \end{bmatrix} \begin{bmatrix} x(k) \\ \sigma_1(k) \\ \sigma_2(k) \end{bmatrix} = \mathbf{e}^\dagger \mathbf{x}(k)$$

gives an augmented plant with feedback having characteristic equation

$$(\lambda - 1)^2 (\lambda - 1 + e_1) = 0$$

so that the eigenvalue of the original plant, which is the controllable part of the augmented plant, can be placed by selecting the plant state gain $e_1$. The disturbance state gains $e_2$ and $e_3$ do not affect this eigenvalue placement.

For the choice

$$\mathbf{e}^\dagger = \begin{bmatrix} \frac{3}{4} & 1 & 0 \end{bmatrix}$$

the eigenvalue of the controllable part of the augmented plant is moved to $\lambda = 1/4$ and the tracking output is related to the augmented plant initial conditions by

$$\bar{y}(k) = \mathbf{c}^\dagger (\mathbf{A} + \mathbf{b}\mathbf{e}^\dagger)^k \mathbf{x}(0) = (\tfrac{1}{4})^k x(0) + 0\sigma_1(0) + 0\sigma_2(0)$$

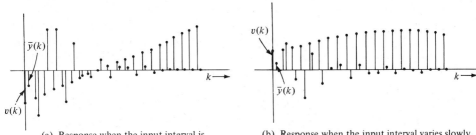

(a) Response when the input interval is a constant plus a ramp sequence.

(b) Response when the input interval varies slowly.

**FIGURE 6-30.   Response of the digital phase-locked loop with a controller based on a second-order disturbance signal model.**

There is then no steady state tracking error for any disturbance that is a constant plus a ramp.

All of the augmented plant state is not available for feedback, so we will design an observer to estimate the state. A full-order state observer of the augmented plant, with all three eigenvalues $\lambda = 1/4$ is

$$\begin{bmatrix} \xi_1(k+1) \\ \xi_2(k+1) \\ \xi_3(k+1) \end{bmatrix} = \begin{bmatrix} -2.75 & 1 & 0 \\ -4.69 & 0 & 1 \\ -6.46 & -1 & 2 \end{bmatrix} \begin{bmatrix} \xi_1(k) \\ \xi_2(k) \\ \xi_3(k) \end{bmatrix} + \begin{bmatrix} 3.75 \\ 4.69 \\ 6.46 \end{bmatrix} y(k) + \begin{bmatrix} -1 \\ 0 \\ 0 \end{bmatrix} u(k)$$

For

$$u(k) = \tfrac{3}{4}\xi_1(k) + \xi_2(k)$$

the original plant with observer feedback has all four eigenvalues at $\lambda = 1/4$ and has zero steady state error to any constant-plus-ramp input sequence. Typical response is shown in Figure 6-30 and is seen to be improved over that of the lower-order observer-controller.

In certain applications, for example data clock recovery from rotating disk drives, the input period $v(k)$ has a small but significant sinusoidal component. For a disk, the frequency of the sinusoidal component is the drive rotation frequency and results mainly from eccentricities in the circular recorded tracks. An appropriate model for $v(k)$ is then an arbitrary constant plus a sinusoidal sequence of arbitrary amplitude and phase.

### 6.6.3 Error Quantization and Measurement Interruption

It is common in a system such as this one for the switching time error measurement $y(k)$ to be made by a counter driven by a high-speed clock. The switching time error is made by counting the clock pulses between the input and output switchings. This error measurement, consisting of a count of clock cycles, could then be highly quantized. The output switching times might also be quantized, synchronized to a master clock. It is then appropriate to consider the measurements $y(k)$ to consist of the accurate switching time error plus a random "noise" component representing the quantization error. Figure 6-31 shows the effect of quantization on the performance of the system with the second-order disturbance input model. Response of the PLL to slowly-varying input intervals is shown when the switching time error measurements are truncated to 8, 6, and 4 binary digits (bits) of accuracy. Under these circumstances, performance would likely be improved by placing the observer and plant eigenvalues still further from the origin of the complex plane so that the reference signal estimate involves greater smoothing of the measurements. The disadvantage of doing this is that the speed of response to changes in $v(k)$ will be slowed.

It is also common for there to be interruptions in the PLL measurements $y(k)$. A PLL used to recover the clock signal from transmitted or recorded data, for instance, can make switching time comparisons only when the data changes from a binary 1 to a 0 or from a 0 to a 1. If the observer-controller is arranged in the form of the augmented plant model driven by measurement error (as in Figure 5-8), new measurement data only need be incorporated when it is available. When it is not available, the plant model predicts the behavior of the plant, including the input model, on the basis of the previous measurements.

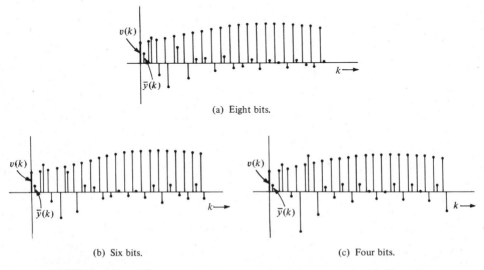

(a) Eight bits.

(b) Six bits.

(c) Four bits.

**FIGURE 6-31. Effects on performance of using quantized switching time error measurements.**

## 6.7 Summary

For a plant

$$\mathbf{x}(k + 1) = \mathbf{A}\mathbf{x}(k) + \mathbf{B}\mathbf{u}(k)$$

we distinguish between the measurement outputs

$$\mathbf{y}(k) = \mathbf{C}\mathbf{x}(k) + \mathbf{D}\mathbf{u}(k)$$

that are available for feedback control and the tracking outputs

$$\bar{\mathbf{y}}(k) = \bar{\mathbf{C}}\mathbf{x}(k) + \bar{\mathbf{D}}\mathbf{u}(k)$$

which are to become and remain nearly equal to externally supplied reference inputs $\mathbf{r}(k)$. The zero-input component of $\bar{\mathbf{y}}(k)$ depends on the initial conditions, which are usually unknown. Having shaped the plant's zero-input response by placing the feedback system eigenvalues with the methods of the previous chapter, the zero-state response of the tracking outputs is now designed. If, instead, the initial conditions were known, the zero-input components of the tracking outputs could be calculated and the system designed to track, instead

$$\bar{\mathbf{r}}(k) = \mathbf{r}(k) - \bar{\mathbf{y}}_{\text{zero-input}}(k)$$

When it can be arranged so that

$$\bar{\mathbf{y}}_{\text{zero-state}}(k) = \mathbf{r}(k)$$

ideal tracking is obtained. The tracking outputs have decaying zero-input response shaped by the selection of feedback system eigenvalues, after which they equal the reference inputs. In terms of transfer function matrices, for a plant with $z$-transfer function matrix $\mathbf{T}(z)$ ideal tracking requires a reference input filter with $z$-transfer function matrix $\mathbf{G}(z)$ such that

$$\mathbf{T}(z)\mathbf{G}(z) = \mathbf{I}$$

and $\mathbf{G}(z)$ is an inverse filter for the plant.

Any reference input filter does not change the feedback system eigenvalues, so the feedback eigenvalue placement part of the design is not affected. The ideal tracking design equations are linear but solutions can, unfortunately, be unstable and noncausal.

Response model tracking is obtained when the reference input filter gives

$$\bar{\mathbf{Y}}_{\text{zero-state}}(z) = \mathbf{\Omega}(z)\mathbf{R}(z)$$

where $\mathbf{\Omega}(z)$ characterizes an acceptable $z$-transfer function matrix relation between the tracking outputs and the reference inputs that is less stringent than the

$$\mathbf{\Omega}(z) = \mathbf{I}$$

for ideal tracking. As with ideal tracking, the response model tracking design equations are linear. Unstable, noncausal, and noise-magnifying filter solutions can be avoided at the expense of less-than-perfect tracking.

The more plant inputs that are available, the more design options there are for a reference input filter. When an observer is used for feedback eigenvalue placement, external inputs can be added to each scalar observer state equation to provide more inputs for the filter.

In reference model tracking, the feedback plant input gains (including gains to feedback observer states) are selected so that the plant is an observer of a designer-selected autonomous (with no input) reference input model. Typical models are of step and step-plus-ramp reference inputs. The zero-state components of the plant tracking outputs track perfectly any reference inputs from the class of modeled inputs. This approach allows the designer to specify those types of inputs the tracking system is to track well. If the order of the reference signal model is so high as to preclude a solution with the number of available inputs to the plant with feedback, the order of the observer used for plant feedback can be raised to provide the needed additional inputs.

Disturbances are inaccessible plant inputs that the designer does not want to have much influence on the tracking outputs. Of the several ways of handling disturbances, we concentrated on the design technique of modeling disturbances as autonomous signal models.* To the extent that the disturbance is accurately modeled, its effects on the plant state can be accounted for and its effects on the tracking outputs can be cancelled. As the disturbance models are autonomous, they are not controllable, so feedback of a disturbance estimate does not affect previously placed feedback system eigenvalues. So far as the model is accurate, its disturbance estimate can be used as a reference input to cancel the actual disturbance's effects on the tracking outputs.

A digital phase-locked loop (PLL) provided an example of tracking system design. In a somewhat unconventional approach, the PLL phase error was modeled as a disturbance. The first controller design incorporated a first-

---

*The "whitening filters" used in Kalman filtering to accommodate noise that is correlated from step to step are precisely deterministic disturbance models driven, in that case, by white noise.

order, arbitrary constant, disturbance model. Then a higher-order controller, having an arbitrary-constant-plus-ramp disturbance model was designed.

Except in very simple situations, one cannot be very specific about most quantization effects except perhaps in a statistical sense. The quantization (e.g., roundoff error) associated with ordinary digital processing is likely to be of diminishing concern in the future because of the easy availability of inexpensive floating-point hardware, particularly in signal processing chips. In the PLL example however, as in similar situations with other systems, the quantization is inherent to the measuring process. Simulation is an important means of study.

There are many other practical systems for which some or all of the measurements are not available at every step. The PLL example demonstrated that a state observer can easily be used to predict the plant state at future steps, providing feedback of the estimated plant state when measurement outputs are not available at those steps.

## REFERENCES

Ideal and response model tracking system design has been used for a long time, sometimes explicitly, sometimes not. State variable viewpoints of inverse filters are the subject of the following papers:

L. M. Silverman, "Properties and Application of Inverse Systems," *IEEE Trans. Automatic Control*, Vol. AC-13, August 1968, pp. 436–437;

M. K. Sain and J. L. Massey, "Invertibility of Linear, Time-Invariant Dynamic Systems," *IEEE Trans. Automatic Control*, Vol. AC-14, April 1969, pp. 141–149;

L. M. Silverman, "Inversion of Multivariable Systems," *IEEE Trans. Automatic Control*, Vol. AC-14, June 1969, pp. 270–276.

The text

C.-T Chen, *Linear System Theory and Design*. New York: Holt, Rinehart and Winston, 1984.

has an extended discussion of these tracking system design methods. Reference model tracking system design, the observation of a reference signal model, was first published in

G. H. Hostetter and J. S. Meditch, "Generalized Inverse Filtering," *Proc. 10th Asilomar Conf. on Circuits, Systems and Computers*, Nov. 1976, pp. 234–239;

G. H. Hostetter, "Controller Design for Exact Signal Model Tracking," *Proc. 18th Asilomar Conf. on Circuits, Systems and Computers*, Nov. 1984, pp. 449–453.

C.-T Chen and G. H. Hostetter, "Design of Two-Input, One-Output Compensators to Achieve Asymptotic Tracking," *Int. J. Control*, to appear, 1987.

Deterministic disturbance models have been used for many years. A modern viewpoint of the estimation of unknown constant disturbances is discussed in

A. E. Bryson and D. G. Luenberger, "The Synthesis of Regulator Logic Using State-Variable Concepts," *Proc. IEEE*, Vol. 58, Nov. 1970, pp. 1803–1811.

More general disturbance models, especially polynomial ones, and their observation are discussed in

G. H. Hostetter and J. S. Meditch, "On the Generalization of Observers to Systems with Unmeasurable, Unknown Inputs," *Automatica*, Vol. 9, July 1973, pp. 721–724;

J. S. Meditch and G. H. Hostetter, "Observers for Systems with Unknown and Inaccessible Inputs," *Int. J. Control*, Vol. 19, March 1974, pp. 473–480.

The text

B. Friedland, *Control System Design*. New York: McGraw-Hill, 1986

also considers deterministic disturbances and reference signal models, using the term "exogenous variables."

The digital phase-locked loop example is based in part on work by Alan H. Ross and the author for Western Digital Corporation. More information about phase-locked loops can be found in

F. M. Gardner, *Phaselock Techniques*, 2nd edition, New York: Wiley, 1979.

## CHAPTER SIX PROBLEMS

**6-1.** Design inverse reference input filters for single-input, single-output plants with the following z-transfer functions. Specify the number of steps in advance, if any, that the reference input must be provided to each filter. Determine whether or not each filter is stable.

**a.** $T(z) = \dfrac{z^2 - \frac{1}{2}z + \frac{1}{2}}{z^3 - \frac{1}{2}z^2 - \frac{1}{2}z}$

**b.** $T(z) = \dfrac{4z^2 + 1}{3z^4 - 2z^3 + z^2 - z + 1}$

**c.** $T(z) = \dfrac{6z^2 - z - 1}{z^3}$

**d.** $T(z) = \dfrac{4z^2 - 1}{(z^2 + 1)(z + 3)}$

**6-2.** Design inverse reference input filters for two-input, single-output plants with the following $z$-transfer functions. In order of importance, the design objectives are

1. Use a stable filter
2. Use a causal filter
3. Use a filter with all poles at $z = 0$

**a.** $T_1(z) = \dfrac{2z}{z^2 - \frac{1}{4}}$

$T_2(z) = \dfrac{z + 1}{z^2 - \frac{1}{4}}$

**b.** $T_1(z) = \dfrac{z^2 + 2}{(2z - 1)(3z + 1)}$

$T_2(z) = \dfrac{z - 1}{(2z - 1)(3z + 1)}$

**c.** $T_1(z) = \dfrac{-2z^3 + 3z - 1}{z^3 - \frac{5}{6}z^2 + \frac{1}{6}z}$

$T_2(z) = \dfrac{z + 3}{z^2 - \frac{1}{2}z}$

**6-3.** For the plant

$$\begin{bmatrix} x_1(k + 1) \\ x_2(k + 1) \end{bmatrix} = \begin{bmatrix} 0 & 1 \\ \frac{1}{3} & \frac{2}{3} \end{bmatrix} \begin{bmatrix} x_1(k) \\ x_2(k) \end{bmatrix} + \begin{bmatrix} 0 \\ 1 \end{bmatrix} u(k)$$

$$y(k) = \begin{bmatrix} 1 & 1 \end{bmatrix} \begin{bmatrix} x_1(k) \\ x_2(k) \end{bmatrix}$$

$$\bar{y}(k) = \begin{bmatrix} 2 & -1 \end{bmatrix} \begin{bmatrix} x_1(k) \\ x_2(k) \end{bmatrix}$$

design feedback with a first-order observer so that all eigenvalues of the feedback system are at $\lambda = 0$. Then, using both the plant and an observer input, design an inverse reference input filter. Specify state variable equations for the controller, which is the combination of the observer and the filter.

**6-4.** Design response model reference input filters for single-input single tracking output plants with the following $z$-transfer functions. The filters must be stable, causal, and must result in systems with zero steady state error to a constant reference input.

**a.** $T(z) = \dfrac{(z - 2)(z^2 - z + \frac{1}{4})}{z^3 - \frac{1}{4}z}$

**b.** $T(z) = \dfrac{3z - 1}{z^2 - z + \frac{1}{4}}$

**c.** $T(z) = \dfrac{3z - 1}{z^2 + 2z + 1}$

**d.** $T(z) = \dfrac{(z + 2)(z - \frac{1}{2})}{z^3}$

**6-5.** Design response model reference input filters for two-input single tracking output plants with the following $z$-transfer functions. The filters must be causal and are to have all poles inside $|z| = 1/2$ on the complex plane. Each overall system must have zero steady state error to a constant reference input.

**a.** $T_1(z) = \dfrac{z + 2}{z - \frac{1}{2}}$

$T_2(z) = \dfrac{z}{z^2 - \frac{1}{4}}$

**b.** $T_2(z) = \dfrac{2z^2 - 4z + 2}{z^2 - z + \frac{1}{4}}$

$T_2(z) = \dfrac{z}{z^2 - z + \frac{1}{4}}$

**c.** $T_1(z) = \dfrac{z^2 - 1}{z^3}$

$T_2(z) = \dfrac{-3z + 1}{z^3}$

**6-6.** Design observer feedback that will place all eigenvalues of the feedback system with plant

$$\begin{bmatrix} x_1(k + 1) \\ x_2(k + 1) \end{bmatrix} = \begin{bmatrix} 0 & 1 \\ -1 & 2 \end{bmatrix} \begin{bmatrix} x_1(k) \\ x_2(k) \end{bmatrix} + \begin{bmatrix} 0 \\ 1 \end{bmatrix} u(k)$$

$$y(k) = \begin{bmatrix} 1 & 1 \end{bmatrix} \begin{bmatrix} x_1(k) \\ x_2(k) \end{bmatrix}$$

$$\bar{y}(k) = \begin{bmatrix} 0 & 1 \end{bmatrix} \begin{bmatrix} x_1(k) \\ x_2(k) \end{bmatrix} + 2u(k)$$

at $\lambda = 0$. Then design an ideal reference input filter for the resulting two-input feedback plant. Specify state equations for the filter.

**6-7.** For the observer feedback system of Problem 6-6, design instead a stable, causal response model reference input filter. Specify state equations for the filter.

**6-8.** A response model tracking system is to be designed for a plant with $z$-transfer function

$$T(z) = \frac{2z - 5}{(z + \frac{2}{3})(z + \frac{1}{3})}$$

using a reference input filter with $z$-transfer function of the form

$$G(z) = \frac{\alpha_1 z^2 + \alpha_2 z + \alpha_3}{(z + \frac{1}{2})^2}$$

The model's zero-input response should decay at least as rapidly as $(3/4)^k$ and it should have zero steady state error to a step input.

**6-9.** There is a duality between plant and reference input filter transfer functions whereby the two can sometimes be interchanged. For example, consider a single-input plant with a single tracking output, having $z$-transfer function $T(z)$. If an acceptable response model results with a filter $z$-transfer function $G(z)$, then the same model is produced if the plant $z$-transfer function is $G(z)$ and the filter is chosen to have the plant $z$-transfer function. Generalize this result to a filter for a two-input, two tracking output plant. Carefully explain and interpret the interchange that is involved.

**6-10.** Design signal models in state variable form having outputs of the following forms, where the $\beta$'s are arbitrary constants:

   **a.** $\beta_1 + \beta_2 k + \beta_3 k^2 + \beta_4 k^3$

   **b.** $\beta_1 + \beta_2 \cos(k/10) + \beta_3 \sin(k/10)$

   **c.** $\beta_1 + \beta_2 e^{-(k/3)} + \beta_3 k e^{-(k/3)}$

   **d.** $\beta_1 e^{-(k/3)} \cos\left[\left(\dfrac{k}{10}\right) + \beta_2\right]$

**6-11.** Find the form of the output of the signal model

$$\begin{bmatrix} \sigma_1(k+1) \\ \sigma_2(k+1) \\ \sigma_3(k+1) \end{bmatrix} = \begin{bmatrix} \frac{1}{2} & 0 & 0 \\ 0 & \frac{1}{2} & 1 \\ 0 & 1 & \frac{1}{2} \end{bmatrix} \begin{bmatrix} \sigma_1(k) \\ \sigma_2(k) \\ \sigma_3(k) \end{bmatrix}$$

$$r(k) = \begin{bmatrix} 1 & 0 & 1 \end{bmatrix} \begin{bmatrix} \sigma_1(k) \\ \sigma_2(k) \\ \sigma_3(k) \end{bmatrix}$$

**6-12.** For each of the following plants, choose the input gains, if possible, so that the plant tracking output $\bar{y}(k)$ observes a reference signal of the form $r(k)$, where the $\beta$'s are arbitrary constants:

**a.**
$$\begin{bmatrix} x_1(k+1) \\ x_2(k+1) \end{bmatrix} = \begin{bmatrix} 0 & 1 \\ \frac{1}{3} & \frac{5}{6} \end{bmatrix} \begin{bmatrix} x_1(k) \\ x_2(k) \end{bmatrix} + \begin{bmatrix} 2 \\ -1 \end{bmatrix} u(k)$$

$$\bar{y}(k) = \begin{bmatrix} 1 & 1 \end{bmatrix} \begin{bmatrix} x_1(k) \\ x_2(k) \end{bmatrix}$$

$$r(k) = \beta_1$$

**b.**
$$\begin{bmatrix} x_1(k+1) \\ x_2(k+1) \end{bmatrix} = \begin{bmatrix} \frac{5}{6} & 1 \\ -\frac{1}{6} & 0 \end{bmatrix} \begin{bmatrix} x_1(k) \\ x_2(k) \end{bmatrix} + \begin{bmatrix} 1 \\ 2 \end{bmatrix} u(k)$$

$$\bar{y}(k) = \begin{bmatrix} 4 & 1 \end{bmatrix} \begin{bmatrix} x_1(k) \\ x_2(k) \end{bmatrix} + u(k)$$

$$r(k) = \beta_1$$

**c.**
$$\begin{bmatrix} x_1(k+1) \\ x_2(k+1) \\ x_3(k+1) \end{bmatrix} = \begin{bmatrix} 0 & 1 & 0 \\ \frac{1}{4} & 0 & 1 \\ 0 & 0 & 0 \end{bmatrix} \begin{bmatrix} x_1(k) \\ x_2(k) \\ x_3(k) \end{bmatrix} + \begin{bmatrix} 0 & 1 \\ -1 & 1 \\ 2 & 0 \end{bmatrix} \begin{bmatrix} u_1(k) \\ u_2(k) \end{bmatrix}$$

$$\bar{y}(k) = \begin{bmatrix} 0 & 2 & -1 \end{bmatrix} \begin{bmatrix} x_1(k) \\ x_2(k) \\ x_3(k) \end{bmatrix}$$

$$r(k) = \beta_1 + \beta_2 k$$

**6-13.** For each of the following plants, design output or observer feedback to place the composite system eigenvalues all at $\lambda = 0$. Then choose the input gains, (including those to any observer) so that the plant tracking output signal $\bar{y}(k)$ observes the highest possible order polynomial signal model.

**a.**
$$\begin{bmatrix} x_1(k+1) \\ x_2(k+1) \end{bmatrix} = \begin{bmatrix} 0 & 1 \\ \frac{1}{2} & -\frac{1}{2} \end{bmatrix} \begin{bmatrix} x_1(k) \\ x_2(k) \end{bmatrix} + \begin{bmatrix} 0 \\ 1 \end{bmatrix} u(k)$$

$$y(k) = \begin{bmatrix} 2 & -1 \end{bmatrix} \begin{bmatrix} x_1(k) \\ x_2(k) \end{bmatrix}$$

$$\bar{y}(k) = x_1(k)$$

**b.**
$$\begin{bmatrix} x_1(k+1) \\ x_2(k+1) \end{bmatrix} = \begin{bmatrix} 0 & 1 \\ -1 & \frac{1}{2} \end{bmatrix} \begin{bmatrix} x_1(k) \\ x_2(k) \end{bmatrix} + \begin{bmatrix} 0 \\ 1 \end{bmatrix} u(k)$$

$$\begin{bmatrix} y_1(k) \\ y_2(k) \end{bmatrix} = \begin{bmatrix} 2 & 1 \\ -1 & 0 \end{bmatrix} \begin{bmatrix} x_1(k) \\ x_2(k) \end{bmatrix}$$

$$\bar{y}(k) = 2x_2(k) + u(k)$$

**c.** $$\begin{bmatrix} x_1(k+1) \\ x_2(k+1) \end{bmatrix} = \begin{bmatrix} 0 & 1 \\ \frac{1}{2} & -\frac{1}{2} \end{bmatrix} \begin{bmatrix} x_1(k+1) \\ x_2(k+1) \end{bmatrix} + \begin{bmatrix} 0 & 1 \\ 1 & -1 \end{bmatrix} \begin{bmatrix} u_1(k) \\ u_2(k) \end{bmatrix}$$

$$y(k) = \begin{bmatrix} 1 & 0 \end{bmatrix} \begin{bmatrix} x_1(k) \\ x_2(k) \end{bmatrix} + \begin{bmatrix} 0 & 1 \end{bmatrix} \begin{bmatrix} u_1(k) \\ u_2(k) \end{bmatrix}$$

$$\bar{y}(k) = 2x_1(k) - x_2(k)$$

**6-14.** Design an observer-controller for the plant

$$\begin{bmatrix} x_1(k+1) \\ x_2(k+1) \\ x_3(k+1) \end{bmatrix} = \begin{bmatrix} 0 & 1 & 0 \\ 0 & 0 & 1 \\ 0 & -\frac{1}{3} & -1 \end{bmatrix} \begin{bmatrix} x_1(k) \\ x_2(k) \\ x_3(k) \end{bmatrix} + \begin{bmatrix} 0 & 0 \\ 0 & 2 \\ 1 & -1 \end{bmatrix} \begin{bmatrix} u_1(k) \\ u_2(k) \end{bmatrix}$$

$$\begin{bmatrix} y_1(k) \\ y_2(k) \end{bmatrix} = \begin{bmatrix} 1 & 2 & -1 \\ 1 & 1 & 0 \end{bmatrix} \begin{bmatrix} x_1(k) \\ x_2(k) \\ x_3(k) \end{bmatrix} + \begin{bmatrix} 0 & 1 \\ -1 & 1 \end{bmatrix} \begin{bmatrix} u_1(k) \\ u_2(k) \end{bmatrix}$$

such that the tracking output

$$\bar{y}(k) = x_1(k) - x_2(k)$$

will track an arbitrary ramp signal and has a zero-input component that decays with step at least as quickly as $\kappa(1/2)^k$, where the constant $\kappa$ depends on the initial conditions.

**6-15.** Design an observer-controller for the plant of Problem 6-14 such that $\bar{y}(k)$ will exactly track any sinusoidal sequence of the form

$$r(k) = \beta_1 \cos\left(\frac{k}{5}\right) + \beta_2 \sin\left(\frac{k}{5}\right)$$

after six steps or less.

**6-16.** Design an observer-controller for the plant of Problem 6-14 with tracking outputs

$$\begin{bmatrix} \bar{y}_1(k) \\ \bar{y}_2(k) \end{bmatrix} = \begin{bmatrix} 0 & 1 & 0 \\ -1 & 2 & 1 \end{bmatrix} \begin{bmatrix} x_1(k) \\ x_2(k) \\ x_3(k) \end{bmatrix} + \begin{bmatrix} 0 & 0 \\ 3 & 0 \end{bmatrix} \begin{bmatrix} u_1(k) \\ u_2(k) \end{bmatrix}$$

instead, such that $\bar{y}(k)$ tracks $r_1(k)$ and $\bar{y}_2(k)$ tracks $r_2(k)$ where $r_1(k)$ and $r_2(k)$ are each modeled as arbitrary constants.

**6-17.** Show that when a single controller gain is to be chosen, the choice that gives zero steady state error to a constant input is the same as the choice for which the tracking output observes an arbitrary constant tracking input.

**6-18.** The term *model algorithmic control* denotes a response model tracking system for which the model plant has all of its eigenvalues at $\lambda = 0$. The model plant is thus a deadbeat system. Show that any input model tracking system for which all of the eigenvalues of the plant with observer feedback have been placed at $\lambda = 0$ is a model algorithmic controller.

**6-19.** Find state equations for disturbance models with responses having the following forms:

**a.** $\beta_1 + \beta_2 e^{-(k/8)} + \beta_3 k e^{-(k/8)}$

**b.** $\beta_1 + \beta_2(\tfrac{1}{2})^k \cos\left(\dfrac{k}{10}\right)$

**6-20.** For each of the following plants, find an autonomous state variable model for disturbances $v(k)$ of the form given, then design a full-order state observer of the augmented plant:

**a.**
$$\begin{bmatrix} x_1(k+1) \\ x_2(k+1) \end{bmatrix} = \begin{bmatrix} \tfrac{1}{2} & 1 \\ 0 & 1 \end{bmatrix}\begin{bmatrix} x_1(k) \\ x_2(k) \end{bmatrix} + \begin{bmatrix} 0 \\ 1 \end{bmatrix} u(k) + \begin{bmatrix} \tfrac{1}{2} \\ -\tfrac{1}{2} \end{bmatrix} v(k)$$

$$y(k) = \begin{bmatrix} 3 & -1 \end{bmatrix}\begin{bmatrix} x_1(k) \\ x_2(k) \end{bmatrix}$$

$$v(k) = \beta_1$$

**b.**
$$\begin{bmatrix} x_1(k+1) \\ x_2(k+1) \end{bmatrix} = \begin{bmatrix} 1 & 1 \\ -\tfrac{1}{4} & 0 \end{bmatrix}\begin{bmatrix} x_1(k) \\ x_2(k) \end{bmatrix} + \begin{bmatrix} 1 & 0 \\ 0 & 1 \end{bmatrix}\begin{bmatrix} u_1(k) \\ u_2(k) \end{bmatrix} + \begin{bmatrix} 1 \\ 0 \end{bmatrix} v(k)$$

$$y(k) = \begin{bmatrix} 1 & 0 \end{bmatrix}\begin{bmatrix} x_1(k) \\ x_2(k) \end{bmatrix} + \begin{bmatrix} 0 & 1 \end{bmatrix}\begin{bmatrix} u_1(k) \\ u_2(k) \end{bmatrix}$$

$$v(k) = \beta_1 + \beta_2 k$$

**c.**
$$\begin{bmatrix} x_1(k+1) \\ x_2(k+1) \end{bmatrix} = \begin{bmatrix} 0 & 1 \\ \tfrac{1}{4} & -1 \end{bmatrix}\begin{bmatrix} x_1(k) \\ x_2(k) \end{bmatrix} + \begin{bmatrix} 0 \\ 1 \end{bmatrix} u(k) + \begin{bmatrix} 1 & 0 \\ -1 & 1 \end{bmatrix}\begin{bmatrix} v_1(k) \\ v_2(k) \end{bmatrix}$$

$$y(k) = \begin{bmatrix} 1 & 2 \end{bmatrix}\begin{bmatrix} x_1(k) \\ x_2(k) \end{bmatrix}$$

$$v_1(k) = \beta_1$$

$$v_2(k) = \beta_2 + \beta_3 k$$

**6-21.** For the plant and disturbance model of Problem 6-20(a), design observer feedback to place the feedback system eigenvalues all at $\lambda = 0$ and to produce zero steady state error to any constant disturbance $v$ in the tracking output

$$\bar{y}(k) = x_2(k) + u(k)$$

**6-22.** Design a controller for the digital phase-locked loop that models the input interval sequence as an arbitrary constant plus an arbitrary ramp and uses a reduced-order observer.

**6-23.** Arrange the higher-order digital phased-locked loop controller of Section 6.6.2 in the form of a plant model driven by observer error feedback. Then carefully explain how the controller should operate if switching-time error measurements $y(k)$ are occasionally not available.

**6-24.** The initial "lock" of the digital phase-locked loop (called its *acquisition* or *capture* performance) can be improved by making the observer-controller deadbeat at first, then changing the observer gains to obtain better smoothing of the VCO period control signal $u(k)$. Design such a controller using the first-order observer structure of Section 6.6.1.

**6-25.** For the digital phase-locked loop design the controller as a tracking system where $s(k)$ in Figure 6-28(a) is to track $r(k)$.

# Controlling Continuous-Time Systems

7

## 7.1 Preview

The first of the two design problems for a tracking system, that of obtaining acceptable digital zero-input response, was solved in Chapter 5. If the designer is willing to provide the needed controller complexity, observer feedback can be used to place the feedback system eigenvalues at any desired locations. Sometimes output feedback will suffice, but in general one is likely to need an observer. The second design problem, obtaining acceptable zero-state tracking performance, was the subject of Chapter 6.

When a digital controller is to control a continuous-time plant, there is a third design problem, that of achieving good between-sample response of the continuous-time plant. That concern is addressed in this chapter. A good discrete-time design will ensure that samples of the plant response are well-behaved, but it is additionally necessary to have satisfactory response between the discrete-time steps. For a fixed plant, this third design concern is met by shaping the plant input waveforms and raising the sample rate as necessary. Significant increases in effective sample rate can be achieved at low cost and without greatly increasing the required controller throughput by updating the plant control signals at a higher rate than that for the bulk of the controller computations.

In this chapter, we first develop computational methods for obtaining discrete-time models of continuous-time plants and for digital computer simulation of continuous-time plant response. In the next section, we discuss the response of continuous-time plants to sampled-and-held inputs. The between-sample response of a continuous-time plant can be improved, if necessary, by changing the plant (perhaps with continuous-time feedback), by increasing the sampling rate, and by changing the shapes of the sampled-and-held plant inputs with a plant input filter. This latter approach is examined in some detail.

The next two sections of this chapter are about basic hardware and software considerations in digital controller design. A wide variety of hardware is now available, including general purpose computers and microprocessors, dedicated signal processing chips, and custom logic. These are assembled in a suitable architecture for the needed processing. Data acquisition and distribution are of key importance to hardware design, so some of the practical aspects of these are discussed at length. Software design might be with a high-level language, or it may be necessary to develop a program in an assembly language or the machine code of a particular processor. In any case, given the hardware architecture, there are usually many options for program, subroutine, and interrupt structures. The final hardware and software design usually must also include extensive alarm, test, and external selection and override provisions.

Finally, the design of two practical discrete-time controllers of continuous-time plants is discussed. The first of these is an advanced elevator positioning controller with a limited speed of travel. The second example is of a highly underdamped torsional positioning mechanism. The otherwise unacceptable between-sample response of the torsional positioner is improved with a continuous-time plant input filter.

# 7.2 Sampled Continuous-Time Systems

The relationship between continuous-time state variable plant models and discrete-time models of plant signal samples is now examined. So far, we have dealt rather exclusively with discrete-time control. When the plant is continuous-time, however, it is important to control its between-sample response as well as its discrete-time response. An important tool in the design process is the computer simulation of discrete-time control of continuous-time plants.

## 7.2.1 Discrete-Time Models of Continuous-Time Systems

Consider a continuous-time system in state variable form

$$\dot{\mathbf{x}}(t) = \mathscr{A}\mathbf{x}(t) + \mathscr{B}\mathbf{u}(t)$$

$$\mathbf{y}(t) = \mathbf{C}\mathbf{x}(t) + \mathbf{D}\mathbf{u}(t) \tag{7-1}$$

Script symbols are now used for the state and input coupling matrices to distinguish between these and the corresponding matrices in discrete-time models. The state as a function of the initial conditions and the input in (7-1) is

$$\mathbf{x(t)} = e^{\mathscr{A}t}\mathbf{x}(0) + \int_0^t e^{\mathscr{A}(t-\tau)}\mathscr{B}\mathbf{u}(\tau)d\tau$$

At the sample times $kT$, $k = 0, 1, 2, \ldots$ the state is

$$\mathbf{x}(kT) = e^{\mathscr{A}kT}\mathbf{x}(0) + \int_0^{kT} e^{\mathscr{A}(kT-\tau)}\mathscr{B}\mathbf{u}(\tau)d\tau$$

The state at the $(k + 1)$th step can be expressed in terms of the state at the $k$th step as follows:

$$\mathbf{x}(kT + T) = e^{\mathscr{A}(kT+T)}\mathbf{x}(0) + \int_0^{kT+T} e^{\mathscr{A}(kT+T-\tau)}\mathscr{B}\mathbf{u}(\tau)d\tau$$

$$= e^{\mathscr{A}T}e^{\mathscr{A}kT}\mathbf{x}(0) + \int_0^{kT} e^{\mathscr{A}(kT+T-\tau)}\mathscr{B}\mathbf{u}(\tau)d\tau$$

$$+ \int_{kT}^{kT+T} e^{\mathscr{A}(kT+T-\tau)}\mathscr{B}\mathbf{u}(\tau)d\tau$$

$$= e^{\mathscr{A}T}\left[ e^{\mathscr{A}kT}\mathbf{x}(0) + \int_0^{kT} e^{\mathscr{A}(kT-\tau)}\mathscr{B}\mathbf{u}(\tau)d\tau \right]$$

$$+ \int_{kT}^{kT+T} e^{\mathscr{A}(kT+T-\tau)}\mathscr{B}\mathbf{u}(\tau)d\tau$$

$$= e^{\mathscr{A}T}\mathbf{x}(kT) + \text{(input term)}$$

The input term, involving as it does a weighted integral of $\mathbf{u}(t)$, is not generally proportional to samples of the input. When the input is constant during each sampling interval, however, as it is when it is driven by sample-and-hold signals, the input term is

$$\int_{kT}^{kT+T} e^{\mathscr{A}(kT+T-\tau)}\mathscr{B}\mathbf{u}(\tau)d\tau = \left[ \int_{kT}^{kT+T} e^{\mathscr{A}(kT+T-\tau)}d\tau \right]\mathscr{B}\mathbf{u}(k)$$

which is proportional to the input samples, the discrete-time input coupling matrix being

$$\mathbf{B} = \left[ \int_{kT}^{kT+T} e^{\mathscr{A}(kT+T-\tau)} d\tau \right] \mathscr{B}$$

Letting

$$\gamma = kT + T - \tau; \qquad d\gamma = -d\tau$$

then

$$\mathbf{B} = \left[ \int_0^T e^{\mathscr{A}\gamma} d\gamma \right] \mathscr{B}$$

Expanding the integrand into a power series

$$e^{\mathscr{A}\gamma} = \mathbf{I} + \frac{\mathscr{A}\gamma}{1!} + \frac{\mathscr{A}^2\gamma^2}{2!} + \cdots + \frac{\mathscr{A}^i\gamma^i}{i!} + \cdots$$

and integrating term by term, there results

$$\mathbf{B} = \left\{ \int_0^T \left[ \mathbf{I} + \frac{\mathscr{A}\gamma}{1!} + \frac{\mathscr{A}^2\gamma^2}{2!} + \cdots + \frac{\mathscr{A}^i\gamma^i}{i!} + \cdots \right] d\gamma \right\} \mathscr{B}$$

$$= \left[ \mathbf{I}T + \frac{\mathscr{A}T^2}{2!} + \frac{\mathscr{A}^2T^3}{3!} + \cdots + \frac{\mathscr{A}^iT^{i+1}}{(i+1)!} + \cdots \right] \mathscr{B} \tag{7-2}$$

Since

$$\mathscr{A}\mathbf{B} = \left[ \frac{\mathscr{A}T}{1!} + \frac{\mathscr{A}^2T^2}{2!} + \cdots + \frac{\mathscr{A}^{i+1}T^{i+1}}{(i+1)1} + \cdots \right] \mathscr{B} = (e^{\mathscr{A}T} - \mathbf{I})\mathscr{B}$$

then if $\mathscr{A}$ is nonsingular

$$\mathbf{B} = \mathscr{A}^{-1}(e^{\mathscr{A}T} - \mathbf{I})\mathscr{B} = (e^{\mathscr{A}T} - \mathbf{I})\mathscr{A}^{-1}\mathscr{B} \tag{7-3}$$

The discrete-time model of (7-1) is then

$$\mathbf{x}[(k+1)T] = \mathbf{A}\mathbf{x}(kT) + \mathbf{B}\mathbf{u}(kT)$$

$$\mathbf{y}(kT) = \mathbf{C}\mathbf{x}(kT) + \mathbf{D}\mathbf{u}(kT)$$

or

$$\mathbf{x}(k+1) = \mathbf{Ax}(k) + \mathbf{Bu}(k)$$

$$\mathbf{y}(k) = \mathbf{Cx}(k) + \mathbf{Du}(k)$$

where

$$\mathbf{A} = e^{\mathscr{A}T} = \mathbf{I} + \frac{\mathscr{A}T}{1!} + \frac{\mathscr{A}^2 T^2}{2!} + \cdots + \frac{\mathscr{A}^i T^i}{i!} + \cdots$$

$$\mathbf{B} = \left[ \mathbf{I}T + \frac{\mathscr{A}T^2}{2!} + \frac{\mathscr{A}^2 T^3}{3!} + \cdots + \frac{\mathscr{A}^i T^{i+1}}{(i+1)!} + \cdots \right] \mathscr{B}$$

and where

$$\mathbf{B} = \mathscr{A}^{-1}[\exp(\mathscr{A}T) - \mathbf{I}]\mathscr{B} = [\exp(\mathscr{A}T) - \mathbf{I}]\mathscr{A}^{-1}\mathscr{B}$$

when $\mathscr{A}$ is nonsingular.

As a numerical example, consider the continuous-time system

$$\begin{bmatrix} \dot{x}_1(t) \\ \dot{x}_2(t) \end{bmatrix} = \begin{bmatrix} -2 & 2 \\ 1 & -3 \end{bmatrix} \begin{bmatrix} x_1(t) \\ x_2(t) \end{bmatrix} + \begin{bmatrix} -1 \\ 5 \end{bmatrix} u(t)$$

$$y(t) = [2 \quad -4] \begin{bmatrix} x_1(t) \\ x_2(t) \end{bmatrix} + 6u(t)$$

with a sampling interval $T = 0.2$. The matrix exponential is

$$e^{\mathscr{A}T} = e^{0.2\mathscr{A}} = \begin{bmatrix} 0.696 & 0.246 \\ 0.123 & 0.572 \end{bmatrix}$$

which can be calculated by truncating the power series:

$$\exp(\mathscr{A}T) \cong \mathbf{I} + \mathscr{A}T + \frac{(\mathscr{A}T)^2}{2!} + \frac{(\mathscr{A}T)^3}{3!} + \cdots + \frac{(\mathscr{A}T)^i}{i!}$$

By examining the finite series as more and more terms are added, it can be decided when to truncate the series. It is good to bear in mind, however, that there are pathological matrices for which the series converges slowly, for which the series seems to converge first to one matrix then to another, and for which numerical rounding can give misleading results.

If the input $u(t)$ is constant in each interval from $kT$ to $kT + T$, the input term in the discrete-time model is proportional to the input samples and has

$$\mathscr{b} = [\exp(\mathscr{A}T) - \mathbf{I}]\mathscr{A}^{-1}\mathscr{b} = \begin{bmatrix} -0.304 & 0.246 \\ 0.123 & -0.428 \end{bmatrix} \begin{bmatrix} -\frac{3}{4} & -\frac{1}{2} \\ -\frac{1}{4} & -\frac{1}{2} \end{bmatrix} \begin{bmatrix} -1 \\ 5 \end{bmatrix}$$

$$= \begin{bmatrix} -0.021 \\ 0.747 \end{bmatrix}$$

which could also have been found using a truncated series (7-2). The discrete-time model of the continuous-time system is thus

$$\begin{bmatrix} x_1(kT + T) \\ x_2(kT + T) \end{bmatrix} = \begin{bmatrix} 0.696 & 0.246 \\ 0.123 & 0.572 \end{bmatrix} \begin{bmatrix} x_1(kT) \\ x_2(kT) \end{bmatrix} + \begin{bmatrix} -0.021 \\ 0.747 \end{bmatrix} u(kT)$$

$$y(kT) = \begin{bmatrix} 2 & -4 \end{bmatrix} \begin{bmatrix} x_1(kT) \\ x_2(kT) \end{bmatrix} + 6u(kT)$$

### 7.2.2 Between-Sample Response

When continuous-time plant inputs are driven by sample-and-hold (S/H) devices, the inputs are constant during each sampling interval, so the plant response during each sampling interval is a step response of the plant *without* the digital controller's feedback. If continuous-time feedback to improve the open-loop plant step response is a design option, it should be considered. When used, the plant to be digitally controlled is then the original plant with the continuous-time feedback. Often, though, continuous-time feedback is not an acceptable option. In this section, it is assumed that any continuous-time feedback around the original plant has been incorporated into the plant model that is now to be digitally controlled.

It is possible for signals in a continuous-time plant to fluctuate wildly, even though discrete-time samples of those signals are very well-behaved. The basic problem is illustrated in Figure 7-1 with the zero-input continuous-time system

$$\begin{bmatrix} \dot{x}_1(t) \\ \dot{x}_2(t) \end{bmatrix} = \begin{bmatrix} -0.2 & 1 \\ -1.01 & 0 \end{bmatrix} \begin{bmatrix} x_1(t) \\ x_2(t) \end{bmatrix} = \mathbf{A}\mathbf{x}(t)$$

$$y(t) = \begin{bmatrix} 1 & 0 \end{bmatrix} \begin{bmatrix} x_1(t) \\ x_2(t) \end{bmatrix} = \mathbf{c}^\dagger \mathbf{x}(t)$$

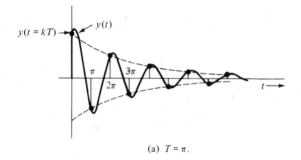

(a) $T = \pi$.

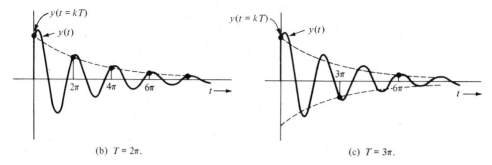

(b) $T = 2\pi$.                                    (c) $T = 3\pi$.

**FIGURE 7-1.   Hidden oscillations in a sampled continuous-time signal.**

This system has characteristic equation

$$s^2 + 0.2s + 1.01 = (s + 0.1 + j)(s + 0.1 - j) = 0$$

and thus response of the form

$$y(t) = Me^{-0.1t} \cos(t + \theta)$$

where the arbitrary constants $M$ and $\theta$ depend on the initial conditions $\mathbf{x}(0)$. When the output of this system is sampled with sampling interval $T = \pi$, the output samples are

$$y(k) = y(t = k\pi) = Me^{-0.1k\pi} \cos(k\pi + \theta)$$
$$= M(e^{-0.1\pi})^k(-1)^k \cos \theta = M \cos \theta(-0.73)^k$$

as shown in Figure 7-1(a). These samples are the response of a *first*-order discrete-time system having a single geometric series model. The wide fluctuations of $y(t)$ between sampling times, termed *hidden oscillations*, cannot be determined from the samples $y(k)$.

As one might expect, the discrete-time model of this continuous-time system,

$$\mathbf{x}(k + 1) = [\exp(\mathscr{A}T)]\mathbf{x}(k)$$
$$y(k) = \mathbf{c}^\dagger\mathbf{x}(k)$$

or

$$\begin{bmatrix} x_1(k + 1) \\ x_2(k + 1) \end{bmatrix} = \begin{bmatrix} -0.73 & 0 \\ 0 & -0.73 \end{bmatrix}\begin{bmatrix} x_1(k) \\ x_2(k) \end{bmatrix} = \mathbf{A}\mathbf{x}(k)$$

$$y(k) = \begin{bmatrix} 1 & 0 \end{bmatrix}\begin{bmatrix} x_1(k) \\ x_2(k) \end{bmatrix} = \mathbf{c}^\dagger\mathbf{x}(k)$$

is not completely observable in this circumstance.

$$\mathbf{M}_0 = \begin{bmatrix} \mathbf{c}^\dagger \\ \hline \mathbf{c}^\dagger\mathbf{A} \end{bmatrix} = \begin{bmatrix} 1 & 0 \\ -0.73 & 0 \end{bmatrix}$$

This phenomenon is called *loss of observability due to sampling.* The discrete-time system would normally have two modes, those given by its characteristic equation

$$\begin{vmatrix} z + 0.73 & 0 \\ 0 & z + 0.73 \end{vmatrix} = (z + 0.73)^2 = 0$$

which are $(-0.73)^k$ and $k(-0.73)^k$. Only the $(-0.73)^k$ mode appears in the output, however.

Hidden oscillations occur at any other integer multiple of the sampling period $T = \pi$ also. Figure 7-1(b) shows sampling with $T = 2\pi$, for which only a $[(-0.73)^2]^k = (0.533)^k$ mode is observable from $y(k)$. In Figure 7-1(c), with $T = 3\pi$, only a $[(-0.73)^3]^k = (-0.39)^k$ mode is observable from $y(k)$. While this illustration is with an autonomous (zero-input) continuous-time system, the situation is the same when the plant has inputs, except that steps in the inputs at the sampling times (from D/A conversion of controller outputs) tend to keep the hidden oscillations excited.

For a slightly different sampling interval, for example $T = 3$, where

$$\begin{bmatrix} x_1(k + 1) \\ x_2(k + 1) \end{bmatrix} = \begin{bmatrix} -0.74 & 0.10 \\ -0.11 & -0.73 \end{bmatrix}\begin{bmatrix} x_1(k) \\ x_2(k) \end{bmatrix}$$

$$y(k) = \begin{bmatrix} 1 & 0 \end{bmatrix}\begin{bmatrix} x_1(k) \\ x_2(k) \end{bmatrix}$$

there are no hidden oscillations, and the discrete-time model is completely observable. Hidden oscillations in a continuous-time system and the accompanying loss of observability of the discrete-time model occurs only when the continuous-time system has oscillatory modes and then only when the sampling interval is half the period of oscillation of an oscillatory mode or an integer multiple of that period. Although it is very unlikely that the sampling interval chosen for a plant control system would be precisely one resulting in hidden oscillations, intervals close to these result in modes in discrete-time models that are "almost unobservable." With limited numerical precision in measurements and in the controller computations, these modes can be difficult to detect and control.

## 7.2.3 Hybrid System Simulation

One of the designer's most important tools is the simulation of control systems and the plants they are to control on a digital computer. It is usually through simulation that difficulties with between-sample plant response are uncovered and solved. It is also good practice to carefully investigate the behavior of the controlled system when the arithmetic precision of the controller is reduced, when disturbance signals are injected into the system at likely points, and when the plant model is changed in ways that might occur in practice.

When a continuous-time plant is simulated on a digital computer, its response is computed at closely-spaced discrete times. It is plotted by joining the closely-spaced calculated response values with straight line segments in approximation of a continuous curve. Thus a digital computer simulation of discrete-time control of a continuous-time system involves at least two sets of discrete-time calculations. One runs at high rate for simulation of the continuous-time plant. The other runs at a lower rate (say once every 50 or 100 of the former calculations) to generate new control signals at each discrete control step.

The structure of a simple simulation program is shown in Figure 7-2, where it is assumed that the user wishes to have 50 steps of continuous-time response calculation during each discrete-time step. The controller begins with zero initial conditions and obtains its first output from the first reference input and the plant measurement output. That controller output (which is to be applied to the plant input via S/H devices) is the constant plant input during the first sampling interval. The loop to the left is then traversed 50 times, and 50 calculations of the plant state are made and plotted, spaced from the beginning to the end of the discrete-time step. The discrete-time step is then incremented, a new controller state and output are calculated, and this controller output becomes the plant input for the next 50 closely-spaced time

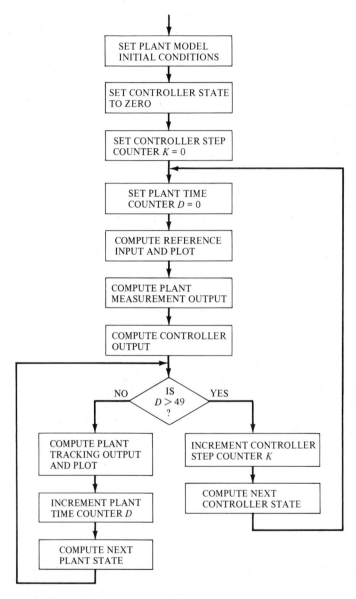

**FIGURE 7-2.**    Computer program structure for simulation of discrete-time control of a continuous-time plant.

steps during the second sampling interval. The process continues until program execution is halted.

An example of a plant and controller simulation is shown in Figure 7-3. The continuous-time plant is

$$\begin{bmatrix} \dot{x}_1(t) \\ \dot{x}_2(t) \end{bmatrix} = \begin{bmatrix} -\frac{3}{2} & 1 \\ -\frac{1}{2} & 0 \end{bmatrix} \begin{bmatrix} x_1(t) \\ x_2(t) \end{bmatrix} + \begin{bmatrix} -1 \\ 1 \end{bmatrix} u(t) = \mathscr{A}\mathbf{x}(t) + \mathscr{b}\mathbf{u}(t)$$

$$\bar{y}(t) = \begin{bmatrix} 1 & 0 \end{bmatrix} \begin{bmatrix} x_1(t) \\ x_2(t) \end{bmatrix} = \bar{\mathbf{c}}^\dagger \mathbf{x}(t) \tag{7-4}$$

The discrete-time controller operates with a sampling interval $T = 0.1$, and a discrete-time model of this plant with that sampling interval and a sampled-and-held input is of the form

$$\mathbf{x}(k + 1) = [\exp(\mathscr{A} T)]\mathbf{x}(k) + [\exp(\mathscr{A} T) - \mathbf{I}]\mathscr{A}^{-1}\mathscr{b}u(k)$$

$$\bar{y}(k) = \bar{\mathbf{c}}^\dagger \mathbf{x}(k)$$

or

$$\begin{bmatrix} x_1(k + 1) \\ x_2(k + 1) \end{bmatrix} = \begin{bmatrix} 0.858 & 0.0928 \\ -0.0464 & 0.998 \end{bmatrix} \begin{bmatrix} x_1(k) \\ x_2(k) \end{bmatrix} + \begin{bmatrix} -0.087 \\ 0.1 \end{bmatrix} u(k)$$

$$\bar{y}(k) = \begin{bmatrix} 1 & 0 \end{bmatrix} \begin{bmatrix} x_1(k) \\ x_2(k) \end{bmatrix}$$

Let

$$u(k) = \alpha r(k) = 0.47r(k) \tag{7-5}$$

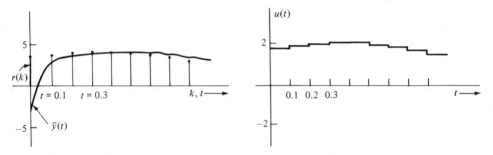

**FIGURE 7-3.** Simulating discrete-time control of a continuous-time plant.

where $r(k)$ is the reference input. The controller gain $\alpha$ is chosen so that the tracking output $\bar{y}(k)$ observes an arbitrary constant reference input.

The simulation shown consists of a plot of the continuous-time tracking output $\bar{y}(t)$ and the discrete-time reference input $r(k)$. The continuous-time input $u(t)$ is also plotted. For the continuous-time plot, 50 values of $\mathbf{x}(t)$ are

**TABLE 7-1 Simulation Program Example in Basic**

```
100   DIM X(2), X1(2)
110   REM SET PLANT MODEL INITIAL CONDITIONS
120   X(1) = −3
130   X(2) = 1
140   REM SET CONTROLLER STEP COUNTER TO ZERO
150   K = 0
160   REM SET PLANT TIME COUNTER TO ZERO
170   T = 0
180   REM COMPUTE REFERENCE INPUT AND PLOT
190   R = 4 * COS(9 * K − 30)
200   PRINT 0.1 * K, R
210   REM COMPUTE CONTROLLER OUTPUT
220   U = 0.47 * R
230   REM CHECK WHETHER ITS TIME FOR A NEW
231   REM DISCRETE-TIME STEP
240   IF T > 49 THEN GOTO 400
250   REM COMPUTE PLANT TRACKING OUTPUT
251   REM AND PLOT
260   Y = X(1)
270   PRINT T,Y
280   REM INCREMENT PLANT TIME COUNTER
290   T = T + 0.002
300   REM COMPUTE NEXT PLANT STATE
310   X1(1) = 0.997 * X(1) + 1.997E − 3 * X(2) − 1.99E − 3 * U
320   X1(2) = −9.985E − 4 * X(1) + X(2) − 2E − 3 * U
330   X(1) = X1(1)
340   X(2) = X1(2)
350   REM LOOP BACK TO CHECK TIME
360   GOTO 240

400   REM INCREMENT CONTROLLER STEP COUNTER
410   K = K + 1
420   REM LOOP BACK TO RESET TIME COUNTER
430   GOTO 170

999   END
```

plotted and connected during each sampling interval $T = 0.1$. The discrete-time model used to plot the continuous-time plant response has sampling interval

$$\Delta t = \frac{T}{50} = 0.002$$

so that its state variable description is

$$\mathbf{x}'(k' + 1) = [\exp(\mathcal{A}\Delta t)]\mathbf{x}'(k') + [\exp(\mathcal{A}\Delta t) - \mathbf{I}]\mathcal{A}^{-1}\mathcal{b}u(k')$$

$$\bar{y}(k') = \bar{\mathbf{c}}^{\dagger}\mathbf{x}'(k')$$

or

$$\begin{bmatrix} x'_1(k' + 1) \\ x'_2(k' + 1) \end{bmatrix} = \begin{bmatrix} 0.997 & 1.997 \times 10^{-3} \\ -9.985 \times 10^{-4} & 1 \end{bmatrix} \begin{bmatrix} x'_1(k') \\ x'_2(k') \end{bmatrix}$$
$$+ \begin{bmatrix} 1.99 \times 10^{-3} \\ -2 \times 10^{-3} \end{bmatrix} u(k')$$

$$\bar{y}(k') = \begin{bmatrix} 1 & 0 \end{bmatrix} \begin{bmatrix} x'_1(k') \\ x'_2(k') \end{bmatrix}$$

Table 7-1 is a digital computer program in the Basic language for the simulation of the continuous-time plant (7-4) and the discrete-time controller (7-5). As plotting commands are peculiar to the computer used, this example program simply prints the coordinates to be plotted. This program follows the structure given in Figure 7-2, but without the need for any controller state calculations.

## 7.3 Designing Between-Sample Response

The character of the between-sample response of a plant driven by sampled-and-held inputs is the step response of the plant without digital feedback. If between-sample plant response is not acceptable, the designer's options are to:

1. *Increase the controller sample rate* so that each step change in the plant input is of smaller amplitude. Often this is undesirable because it requires a major increase in hardware cost.

2. *Change the plant,* perhaps by adding continuous-time feedback. This too is often undesirable because of its susceptibility to noise and drift and the expense of routing analog signals.
3. *Change the shapes of the plant input signals* from having step changes at the controller sample rate to a shape that gives improved plant response.

It is straightforward to raise the sampling rate and redesign a controller for the higher rate, if necessary. It is also straightforward to incorporate analog feedback to improve the plant's step response by placing the continuous-time plant eigenvalues to achieve acceptable zero-input response. The continuous-time plant with feedback, rather than the original plant, then becomes the plant to be controlled digitally. The third option, that of changing the shape of the plant input signals is now examined. First, input signal shaping with analog filters is considered, then shaping with high-speed dedicated digital filters is discussed.

### 7.3.1 Analog Plant Input Filtering

Analog filters between the D/A converters and the plant inputs, particularly if they are relatively simple and composed of reliable and stable components, are usually acceptable in a controller design. As indicated in Figure 7-4, the idea is to use a filter or filters to smooth or shape the plant inputs so that the undesirable modes of the plant's open loop response are not excited as much as they would be with abrupt changes in the plant inputs at each step.

Figure 7-5(a) shows simulation results for the continuous-time plant

$$\begin{bmatrix} \dot{x}_1(t) \\ \dot{x}_2(t) \end{bmatrix} = \begin{bmatrix} -0.6 & 1 \\ -9 & 0 \end{bmatrix} \begin{bmatrix} x_1(t) \\ x_2(t) \end{bmatrix} + \begin{bmatrix} -1 \\ 1 \end{bmatrix} u(t) = \mathscr{A}\mathbf{x}(t) + \mathscr{b}u(t)$$

$$\bar{y}(t) = \begin{bmatrix} 1 & 0 \end{bmatrix} \begin{bmatrix} x_1(t) \\ x_2(t) \end{bmatrix} = \bar{\mathbf{c}}^\dagger \mathbf{x}(t) \tag{7-6}$$

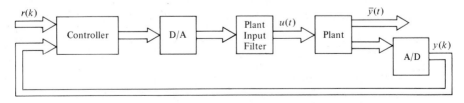

**FIGURE 7-4.**   Use of an analog plant input filter to improve between-sample response.

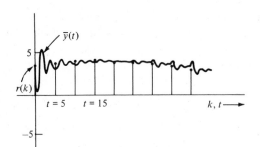
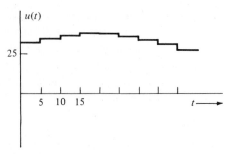

(a) Response of a system without a plant input filter.

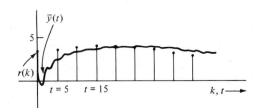
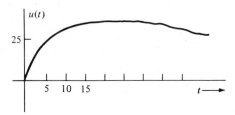

(b) Response with an added first-order analog plant input filter.

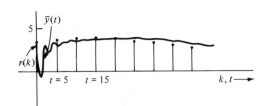
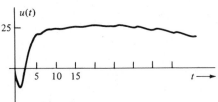

(c) Response with a better analog plant input filter.

**FIGURE 7-5.   Improvement of between-sample response with analog plant input filtering.**

driven by a discrete-time control system

$$u(k) = -9r(k)$$

where $r(k)$ is the reference input and where the sampling interval is $T = 5$. The plant characteristic equation is

$$s^2 + 0.6s + 9 = (s + 0.3 + j2.98)(s + 0.3 - j2.98) = 0$$

which means that its zero-input response is of the form

$$\bar{y}_{\text{zero-input}}(t) = Me^{-0.3t}\cos(2.98t + \theta)$$

where $M$ and $\theta$ are arbitrary constants. While for the sampling interval $T = 5$ there are no hidden oscillations, the highly undamped zero-input plant response results in large fluctuations ("ringing") of the tracking output each time there is a step change in the plant input by the controller.

The plant response is improved considerably by the insertion of a plant input filter with transfer function

$$G(s) = \frac{\frac{1}{3}}{s + \frac{1}{3}}$$

as is shown in Figure 7-5(b). This first-order filter was designed heuristically; its 3-second time constant was chosen to smooth the plant input waveform during each five-second sampling interval, resulting in much less ringing of the tracking output. This filter is realized by the state variable equations

$$\dot{\varepsilon}(t) = -\tfrac{1}{3}\varepsilon(t) + \tfrac{1}{3}w(t)$$

$$u(t) = \varepsilon(t)$$

and now it is the composite third-order system

$$\begin{bmatrix} \dot{x}_1(t) \\ \dot{x}_2(t) \\ \dot{\varepsilon}(t) \end{bmatrix} = \begin{bmatrix} -0.6 & 1 & -1 \\ -9 & 0 & 1 \\ 0 & 0 & -\frac{1}{3} \end{bmatrix} \begin{bmatrix} x_1(t) \\ x_2(t) \\ \varepsilon(t) \end{bmatrix} + \begin{bmatrix} 0 \\ 0 \\ \frac{1}{3} \end{bmatrix} w(t)$$

$$\bar{y}(t) = \begin{bmatrix} 1 & 0 & 0 \end{bmatrix} \begin{bmatrix} x_1(t) \\ x_2(t) \\ \varepsilon(t) \end{bmatrix}$$

that the controller must control. Here,

$$w(k) = -9r(k)$$

In general, insertion of a plant input filter with transfer function matrix $\mathbf{G}(s)$ before a plant with transfer function matrix $\mathbf{T}(s)$ results in a composite continuous-time *model plant* with transfer function matrix

$$\mathbf{M}(s) = \mathbf{G}(s)\mathbf{T}(s)$$

Designing analog plant input filters is quite similar to designing discrete-time reference input filters, although the former are continuous-time. The objective of the design is to improve the between-sample plant response, and this is done by obtaining a model plant with acceptable step response. With a plant input filter, the order of the continuous-time plant is raised, which might result in a different controller design than for the plant without the input filter.

As a simple example of analog plant input filter design, consider again the continuous-time plant (7-6) with transfer function

$$T(s) = \bar{\mathbf{c}}^\dagger(s\mathbf{I} - \mathscr{A})^{-1}\boldsymbol{b} = \frac{-s + 1}{s^2 + 0.6s + 9}$$

A plant input filter with transfer function

$$G(s) = \frac{s^2 + 0.6s + 9}{(s + 1)^2} = 1 + \frac{-1.4s + 8}{s^2 + 2s + 1}$$

cancels the plant poles and results in a model plant transfer function

$$M(s) = G(s)T(s) = \frac{-s + 1}{(s + 1)^2}$$

If the plant model is imperfectly known, exact pole cancellation is not possible, but approximate cancellation will still reduce the effects of those poles on the plant's step response. This plant input filter is realized by the state equations (in observable form for convenience)

$$\begin{bmatrix} \dot{\varepsilon}_1(t) \\ \dot{\varepsilon}_2(t) \end{bmatrix} = \begin{bmatrix} -2 & 1 \\ -1 & 0 \end{bmatrix} \begin{bmatrix} \varepsilon_1(t) \\ \varepsilon_2(t) \end{bmatrix} + \begin{bmatrix} -1.4 \\ 8 \end{bmatrix} w(t)$$

$$u(t) = \begin{bmatrix} 1 & 0 \end{bmatrix} \begin{bmatrix} \varepsilon_1(t) \\ \varepsilon_2(t) \end{bmatrix} + w(t)$$

so that the combination of plant and filter are described by

$$\begin{bmatrix} \dot{x}_1(t) \\ \dot{x}_2(t) \\ \dot{\varepsilon}_1(t) \\ \dot{\varepsilon}_2(t) \end{bmatrix} = \begin{bmatrix} -0.6 & 1 & -1 & 0 \\ -9 & 0 & 1 & 0 \\ 0 & 0 & -2 & 1 \\ 0 & 0 & -1 & 0 \end{bmatrix} \begin{bmatrix} x_1(t) \\ x_2(t) \\ \varepsilon_1(t) \\ \varepsilon_2(t) \end{bmatrix} + \begin{bmatrix} -1 \\ 1 \\ -1.4 \\ 8 \end{bmatrix} w(t)$$

$$\bar{y}(t) = \begin{bmatrix} 1 & 0 & 0 & 0 \end{bmatrix} \begin{bmatrix} x_1(t) \\ x_2(t) \\ \varepsilon_1(t) \\ \varepsilon_2(t) \end{bmatrix}$$

A discrete-time controller

$$w(k) = -r(k)$$

like the previous ones, makes the plant an observer of any constant reference input. The resulting response is shown in Figure 7-5(c). The original plant's zero-input response, excited by nonzero plant initial conditions, is apparent at first but eventually decays to zero.

## 7.3.2 Higher-Rate Digital Filtering and Feedback

Another way of doing plant input filtering is to use a digital filter that operates at many times the rate of the controller, as indicated in Figure 7-6. Analog-to-digital conversion is usually done with repeated approximations, one for each bit. With a given technology, one can do several D/A conversions as fast as one A/D conversion can be done. The cost of a digital plant input filter is thus relatively low because it requires higher D/A, not A/D, speed.

As an example, consider the continuous-time plant (7-6) again. The discrete-time controller for this plant operates with a sampling interval $T = 5$. An analog filter with transfer function

$$G(s) = \frac{\frac{1}{3}}{s + \frac{1}{3}}$$

was earlier found to improve the plant's between-sample behavior. The step response of the plant alone and the response of the plant with this input filter are shown in Figure 7-7(a).

A state variable realization of the analog filter is

$$\dot{\varepsilon}(t) = -\tfrac{1}{3}\varepsilon(t) + \tfrac{1}{3}w(t)$$

$$u(t) = \varepsilon(t)$$

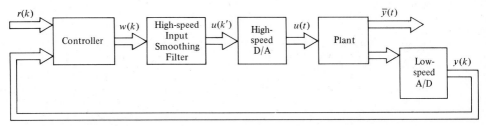

**FIGURE 7-6.** Use of high-speed digital plant input filtering to improve between-sample response.

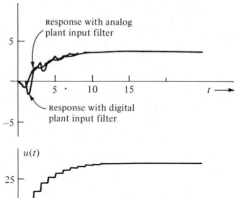

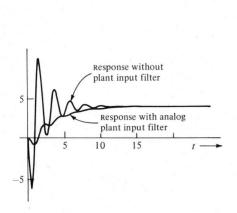

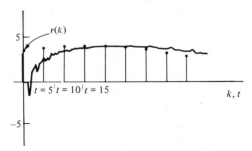

(a)  Step response of the example system, with and without an analog input filter.

(b)  Step response with the analog input filter and with a digital input filter.

(c)  Tracking response of the system with the digital plant input filter.

**FIGURE 7-7.   Improvement of between-sample plant response with high-speed digital input filtering.**

A discrete-time model of this filter with sampling interval $\Delta t = 1$, one-fifth the controller interval, is

$$\varepsilon(k' + 1) = 0.717\varepsilon(k') + 0.283w(k')$$

$$u(k') = \varepsilon(k')$$

where $k'$ is the index for steps of size $\Delta t$. The step response of the plant with the digital filter that approximates the continuous-time filter is shown in Figure 7-7(b). Figure 7-7(c) is a tracking response plot for the combination of plant, high-speed digital plant input filter, and lower-speed digital controller.

A discrete-time model for the plant with sampling interval $\Delta t = 1$ is

$$\mathbf{x}(k' + 1) = [\exp(\mathscr{A}\Delta t)]\mathbf{x}(k') + [\exp(\mathscr{A}\Delta t) - \mathbf{I}]\mathscr{A}^{-1}\mathcal{b}u(k')$$

$$y(k') = \bar{\mathbf{c}}^{\dagger}\mathbf{x}(k')$$

or

$$\begin{bmatrix} x_1(k' + 1) \\ x_2(k' + 1) \end{bmatrix} = \begin{bmatrix} -0.743 & 0.0387 \\ -0.348 & -0.720 \end{bmatrix} \begin{bmatrix} x_1(k') \\ x_2(k') \end{bmatrix} + \begin{bmatrix} 0.152 \\ 1.87 \end{bmatrix} u(k')$$

The composite system consisting of this model and the digital filter is

$$\begin{bmatrix} x_1(k' + 1) \\ x_2(k' + 1) \\ \varepsilon(k' + 1) \end{bmatrix} = \begin{bmatrix} -0.743 & 0.0387 & 0.152 \\ -0.348 & 0.720 & 1.87 \\ 0 & 0 & 0.717 \end{bmatrix} \begin{bmatrix} x_1(k') \\ x_2(k') \\ \varepsilon(k') \end{bmatrix} + \begin{bmatrix} 0 \\ 0 \\ 0.283 \end{bmatrix} w(k')$$

$$= \mathbf{A}\mathbf{x}(k') + \mathbf{b}w(k')$$

$$\bar{y}(k') = \begin{bmatrix} 1 & 0 & 0 \end{bmatrix} \begin{bmatrix} x_1(k') \\ x_2(k') \\ \varepsilon(k') \end{bmatrix} = \bar{\mathbf{c}}^{\dagger}\mathbf{x}(k')$$

The discrete-time model of the plant and filter with steps $k$ and the sampling interval $T = 5\Delta t$ is given by

$$\mathbf{x}(k' + 5) = \mathbf{A}^5\mathbf{x}(k') + \mathbf{A}^4\mathbf{b}w(k') + \mathbf{A}^3\mathbf{b}w(k' + 1)$$
$$+ \mathbf{A}^2\mathbf{b}w(k' + 2) + \mathbf{A}\mathbf{b}w(k' + 3) + \mathbf{b}w(k' + 4)$$

$$\bar{y}(k' + 5) = \bar{\mathbf{c}}^{\dagger}\mathbf{x}(k')$$

but since the controller output $w(k')$ changes only every fifth $k'$ step,

$$\mathbf{x}(k' + 5) = \mathbf{x}(k + 1) = \mathbf{A}^5\mathbf{x}(k) + [\mathbf{A}^4 + \mathbf{A}^3 + \mathbf{A}^2 + \mathbf{A} + \mathbf{I}]\mathbf{b}w(k)$$

$$\bar{y}(k) = \bar{\mathbf{c}}^{\dagger}\mathbf{x}(k)$$

This is now the discrete-time plant model to be used for the controller design.

Higher-rate digital plant feedback can also be used to improve a plant's between-sample response, but this requires high-rate A/D as well as high-rate

D/A conversion. Another possibility is to sample the plant measurement outputs at the lower rate, but estimate the plant state at a high rate, feeding the state estimate back at high rate.

### 7.3.3 Higher-Order Holds

A traditional approach to improving reconstruction is to employ higher-order holds than the zeroth-order one. An $n$th-order hold produces a piecewise $n$th-degree polynomial output that passes through the most recent $n + 1$ input samples. It can be shown that, as the order of the hold is increased, a well-behaved signal is reconstructed with increasing accuracy. Several holds and their typical response are shown in Figure 7-8.

While higher-order holds do have a smoothing effect on the plant inputs, the resulting improvement of plant between-sample response is generally poor compared to that possible with a conventional filter of comparable complexity. Hardware for holds of higher than zero-order (which is the sample-and-hold operation) is not routinely available from manufacturers. One approach is to employ high-speed digital devices and D/A conversion, as in the technique of Figure 7-6, but where the high-speed input smoothing filter performs the interpolation calculations for a hold.

## 7.4 Digital Hardware for Control

The specifics of the hardware used for realization of a digital control system are highly dependent on the application involved and the state of technology. Nonetheless, it will be helpful to now discuss some general hardware considerations that are not likely to be obsolete in the near future. On the horizon, but not yet sufficiently developed for enduringly relevant discussion here are efficient use of the enormous processing capacity of VLSI chips, the blinding speed promised by massively parallel architectures, and the seemingly limitless storage capacity of laser disks and similar devices. All of these may greatly influence future directions in digital control.

### 7.4.1 Processing with General-Purpose Computers

The hardware available for the computations involved in digital control includes the following:

large mainframe computers,
minicomputers,

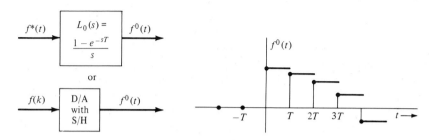

(a) Zeroth-order hold.

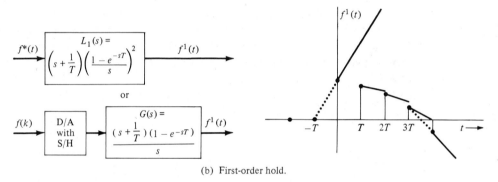

(b) First-order hold.

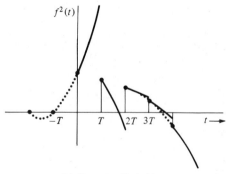

(c) Second-order hold.

**FIGURE 7-8. Typical response of holds.**

desktop (personal) computers,
microprocessors,
special-purpose devices such as signal processing, and multiplier-accumulator chips.

In addition, some manufacturers offer computers that are especially designed for control applications.

Figure 7-9 shows a general-purpose computer architecture similar to that of many IBM mainframe computers and of Intel microprocessors in the 8080A and the 8086 through 8286 and 80386 series. The *central processor unit* (CPU) accesses memory and peripherial devices through separate channels. *Read-only memory* (ROM), which cannot be erased or changed electronically, is used for the *bootstrap* instructions that begin processing and perhaps for other instructions. *Random access memory* (RAM) is used for temporary high-speed storage. Its contents are probably destroyed whenever the computer power is turned off.

In small microprocessor-based control systems, the main program is usually stored in ROM so that it cannot be inadvertently changed or erased. For larger control systems, the main program is commonly stored on disk memory and is transferred to the faster-operating RAM by bootstrap instructions just after the computer system is turned on. In the system shown,

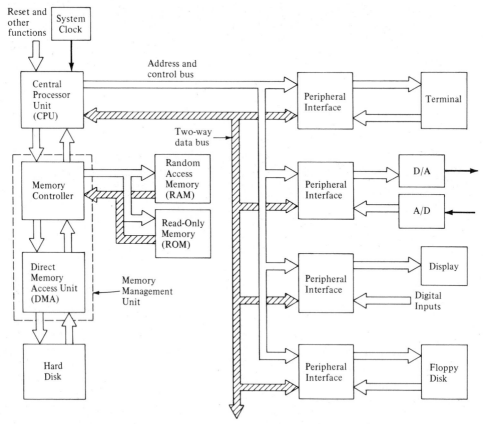

**FIGURE 7-9.    A general-purpose computer architecture where the CPU separately controls memory and peripheral devices.**

the disk memory can access the RAM directly, without having to pass through (and tie up) the CPU. This capability is called *direct memory access* (DMA). It allows blocks of data to be transferred very rapidly between disk and RAM, usually interleaved between RAM memory accesses by the CPU. The combination of the memory circuits and any DMA circuitry is called the computer's *memory controller*. In microprocessor systems, the CPU, memory controller, perhaps even with some DMA capability, might be combined on the same chip.

Input and output from this computer is via *peripheral interface* circuits. These receive data from external devices, store it, and send it to the CPU when it is needed. They also receive data from the CPU for transmission to external devices. In most computers, the peripheral interfaces share common sets of wires, called *busses*, for communicating with the CPU. One bus is an address and control bus from the CPU to the peripheral interfaces, used for designating an interface and transmitting an instruction to it. The other is two-way data bus for transferring data to and from the CPU.

In the general-purpose computer architecture of Figure 7-10, memory and peripheral devices share the same address and data busses, an arrangement termed *memory-mapped input/output* (I/O). The peripheral interfaces contain registers for instructions and to transfer data to and from the CPU. These registers are addressed as if they were memory locations. This architecture is similar to that of many DEC computers and of Motorola microprocessors in the 6800 and 68000 series.

Multiprocessor architectures are common, particularly for micro-processor-based digital control systems. Figure 7-11 describes a system with separate processors for program control and for computation. The program control processor executes the main program for control, but passes the required lengthy observer-controller state and output calculations to a second processor. The second processor is, in turn, aided by a *coprocessor*, which is a device that performs precision arithmetic computations at high speed. The data acquisition and distribution system might involve a third processor. The advantages of multiprocessing include increased effective processing speed and the ability to gain and build long-term experience with subsystems for standardized functions.

Another common multiprocessor arrangement is one in which individual processors are placed in several different locations, each near a cluster of plant sensors and actuators. Figure 7-12(a) shows a diagram of such an arrangement. Often, the local computers each constitute smaller control systems. These subsystems are then joined and controlled overall by the central computer. Complicated plants, such as those for manufacturing, can thus be divided into smaller, more tractable subsystems to be controlled. Once locally controlled, control of the collection of subsystems is generally much simplified. Changes in subsystem hardware and software are usually

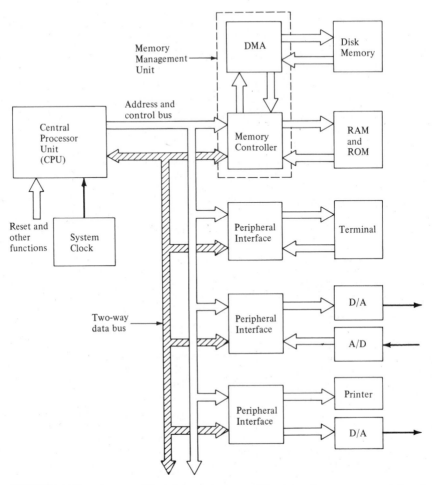

**FIGURE 7-10.** **A general-purpose computer architecture where memory and peripheral devices share the same address space.**

easier to make than in a wholly central system because it is easier to isolate each subsystem and its interface.

In a *distributed control system,* all of the control is done by a collection of local computers that share information; there is no central controller. Figure 7-12(b) describes such a system. In this example, additional storage and computational ability is available to the local computers from a shared resource. It may be possible to design distributed systems that will withstand component failures and have a flexibility and adaptability similar to that exhibited by some organisms and social systems. Each local computer would

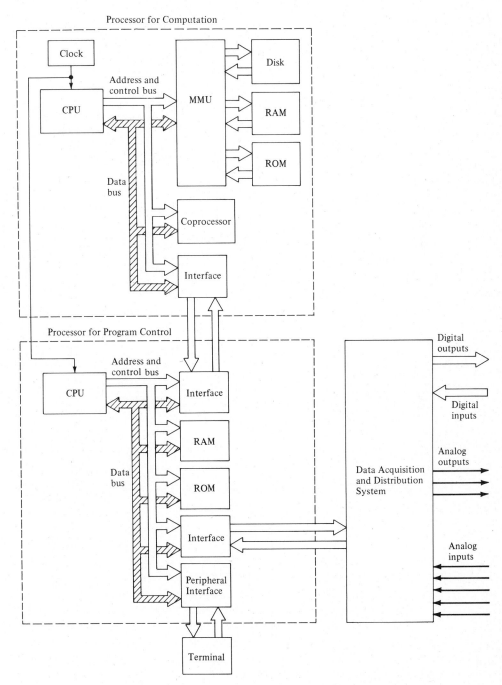

**FIGURE 7-11.  A multiprocessor architecture for a centralized controller.**

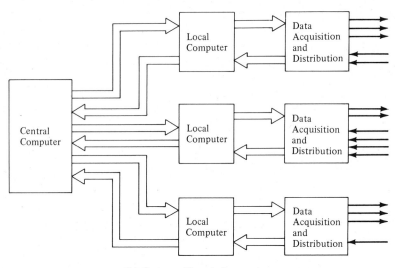

(a)  System with central computer.

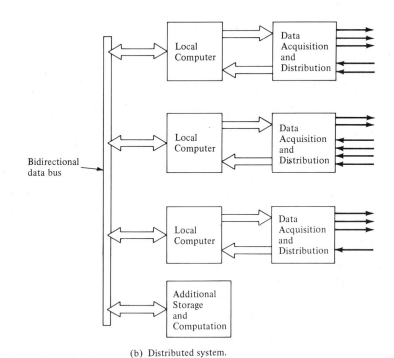

(b)  Distributed system.

**FIGURE 7-12.   Multiprocessor arrangements.**

operate according to local principles and objectives, the collection of which gives good overall system control. A distributed control system's parts can be linked by a *local area network* (LAN).

## 7.4.2 Data Acquisition and Distribution

Digital control systems require that signal samples be collected from sensors of plant outputs and that samples be delivered to actuators at plant inputs. Most often in practice, the sensors and actuators are analog devices so that analog-to-digital (A/D) and digital-to-analog (D/A) conversion is needed. Data acquisition is the A/D conversion of a set of analog sensor signals and the transmission of their samples to a digital processor. Usually, samples from several sensors are collected and sent one at a time, reducing the number of needed wires and connections to the processor. One type of data acquisition system is shown in Figure 7-13(a). To obtain signal samples all at the same time, the sensor signals are sampled by individual sample-and-hold (S/H) devices and converted to binary digital representations by individual A/D converters. The processor provides a sequence of digital codes that cause a digital multiplexer to transmit the sensor samples, one after the other, to the processor.

A single A/D converter is shared for each of the sensor signal conversions in the configuration of Figure 7-13(b). As before, separate S/H devices are used so that all samples are taken at the same time. An analog multiplexer selects one then the next signal sample for conversion to binary code. To sequentially convert $m$ sensor signals during each sampling interval, the A/D converter in this configuration must operate $m$ times as rapidly as each A/D converter must in the configuration of Figure 7-13(a).

The arrangement of Figure 7-13(c) is more common than either of the other two because its hardware is simpler. A single S/H and a single A/D converter are shared by each of the signals to be converted. The resulting samples are taken at different instants of time during each sampling interval. These *time offsets* complicate the control system design only to the extent of needing a modified discrete-time model of the continuous-time system to be controlled. With time offsets, the discrete-time model can be of higher order because parts of two successive sampled-and-held inputs can affect the plant state at each step.

Several multiple-output data distribution systems are shown in Figure 7-14. In the first, Figure 7-14(a), binary digital samples are sent from the processor, one set at a time, and stored in digital registers. The contents of the registers are converted by individual D/A converters, then individual S/H devices are used so that each of the analog output signals changes only at the sampling times. A single D/A converter is shared by each of the actuator

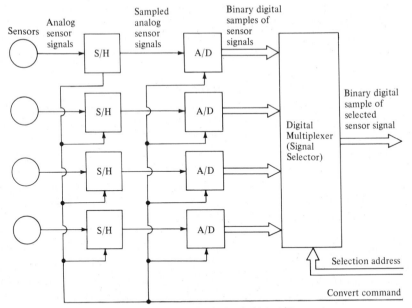

(a)  Simultaneous input sampling using multiple A/D converters.

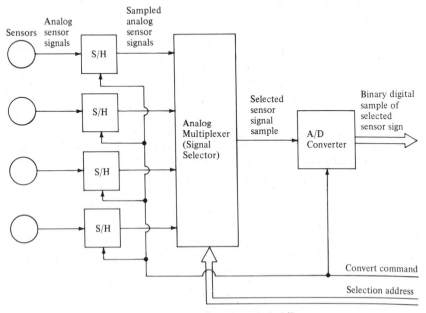

(b)  Simultaneous input sampling using a single A/D converter.

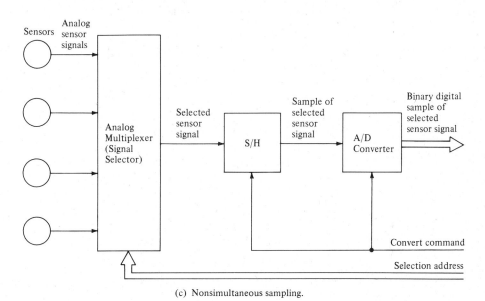

(c) Nonsimultaneous sampling.

**FIGURE 7-13.** **Some multiple-input data acquisition arrangements.**

signals in the configuration of Figure 7-14(b), where an analog demultiplexer is used to distribute the sequentially converted signals for storage in individual S/H circuits. For $m$ signals converted during each sampling interval, the single shared D/A converter must operate $m$ times as rapidly as individual D/A converters. So that the analog output signals each change only at the sampling times, a second set of S/H circuits is used.

The most common data distribution arrangement is that of Figure 7-14(c), which uses a single D/A converter and only one S/H device for each output. The output signals change one at a time, as each conversion is completed, not all at the same time. It is straightforward to account for this nonsimultaneous reconstruction when deriving the discrete-time model of the continuous-time plant.

Data acquisition and distribution systems also commonly contain analog *prefilters* and *postfilters*. The prefilters attenuate unwanted high frequencies from incoming continuous-time signals before they are sampled and A/D converted; usually those frequencies above half the sampling rate are removed so that the converted signal is uniquely described by its samples. Postfiltering is analog plant input filtering to smooth changes in the plant inputs after D/A conversion of the plant input samples.

The time used to process incoming and outgoing samples cannot exceed the sampling interval. Similarly, a cycle of data transmissions, A/D, and D/A conversions must be completed during each sampling interval. Even so,

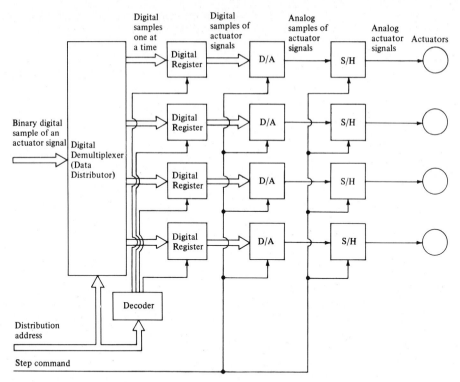

(a) Simultaneous output changes using multiple D/A converters.

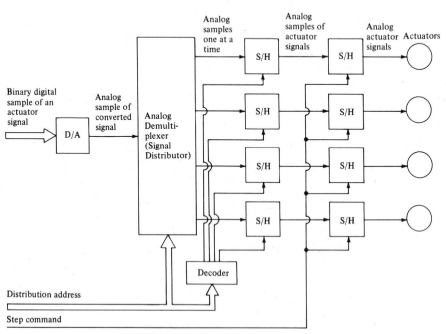

(b) Simultaneous output changes using a single D/A converter.

**436**

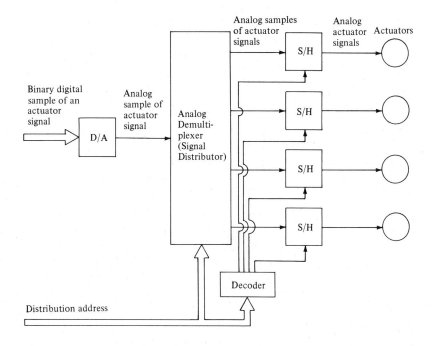

(c) Non-simultaneous output changes.

**FIGURE 7-14. Some multiple-output data distribution arrangements.**

especially in high-rate systems, the total time needed to do both the processing and conversions can be more than one sampling interval, in which event one must account for a *processing delay* in the system model.

### 7.4.3 Processing with Special Purpose Hardware

General-purpose computer hardware has the advantages of low cost for the functions provided, a base of application experience, and the availability of sophisticated programming tools. Special-purpose hardware is also available for the designer who needs higher-speed operation and for high-volume applications where the hardware development and manufacturing costs are justified. Among the special-purpose devices available are microprocessors designed especially for certain types of signal processing and chips for specific signal processing functions such as multiplication.

A multiplier-accumulator is a device for rapidly calculating sums of products of numbers, a function that is central to the implementation of difference equations. It typically has two sets of input connections, called input *ports*, one for each binary representation of the two numbers to be multiplied. The product of the two incoming numbers is added to any previous result and stored in an accumulator register connected to an output port. Additional connections control the chip's timing and allow the user to reset the accumulator contents to zero.

Figure 7-15 is a diagram of the hardware for a second-order controller

$$\begin{bmatrix} \xi_1(k+1) \\ \xi_2(k+1) \end{bmatrix} = \begin{bmatrix} 0 & 1 \\ -\frac{5}{6} & -\frac{1}{6} \end{bmatrix} \begin{bmatrix} \xi_1(k) \\ \xi_2(k) \end{bmatrix} + \begin{bmatrix} 0 \\ 1 \end{bmatrix} r(k)$$

$$u(k) = \begin{bmatrix} \frac{1}{2} & -\frac{3}{5} \end{bmatrix} \begin{bmatrix} \xi_1(k) \\ \xi_2(k) \end{bmatrix} + r(k) \tag{7-7}$$

using a multiplier-accumulator (M/A) chip. The clock and counter generate a sequence of ROM addresses, the contents of which control which of several digital signals is applied to one port of the M/A, the coefficient that is applied to the other M/A port, and where the M/A output is to be sent. The ROM additionally provides a signal that can reset the accumulator to zero and a signal that can activate the shift registers.

At the first count, the accumulator is reset and the binary signal representing $r$ is multiplied by unity and added to the accumulator. At the second count, $\xi_1$ is selected, multiplied by 1/2 and added to the accumulator. At count three, $\xi_2$ is selected, multiplied by $-3/5$, and added to the accumulator. The M/A output now is the new value of the output $u$, which is transferred to the D/A converter.

At count four, the accumulator is reset to zero, $r$ is selected, multiplied by unity, and added to the accumulator. At count five, $\xi_1$ is selected, multiplied by $-5/6$, and added to the accumulator. The binary signal representing $\xi_2$ is selected at count six, multiplied by $-1/6$, and added to the accumulator so that the M/A output now holds the new value of $\xi_2$. The shift registers are clocked, and this new value of $\xi_2$ is stored in the register to the left while the new $\xi_1$, which is the old $\xi_2$ is moved to the rightmost shift register. The output generation and state updating cycle then repeats.

This hardware arrangement constitutes a special-purpose stored program computer that executes the same cycle of instructions over and over. The counter specifies the address of the current instruction and the ROM output is the instruction code.

Another dedicated hardware option for the controller (7-7) is shown in Figure 7-16. Here, individual multipliers and adders are interconnected to generate the needed signals. As in the previous example, these are represented by *fixed-point* binary numbers. The adders and multipliers are arranged to accommodate both negative and positive numbers. The controller state variables $\xi_1$ and $\xi_2$ are stored in shift registers as before. Each clock cycle, the

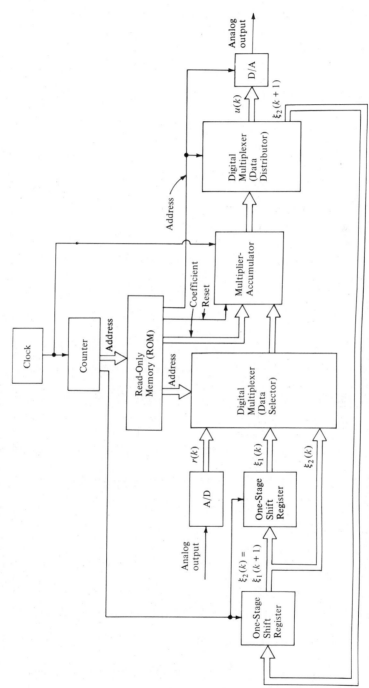

**FIGURE 7-15.** Hardware for a second-order single-input, single-output digital controller using a multiplier-accumulator controlled by a sequencer.

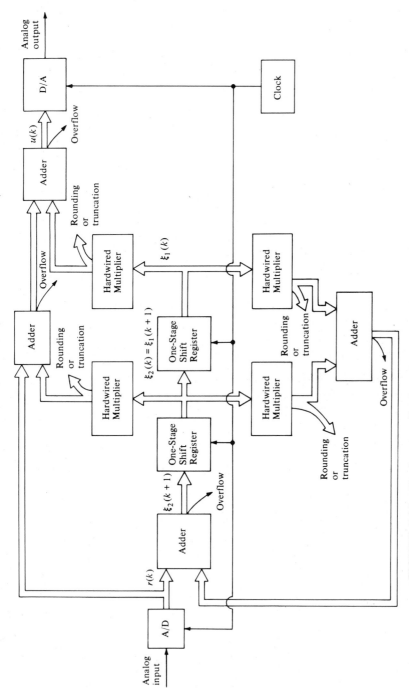

**FIGURE 7-16. Hardware realization of a second-order single-input, single-output digital controller using hardwired multipliers. No software is involved.**

old $\xi_2$, is shifted into the right register to become the new $\xi_1$ and the new $\xi_2$ is shifted into the left register. The new $\xi_2$ is formed by multiplying the old $\xi_1$ by $-5/6$, multiplying the old $\xi_2$ by $-1/6$, adding, and adding to $r$, as shown. To form the output, $\xi_2$ is multiplied by $-3/5$, added to $r$, then added to $(1/2)\,\xi_1$. Because this design doesn't share a multiplier-adder, it has the potential of higher-speed operation than the previous hardware.

If the number of bits representing each signal is not to grow as the computations proceed, the results of multiplications must be rounded or truncated, since the product of two $m$-bit binary numbers is a $2m$-bit number. Similarly, the sum of two $m$-bit binary numbers can require $m + 1$ bits, so there is the possibility of an *overflow* condition at each adder. The design in Figure 7-16 shows the roundings or truncations and the possible overflows in the design.

Controller hardware can alternatively be configured for *floating-point* representations and arithmetic. Inaccuracies due to numerical truncations or roundings still occur, but a wider range of numbers can be accommodated with the same number of bits than when the position of the binary point is fixed. Floating-point multiplication involves multiplication of mantissas, addition of exponents, and shifting of the result as necessary to keep the binary point of the mantissa of the product at a fixed position. Floating-point addition requires mantissa addition and possibly shifting. Multiplier, adder, and multiplier-accumulator chips that perform floating-point computations are available. They are generally more complicated (and thus more expensive) and somewhat slower in operation than their fixed-point counterparts.

# 7.5 Computer Software for Control

Like digital hardware, software needs for computer control are likely to continue to evolve rapidly in the foreseeable future. In this section, some general software considerations are discussed that complement the discussion of digital control system hardware in the previous section. Standard networking interfaces and protocols, virtual memory, expert systems, artificial intelligence, and increasingly capable and sophisticated dedicated signal processing chips promise much for the future.

## 7.5.1 Main Program Structures

As the art of computer programming has matured, the sophistication of programming languages and other available aid has increased. At the most primitive level, that of *binary machine code*, each string of ones and zeros representing an instruction is stored in memory. It is unusual for a designer to deal directly with binary codes because it is a simple matter to use another computer for aid in translating a more human-friendly alphanumeric *mnemonic machine code* to the binary code equivalents. When the programmer can use symbols to represent addresses and other quantities in a machine code program, the program is said to be written in an *assembly language*, which requires the use of a more sophisticated assembler program to generate the corresponding binary machine code.

High-level languages deal with more abstract instructions and divorce the programmer from the underlying machine code. The needed machine code is obtained with a program that *compiles* the higher-level statements into machine language instructions. The same Basic, Pascal, or other high-level language program can run on computers with different sets of machine instructions if each has a compiler that converts high-level instructions to the machine instructions peculiar to each computer.

High-level languages are usually less efficient than lower-level ones; that is, they tend to produce machine language programs that take longer to execute than when the program is written directly in machine language. However, when the required hardware and speed of operation is adequate, use of a higher-level language is greatly preferred because the entire program is far easier and faster to develop, debug, and modify. There is the possibility, too, that a high-level language program will be *portable*; that is, it will also run on other computers with different machine language instruction sets.

Programs for digital control are said to operate in *real time*, meaning that the computer processes data as it arrives, not as a "batch." The structure of a simple digital controller program is shown in Figure 7-17. The sampling rate is maintained by a periodic signal called the step clock (perhaps generated externally) that informs the processor each time a new set of measurement and reference samples are to be processed and a new set of plant input samples are to be produced. The program begins with initialization. Each controller state variable is set to zero, and other variables used in the program are given initial values. Possibly, digital signals are sent to turn on external equipment and to test whether it is functioning properly.

When the initialization is complete, the program waits for the step clock to indicate that a new set of measurement and reference samples is to be processed. Then, those samples are transferred, under program control, to specific processor memory locations. The new controller states and outputs are computed and the outputs are transferred for data distribution to the plant inputs. This program then checks to see if shutdown of the system is to be done. If so, it executes a series of instructions to turn off the system in an orderly manner. These might involve, for example, a gradual tapering to zero of some, or all, of the plant inputs. If shutdown is not to be done, the program again waits for the step clock to indicate that new measurement and reference samples are to be processed.

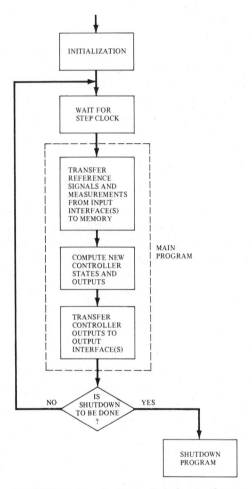

**FIGURE 7-17.   A simple digital control program structure.**

Computers for control are often also used to collect data about system performance and to carry out routine testing and other functions. These "housekeeping" tasks are done when there is otherwise unused processing time available, as when the program is waiting to begin the next discrete-time step. These tasks can be *stacked* so that when the processor is available for them it resumes processing where it last left off, continuing until it must return to its control function. When it must return, the contents of all CPU registers needed, including the one containing the address of the next "housekeeping" instruction, are stored in memory, to be recalled later.

Instead of controlling the sampling times with a step clock, the input, output, and computation operations can be interleaved and the CPU clock used to control the rate and timing of sampling. For a given CPU clock frequency, the time spacing of data transfers and the rate at which the entire loop of the program is traversed depends on the number of instructions executed and the number of CPU clock cycles needed for each instruction. This kind of program structure is simple, but it is difficult to modify because any modification of the program can change the program's timing. It is usually necessary to do the programming in assembly language rather than a higher-level language.

## 7.5.2 *Subroutines and Interrupt Structures*

Instead of stringing all the instructions in the order of their execution in a complicated program, an experienced programmer will likely decompose the program into coherent parts and code each of the parts as a subroutine. The main program will then consist mostly of subroutine calls, as in the example program structure in Figure 7-18. When a subroutine is called, the CPU saves the address of the next instruction in the main program and any other CPU register contents being used before it executes the series of instructions in the subroutine. When the subroutine is completed, the CPU returns to execution of the main program. It is a simple matter to arrange things so that subroutines can call other subroutines. One advantage of using subroutines is that the individual parts of a program can be developed and modified separately. Another advantage is that repetitive portions of the code need be included only once. Also, the main program, consisting as it does mostly of subroutine calls, is easier to follow.

An *interrupt* is a method for an external device to easily and quickly signal its need for attention to the CPU. When the CPU receives an interrupt, it completes execution of the current instruction, stores the address of the next instruction in memory, then jumps to the execution of an interrupt service routine. The interrupt service routine saves the contents of any CPU registers that should later be restored, determines which device sent the interrupt, and does the necessary processing required by that interrupt. When the interrupt processing has been completed, the CPU returns to processing the original stream of instructions.

A very useful interrupt device is the *timer* which consists of a counter driven by the system clock. The CPU is able to load the counter with a number specifying the number of clock cycles until a new interrupt signal is to be sent. A timer would likely be used for the step clock in the program structures of Figures 7-17 and 7-18.

A *nonmaskable interrupt* is one that will not be ignored by the CPU. Upon its receipt, without fail, a jump is made to the interrupt service routine after execution of the current instruction. A *maskable interrupt* is one that can be

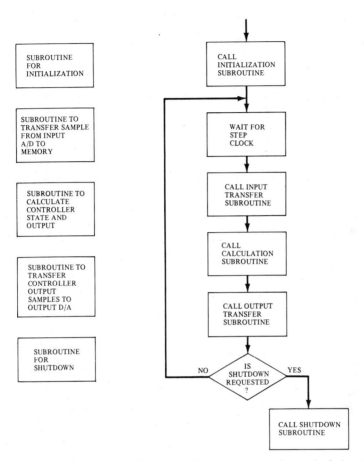

**FIGURE 7-18.   A simple subroutine arrangement for a single-input, single-output digital controller.**

turned off (or masked) by the program until an appropriate time for its service. A computer power failure in progress and emergency shutdown commands would likely be arranged as unmaskable interrupts. The signal that a new sample is available from a data acquisition system might be masked until it is time for the sample to be incorporated into the calculations.

Figure 7-19 shows hardware connections for interrupts. In the arrangement of Figure 7-19(a), the interrupts from each of several devices are separately wired to the CPU. When the interrupt is being serviced, the CPU sends an interrupt acknowledge signal back to the device. Upon receipt of the acknowledge signal, the device transfers data via a common data bus. For more than a very few devices, this arrangement uses many wires, so the configuration of Figure 7-19(b) is often preferable. Here, single interrupt

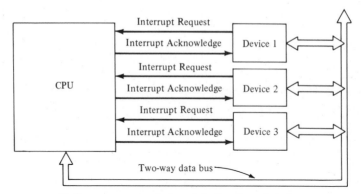

(a) Separate request and acknowledge lines for each device.

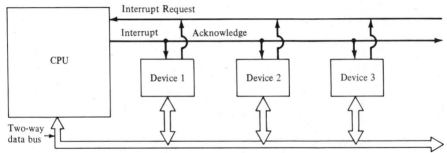

(b) Common request and acknowledge lines. After reception of a request, the processor polls the devices to determine the highest-priority device that has requested an interrupt.

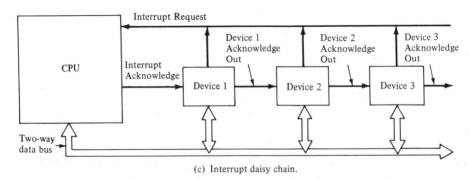

(c) Interrupt daisy chain.

**FIGURE 7-19. Some interrupt hardware arrangements.**

request and interrupt acknowledge lines are shared by all the devices. When an interrupt request is received by the CPU, it acknowledges the request, which temporarily prevents the sending of new requests. The CPU then addresses the devices, in order of their priority, via the data bus to determine the highest-priority device that has requested an interrupt, a procedure called *polling*. An interrupting device can identify itself by sending a second interrupt request signal when its address appears on the data bus.

A third hardware connection for interrupts, the daisy chain, is described in Figure 7-19(c). Devices send their interrupt requests on a common line, but the interrupt acknowledge signal is passed on to the next device only if the previous device has not requested an interrupt. Eventually the acknowledge signal reaches an interrupting device which does not pass it on, and the interrupting device identifies itself to the CPU via the data bus. The order of priority of the interrupts is their order in the chain from the CPU.

An example of the structure of a program for a single-input, single-output digital controller that uses subroutines and interrupts is given in Figure 7-20. Emergency shutdown and power loss conditions are serviced immediately. Each discrete-time step is timed by an external clock that also drives the A/D and D/A converters. When this program is ready to process an input sample, it temporarily unmasks the A/D interrupt and waits until the sample is ready. Similarly, when the program is ready to send a new controller output sample, it temporarily unmasks the D/A interrupt and waits until the sample can be received.

### 7.5.3 Software Design, Test and Modification

Every experienced programmer knows the importance of *designing* software, using many of the same steps that are used in good hardware design. It is particularly important to carefully structure the program at several levels, from the initial "large blocks," to the interrupt structure and subroutines, to the detailed sequences of instructions. Each level of design is modified as conflicts are resolved and as improvements are developed. As there is a high probability that the designer and others will need to understand and perhaps modify the program at a later time, contrary as it is to human nature, clear and complete documentation is essential.

Control system hardware and software is usually tested by simulation in several ways before it is connected to the plant it is to control. At first, the basic controller equations are tested in much the same way as the typical response figures were produced for the design examples in this chapter. The idea is to verify expected properties of the design (such as speed of response and steady state error) and to uncover shortcomings (such as the need for an unreasonably large control signal or high susceptibility to small errors)

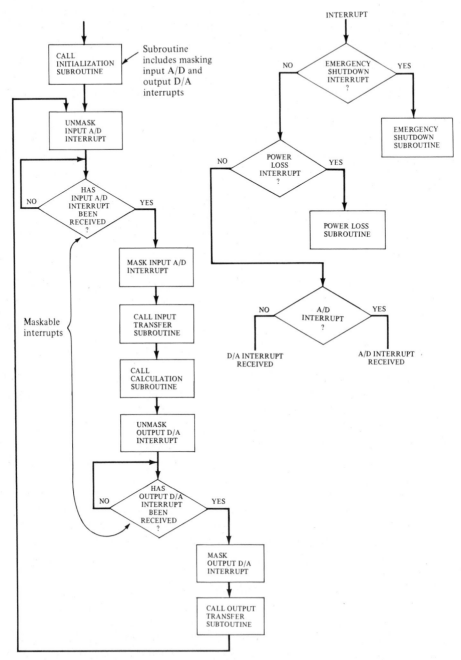

**FIGURE 7-20.   A subroutine and interrupt arrangement for a single-input, single-output digital controller.**

before proceeding further. Later, most of the complete program is tested using simulated measurement samples. Then the controller hardware-software combination can be tested with simulated analog sensor signals.

A particularly intriguing problem is that of designing hardware and software for control that is able to automatically adapt to failures of some sensors and actuators, still maintaining good control of the plant. Sensor failures usually result in unreasonable (such as zero) or inconsistent measurements. Actuator failures might be inferred from measurements by nearby sensors or from the errors between actual and calculated plant performance. If these failures are identified by the control program, then the controller can be changed to ignore measurements from defective sensors and not to depend on defective actuators.

The design of a program that adapts to failures in a large system such as a power plant is formidable. If there can be 100 different failures and, say up to four failures can be present at once, then the program might be required to have as many as

$$N = 1 + 100 + \tfrac{1}{2}(100)(99) + \tfrac{1}{6}(100)(99)(98) + \tfrac{1}{24}(100)(99)(98)(97)$$

different possibilities for the controller. The program might have only 100 different branches, one for each individual failure, but there could be on the order of 4 million different combinations possible. Testing all of these is probably quite impractical, and the alternative is using an untested system for control.

The results of simulation and operation almost invariably lead to hardware and software modifications; this observation underscores the need for well-documented, easily read programs.

# 7.6 Design Examples

We now consider discrete-time control of two example continuous-time systems. Although these system are of relatively low order, there is much to learn from each. The first system, a sophisticated elevator position controller, includes a saturation nonlinearity. This kind of model and the control strategy used is quite common in practice. The second example system, a simplified version of an undersea robotic torsional positioning mechanism, has a highly oscillatory continuous-time step response. This response is indicative of poor between-sample tracking, especially at the expected low sample rate that is to be used. A continuous-time plant input filter is used to improve the between-sample response and, since the filter zeros are intended to cancel plant poles, the overall model of the plant and filter has uncontrollable modes.

The discussion of each example system is carried to the point where discrete-time controllers are to be designed, using the methods of previous chapters. For the elevator controller, the effect of the nonlinearity is taken into account in an observer's state estimate. It is decided that, although the observer might be deadbeat, initially converging quickly to the plant state, the other eigenvalues of the discrete-time feedback system should give a more gradual zero-input response decay. For the torsional positioning mechanism, having designed a continuous-time plant input filter, the designer might elect to ignore the uncontrollable plant modes which, ideally, decay to zero and stay there. Or, recognizing that with errors in the plant model these modes will continue to be excited, the modes can be estimated and the estimates used to improve tracking performance.

Some of the problems associated with this section involve simulation, but none concerns hardware or software design. Readers may wish to extend the problems' scope to include hardware and software design that is compatible with their specific facilities.

### 7.6.1 An Elevator Controller

A simplified block diagram for elevator positioning is shown in Figure 7-21(a). The elevator drive motor armature voltage is supplied by a power amplifier with the saturation characteristic shown in Figure 7-21(b). The armature voltage $v$ is not allowed to exceed $\pm 200$ volts which, in steady state, results in an elevator speed of

$$x_1 = \left( \frac{0.001}{s + 0.2} \right)\bigg|_{s=0} (200) = 1 \text{ m/sec}$$

The elevator drive motor and cable drum dynamics are modeled as a first-order subsystem with a $1/0.2 = 5$ sec time constant. The elevator speed and position are each sensed separately. The speed sensor, a tachometer on the drive motor shaft with an electrical filter for noise reduction, has a 0.5 sec time constant. The position sensor has a 0.2 sec time constant.

Between floors, the power amplifier is in saturation, supplying either $+200$ volts or $-200$ volts to the motor, depending on whether the elevator is moving up or down. As the elevator approaches the floor where it is to stop, the amplifier output voltage comes out of saturation, into the linear region where a controller, using the sensed speed and position, is to control $u(t)$ in such a way as to bring the elevator smoothly and accurately to rest at the floor. The drive motor armature voltage, after the saturation nonlinearity, is easy to measure and is also available to the controller.

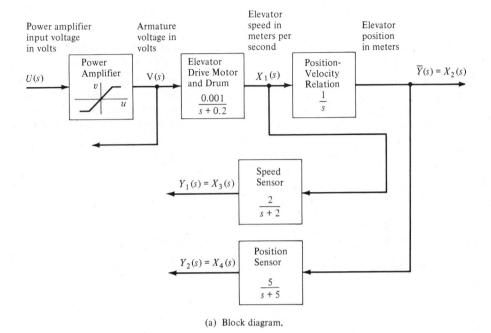

(a) Block diagram.

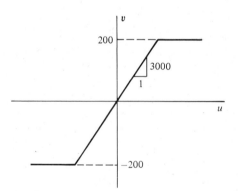

(b) Power amplifier input-output characteristic.

**FIGURE 7-21. Elevator positioning components.**

When the elevator is to move from one floor to another, the position sensor is switched so that it measures position to the floor at which the elevator is to stop. The controller is thus to act as a regulator for each movement between floors. The position sensor hardware consists of a subsystem that uses coarse elevator position information derived from electrical switch closures, medium-accuracy position information from an electro-optic range sensor, and short-range fine position information from a differential magnetic sensor on the elevator that is activated by soft iron target strips at each floor.

Figure 7-22(a) shows a diagram of the plant to be controlled, together with a digital controller. A 0.2 sec sampling interval has been chosen for the initial design, based on A/D and D/A hardware costs and the fact that the shortest plant time constant, that associated with the position sensor, is 0.2 sec. The data acquisition subsystem is then required to sample three signals, each at this five-sample-per-second rate. The rate is well within the capability of inexpensive dual slope integrating A/D converters such as those used in most digital voltmeters. With this sampling rate, the between-sample response of the elevator is expected to be adequate, as can be judged from the elevator velocity unit step response in Figure 7-22(b). The position step response is the integral of this curve.

A control strategy is illustrated in Figure 7-23. The state of the elevator drive and sensor is observed and a linear transformation of this observed elevator drive and state drives the power amplifier. When this observer-controller attempts to supply the elevator drive motor with more than 200

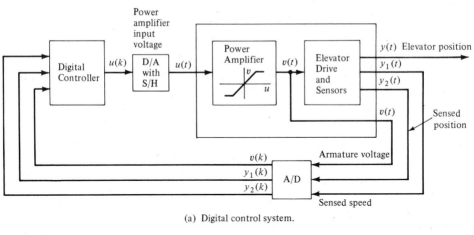

(a) Digital control system.

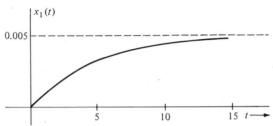

(b) Elevator velocity unit step response.

**FIGURE 7-22.    Digital control of elevator positioning.**

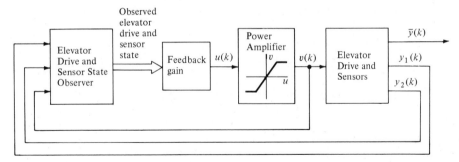

**FIGURE 7-23.   Controller arrangement.**

volts, the power amplifier limiting comes into play, but the observer still calculates the proper state because it uses the actual input to the elevator drive. This kind of plant control is common. In a fighter plane's climb control for example, the aircraft should be allowed to climb no faster than a certain safe rate. When commanded to change altitude quickly, the control system has the aircraft climb at the maximum rate until it nears the new desired altitude.

Continuous-time state equations for the plant consisting of elevator drive and sensors are

$$
\begin{bmatrix} \dot{x}_1(t) \\ \dot{x}_2(t) \\ \dot{x}_3(t) \\ \dot{x}_4(t) \end{bmatrix} = \begin{bmatrix} -0.2 & 0 & 0 & 0 \\ 1 & 0 & 0 & 0 \\ 2 & 0 & -2 & 0 \\ 5 & 0 & 0 & -5 \end{bmatrix} \begin{bmatrix} x_1(t) \\ x_2(t) \\ x_3(t) \\ x_4(t) \end{bmatrix} + \begin{bmatrix} 10^{-3} \\ 0 \\ 0 \\ 0 \end{bmatrix} v(t)
$$

$$
= \mathscr{A}\mathbf{x}(t) + \mathscr{b}v(t)
$$

$$
\begin{bmatrix} y_1(t) \\ y_2(t) \end{bmatrix} = \begin{bmatrix} 0 & 0 & 1 & 0 \\ 0 & 0 & 0 & 1 \end{bmatrix} \begin{bmatrix} x_1(t) \\ x_2(t) \\ x_3(t) \\ x_4(t) \end{bmatrix} = \mathbf{C}\mathbf{x}(t)
$$

$$
\bar{y}(t) = \begin{bmatrix} 0 & 1 & 0 & 0 \end{bmatrix} \begin{bmatrix} x_1(t) \\ x_2(t) \\ x_3(t) \\ x_4(t) \end{bmatrix} = \bar{\mathbf{C}}\mathbf{x}(t)
$$

When the signals of this plant are sampled with sampling interval $T = 0.2$

second, a discrete-time plant model is

$$
\begin{bmatrix} x_1(k+1) \\ x_2(k+1) \\ x_3(k+1) \\ x_4(k+1) \end{bmatrix} = \begin{bmatrix} 0.961 & 0 & 0 & 0 \\ 0.196 & 1 & 0 & 0 \\ 0.323 & 0 & 0.670 & 0 \\ 0.618 & 0 & 0 & 0.368 \end{bmatrix} \begin{bmatrix} x_1(k) \\ x_2(k) \\ x_3(k) \\ x_4(k) \end{bmatrix} + \begin{bmatrix} 0.19 \times 10^{-3} \\ 0.02 \times 10^{-3} \\ 0.035 \times 10^{-3} \\ 0.072 \times 10^{-3} \end{bmatrix} v(k)
$$

$$
= \mathbf{A}\mathbf{x}(k) + \mathbf{b}v(k)
$$

$$
\begin{bmatrix} y_1(k) \\ y_2(k) \end{bmatrix} = \begin{bmatrix} 0 & 0 & 1 & 0 \\ 0 & 0 & 0 & 1 \end{bmatrix} \begin{bmatrix} x_1(k) \\ x_2(k) \\ x_3(k) \\ x_4(k) \end{bmatrix} = \mathbf{C}\mathbf{x}(k)
$$

$$
\bar{y}(k) = \begin{bmatrix} 0 & 1 & 0 & 0 \end{bmatrix} \begin{bmatrix} x_1(k) \\ x_2(k) \\ x_3(k) \\ x_4(k) \end{bmatrix} = \bar{\mathbf{C}}\mathbf{x}(k)
$$

Numerical values for the elements of $\mathbf{A}$ and $\mathbf{b}$ are found using truncated series as in Section 7.2. Twenty terms of each series give results that are accurate to at least 10 significant figures.

State feedback can be designed to place the plant's eigenvalues at any desired locations. The locations desired depend on how quickly one wishes the zero-input component of the plant response to decay with step. Decay by a factor of one-half in each one-second interval might be desirable, requiring eigenvalue locations with radius $c$ from the origin of the complex plane such that

$$
c^5 = \tfrac{1}{2}; \qquad c = 0.87
$$

since there are five discrete-time steps each second. One possibility is to choose all four feedback system eigenvalues to be real and equal to 0.87.

For this plant with two measurement outputs, a second-order observer will observe the plant state. However, only a first-order observer is necessary for observation of a single scalar state transformation $\mathbf{e}^{\dagger}\mathbf{x}$. The choice of observer eigenvalue(s) will depend on the accuracy of the individual measurements. The choice of eigenvalues that give a slow decay of the observer error produce estimates that depend on past measurements as well as the most recent ones; this can have a smoothing effect on the estimates that reduces the influence of measurement "noise". If individual measurement samples are sufficiently accurate, deadbeat design, with all eigenvalues at $\lambda = 0$, is workable. The deadbeat observer uses only the most recent measurements to produce its estimates.

## 7.6.2 *Positioning Mechanism Tracking*

A torsional positioning mechanism that is part of an undersea robotic manipulator is described by an input-output differential equation of the form

$$J \frac{d^2\Theta}{dt^2} + D \frac{d\Theta}{dt} + K\Theta(t) = \tau(t) = Li(t)$$

$J$ is the manipulator's moment of inertia, $D$ is its damping constant, $K$ is its spring constant, and $\tau(t)$ is the applied torque, supplied by an electromagnetic actuator. This torque is, in turn, proportional to the actuator drive current $i(t)$. For

$$J = \frac{1}{100} \text{ N} \cdot \text{m sec}^2/\text{rad}$$

$$D = \frac{2}{100} \text{ N} \cdot \text{m sec}/\text{rad}$$

$$K = 1 \text{ N} \cdot \text{m}/\text{rad}$$

$$L = 1 \text{ N} \cdot \text{m}/\text{a}$$

the input-output equation is

$$\frac{d^2\Theta}{dt^2} + \frac{D}{J} \frac{d\Theta}{dt} + \frac{K}{J} \Theta(t) = \frac{L}{J} i(t)$$

or

$$\frac{d^2\Theta}{dt^2} + 2 \frac{d\Theta}{dt} + 100\Theta(t) = 100i(t)$$

Letting the state variables $x_1(t)$ and $x_2(t)$ be, respectively, rotational position and rotational velocity

$$x_1(t) = \Theta(t)$$

$$x_2(t) = \frac{d\Theta}{dt}$$

and letting the input be the drive current

$$u(t) = i(t)$$

state equations for the mechanism are

$$
\begin{bmatrix} \dot{x}_1(t) \\ \dot{x}_2(t) \end{bmatrix} = \begin{bmatrix} 0 & 1 \\ -100 & -2 \end{bmatrix} \begin{bmatrix} x_1(t) \\ x_2(t) \end{bmatrix} + \begin{bmatrix} 0 \\ 100 \end{bmatrix} u(t)
$$

$$= \mathscr{A}\mathbf{x}(t) + \mathscr{b}u(t)$$

$\qquad\qquad$ (7-8)

Rotational position is sensed with an electrical strain gauge and rotational velocity is sensed with a magnetic motion detector, so the measurement outputs are

$$
\begin{bmatrix} y_1(t) \\ y_2(t) \end{bmatrix} = \begin{bmatrix} 1 & 0 \\ 0 & 1 \end{bmatrix} \begin{bmatrix} x_1(t) \\ x_2(t) \end{bmatrix} = \mathbf{C}\mathbf{x}(t)
$$

$\qquad\qquad$ (7-9)

The position is to be controlled in this tracking system, so the tracking output is

$$
\bar{y}(t) = y_1(t) = \begin{bmatrix} 1 & 0 \end{bmatrix} \begin{bmatrix} x_1(t) \\ x_2(t) \end{bmatrix} = \bar{\mathbf{c}}^\dagger \mathbf{x}(t)
$$

$\qquad\qquad$ (7-10)

The transfer function relating the tracking output $\bar{y}(t)$ to the control input $u(t)$ is

$$T(s) = \bar{\mathbf{c}}^\dagger (s\mathbf{I} - \mathscr{A})^{-1} \mathscr{b} = \frac{100}{s^2 + 2s + 100}$$

as indicated in Figure 7-24(a), where this plant's step response is shown. The plant eigenvalues (or poles) are at $-1 \pm j\sqrt{99}$. Mechanical losses of the manipulator were deliberately kept low, with the result that its zero-input response (and thus its step response) is highly oscillatory. If the input $u(t)$ is a sampled-and-held waveform from a digital controller, the between-sample response of $\bar{y}(t)$ will exhibit this character. As a sampling interval no shorter than $T = 0.5$ second is contemplated, between-sample oscillations in $\bar{y}(t)$ are likely to be substantial.

Figure 7-24(b) shows a plant input filter to improve the between-sample tracking response, with transfer function

$$G(s) = \frac{s^2 + 2s + 100}{s^2 + 20s + 100}$$

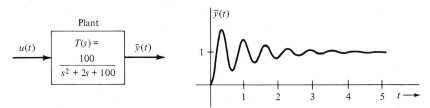

(a) Step response of the plant tracking output.

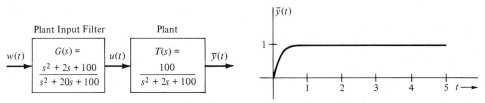

(b) Step response with a plant input filter.

**FIGURE 7-24.    Improving between-sample response with a plant input filter.**

The combination of plant and filter have model transfer function

$$M(s) = T(s)G(s) = \frac{100}{s^2 + 20s + 100}$$

The filter's zeros cancel the plant poles and the filter's two poles are repeated, resulting in critically damped step response. A portion of a simulation study to evaluate the effects of inaccuracies in the plant model is shown in Figure 7-25. Precise pole-zero cancellation is not needed for the filter to be effective;

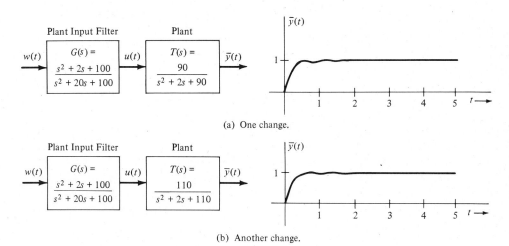

(a) One change.

(b) Another change.

**FIGURE 7-25.    Simulation of step response with a plant parameter change.**

when the filter's zeros are sufficiently close to the unwanted plant poles, the amplitude of the original plant's zero-input response is low. A state variable model of the filter, in upper Jordan form, is

$$\begin{bmatrix} \dot{x}_3(t) \\ \dot{x}_4(t) \end{bmatrix} = \begin{bmatrix} -10 & 1 \\ 0 & -10 \end{bmatrix} \begin{bmatrix} x_3(t) \\ x_4(t) \end{bmatrix} + \begin{bmatrix} -18 \\ 180 \end{bmatrix} w(t)$$

$$u(t) = \begin{bmatrix} 1 & 0 \end{bmatrix} \begin{bmatrix} x_3(t) \\ x_4(t) \end{bmatrix} + w(t) \tag{7-11}$$

where $w(t)$ is the filter input.

The combined state variable equations of the original plant (7-8) to (7-10) and the plant input filter (7-11) are

$$\begin{bmatrix} \dot{x}_1(t) \\ \dot{x}_2(t) \\ \dot{x}_3(t) \\ \dot{x}_4(t) \end{bmatrix} = \begin{bmatrix} 0 & 1 & 0 & 0 \\ -100 & -2 & 100 & 0 \\ 0 & 0 & -10 & 1 \\ 0 & 0 & 0 & -10 \end{bmatrix} \begin{bmatrix} x_1(t) \\ x_2(t) \\ x_3(t) \\ x_4(t) \end{bmatrix} + \begin{bmatrix} 0 \\ 100 \\ -18 \\ 180 \end{bmatrix} w(t)$$

$$\begin{bmatrix} y_1(t) \\ y_2(t) \end{bmatrix} = \begin{bmatrix} 1 & 0 & 0 & 0 \\ 0 & 1 & 0 & 0 \end{bmatrix} \begin{bmatrix} x_1(t) \\ x_2(t) \\ x_3(t) \\ x_4(t) \end{bmatrix}$$

$$\bar{y}(t) = \begin{bmatrix} 1 & 0 & 0 & 0 \end{bmatrix} \begin{bmatrix} x_1(t) \\ x_2(t) \\ x_3(t) \\ x_4(t) \end{bmatrix} \tag{7-12}$$

The original plant modes with eigenvalues $-1 \pm j\sqrt{99}$ are not controllable because of the pole-zero cancellations of the filter. All four modes are observable from each of the outputs.

If the cancellation of plant poles by the plant input filter is sufficiently precise, the completely controllable and observable part of (7-12) can be used as the plant and input filter model for digital controller design. If the initial conditions are zero, the amplitude of the uncontrollable plant modes in $\bar{y}(t)$ will be zero. For nonzero initial conditions, the uncontrollable modes will contribute a transient of the form

$$\bar{y}_{\text{zero-input}}(t) = K e^{-t} \cos(\sqrt{99}t + \phi)$$

where $K$ and $\phi$ are constants. This term will decay with a one-second time constant, never to be seen again. The continuous-time plant is then described by the state variable equations

$$\begin{bmatrix} \dot{x}_1(t) \\ \dot{x}_2(t) \end{bmatrix} = \begin{bmatrix} 0 & 0 \\ -100 & -20 \end{bmatrix} \begin{bmatrix} x_1(t) \\ x_2(t) \end{bmatrix} + \begin{bmatrix} 0 \\ 100 \end{bmatrix} w(t)$$

$$\begin{bmatrix} y_1(t) \\ y_2(t) \end{bmatrix} = \begin{bmatrix} 1 & 0 \\ 0 & 1 \end{bmatrix} \begin{bmatrix} x_1(t) \\ x_2(t) \end{bmatrix}$$

$$\bar{y}(t) = \begin{bmatrix} 1 & 0 \end{bmatrix} \begin{bmatrix} x_1(t) \\ x_2(t) \end{bmatrix} \tag{7-13}$$

Digital controller design will be relatively easy because the state is available for feedback. Using the series methods of Section 7.2, a discrete-time model of (7-13) with sampling interval $T = 1/2$ is

$$\begin{bmatrix} x_1(k+1) \\ x_2(k+1) \end{bmatrix} = \begin{bmatrix} 0.040 & 3.37 \times 10^{-3} \\ -0.337 & -2.70 \times 10^{-2} \end{bmatrix} \begin{bmatrix} x_1(k) \\ x_2(k) \end{bmatrix} + \begin{bmatrix} 2.05 \\ -62.3 \end{bmatrix} w(k)$$

$$\begin{bmatrix} y_1(k) \\ y_2(k) \end{bmatrix} = \begin{bmatrix} 1 & 0 \\ 0 & 1 \end{bmatrix} \begin{bmatrix} x_1(k) \\ x_2(k) \end{bmatrix}$$

$$\bar{y}(k) = \begin{bmatrix} 1 & 0 \end{bmatrix} \begin{bmatrix} x_1(k) \\ x_2(k) \end{bmatrix} \tag{7-14}$$

If the plant pole cancellation by the filter is not so accurate, the full model of the plant and filter can be used to advantage. The effects of the modes that would ideally be uncontrollable can be estimated and these used to improve the plant state estimate. Effects of the uncontrollable modes on the tracking output might even be cancelled. A discrete-time model of the plant and filter (7-12) with sampling interval $T = 1/2$, computed using series as in Section 7.2, is

$$\begin{bmatrix} x_1(k+1) \\ x_2(k+1) \\ x_3(k+1) \\ x_4(k+1) \end{bmatrix} = \begin{bmatrix} 0.0986 & -0.0589 & -0.378 & -3.23 \times 10^{-3} \\ 5.89 & 0.216 & -2.11 & -0.346 \\ 0 & 0 & 6.74 \times 10^{-3} & 3.37 \times 10^{-3} \\ 0 & 0 & 0 & 6.74 \times 10^{-3} \end{bmatrix} \begin{bmatrix} x_1(k) \\ x_2(k) \\ x_3(k) \\ x_4(k) \end{bmatrix}$$

$$+ \begin{bmatrix} 1.28 \\ -45.4 \\ 11.2 \\ -75.2 \end{bmatrix} w(k)$$

$$\begin{bmatrix} y_1(k) \\ y_2(k) \end{bmatrix} = \begin{bmatrix} 1 & 0 & 0 & 0 \\ 0 & 1 & 0 & 0 \end{bmatrix} \begin{bmatrix} x_1(k) \\ x_2(k) \\ x_3(k) \\ x_4(k) \end{bmatrix}$$

$$\bar{y}(k) = \begin{bmatrix} 1 & 0 & 0 & 0 \end{bmatrix} \begin{bmatrix} x_1(k) \\ x_2(k) \\ x_3(k) \\ x_4(k) \end{bmatrix} \tag{7-15}$$

The eigenvalues of the continuous-time system (7-12)

$$-1 \pm j\sqrt{99}, \qquad -10, \qquad -10$$

translate to

$$\exp[(-1 \pm j\sqrt{99})T], \qquad \exp(-10T), \qquad \exp(-10T)$$

or

$$0.157 \pm j0.59, \qquad 6.74 \times 10^{-3}, \qquad 6.74 \times 10^{-3}$$

in the discrete-time model.

The continuous-time model assumes plant pole cancellation by the filter, so the original plant modes $-1 \pm j\sqrt{99}$ are uncontrollable. They affect the system (7-14) as if they were produced by an autonomous disturbance model as in Section 6.5. Even though these modes are actually excited by small unmodeled couplings from the input $w(k)$, they can be treated as if they were produced by initial conditions.

## 7.7 Summary

The relationship between a linear, time-invariant continuous-time plant driven by sampled-and-held inputs

$$\dot{x}(t) = \mathscr{A}x(t) + \mathscr{B}u(t)$$

$$y(t) = Cx(t) + Du(t)$$

and the linear, step-invariant discrete-time model of its evenly spaced samples at intervals $T$

$$\mathbf{x}(k + 1) = \mathbf{A}\mathbf{x}(k) + \mathbf{B}\mathbf{u}(k)$$

$$\mathbf{y}(k) = \mathbf{C}\mathbf{x}(k) + \mathbf{D}\mathbf{u}(k)$$

is

$$\mathbf{A} = e^{\mathscr{A}T} = \left[\mathbf{I} + \frac{\mathscr{A}T}{1!} + \frac{\mathscr{A}^2 T^2}{2!} + \cdots + \frac{\mathscr{A}^i T^i}{i!} + \cdots\right]$$

and

$$\mathbf{B} = \left[\mathbf{I}T + \frac{\mathscr{A}T^2}{2!} + \frac{\mathscr{A}^2 T^3}{3!} + \cdots + \frac{\mathscr{A}^i T^{i+1}}{(i + 1)!} + \cdots\right]\mathscr{B}$$

Truncated power series are a convenient computational method. Computer simulation of the plant and controller is an important design tool.

When a continuous-time plant is driven by sampled-and-held input signals from a digital controller, the character of the plant's continuous-time response between samples is the plant step response without feedback. It sometimes happens that, although tracking is quite good at the sample times, the plant response is highly oscillatory or in some other way undesirable between samples. If it is feasible to change the plant with analog feedback, this option should be explored.

Raising the sample rate will tend to decrease the amplitude of each step input change and thus reduce the amplitude of the undesirable between-sample response, but it is usually expensive to increase the sample rate greatly. If the plant model is sufficiently well known, a continuous-time filter between the controller's D/A conversion and the plant inputs can be designed to improve the plant between-sample response.

Designing filters at the analog plant inputs to improve plant between-sample response is a continuous-time plant input filter design problem similar to the reference input filters for discrete-time tracking discussed in Chapter 6. For a continuous-time plant with transfer function matrix $\mathbf{T}(s)$ relating the tracking outputs to the plant inputs, an analog plant input filter with transfer function matrix $\mathbf{G}(s)$ is designed such that the model plant

$$\mathbf{M}(s) = \mathbf{T}(s)\mathbf{G}(s)$$

responds in an acceptable way to sampled-and-held inputs. Usually, but not always, $\mathbf{G}(s)$ is required to be stable and proper. If $\mathbf{G}(s)$ is an inverse filter, so that

$$\mathbf{T}(s)\mathbf{G}(s) = \mathbf{I}$$

then the forced tracking outputs will, like the filter inputs, be piecewise constant between sample times. Other choices of $G(s)$ will give other, perhaps more desirable, response.

When an analog plant input filter is used, it becomes part of the plant to be controlled by the discrete-time controller. Analog plant input filtering should thus be designed first, obtaining acceptable open-loop plant step response, before the discrete-time control design.

If adequate analog plant input filtering is undesirable, the designer might elect to instead use high-speed digital filters at the plant inputs. The higher filter speed is generally feasible and attractive because it requires an increased D/A but not A/D rate. A higher-rate digital plant input filter can be incorporated as part of a lower-rate discrete-time model by including the filter state as well as the original plant state in the model.

Some ideas relating to hardware and software for digital control were then discussed. The hardware/software options range from dedicated hardwired processing, involving no software, to more general signal processing hardware programmed by ROM "firmware", to highly flexible general-purpose hardware with software derived from a high-level language. The timing of digital control is done in some simple programmed systems by arranging instructions in a loop that executes once each sample period. In more sophisticated systems, timing is controlled by interrupts from an external clock or from timers driven by the CPU clock.

Practical data acquisition and distribution subsystems often share single A/D and D/A converters and a data transmission bus. They commonly convert several different signals sequentially rather than all at the same time. It is straightforward to account for the resulting time offsets in the discrete-time model, but doing so generally results in an increased model order because two successive input samples, not just one, can affect the plant state at each step.

The chapter concluded with two open-ended examples of design of discrete-time controllers of continuous-time systems, an elevator positioning controller and a torsional position mechanism. Like many other practical systems, the elevator's speed is not to exceed a certain maximum amount, so the control voltage to its drive motor was limited. This limiting constitutes an important kind of nonlinearity. The elevator moves at the maximum rate until the motor drive voltage falls below its maximum value as the elevator nears the floor where it is to stop. The observer's state estimate was kept correct during the time of limiting by sensing and using the limited signal to drive the observer. In the torsional positioner example, a continuous-time plant input filter was used to improve between-sample tracking response. The combined system consisting of filter and plant had uncontrollable modes because of the cancellation of plant poles by the filter. It was the designer's option whether to ignore the uncontrollable modes or to observe them and use their estimates to improve tracking performance.

# REFERENCES

Little has been written in the control literature about improving continuous-time system between-sample response with a fixed sample rate. Discussion of interpolation methods and higher-order holds is in

S. A. Tretter, *Introduction to Discrete-Time Signal Processing.* New York: Wiley, 1976

and in an occasional paper such as

G. H. Hostetter and A. R. Stubberud, "High-Order Holds Using Polynomial Spectral Observation, *Computers and Electrical Engineering,* Vol. 9, Dec. 1982, pp. 11–18.

More material on some of the hardware and software considerations in digital control system design can be found in

J. A. Cadzow and H. R. Martens, *Discrete-Time and Computer Control Systems.* Englewood Cliffs, NJ: Prentice-Hall, 1970;

P. Katz, *Digital Control Using Microprocessors.* Englewood Cliffs, NJ: Prentice-Hall, 1981;

K. J. Åström and B. Wittenmark, *Computer Controlled Systems.* Englewood Cliffs, NJ: Prentice-Hall, 1984;

C. H. Houpis and G. B. Lamont, *Digital Control Systems.* New York: McGraw-Hill, 1985.

The two example systems of Section 7.7 are based on research work by the author and others for Battelle Institute and for the Office of Naval Research.

# CHAPTER SEVEN PROBLEMS

**7-1.** Find discrete-time models of each of the following continuous-time systems. The inputs are all piecewise constant during each sampling interval, $T$.

**a.** $\dot{x}(t) = -3x(t) + 4u(t)$

$y(t) = 2x(t) - u(t)$

$T = 0.2$

**b.** $\begin{bmatrix} \dot{x}_1(t) \\ \dot{x}_2(t) \end{bmatrix} = \begin{bmatrix} -2 & 1 \\ 1 & -2 \end{bmatrix} \begin{bmatrix} x_1(t) \\ x_2(t) \end{bmatrix} + \begin{bmatrix} 3 \\ -1 \end{bmatrix} u(t)$

$\begin{bmatrix} y_1(t) \\ y_2(t) \end{bmatrix} = \begin{bmatrix} 1 & 0 \\ 2 & -3 \end{bmatrix} \begin{bmatrix} x_1(t) \\ x_2(t) \end{bmatrix} + \begin{bmatrix} 0 \\ -2 \end{bmatrix} u(t)$

$T = 0.3$

c. $\begin{bmatrix} \dot{x}_1(t) \\ \dot{x}_2(t) \\ \dot{x}_3(t) \end{bmatrix} = \begin{bmatrix} 0 & 1 & 0 \\ 0 & 0 & 1 \\ -12 & -4 & -3 \end{bmatrix} \begin{bmatrix} x_1(t) \\ x_2(t) \\ x_3(t) \end{bmatrix} + \begin{bmatrix} 0 & 0 \\ 2 & -1 \\ 1 & 3 \end{bmatrix} \begin{bmatrix} u_1(t) \\ u_2(t) \end{bmatrix}$

$y(t) = \begin{bmatrix} 1 & 0 & -1 \end{bmatrix} \begin{bmatrix} x_1(t) \\ x_2(t) \\ x_3(t) \end{bmatrix} + \begin{bmatrix} 0 & \frac{1}{2} \end{bmatrix} \begin{bmatrix} u_1(t) \\ u_2(t) \end{bmatrix}$

$T = 0.02$

**7-2.** Modify the program of Table 7-1 so that the controller output is truncated to give only three decimal digits of precision. Repeat, so that the controller output is rounded and has only one significant decimal digit.

**7-3.** Find *continuous-time* state equation models for plants with the following discrete-time state models with the indicated sampling intervals, $T$:

a. $\begin{bmatrix} x_1(k+1) \\ x_2(k+1) \end{bmatrix} = \begin{bmatrix} -\frac{3}{4} & 1 \\ -\frac{1}{8} & 0 \end{bmatrix} \begin{bmatrix} x_1(k) \\ x_2(k) \end{bmatrix} + \begin{bmatrix} 2 \\ -1 \end{bmatrix} u(k)$

$T = 0.5$

b. $\begin{bmatrix} x_1(k+1) \\ x_2(k+1) \end{bmatrix} = \begin{bmatrix} 0.2 & 1.1 \\ -0.3 & 0.1 \end{bmatrix} \begin{bmatrix} x_1(k) \\ x_2(k) \end{bmatrix} + \begin{bmatrix} 0 & -1 \\ 1 & 3 \end{bmatrix} \begin{bmatrix} u_1(k) \\ u_2(k) \end{bmatrix}$

$T = 2$

c. $\begin{bmatrix} x_1(k+1) \\ x_2(k+1) \\ x_3(k+1) \end{bmatrix} = \begin{bmatrix} 0 & 1 & 0 \\ 0 & 0 & 0 \\ \frac{1}{4} & 0 & 0 \end{bmatrix} \begin{bmatrix} x_1(k) \\ x_2(k) \\ x_3(k) \end{bmatrix} + \begin{bmatrix} 1 \\ -1 \\ 3 \end{bmatrix} u(k)$

$T = 0.2$

**7-4.** Design analog plant input filters for plants with the following transfer functions, specifying state variable equations for each filter realization. The filter time constants should be no larger than about one-half of the sampling interval $T$ so that the controlled system can easily respond to significant changes in the tracking input from sample to sample.

a. $T(s) = \dfrac{20s^2 + 10}{(s+2)^3(s^2 + 0.1s + 1)}; \qquad T = 4$

b. $T(s) = \dfrac{10^6(s+1)}{s^4 + 100s^3 + 10^6s^2}; \qquad T = 10^{-3}$

c. A two-input plant with a single tracking output, with

$$T_1(s) = \frac{s + 1000}{(s^2 + 20s + 100)(s^2 + 10s + 100)}$$

$$T_2(s) = \frac{s^3 + 5s^2 - 30s + 1000}{(s^2 + 10s + 100)(s + 20)}$$

and $T = 0.5$

**7-5.**   Design a high-speed discrete-time plant input filter for the system

$$\begin{bmatrix} \dot{x}_1(t) \\ \dot{x}_2(t) \end{bmatrix} = \begin{bmatrix} -1 & 1 \\ -10 & 0 \end{bmatrix} \begin{bmatrix} x_1(t) \\ x_2(t) \end{bmatrix} + \begin{bmatrix} -1 \\ 2 \end{bmatrix} u(t)$$

$$y(t) = \begin{bmatrix} 1 & 0 \end{bmatrix} \begin{bmatrix} x_1(t) \\ x_2(t) \end{bmatrix}$$

with a sampling interval $\Delta t = 0.1$, that improves the plant step response. Then find a discrete-time model of the system with sampling interval $T = 5\Delta t = 0.5$, where the discrete-time filter input changes at the lower rate.

**7-6.**   Design high-speed discrete-time measurement output feedback for the system

$$\begin{bmatrix} \dot{x}_1(t) \\ \dot{x}_2(t) \end{bmatrix} = \begin{bmatrix} 0 & 1 \\ -10 & -1 \end{bmatrix} \begin{bmatrix} x_1(t) \\ x_2(t) \end{bmatrix} + \begin{bmatrix} 0 \\ 1 \end{bmatrix} u(t)$$

$$y(t) = \begin{bmatrix} 2 & -1 \end{bmatrix} \begin{bmatrix} x_1(t) \\ x_2(t) \end{bmatrix}$$

with a sampling interval $\Delta t = 0.1$, that improves the plant step response over that without the feedback. Then find a discrete-time model of the system with sampling interval $T = 5\Delta t = 0.5$, where the plant consists of the sum of the high-speed output feedback and a sampled-and-held external input that changes at the lower rate.

**7-7.**   At the level of Figure 7-11, specify a multiprocessor computer architecture where separate processors are used for

1. data acquisition,
2. program control and computation, and
3. high-speed output signal generation.

**7-8.**   At the level of Figure 7-12, specify a multiprocessor computer architecture for a decentralized distributed system with three local computers. Discuss in some detail how the local computers are to communicate with one another, especially in those situations where more than one processor wants to communicate with others at the same time.

**7-9.** At the level of Figure 7-13, specify a data acquisition arrangement where there is simultaneous input sampling of a pressure sensor, a voltage sensor, and a temperature sensor and where there are two additional temperature sensors, either one of which can be substituted for the temperature sensor currently being used. The substitution should be controllable with an external command. There is time for only three measurements to be sent from the data acquisition system each step.

**7-10.** At the level of Figure 7-14, specify a data distribution arrangement for three actuators. Two of the actuator samples are sent to this system each step, and one of the actuator samples is sent every other step. On in-between steps, the latter actuator is to be driven by the average of the previous two samples received.

**7-11.** At the level of Figure 7-15 or 7-16, specify a hardware design for a single-input, single-output controller with input $r(k)$ and output $u(k)$, for which

$$\begin{bmatrix} \xi_1(k+1) \\ \xi_2(k+1) \\ \xi_3(k+1) \end{bmatrix} = \begin{bmatrix} 0 & 1 & 0 \\ -1 & \frac{1}{3} & \frac{4}{3} \\ 1 & 1 & \frac{1}{4} \end{bmatrix} \begin{bmatrix} \xi_1(k) \\ \xi_2(k) \\ \xi_3(k) \end{bmatrix} + \begin{bmatrix} 0 \\ 1 \\ -1 \end{bmatrix} r(k)$$

$$u(k) = \begin{bmatrix} 2 & 0 & \frac{1}{3} \end{bmatrix} \begin{bmatrix} \xi_1(k) \\ \xi_2(k) \\ \xi_3(k) \end{bmatrix} + 3r(k)$$

**7-12.** Digital controllers are sometimes designed so that they accumulate the error between a desired output and its measured samples and feed this sum of errors back to a plant input. The first-order plant

$$x(k+1) = -\tfrac{1}{2}x(k) + u(k)$$

$$\bar{y}(k) = y(k) = x(k)$$

with first-order controller

$$\xi(k+1) = \xi(k) + [r(k) - y(k)]$$

$$u(k) = \tfrac{1}{16}\xi(k)$$

is a simple example of such a system. Should the measurement sensor fail, the accumulated error signal $\xi$ can become very large. Once the problem is corrected, it may therefore take a very long time for the accumulated error to return to realistic values. Digital control systems using error accumulation are thus usually designed with provision for resetting accumulators to zero. This provision is called *antiwindup reset*.

Design hardware for the above controller in the form of Figure 7-16 and include an antiwindup reset switch.

**7-13.** Write a controller program in the Basic language that will realize

$$
\begin{bmatrix} \xi_1(k+1) \\ \xi_2(k+1) \\ \xi_3(k+1) \end{bmatrix} = \begin{bmatrix} \tfrac{3}{4} & 1 & 0 \\ -\tfrac{1}{2} & 0 & 1 \\ \tfrac{1}{2} & 0 & 0 \end{bmatrix} \begin{bmatrix} \xi_1(k) \\ \xi_2(k) \\ \xi_3(k) \end{bmatrix} + \begin{bmatrix} -3 \\ 4 \\ 6 \end{bmatrix} r(k)
$$

$$
u(k) = \begin{bmatrix} 1 & 0 & 0 \end{bmatrix} \begin{bmatrix} \xi_1(k) \\ \xi_2(k) \\ \xi_3(k) \end{bmatrix} + \tfrac{1}{2}r(k)
$$

Assume that an INPUT R instruction causes the program to wait until a new input sample is available from the input A/D converter, then assigns that sample to the variable R. Assume, too, that a PRINT U instruction causes transfer of the value of the variable U to the output D/A converter. This is essentially as if the samples were received from and delivered to a terminal.

**7-14.** For the two-input, two-output controller

$$
\begin{bmatrix} \xi_1(k+1) \\ \xi_2(k+1) \\ \xi_3(k+1) \end{bmatrix} = \begin{bmatrix} 0.25 & 0.3 & -1.0 \\ 1.25 & -1.2 & 0 \\ 0 & 0.33 & 1.0 \end{bmatrix} \begin{bmatrix} \xi_1(k) \\ \xi_2(k) \\ \xi_3(k) \end{bmatrix} + \begin{bmatrix} 6.25 \\ -0.4 \\ -0.7 \end{bmatrix} \begin{bmatrix} r(k) \\ y(k) \end{bmatrix}
$$

$$
\begin{bmatrix} u_1(k) \\ u_2(k) \end{bmatrix} = \begin{bmatrix} 1.0 & 2.0 & 0 \\ 0 & -1.5 & 5.5 \end{bmatrix} \begin{bmatrix} \xi_2(k) \\ \xi_2(k) \\ \xi_3(k) \end{bmatrix} + \begin{bmatrix} 0 & 0.5 \\ -0.5 & 0.2 \end{bmatrix} \begin{bmatrix} r(k) \\ y(k) \end{bmatrix}
$$

write software in the Basic language. The variables R and Y, representing the signal samples $r(k)$ and $y(k)$ respectively, are the contents of certain memory locations that are automatically changed by the data acquisition system whenever new samples are available. When the new samples of each have been entered, the data acquisition system sets the variable P to unity. The program should test to see if P equals one. When it does, the program should set P to zero, then process the new input samples.

Similarly, the data distribution system uses as samples $u_1(k)$ and $u_2(k)$ the contents of the memory locations where the variables U1 and U2 are stored. The program signals to the data distribution system that new output samples are available by setting the variable Q to unity. When the data distribution system has transferred the samples to its D/A converters, it sets Q to zero.

**7-15.** Design a detailed program flow chart for realizing the controller

$$
\begin{bmatrix} \xi_1(k+1) \\ \xi_2(k+1) \\ \xi_3(k+1) \end{bmatrix} = \begin{bmatrix} 0 & 1 & 0 \\ 0 & 0 & 1 \\ -1 & -\tfrac{1}{2} & \tfrac{1}{3} \end{bmatrix} \begin{bmatrix} \xi_1(k) \\ \xi_2(k) \\ \xi_3(k) \end{bmatrix} + \begin{bmatrix} 3 \\ -4 \\ 0 \end{bmatrix} r(k)
$$

$$
\begin{bmatrix} u_1(k) \\ u_2(k) \end{bmatrix} = \begin{bmatrix} 1 & 1 & 0 \\ -1 & 1 & 0 \end{bmatrix} \begin{bmatrix} \xi_1(k) \\ \xi_2(k) \\ \xi_3(k) \end{bmatrix} + \begin{bmatrix} 0 \\ 2 \end{bmatrix} r(k)
$$

Assume that there is a step clock to indicate when new samples are to be processed and that a loop of the program executes in less than one clock period. Do not use subroutines or interrupts.

**7-16.** Repeat problem 7-15 but use a subroutine structure similar to that shown in Figure 7-18. Do not use interrupts.

**7-17.** Write a controller program in the Basic language that will realize

$$
\begin{bmatrix} \xi_1(k+1) \\ \xi_2(k+1) \end{bmatrix} = \begin{bmatrix} 0 & 1 \\ -\frac{1}{2} & -\frac{3}{2} \end{bmatrix} \begin{bmatrix} \xi_1(k) \\ \xi_2(k) \end{bmatrix} + \begin{bmatrix} 3 & 1 \\ 0 & -1 \end{bmatrix} \begin{bmatrix} y_1(k) \\ y_2(k) \end{bmatrix}
$$

$$
u(k) = \begin{bmatrix} 5 & 4 \end{bmatrix} \begin{bmatrix} \xi_1(k) \\ \xi_2(k) \end{bmatrix}
$$

when both the $y_1$ and $y_2$ sensors are working properly,

$$\xi(k+1) = (\tfrac{3}{8})\xi(k) + 2y_2(k)$$

$$u(k) = (\tfrac{5}{2})\xi(k)$$

when the $y_1$ sensor is not working, and

$$\xi(k+1) = (\tfrac{9}{10})\xi(k) + 3y_1(k)$$

$$u(k) = -5\xi(k) + (\tfrac{3}{10})y_1(k)$$

when the $y_2$ sensor is inoperative. The INPUT A, B, C command (where $A, B, C$ are any variables) causes the program to wait until new samples of $y_1$ and $y_2$ are available, then assigns the $y_1$ sample to A and the $y_2$ sample to B. When a sensor is not working, input samples are provided, but they are meaningless. The third INPUT variable ($C$ here) indicates which sensors are working properly, as follows:

$0 \leqslant C < 0.5$:     $y_1$ working, $y_2$ not working

$0.5 \leqslant C < 1.5$:     both $y_1$ and $y_2$ working

$1.5 \leqslant C < 2.0$:     $y_1$ not working, $y_2$ working

Output samples are transferred to the data distribution hardware using a PRINT command.

**7-18.** Write, debug and test controller and plant simulation programs for the tracking systems in the following figures:

    **a.** Figure 6-2        **d.** Figure 6-10
    **b.** Figure 6-3        **e.** Figure 6-11
    **c.** Figure 6-9

**7-19.** Write, debug, and test controller and plant simulation programs for the tracking systems in the following figures:

    **a.** Figure 7-5(a)
    **b.** Figure 7-5(b)
    **c.** Figure 7-5(c)

**7-20.** Write, debug, and test a controller and plant simulation program for the tracking system with high-speed plant input filter in Figure 7-7(c).

**7-21.** Write a controller program in the Basic language for the two-input, two-output controller

$$\begin{bmatrix} \xi_1(k+1) \\ \xi_2(k+1) \end{bmatrix} = \begin{bmatrix} 0.25 & 1 \\ 0.47 & 0 \end{bmatrix} \begin{bmatrix} \xi_1(k) \\ \xi_2(k) \end{bmatrix} + \begin{bmatrix} 1.3 & 4 \\ -0.3 & -1 \end{bmatrix} \begin{bmatrix} y(k) \\ r(k) \end{bmatrix}$$

$$\begin{bmatrix} u_1(k) \\ u_2(k) \end{bmatrix} = \begin{bmatrix} 1 & 0 \\ 0.5 & -2 \end{bmatrix} \begin{bmatrix} \xi_1(k) \\ \xi_2(k) \end{bmatrix} + \begin{bmatrix} 0 & 1 \\ -0.2 & 0 \end{bmatrix} \begin{bmatrix} y(k) \\ r(k) \end{bmatrix}$$

Assume that at each step, new samples of the plant output $y(k)$ and the reference input $r(k)$ are automatically stored, as the variables $Y$ and $R$ respectively, by the computer hardware. Similarly, the stored value of $U$ is automatically transferred to the plant input D/A at each step. There is also hardware that causes execution of the program to wait until new input samples are available at each step.

**7-22.** Provision is usually made in a digital control system for manual control. (There may also be an alternate, simpler backup controller standing by.) When control is switched between manual and the computer, it is undesirable to have the system undergo large transients, behaving as if it were just being started up. As the controller-generated plant inputs and those produced manually may differ substantially, there can be large step changes in the plant inputs in changing between manual and computer control. When provision has been made to avoid this problem, the control system is said to be capable of *bumpless transfer*. Write a controller program in the Basic language for a two-input, single-output controller

$$\begin{bmatrix} \xi_1(k+1) \\ \xi_2(k+1) \end{bmatrix} = \begin{bmatrix} -0.3 & 0.55 \\ 1.7 & -0.02 \end{bmatrix} \begin{bmatrix} \xi_1(k) \\ \xi_2(k) \end{bmatrix} + \begin{bmatrix} 0 & -0.22 \\ 1.0 & 2.14 \end{bmatrix} \begin{bmatrix} y(k) \\ r(k) \end{bmatrix}$$

$$w(k) = \begin{bmatrix} 1 & 6.2 \end{bmatrix} \begin{bmatrix} \xi_2(k) \\ \xi_2(k) \end{bmatrix} + \begin{bmatrix} 1.8 & -0.7 \end{bmatrix} \begin{bmatrix} y(k) \\ r(k) \end{bmatrix}$$

and arrange for bumpless transfer between manual and computer control. Assume that at each step, new samples of the plant output $y(k)$, the reference input $r(k)$, and the manual plant input $m(k)$ are automatically stored, as the variables $Y$, $R$, and $M$ respectively, by the computer hardware. Similarly, the stored value of $U$ is automatically transferred to the plant input D/A at each step. Just before the input signals are to be automatically updated, there is to be an INPUT L statement, through which the program determines whether the plant input is to be from the controller $w(k)$ or from the manual signal $m(k)$. If $L = 0$, plant control is to be by the controller; otherwise, plant control is to be manual. Rather than immediately switching the plant input between $w(k)$ and $m(k)$, make the transitions between the two a ramp of appropriate slope.

**7-23.** Design a second-order deadbeat observer of the four state variables describing the discrete-time model of the elevator drive and sensors. Simulate and compare the plant and observer signals for various power amplifier inputs $u(k)$.

**7-24.** Design state feedback gains **e** for the digital controller arrangement of Figure 7-23 so that the plant with state feedback has characteristic equation $(\lambda - 0.87)^4 = 0$. For these gains, design a first-order deadbeat observer of $\mathbf{e}^\dagger \mathbf{x}$ for feedback. Simulate this discrete-time control of the continuous-time elevator position for various reasonable initial elevator positions and velocities. Be sure to include the power amplifier nonlinearity.

**7-25.** Design a discrete-time deadbeat regulator of the positioning mechanism, using the models of (7-13) and (7-14). Simulate $\bar{y}(t)$ with this discrete-time control of the plant and plant input filter for various plant initial conditions. Then vary the plant (but not the filter) to give each of the two situations of Figure 7-25.

**7-26.** Using the models (7-13) and (7-14), design a discrete-time tracking controller for the positioning mechanism. Choose the discrete-time feedback eigenvalues to be other than at the origin and have the tracking output $\bar{y}(k)$ observe any constant-plus-ramp reference input $r(k)$.

**7-27.** Using the models (7-13) and (7-14), design a deadbeat discrete-time tracking controller for the positioning mechanism. Have the tracking output observe any constant reference input $r(k)$. Simulate this discrete-time control of the continuous-time plant and filter with various plant initial conditions and reference inputs, including sinusoidal ones. Through simulation, investigate the controller's performance with changed plant parameters as in Figure 7-25.

**7-28.** Using the models (7-12) and (7-15), design a deadbeat tracking controller for the positioning mechanism. Take the uncontrollable modes into account, and have the tracking output observe any constant-plus-ramp reference input $r(k)$.

# Step-Varying Control

8

## 8.1 Preview

In this final chapter, we extend each of the main ideas of tracking system design to the step-varying case. This requires only relatively small additions to the knowledge already gained in connection with step-invariant systems. In most practical situations, implementation of step-varying control involves only a slight increase in complexity compared to step-invariant control. By extending the scope of design skills to step-varying systems, we include the ability to control step-varying plants. For step-invariant plants, the additional design freedom can be used to substantially improve controller performance.

First, we introduce step-varying state equations, their recursive solution, and some ideas about linear discrete-time system stability. Then, concepts of controllability and observability are extended to the step-varying case. Next, step-varying observer theory is developed, and observers are used for step-varying plant state estimation. Dual to the observer design problem is the design of step-varying state feedback. That problem is considered in some detail, particularly for the case of step-varying deadbeat feedback. Disturbance modeling and tracking system design are also carried over to the step-varying case.

Recursive least squares state estimation, an attractive alternative method of choosing step-varying observer gains is then developed, yielding the Kalman filter. The previous step-varying observer design methods choose the observer convergence properties directly. In the recursive least squares approach, the observer gains are chosen to minimize a designer-selected weighted sum of squares of errors, indirectly resulting in the observer's convergence.

The final section of the chapter concerns quadratic optimal control. In the previous design methods, the zero-input response convergence properties of the plant with state feedback are selected directly. In the optimal control approach, state feedback is chosen to minimize a designer-selected performance measure, indirectly resulting in a certain zero-input response. The optimal quadratic solution is derived via dynamic programming and examples are given.

## 8.2 Step-Varying Systems

### 8.2.1 State Equations and Response

A step-varying discrete-time system has state equations of the form

$$\mathbf{x}(k + 1) = \mathbf{A}(k)\mathbf{x}(k) + \mathbf{B}(k)\mathbf{u}(k)$$

$$\mathbf{y}(k) = \mathbf{C}(k)\mathbf{x}(k) + \mathbf{D}(k)\mathbf{u}(k) \tag{8-1}$$

The **A**, **B**, **C**, and **D** matrices each might vary with step, as is indicated in the vector signal delay diagram of Figure 8-1. Most of the ideas and results for step-invariant systems have counterparts for step-varying systems. The $z$-transform is generally of no help in finding the response of a step-varying system, though, and matrix eigenvalues do not have the same significance for step-varying systems as they do for step-invariant ones. The response of a

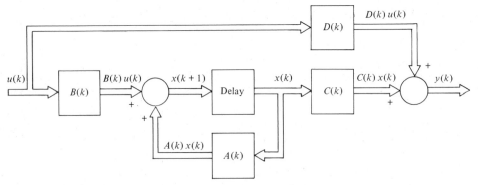

**FIGURE 8-1.** Delay diagram representation of a step-varying system. The signals are vectors.

step-varying discrete-time system can be calculated recursively from the state equations (8-1), the initial state $\mathbf{x}(0)$, and the input $\mathbf{u}(k)$ as follows:

$$\mathbf{x}(1) = \mathbf{A}(0)\mathbf{x}(0) + \mathbf{B}(0)\mathbf{u}(0)$$

$$\mathbf{x}(2) = \mathbf{A}(1)\mathbf{x}(1) + \mathbf{B}(1)\mathbf{u}(1)$$
$$= \mathbf{A}(1)\mathbf{A}(0)\mathbf{x}(0) + \mathbf{A}(1)\mathbf{B}(0)\mathbf{u}(0) + \mathbf{B}(1)\mathbf{u}(1)$$

$$\mathbf{x}(3) = \mathbf{A}(2)\mathbf{x}(2) + \mathbf{B}(2)\mathbf{u}(2)$$
$$= \mathbf{A}(2)\mathbf{A}(1)\mathbf{A}(0)\mathbf{x}(0) + \mathbf{A}(2)\mathbf{A}(1)\mathbf{B}(0)\mathbf{u}(0) + \mathbf{A}(2)\mathbf{B}(1)\mathbf{u}(1) + \mathbf{B}(2)\mathbf{u}(2)$$

$$\vdots$$

$$\mathbf{x}(k) = \mathbf{A}(k-1)\mathbf{A}(k-2)\cdots\mathbf{A}(0)\mathbf{x}(0) + \mathbf{A}(k-1)\cdots\mathbf{A}(1)\mathbf{B}(0)\mathbf{u}(0)$$
$$+ \mathbf{A}(k-1)\cdots\mathbf{A}(2)\mathbf{B}(1)\mathbf{u}(1) + \cdots$$
$$+ \mathbf{A}(k-1)\mathbf{B}(k-2)\mathbf{u}(k-2) + \mathbf{B}(k-1)\mathbf{u}(k-1)$$

$$\vdots$$

A product of state coupling matrices

$$\mathbf{\Phi}(j, i) = \mathbf{A}(i-1)\mathbf{A}(i-2)\cdots\mathbf{A}(j)$$

is the state transition matrix of the system.

The definitions of stability for step-varying linear discrete-time systems are many and varied. Perhaps the best general definition is the following: a system with state equations

$$\mathbf{x}(k+1) = \mathbf{A}(k)\mathbf{x}(k) + \mathbf{B}(k)\mathbf{u}(k)$$

is *zero-input stable* if and only if for every set of finite initial conditions $\mathbf{x}_{\text{zero-input}}(0)$, the zero-input component of the state, governed by

$$\mathbf{x}_{\text{zero-input}}(k+1) = \mathbf{A}(k)\mathbf{x}_{\text{zero-input}}(k)$$

approaches zero with step:

$$\lim_{k \to \infty} \|\mathbf{x}_{\text{zero-input}}(k)\| = 0$$

The system is *zero-state stable* if and only if for zero initial conditions and every bounded input

$$\|\mathbf{u}(k)\| < \delta; \qquad k = 0, 1, 2, \ldots$$

the zero-state component of the state, governed by

$$\begin{cases} \mathbf{x}_{\text{zero-state}}(k+1) = \mathbf{A}(k)\mathbf{x}_{\text{zero-state}}(k) + \mathbf{B}(k)\mathbf{u}(k) \\ \mathbf{x}_{\text{zero-state}}(0) = \mathbf{0} \end{cases}$$

is bounded:

$$\|\mathbf{x}_{\text{zero-state}}(k)\| < \sigma, \qquad k = 0, 1, 2, \ldots$$

A linear discrete-time system is *stable* if it is both zero-input stable and zero-state stable.

The system with state equations

$$\begin{bmatrix} x_1(k+1) \\ x_2(k+1) \end{bmatrix} = \begin{bmatrix} k & 0 \\ 0 & \frac{1}{2} \end{bmatrix} \begin{bmatrix} x_1(k) \\ x_2(k) \end{bmatrix} + \begin{bmatrix} 0 \\ 1 \end{bmatrix} u(k)$$

is zero-state stable but not zero-input stable. The system

$$\begin{bmatrix} x_1(k+1) \\ x_2(k+1) \end{bmatrix} = \begin{bmatrix} \frac{1}{3} & 0 \\ 0 & \frac{1}{2} \end{bmatrix} \begin{bmatrix} x_1(k) \\ x_2(k) \end{bmatrix} + \begin{bmatrix} k! \\ 1 \end{bmatrix} u(k)$$

is zero-input stable but not zero-state stable. Although these examples are somewhat contrived, they serve to illustrate the ideas involved. Having defined stability, it may not be an easy matter to determine whether a given step-varying system is stable. There is the possibility though, whether the system is stable or not, of using feedback to obtain acceptable response.

When a nonsingular change of state variables, possibly step-varying,

$$\mathbf{x}(k) = \mathbf{P}(k)\mathbf{x}'(k); \qquad \mathbf{x}'(k) = \mathbf{P}^{-1}(k)\mathbf{x}(k)$$

is made for a step-varying system (8-1) the result is

$$\mathbf{P}(k+1)\mathbf{x}'(k+1) = \mathbf{A}(k)\mathbf{P}(k)\mathbf{x}'(k) + \mathbf{B}(k)\mathbf{u}(k)$$

or

$$\mathbf{x}'(k+1) = [\mathbf{P}^{-1}(k+1)\mathbf{A}(k)\mathbf{P}(k)]\mathbf{x}'(k) + [\mathbf{P}^{-1}(k+1)\mathbf{B}(k)]\mathbf{u}(k)$$

$$= \mathbf{A}'(k)\mathbf{x}'(k) + \mathbf{B}'(k)\mathbf{u}(k)$$

$$\mathbf{y}(k) = [\mathbf{C}(k)\mathbf{P}(k)]\mathbf{x}'(k) + \mathbf{D}(k)\mathbf{u}(k) = \mathbf{C}'(k)\mathbf{x}'(k) + \mathbf{D}'(k)\mathbf{u}(k)$$

which is also in the state variable form. Unlike the step-invariant case, the new state coupling matrix

$$\mathbf{A}'(k) = \mathbf{P}^{-1}(k+1)\mathbf{A}(k)\mathbf{P}(k)$$

is not a similarity transformation of $\mathbf{A}(k)$ unless the transformation $\mathbf{P}$ does not change with step.

A particularly interesting change of state variables is the one for which

$$P(k + 1) = A(k)P(k); \qquad P(0) = I; \qquad P(k) = \prod_{i=1}^{k} A(k - i)$$

When $A(k)$ is nonsingular, as it always is when (8-1) is a discrete-time model of a time-invariant plant, the new state variable equations are

$$x'(k + 1) = x'(k) + P^{-1}(k + 1)B(k)u(k)$$

$$y(k) = C(k)P(k)x'(k) + D(k)u(k)$$

In this form, the state equations simply accumulate the effects of the inputs, while the rest of the state dynamics have been transferred to the output equations. If the $n \times n$ state coupling matrix $A(k)$ is singular at any step, then at that step, the system can be described by less than $n$ state variables.

## 8.2.2 Observability and State Determination

A step-varying system (8-1) is *observable at step 0* if $x(0)$ can be determined from the system outputs, $y(0), y(1), \ldots, y(N - 1)$ and $u(0), u(1), \ldots, u(N - 1)$ for some finite number of steps, $N$. From $x(0)$ and the inputs and outputs, the system state at any later step can be found. A system (8-1) is *observable at step k* if $x(k)$ can be determined from the outputs $y(k), y(k + 1), \ldots, y(k + N - 1)$ and inputs $u(k), u(k + 1), \ldots, u(k + N - 1)$ for some finite number of steps, $N$. If the system is observable at every step, it is termed *uniformly observable*.

The observability of a system rests upon whether or not there is a unique solution for the state given the outputs and inputs. For a general step-varying system (8-1) the state at step 0, in terms of outputs and inputs from step 0 through step $N - 1$, satisfies

$$
\begin{cases}
y(0) = C(0)x(0) + D(0)u(0) \\
y(1) = C(1)x(1) + D(1)u(1) = C(1)A(0)x(0) + C(1)B(0)u(0) + D(1)u(1) \\
y(2) = C(2)A(1)A(0)x(0) + C(2)A(1)B(0)u(0) + C(2)B(1)u(1) + D(2)u(2) \\
\quad \vdots \\
y(N - 1) = C(N - 1)A(N - 2) \cdots A(0)x(0) \\
\qquad + C(N - 1)A(N - 2) \cdots A(1)B(0)u(0) \\
\qquad + C(N - 1)A(N - 2) \cdots A(2)B(1)u(1) + \cdots \\
\qquad + C(N - 1)A(N - 2)B(N - 3)u(N - 3) \\
\qquad + C(N - 1)B(N - 2)u(N - 2) + D(N - 1)u(N - 1)
\end{cases}
$$

or

$$\begin{bmatrix} C(0) \\ \hline C(1)A(0) \\ \hline C(2)A(1)A(0) \\ \hline \vdots \\ \hline C(N-1)A(N-2)\cdots A(0) \end{bmatrix} x(0) = M_0(0,\ N-1)x(0) = \begin{bmatrix} known \\ quantities \end{bmatrix}$$

If, for some finite $N$, the observability matrix $M_0(0, N-1)$ is of full rank (that is, if its $n$ columns are linearly independent), the system is observable at step 0; otherwise, it is not. Similarly, the system is observable at step $k$ if and only if the observability matrix

$$M_0(k,\ k+N-1) = \begin{bmatrix} C(k) \\ \hline C(k+1)A(k) \\ \hline C(k+2)A(k+1)A(k) \\ \hline \vdots \\ \hline C(k+N-1)A(k+N-2)\cdots A(k) \end{bmatrix}$$

is of full rank for some finite $N$.

In the step-invariant case, the matrices $A$ and $C$ do not vary with step. Since powers of the $n \times n$ matrix $A$ above $A^{n-1}$ can be expressed in terms of $A^{n-1}$ and lower powers of $A$, there is no need to use outputs from more than $N = n$ consecutive steps. And, in the step-invariant case, observability at any step means that the system is observable at any other step because the equations to be solved for the initial state are unchanged by a translation in step. Neither of these properties necessarily holds for a step-varying system.

### 8.2.3 Controllability and State Control

A step-varying system (8-1) is *controllable at step 0* if there exists a finite-length input sequence $u(0), u(1), \ldots, u(N-1)$, depending on $x(0)$ and $x(N)$ that will take the system from any known state $x(0)$ to any desired state $x(N)$. A system is *controllable at step $k$* if a finite-length input sequence $u(k)$, $u(k+1), \ldots, u(k+N-1)$ exists such that the state can be moved from any known $x(k)$ to any desired $x(N)$. If the system is controllable at every step, it is termed *uniformly controllable*.

For a general step-varying system (8-1), the state at step $N$ in terms of the state at step 0 and the inputs $\mathbf{u}(0), \mathbf{u}(1), \ldots, \mathbf{u}(N-1)$ is given by

$$\mathbf{x}(N) = \mathbf{A}(N-1) \ldots \mathbf{A}(0)\mathbf{x}(0) + \mathbf{A}(N-1) \ldots \mathbf{A}(1)\mathbf{B}(0)\mathbf{u}(0)$$
$$+ \mathbf{A}(N-1) \ldots \mathbf{A}(2)\mathbf{B}(1)\mathbf{u}(1) + \cdots$$
$$+ \mathbf{A}(N-1)\mathbf{B}(N-2)\mathbf{u}(N-2) + \mathbf{B}(N-1)\mathbf{u}(N-1)$$

Taking the initial state $\mathbf{x}(0)$ and the desired state $\mathbf{x}(N)$ to be known, these are of the form

$$[\mathbf{B}(N-1) \vert \mathbf{A}(N-1)\mathbf{B}(N-2) \vert \cdots \vert \mathbf{A}(N-1) \ldots \mathbf{A}(2)\mathbf{B}(1) \vert \mathbf{A}(N-1) \ldots \mathbf{A}(1)\mathbf{B}(0)]$$

$$\times \begin{bmatrix} \mathbf{u}(N-1) \\ \hline \mathbf{u}(N-2) \\ \hline \vdots \\ \hline \mathbf{u}(1) \\ \hline \mathbf{u}(0) \end{bmatrix} = \mathbf{M}_c(0, N-1) \begin{bmatrix} \mathbf{u}(N-1) \\ \hline \vdots \\ \hline \mathbf{u}(0) \end{bmatrix} = \begin{bmatrix} \text{known} \\ \text{quantities} \end{bmatrix}$$

If, for some finite $N$, the controllability matrix, $\mathbf{M}_c(0, N-1)$ is of full rank (that is, if its $n$ rows are linearly independent), the system is controllable at step 0; otherwise, it is not. The system is controllable at step $k$ if and only if the controllability matrix

$$\mathbf{M}_c(k, k+N-1)$$
$$= [\mathbf{B}(k+N-1) \vert \mathbf{A}(k+N-1)\mathbf{B}(k+N-2) \vert \cdots \vert \mathbf{A}(k+N-1) \ldots \mathbf{A}(k+1)\mathbf{B}(k)]$$

is of full rank for some finite $N$.

## 8.3 Step-Varying Observers

The observer concept generalizes nicely for the linear, step-varying case. However, eigenvalue placement is no longer of direct interest because the observer error is not generally governed by powers of a matrix. We concentrate in this section on deadbeat step-varying observer design, although other observer error responses can be obtained if desired. Methods for observing linear state transformations, paralleling those for step-invariant observers, allow state observer order reduction and direct observation of a state transformation needed for feedback. In the step-invariant case, continuing convergence of the observer is guaranteed. That is, for a $p$th order observer with state $\xi(k)$ and a plant with state $x(k)$, if

$$\mathbf{Mx}(p) - \xi(p) = \mathbf{F}^p[\mathbf{Mx}(0) - \xi(0)]$$

then

$$\mathbf{Mx}(p+1) - \xi(p+1) = \mathbf{F}^p[\mathbf{Mx}(1) - \xi(1)]$$

and so on. For step-varying observers, we must specifically design continued convergence; it is not automatic.

Step-varying observation is desirable for step-invariant plants, too, because it can give an error response with a relatively small transient response amplitude.

## 8.3.1 *State Observation*

For an *n*th order linear, step-varying plant

$$\mathbf{x}(k+1) = \mathbf{A}(k)\mathbf{x}(k) + \mathbf{B}(k)\mathbf{u}(k)$$

$$\mathbf{y}(k) = \mathbf{C}(k)\mathbf{x}(k) + \mathbf{D}(k)\mathbf{u}(k)$$

a full-order state observer is another *n*th-order linear, step-varying system of the form

$$\xi(k+1) = \mathbf{F}(k)\xi(k) + \mathbf{G}(k)\mathbf{y}(k) + \mathbf{H}(k)\mathbf{u}(k) \tag{8-2}$$

as shown in Figure 8-2. The error between the plant state and the observer state is governed by

$$\mathbf{x}(k+1) - \xi(k+1)$$
$$= [\mathbf{A}(k) - \mathbf{G}(k)\mathbf{C}(k)]\mathbf{x}(k) - \mathbf{F}(k)\xi(k) + [\mathbf{B}(k) - \mathbf{H}(k) - \mathbf{G}(k)\mathbf{D}(k)]\mathbf{u}(k)$$

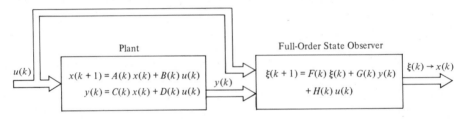

**FIGURE 8-2.** **Plant and step-varying observer.**

Requiring that the error equation be autonomous

$$F(k) = A(k) - G(k)C(k)$$

$$H(k) = B(k) - G(k)D(k) \tag{8-3}$$

where the step-varying matrix $G(k)$ is arbitrary. The observer error is then governed by

$$x(k + 1) - \xi(k + 1) = F(k)[x(k) - \xi(k)]$$

or

$$x(k) - \xi(k) = F(k - 1)F(k - 2) \ldots F(0)[x(0) - \xi(0)]$$

Rewriting the observer state equation (8-2) using (8-3) and the observer estimate of the plant outputs

$$w(k) = C(k)\xi(k) + D(k)u(k)$$

there results

$$\xi(k + 1) = A(k)\xi(k) + B(k)u(k) + G(k)[y(k) - w(k)]$$

which demonstrates that the full-order state observer can be viewed as a model of the plant, driven by the difference between the actual plant output and the model plant output. This arrangement is illustrated in Figure 8-3.

## 8.3.2 Gain Calculations for Single-Output Plants

Although the observer gain sequence $G(k)$ can be chosen to place eigenvalues of the observer state coupling matrices $F(k)$, this is of little direct help in designing the observer so that its state converges to that of the plant unless $F$ does not vary with step. A particularly simple and effective general method for achieving convergence is the following: for a single-output $n$th-order plant

$$x(k + 1) = A(x)x(k) + B(k)u(k)$$

$$y(k) = c^\dagger(k)x(k) + d^\dagger(k)u(k) \tag{8-4}$$

and full order state observer

$$\xi(k + 1) = F(k)\xi(k) + g(k)y(k) + H(k)u(k)$$

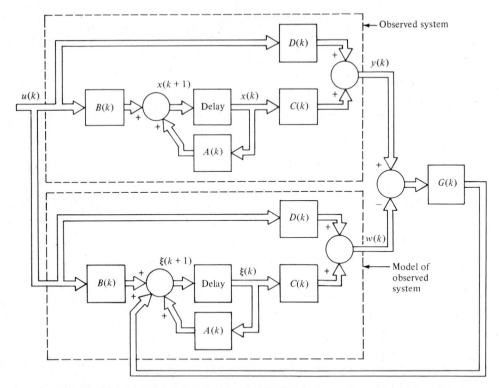

**FIGURE 8-3. State observer as a plant model driven by the output estimate error through a step-varying gain.**

the error between the plant state and the observer state at the $n$th step is

$$\mathbf{x}(n) - \boldsymbol{\xi}(n) = \mathbf{F}(n-1)\mathbf{F}(n-2)\ldots \mathbf{F}(1)\mathbf{F}(0)[\mathbf{x}(0) - \boldsymbol{\xi}(0)]$$

If $\mathbf{g}(0), \mathbf{g}(1), \ldots, \mathbf{g}(n-1)$ can be chosen so that

$$\mathbf{F}(n-1)\mathbf{F}(n-2)\cdots \mathbf{F}(1)\mathbf{F}(0) = \mathbf{0} \tag{8-5}$$

then the observer state will equal the plant state at the $n$th step and beyond.
    The desired relation (8-5) is obtained if

$$\begin{cases} \mathbf{F}(n-1)\mathbf{F}(n-2)\ldots \mathbf{F}(1)\mathbf{F}(0)\mathbf{j}_1 = \mathbf{0} \\ \mathbf{F}(n-1)\mathbf{F}(n-2)\ldots \mathbf{F}(1)\mathbf{F}(0)\mathbf{j}_2 = \mathbf{0} \\ \quad \vdots \\ \mathbf{F}(n-1)\mathbf{F}(n-2)\ldots \mathbf{F}(1)\mathbf{F}(0)\mathbf{j}_{n-1} = \mathbf{0} \\ \mathbf{F}(n-1)\mathbf{F}(n-2)\ldots \mathbf{F}(1)\mathbf{F}(0)\mathbf{j}_n = \mathbf{0} \end{cases} \tag{8-6}$$

where $\mathbf{j}_1, \mathbf{j}_2, \ldots, \mathbf{j}_n$ are any $n$ linearly independent $n$-vectors. These will be called *basis vectors* because they span the $n$ dimensional space. Relations (8-6) are, in turn, obtained if

$$\begin{cases} \mathbf{F}(0)\mathbf{j}_1 = \mathbf{0} \\ \mathbf{F}(1)\mathbf{F}(0)\mathbf{j}_2 = \mathbf{0} \\ \vdots \\ \mathbf{F}(n-2)\mathbf{F}(n-3)\ldots\mathbf{F}(1)\mathbf{F}(0)\mathbf{j}_{n-1} = \mathbf{0} \\ \mathbf{F}(n-1)\mathbf{F}(n-2)\ldots\mathbf{F}(1)\mathbf{F}(0)\mathbf{j}_n = \mathbf{0} \end{cases} \qquad (8\text{-}7)$$

The observer state coupling matrix is, at step zero

$$\mathbf{F}(0) = \mathbf{A}(0) - \mathbf{g}(0)\mathbf{c}^\dagger(0)$$

where the observer gain $\mathbf{g}(0)$ is an $n$-vector. Substituting into the first equation of (8-7)

$$\mathbf{A}(0)\mathbf{j}_1 - \mathbf{g}(0)\mathbf{c}^\dagger(0)\mathbf{j}_1 = \mathbf{0}$$

$$\mathbf{g}(0) = \frac{\mathbf{A}(0)\mathbf{j}_1}{\mathbf{c}^\dagger(0)\mathbf{j}_1}$$

where the quantity in the denominator of $\mathbf{g}(0)$ is a scalar. Similarly, given $\mathbf{g}(0)$ and thus $\mathbf{F}(0)$, the second equation of (8-7) is

$$[\mathbf{A}(1) - \mathbf{g}(1)\mathbf{c}^\dagger(1)]\mathbf{F}(0)\mathbf{j}_2 = \mathbf{0}$$

$$\mathbf{g}(1) = \frac{\mathbf{A}(1)\mathbf{F}(0)\mathbf{j}_2}{\mathbf{c}^\dagger(1)\mathbf{F}(0)\mathbf{j}_2}$$

In general

$$\mathbf{g}(k) = \frac{\mathbf{A}(k)\mathbf{F}(k-1)\ldots\mathbf{F}(1)\mathbf{F}(0)\mathbf{j}_{k+1}}{\mathbf{c}^\dagger(k)\mathbf{F}(k-1)\ldots\mathbf{F}(1)\mathbf{F}(0)\mathbf{j}_{k+1}} \qquad (8\text{-}8)$$

Table 8-1 summarizes this recursive process of determining observer gain vectors $\mathbf{g}(0), \mathbf{g}(1), \ldots, \mathbf{g}(n-1)$. The resulting observer is termed *deadbeat*. Like the case of a deadbeat step-invariant system, its error is zero in $n$ steps or less.

Each observer gain vector $\mathbf{g}(i)$ is that needed to drive the observer error due to a nonzero initial error in the $\mathbf{j}_{i+1}$ direction to zero. The transients in this step-varying observer's error response tend to be much smaller in amplitude than those typical for step-invariant observers.

---

**TABLE 8-1   Deadbeat Observer Design for Single-Output Plants**

---

## Plant Model

$\mathbf{x}(k + 1) = \mathbf{A}(k)\mathbf{x}(k) + \mathbf{B}(k)\mathbf{u}(k)$

$y(k) = \mathbf{c}^\dagger(k)\mathbf{x}(k) + \mathbf{d}^\dagger(k)\mathbf{u}(k)$

where $\mathbf{x}(k)$ is an $n$-vector and $y(k)$ is a scalar.

## Observer Structure

$\xi(k + 1) = \mathbf{F}(k)\xi(k) + \mathbf{g}(k)y(k) + \mathbf{H}(k)\mathbf{u}(k)$

where

$\mathbf{F}(k) = \mathbf{A}(k) - \mathbf{g}(k)\mathbf{c}^\dagger(k)$

$\mathbf{H}(k) = \mathbf{B}(k) - \mathbf{g}(k)\mathbf{d}^\dagger(k)$

## Observer Gain Calculation

Choose any set of linearly independent $n$-vectors (basis vectors)

$\mathbf{j}_1, \mathbf{j}_2, \cdots, \mathbf{j}_n.$

Then

$$\begin{cases} \mathbf{g}(0) = \dfrac{\mathbf{A}(0)\mathbf{j}_1}{\mathbf{c}^\dagger(0)\mathbf{j}_1} \\[2mm] \mathbf{F}(0) = \mathbf{A}(0) - \mathbf{g}(0)\mathbf{c}^\dagger(0) \\[2mm] \mathbf{H}(0) = \mathbf{B}(0) - \mathbf{g}(0)\mathbf{d}^\dagger(0) \end{cases}$$

$$\begin{cases} \mathbf{g}(1) = \dfrac{\mathbf{A}(1)\mathbf{F}(0)\mathbf{j}_2}{\mathbf{c}^\dagger(1)\mathbf{F}(0)\mathbf{j}_2} \\[2mm] \mathbf{F}(1) = \mathbf{A}(1) - \mathbf{g}(1)\mathbf{c}^\dagger(1) \\[2mm] \mathbf{H}(1) = \mathbf{B}(1) - \mathbf{g}(1)\mathbf{d}^\dagger(1) \end{cases}$$

$\vdots$

**TABLE 8-1** (cont)

$$\begin{cases} g(k) = \dfrac{A(k)F(k-1)\ldots F(1)F(0)j_{k+1}}{c^\dagger(k)F(k-1)\ldots F(1)F(0)j_{k+1}} \\[2mm] F(k) = A(k) - g(k)c^\dagger(k) \\[2mm] H(k) = B(k) - g(k)d^\dagger(k) \end{cases}$$

$$\vdots$$

$$g(n-1) = \frac{A(n-1)F(n-2)\ldots F(1)F(0)j_n}{c^\dagger(n-1)F(n-2)\ldots F(1)F(0)j_n}$$

If, for any gain calculation $g(k)$, the scalar divisor involved is zero

$$c^\dagger(k)F(k-1)\ldots F(1)F(0)j_{k+1} = 0$$

reordering the *remaining* $n$-vectors $j_{k+1}, j_{k+2}, \ldots, j_n$ will give a solution whenever one exists. If all remaining $n$-vectors give a zero scalar divisor, the plant output at this step is not linearly independent of previously used outputs, and can be discarded.

---

After $n$ steps, the observer error will have ideally been driven to zero. However, if there are inaccuracies, it is expedient to attempt to drive any remaining error toward zero on succeeding steps. One strategy is to restart the previous observer gain calculation algorithm by computing

$$g(n+1) = \frac{A(n+1)j_1}{c^\dagger(n+1)j_1}$$

$$F(n+1) = A(n+1) - g(n+1)c^\dagger(n+1)$$

$$g(n+2) = \frac{A(n+2)F(n+1)j_2}{c^\dagger(n+2)F(n+1)j_2}$$

and so on. Another strategy is to require *ongoing* observer convergence, where for each successive step after step $n-1$, the next observer gain is chosen so that

$$F(n-1+i)F(n-2+i)\ldots F(i) = 0, \qquad i = 1, 2, \ldots$$

The observer gain needed is

$$\mathbf{g}(n - 1 + i) = \frac{\mathbf{A}(n - 1 + i)\mathbf{F}(n - 2 + i) \ldots \mathbf{F}(i)\mathbf{j}_v}{\mathbf{c}^\dagger(n - 1 + i)\mathbf{F}(n - 2 + i) \ldots \mathbf{F}(i)\mathbf{j}_v}, \qquad i = 1, 2, \ldots$$

where $\mathbf{j}_v$ is any basis vector for which the scalar denominator is nonzero. The combination of the initial and ongoing observer gain algorithms is summarized in Table 8-2.

As a numerical example of deadbeat observer gain calculation, consider the single-output step-varying system

$$\begin{bmatrix} x_1(k + 1) \\ x_2(k + 1) \end{bmatrix} = \begin{bmatrix} k & 2 \\ 1 & -1 \end{bmatrix} \begin{bmatrix} x_1(k) \\ x_2(k) \end{bmatrix} + \begin{bmatrix} -1 \\ 1 \\ k + 1 \end{bmatrix} u(k) = \mathbf{A}(k)\mathbf{x}(k) + \mathbf{b}(k)u(k)$$

$$y(k) = [(\tfrac{1}{2})^k \quad 0] \begin{bmatrix} x_1(k) \\ x_2(k) \end{bmatrix} + u(k) = \mathbf{c}^\dagger(k)\mathbf{x}(k) + d(k)u(k)$$

For a deadbeat state observer of this plant

$$\boldsymbol{\xi}(k + 1) = \mathbf{F}(k)\boldsymbol{\xi}(k) + \mathbf{g}(k)y(k) + \mathbf{h}(k)u(k)$$

choosing the basis vectors $\mathbf{j}_1$ and $\mathbf{j}_2$ to be unit coordinate vectors

$$\mathbf{j}_1^\dagger = [1 \quad 0]; \qquad \mathbf{j}_2^\dagger = [0 \quad 1]$$

## TABLE 8-2    Initial and Ongoing Deadbeat Observer Design

Choose any set of linearly independent $n$-vectors (basis vectors) $\mathbf{j}_1, \mathbf{j}_2, \ldots, \mathbf{j}_n$. Then

$$\mathbf{g}(k) = \frac{\mathbf{A}(k)\mathbf{F}(k - 1) \ldots \mathbf{F}(k - n + 2)\mathbf{F}(k - n + 1)\mathbf{j}_i}{\mathbf{c}^\dagger(k)\mathbf{F}(k - 1) \ldots \mathbf{F}(k - n + 2)\mathbf{F}(k - n + 1)\mathbf{j}_i}$$

where $\mathbf{j}_i$ is any vector for which the scalar divisor in the above is nonzero and where

$$\mathbf{F}(i) = \begin{cases} \mathbf{A}(i) - \mathbf{g}(i)\mathbf{c}^\dagger(i) & i = 0, 1, 2, \ldots \\ \mathbf{I} & i = -1, -2, \ldots \end{cases}$$

If the scalar divisor is zero for all of the $n$-vectors $\mathbf{j}_1, \mathbf{j}_2, \ldots, \mathbf{j}_n$, the plant output at this step is not linearly independent of previously used outputs, and can be ignored.

give the following two deadbeat observer gains and plant input couplings:

$$g(0) = \frac{A(0)j_1}{c^\dagger(0)j_1} = \frac{\begin{bmatrix} 0 & 2 \\ 1 & -1 \end{bmatrix}\begin{bmatrix} 1 \\ 0 \end{bmatrix}}{[1 \quad 0]\begin{bmatrix} 1 \\ 0 \end{bmatrix}} = \begin{bmatrix} 0 \\ 1 \end{bmatrix}$$

$$F(0) = A(0) - g(0)c^\dagger(0) = \begin{bmatrix} 0 & 2 \\ 1 & -1 \end{bmatrix} - \begin{bmatrix} 0 \\ 1 \end{bmatrix}[1 \quad 0] = \begin{bmatrix} 0 & 2 \\ 0 & -1 \end{bmatrix}$$

$$h(0) = b(0) - g(0)d(0) = \begin{bmatrix} -1 \\ 1 \end{bmatrix} - \begin{bmatrix} 0 \\ 1 \end{bmatrix} = \begin{bmatrix} -1 \\ 0 \end{bmatrix}$$

$$g(1) = \frac{A(1)F(0)j_2}{c^\dagger(1)F(0)j_2} = \frac{\begin{bmatrix} 1 & 2 \\ 1 & -1 \end{bmatrix}\begin{bmatrix} 0 & 2 \\ 0 & -1 \end{bmatrix}\begin{bmatrix} 0 \\ 1 \end{bmatrix}}{[\frac{1}{2} \quad 0]\begin{bmatrix} 0 & 2 \\ 0 & -1 \end{bmatrix}\begin{bmatrix} 0 \\ 1 \end{bmatrix}} = \begin{bmatrix} 0 \\ 3 \end{bmatrix}$$

$$F(1) = A(1) - g(1)c^\dagger(1) = \begin{bmatrix} 1 & 2 \\ 1 & -1 \end{bmatrix} - \begin{bmatrix} 0 \\ 3 \end{bmatrix}[\frac{1}{2} \quad 0] = \begin{bmatrix} 1 & 2 \\ -\frac{1}{2} & -1 \end{bmatrix}$$

$$h(1) = b(1) - g(1)d(1) = \begin{bmatrix} -1 \\ \frac{1}{2} \end{bmatrix} - \begin{bmatrix} 0 \\ 3 \end{bmatrix} = \begin{bmatrix} -1 \\ -\frac{5}{2} \end{bmatrix}$$

For ongoing deadbeat observation with the same basis vector ordering, the next observer gain is

$$g(2) = \frac{A(2)F(1)j_1}{c^\dagger(2)F(1)j_1} = \frac{\begin{bmatrix} 2 & 2 \\ 1 & -1 \end{bmatrix}\begin{bmatrix} 1 & 2 \\ -\frac{1}{2} & -1 \end{bmatrix}\begin{bmatrix} 1 \\ 0 \end{bmatrix}}{[\frac{1}{4} \quad 0]\begin{bmatrix} 1 & 2 \\ -\frac{1}{2} & -1 \end{bmatrix}\begin{bmatrix} 1 \\ 0 \end{bmatrix}} = \begin{bmatrix} 4 \\ 6 \end{bmatrix}$$

and so on.

Other observer error responses besides deadbeat ones can be obtained, if desired. For example, the algorithm for which

$$\begin{cases} F(0)j_1 = \alpha j_1 \\ F(1)F(0)j_2 = \alpha j_2 \\ F(2)F(1)F(0)j_3 = \alpha j_3 \\ \quad \vdots \end{cases} \tag{8-9}$$

where

$$|\alpha| < 1$$

will progressively reduce, but not drive to zero, the observer error. Observer gains that give (8-9) are

$$
\begin{cases}
\mathbf{g}(0) = \dfrac{\mathbf{A}(0)\mathbf{j}_1 - \alpha\mathbf{j}_1}{\mathbf{c}^\dagger(0)\mathbf{j}_1} \\[3mm]
\mathbf{F}(0) = \mathbf{A}(0) - \mathbf{g}(0)\mathbf{c}^\dagger(0)
\end{cases}
$$

$$
\begin{cases}
\mathbf{g}(1) = \dfrac{\mathbf{A}(1)\mathbf{F}(0)\mathbf{j}_2 - \alpha\mathbf{j}_2}{\mathbf{c}^\dagger(1)\mathbf{F}(0)\mathbf{j}_2} \\[3mm]
\mathbf{F}(1) = \mathbf{A}(1) - \mathbf{g}(1)\mathbf{c}^\dagger(1)
\end{cases}
$$

$$
\mathbf{g}(2) = \dfrac{\mathbf{A}(2)\mathbf{F}(1)\mathbf{F}(0)\mathbf{j}_3 - \alpha\mathbf{j}_3}{\mathbf{c}^\dagger(2)\mathbf{F}(1)\mathbf{F}(0)\mathbf{j}_3}
$$

$$\vdots$$

When the deadbeat observer gain algorithm (8-8) is used for observation of a plant (8-4) with matrices $\mathbf{A}$ and $\mathbf{c}$ constant, the last observer gain obtained, $\mathbf{g}(n-1)$, is the constant gain for which all the eigenvalues of

$$\mathbf{F} = \mathbf{F}(n-1) = \mathbf{A} - \mathbf{g}(n-1)\mathbf{c}^\dagger$$

are at $\lambda = 0$. That gain can simply be held for steps beyond the $(n-1)$th to obtain ongoing observer convergence. For example, for the step-invariant system

$$
\begin{bmatrix} x_1(k+1) \\ x_2(k+1) \end{bmatrix} = \begin{bmatrix} 1 & 2 \\ 0 & -1 \end{bmatrix}\begin{bmatrix} x_1(k) \\ x_2(k) \end{bmatrix} + \begin{bmatrix} 1 \\ 2 \end{bmatrix} u(k)
$$

$$
y(k) = \begin{bmatrix} 1 & -1 \end{bmatrix}\begin{bmatrix} x_1(k) \\ x_2(k) \end{bmatrix}
$$

and unit coordinate basis vectors $\mathbf{j}_1$ and $\mathbf{j}_2$ as before, (8-8) gives

$$
\mathbf{g}(0) = \frac{\begin{bmatrix} 1 & 2 \\ 0 & -1 \end{bmatrix}\begin{bmatrix} 1 \\ 0 \end{bmatrix}}{\begin{bmatrix} 1 & -1 \end{bmatrix}\begin{bmatrix} 1 \\ 0 \end{bmatrix}} = \begin{bmatrix} 1 \\ 0 \end{bmatrix}
$$

$$F(0) = \begin{bmatrix} 1 & 2 \\ 0 & -1 \end{bmatrix} - \begin{bmatrix} 1 \\ 0 \end{bmatrix} [1 \quad -1] = \begin{bmatrix} 0 & 3 \\ 0 & -1 \end{bmatrix}$$

$$g(1) = \frac{\begin{bmatrix} 1 & 2 \\ 0 & -1 \end{bmatrix} \begin{bmatrix} 0 & 3 \\ 0 & -1 \end{bmatrix} \begin{bmatrix} 0 \\ 1 \end{bmatrix}}{[1 \quad -1] \begin{bmatrix} 0 & 3 \\ 0 & -1 \end{bmatrix} \begin{bmatrix} 0 \\ 1 \end{bmatrix}} = \begin{bmatrix} \frac{1}{4} \\ \frac{1}{4} \end{bmatrix}$$

$$F(1) = \begin{bmatrix} 1 & 2 \\ 0 & -1 \end{bmatrix} - \begin{bmatrix} \frac{1}{4} \\ \frac{1}{4} \end{bmatrix} [1 \quad -1] = \begin{bmatrix} \frac{3}{4} & \frac{9}{4} \\ -\frac{1}{4} & -\frac{3}{4} \end{bmatrix}$$

The observer state coupling matrix $F(1)$ has characteristic equation

$$\lambda^2 = 0$$

Using the algorithm (8-8) is also a handy way of calculating step-invariant deadbeat observer gains.

### 8.3.3 Gain Calculations for Multiple-Output Plants

The same general approach to observer design can be used for multiple-output plants. To illustrate the ideas involved, we consider the initial deadbeat gain sequence for a two-output plant. Extensions to plants with more than two outputs and to ongoing observation are straightforward.

For an $n$th-order two-output plant

$$x(k + 1) = A(k)x(k) + B(k)u(k)$$

$$y(k) = \begin{bmatrix} y_1(k) \\ y_2(k) \end{bmatrix} = \begin{bmatrix} c_1^\dagger(k) \\ c_2^\dagger(k) \end{bmatrix} x(k) + \begin{bmatrix} d_1^\dagger(k) \\ d_2^\dagger(k) \end{bmatrix} u(k) = C(k)x(k) + D(k)u(k)$$

a full-order state observer has the form

$$\xi(k + 1) = F(k)\xi(k) + [g_1(k) \mid g_2(k)]y(k) + H(k)u(k) \tag{8-10}$$

where

$$F(k) = A(k) - g_1(k)c_1^\dagger(k) - g_2(k)c_2^\dagger(k)$$

$$H(k) = B(k) - g_1(k)d_1^\dagger(k) - g_2(k)d_2^\dagger(k) \tag{8-11}$$

The error between the plant state and the observer state is governed by

$$\mathbf{x}(k) - \xi(k) = \mathbf{F}(k-1)\mathbf{F}(k-2)\ldots\mathbf{F}(1)\mathbf{F}(0)[\mathbf{x}(0) - \xi(0)]$$

Choosing $n$ linearly independent basis vectors $\mathbf{j}_1, \mathbf{j}_2, \ldots, \mathbf{j}_n$ and requiring that

$$\begin{cases} \mathbf{F}(0)\mathbf{j}_1 = \mathbf{0} \\ \mathbf{F}(0)\mathbf{j}_2 = \mathbf{0} \\ \mathbf{F}(1)\mathbf{F}(0)\mathbf{j}_3 = \mathbf{0} \\ \mathbf{F}(1)\mathbf{F}(0)\mathbf{j}_4 = \mathbf{0} \\ \mathbf{F}(2)\mathbf{F}(1)\mathbf{F}(0)\mathbf{j}_5 = \mathbf{0} \\ \quad\vdots \end{cases}$$

gives

$$\begin{cases} [\mathbf{A}(0) - \mathbf{g}_1(0)\mathbf{c}_1^\dagger(0) - \mathbf{g}_2(0)\mathbf{c}_2^\dagger(0)]\mathbf{j}_1 = \mathbf{0} \\ [\mathbf{A}(0) - \mathbf{g}_1(0)\mathbf{c}_1^\dagger(0) - \mathbf{g}_2(0)\mathbf{c}_2^\dagger(0)]\mathbf{j}_2 = \mathbf{0} \end{cases}$$

$$\begin{cases} [\mathbf{A}(1) - \mathbf{g}_1(1)\mathbf{c}_1^\dagger(1) - \mathbf{g}_2(1)\mathbf{c}_2^\dagger(1)]\mathbf{F}(0)\mathbf{j}_3 = \mathbf{0} \\ [\mathbf{A}(1) - \mathbf{g}_1(1)\mathbf{c}_1^\dagger(1) - \mathbf{g}_2(1)\mathbf{c}_2^\dagger(1)]\mathbf{F}(0)\mathbf{j}_4 = \mathbf{0} \end{cases}$$

$$\begin{cases} [\mathbf{A}(2) - \mathbf{g}_1(2)\mathbf{c}_1^\dagger(2) - \mathbf{g}_2(2)\mathbf{c}_2^\dagger(2)]\mathbf{F}(1)\mathbf{F}(0)\mathbf{j}_5 = \mathbf{0} \\ [\mathbf{A}(2) - \mathbf{g}_1(2)\mathbf{c}_1^\dagger(2) - \mathbf{g}_2(2)\mathbf{c}_2^\dagger(2)]\mathbf{F}(1)\mathbf{F}(0)\mathbf{j}_6 = \mathbf{0} \end{cases}$$

$$\vdots$$

and so on.

Each pair of simultaneous vector equations is a set of $2n$ linear algebraic equations in the $2n$ unknown elements of two observer gain vectors, of the form

$$\begin{cases} \delta_{11}\mathbf{g}_1(k) + \delta_{12}\mathbf{g}_2(k) = \mathbf{A}(k)\mathbf{F}(k-1)\ldots\mathbf{F}(0)\mathbf{j}_a \\ \delta_{21}\mathbf{g}_1(k) + \delta_{22}\mathbf{g}_2(k) = \mathbf{A}(k)\mathbf{F}(k-1)\ldots\mathbf{F}(0)\mathbf{j}_b \end{cases}$$

where $\mathbf{j}_a$ and $\mathbf{j}_b$ are the two $n$-vectors involved. Defining the $2 \times 2$ matrix

$$\Delta = \begin{bmatrix} \delta_{11} & \delta_{12} \\ \delta_{21} & \delta_{22} \end{bmatrix}$$

then

$$\begin{bmatrix} \{\mathbf{g}_1(k)\}\text{ith element} \\ \{\mathbf{g}_2(k)\}\text{ith element} \end{bmatrix} = \Delta^{-1} \begin{bmatrix} \{\mathbf{A}(k)\mathbf{F}(k-1)\ldots\mathbf{F}(0)\mathbf{j}_a\}\text{ith element} \\ \{\mathbf{A}(k)\mathbf{F}(k-1)\ldots\mathbf{F}(0)\mathbf{j}_b\}\text{ith element} \end{bmatrix}$$

or

$$
\begin{bmatrix} \mathbf{g}_1^\dagger(k) \\ \hline \mathbf{g}_2^\dagger(k) \end{bmatrix} = \Delta^{-1} \begin{bmatrix} \{\mathbf{A}(k)\mathbf{F}(k-1)\ldots\mathbf{F}(0)\mathbf{j}_a\}^\dagger \\ \{\mathbf{A}(k)\mathbf{F}(k-1)\ldots\mathbf{F}(0)\mathbf{j}_b\}^\dagger \end{bmatrix}
$$

Only a 2 × 2 matrix need be inverted to find each pair of observer gains. Consider, for example, the third-order, two-output plant

$$
\begin{bmatrix} x_1(k+1) \\ x_2(k+1) \\ x_3(k+1) \end{bmatrix} = \begin{bmatrix} (\tfrac{1}{2})^k & 0 & 1 \\ -1 & -1 & 0 \\ 2 & 0 & k \end{bmatrix} \begin{bmatrix} x_1(k) \\ x_2(k) \\ x_3(k) \end{bmatrix} + \begin{bmatrix} 1 \\ 1 \\ 1 \end{bmatrix} u(k)
$$

$$
\begin{bmatrix} y_1(k) \\ y_2(k) \end{bmatrix} = \begin{bmatrix} 0 & (k-2) & 1 \\ -1 & 3 & 0 \end{bmatrix} \begin{bmatrix} x_1(k) \\ x_2(k) \\ x_3(k) \end{bmatrix} + \begin{bmatrix} 0 \\ 4 \end{bmatrix} u(k)
$$

and a third-order state observer of the form (8-10) with (8-11). Choosing the basis vectors to be unit coordinate vectors

$$
\mathbf{j}_1 = \begin{bmatrix} 1 \\ 0 \\ 0 \end{bmatrix}; \qquad \mathbf{j}_2 = \begin{bmatrix} 0 \\ 1 \\ 0 \end{bmatrix}; \qquad \mathbf{j}_3 = \begin{bmatrix} 0 \\ 0 \\ 1 \end{bmatrix}
$$

and requiring that the observer gain vector at step 0 satisfy

$$
\left\{ \left( \begin{bmatrix} 1 & 0 & 1 \\ -1 & -1 & 0 \\ 2 & 0 & 0 \end{bmatrix} - \begin{bmatrix} g_{11}(0) \\ g_{21}(0) \\ g_{31}(0) \end{bmatrix} [0 \ -2 \ 1] \right) \begin{bmatrix} g_{12}(0) \\ g_{22}(0) \\ g_{32}(0) \end{bmatrix} [-1 \ 3 \ 0] \right\} \begin{bmatrix} 1 \\ 0 \\ 0 \end{bmatrix} = \begin{bmatrix} 0 \\ 0 \\ 0 \end{bmatrix}
$$

$$
\left\{ \left( \begin{bmatrix} 1 & 0 & 1 \\ -1 & -1 & 0 \\ 2 & 0 & 0 \end{bmatrix} - \begin{bmatrix} g_{11}(0) \\ g_{21}(0) \\ g_{31}(0) \end{bmatrix} [0 \ -2 \ 1] \right) \begin{bmatrix} g_{12}(0) \\ g_{22}(0) \\ g_{32}(0) \end{bmatrix} [-1 \ 3 \ 0] \right\} \begin{bmatrix} 0 \\ 1 \\ 0 \end{bmatrix} = \begin{bmatrix} 0 \\ 0 \\ 0 \end{bmatrix}
$$

gives

$$
\mathbf{G}(0) = \begin{bmatrix} g_{11}(0) & g_{12}(0) \\ g_{21}(0) & g_{22}(0) \\ g_{31}(0) & g_{32}(0) \end{bmatrix} = \begin{bmatrix} -\tfrac{3}{2} & -1 \\ 2 & 1 \\ -3 & -2 \end{bmatrix}
$$

and

$$
\mathbf{F}(0) = \begin{bmatrix} 1 & 0 & 1 \\ -1 & -1 & 0 \\ 2 & 0 & 0 \end{bmatrix} - \begin{bmatrix} -\tfrac{3}{2} & -1 \\ 2 & 1 \\ -3 & -2 \end{bmatrix} \begin{bmatrix} 0 & -2 & 1 \\ -1 & 3 & 0 \end{bmatrix} = \begin{bmatrix} 0 & 0 & \tfrac{3}{2} \\ 0 & 0 & -2 \\ 0 & 0 & 3 \end{bmatrix}
$$

Requiring that, on step 1,

$$\begin{cases} [\mathbf{A}(1) - \mathbf{g}_1(1)\mathbf{c}_1^\dagger(1) - \mathbf{g}_2(1)\mathbf{c}_2^\dagger(1)]\mathbf{F}(0)\mathbf{j}_3 = \mathbf{0} \\ [\mathbf{A}(1) - \mathbf{g}_1(1)\mathbf{c}_1^\dagger(1) - \mathbf{g}_2(1)\mathbf{c}_2^\dagger(1)]\mathbf{j}_1 = \mathbf{0} \end{cases}$$

will drive the observer error to zero as well as zeroing again any residual observer error in the $\mathbf{j}_1$ direction.

## 8.3.4 Observing Linear State Transformations

When the state of a step-varying observer, which is not necessarily of the same order as the plant, observes a linear transformation of the plant state

$$\xi(k) \rightarrow \mathbf{M}(k)\mathbf{x}(k)$$

## TABLE 8-3   Step-Varying Observers of Plant State Transformations

### Plant Model

$$\mathbf{x}(k + 1) = \mathbf{A}(k)\mathbf{x}(k) + \mathbf{B}(k)\mathbf{u}(k)$$

$$\mathbf{y}(k) = \mathbf{C}(k)\mathbf{x}(k) + \mathbf{D}(k)\mathbf{u}(k)$$

### Observer

$$\xi(k + 1) = \mathbf{F}(k)\xi(k) + \mathbf{G}(k)\mathbf{y}(k) + \mathbf{H}(k)\mathbf{u}(k)$$

$$\xi(k) \rightarrow \mathbf{M}(k)\mathbf{x}(k)$$

where

$$\mathbf{F}(k)\mathbf{M}(k) = \mathbf{M}(k + 1)\mathbf{A}(k) - \mathbf{G}(k)\mathbf{C}(k)$$

$$\mathbf{H}(k) = \mathbf{M}(k + 1)\mathbf{B}(k) - \mathbf{G}(k)\mathbf{D}(k)$$

### Observer Error

$$\mathbf{M}(k + 1)\mathbf{x}(k + 1) - \xi(k + 1) = \mathbf{F}(k)[\mathbf{M}(k)\mathbf{x}(k) - \xi(k)]$$

$$\mathbf{M}(k)\mathbf{x}(k) - \xi(k) = \mathbf{F}(k - 1)\mathbf{F}(k - 2)\ldots\mathbf{F}(0)[\mathbf{M}(0)\mathbf{x}(0) - \xi(0)]$$

the observer error is governed by

$$\mathbf{M}(k+1)\mathbf{x}(k+1) - \xi(k+1) = [\mathbf{M}(k+1)\mathbf{A}(k) - \mathbf{G}(k)\mathbf{C}(k)]\mathbf{x}(k) - \mathbf{F}(k)\xi(k)$$
$$+ [\mathbf{M}(k+1)\mathbf{B}(k) - \mathbf{G}(k)\mathbf{D}(k) - \mathbf{H}(k)]\mathbf{u}(k)$$

Requiring that the error be autonomous, with

$$\mathbf{M}(k+1)\mathbf{x}(k+1) - \xi(k+1) = \mathbf{F}(k)[\mathbf{M}(k)\mathbf{x}(k) - \xi(k)]$$

gives

$$\mathbf{F}(k)\mathbf{M}(k) = \mathbf{M}(k+1)\mathbf{A}(k) - \mathbf{G}(k)\mathbf{C}(k)$$

$$\mathbf{H}(k) = \mathbf{M}(k+1)\mathbf{B}(k) - \mathbf{G}(k)\mathbf{D}(k) \tag{8-12}$$

The observer error is then governed by

$$\mathbf{M}(k)\mathbf{x}(k) - \xi(k) = \mathbf{F}(k-1)\mathbf{F}(k-2)\cdots\mathbf{F}(0)[\mathbf{M}(0)\mathbf{x}(0) - \xi(0)]$$

These relations are summarized in Table 8-3. As with their counterparts in the step-invariant case, these equations can be used to design state observers of reduced order and observers of linear plant state transformations.

# 8.4 Tracking System Controller Design

Most of the step-invariant tracking system design principles also carry over nicely to step-varying tracking system design. Although eigenvalue placement is no longer of direct interest, the same methods used for step-varying deadbeat observer design can be applied to obtain deadbeat plant response (or some other response, if needed) with step-varying state feedback. When a deadbeat observer state estimate is substituted for the plant state with deadbeat state feedback, the resulting overall system is deadbeat.

Each of the three basic tracking system design methods

1. Ideal tracking
2. Response model
3. Reference input model

can be generalized to step-varying systems. Existence of an ideal tracking filter rests on whether the plant with feedback has a suitable step-varying inverse filter. Design using a response model requires, as before, selecting a response model that is both suitable and feasible, a process that, in general, is even more difficult than in the step-invariant case. In reference input model design, the plant to be controlled is made to be an observer of a model of the reference signals of particular interest. The system then tracks ideally all reference inputs that are modeled.

## 8.4.1 State Feedback

Deadbeat or perhaps some other shaping of a step-varying plant's zero-input response with state feedback is dual to step-varying observer design. For a single-input $n$th-order plant with state equations

$$\mathbf{x}(k + 1) = \mathbf{A}(k)\mathbf{x}(k) + \mathbf{b}(k)u(k)$$

the state feedback

$$u(k) = \mathbf{e}^\dagger(k)\mathbf{x}(k) + \rho(k)$$

where $\rho(k)$ is an external input, gives feedback system state equations

$$\mathbf{x}(k + 1) = [\mathbf{A}(k) + \mathbf{b}(k)\mathbf{e}^\dagger(k)]\mathbf{x}(k) + \mathbf{b}(k)\rho(k) \tag{8-13}$$

This arrangement is shown in Figure 8-4. The zero-input response of the feedback system (8-13) is

$$\mathbf{x}_{\text{zero-input}}(k) = \mathbf{\Phi}(k - 1)\mathbf{\Phi}(k - 2) \cdots \mathbf{\Phi}(0)\mathbf{x}(0)$$

where

$$\mathbf{\Phi}(i) = \mathbf{A}(i) + \mathbf{b}(i)\mathbf{e}^\dagger(i)$$

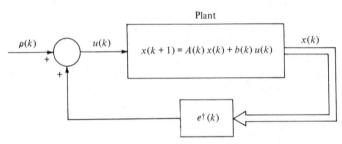

**FIGURE 8-4.   Step-varying state feedback for a single-input plant.**

Let

$$\mathbf{j}_1, \mathbf{j}_2, \ldots, \mathbf{j}_n$$

be any linearly independent set of $n$-vectors. Requiring that

$$\mathbf{\Phi}(n - 1)\mathbf{\Phi}(n - 2) \cdots \mathbf{\Phi}(0) = \mathbf{0} \qquad (8\text{-}14)$$

so that the zero-input response of the state feedback system is zero at step $n$ and beyond is equivalent to requiring that

$$\mathbf{\Phi}^\dagger(0) \cdots \mathbf{\Phi}^\dagger(n - 2)\mathbf{\Phi}^\dagger(n - 1) = \mathbf{0}$$

or

$$\begin{cases} \mathbf{\Phi}^\dagger(0) \cdots \mathbf{\Phi}^\dagger(n - 2)\mathbf{\Phi}^\dagger(n - 1)\mathbf{j}_1 = \mathbf{0} \\ \mathbf{\Phi}^\dagger(0) \cdots \mathbf{\Phi}^\dagger(n - 2)\mathbf{\Phi}^\dagger(n - 1)\mathbf{j}_2 = \mathbf{0} \\ \quad \vdots \\ \mathbf{\Phi}^\dagger(0) \cdots \mathbf{\Phi}^\dagger(n - 2)\mathbf{\Phi}^\dagger(n - 1)\mathbf{j}_n = \mathbf{0} \end{cases} \qquad (8\text{-}15)$$

In turn, the following requirements assure (8-15) and thus (8-14):

$$\begin{cases} \mathbf{\Phi}^\dagger(n - 1)\mathbf{j}_1 = \mathbf{0} \\ \mathbf{\Phi}^\dagger(n - 2)\mathbf{\Phi}^\dagger(n - 1)\mathbf{j}_2 = \mathbf{0} \\ \quad \vdots \\ \mathbf{\Phi}^\dagger(0) \cdots \mathbf{\Phi}^\dagger(n - 2)\mathbf{\Phi}^\dagger(n - 1)\mathbf{j}_n = \mathbf{0} \end{cases} \qquad (8\text{-}16)$$

The first equation of (8-16) is, in terms of the feedback gain $\mathbf{e}(n - 1)$

$$\mathbf{A}^\dagger(n - 1)\mathbf{j}_1 + \mathbf{e}(n - 1)\mathbf{b}^\dagger(n - 1)\mathbf{j}_1 = \mathbf{0}$$

or

$$\mathbf{e}(n - 1) = -\frac{\mathbf{A}^\dagger(n - 1)\mathbf{j}_1}{\mathbf{b}^\dagger(n - 1)\mathbf{j}_1}$$

Similarly, the second equation of (8-16) gives

$$\mathbf{e}(n - 2) = -\frac{\mathbf{A}^\dagger(n - 2)\mathbf{\Phi}^\dagger(n - 1)\mathbf{j}_2}{\mathbf{b}^\dagger(n - 2)\mathbf{\Phi}^\dagger(n - 1)\mathbf{j}_2}$$

where

$$\mathbf{\Phi}(n - 1) = \mathbf{A}(n - 1) + \mathbf{b}(n - 1)\mathbf{e}^\dagger(n - 1)$$

and in general

$$\mathbf{e}(k) = -\frac{\mathbf{A}^\dagger(k)\mathbf{\Phi}^\dagger(k+1)\cdots\mathbf{\Phi}^\dagger(n-1)\mathbf{j}_{n-k}}{\mathbf{b}^\dagger(k)\mathbf{\Phi}^\dagger(k+1)\cdots\mathbf{\Phi}^\dagger(n-1)\mathbf{j}_{n-k}} \tag{8-17}$$

where

$$\mathbf{\Phi}(i) = \mathbf{A}(i) + \mathbf{b}(i)\mathbf{e}^\dagger(i) \tag{8-18}$$

The computational procedure is summarized in Table 8-4. The calculations are inherently backward-in-step, in contrast to the forward-in-step procedure for observers.

Consider the plant

$$\begin{bmatrix} x_1(k+1) \\ x_2(k+1) \end{bmatrix} = \begin{bmatrix} k & 2 \\ 1 & -1 \end{bmatrix}\begin{bmatrix} x_1(k) \\ x_2(k) \end{bmatrix} + \begin{bmatrix} -1 \\ 1 \\ \overline{k+1} \end{bmatrix} u(k) = \mathbf{A}(k)\mathbf{x}(k) + \mathbf{b}(k)u(k)$$

with state feedback

$$u(k) = [e_1(k) \quad e_2(k)]\begin{bmatrix} x_1(k) \\ x_2(k) \end{bmatrix} + \rho(k) = \mathbf{e}^\dagger(k)\mathbf{x}(k) + \rho(k)$$

Relations (8-17) and (8-18) and the choices of basis vectors $\mathbf{j}_1$ and $\mathbf{j}_2$ as unit coordinate vectors

$$\mathbf{j}_1^\dagger = [1 \quad 0]; \qquad \mathbf{j}_2^\dagger = [0 \quad 1]$$

give the following feedback gains for deadbeat zero-input response:

$$\mathbf{e}(1) = -\frac{\mathbf{A}^\dagger(1)\mathbf{j}_1}{\mathbf{b}^\dagger(1)\mathbf{j}_1} = \begin{bmatrix} 1 \\ 2 \end{bmatrix}$$

$$\mathbf{\Phi}(1) = \mathbf{A}(1) + \mathbf{b}(1)\mathbf{e}^\dagger(1) = \begin{bmatrix} 0 & 0 \\ \frac{3}{2} & 0 \end{bmatrix}$$

$$\mathbf{e}(0) = -\frac{\mathbf{A}^\dagger(0)\mathbf{\Phi}^\dagger(1)\mathbf{j}_2}{\mathbf{b}^\dagger(0)\mathbf{\Phi}^\dagger(1)\mathbf{j}_2} = \begin{bmatrix} 0 \\ 2 \end{bmatrix}$$

For continued (but not *ongoing*) deadbeat state feedback, this computational procedure can simply be repeated to obtain $\mathbf{e}(3)$ and $\mathbf{e}(2)$, then $\mathbf{e}(5)$ and $\mathbf{e}(4)$, and so on. Different pairs of gain vectors will generally result

## TABLE 8-4 Deadbeat State Feedback for Single-Input Plants

### Plant With State Feedback

$$u(k) = \mathbf{e}^\dagger(k)\mathbf{x}(k) + \rho(k)$$

in

$$\mathbf{x}(k + 1) = \mathbf{A}(k)\mathbf{x}(k) + \mathbf{b}(k)u(k) = [\mathbf{A}(k) + \mathbf{b}(k)\mathbf{e}^\dagger(k)]\mathbf{x}(k) + \mathbf{b}(k)\rho(k)$$

### Feedback Gain Calculation

Choose any set of linearly independent $n$-vectors (basis vectors) $\mathbf{j}_1, \mathbf{j}_2, \ldots, \mathbf{j}_n$. Then

$$\begin{cases} \mathbf{e}(n - 1) = -\dfrac{\mathbf{A}^\dagger(n - 1)\mathbf{j}_1}{\mathbf{b}^\dagger(n - 2)\mathbf{j}_1} \\[2mm] \mathbf{\Phi}(n - 1) = \mathbf{A}(n - 1) + \mathbf{b}(n - 1)\mathbf{e}^\dagger(n - 1) \end{cases}$$

$$\begin{cases} \mathbf{e}(n - 2) = -\dfrac{\mathbf{A}^\dagger(n - 2)\mathbf{\Phi}^\dagger(n - 1)\mathbf{j}_2}{\mathbf{b}^\dagger(n - 2)\mathbf{\Phi}^\dagger(n - 1)\mathbf{j}_2} \\[2mm] \mathbf{\Phi}(n - 2) = \mathbf{A}(n - 2) + \mathbf{b}(n - 2)\mathbf{e}^\dagger(n - 2) \end{cases}$$

$$\vdots$$

$$\begin{cases} \mathbf{e}(k) = -\dfrac{\mathbf{A}^\dagger(k)\mathbf{\Phi}^\dagger(k + 1)\ldots\mathbf{\Phi}^\dagger(n - 1)\mathbf{j}_{n-k}}{\mathbf{b}^\dagger(k)\mathbf{\Phi}^\dagger(k + 1)\ldots\mathbf{\Phi}^\dagger(n - 1)\mathbf{j}_{n-k}} \\[2mm] \mathbf{\Phi}(k) = \mathbf{A}(k) + \mathbf{b}(k)\mathbf{e}^\dagger(k) \end{cases}$$

$$\vdots$$

$$\begin{cases} \mathbf{e}(0) = -\dfrac{\mathbf{A}^\dagger(0)\mathbf{\Phi}^\dagger(1)\ldots\mathbf{\Phi}^\dagger(n - 1)\mathbf{j}_n}{\mathbf{b}^\dagger(0)\mathbf{\Phi}^\dagger(1)\ldots\mathbf{\Phi}^\dagger(n - 1)\mathbf{j}_n} \\[2mm] \mathbf{\Phi}(0) = \mathbf{A}(0) + \mathbf{b}(0)\mathbf{e}^\dagger(0) \end{cases}$$

If for any gain calculation $\mathbf{e}(k)$, the scalar divisor involved is zero

$$\mathbf{b}^\dagger(k)\mathbf{\Phi}^\dagger(k + 1)\ldots\mathbf{\Phi}^\dagger(n - 1)\mathbf{j}_{n-k} = 0$$

a special situation has occurred for which the state of the plant cannot be controlled in the $\mathbf{j}_{n-k}$ direction at that step. Reordering the *remaining* basis vectors will give a solution whenever one exists. If all remaining basis vectors give a zero scalar divisor, the plant state cannot be changed by the input as desired at this step.

because $\mathbf{A}(k)$ and $\mathbf{b}(k)$ can change with step. The next two gains calculated in this way are

$$\mathbf{e}(3) = -\frac{\mathbf{A}^{\dagger}(3)\mathbf{j}_1}{\mathbf{b}^{\dagger}(3)\mathbf{j}_1} = \begin{bmatrix} 3 \\ 2 \end{bmatrix}$$

$$\boldsymbol{\Phi}(3) = \mathbf{A}(3) + \mathbf{b}(3)\mathbf{e}^{\dagger}(3) = \begin{bmatrix} 0 & 0 \\ \frac{7}{4} & -\frac{1}{2} \end{bmatrix}$$

$$\mathbf{e}(2) = -\frac{\mathbf{A}^{\dagger}(2)\boldsymbol{\Phi}^{\dagger}(3)\mathbf{j}_2}{\mathbf{b}^{\dagger}(2)\boldsymbol{\Phi}^{\dagger}(3)\mathbf{j}_2} = \begin{bmatrix} -3 \\ 3 \end{bmatrix}$$

Analogous to the situation with step-varying observers, if the plant has multiple inputs, a scalar feedback signal can be distributed to the inputs and the feedback designed as if the plant were single-input. Better, the state feedback to each of the inputs can be designed to drive the state vector to zero in more than one direction at each step, as was done for observer error in Section 8.3.3.

## 8.4.2 Observer Feedback

Suppose that state estimates from a $p$th-order deadbeat observer are substituted for the state in a plant feedback arrangement as in Figure 8-5. The character of the observer feedback system's zero-input response is the same as the zero-input response of the state feedback system after $p$ steps because, then, the observer state and the plant state are identical. The observer feedback system will have a $p$-step initial transient interval during which the observer is converging to the plant state. Thereafter, the feedback system will behave as if it had state feedback. If the plant is $n$th-order and the state feedback has also been designed for deadbeat response, the $(n + p)$th-order observer feedback system will be deadbeat.

## 8.4.3 Disturbance Models

The approaches to tracking system disturbance rejection,

1. Ignoring the disturbances;
2. Structuring the plant and controller (when possible) to reduce the undesirable effects of disturbances;
3. Modeling disturbances as stochastic processes;
4. Modeling disturbances as the output of an autonomous system

Plant with Observer Feedback

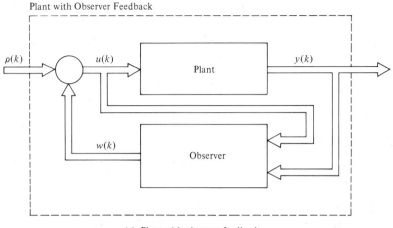

(a) Plant with observer feedback.

Plant with Observer Feedback

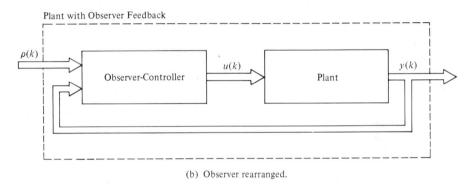

(b) Observer rearranged.

**FIGURE 8-5.   Step-varying plant with observer feedback in place of state feedback.**

apply also to step-varying tracking system design. As always, simulation studies are helpful for evaluating choice 1. Choice 2 is difficult to discuss in general because system configurations have highly individual costs and constraints. We touch upon the third choice in the next section, in connection with producing least squares estimates of a plant's state from its control inputs and measurement outputs. However, only an overview of the approach is given here because a background in the study of stochastic processes has not been assumed.

The fourth choice, which is especially suitable for disturbances that are highly correlated from step to step, is pictured in Figure 8-6. It is actually easier to design step-varying state models of disturbances than step-invariant

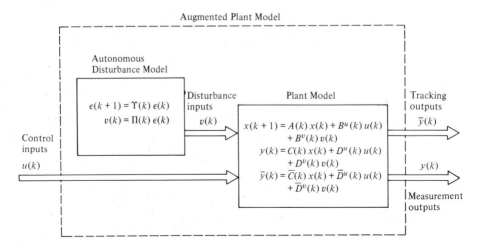

**FIGURE 8-6. Incorporating a disturbance model.**

ones. For example, any scalar disturbance of the form

$$v(k) = \beta_1 f_1(k) + \beta_2 f_2(k) + \cdots + \beta_i f_i(k)$$

with constants $\beta_1, \beta_2, \ldots, \beta_i$ arbitrary and $f_1(k), f_2(k), \ldots, f_i(k)$ any functions is easily modeled with an $i$th-order linear, step-varying system

$$\varepsilon(k+1) = \gamma(k)\varepsilon(k)$$

$$v(k) = \pi^\dagger(k)\varepsilon(k)$$

by choosing

$$\gamma(k) = \mathbf{I}$$

and

$$\pi^\dagger(k) = [f_1(k) \quad f_2(k) \quad \cdots \quad f_i(k)]$$

For these choices, the model state $\varepsilon(k) = \varepsilon(0)$ is constant and equal to the initial conditions:

$$v(k) = \varepsilon_1(0)f_1(k) + \varepsilon_2(0)f_2(k) + \cdots + \varepsilon_i(0)f_i(k)$$

For example, a disturbance of the form

$$v(k) = \beta_1 e^{-0.1k^2} + \beta_2 \left(\frac{1}{k!}\right)$$

can only be modeled approximately with a step-invariant system, even one of very high order. It is modeled exactly by the linear, step-varying model.

$$\begin{bmatrix} \varepsilon_1(k+1) \\ \varepsilon_2(k+1) \end{bmatrix} = \begin{bmatrix} \varepsilon_1(k) \\ \varepsilon_2(k) \end{bmatrix}$$

$$v(k) = \begin{bmatrix} e^{-0.1k^2} & \dfrac{1}{k!} \end{bmatrix} \begin{bmatrix} \varepsilon_1(k) \\ \varepsilon_2(k) \end{bmatrix}$$

As with step-invariant systems, observer estimates of disturbances, obtained by observing a plant augmented with a state disturbance model, can be used to cancel the effect of a disturbance on a tracking output, to the extent that the model is accurate.

### 8.4.4 Observing Tracking Signal Models

Having designed an acceptable zero-input response, the zero-state response of a tracking system can be designed by requiring that the tracking outputs observe signals from a suitable reference signal model, as in Figure 8-7. In the step-varying case, observation of a signal model

$$\sigma(k+1) = \mathbf{\Psi}(k)\sigma(k)$$

$$\mathbf{r}(k) = \mathbf{\Theta}(k)\sigma(k) \tag{8-19}$$

by the plant

$$\mathbf{x}(k+1) = \mathbf{A}(k)\mathbf{x}(k) + \mathbf{B}(k)\mathbf{r}(k)$$

$$\bar{\mathbf{y}}(k) = \bar{\mathbf{C}}(k)\mathbf{x}(k) + \bar{\mathbf{D}}(k)\mathbf{r}(k)$$

where

$$\mathbf{x}(k) \rightarrow \mathbf{M}(k)\sigma(k)$$

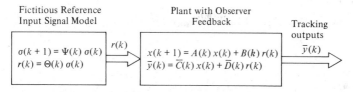

**FIGURE 8-7.** Observation of a step-varying reference input signal model.

requires that (translating (8-12) to this situation)

$$\mathbf{A}(k)\mathbf{M}(k) = \mathbf{M}(k+1)\mathbf{\Psi}(k) - \mathbf{B}(k)\mathbf{\Theta}(k)$$

For the plant tracking outputs to observe the model reference signal

$$\bar{\mathbf{y}}(k) \rightarrow \mathbf{r}(k)$$

constrains the observation transformation matrices $\mathbf{M}(k)$ according to

$$\bar{\mathbf{y}}(k) = \bar{\mathbf{C}}(k)\mathbf{x}(k) + \bar{\mathbf{D}}(k)\mathbf{r}(k) \rightarrow \bar{\mathbf{C}}(k)\mathbf{M}(k)\mathbf{\sigma}(k) + \bar{\mathbf{D}}(k)\mathbf{r}(k) = \mathbf{r}(k)$$

Substituting from (8-19):

$$\mathbf{C}(k)\mathbf{M}(k)\mathbf{\sigma}(k) = [\mathbf{I} - \bar{\mathbf{D}}(k)]\mathbf{\Theta}(k)\mathbf{\sigma}(k)$$

or

$$\mathbf{C}(k)\mathbf{M}(k) = [\mathbf{I} - \bar{\mathbf{D}}(k)]\mathbf{\Theta}(k)$$

As an example, consider the plant

$$\begin{bmatrix} x_1(k+1) \\ x_2(k+1) \end{bmatrix} = \begin{bmatrix} \frac{1}{2} & 1 \\ 0 & \frac{1}{k+1} \end{bmatrix} \begin{bmatrix} x_1(k) \\ x_2(k) \end{bmatrix} + \begin{bmatrix} \alpha(k) \\ 2\alpha(k) \end{bmatrix} r(k)$$

$$= \mathbf{A}(k)\mathbf{x}(k) + \mathbf{b}(k)r(k)$$

$$\bar{y}(k) = \begin{bmatrix} 1 & k \end{bmatrix} \begin{bmatrix} x_1(k) \\ x_2(k) \end{bmatrix} = \bar{\mathbf{c}}^\dagger(k)\mathbf{x}(k)$$

which includes output or observer feedback, if used, and has a scalar control input gain sequence $\alpha(k)$ to be selected. Suppose it is desired that the zero-state component of the plant's tracking output $\bar{y}(k)$ track an alternating reference input of the form

$$r(k) = \beta(-1)^k$$

where $\beta$ is any constant. A model for this class of reference input signals is the first-order system

$$\sigma(k+1) = \sigma(k) = \mathbf{\Psi}\sigma(k)$$

$$r(k) = (-1)^k\sigma(k) = \theta(k)\sigma(k)$$

Denoting the state transformation of $\sigma(k)$ observed by $\mathbf{x}(k)$ as

$$\mathbf{x}(k) \rightarrow \mathbf{m}(k)\sigma(k)$$

for the plant to be an observer of the reference signal model requires that

$$A(k)\mathbf{m}(k) = \mathbf{m}(k + 1)\Psi - \mathbf{b}(k)\theta(k)$$

or

$$A\begin{bmatrix} m_1(k) \\ m_2(k) \end{bmatrix} = \begin{bmatrix} m_1(k + 1) \\ m_2(k + 1) \end{bmatrix} - \begin{bmatrix} \alpha(k) \\ 2\alpha(k) \end{bmatrix}(-1)^k \qquad (8\text{-}20)$$

If

$$\bar{y}(k) \rightarrow r(k)$$

it is also required that

$$\bar{y}(k) = \bar{\mathbf{c}}^\dagger(k)\mathbf{x}(k) \rightarrow \bar{\mathbf{c}}^\dagger(k)\mathbf{m}(k)\sigma(k) = r(k)$$

or

$$\mathbf{c}^\dagger(k)\mathbf{m}(k) = \theta(k)$$

or

$$[1 \quad k]\begin{bmatrix} m_1(k) \\ m_2(k) \end{bmatrix} = m_1(k) + km_2(k) = (-1)^k \qquad (8\text{-}21)$$

At each step $k$, (8-21) constrains the two components of the observation matrix $m$ such that

$$m_1(k) = (-1)^k - km_2(k) \qquad (8\text{-}22)$$

Combining this constraint at step $k + 1$ with the other two linear algebraic equations (8-20) gives

$$\begin{cases} m_1(k + 1) + (k + 1)m_2(k + 1) = (-1)^{k+1} \\ m_1(k + 1) - (-1)^k\alpha(k) = \tfrac{1}{2}m_1(k) + m_2(k) \\ m_2(k + 1) - 2(-1)^k\alpha(k) = \dfrac{1}{k + 1}m_2(k) \end{cases} \qquad (8\text{-}23)$$

which is a recursive arrangement for computing $\mathbf{m}(k + 1)$ and $\alpha(k)$ from any initial $\mathbf{m}(0)$ satisfying (8-22). Arbitrarily choosing

$$\mathbf{m}(0) = \begin{bmatrix} 1 \\ 0 \end{bmatrix}$$

then (8-23) with $k = 0$ gives

$$\begin{cases} m_1(1) + 2m_2(1) = -1 \\ m_1(1) - \alpha(0) = \frac{1}{2} \\ m_2(1) - 2\alpha(0) = 0 \end{cases}$$

which has solution

$$\mathbf{m}(1) = \begin{bmatrix} 0 \\ -1 \end{bmatrix}; \qquad \alpha(0) = -\frac{1}{2}$$

Then, (8-23) with $k = 1$ gives

$$\begin{cases} m_1(2) + 2m_2(2) = 1 \\ m_1(2) + \alpha(1) = \frac{1}{2}m_1(1) + m_2(1) = -1 \\ m_2(2) + 2\alpha(1) = \frac{1}{2}m_2(1) = -\frac{1}{2} \end{cases}$$

which has solution

$$\mathbf{m}(2) = \begin{bmatrix} -0.4 \\ 0.7 \end{bmatrix}; \qquad \alpha(1) = -0.6$$

and so on. The gains $\alpha(k)$ make the plant's zero-state response track any alternating sequence perfectly.

## 8.5 Least Squares Estimation

In this section, we discuss some of the properties of quadratic forms and we develop the weighted least squares estimate. A recursive formulation of least squares state estimation is then derived in which each additional measurement is incorporated sequentially, as it is available, modifying the previous estimate to produce a new estimate based on the previous measurements and the one additional new measurement. Finally, we apply these results to the recursive estimation of a system's state. The result is in the form of an observer, and recursive least squares is often a convenient way of choosing a full-order step-varying state observer's gain sequence. This topic forms a nice introduction to more advanced study of Kalman filtering and stochastic estimation.

## 8.5.1 Quadratic Forms

A quadratic form is a scalar function of the form

$$f(x_1, x_2, \ldots, x_n) = f(\mathbf{x}) = \mathbf{x}^t \mathbf{S} \mathbf{x} = [x_1 x_2 \ldots x_n] \begin{bmatrix} s_{11} & s_{12} & \cdots & s_{1n} \\ s_{21} & s_{22} & \cdots & s_{2n} \\ \vdots & & & \\ s_{n1} & s_{n2} & \cdots & s_{nn} \end{bmatrix} \begin{bmatrix} x_1 \\ x_2 \\ \vdots \\ x_n \end{bmatrix}$$

$$= s_{11}x_1^2 + s_{12}x_1x_2 + s_{13}x_1x_3 + \cdots + s_{1n}x_1x_n$$
$$+ s_{21}x_2x_1 + s_{22}x_2^2 + s_{23}x_2x_3 + \cdots + s_{2n}x_2x_n + \cdots$$
$$+ s_{n1}x_nx_1 + s_{n2}x_nx_2 + \cdots + s_{nn}x_n^2$$

A quadratic form is a linear combination of the products $x_ix_j$, including the squares of each variable. For example,

$$f(\mathbf{x}) = x_1^2 + 2x_1x_2 - 8x_1x_3 + 4x_2^2 + 4x_2x_3$$

$$= [x_1 \quad x_2 \quad x_3] \begin{bmatrix} 1 & 1 & -4 \\ 1 & 4 & 2 \\ -4 & 2 & 0 \end{bmatrix} \begin{bmatrix} x_1 \\ x_2 \\ x_3 \end{bmatrix}$$

is a three-variable quadratic form. A quadratic form can be expressed in terms of many different matrices $\mathbf{S}$. However, it is always possible to choose $\mathbf{S}$ to be a symmetric matrix.

Symmetric matrices have three key properties that are of special importance for quadratic forms:

1. The eigenvalues of a symmetric matrix with real elements are real numbers. In consequence, the corresponding eigenvectors are always real.
2. Any two eigenvectors corresponding to different eigenvalues are orthogonal to one another.
3. If, for a real, symmetric matrix $\mathbf{S}$, an eigenvalue $\lambda_i$ is repeated, the rank of $\lambda_i\mathbf{I} - \mathbf{S}$ is always reduced by the number of occurrences of the root $\lambda_i$.

Thus it is always possible to find $n$ linearly independent eigenvectors and hence a nonsingular modal matrix. Even with repeated roots, the eigenvectors can always be chosen to be orthogonal.

As a numerical example, consider the symmetric matrix

$$S = \begin{bmatrix} 2 & -36 & 0 \\ -36 & 23 & 0 \\ 0 & 0 & -75 \end{bmatrix} \tag{8-24}$$

which has characteristic equation

$$\begin{vmatrix} (\lambda - 2) & 36 & 0 \\ 36 & (\lambda - 23) & 0 \\ 0 & 0 & (\lambda + 75) \end{vmatrix} = (\lambda + 75)(\lambda - 50)(\lambda + 25) = 0$$

The eigenvalues of $S$ are

$$\lambda_1 = -25; \qquad \lambda_2 = 50; \qquad \lambda_3 = -75$$

which are real, as they should be. The corresponding eigenvectors (with convenient scaling) are

$$\mathbf{p}^1 = \begin{bmatrix} 4 \\ 3 \\ 0 \end{bmatrix}; \qquad \mathbf{p}^2 = \begin{bmatrix} 3 \\ -4 \\ 0 \end{bmatrix}; \qquad \mathbf{p}^3 = \begin{bmatrix} 0 \\ 0 \\ 1 \end{bmatrix}$$

and these are mutually orthogonal. Normalizing them (so that each eigenvector has unit norm) and forming a modal matrix, there results

$$\mathbf{P}_0 = \begin{bmatrix} \frac{4}{5} & \frac{3}{5} & 0 \\ \frac{3}{5} & -\frac{4}{5} & 0 \\ 0 & 0 & 1 \end{bmatrix} \tag{8-25}$$

which is an orthogonal matrix

$$\mathbf{P}_0^{-1} = \mathbf{P}_0^{\dagger}$$

and for which

$$\mathbf{P}_0^{-1}\mathbf{S}\mathbf{P}_0 = \mathbf{P}_0^{\dagger}\mathbf{S}\mathbf{P}_0 = \begin{bmatrix} -25 & 0 & 0 \\ 0 & 50 & 0 \\ 0 & 0 & -75 \end{bmatrix} = \mathbf{S}_0$$

For a quadratic form

$$f(\mathbf{x}) = \mathbf{x}^t \mathbf{S} \mathbf{x}$$

expressed in terms of a symmetric matrix $\mathbf{S}$ it is always possible to find an orthogonal change of variables

$$\mathbf{x} = \mathbf{P}_0 \mathbf{x}'; \qquad \mathbf{x}' = \mathbf{P}_0^t \mathbf{x}$$

such that

$$f(\mathbf{x}) = \mathbf{x}^t \mathbf{S} \mathbf{x} = \mathbf{x}'^t (\mathbf{P}_0^t \mathbf{S} \mathbf{P}_0) \mathbf{x}' = \mathbf{x}'^t (\mathbf{P}_0^{-1} \mathbf{S} \mathbf{P}_0) \mathbf{x}' = \mathbf{x}'^t \mathbf{S}_0 \mathbf{x}'$$
$$= \lambda_1 x_1'^2 + \lambda_2 x_2'^2 + \cdots + \lambda_n x_n'^2$$

where $\mathbf{S}_0$ is diagonal. In terms of the new variables, the quadratic form is a sum of squares, with no cross-product terms. The eigenvalues of $\mathbf{S}$ and thus of $\mathbf{S}_0$ are coefficients of the squares of the new variables. For the quadratic form defined by the symmetric matrix (8-24),

$$f(\mathbf{x}) = \begin{bmatrix} x_1 & x_2 & x_3 \end{bmatrix} \begin{bmatrix} 2 & -36 & 0 \\ -36 & 23 & 0 \\ 0 & 0 & -75 \end{bmatrix} \begin{bmatrix} x_1 \\ x_2 \\ x_3 \end{bmatrix}$$
$$= 2x_1^2 - 72x_1 x_2 + 23x_2^2 - 75x_3^2$$

the orthogonal change of variables,

$$\mathbf{x} = \mathbf{P}_0 \mathbf{x}'; \qquad \mathbf{x}' = \mathbf{P}_0^{-1} \mathbf{x} = \mathbf{P}_0^t \mathbf{x} \qquad\qquad (8\text{-}26)$$

using (8-25) gives

$$f(\mathbf{x}') = (\mathbf{P}_0 \mathbf{x}')^t \mathbf{S} (\mathbf{P}_0 \mathbf{x}') = \mathbf{x}'^t (\mathbf{P}_0^t \mathbf{S} \mathbf{P}_0) \mathbf{x}'$$
$$= \mathbf{x}'^t \mathbf{S}_0 \mathbf{x}' = \begin{bmatrix} x_1' & x_2' & x_3' \end{bmatrix} \begin{bmatrix} -25 & 0 & 0 \\ 0 & 50 & 0 \\ 0 & 0 & -75 \end{bmatrix} \begin{bmatrix} x_1' \\ x_2' \\ x_3' \end{bmatrix}$$
$$= -25x_1'^2 + 50x_2'^2 - 75x_3'^2$$

which is a pure sum of squares.
    A quadratic form

$$f(\mathbf{x}) = \mathbf{x}^t \mathbf{S} \mathbf{x}$$

and its associated symmetric matrix $\mathbf{S}$ is classified as sign definite as follows:

**1.** If for all nonzero real vectors $\mathbf{x}$

$$\mathbf{x}^\dagger \mathbf{S} \mathbf{x} > 0$$

the quadratic form is *positive definite*.
**2.** If for all nonzero real vectors $\mathbf{x}$

$$\mathbf{x}^\dagger \mathbf{S} \mathbf{x} \geqslant 0$$

the quadratic form is *positive semidefinite*.
**3.** If for all nonzero real vectors $\mathbf{x}$

$$\mathbf{x}^\dagger \mathbf{S} \mathbf{x} < 0$$

the quadratic form is *negative definite*.
**4.** If for all nonzero real vectors $\mathbf{x}$

$$\mathbf{x}^\dagger \mathbf{S} \mathbf{x} \leqslant 0$$

the quadratic form is *negative semidefinite*.

Otherwise, the quadratic form is not sign definite.

Sign definiteness of a quadratic form is unchanged by a nonsingular transformations of variables (8-26). For $\mathbf{S}$ to be positive definite, it is necessary and sufficient for all of the eigenvalues $\lambda_1, \lambda_2, \ldots, \lambda_n$ of $\mathbf{S}$ (which are real for $\mathbf{S}$ symmetric) to be positive. If all of the eigenvalues of $\mathbf{S}$ are nonnegative, with one or more roots equal to zero, the quadratic form is positive semidefinite. If all of the characteristic roots of $\mathbf{S}$ are negative, $f$ is negative definite and so forth. The quadratic form (8-24) is not sign definite because it has both positive and negative eigenvalues.

Every symmetric matrix $\mathbf{S}$ can be factored in a form

$$\mathbf{S} = \mathbf{\Psi}^\dagger \mathbf{\Psi}$$

where $\mathbf{\Psi}$ is termed a *square root* of $\mathbf{S}$. Generally, square roots of symmetric matrices are not unique and they can involve complex elements. A positive definite symmetric matrix $\mathbf{S}$ has a square root involving real numbers that is especially simple to visualize. If, when diagonalized, $\mathbf{S}$ becomes

$$\mathbf{S}_0 = \begin{bmatrix} s_1 & 0 & \cdots & \\ 0 & s_2 & \cdots & \\ \vdots & & & \\ 0 & 0 & \cdots & s_n \end{bmatrix}$$

then

$$S = P_0 S_0 P_0^{-1} = P_0 S_0 P_0^{\dagger}$$

Defining the real, diagonal matrix

$$\Psi_0 = \Psi_0^{\dagger} = \begin{bmatrix} \sqrt{s_1} & 0 & \cdots & 0 \\ 0 & \sqrt{s_2} & \cdots & 0 \\ 0 & 0 & \cdots & \sqrt{s_n} \end{bmatrix}$$

so that

$$S_0 = \Psi_0^{\dagger} \Psi_0$$

then

$$S = P_0 \Psi_0^{\dagger} \Psi_0 P_0^{\dagger} = \Psi^{\dagger} \Psi$$

where

$$\Psi = \Psi_0 P_0^{\dagger}$$

## 8.5.2 Weighted Least Squares

The basic least squares problem, solved in Section 4.3, involves an overdetermined set of linear algebraic equations

$$Hx = z$$

for which there is no solution. An estimate $\hat{x}$ that is the solution of

$$H\hat{x} + v = z$$

is found, for which

$$J(\hat{x}) = (z - H\hat{x})^{\dagger}(z - H\hat{x}) = v^{\dagger}v = v_1^2 + v_2^2 + \cdots \tag{8-27}$$

is minimum. To find the minimum, the partial derivatives of $J$ with respect to each of the elements of $\hat{x}$ are taken and equated to zero, which gives

$$H^{\dagger}H\hat{x} = H^{\dagger}z$$

$$\hat{x} = (H^{\dagger}H)^{-1}H^{\dagger}z \tag{8-28}$$

It can be shown that the matrix of second derivatives of $J$

$$\frac{\partial^2 J}{\partial \hat{\mathbf{x}}^2} = \mathbf{H}^\dagger \mathbf{H}$$

which is symmetric, is positive definite if $\mathbf{H}$ is of full rank, so the solution is unique and a minimum. $\mathbf{H}^\dagger \mathbf{H}$ being positive definite, then $(\mathbf{H}^\dagger \mathbf{H})^{-1}$ exists.

When a least squares estimate is interpreted as yielding the "best" or "most likely" value of the estimated quantity, probabilistic assumptions are being made about the measurement errors $v_1, v_2, \ldots$, as Gauss knew and discussed. In the basic least squares problem, equal weightings of the squares of the measurement errors in the performance measure $J$ implies that each measurement has equal likelihood of error and that the errors are independent of each other.

A more general least squares problem minimizes

$$J(\hat{\mathbf{x}}) = (\mathbf{z} - \mathbf{H}\hat{\mathbf{x}})^\dagger \mathbf{W}(\mathbf{z} - \mathbf{H}\hat{\mathbf{x}}) = \mathbf{v}^\dagger \mathbf{W} \mathbf{v}$$

where $\mathbf{W}$ is a symmetric, positive definite weighting matrix. $J$ is then a quadratic form in the measurement errors $\mathbf{v}$. When one is more confident in the accuracy of some of the measurements than of others, the elements of $\mathbf{W}$ can be chosen to weigh them more heavily than others. If the errors $\mathbf{v}$ are zero-mean

$$E[\mathbf{v}] = \mathbf{0}$$

with known positive definite covariance matrix

$$E[\mathbf{v}\mathbf{v}^\dagger] = \mathbf{R}$$

it is natural to choose

$$\mathbf{W} = \mathbf{R}^{-1}$$

For a set of overdetermined equations

$$\mathbf{H}\mathbf{x} = \mathbf{z}$$

the estimate $\hat{\mathbf{x}}$ in

$$\mathbf{H}\hat{\mathbf{x}} + \mathbf{v} = \mathbf{z}$$

that results in minimum weighted sum of squares of measurement error

$$J(\hat{\mathbf{x}}) = (\mathbf{z} - \mathbf{H}\hat{\mathbf{x}})^\dagger \mathbf{W}(\mathbf{z} - \mathbf{H}\hat{\mathbf{x}}) = \mathbf{v}^\dagger \mathbf{W}\mathbf{v}$$

is

$$\hat{\mathbf{x}} = (\mathbf{H}^\dagger \mathbf{W}\mathbf{H})^{-1}\mathbf{H}^\dagger \mathbf{W}\mathbf{z} \tag{8-29}$$

This result is derived by expressing the positive definite symmetric weighting matrix $\mathbf{W}$ as

$$\mathbf{W} = \mathbf{\Psi}^\dagger \mathbf{\Psi}$$

Then

$$J(\hat{\mathbf{x}}) = [(\mathbf{\Psi}\mathbf{z}) - (\mathbf{\Psi}\mathbf{H})\hat{\mathbf{x}}]^\dagger [\mathbf{\Psi}\mathbf{z} - (\mathbf{\Psi}\mathbf{H})\hat{\mathbf{x}}]$$

which is in the form of (8-27) with $\mathbf{z}$ replaced by $\mathbf{\Psi}\mathbf{z}$ and $\mathbf{H}$ replaced by $\mathbf{\Psi}\mathbf{H}$. Making these substitutions into the basic least squares result (8-28)

$$\hat{\mathbf{x}} = [(\mathbf{H}^\dagger \mathbf{\Psi}^\dagger)(\mathbf{\Psi}\mathbf{H})]^{-1}(\mathbf{H}^\dagger \mathbf{\Psi}^\dagger)(\mathbf{\Psi}\mathbf{z})$$

gives (8-29).

For the equations

$$\begin{bmatrix} 3 & -1 \\ 2 & 1 \\ 1 & -2 \\ 2 & 2 \end{bmatrix} \begin{bmatrix} x_1 \\ x_2 \end{bmatrix} = \mathbf{Hx} = \begin{bmatrix} -4 \\ 1 \\ -5 \\ 1 \end{bmatrix} = \mathbf{z}$$

for example, suppose that it is desired to weight with

$$\mathbf{W} = \begin{bmatrix} 4 & 0 & 0 & 0 \\ 0 & 3 & 0 & 0 \\ 0 & 0 & 2 & 0 \\ 0 & 0 & 0 & 1 \end{bmatrix}$$

In other words, suppose we have the most confidence in the first equation and decreasing confidence in later equations. In general, $\mathbf{W}$ need not be diagonal, but in this simple example, it is particularly easy to interpret the meaning of $\mathbf{W}$ when it is diagonal: we expect the square error in the first equation to be 3/4 as large as the square error in the second equation, and so on. The weighted least squares estimate is

$$
\hat{x} = \left( \begin{bmatrix} 3 & 2 & 1 & 2 \\ -1 & 1 & -2 & 2 \end{bmatrix} \begin{bmatrix} 4 & 0 & 0 & 0 \\ 0 & 3 & 0 & 0 \\ 0 & 0 & 2 & 0 \\ 0 & 0 & 0 & 1 \end{bmatrix} \begin{bmatrix} 3 & -1 \\ 2 & 1 \\ 1 & -2 \\ 2 & 2 \end{bmatrix} \right)^{-1}
$$

$$
\times \begin{bmatrix} 3 & 2 & 1 & 2 \\ -1 & 1 & -2 & 2 \end{bmatrix} \begin{bmatrix} 4 & 0 & 0 & 0 \\ 0 & 3 & 0 & 0 \\ 0 & 0 & 2 & 0 \\ 0 & 0 & 0 & 1 \end{bmatrix} \begin{bmatrix} -4 \\ 1 \\ -5 \\ 1 \end{bmatrix}
$$

$$
= \begin{bmatrix} 54 & -6 \\ -6 & 19 \end{bmatrix}^{-1} \begin{bmatrix} -50 \\ 41 \end{bmatrix} = \frac{1}{990} \begin{bmatrix} 19 & 6 \\ 6 & 54 \end{bmatrix} \begin{bmatrix} -50 \\ 41 \end{bmatrix}
$$

$$
= \begin{bmatrix} -704/990 \\ 1914/990 \end{bmatrix} = \begin{bmatrix} -0.71 \\ 1.93 \end{bmatrix}
$$

### 8.5.3  Recursive Least Squares

Recursive least squares is an arrangement of the least squares solution in which each new measurement is used to update the previous least squares estimate that was based on previous measurements. Instead of processing all of the measurement data at once, the measurements are processed one at a time, with each new measurement causing a modification in the current estimate. Least squares estimates are linear transformations of the measurements. The least squares estimate based on the first $k + 1$ equations can therefore be expressed as a linear transformation of the least squares estimate based on the first $k$ measurements plus a linear correction term based on the $(k + 1)$th measurement alone.

Denoting the number of measurements used by arguments, the least squares estimate based on $k$ measurements is

$$
\hat{x}(k) = [H^\dagger(k)H(k)]^{-1}H^\dagger(k)z(k)
$$

The least squares estimate based on $k + 1$ measurements is

$$
\hat{x}(k + 1) = [H^\dagger(k + 1)H(k + 1)]^{-1}H^\dagger(k + 1)z(k + 1)
$$

where $H(k + 1)$ is $H(k)$ with an additional row, $h^\dagger(k + 1)$,

$$
H(k + 1) = \begin{bmatrix} H(k) \\ \hline h^\dagger(k + 1) \end{bmatrix}
$$

and the vector of measurements $\mathbf{z}(k + 1)$ is the measurement vector $\mathbf{z}(k)$ with one additional scalar measurement $z_{k+1}$:

$$\mathbf{z}(k + 1) = \begin{bmatrix} \mathbf{z}(k) \\ \hdashline z_{k+1} \end{bmatrix}$$

Then

$$\mathbf{H}^\dagger(k + 1)\mathbf{H}(k + 1) = [\mathbf{H}^\dagger(k) \mid \mathbf{h}(k + 1)] \begin{bmatrix} \mathbf{H}(k) \\ \hdashline \mathbf{h}^\dagger(k + 1) \end{bmatrix}$$

$$= \mathbf{H}^\dagger(k)\mathbf{H}(k) + \mathbf{h}(k + 1)\mathbf{h}^\dagger(k + 1)$$

Defining

$$\mathbf{P}(k) = [\mathbf{H}^\dagger(k)\mathbf{H}(k)]^{-1}$$

then

$$\mathbf{P}(k + 1) = [\mathbf{H}^\dagger(k + 1)\mathbf{H}(k + 1)]^{-1} = [\mathbf{H}^\dagger(k)\mathbf{H}(k) + \mathbf{h}(k + 1)\mathbf{h}^\dagger(k + 1)]^{-1}$$

$$= [\mathbf{P}^{-1}(k) + \mathbf{h}(k + 1)\mathbf{h}^\dagger(k + 1)]^{-1} \tag{8-30}$$

Relation (8-30) is in a form for which the matrix inversion lemma

$$(\mathbf{\Gamma} + \mathbf{u}\mathbf{v}^\dagger)^{-1} = \mathbf{\Gamma}^{-1} - \frac{\mathbf{\Gamma}^{-1}\mathbf{u}\mathbf{v}^\dagger\mathbf{\Gamma}^{-1}}{1 + \mathbf{v}^\dagger\mathbf{\Gamma}^{-1}\mathbf{u}} \tag{8-31}$$

applies. The lemma is verified by multiplying both sides of (8-31) by $\mathbf{\Gamma} + \mathbf{u}\mathbf{v}^\dagger$ to obtain the identity matrix. Using the matrix inversion lemma on (8-30) gives

$$\mathbf{P}(k + 1) = \mathbf{P}(k) - \frac{\mathbf{P}(k)\mathbf{h}(k + 1)\mathbf{h}^\dagger(k + 1)\mathbf{P}(k)}{1 + \mathbf{h}^\dagger(k + 1)\mathbf{P}(k)\mathbf{h}(k + 1)}$$

which is an update equation for $\mathbf{P}(k + 1)$ in terms of $\mathbf{P}(k)$ and the next measurement equation coefficients, $\mathbf{h}(k + 1)$. Defining

$$\delta(k + 1) = 1 + \mathbf{h}^\dagger(k + 1)\mathbf{P}(k)\mathbf{h}(k + 1)$$

$$\mathbf{\kappa}(k + 1) = \mathbf{P}(k)\mathbf{h}(k + 1)\delta^{-1}(k + 1)$$

then this update equation becomes

$$\mathbf{P}(k + 1) = \mathbf{P}(k) - \mathbf{P}(k)\mathbf{h}(k + 1)\delta^{-1}(k + 1)\mathbf{h}^\dagger(k + 1)\mathbf{P}(k)$$

$$= [\mathbf{I} - \mathbf{\kappa}(k + 1)\mathbf{h}^\dagger(k + 1)]\mathbf{P}(k) \tag{8-32}$$

The least squares estimate at step $k + 1$ is

$$\hat{\mathbf{x}}(k + 1) = \mathbf{P}(k + 1)\mathbf{H}^{\dagger}(k + 1)\mathbf{z}(k + 1) = \mathbf{P}(k + 1)[\mathbf{H}^{\dagger}(k) \mid \mathbf{h}(k + 1)]\begin{bmatrix} \mathbf{z}(k) \\ \hline z_{k+1} \end{bmatrix}$$

$$= \mathbf{P}(k + 1)[\mathbf{H}^{\dagger}(k)\mathbf{z}(k) + \mathbf{h}(k + 1)z_{k+1}]$$

$$= [\mathbf{P}(k) - \mathbf{P}(k)\mathbf{h}(k + 1)\delta^{-1}(k + 1)\mathbf{h}^{\dagger}(k + 1)\mathbf{P}(k)]$$

$$\times [\mathbf{H}^{\dagger}(k)\mathbf{z}(k) + \mathbf{h}(k + 1)z_{k+1}]$$

$$= \mathbf{P}(k)\mathbf{H}^{\dagger}(k)\mathbf{z}(k) + \mathbf{P}(k)\mathbf{h}(k + 1)z_{k+1}$$

$$- \mathbf{P}(k)\mathbf{h}(k + 1)\delta^{-1}(k + 1)\mathbf{h}^{\dagger}(k + 1)\mathbf{P}(k)\mathbf{H}^{\dagger}(k)\mathbf{z}(k)$$

$$- \mathbf{P}(k)\mathbf{h}(k + 1)\delta^{-1}(k + 1)\mathbf{h}^{\dagger}(k + 1)\mathbf{P}(k)\mathbf{h}(k + 1)z_{k+1}$$

$$= \hat{\mathbf{x}}(k) + \mathbf{P}(k)\mathbf{h}(k + 1)\delta^{-1}(k + 1)[z_{k+1} - \mathbf{h}^{\dagger}(k + 1)\hat{\mathbf{x}}(k)]$$

$$= \hat{\mathbf{x}}(k) + \mathbf{\kappa}(k + 1)[z_{k+1} - \mathbf{h}^{\dagger}(k + 1)\hat{\mathbf{x}}(k)] \tag{8-33}$$

The least squares estimate based on $k + 1$ measurements, $\hat{\mathbf{x}}(k + 1)$, is the estimate based on $k$ measurements, $\hat{\mathbf{x}}(k)$, plus a gain (which does not depend on the measurements)

$$\mathbf{\kappa}(k + 1) = \mathbf{P}(k)\mathbf{h}(k + 1)\delta^{-1}(k + 1)$$

times the difference between the new measurement and the predicted measurement

$$\mathbf{h}^{\dagger}(k + 1)\hat{\mathbf{x}}(k)$$

based on the previous estimate.

These equations for recursive least squares estimation are collected in Table 8-5. A block diagram of the recursive least squares estimator is given in Figure 8-8. The filter shown processes one scalar measurement at a time and

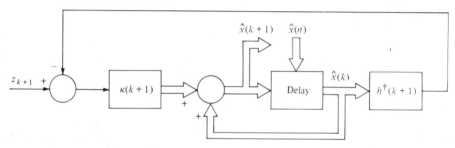

**FIGURE 8-8.** Block diagram of the recursive least squares estimator.

## TABLE 8-5    Recursive Least Squares Computation

### Measurement Model and Problem Statement

$$z_i = \mathbf{h}^\dagger(i)\mathbf{x}; \qquad i = 1, 2, 3, \ldots$$

where the unknown quantity $\mathbf{x}$ is an $n$-vector and where the scalar measurements $z$ have errors. The least squares solution based on $k$ measurements, $\hat{\mathbf{x}}(k)$ satisfies

$$z_i = \mathbf{h}^\dagger(i)\hat{\mathbf{x}}(k) + v_i, \qquad i = 1, 2, \ldots, k$$

where the sum of squares of errors

$$J(k) = v_1^2 + v_2^2 + \cdots + v_k^2 = \sum_{i=1}^{k} v_i^2$$

is minimum.

### Initialization

$$\mathbf{P}(n) = [\mathbf{H}^\dagger(n)\mathbf{H}(n)]^{-1}$$

$$\hat{\mathbf{x}}(n) = \mathbf{P}(n)\mathbf{H}^\dagger(n)\mathbf{z}(n)$$

where

$$\mathbf{H}(n) = \begin{bmatrix} \mathbf{h}^\dagger(1) \\ \vdots \\ \mathbf{h}^\dagger(n) \end{bmatrix}; \qquad \mathbf{z}(n) = \begin{bmatrix} z_1 \\ \vdots \\ z_n \end{bmatrix}$$

### Corrector Gain

$$\delta(k + 1) = \mathbf{h}^\dagger(k + 1)\mathbf{P}(k)\mathbf{h}(k + 1) + 1$$

$$\boldsymbol{\kappa}(k + 1) = \mathbf{P}(k)\mathbf{h}(k + 1)\delta^{-1}(k + 1)$$

$$\mathbf{P}(k + 1) = [\mathbf{I} - \boldsymbol{\kappa}(k + 1)\mathbf{h}^\dagger(k + 1)]\mathbf{P}(k) \tag{8-32}$$

### Predictor-Corrector

$$\hat{\mathbf{x}}(k + 1) = \hat{\mathbf{x}}(k) + \boldsymbol{\kappa}(k + 1)[z_{k+1} - \mathbf{h}^\dagger(k + 1)\hat{\mathbf{x}}(k)] \tag{8-33}$$

produces the least squares estimate based on that and all preceding measurements. There are many variations on this basic result, including those where vector, rather than scalar, measurements are processed at each step.

To estimate an $n$-vector $\mathbf{x}$ with recursive least squares, one first obtains an initial estimate based on the first $n$ linearly independent measurements

$$\hat{\mathbf{x}}(n) = [\mathbf{H}^\dagger(n)\mathbf{H}(n)]^{-1}\mathbf{H}^\dagger(n)\mathbf{z}(n)$$

and the initial $\mathbf{P}$ matrix

$$\mathbf{P}(n) = [\mathbf{H}^\dagger(n)\mathbf{H}(n)]^{-1}$$

Thereafter, the least squares estimate is updated with each new scalar measurement. Except in the first-order case, one cannot begin this recursive least squares algorithm with the first measurement, using

$$\hat{\mathbf{x}}(1) = [\mathbf{H}^\dagger(1)\mathbf{H}(1)]^{-1}\mathbf{H}^\dagger(1)\mathbf{z}(1) = [\mathbf{h}(1)\mathbf{h}^\dagger(1)]^{-1}\mathbf{h}(1)\mathbf{z}(1)$$

$$\mathbf{P}(1) = [\mathbf{H}^\dagger(1)\mathbf{H}(1)]^{-1} = [\mathbf{h}(1)\mathbf{h}^\dagger(1)]^{-1}$$

because $\mathbf{h}(1)\mathbf{h}^\dagger(1)$ is singular. The initial estimate can be obtained recursively (for example, with a deadbeat observer), but not with (8-32) and (8-33).

As a simple example of recursive least squares, consider the estimation of a two-vector

$$\mathbf{x} = \begin{bmatrix} x_1 \\ x_2 \end{bmatrix}$$

from the following four measurements:

$$\begin{cases} z_1 = 3 = 2x_1 = \mathbf{h}^\dagger(1)\mathbf{x} \\ z_2 = 5 = x_1 - x_2 = \mathbf{h}^\dagger(2)\mathbf{x} \\ z_3 = 4 = 3x_1 + x_2 = \mathbf{h}^\dagger(3)\mathbf{x} \\ z_4 = -4 = x_1 + 2x_2 = \mathbf{h}^\dagger(4)\mathbf{x} \end{cases}$$

The initialization step uses the first two of these measurements to obtain an initial estimate of $\mathbf{x}$. Using

$$\mathbf{P}(2) = [\mathbf{H}^\dagger(2)\mathbf{H}(2)]^{-1} \left\{ \begin{bmatrix} 2 & 1 \\ 0 & -1 \end{bmatrix} \begin{bmatrix} 2 & 0 \\ 1 & -1 \end{bmatrix} \right\}^{-1} = \begin{bmatrix} \frac{1}{4} & \frac{1}{4} \\ \frac{1}{4} & \frac{5}{4} \end{bmatrix}$$

then

$$\mathbf{x}(2) = \mathbf{H}^{-1}(2)\mathbf{H}^{\dagger-1}(2)\mathbf{H}^{\dagger}(2)\mathbf{z}(2)$$

$$= \mathbf{P}(2)\mathbf{H}^{\dagger}(2)\mathbf{z}(2) = \begin{bmatrix} \frac{1}{4} & \frac{1}{4} \\ \frac{1}{4} & \frac{5}{4} \end{bmatrix}\begin{bmatrix} 2 & 1 \\ 0 & -1 \end{bmatrix}\begin{bmatrix} 3 \\ 5 \end{bmatrix} = \begin{bmatrix} \frac{3}{2} \\ -\frac{7}{2} \end{bmatrix}$$

Hereafter, the recursive relations are used. For step 3

$$\delta(3) = 1 + \mathbf{h}^{\dagger}(3)\mathbf{P}(2)\mathbf{h}(3) = 1 + \begin{bmatrix} 3 & 1 \end{bmatrix}\begin{bmatrix} \frac{1}{4} & \frac{1}{4} \\ \frac{1}{4} & \frac{5}{4} \end{bmatrix}\begin{bmatrix} 3 \\ 1 \end{bmatrix} = 6$$

$$\kappa(3) = \mathbf{P}(2)h(3)\delta^{-1}(3) = \begin{bmatrix} \frac{1}{4} & \frac{1}{4} \\ \frac{1}{4} & \frac{5}{4} \end{bmatrix}\begin{bmatrix} 3 \\ 1 \end{bmatrix}\frac{1}{6} = \begin{bmatrix} \frac{1}{6} \\ \frac{1}{3} \end{bmatrix}$$

$$\mathbf{P}(3) = [\mathbf{I} - \kappa(3)\mathbf{h}^{\dagger}(3)]\mathbf{P}(2) = \left\{\begin{bmatrix} 1 & 0 \\ 0 & 1 \end{bmatrix} - \begin{bmatrix} \frac{1}{6} \\ \frac{1}{3} \end{bmatrix}\begin{bmatrix} 3 & 1 \end{bmatrix}\right\}\begin{bmatrix} \frac{1}{4} & \frac{1}{4} \\ \frac{1}{4} & \frac{5}{4} \end{bmatrix} = \begin{bmatrix} \frac{1}{12} & -\frac{1}{12} \\ -\frac{1}{12} & \frac{7}{12} \end{bmatrix}$$

$$\hat{\mathbf{x}}(3) = \hat{\mathbf{x}}(2) + \kappa(3)[z_3 - \mathbf{h}^{\dagger}(3)\hat{\mathbf{x}}(2)] = \begin{bmatrix} 2 \\ -\frac{5}{2} \end{bmatrix}$$

and so on.

## 8.5.4 State Estimation and Kalman Filtering

It is straightforward to recursively estimate the initial state of a system from its outputs and inputs, using least squares. For a single-output plant

$$\mathbf{x}(k + 1) = \mathbf{A}(k)\mathbf{x}(k) + \mathbf{B}(k)\mathbf{u}(k)$$

$$y(k) = \mathbf{c}^{\dagger}(k)\mathbf{x}(k) + \mathbf{d}^{\dagger}(k)\mathbf{u}(k)$$

the measurements are expressed in terms of the unknown initial state $\mathbf{x}(0)$:

$$\begin{cases} y(0) = \mathbf{c}^{\dagger}(0)\mathbf{x}(0) + \mathbf{d}^{\dagger}(0)\mathbf{u}(0) \\ y(1) = \mathbf{c}^{\dagger}(1)\mathbf{x}(1) + \mathbf{d}^{\dagger}(1)\mathbf{u}(1) = \mathbf{c}^{\dagger}(1)\mathbf{A}(0)\mathbf{x}(0) + \mathbf{c}^{\dagger}(1)\mathbf{B}(0)\mathbf{u}(0) + \mathbf{d}^{\dagger}(1)\mathbf{u}(1) \\ y(2) = \mathbf{c}^{\dagger}(2)\mathbf{x}(2) + \mathbf{d}^{\dagger}(2)\mathbf{u}(2) = \mathbf{c}^{\dagger}(2)\mathbf{A}(0)\mathbf{x}(0) + \mathbf{c}^{\dagger}(2)\mathbf{A}(1)\mathbf{B}(0)\mathbf{u}(0) \\ \qquad\qquad + \mathbf{c}^{\dagger}(2)\mathbf{B}(1)\mathbf{u}(1) + \mathbf{d}^{\dagger}(2)\mathbf{u}(2) \\ \vdots \end{cases}$$

which can be put in the form

$$\begin{cases} \mathbf{h}^\dagger(1)\mathbf{x}(0) = z_1 \\ \mathbf{h}^\dagger(2)\mathbf{x}(0) = z_2 \\ \mathbf{h}^\dagger(3)\mathbf{x}(0) = z_3 \\ \quad \vdots \end{cases}$$

and to which the previous results apply directly. If the plant is multiple-output, the outputs can be processed one at a time or the recursive least squares algorithm can be expressed in terms of updating with vector measurements.

Usually, though, we want to have an estimate of the *present* plant state, not the initial state, at each step. While this could be calculated from the estimated initial state, it is awkward to do so; it is very useful to reformulate the recursive least squares solution to produce present state estimates. The previous least squares algorithm is recursive and the plant state equations are recursive, so the two can be combined into a single recursive solution. For the plant

$$\mathbf{x}(k + 1) = \mathbf{A}(k)\mathbf{x}(k) + \mathbf{B}(k)\mathbf{u}(k)$$

$$\mathbf{y}(k) = \mathbf{C}(k)\mathbf{x}(k) + \mathbf{D}(k)\mathbf{u}(k)$$

the sequence of least squares state estimates $\hat{\mathbf{x}}(k)$ satisfying

$$\hat{\mathbf{x}}(k + 1) = \mathbf{A}(k)\hat{\mathbf{x}}(k) + \mathbf{B}(k)\mathbf{u}(k) + \mathbf{w}(k)$$

$$\mathbf{y}(k) = \mathbf{C}(k)\hat{\mathbf{x}}(k) + \mathbf{D}(k)\mathbf{u}(k) + \mathbf{v}(k)$$

with

$$\hat{\mathbf{x}}(0) = \mathbf{0}$$

that results in minimum sum of squares of errors

$$J(k) = \sum_{i=0}^{k-1} \mathbf{w}^\dagger(i)\mathbf{Q}^{-1}(i)\mathbf{w}(i) + \sum_{i=0}^{k} \mathbf{v}^\dagger(i)\mathbf{R}^{-1}(i)\mathbf{v}(i) \tag{8-34}$$

can be calculated as indicated in Table 8-6. The sequence $\mathbf{w}(k)$ is the state error and $\mathbf{v}(k)$ is the measurement error. The symmetric positive definite weighting matrices $\mathbf{Q}^{-1}$ and $\mathbf{R}^{-1}$ are expressed in $J$ as inverses, for convenience. That way, $\mathbf{Q}$ and $\mathbf{R}$, rather than their inverses, appear in the corrector gain equations. The algorithm is begun with an initial state estimate

**TABLE 8-6    Recursive Least Squares State Estimation and Kalman Filtering**

## *Model and Problem Statement*

$$\mathbf{x}(k + 1) = \mathbf{A}(k)\mathbf{x}(k) + \mathbf{B}(k)\mathbf{u}(k)$$

$$\mathbf{y}(k) = \mathbf{C}(k)\mathbf{x}(k) + \mathbf{D}(k)\mathbf{u}(k); \qquad k = 0, 1, 2, \ldots$$

where the unknown quantities $\mathbf{x}(k)$ are $n$-vectors, the measurements $\mathbf{y}(k)$ are $m$-vectors, and both the states and the measurements have errors. The least squares solution $\hat{\mathbf{x}}(k)$, which is the estimate of $\mathbf{x}(k)$ based on measurements $\mathbf{y}(0), \mathbf{y}(1), \ldots, \mathbf{y}(k)$, satisfies

$$\hat{\mathbf{x}}(k + 1) = \mathbf{A}(k)\hat{\mathbf{x}}(k) + \mathbf{B}(k)\mathbf{u}(k) + \mathbf{w}(k)$$

$$\mathbf{y}(k) = \mathbf{C}(k)\hat{\mathbf{x}}(k) + \mathbf{D}(k)\mathbf{u}(k) + \mathbf{v}(k)$$

with

$$\hat{\mathbf{x}}(0) = \mathbf{0}$$

where the sum of squares of errors

$$J(k) = \sum_{i=0}^{k-1} \mathbf{w}^{\dagger}(i)\mathbf{Q}^{-1}(i)\mathbf{w}(i) + \sum_{i=0}^{k} \mathbf{v}^{\dagger}(i)\mathbf{R}^{-1}(i)\mathbf{v}(i)$$

is minimum at each step $k$.

## *Corrector Gain*

$$\mathscr{P}(k + 1) = \mathbf{A}(k)\mathbf{P}(k)\mathbf{A}^{\dagger}(k) + \mathbf{Q}(k)$$

$$\mathbf{K}(k + 1) = \mathbf{P}(k + 1)\mathbf{C}^{\dagger}(k + 1)[\mathbf{C}(k + 1)\mathbf{P}(k + 1)\mathbf{C}^{\dagger}(k + 1) + \mathbf{R}(k)]^{-1}$$

$$\mathbf{P}(k + 1) = [\mathbf{I} - \mathbf{K}(k + 1)\mathbf{C}(k + 1)]\mathscr{P}(k + 1)$$

## *Predictor-Corrector*

$$\hat{\mathbf{x}}(k + 1) = \mathbf{A}(k)\hat{\mathbf{x}}(k) + \mathbf{B}(k)\mathbf{u}(k)$$
$$+ \mathbf{K}(k + 1)\{\mathbf{y}(k + 1) - \mathbf{C}(k + 1)[\mathbf{A}(k)\hat{\mathbf{x}}(k) + \mathbf{B}(k)\mathbf{u}(k)] - \mathbf{D}(k + 1)\mathbf{u}(k + 1)\}$$

## *Predictor-Corrector Using Measurements Only to Step k*

$$\hat{\hat{\mathbf{x}}}(k + 1) = \mathbf{A}(k)\hat{\hat{\mathbf{x}}}(k) + \mathbf{B}(k)\mathbf{u}(k) + \mathbf{A}(k)\mathbf{K}(k)[\mathbf{y}(k) - \mathbf{C}(k)\hat{\hat{\mathbf{x}}}(k) - \mathbf{D}(k)\mathbf{u}(k)]$$

$\mathbf{x}(0)$ and an initial $\mathbf{P}$ matrix

$$\mathbf{P}(0) = [\mathbf{H}^\dagger(0)\mathbf{H}(0)]^{-1}$$

perhaps based on measurements before step 0.

Figure 8-9 shows the structure of this recursive least squares state estimator. It differs from an ordinary state observer only in that it is driven with the measurement error at step $k + 1$ rather than at step $k$. In the ordinary observer, the observer state at step $k + 1$ is influenced by measurements through step $k$, not through step $k + 1$. For feedback control, it may not be possible to use the step $k + 1$ measurement to help in the estimation of the state at step $k + 1$ because of the time needed to perform the calculations. If it is possible, then so much the better. The previous observer equations could be modified to involve step $k + 1$ measurements, if desired.

Suppose that the least squares estimator must use only the plant measurements through step $k$ to estimate the plant state at step $k + 1$. Then this least squares estimate, which we will denote by $\hat{\hat{\mathbf{x}}}(k + 1)$, is given by

$$\hat{\hat{\mathbf{x}}}(k + 1) = \mathbf{A}(k)\hat{\mathbf{x}}(k) + \mathbf{B}(k)\mathbf{u}(k)$$

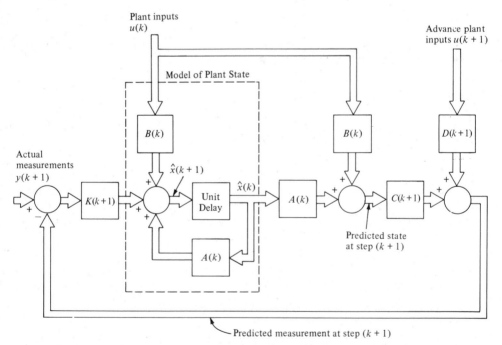

**FIGURE 8-9.** Structure of the recursive least squares state estimator (or Kalman filter).

Substituting into the predictor-corrector relation

$$\hat{x}(k) = A(k-1)\hat{x}(k+1) + B(k-1)u(k-1)$$
$$+ K(k)\{y(k) - C(k)[A(k-1)\hat{x}(k-1) + B(k-1)u(k-1)] - D(k)u(k)\}$$

there results

$$\hat{x}(k+1) = A(k)[A(k-1)\hat{x}(k-1) + B(k-1)u(k-1)] + Bu(k)$$
$$+ A(k)K(k)\{y(k) - C(k)[A(k-1)\hat{x}(k-1)$$
$$+ B(k-1)u(k-1)] - D(k)u(k)\}$$
$$= A(k)\hat{x}(k) + A(k)K(k)[y(k) - C(k)\hat{x}(k) - D(k)u(k)]$$

The structure of this solution is identical to that for a full-order state observer. That is, if the observer's gain sequence is chosen to be

$$G(k) = A(k)K(k)$$

the observer is a least squares state estimator.

It should not be inferred that the recursive least squares (or Kalman filter) approach to determining observer gains for state estimation is necessarily superior or inferior to determining the gain by selecting the desired estimator convergence properties. For some kinds of state and measurement errors, white noise, the Kalman filter is the best we can do using linear operations. In many applications, it is a good approach even when the error model is imprecise. In other situations, it is more sensible to specify observer convergence properties directly.

Any full-order state observer is a recursive least squares state estimator with some set of weighting matrices $Q(k)$ and $R(k)$. And, a recursive least squares state estimator is a full-order state observer with some set of state transition matrices $F(k)$. When the weighting matrices can be sensibly chosen, the least squares approach to designing the observer gains is excellent. When it is more reasonable to select observer convergence properties directly, the other approach is better.

One can, and perhaps should, view state estimation with step-varying observers as a continuum of possibilities. At one extreme, ordinary recursive least squares uses all the available data, without any weighting as to the time it occurred, in estimating the present plant state at each step. At the other extreme is deadbeat observation where only the minimum amount of the most recent data is used to calculate the present state estimate. In between these extremes are recursive least squares state estimation with "fading memory" and observers with specific convergence properties.

The least squares result is also the solution to a key stochastic optimal estimation problem. The stochastic problem was solved by Kalman during a boring train trip in late 1958, and published in 1960. It is termed the *Kalman filter*. The gain sequence $\mathbf{K}(k)$ is commonly called the *Kalman gain*. The estimate $\hat{\mathbf{x}}(k)$ also minimizes the expectation of the sum of squares of errors between the actual and estimated states

$$\mathscr{J}(k) = E\{[\mathbf{x}(k) - \hat{\mathbf{x}}(k)]^{\dagger}[\mathbf{x}(k) - \hat{\mathbf{x}}(k)]\}$$

when the state errors $\mathbf{w}(k)$ and measurement errors $\mathbf{v}(k)$ are white noise sequences that are zero-mean, uncorrelated with one another and the initial state, and have covariances

$$E[\mathbf{w}(k)\mathbf{w}^{\dagger}(k)] = \mathbf{Q}(k)$$

$$E[\mathbf{v}(k)\mathbf{v}^{\dagger}(k)] = \mathbf{R}(k)$$

which are positive semidefinite. $\mathbf{P}(k)$ is then the covariance of the estimate error

$$\mathbf{P}(k) = E\{[\mathbf{x}(k) - \hat{\mathbf{x}}(k)][\mathbf{x}(k) - \hat{\mathbf{x}}(k)]^{\dagger}\}$$

and the computations are begun with the covariance of the initial state. This nicely bypasses the complication of obtaining an initial state estimate and $\mathbf{P}$ matrix for least squares. $\mathscr{P}(k)$ is the covariance of the predicted state

$$\mathscr{P}(k) = E\{[\mathbf{x}(k) - \mathbf{A}(k-1)\hat{\mathbf{x}}(k-1)][\mathbf{x}(k) - \mathbf{A}(k-1)\hat{\mathbf{x}}(k-1)]^{\dagger}\}$$

For a step-invariant linear plant and constant $\mathbf{Q}$ and $\mathbf{R}$ matrices, the Kalman gain matrix $\mathbf{K}(k)$ approaches a limit as $k$ becomes large. This steady state Kalman gain is sometimes used for step-invariant observer eigenvalue placement.

There are strong parallels between these results and those for optimal control which will be discussed in the next section.

# 8.6  Quadratic Optimal Regulation

Another approach to the state feedback portion of tracking system design is that of *optimal regulation*, in which the plant feedback is chosen to minimize a scalar performance measure that weights the control input and the error from zero of the plant state at each step. Instead of choosing state feedback gains to give zero-input response convergence properties directly, the gains are selected to minimize a performance measure, indirectly resulting in whatever convergence results from the minimization. The designer trades selecting the nature of the decay of the feedback system's zero-input response at each step for selection of step-varying weighting matrices in the performance measure.

The discrete-time linear-quadratic optimal control problem is to find the inputs $\mathbf{u}(0), \mathbf{u}(1), \ldots, \mathbf{u}(N-1)$ to the plant with linear state equations

$$\mathbf{x}(k+1) = \mathbf{A}(k)\mathbf{x}(k) + \mathbf{B}(k)\mathbf{u}(k)$$

such that a scalar quadratic performance measure (or *cost function*)

$$J = \mathbf{x}^\dagger(N)\mathbf{P}(N)\mathbf{x}(N) + \sum_{k=0}^{N-1} [\mathbf{x}^\dagger(k)\mathbf{Q}(k)\mathbf{x}(k) + \mathbf{u}^\dagger(k)\mathbf{R}(k)\mathbf{u}(k)] \qquad (8\text{-}35)$$

is minimized. The matrix $\mathbf{P}(N)$, the matrices $\mathbf{Q}(0), \mathbf{Q}(1), \ldots, \mathbf{Q}(N-1)$ and the matrices $\mathbf{R}(0), \mathbf{R}(1), \ldots, \mathbf{R}(N-1)$ are each taken to be symmetric, since each defines a quadratic form. Each are assumed to be positive semidefinite, which means that contributions to $J$ by each of the individual terms are never negative.

The minimization of $J$ in equation (8-35), which can be written as

$$J = \sum_{i=0}^{N-1} \mathbf{u}^\dagger(i)\mathbf{R}(i)\mathbf{u}(i) + \sum_{i=0}^{N} \mathbf{x}^\dagger(i)\mathbf{Q}(i)\mathbf{x}(i)$$

with $\mathbf{Q}(N) = \mathbf{P}(N)$, is the solution of a related recursive least squares state estimation problem where the performance measure to be minimized is (8-34):

$$J = \sum_{i=0}^{k-1} \mathbf{w}^\dagger(i)\mathbf{Q}^{-1}(i)\mathbf{w}(i) + \sum_{i=0}^{k} \mathbf{v}^\dagger(i)\mathbf{R}^{-1}(i)\mathbf{v}(i)$$

Kalman, by applying this duality to the discrete-time Kalman filter, was the first to obtain the solution.

## 8.6.1 *State Feedback Solution*

Solution of the linear-quadratic optimal control problem is also obtained easily by applying the *principle of optimality*, a technique developed by Richard Bellman in the 1950s in connection with his invention of *dynamic programming*. This method also offers insight as to the backward-in-step nature of the solution. To solve the problem, we use the partial performance measures $J(i, j)$ which are the costs of control from step $i$ to a later step $j$,

$$J(i, j) = \sum_{k=i}^{j-1} [\mathbf{x}^\dagger(k)\mathbf{Q}(k)\mathbf{x}(k) + \mathbf{u}^\dagger(k)\mathbf{R}(k)\mathbf{u}(k)]$$

when step $j$ is not the last step $N$, and

$$J(i, N) = \mathbf{x}^\dagger(N)\mathbf{P}(N)\mathbf{x}(N) + \sum_{k=i}^{N-1} [\mathbf{x}^\dagger(k)\mathbf{Q}(k)\mathbf{x}(k) + \mathbf{u}^\dagger(k)\mathbf{R}(k)\mathbf{u}(k)]$$

when the last step is $N$.

The problem at hand is to find, as a function of the initial state $\mathbf{x}(0)$, the sequence of inputs $\mathbf{u}(0), \mathbf{u}(1), \ldots, \mathbf{u}(N-1)$ that results in minimal cost from the zeroth step to the $N$th step:

$$\underset{\mathbf{u}(0), \ldots, \mathbf{u}(N-1)}{\text{minimum with respect to}} \{J(0, N)\}$$

$$= \underset{\mathbf{u}(0), \ldots, \mathbf{u}(N-1)}{\text{minimum with respect to}} \left\{ \mathbf{x}^\dagger(N)\mathbf{P}(N)\mathbf{x}(N) \right.$$

$$\left. + \sum_{k=1}^{N-1} [\mathbf{x}^\dagger(k)\mathbf{Q}(k)\mathbf{x}(k) + \mathbf{u}^\dagger(k)\mathbf{R}(k)\mathbf{u}(k)] \right\}$$

Separating the cost of the last control $\mathbf{u}(N-1)$ from the rest of the cost

$$\underset{\mathbf{u}(0), \ldots, \mathbf{u}(N-1)}{\text{minimum with respect to}} \{J(0, N)\}$$

$$= \underset{\mathbf{u}(0), \ldots, \mathbf{u}(N-1)}{\text{minimum with respect to}} \{J(0, N-1) + J(N-1, N)\}$$

we note that $\mathbf{u}(N-1)$ does not affect $J(0, N-1)$ so that

$$\underset{\mathbf{u}(0), \ldots, \mathbf{u}(N-1)}{\text{minimum with respect to}} \{J(0, N)\}$$

$$= \underset{\mathbf{u}(0), \ldots, \mathbf{u}(N-2)}{\text{minimum with respect to}} \{J(0, N-1)\}$$

$$+ \underset{\mathbf{u}(0), \ldots, \mathbf{u}(N-1)}{\text{minimum with respect to}} \{J(N-1, N)\}$$

$$= \underset{\mathbf{u}(0), \ldots, \mathbf{u}(N-2)}{\min} \left\{ J(0, N-1) + \underset{\mathbf{u}(N-1)}{\min} [J(N-1), N)] \right\}$$

In general:

$$\min_{\mathbf{u}(0), \ldots, \mathbf{u}(N-1)} \{J(0, N)\}$$

$$= \min_{\mathbf{u}(0), \ldots, \mathbf{u}(i-1)} \left\{ J(0, i) + \min_{\mathbf{u}(i), \ldots, \mathbf{u}(N-1)} [J(i, N)] \right\} \qquad (8\text{-}36)$$

The term involving $J(i, N)$ is a minimization problem of the same type. It begins at step $i$ with the initial state $\mathbf{x}(i)$. Relation (8-36) is a statement of the principle of optimality which is in words: whatever the initial state $\mathbf{x}(0)$ of the system and the initial control sequence $\mathbf{u}(0), \ldots, \mathbf{u}(i-1)$, the remaining control sequence $\mathbf{u}(i), \ldots, \mathbf{u}(N-1)$ is optimal with regard to the state $\mathbf{x}(i)$ that results from the initial control sequence.

To apply the principle of optimality, one begins at the next-to-last step, $N-1$, and finds the last input, $\mathbf{u}(N-1)$, that minimizes the cost of control from step $N-1$ to step $N$, $J(N-1, N)$, as a function of the beginning state for that step, $\mathbf{x}(N-1)$. Then, the input $\mathbf{u}(N-2)$ is found that minimizes $J(N-2, N)$ when $\mathbf{u}(N-1)$ is as previously determined. One proceeds in this manner finding one control vector at a time, from the last to the first, as a function of the system's state. In consequence of the quadratic nature of the cost function, the optimal input at each step will turn out to be a linear transformation of the system state at that step, so the result will be in the form of state feedback. The transformation will generally not be the same at each step, so the optimal control solution is step-varying feedback, whether or not the controlled system is step-invariant.

At the next-to-last step, substituting

$$\mathbf{x}(N) = \mathbf{A}(N-1)\mathbf{x}(N-1) + \mathbf{B}(N-1)\mathbf{u}(N-1)$$

the cost of control to the last step is

$$
\begin{aligned}
J(N-1, N) = {}& \mathbf{x}^\dagger(N)\mathbf{P}(N)\mathbf{x}(N) + \mathbf{x}^\dagger(N-1)\mathbf{Q}(N-1)\mathbf{x}(N-1) \\
& + \mathbf{u}^\dagger(N-1)\mathbf{R}(N-1)\mathbf{u}(N-1) \\
= {}& \mathbf{x}^\dagger(N-1)[\mathbf{A}^\dagger(N-1)\mathbf{P}(N)\mathbf{A}(N-1) + \mathbf{Q}(N-1)]\mathbf{x}(N-1) \\
& + \mathbf{x}^\dagger(N-1)\mathbf{A}^\dagger(N-1)\mathbf{P}(N)\mathbf{B}(N-1)\mathbf{u}(N-1) \\
& + \mathbf{u}^\dagger(N-1)\mathbf{B}^\dagger(N-1)\mathbf{P}(N)\mathbf{A}(N-1)\mathbf{x}(N-1) \\
& + \mathbf{u}^\dagger(N-1)[\mathbf{B}^\dagger(N-1)\mathbf{P}(N)\mathbf{B}(N-1) + \mathbf{R}(N-1)]\mathbf{u}(N-1)
\end{aligned}
$$

Taking the partial derivatives of this expression with respect to each of the $r$

scalar components of $\mathbf{u}(N - 1)$ gives

$$
\left[\frac{\partial J}{\partial \mathbf{u}(N - 1)}\right]^{\dagger} = \begin{bmatrix} \dfrac{\partial J}{\partial u_1(N - 1)} \\ \dfrac{\partial J}{\partial u_2(N - 1)} \\ \vdots \\ \dfrac{\partial J}{\partial u_r(N - 1)} \end{bmatrix}
$$

$$
\begin{aligned}
= \, &0 + \mathbf{B}^{\dagger}(N - 1)\mathbf{P}^{\dagger}(N)\mathbf{A}(N - 1)\mathbf{x}(N - 1) \\
&+ \mathbf{B}^{\dagger}(N - 1)\mathbf{P}(N)\mathbf{A}(N - 1)\mathbf{x}(N - 1) \\
&+ [\mathbf{B}^{\dagger}(N - 1)\mathbf{P}(N)\mathbf{B}(N - 1) + \mathbf{R}(N - 1)]\mathbf{u}(N - 1) \\
&+ [\mathbf{B}^{\dagger}(N - 1)\mathbf{P}^{\dagger}(N)\mathbf{B}(N - 1) + \mathbf{R}^{\dagger}(N - 1)]\mathbf{u}(N - 1) \\
= \, &2\mathbf{B}^{\dagger}(N - 1)\mathbf{P}(N)\mathbf{A}(N - 1)\mathbf{x}(N - 1) \\
&+ 2[\mathbf{B}^{\dagger}(N - 1)\mathbf{P}(N)\mathbf{B}(N - 1) + \mathbf{R}(N - 1)]\mathbf{u}(N - 1)
\end{aligned}
$$

using partial derivative identities from Table 1-1 and

$$\mathbf{P}^{\dagger}(N) = \mathbf{P}(N); \qquad \mathbf{R}^{\dagger}(N - 1) = \mathbf{R}(N - 1)$$

because of the symmetry of $\mathbf{P}$ and $\mathbf{R}$. Equating this result to zero,

$$
\begin{aligned}
\mathbf{u}(N - 1) &= -[\mathbf{B}^{\dagger}(N - 1)\mathbf{P}(N)\mathbf{B}(N - 1) + \mathbf{R}(N - 1)]^{-1} \\
&\quad \times \mathbf{B}^{\dagger}(N - 1)\mathbf{P}(N)\mathbf{A}(N - 1)\mathbf{x}(N - 1) \\
&= \mathbf{K}(N - 1)\mathbf{x}(N - 1)
\end{aligned}
$$

where

$$
\begin{aligned}
\mathbf{K}(N - 1) &= -[\mathbf{B}^{\dagger}(N - 1)\mathbf{P}(N)\mathbf{B}(N - 1) + \mathbf{R}(N - 1)]^{-1} \\
&\quad \times \mathbf{B}^{\dagger}(N - 1)\mathbf{P}(N)\mathbf{A}(N - 1)
\end{aligned} \tag{8-37}
$$

Because of the quadratic nature of the performance measure, the solution is a global minimum.

The optimal last-step input $\mathbf{u}(N - 1)$ is a linear transformation of the state $\mathbf{x}(N - 1)$. The transformation (or gain) $\mathbf{K}(N - 1)$ of the state feedback is given by the complicated but straightforward expression (8-37). The matrix inversion involved is of an $r \times r$ matrix, where $r$ is the number of plant inputs. The number $r$ is usually not as large as $n$, the plant order. Existence of the inverse in (8-37) is guaranteed if $\mathbf{R}(N - 1)$ is positive definite rather than the assumed positive semidefinite; that is, when any nonzero control input contributes to the performance measure. Its existence is also guaranteed under other conditions such as when $\mathbf{P}(N)$ is positive definite and the columns of $\mathbf{B}(N - 1)$ are linearly independent. If the inverse does not exist, it means that the solution for the optimal control input is not unique.

When the optimal last-step input $\mathbf{u}(N - 1)$ is used, the cost of control from the next-to-last step to the last step is

$$
\begin{aligned}
\min_{\mathbf{u}(N-1)} &\{J(N - 1, N\} \\
&= \mathbf{x}^{\dagger}(N)\mathbf{P}(N)\mathbf{x}(N) + \mathbf{x}^{\dagger}(N - 1)\mathbf{Q}(N - 1)\mathbf{x}(N - 1) \\
&\quad + \mathbf{u}^{\dagger}(N - 1)\mathbf{R}(N - 1)\mathbf{u}(N - 1) \\
&= \mathbf{x}^{\dagger}(N - 1)[\mathbf{A}^{\dagger}(N - 1)\mathbf{P}(N)\mathbf{A}(N - 1) + \mathbf{Q}(N - 1)]\mathbf{x}(N - 1) \\
&\quad + \mathbf{x}^{\dagger}(N - 1)\mathbf{A}^{\dagger}(N - 1)\mathbf{P}(N)\mathbf{B}(N - 1)\mathbf{K}(N - 1)\mathbf{x}(N - 1) \\
&\quad + \mathbf{x}^{\dagger}(N - 1)\mathbf{K}^{\dagger}(N - 1)\mathbf{B}^{\dagger}(N - 1)\mathbf{P}(N)\mathbf{A}(N - 1)\mathbf{x}(N - 1) \\
&\quad + \mathbf{x}^{\dagger}(N - 1)\mathbf{K}^{\dagger}(N - 1)[\mathbf{B}^{\dagger}(N - 1)\mathbf{P}(N)\mathbf{B}(N - 1) + \mathbf{R}(N - 1)] \\
&\quad \times \mathbf{K}(N - 1)\mathbf{x}(N - 1) \\
&= \mathbf{x}^{\dagger}(N - 1)\{[\mathbf{A}(N - 1) + \mathbf{B}(N - 1)\mathbf{K}(N - 1)]^{\dagger}\mathbf{P}(N)] \\
&\quad \times [\mathbf{A}(N - 1) + \mathbf{B}(N - 1)\mathbf{K}(N - 1)] \\
&\quad + \mathbf{K}^{\dagger}(N - 1)\mathbf{R}(N - 1)\mathbf{K}(N - 1) + \mathbf{Q}(N - 1)\}\mathbf{x}(N - 1) \\
&= \mathbf{x}^{\dagger}(N - 1)\mathbf{P}(N - 1)\mathbf{x}(N - 1)
\end{aligned}
$$

where

$$
\begin{aligned}
\mathbf{P}(N - 1) = &[\mathbf{A}(N - 1) + \mathbf{B}(N - 1)\mathbf{K}(N - 1)]^{\dagger}\mathbf{P}(N)[\mathbf{A}(N - 1) \\
&\quad + \mathbf{B}(N - 1)\mathbf{K}(N - 1)] \\
&\quad + \mathbf{K}^{\dagger}(N - 1)\mathbf{R}(N - 1)\mathbf{K}(N - 1) + \mathbf{Q}(N - 1)
\end{aligned}
$$

It is significant that the minimum cost is quadratic in $\mathbf{x}(N - 1)$ because this means that finding the optimal input $\mathbf{u}(N - 2)$ is another problem of exactly the same form as the last-step problem.

Applying the principle of optimality, the optimum input $\mathbf{u}(N - 2)$ is given by

$$
\begin{aligned}
\min_{\mathbf{u}(N-2),\, \mathbf{u}(N-1)} &\{J(N - 2, N)\} \\
&= \min_{\mathbf{u}(N-2)} \left\{ J(N - 2, N - 1) + \min_{\mathbf{u}(N-1)} [J(N - 1, N]\right\} \\
&= \min_{\mathbf{u}(N-2)} \{\mathbf{x}^{\dagger}(N - 2)\mathbf{Q}(N - 2)\mathbf{x}(N - 2) + \mathbf{u}^{\dagger}(N - 2)\mathbf{u}(N - 2) \\
&\quad + \mathbf{x}^{\dagger}(N - 1)\mathbf{P}(N - 1)\mathbf{x}(N - 1)\}
\end{aligned}
$$

which is of the form of the previous problem, with the indices of each of the quantities moved back one step, to $N - 2$. Using the previous results, the optimal input is given by

$$\mathbf{u}(N - 2) = \mathbf{K}(N - 2)\mathbf{x}(N - 2)$$

where

$$\mathbf{K}(N - 2) = -[\mathbf{B}^\dagger(N - 2)\mathbf{P}(N - 1)\mathbf{B}(N - 2) + \mathbf{R}(N - 2)]^{-1}$$
$$\times \mathbf{B}^\dagger(N - 2)\mathbf{P}(N - 1)\mathbf{A}(N - 2)$$

and where $\mathbf{P}(N - 1)$ is as given above. The cost of using the optimal controls $\mathbf{u}(N - 2)$ and $\mathbf{u}(N - 1)$ is

$$\min_{\mathbf{u}(N - 2),\, \mathbf{u}(N - 1)} \{J(N - 2, N\} = \mathbf{x}^\dagger(N - 2)\mathbf{P}(N - 2)\mathbf{x}(N - 2)$$

where

$$\mathbf{P}(N - 2) = [\mathbf{A}(N - 2) + \mathbf{B}(N - 2)\mathbf{K}(N - 2)]^\dagger \, \mathbf{P}(N - 1)[\mathbf{A}(N - 2)$$
$$+ \mathbf{B}(N - 2)\mathbf{K}(N - 2)]$$
$$+ \mathbf{K}^\dagger(N - 2)\mathbf{R}(N - 2)\mathbf{K}(N - 2) + \mathbf{Q}(N - 2)$$

The optimal input $\mathbf{u}(N - 3)$ is the solution to a problem of the same form, and so on.

This recursive calculation of the optimal feedback gains for the linear-quadratic regulator is summarized in Table 8-7. Beginning with $\mathbf{P}(N)$, the last feedback gain matrix $\mathbf{K}(N - 1)$ is calculated. Using $\mathbf{K}(N - 1)$, the matrix $\mathbf{P}(N - 1)$ is computed. Then all of the indices are stepped backward one step and, with $\mathbf{P}(N - 1)$, the feedback gain matrix $\mathbf{K}(N - 2)$ is calculated. Using $\mathbf{K}(N - 2)$, $\mathbf{P}(N - 2)$ is calculated. The cycle is continued until $\mathbf{K}(0)$ is found. A formidable amount of algebraic computation is required, so that the user should have digital computer aid for all but the lowest-order problems.

## 8.6.2 First-Order Examples

A program in the Basic language for computing the optimal feedback control gains for a first-order step-invariant plant

$$x(k + 1) = ax(k) + bu(k)$$

$$u(k) = K(k)x(k)$$

## TABLE 8-7   Procedure for Backwards-in-Time Calculation of Optimal Quadratic Regulator Gains

For the plant

$$\mathbf{x}(k + 1) = \mathbf{A}(k)\mathbf{x}(k) + \mathbf{B}(k)\mathbf{u}(k)$$

with state feedback

$$\mathbf{u}(k) = \mathbf{K}(k)\mathbf{x}(k)$$

and performance measure

$$J = \mathbf{x}^{\dagger}(N)\mathbf{P}(N)\mathbf{x}(N) + \sum_{i=0}^{N-1} [\mathbf{x}^{\dagger}(i)\mathbf{Q}(i)\mathbf{x}(i) + \mathbf{u}^{\dagger}(i)\mathbf{R}(i)\mathbf{u}(i)]$$

begin with $i = 1$ and the known $\mathbf{P}(N)$:

1. $\mathbf{K}(N - i) = -[\mathbf{B}^{\dagger}(N - i)\mathbf{P}(N + 1 - i)\mathbf{B}(N - i) + \mathbf{R}(N - i)]^{-1}$
   $\times \mathbf{B}^{\dagger}(N - i)\mathbf{P}(N + 1 - i)\mathbf{A}(N - i)$     (8-38)

2. $\mathbf{P}(N - i) = [\mathbf{A}(N - i) + \mathbf{B}(N - i)\mathbf{K}(N - i)]^{\dagger}\mathbf{P}(N + 1 - i)$
   $\times [\mathbf{A}(N - i) + \mathbf{B}(N - i)\mathbf{K}(N - i)]$
   $+ \mathbf{K}^{\dagger}(N - i)\mathbf{R}(N - i)\mathbf{K}(N - i) + \mathbf{Q}(N - i)$     (8-39)

3. Increment $i$ and repeat steps 1, 2, and 3 until $\mathbf{K}(0)$ and (if desired) $\mathbf{P}(0)$ have been calculated.

The minimum performance measure is

$$\min_{\mathbf{u}(0),\,\ldots,\,\mathbf{u}(N-1)} \{J\} = \mathbf{x}^{\dagger}(0)\mathbf{P}(0)\mathbf{x}(0)$$

---

with performance measure of the form

$$J = Px^2(N) + \sum_{i=0}^{N-1} [Qx^2(i) + Ru^2(i)]$$

is listed in Table 8-8. The solution for the specific plant

$$x(k + 1) = 0.5x(k) + 3u(k)$$

**TABLE 8-8  Program in Basic to Calculate Optimal Control Gains for a Step-Invariant System and Cost Measure**

```
100   PRINT "SCALAR OPTIMAL CONTROL CALCULATION"
120   A = 0.5
130   B = 3
140   P = 10
150   Q = 1
160   R = 4
170   N = 10
180   FOR I = 1 to N
190   K = - B*P*A/(B*P*B + R)
200   P = (A + B*K)*P*(A + B*K) + K*R*K + Q
210   PRINT " "
220   PRINT "AT STEP ";I – I
230   PRINT "K = ";K
240   PRINT "P = ";P
250   NEXT I
260   END
```

with

$$N = 10; \quad P = 10; \quad Q = 1; \quad R = 4$$

is listed and plotted in Figure 8-10 for $x(0) = 100$. The feedback gain is step-varying. Moving backward in time, from step $k = N$ toward $k = 0$, there is an initial transient, after which the gain is very nearly constant.

For a step-invariant plant, the optimum feedback gains, from $K(N)$ backwards, are not changed if the final step $N$ is changed. An example, when $N$ is changed from 10 to 4 is shown in Figure 8-11. When $Q = 0$ so that there is no weighting of the state error except at the last step, as in Figure 8-12, the feedback gains tend to be very small at first. This lets the plant state decay as much as it can without feedback (and without cost). This would not be the case, of course, if the plant were unstable. When $R = 0$ so that there is no weighting of the control effort in the performance measure, the feedback gains make the system deadbeat, as shown in Figure 8-13. The plant state is driven to zero right away so that there is no state error cost on succeeding steps.

These simple examples serve to demonstrate that an optimal quadratic feedback regulator performs reasonably and relatively well. In this approach, the designer selects the performance measure instead of choosing state feedback convergence properties directly.

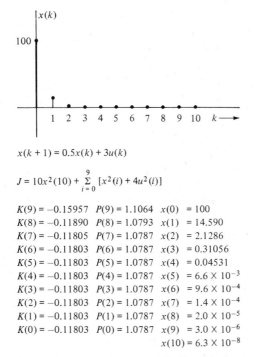

$$x(k + 1) = 0.5x(k) + 3u(k)$$

$$J = 10x^2(10) + \sum_{i=0}^{9} [x^2(i) + 4u^2(i)]$$

| | | |
|---|---|---|
| $K(9) = -0.15957$ | $P(9) = 1.1064$ | $x(0) = 100$ |
| $K(8) = -0.11890$ | $P(8) = 1.0793$ | $x(1) = 14.590$ |
| $K(7) = -0.11805$ | $P(7) = 1.0787$ | $x(2) = 2.1286$ |
| $K(6) = -0.11803$ | $P(6) = 1.0787$ | $x(3) = 0.31056$ |
| $K(5) = -0.11803$ | $P(5) = 1.0787$ | $x(4) = 0.04531$ |
| $K(4) = -0.11803$ | $P(4) = 1.0787$ | $x(5) = 6.6 \times 10^{-3}$ |
| $K(3) = -0.11803$ | $P(3) = 1.0787$ | $x(6) = 9.6 \times 10^{-4}$ |
| $K(2) = -0.11803$ | $P(2) = 1.0787$ | $x(7) = 1.4 \times 10^{-4}$ |
| $K(1) = -0.11803$ | $P(1) = 1.0787$ | $x(8) = 2.0 \times 10^{-5}$ |
| $K(0) = -0.11803$ | $P(0) = 1.0787$ | $x(9) = 3.0 \times 10^{-6}$ |
| | | $x(10) = 6.3 \times 10^{-8}$ |

**FIGURE 8-10.   A scalar optimal regulation example.**

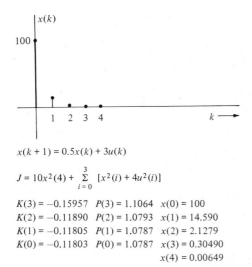

$$x(k + 1) = 0.5x(k) + 3u(k)$$

$$J = 10x^2(4) + \sum_{i=0}^{3} [x^2(i) + 4u^2(i)]$$

| | | |
|---|---|---|
| $K(3) = -0.15957$ | $P(3) = 1.1064$ | $x(0) = 100$ |
| $K(2) = -0.11890$ | $P(2) = 1.0793$ | $x(1) = 14.590$ |
| $K(1) = -0.11805$ | $P(1) = 1.0787$ | $x(2) = 2.1279$ |
| $K(0) = -0.11803$ | $P(0) = 1.0787$ | $x(3) = 0.30490$ |
| | | $x(4) = 0.00649$ |

**FIGURE 8-11.   Scalar optimal regulation example with a different number of steps, $N = 4$.**

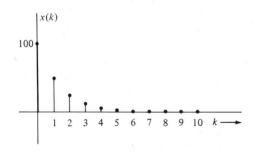

$$x(k + 1) = 0.5x(k) + 3u(k)$$

$$J = 10x^2(10) + \sum_{i=0}^{9} 4u^2(i)$$

| | | |
|---|---|---|
| $K(9) = -0.15957$ | $P(9) = 0.1064$ | $x(0) = 100$ |
| $K(8) = -3.21888 \times 10^{-2}$ | $P(8) = 2.146 \times 10^{-2}$ | $x(1) = 50.000$ |
| $K(7) = -7.67656 \times 10^{-3}$ | $P(7) = 5.118 \times 10^{-3}$ | $x(2) = 25.000$ |
| $K(6) = -1.89729 \times 10^{-3}$ | $P(6) = 1.265 \times 10^{-3}$ | $x(3) = 12.500$ |
| $K(5) = -4.72977 \times 10^{-4}$ | $P(5) = 3.153 \times 10^{-4}$ | $x(4) = 6.249$ |
| $K(4) = -1.18160 \times 10^{-5}$ | $P(4) = 7.877 \times 10^{-5}$ | $x(5) = 3.122$ |
| $K(3) = -2.95349 \times 10^{-5}$ | $P(3) = 1.969 \times 10^{-5}$ | $x(6) = 1.557$ |
| $K(2) = -7.38339 \times 10^{-6}$ | $P(2) = 4.922 \times 10^{-6}$ | $x(7) = 0.769$ |
| $K(1) = -1.84583 \times 10^{-6}$ | $P(1) = 1.231 \times 10^{-6}$ | $x(8) = 0.367$ |
| $K(0) = -4.61456 \times 10^{-7}$ | $P(0) = 3.076 \times 10^{-7}$ | $x(9) = 0.148$ |
| | | $x(10) = 3.15 \times 10^{-3}$ |

**FIGURE 8-12.   Optimal regulation when there is no state error cost except at the last step.**

## 8.6.3 *Spacecraft Roll Attitude Control*

The formulation of an optimal control problem sometimes is a natural consequence of the objectives of a control system design. A simplified discrete-time model for the roll attitude control of a spacecraft is

$$\begin{bmatrix} x_1(k + 1) \\ x_2(k + 1) \end{bmatrix} = \begin{bmatrix} 1 & T \\ 0 & 1 \end{bmatrix} \begin{bmatrix} x_1(k) \\ x_2(k) \end{bmatrix} + \begin{bmatrix} 0 \\ \alpha T \end{bmatrix} u(k)$$

where

$x_1$ = roll attitude in degrees

$x_2$ = roll rate in degrees per second

$u$ = roll thrust jet impulse in newton-seconds

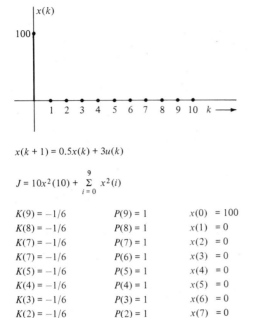

$x(k+1) = 0.5x(k) + 3u(k)$

$$J = 10x^2(10) + \sum_{i=0}^{9} x^2(i)$$

| | | |
|---|---|---|
| $K(9) = -1/6$ | $P(9) = 1$ | $x(0)\ = 100$ |
| $K(8) = -1/6$ | $P(8) = 1$ | $x(1)\ = 0$ |
| $K(7) = -1/6$ | $P(7) = 1$ | $x(2)\ = 0$ |
| $K(7) = -1/6$ | $P(6) = 1$ | $x(3)\ = 0$ |
| $K(5) = -1/6$ | $P(5) = 1$ | $x(4)\ = 0$ |
| $K(4) = -1/6$ | $P(4) = 1$ | $x(5)\ = 0$ |
| $K(3) = -1/6$ | $P(3) = 1$ | $x(6)\ = 0$ |
| $K(2) = -1/6$ | $P(2) = 1$ | $x(7)\ = 0$ |
| $K(1) = -1/6$ | $P(1) = 1$ | $x(8)\ = 0$ |
| $K(0) = -1/6$ | $P(0) = 1$ | $x(9)\ = 0$ |
| | | $x(10) = 0$ |

**FIGURE 8-13.   Optimal regulation when there is no control cost.**

and where $T$ is the sampling interval and $\alpha$ is the thrust coefficient. The roll rate at step $k + 1$ is the rate at step $k$ plus the rate change caused by the thrust jet:

$$x_2(k + 1) = x_2(k) + \alpha Tu(k)$$

The roll attitude at step $k + 1$ is the attitude at step $k$ plus the roll rate times the time interval:

$$x_1(k + 1) = x_1(k) + Tx_2(k)$$

For a one-tenth second sampling rate, $T = 1/10$, and $\alpha = 20$ the model becomes

$$\begin{bmatrix} x_1(k + 1) \\ x_2(k + 1) \end{bmatrix} = \begin{bmatrix} 1 & 0.1 \\ 0 & 1 \end{bmatrix} \begin{bmatrix} x_1(k) \\ x_2(k) \end{bmatrix} + \begin{bmatrix} 0 \\ 2 \end{bmatrix} u(k) = \mathbf{A}\mathbf{x}(k) + \mathbf{b}u(k) \tag{8-40}$$

When it is desired to bring the spacecraft from an initial roll attitude and rate to near zero attitude and rate in a fixed number of steps, the optimal regulator solution is attractive. The state variables can be defined so that the zero attitude is any angle desired. The performance measure

$$J = 10x_1^2(10) + 20x_2(10) + \sum_{i=0}^{9} [x_1^2(i) + 2x_2^2(i) + 5u^2(i)]$$

is for an 11-step interval from step 0 through step 10 with the control input $u$ applied at steps 0 through 9. Errors in rate are weighted twice as heavily as those of attitude, and squares of the control input have five times that weight. The final penalties, at step 10, for attitude and rate errors have weights of 1000 and 100, respectively. In terms of matrices:

$$J = \mathbf{x}^\dagger(10)\mathbf{P}(10)\mathbf{x}(10) + \sum_{i=0}^{9} [\mathbf{x}^\dagger(i)\mathbf{Q}\mathbf{x}(i) + u^\dagger(i)Ru(i)]$$

where

$$\mathbf{P}(10) = \begin{bmatrix} 1000 & 0 \\ 0 & 100 \end{bmatrix}; \qquad \mathbf{Q} = \begin{bmatrix} 1 & 0 \\ 0 & 2 \end{bmatrix}; \qquad R = 3$$

The optimal quadratic regulator gains are given by

$$\mathbf{k}^\dagger(9) = -[\mathbf{b}^\dagger\mathbf{P}(10)\mathbf{b} + R]^{-1}\mathbf{b}^\dagger\mathbf{P}(10)\mathbf{A}$$

$$\mathbf{P}(9) = [\mathbf{A} + \mathbf{b}\mathbf{k}^\dagger(9)]^\dagger\mathbf{P}(10)[\mathbf{A} + \mathbf{b}\mathbf{k}^\dagger(9)] + \mathbf{k}R\mathbf{k}^\dagger + \mathbf{Q}$$

$$\mathbf{k}^\dagger(8) = -[\mathbf{b}^\dagger\mathbf{P}(9)\mathbf{b} + R]^{-1}\mathbf{b}^\dagger\mathbf{P}(9)\mathbf{A}$$

$$\mathbf{P}(8) = [\mathbf{A} + \mathbf{b}\mathbf{k}^\dagger(8)]\mathbf{P}(9)[\mathbf{A} + \mathbf{b}\mathbf{k}^\dagger(8)] + \mathbf{k}R\mathbf{k}^\dagger + \mathbf{Q}$$

and so on, through

$$\mathbf{k}^\dagger(0) = -[\mathbf{b}^\dagger\mathbf{P}(1)\mathbf{b} + R]^{-1}\mathbf{b}^\dagger\mathbf{P}(1)\mathbf{A}$$

Tables 8-9 gives numerical results for the gains $\mathbf{k}$. For the initial conditions

$$x_1(0) = 100$$

$$x_2(0) = -50$$

the performance of this regulator is shown in Figure 8-14.

**TABLE 8-9    Optimal Feedback Gains for the Spacecraft Roll Attitude Control**

| Step | $k_1$ | $k_2$ |
|------|-------|-------|
| 9 | 0 | $-0.496$ |
| 8 | $-3.71$ | $-0.843$ |
| 7 | $-2.20$ | $-0.668$ |
| 6 | $-1.46$ | $-0.576$ |
| 5 | $-1.08$ | $-0.526$ |
| 4 | $-0.859$ | $-0.498$ |
| 3 | $-0.716$ | $-0.480$ |
| 2 | $-0.618$ | $-0.467$ |
| 1 | $-0.547$ | $-0.458$ |
| 0 | $-0.494$ | $-0.451$ |

## 8.6.4 Steady State Regulation

For a completely controllable, step-invariant plant and constant cost weighting matrices $\mathbf{Q}$ and $\mathbf{R}$, the optimal quadratic regulator solution approaches a constant feedback gain matrix as one proceeds backwards from the final step $k = N$. Figure 8-15 illustrates this property for the spacecraft roll attitude control. As the final step $N$ goes to infinity, in what is termed the "infinite horizon" problem, these steady state gains become optimal. Steady

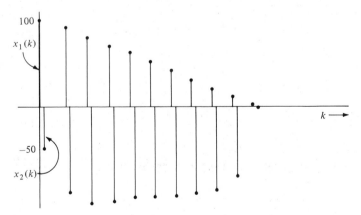

**FIGURE 8-14.    Representative performance of the optimal spacecraft roll attitude control.**

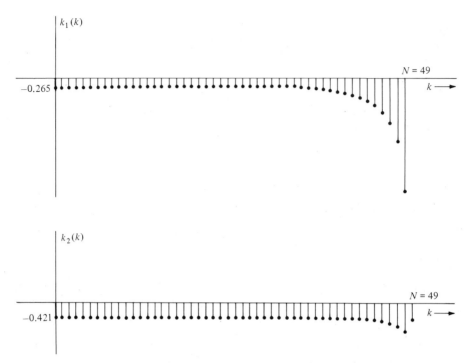

**FIGURE 8-15.   Optimal feedback gains approaching a constant steady state, backwards from the final time.**

state optimal (with regard to some performance measure) gains are occasionally used in lieu of state feedback eigenvalue placement for step-invariant regulator design. Of course, the steady state optimal gains result in *some* certain eigenvalue placement, just as any eigenvalue placement minimizes some quadratic performance measure. The designer's choice is whether to

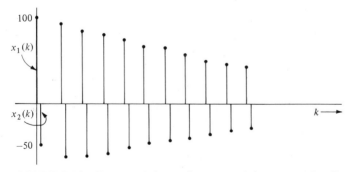

**FIGURE 8-16.   Representative performance of the spacecraft roll attitude when the constant steady state feedback gains are used.**

select the system eigenvalues or the weighting matrices $\mathbf{Q}$ and $\mathbf{R}$. Figure 8-16 shows performance of the spacecraft roll attitude control when the steady state gains are used.

## 8.7 Summary

State equations for linear, step-varying systems are of the form

$$\mathbf{x}(k + 1) = \mathbf{A}(k)\mathbf{x}(k) + \mathbf{B}(k)\mathbf{u}(k)$$

$$\mathbf{y}(k) = \mathbf{C}(k)\mathbf{x}(k) + \mathbf{D}(k)\mathbf{u}(k)$$

For any initial state $\mathbf{x}(0)$, the state thereafter is composed of the zero-input component and the zero-state component

$$\mathbf{x}(k) = \mathbf{x}_{\text{zero-input}}(k) + \mathbf{x}_{\text{zero-state}}(k)$$

where

$$\begin{cases} \mathbf{x}_{\text{zero-input}}(k + 1) = \mathbf{A}(k)\mathbf{x}_{\text{zero-input}}(k) \\ \mathbf{x}_{\text{zero-input}}(0) = \mathbf{x}(0) \end{cases}$$

and

$$\begin{cases} \mathbf{x}_{\text{zero-state}}(k + 1) = \mathbf{A}(k)\mathbf{x}_{\text{zero-state}}(k) + \mathbf{B}(k)\mathbf{u}(k) \\ \mathbf{x}_{\text{zero-state}}(0) = \mathbf{0} \end{cases}$$

A linear, step-varying system is stable if the zero-input component of its state decays to zero as $k$ becomes large

$$\lim_{k \to \infty} \mathbf{x}_{\text{zero-input}}(k) = \mathbf{0}$$

and if the zero-state component of its state is bounded for any bounded input.
A step-varying system is observable at step $k$ if $\mathbf{x}(k)$ can be determined from the system outputs $\mathbf{y}(k)$, $\mathbf{y}(k + 1), \ldots,$ $\mathbf{y}(k + N - 1)$ and inputs $\mathbf{u}(k)$, $\mathbf{u}(k + 1), \ldots, \mathbf{u}(k + N - 1)$ for some finite number of steps, $N$. It is uniformly observable if it is observable at every step. Similarly, a step-varying system is controllable at step $k$ if there are input sequences $\mathbf{u}(k)$, $\mathbf{u}(k + 1), \ldots,$ $\mathbf{u}(k + N - 1)$ that will move the state from any known $\mathbf{x}(k)$ to any desired $\mathbf{x}(N)$ in some finite number of steps, $N$. It is uniformly controllable if it is controllable at every step. More general observability and controllability

matrices than those for step-invariant systems can be used to test observability and controllability of step-varying systems.

Step-varying observers recursively estimate the state of a plant, step-varying or not. A full-order state observer of the form

$$\xi(k + 1) = \mathbf{F}(k)\xi(k) + \mathbf{G}(k)\mathbf{y}(k) + \mathbf{H}(k)\mathbf{u}(k)$$

is governed by

$$\mathbf{F}(k) = \mathbf{A}(k) - \mathbf{G}(k)\mathbf{C}(k)$$

$$\mathbf{H}(k) = \mathbf{B}(k) - \mathbf{G}(k)\mathbf{D}(k)$$

where $\mathbf{G}(k)$ is arbitrary. It has error given by

$$\mathbf{x}(k) - \xi(k) = \mathbf{F}(k - 1)\mathbf{F}(k - 2) \ldots \mathbf{F}(0)[\mathbf{x}(0) - \xi(0)]$$

The algorithm of Table 8-1 gives gains for a deadbeat observer. For an $n$th-order plant

$$\mathbf{F}(n - 1)\mathbf{F}(n - 2) \ldots \mathbf{F}(0) = \mathbf{0}$$

so that

$$\xi(n) = \mathbf{x}(n)$$

For ongoing deadbeat convergence

$$\mathbf{F}(n + i)\mathbf{F}(n + i - 1) \ldots \mathbf{F}(i) = \mathbf{0}; \qquad i = 0, 1, 2, \ldots$$

the observer gain calculation summarized in Table 8-2 can be used. Reduced-order observers and observers of state transformations (Table 8-3) also have their step-varying counterparts.

State feedback regulation

$$\mathbf{u}(k) = \mathbf{E}(k)\mathbf{x}(k)$$

so that

$$\mathbf{x}(k + 1) = [\mathbf{A}(k) + \mathbf{B}(k)\mathbf{E}(k)]\mathbf{x}(k) = \mathbf{\Phi}(k)\mathbf{x}(k)$$

and

$$\mathbf{x}(k) = \mathbf{\Phi}(k - 1)\mathbf{\Phi}(k - 2) \ldots \mathbf{\Phi}(0)\mathbf{x}(0)$$

is characterized by backward-in-step gain calculations. The algorithm of Table 8-4 is for step-varying deadbeat state feedback, for which

$$\mathbf{\Phi}(n-1)\mathbf{\Phi}(n-2)\ldots\mathbf{\Phi}(0) = \mathbf{0}$$

Step-varying disturbance modeling and tracking system design parallels that for the step-invariant case. Even for a step-invariant plant, the additional design freedom in step-varying observation and feedback can result in better performance.

   If more than the minimal number of measurements necessary to determine the state of a plant are available, a least squares state estimate can be used. After a summary of properties of quadratic forms, we generalized the basic least squares solution to weighted least squares. Then the least squares calculations were arranged recursively so that the estimate is not completely recomputed whenever new, additional data is available. Instead, the previous least squares estimate is corrected to produce the new least squares estimate based on the previous estimate and the new data. The result for the case of scalar measurements is summarized in Table 8-5. When the present state of a plant is estimated with recursive least squares, with possible weighted state errors and weighted measurement errors, the Kalman filter results.

   The Kalman filter (Table 8-6) is a full-order state observer with a gain sequence that results in minimum weighted sum of squares of state and measurement errors at each step. When the errors are uncorrelated from step to step and when enough is known about the errors to sensibly choose the weighting matrices, the Kalman gain sequence is an attractive alternative to deriving observer gains from specific desired convergence properties.

   Quadratic optimal regulation (Table 8-7) is dual to the weighted recursive least squares observation done by the Kalman filter. It is the filter's counterpart for selecting step-varying state feedback gains on the basis of a quadratic error criterion rather than giving a desired state convergence directly. Although the Kalman filter results could have simply been translated to give the solution of this problem, we elected to derive it by applying the principle of optimality. This approach gives added insight with regard to the solution and as to why the result is backward-in-step. First-order examples were seen to give reasonable and expected results, and an example of optimal roll attitude control of a spacecraft provided a more involved example.

   There you have it. Eight chapters beginning with a review and overview of classical control system design and ending with modern, state space-based time-varying discrete time control. I sincerely hope that you enjoyed the tour as much as I have and that you will find the design philosophy and methods highly useful now and in the future.

## REFERENCES

A comprehensive treatment of the elements of linear system theory for both continuous-time and discrete-time systems is

L. A. Zadeh and C. A. Desoer, *Linear System Theory*. New York: McGraw-Hill, 1963.

Step-varying observer design is discussed in the papers

E. Tse and M. Athans, "Optimal Minimum-Order Observer-Estimators for Discrete Linear Time-Varying Systems," *IEEE Trans. Automatic Control*, Vol. AC-15, Aug. 1970, pp. 416–426;

G. H. Hostetter, "Robust Projector Matrix Decomposition in Time-Varying Observer Design," *Proc. 1983 IEEE Conf. on Decision and Control*, Dec. 1983, pp. 331–334;

G. H. Hostetter, "Recursive Discrete Functional Expansion," *IEEE Trans. Automatic Control*, Vol. AC-29, July 1984, pp. 654–656.

More about recursive least squares estimation and Kalman filtering can be found in the following books:

R. C. K. Lee, *Optimal Estimation, Identification and Control*. Cambridge, MA: M.I.T. Press, 1964;

J. S. Meditch, *Stochastic Optimal Linear Estimation and Control*. New York: McGraw-Hill, 1969;

A. P. Sage and J. L. Melsa, *Estimation Theory with Applications to Communications and Control*. New York: McGraw-Hill, 1971;

F. C. Schweppe, *Uncertain Dynamic Systems*. Englewood Cliffs, NJ: Prentice-Hall, 1973;

T. P. McGarty, *Stochastic Systems and State Estimation*. New York: Wiley, 1974;

A. Gelb, Editor, *Applied Optimal Estimation*. Cambridge, MA: M.I.T. Press, 1974;

B. D. O. Anderson and J. B. Moore, *Optimal Filtering*. Englewood Cliffs, NJ: Prentice-Hall, 1979;

H. W. Sorenson, *Parameter Estimation*. New York: Marcel Dekker, 1980;

R. G. Brown, *Introduction to Random Signal Analysis and Kalman Filtering*. New York: Wiley, 1983.

The original paper on what is now known as Kalman filtering is

R. E. Kalman and R. S. Bucy, "New Results in Linear Filtering and Prediction Theory," *Trans. ASME, J. Basic Eng.*, Ser. D, 83, Dec. 1961, pp. 95–107.

The paper

T. Kailath, "A View of Three Decades of Linear Filtering Theory," *IEEE Trans. Information Theory*, Vol. IT-20, March 1974, pp. 146–181

is a good survey of the subject, and the book

G. Bierman, *Factorization Methods for Discrete Estimation*. New York: Academic Press, 1977

gives important computational considerations.
     Both continuous-time and discrete-time optimal control are covered in

M. Athans and P. L. Falb, *Optimal Control: An Introduction to the Theory and Its Applications*. New York: McGraw-Hill, 1966;

D. E. Kirk, *Optimal Control Theory*. Englewood Cliffs, N.J.: Prentice-Hall, 1970;

A. P. Sage and C. C. White, *Optimum Systems Control*, 2nd edition. Englewood Cliffs, NJ: Prentice-Hall, 1977,

and a comprehensive survey of most of the subject is

M. Athans, "The Status of Optimal Control Theory and Applications for Deterministic Systems," *IEEE Trans. Automatic Control*, Vol. AC-11, July 1966, pp. 580–596

Dynamic programming is discussed in detail in

R. E. Bellman, *Dynamic Programming*. Princeton, NJ: Princeton University Press, 1957,

and

R. E. Bellman and R. E. Kalaba, *Dynamic Programming and Modern Control Theory*. New York: Academic Press, 1965.

The equivalence of eigenvalue placement and steady state optimal control was first given in

R. E. Kalman, "When is a Linear Control System Optimal?" *Trans. ASME J. Basic Eng.*, Ser. D, 86, March 1964, pp. 1–10.

## CHAPTER EIGHT PROBLEMS

**8-1.** Find the state and output of the system

$$
\begin{bmatrix} x_1(k+1) \\ x_2(k+1) \end{bmatrix} = \begin{bmatrix} (-1)^k & -1 \\ 0 & 1 \end{bmatrix} \begin{bmatrix} x_1(k) \\ x_2(k) \end{bmatrix} + \begin{bmatrix} k \\ 2 \end{bmatrix} u(k)
$$

$$
y(k) = \begin{bmatrix} \dfrac{1}{k+1} & 0 \end{bmatrix} \begin{bmatrix} x_1(k) \\ x_2(k) \end{bmatrix} - u(k)
$$

for steps 1, 2, and 3 if

$$
\mathbf{x}(0) = \begin{bmatrix} 3 \\ -4 \end{bmatrix} \quad \text{and} \quad u(k) = 4 - k
$$

**8-2.** Find the new state and output equations in terms of

$$
\mathbf{x}'(k) = \begin{bmatrix} 1 & k \\ 0 & -1 \end{bmatrix} \mathbf{x}(k)
$$

for the system of Problem 8-1.

**8-3.** For the system of Problem 8-1, find $\mathbf{x}(0)$, $\mathbf{x}(1)$, and $\mathbf{x}(2)$ if

$$y(0) = -1; \qquad u(0) = 0$$

$$y(1) = -0.5; \qquad u(1) = -1$$

$$y(2) = -2; \qquad u(2) = 2$$

$$y(3) = 3.5; \qquad u(3) = -3$$

**8-4.** For the system of problem 8-1, find $u(0)$, $u(1)$, and $u(2)$ that will take the state from

$$
\mathbf{x}(0) = \begin{bmatrix} 0 \\ -2 \end{bmatrix} \quad \text{to} \quad \mathbf{x}(3) = \begin{bmatrix} 3 \\ 0 \end{bmatrix}
$$

The solution to this problem is not unique.

**8-5.** Find second-order step-varying systems that are

    **a.** observable at step 0 but not observable at step 1

    **b.** observable at step 1 but not observable at step 0

    **c.** observable at step 0 and step 2 but not observable at step 1.

**8-6.** For the plant

$$
\begin{bmatrix} x_1(k+1) \\ x_2(k+1) \\ x_3(k+1) \end{bmatrix} = \begin{bmatrix} 1 & -1 & 0 \\ k & 1 & 2 \\ -2 & 0 & 0 \end{bmatrix} \begin{bmatrix} x_1(k) \\ x_2(k) \\ x_3(k) \end{bmatrix} + \begin{bmatrix} 1 \\ k+1 \\ 0 \\ -2 \end{bmatrix} u(k)
$$

$$
y(k) = \begin{bmatrix} 2 & (-1)^k & 0 \end{bmatrix} \begin{bmatrix} x_1(k) \\ x_2(k) \\ x_3(k) \end{bmatrix} - u(k)
$$

design a deadbeat state observer and find the observer gains $g(0)$, $g(1)$, and $g(2)$. The solution obtained will depend on your choice of basis vectors.

**8-7.** For the plant and observer of Problem 8-6, find the next three observer gains, $g(3)$, $g(4)$, and $g(5)$ by

    **a.** restarting the initial observer gain algorithm;
    **b.** using the ongoing algorithm;
    **c.** using the ongoing algorithm with a different ordering of the basis vectors.

**8-8.** Repeat Problem 8-6 for the step-invariant plant

$$
\begin{bmatrix} x_1(k+1) \\ x_2(k+1) \\ x_3(k+1) \end{bmatrix} = \begin{bmatrix} 1 & 1 & 0 \\ 0 & -1 & -1 \\ 3 & 0 & 2 \end{bmatrix} \begin{bmatrix} x_1(k) \\ x_2(k) \\ x_3(k) \end{bmatrix} + \begin{bmatrix} 2 \\ 1 \\ 0 \end{bmatrix} u(k)
$$

$$
y(k) = \begin{bmatrix} -2 & 0 & 1 \end{bmatrix} \begin{bmatrix} x_1(k) \\ x_2(k) \\ x_3(k) \end{bmatrix}
$$

Verify that the gain $g(2)$ places all the eigenvalues of

$$ F = A - g(2)c^\dagger $$

at $\lambda = 0$.

**8-9.** For the plant with state equations in Problem 8-6 but outputs

$$
\begin{bmatrix} y_1(k) \\ y_2(k) \end{bmatrix} = \begin{bmatrix} 2 & (-1)^k & 0 \\ 0 & 1 & k \end{bmatrix} \begin{bmatrix} x_1(k) \\ x_2(k) \\ x_3(k) \end{bmatrix} + \begin{bmatrix} 0 \\ 1 \end{bmatrix} u(k)
$$

design a deadbeat state observer that converges in two steps. Find an ongoing observer gain for the next step, also.

**8-10.** For the plant of Problem 8-6, specify the various matrices defining a reduced-order deadbeat state observer for steps 0 through 4.

**8-11.** Find state feedback gains e(0), e(1), and e(2) that make the system with state equations

$$
\begin{bmatrix} x_1(k+1) \\ x_2(k+1) \\ x_3(k+1) \end{bmatrix} = \begin{bmatrix} \frac{1}{2} & (-1)^k & 0 \\ 0 & 0 & 0 \\ 0 & \frac{1}{2} & -\frac{1}{2} \end{bmatrix} \begin{bmatrix} x_1(k) \\ x_2(k) \\ x_3(k) \end{bmatrix} + \begin{bmatrix} 0 \\ 1 \\ 0 \end{bmatrix} u(k)
$$

and input

$$ u(k) = e^\dagger(k)x(k) + \rho(k) $$

where $\rho$ is an external input, deadbeat.

**8-12.** Find state feedback gains E(0) and E(1) that make the system with state equations

$$
\begin{bmatrix} x_1(k+1) \\ x_2(k+1) \\ x_3(k+1) \end{bmatrix} = \begin{bmatrix} \frac{1}{2} & k & 0 \\ 0 & -1 & 1 \\ 0 & (-1)^k & \frac{1}{2} \end{bmatrix} \begin{bmatrix} x_1(k) \\ x_2(k) \\ x_3(k) \end{bmatrix} + \begin{bmatrix} 1 & 0 \\ k & -1 \\ 0 & 0 \end{bmatrix} \begin{bmatrix} u_1(k) \\ u_2(k) \end{bmatrix}
$$

and input

$$ \mathbf{u}(k) = \mathbf{E}(k)\mathbf{x}(k) + \boldsymbol{\rho}(k) $$

deadbeat in two steps, $\boldsymbol{\rho}(k)$ is an external input.

**8-13.** Design observer feedback so that the plant

$$
\begin{bmatrix} x_1(k+1) \\ x_2(k+1) \end{bmatrix} = \begin{bmatrix} \frac{1}{k+1} & 1 \\ 0 & \frac{1}{2} \end{bmatrix} \begin{bmatrix} x_1(k) \\ x_2(k) \end{bmatrix} + \begin{bmatrix} 2 \\ k-1 \end{bmatrix} u(k)
$$

$$
y(k) = \begin{bmatrix} 1 & -3 \end{bmatrix} \begin{bmatrix} x_1(k) \\ x_2(k) \end{bmatrix} + \tfrac{1}{3}u(k)
$$

with the feedback is deadbeat. Specify the various matrices involved for steps 0 through 4. Find also the state equations that describe the composite feedback system.

**8-14.** Design a linear, step-varying model of the vector of disturbance signals

$$
\begin{bmatrix} v_1(k) \\ v_2(k) \end{bmatrix} = \begin{bmatrix} \beta_1 \sin(k^2) + \beta_2(-1)^k \\ 2\beta_2 \sin(k^2) + \beta_3 \ln(k+1) \end{bmatrix}
$$

where $\beta_1$, $\beta_2$, and $\beta_3$ are arbitrary constants.

**8-15.** For the plant

$$
\begin{bmatrix} x_1(k+1) \\ x_2(k+1) \end{bmatrix} = \begin{bmatrix} \frac{1}{2} & 1 \\ 0 & \frac{1}{k+1} \end{bmatrix} \begin{bmatrix} x_1(k) \\ x_2(k) \end{bmatrix} + \begin{bmatrix} \alpha(k) \\ 1+\alpha(k) \end{bmatrix} r(k)
$$

$$\bar{y}(k) = [4(\tfrac{1}{2})^k \quad 1]\begin{bmatrix} x_1(k) \\ x_2(k) \end{bmatrix}$$

find a control input gain sequence $\alpha(k)$ for which $\bar{y}(k)$ observes any constant reference input $r$. Find $\alpha(k)$ for steps 0 through 4.

**8-16.** Repeat Problem 8-15, but find a control input gain sequence $\alpha(k)$ for which $\bar{y}(k)$ observes any alternating reference input sequence of the form

$$r(k) = \beta(-1)^k$$

where $\beta$ is a constant.

**8-17.** Express the following quadratic forms in terms of symmetric matrices $S$ in $f(\mathbf{x}) = \mathbf{x}^t S \mathbf{x}$.

  **a.** $f(x_1, x_2, x_3) = 3x_1^2 - 2x_1x_2 + 8x_1x_3 + 5x_2^2 + 4x_2x_3 - x_3^2$
  **b.** $f(x_1, x_2, x_3, x_4, x_5) = 6x_1^2 + 3x_1x_2 - 2x_1x_3 + 4x_1x_4$
  $+ 8x_2^2 + 7x_2x_3 - x_2x_4 + x_2x_5 + 10x_3^2 - 6x_3x_4 - 8x_3x_5 - 16x_4^2 + 5x_4x_5 - x_5^2$

**8-18.** For the following symmetric matrices, find an orthogonal modal matrix $P_0$ and the corresponding spectral matrix $S_0$. Verify that $P_0^t S P_0 = S_0$.

  **a.** $\begin{bmatrix} 3 & -1 \\ -1 & 3 \end{bmatrix}$

  **b.** $\begin{bmatrix} 3 & 0 & 0 \\ 0 & 3 & -1 \\ 0 & -1 & 3 \end{bmatrix}$

  **c.** $\begin{bmatrix} -1 & 0 & -3 \\ 0 & 3 & 0 \\ -3 & 0 & -1 \end{bmatrix}$

**8-19.** For each of the following quadratic forms, find orthogonal matrices $P_0$ that transform the function to a sum of squares through

$$\mathbf{x} = P_0 \mathbf{x}'; \qquad \mathbf{x}' = P_0^{-1} \mathbf{x}.$$

  **a.** $f(\mathbf{x}) = \mathbf{x}^t \begin{bmatrix} 2 & 1 \\ 1 & 2 \end{bmatrix} \mathbf{x}$

  **b.** $f(\mathbf{x}) = \mathbf{x}^t \begin{bmatrix} 2 & -1 & 0 \\ -1 & 3 & -1 \\ 0 & -1 & 2 \end{bmatrix} \mathbf{x}$

**8-20.** Determine the sign definiteness, if any, of the following symmetric matrices:

a. $\mathbf{A}_1 = \begin{bmatrix} 2 & -1 \\ -1 & 3 \end{bmatrix}$

b. $\mathbf{A}_2 = \begin{bmatrix} 1 & 1 & 2 \\ 1 & 3 & 1 \\ 2 & 1 & 8 \end{bmatrix}$

c. $\mathbf{A}_3 = \begin{bmatrix} -3 & 1 & 0 \\ 1 & -4 & -2 \\ 0 & -2 & -5 \end{bmatrix}$

**8-21.** Find weighted least squares estimates for the following sets of equations, using the given weighting matrix $\mathbf{W}$:

a. $\begin{bmatrix} 1 \\ 1 \\ 2 \\ -3 \end{bmatrix} x = \begin{bmatrix} -1 \\ -2 \\ -3 \\ 7 \end{bmatrix}; \quad \mathbf{W} = \begin{bmatrix} 3 & 1 & 0 & 0 \\ 1 & 2 & 0 & 0 \\ 0 & 0 & 4 & 1 \\ 0 & 0 & 1 & 1 \end{bmatrix}$

b. $\begin{bmatrix} 1 & 1 \\ 2 & -1 \\ -2 & 2 \end{bmatrix} \begin{bmatrix} x_1 \\ x_2 \end{bmatrix} = \begin{bmatrix} 3 \\ -2 \\ 5 \end{bmatrix}; \quad \mathbf{W} = \begin{bmatrix} 1 & 0 & 0 \\ 0 & 2 & 0 \\ 0 & 0 & 2 \end{bmatrix}$

**8-22.** By expressing positive weighting coefficients $\sigma_i$ as

$$\sigma_i = e_i^2$$

generalize the unweighted least squares estimate of equation (8-28) to obtain the solution that minimizes the weighted sum of squares

$$J = \sigma_1 v_1^2 + \sigma_2 v_2^2 + \cdots + \sigma_k v_k^2 = \sum_{i=1}^{k} \sigma_i v_i^2$$

**8-23.** Use recursive least squares to find least squares estimates for the equations

a. $\begin{bmatrix} 2 \\ -1 \\ 3 \\ -2 \end{bmatrix} x = \begin{bmatrix} 5 \\ -2 \\ 5 \\ -6 \end{bmatrix}$

b. $\begin{bmatrix} 3 & -1 \\ 0 & 2 \\ 1 & 1 \\ 2 & -2 \end{bmatrix} \begin{bmatrix} x_1 \\ x_2 \end{bmatrix} = \begin{bmatrix} -5 \\ 4 \\ 2 \\ -5 \end{bmatrix}$

**8-24.** Find the gain sequence for the first ten steps of the Kalman filter for state estimation for the systems

**a.**
$$\begin{bmatrix} x_1(k+1) \\ x_2(k+1) \end{bmatrix} = \begin{bmatrix} -\frac{1}{2} & 1 \\ \frac{1}{2} & 0 \end{bmatrix} \begin{bmatrix} x_1(k) \\ x_2(k) \end{bmatrix} + \begin{bmatrix} 0 \\ 1 \end{bmatrix} u(k)$$

$$y(k) = \begin{bmatrix} 2 & 1 \end{bmatrix} \begin{bmatrix} x_1(k) \\ x_2(k) \end{bmatrix}$$

$$\mathbf{Q} = \mathbf{I}; \qquad R = 5$$

**b.**
$$\begin{bmatrix} x_1(k+1) \\ x_2(k+1) \\ x_3(k+1) \end{bmatrix} = \begin{bmatrix} 0 & 1 & 0 \\ \frac{1}{4} & 0 & 1 \\ 0 & 0 & 0 \end{bmatrix} \begin{bmatrix} x_1(k) \\ x_2(k) \\ x_3(k) \end{bmatrix} + \begin{bmatrix} 2 \\ 0 \\ 1 \end{bmatrix} u(k)$$

$$\begin{bmatrix} y_1(k) \\ y_2(k) \end{bmatrix} = \begin{bmatrix} 1 & 0 & 0 \\ 1 & -1 & 1 \end{bmatrix} \begin{bmatrix} x_1(k) \\ x_2(k) \\ x_3(k) \end{bmatrix} + \begin{bmatrix} 1 \\ 0 \end{bmatrix} u(k)$$

$$\mathbf{Q} = 5\mathbf{I}; \qquad \mathbf{R} = \begin{bmatrix} 2 & 0 \\ 0 & 3 \end{bmatrix}$$

**8-25.** For the first-order plant

$$x(k+1) = 0.8x(k) + u(k)$$

calculate the optimal state feedback gains for each of the following performance measures:

**a.** $J = 10x^2(4) + \displaystyle\sum_{i=u}^{3} u^2(i)$

**b.** $J = 10x^2(4) + \displaystyle\sum_{i=0}^{3} 5x^2(i)$

**c.** $J = 10x^2(4) = \displaystyle\sum_{i=0}^{3} [5x^2(i) + u^2(i)]$

**d.** $J = 10x^2(4) + \displaystyle\sum_{i=0}^{3} [x^2(i) + 5u^2(i)]$

**8-26.** Repeat Problem 8-25 for the unstable plant

$$x(k+1) = 1.5x(k) + u(k)$$

**8-27.** Find the optimal steady state feedback gain for the first-order plant

$$x(k+1) = 0.9x(k) + u(k)$$

corresponding to the performance measure

$$J = \sum_{i=0}^{\infty} [x^2(i) + 3u^2(i)]$$

**a.** Find $K$ to three significant figures by calculating $K$, with the aid of a computer or calculator, for enough backward-in-step iterations.

**b.** Find $K$ by letting $K$ and $P$ in (8-38) and (8-39) be constant and solving the resulting quadratic equation.

**8-28.** For the spacecraft roll attitude (8-40), suppose that only the attitude, but not the rate, is measured with a sensor:

$$y(k) = [1 \quad 0] \begin{bmatrix} x_1(k) \\ x_2(k) \end{bmatrix}$$

Design a deadbeat observer to estimate the state. Investigate the control system's performance when the estimated state is fed back through the quadratic optimal feedback gains.

# Index